KRLA ARCHIVES

KRLA
Chronological Archives
Volume 8
September 23, 1967, to May 4, 1967

KRLA ARCHIVES

This final archive collects the KRLA Beat running from Sept 23, 1967 to May 4, 1968.

The Beat showed more counter-culture coverage toward the end of its run, including the drug culture as it influenced popular music. The publication seemed to delight in reporting on various pop-artist arrests, which were becoming more commonplace. Their coverage of other culture focuses, like the Smothers Brothers and censorship, and the Beatles discussing religion reflected the changing of society on many levels.

Readers of the September 23rd 1967 issue were thrilled to see Paul McCarney and Mick Jagger in the same cover photo and an internal story hinting at a possible joint venture between The Beatles and The Stones. But in that same issue, (indeed, on the same page 2), they would also read about Brian Epstein's death.

The Rolling Stones, The Beatles, The Mamas and The Papas, The Turtles, Bob Dylan, and the Association continued to see coverage.

Bands like the Rascals, Jimi Hendrix, Jay and the Techniques, Don Ho, The Doors, Buffalo Springfield, Spanky and Our Gang, the Cowsills, Sunshine Company and Van Morrison began getting coverage as well.

For many, the end of the publication came too soon. Still on a bi-weekly schedule, to save money some of the news items were written from the wire service and press releases. The magic started to fade and the ad revenue became weaker. May 3, 1968 was the final issue to see publication.

In presenting these original issues, we've moved a few of the pages around to ensure that the spreads still lined up. Not a big deal to most people unless you are severly OCD and have access to the original issues.

Copyright © 2016 White Lightning Publishing

KRLA ARCHIVES

BEATLES, STONE TRAIL HIS HOLINESS 25¢

KRLA *Edition* BEAT
SEPTEMBER 23, 1967

KRLA ARCHIVES

KRLA BEAT

Volume 3, Number 14   September 23, 1967

IN THE BACKGROUND HERE, manager Epstein was at the forefront of the Beatles startling success.

BRIAN EPSTEIN took Beatles from Liverpool club to World fame!

Epstein Death Shocks India-Bound Beatles

LONDON — Although the official inquest into the death of Beatle manager Brian Epstein has been postponed, authorities are certain that no foul play was involved in the unexpected passing of the 32-year-old financial genius.

A routine autopsy failed to reveal the cause of death, so the inquest was adjourned to Sept. 8 to allow time for laboratory tests.

Epstein was found in the bedroom of his Belgravia town house with several bottles of pills reportedly at his side. Police said he had been taking the pills for "various ailments, and a friend later disclosed that Epstein had been unwell for some months.

The laboratory tests were ordered to determine if a lethal mixture of the pills and any liquor Epstein had consumed the night before at a party might have killed him.

The Beatles were in Bangor, Wales, on a meditation retreat with Indian mystic Maharishi Mahesh Yogi when they heard about the death of their manager.

"It's a great shock," said Paul McCartney when he was told the news.

The Maharishi broke the news to the Beatles after newsmen brought word to the retreat.

Later in the week the Beatles announced that they would be spending at least two months in India where they would "learn how to meditate better."

Meanwhile reports began circulating that the copyrights to the Beatles' music might be sold to pay an estimated $14 to $16.8 million taxes on Epstein's estate. The eldest son of a furniture store owner, Epstein left an estimated $19.8 million fortune, and according to British tax law, 80 per cent of it must be confiscated by the government.

Rumors were that the copyrights would be sold to an American concern. A year ago, an American consortium offered $9.8 for Epstein's Nems Enterprises, but he rejected the offer.

Bee Gees May Move To U.S.

LONDON—The Bee Gees are considering setting up permanent residence in the United States as a result of the British government not granting work permits to two Australian members of the group.

The action against Colin Peterson and Vince Melouney will definitely force the group to move elsewhere unless the two decide to change their citizenship and live in Spain or Italy. Another possibility being considered is to move the entire group to Germany.

Although Vince and Colin are members of a British Commonwealth country, the British Home Office has refused to grant them permits. Residents of other European nations as well as America have a better chance of getting the permit, however.

Beatles, Stones Joining Voices?

LONDON—Have the two top British rock groups teamed up for a single release? The question is being asked here as the new Rolling Stones recording, "We Love You," hits the record racks. The cut features the Stones and some unidentified "friends," and these friends sound suspiciously like the Beatles.

Whether John, Paul, George and Ringo did or did not back up the Stones, Jagger and Co. are going more and more into the Beatle groove, not only sounding like them but using a similar lyric theme—love.

Revere Breaks Illinois Mark

SPRINGFIELD, Ill.—Paul Revere and the Raiders broke a century-old attendance mark at the Illinois State Fair when they opened before a crowd of 27,000.

Governor Otto Kerner presented the Raiders with a trophy after the performance, telling them that in the fair's 115-year history there had never been a bigger opening.

Revere and his Raiders used the Springfield concert as the springboard for their tenth national concert tour.

Hendrix Drummer Collapses On Stage

WASHINGTON — Jimi Hendrix drummer Mitch Mitchell collapsed on stage while playing at the Ambassador Theatre in Washington, D.C. He was rushed to a hospital where it was reported that he had appendix trouble.

The Experience had been playing at a special benefit at the theatre for the Keep The Faith For Washington Youth fund.

AROUND the WORLD

A NEW STARR ENTERS THE WORLD

By Tony Barrow

Jason Starkey, weighing 8 pounds 5½ ounces, was born to Maureen and Richard at 3:25 p.m. on Saturday, August 19 in Queen Charlotte's Maternity Hospital, Hammersmith, West London.

"It's just like going back two years," commented Ringo. "It's like Zak being born all over again."

Maureen had chosen the name Jason. "It was her turn. Zak was my idea," said the proud father.

Less than four hours before the birth, Ringo drove Maureen up to London from their Weybridge, Surrey, home. He stayed at the hospital until four thirty, returning at eight the same evening with Maureen's mother, Mrs. Florence Cox, who had been staying with them all out at Weybridge throughout the final weeks of her daughter's second pregnancy.

Gift of Flowers

Maureen was in hospital precisely one week — to the very hour. She occupied a pleasant little private room — ward D — in the West Wing of the hospital's fourth floor. For company she had radio, television, telephone, at least a hundred cables of congratulations plus a splendid selection of floral tributes including a teddy bear made entirely from golden colored flowers. There was a beautiful cradle, also made with flowers, from Mick and Marianne.

Tiny Jason, a neat little mop of dark brown hair curling about his head and an identity tape stitched round one wrist in regulation fashion, made his photographic press debut at the age of 5 days. London photographer Jon Kelly took the only hospital shots of Ringo, Maureen and the new baby. Unfortunately Jason slept peacefully through the photo session, his eyes closely tight in every shot!

Eyes Open

Afterwards Nurse McGlasson held him in her arms for the final set of pictures to be taken. And for a few moments Jason, affected by the strong sunlight in the corridor outside his mother's room, opened his eyes wide and appeared to stare straight into Kelly's camera lenses for the first time.

On Saturday, August 26 Zak, 23½ months old at the time, saw his new brother for the first time when Mrs. Cox collected Maureen and Jason from Hammersmith and took them home. And a day or two later Ringo's parents travelled from Liverpool to join the family gathering at Welbridge. By now Ringo had returned from his long weekend in Nortl Wales with the other Beatles.

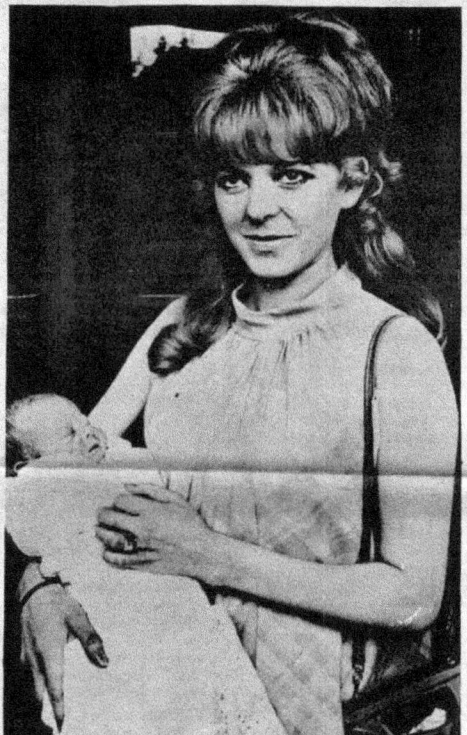

UPI Photo
"It's like going back two years, it's Zak being born all over again."

Bans Rock

HONOLULU — Complaints from residents around the outdoor Waikiki Shell have forced city officials to ban the concert bowl from further rock and roll performances.

Dylan Signs With Columbia

Bob Dylan has signed a long-term contract with Columbia Records, and the feeling is that the folk-rock singer will resume recording early this fall.

Dylan hasn't cut a recording for nearly a year after a motorcycle accident. He has reportedly been composing songs and working on several film projects in his Woodstock, New York, home.

New sound for long silent Dylan

Hippie Shoulder Strap Bag - $2.00 P.P.

I'm Not Just a Negro—Poitier

ATLANTA — Sidney Poitier denounced reporters at a press conference here for "only asking me questions that relate to my Negro-ness."

The actor had been asked a number of questions concerning his politics as a Negro. Poitier refused to answer any more such questions and told reporters, "I am many other things aside from a Negro. I am an artist, an actor, an American."

Staples Nab Top Gospel

ATLANTA—The Staple Singers received a Golden Mike Award as the Best Gospel Group of the Year from the National Association of Radio and Television Announcers. The award was made at the Association's annual convention here.

'I am an artist... an American'

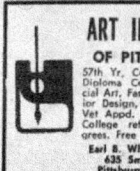

ART INSTITUTE OF PITTSBURGH
57th Yr, Coed. & 24 mo. Diploma Course, Commercial Art, Fashion Art, Interior Design, Begin. & Adv. Vet Appd. Dorm facilities. College referrals for degrees. Free Illus. brochure.
Earl B. Wheeler, Director
635 Smithfield St.
Pittsburgh, Pa. 15222

HARK! A WORTHWHILE CAUSE!

JOIN THE JBL CAUSE!

IRVING MENDELSOHN SWINGS

LOYAL FANS OF "THE MENDELSOHN QUINTETTE CLUB OF BOSTON" HELP BRING JOY TO ONE AND ALL...MAKE YOUR FELLOW MAN HAPPY...LET THE WORLD KNOW THAT "IRVING MENDELSOHN SWINGS"!!!
Get your bumper sticker and button now! Friends will gather around you... Strangers will rush to greet you... Cars will stop behind you at red lights. HANDSOMELY ILLUSTRATED... CHEAPEST ON EARTH!

ONLY 25¢ FOR BOTH!

No Deposit...no references ...just send your money along with this coupon.

COUPON
Enclosed is 25¢. Please send me my "IRVING MENDELSOHN SWINGS" bumper sticker and button.
Name
Address
City   State
Postal Zone
JAMES B. LANSING SOUND, INC.
3249 CASITAS AVE., LOS ANGELES, CALIFORNIA 90039
BEATE

KRLA ARCHIVES

ON THE BEAT
BY LOUISE CRISCIONE

The Ringo Starrs' were not the only ones in the pop world to welcome a new addition to their family. Mark Volman, of the Turtles, and his wife, Patricia, are now the proud parents of a daughter, Sarina, born at St. John's Hospital in Santa Monica, California and weighing in at 6 lbs., 12 ozs.

Talks and scripts are still going back and forth between the Beatles and film producer, Walter Shenson. However, nothing is even remotely scheduled. Says Shenson: "Let's face it—they need another picture like a hole in the head. They're young and rich and enjoying life." Which is where the situation stood last year as well.

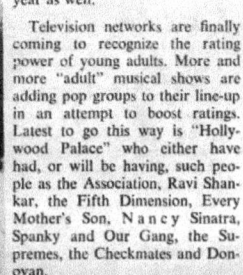

Television networks are finally coming to recognize the rating power of young adults. More and more "adult" musical shows are adding pop groups to their line-up in an attempt to boost ratings. Latest to go this way is "Hollywood Palace" who either have had, or will be having, such people as the Association, Ravi Shankar, the Fifth Dimension, Every Mother's Son, Nancy Sinatra, Spanky and Our Gang, the Supremes, the Checkmates and Donovan.

The Young Rascals always keep themselves busy—you can count on that. So, on September 22 they'll play the University of Louisville in Louisville, Ky.; September 29, Duke University in Durham, N.C.; September 30, the University of North Carolina in Chapel Hill, N.C.; and then it's off to England on October 4. Their latest single is a gas, isn't it?

Would you believe that Vice President Hubert H. Humphrey has written the liner notes for the "Stay In School" campaign album put out by the Stax/Volt family of recording artists? Believe it because the man has done it. The album features the sounds of Otis Redding, Carla Thomas, Sam and Dave, Booker T and the MG's, etc. The purpose of the album is to convince teens the value of education and contains both "talks" by the artists as well as previously unreleased song cuts.

I think I'll devote the rest of my column to listing the tour schedules of some of the pop groups because of an overwhelming amount of mail asking when . . . . . is going to play South Orange or Salt Lake City. So, here goes:

The FOUR SEASONS: September 30, Bloomington, Indiana, Indiana University; Oct. 1, Manchester, Michigan; Oct. 6, Cleveland, Ohio; Oct. 8, Detroit, Michigan, Masonic Temple; Oct. 11, I.M.A. Auditorium, Flint, Michigan; Oct. 12, Lansing, Michigan, Civic Center; Oct. 13, South Bend, Indiana, Morris Civic Auditorium.

SPANKY & OUR GANG: September 30, New Pauls, New York, State University of New York; Oct. 6, Lubbock, Texas, Texas A&M; Oct. 13, Chicago, Ill., Orchestra Hall; Oct. 14, Grand Rapids, Michigan, Civic Auditorium; Oct. 20, Washington, D.C., American University; Oct. 25, Homecoming Special, television show.

JAY & THE TECHNIQUES: September 22-24, Cleveland, Ohio; September 29-30, Miami, Florida.

NEW VAUDEVILLE BAND: September 15-28, Lake Tahoe, Nevada; September 20-Oct. 7, British Columbia, Isy's in Vancouver; Oct. 13-26, Las Vegas, Nevada, Tropicana Hotel.

One more thing before I sign off—we're all really excited to have Dr. Bolter working with us because we feel it will be a great opportunity for you to ask any questions which have been bothering you by simply writing them down and sending them in. What could be easier?

Spencer Falls For America

CHICAGO — Spencer Davis opened his American tour here and promptly fell off a stage and injured his leg. The fall required three stitches.

Pitney Tour Scores A Hit

Gene Pitney's touring caravan broke two house records in the South recently at Memorial Auditorium in Greenville, S.C., and Dorton Arena in Raleigh, N.C. With Pitney on the tour are The Buckinghams, the Easybeats, the Fifth Estate, The Happenings, and the Music Explosion.

Chubby Drops Suit vs. Cameo

NEW YORK—Chubby Checker has dropped his suit against Cameo/Parkway Records. He was suing for $110,000 which he alleged the company owed him in royalties. A spokesman simply said Chubby had come to terms with the label.

Doctor To Pen BEAT Column

Beginning with our next issue, The BEAT is proud to have a new column written by Arthur Bolten, M.D. Dr. Bolter will be answering any medical or social problems which you may have.

Please send any questions you'd like Dr. Bolter to answer to: Dr. Bolter, Beat Publications, 9121 Sunset Blvd, Los Angeles, California 90069.

The Wilson's Dad Makes A Donation

LOS ANGELES — Murry Wilson, father of the Beach Boys, donated $5,000 to Synanon, a well-known re-education center for drug addicts and derelicts. Mr. Wilson is a songwriter for Capitol Records.

Beat Publications, Inc.

Executive Editor .... Cecil I. Tuck
Publisher .... Gayle Tuck
Editor .... Louise Criscione
Assistant Editor .... Greg Kieselmann

Staff Writers
Jacoba Atlas   Bobby Farrow
Ron Koslow   Shirley Poston

Contributing Writers
Tony Barrow   Sue Barry
Lawrence Charles   Eden
Bob Levinson   Jamie McCluskey, III

Photographers
Ed Caraeff
Howard L. Bingham   Jerry Haas

Advertising
Sam Chase   Dick Stricklin
Business Manager   Judy Felice
Subscriptions .... Diane Clatworthy

Distribution
Miller Freeman Publications
500 Howard Street, San Francisco, Calif.
The BEAT is published bi-weekly by BEAT Publications, Inc., editorial and advertising offices at 9121 Sunset Blvd., Los Angeles, California 90069. U.S. bureaus in Hollywood, San Francisco, New York, Chicago and Nashville; overseas correspondents in London, Liverpool and Manchester, England. Sale price 25 cents. Subscription price: U.S. and sessions $5 per year; Canada and foreign rates, $9 per year. Second class postage prepaid at Los Angeles, California.

BILL COSBY brought his "silver throat" to Los Angeles.

A NEW FIRST: COSBY SINGS!

HOLLYWOOD — Bill Cosby, super cool star of TVs "I Spy" has branched out into the singing field. To promote his new Warner Bros. album "Silver Throat" Cosby played nine standing room only performances at the Whisky A Go-Go over the weekend.

His performance lasted 55 minutes. Backed by the Watt's 103rd Street Band, Cosby when not singing, played the washboard and drums, mugged and clowned.

Although his voice is something less than "silver" he did very well with his material, and the audience, of course, thought he could do no wrong. Singing, "I Got A Woman," "Spreading Honey" and "Why Am I Treated So Bad" among others, Cosby proved that he might just have another important talent to add to his already staggering list of accomplishments.

Cosby also gave the Watt's 103rd Street Band every opportunity to show their ability. He was also accompanied by Delores Hall on "Big Boss Man" and "Baby What You Want Me To Do." After Miss Hall, Jackie Lee came on to keep things rolling.

"The Standel Sound"

"The Grass Roots"

Professional musicians throughout the world choose the "Standel Sound," the accepted standard for professional musicians who demand professional performance.
(Dept. B)

A. P.A. Speaker Column Amplifier
B. P.A. Master Control with Reverb
C. Imperial Line Amplifier — Solid State, Dual Channel

Standel
Solid State Music Systems
4918 DOUBLE DRIVE • EL MONTE, CALIF. 91731

Bobby Gentry Now!

...An Urgent And Welcomed

Chapter In Contemporary

History At

Its Best...

BEATLES John, George and Paul with His Holiness Marharishi Mahesh Yogi.
UPI Photos

Beatles And A Stone To Wales With Mystic

MICK AND MARIANNE board the "Love" train for Bangor.

PATTI HARRISON and sister, Jenny, try to pull Cyn aboard.

By Tony Barrow

Any good groupie and, indeed, any teenybopper of average intellect would assure you that one of the least likely places top pop people are to be found is a busy city rail terminal at holiday time. But there's always the exception to the general rule.

The date was Friday, August 25, the beginning of Britain's August Bank Holiday Weekend.

The time was just after three o'clock in the afternoon.

The place was London's crowded Euston rail terminal with thousands of vacationing families bustling about with their baggage and their infant children.

Suddenly, without warning, there were Beatles and a Rolling Stone right there in the midst of the holiday crowds. Suddenly the 3:05 p.m. London to North Wales Express became the grooviest Bank Holiday train to pull out of Euston Station that day, this year or this decade!

Meditation Lecture

But I'd better start at the beginning. The previous day, Thursday, Aug. 24, a 56-year-old Himalayan mystic named Maharishi Mahesh Yogi (alias His Holiness The Master) gave a two-hour evening "transcendental meditation" lecture at the London Hilton Hotel. A few hours before the lecture was due to begin George Harrison decided he'd like to buy a couple of tickets—a dollar each—to hear the saintly, tiny, white-whiskered old man of the East preach his doctrine. Eventually Paul and John went along too and all seemed thoroughly impressed by the theories expounded by the leader of the Kashmir cult.

After joining 1500 other believers and intrigued spectators for the lengthy lecture, the three Beatles had a special audience with The Master who sat cross-legged before them in a fine white cloak and brightly colored beads with a little bunch of red roses and carnations clutched in his dark brown hands. He told the Beatles many things. "If you go into your garden and sit down to meditate," Maharishi Mahesh Yogi explained to Paul, "you must not keep your eyes closed all of the time or you will miss the great beauty of your garden."

Invitation to Wales

Before they left the Maharishi invited John, Paul and George to be guests at University College, Bangor, North Wales for the next four or five days. Over the August Bank Holiday Weekend the mystic was to give a further series of meditation lectures and the Beatles would be welcome to attend.

At first it didn't seem likely that they would. For one thing the Beattles had a recording session scheduled.

Twelve hours later, at noon on Friday, John and George determined to postpone all other activities and accompany His Holiness to the North Wales coastal town of Bangor, a 300-mile train ride from London. They contacted Paul who was equally enthusiastic. Ringo decided to delay his journey to Bangor in order to bring Maureen and the week-old baby Jason out of the hospital on Saturday morning. But at the very last moment he switched his plans, after talking to Maureen, and left from Euston station with the rest.

Just before three o'clock, Mick Jagger and Marianne Faithfull arrived at Euston, an unexpected addition to the colorful party of disciples. Everything had been fixed in such a rush that nobody had reserved seats for the train. Mick and Marianne hadn't even bought tickets for the trip.

Paul Arrives

Next to arrive was Paul, riding in Neil Aspinall's elegant pale blue Jaguar. But there was no sign of the others and the train was due to pull out. So Paul, Mick and Marianne got onto the train — along with their silver-haired master and one or two of his Eastern followers.

At seven minutes after three John's beautiful Rolls Royce drew in beside Euston's departure entrance. Out piled George and Patti plus Patti's young sister, Jenny, John and Cynthia and Ringo. Grasping multi-colored Greek bags and a small assortment of musical instruments shrouded in flower-painted cloth covers, the six walked and then ran through the crowds, past the ticket barrier and onto Platform 13. As they drew alongside the first part of the train, everyone realized that there was no time to look for any particular section. It was a matter of leaping aboard blindly. As they do this the train began to move.

A cop thought he'd be helpful by closing the door on the last of the party. But, by coincidence rather than design, he prevented Cynthia Lennon getting on. Poor Cyn was left all alone on the platform as the train disappeared from the station. John's frantic

(Continued on Page 9)

LEFT BEHIND, Cynthia Lennon wipes tears from her eyes.

The Bee Gees First Album

Now Available At:
MONTGOMERY WARD DEPARTMENT STORES

Nancy Heads For Jackson!

RASCALS PEACE TOUR ALL SET

THE RASCALS—Gene, Eddie, Felix and Dino—are one of the most well-travelled r 'n r groups around today. They've appeared in England, in Japan, in France, in every major city of the U.S. and Canada—and most recently Hawaii! Everywhere they go, they hold teen press conferences, dance, write, compose, groove — all the frantic antics of a Rascals tour!

And guess what's coming up—in January, 1968, they begin a world-peace tour — appearing in every major country and possibly Russia!

Moving Fast

The Rascals have always been moving fast and frantic—the story of their beginnings is crazy, clipped, slapstick and stop-motion—just like a Keystone Kop Chase Scene. Before their whirlwind world scene, two Rascals were in New Jersey, two in New York (playing separate gigs in different parts of the city) — and then—POW' — they met and linked forces in 1965. Gene, the guitarist, left his own group to join this new and exciting formation; Dino, suddenly a Rascal after playing drums with every great jazz star that ever was; Felix, coming from a pre-med course at Syracuse and a stint as organist for "Sandu Scott and Her Scotties;" and Eddie, jumping and skating in after working as a percussionist with Joey Dee's Band. SHAZAM!! They were there! Working and playing like they had worked and played together all their lives!

Now The Rascals are branching out even further—Dino into painting and acting; Felix, into writing and composing material for all the Rascals' albums and singles; Eddie, writing lyrics, building homes; and Gene, producing (a new rock group from Rochester, N.Y., called "The Brass Buttons") and arranging Rascals' material.

Where do they go from here? Nobody Really Knows . . . but The Rascals do have an idea or two about where they *want* to go . . .

For one thing, they'd like to make a movie about themselves (produced, of course, by their manager Sid Bernstein).

More Writing

For another thing, they'd like to keep on working out their own material—for Rascals' use *and* for other name performers, too.

After "Groovin' " was number one for eight weeks, they discovered they matched a record for a top hit held previously only by The Beatles! More Gold Records—that's another Rascals' goal.

As far as Dino, Eddie, Gene and Felix are concerned, there's no limit to the new directions their career as a r 'n r group can go . . . but if you had a plan for your favorite group, what would it be?

EDDIE backstage before show.

GENE waits for end of applause before going on with more.

FELIX smiles at "A Girl Like You".

DINO plants earphones securely.

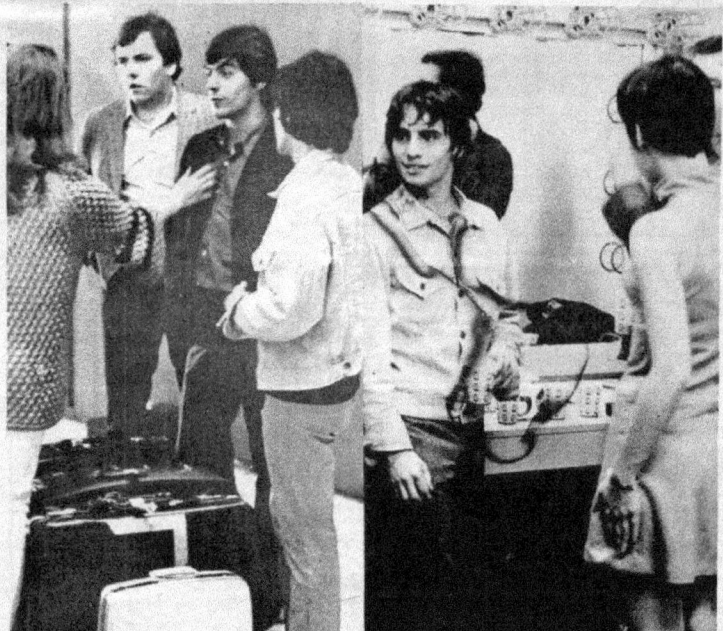
YOU CAN ALWAYS be sure of one thing—wherever the Rascals go so go the girls!
BEAT Photos: Judy Eldridge

BEAT EXCLUSIVE
The News From The Rascals

By Gene Cornish

You know, there's nothing like a cool dip in the ocean—when the ocean is the Pacific and the place is Waikiki Beach. Felix, Dino, Eddie and I just returned from a flip-out tour of the West Coast and Hawaiian Islands! (Eddie's still doing the dog-paddle, I discovered). We met thousands of our fans along the way and played with The Beard — but it's sure good to be home, in the air-conditioned towers of NYC!

World Tour

We're going on a trip again—in October—back to Mod Country and the birthplace of Zak Starr. And then we're off again! This time—in February—all OVER THE WORLD—a peace tour of the globe. If you see us, please have flowers ready!

Hey! I'm producing a new r 'n r group you'll probably be hearing about—they're called "The Brass Buttons" and they're from Rochester, New York. Look for 'em!

By the way, have you noticed the drawings on the cover of our album, "Groovin' "—they're done by Lynn Rubin—and it was Dino's idea to use them on the outside cover. I hope you dig the four pin-ups (how sweet!) inside. We're already working on the material for our next album—writing the lyrics and music for *all* the songs ourselves!

I saw a friend of mine the other day—sipping a soda on a corner—Janis Ian. Have you heard her "Society's Child"? What a sound-off!

I'm writing to you from my apartment in Manhattan — and I've just been invaded by three familiar faces. Eddie's got a hold of the chandelier again, Dino's taken all the silverware and is pounding out "A Girl Like You" on a glass table top—and Felix—he's got a hold of Eddie—and here they come, swinging toward the desk—BYE!—Ahhhhhhhh!

September 23, 1967 — THE BEAT — Page 9

U.K. Pop News Round-Up

Flower Festival Hits Britain

By Tony Barrow

Over Britain's August Bank Holiday Weekend, while The Beatles went into semi-secluded meditation with a Himalayan mystic in North Wales, an estimated 50,000 people paid about 3 dollars to attend the world's first Duke-in, a 3 day "Festival of the Flower Children" in the grounds of Woburn Abbey, home of His Grace the 13th Duke of Bedford, spread over part of a beautiful 3,000 acre estate. For permitting his stately lawns and woodlands to be invaded by 21 groups plus so many of his followers His Grace took 10 per cent of the gate money, a handsome sum in excess of 15,000 dollars. Woburn Abbey, built 200 years ago, has the reputation of being the most commercially successful of Britain's stately homes, the present Duke having decided to accumulate as much cash as possible from visitors in order to offset inherited death duties which ran into many millions.

Highlights

A highlight of the Festival was the dropping of 5,000 carnations from an air balloon by Mr. Don Piccard, a 41-year-old American. Musically, the highlights included appearances by THE SMALL FACES, THE MOVE, ERIC BURDON, JEFF BECK, THE ALAN PRICE SET, TOMORROW FEATURING KEITH WEST, THE DREAM, and ZOOT MOBEY'S new group called DANTALLIN'S CHARIOT.

Also in Holiday Weekend attendance at Woburn were 300 security men equipped with jeeps, many gallons of two-per-cent alcohol lager, several tons of hot dogs and 20-year-old hippie Steve Brody who had hitch-hiked from San Francisco to be amongst Britain's beautiful Flower Children.

For "The Anniversary" movie starring Bette Davis NEW VAUDEVILLE BAND recording Al Jolson oldie "The Anniversary Song." N.V.B. will be heard singing over opening credits and title will be issued as the top deck of a single ... Many future records produced by Denny Cordell will be issued in Britain via the Regal Zonophone label, until now a specialist outlet for Salvation Army records. First artists affected include THE MOVE ("Flowers in the Rain") and THE PROCOL HARUM ("Homburg Hat") both of whom have been with Decca's Deram label until now ... Latest single by the BEE GEES couples another of two of the group's own original compositions — "Massachusetts" and "Barker of the U.F.O." ... My private Sirip Chick Spy denies that HARRY PULES is best friend of SCOTT MACKENZIE and THE BYRDS but confirms that he has 3 sons, 2 daughters and 1 wife.

Solo Hendrix

Solo guitar performance by JIMI HENDRIX at London's Royal Festival Hall this month in "Festival of Guitar Music" ... fourth postponement of American trip by THE MOVE who are not expected to tour before next February ... Sunday, September 25 marks U.K. concert debut Stevie Winwood's group TRAFFIC at Saville Theatre in London's West End ... MGM recording sessions for PAUL and BARRY RYAN cancelled when both twins entered the London Clinic for tonsil operations.

For "Two A Penny", the movie he made with Billy Graham, CLIFF RICHARD penning title number. Meanwhile Cliff begins shooting his fifth feature-length screen musical with THE SHADOWS in October ... "Huff Puff" by MICKEY DLENZ issued via Decca's London label in U.K. ... On Fontana THE MINDBENDERS have covered THE BOX TOPS' "The Letter."

Beatles Take Mystic Train

(Continued from Page 5)

cries as he poked his head from a window and yelled "Jump, Cyn, jump!" were all too late. Cyn burst into tears and the press and TV cameramen went to work again with a great whirling and much clicking.

Too Beautiful

The grooviest train took nearly five hours to reach Bangor. By that time radio and press news had told the Welsh population what as happening.

"It is all too beautiful" murmured His Holiness accepting a bunch of carnations from a Bangor inhabitant.

"Its all intriguing but I don't know a lot about it," replied Mick Jagger when a Welsh reporter demanded to know the Stone's motives.

"One of the most illuminating and exciting experiences I have had," Paul summed up when cross-examined about the transcendental meditation thing.

So, the Beatles and their closest friends stayed on in Bangor, turning on to the words of their robed and bearded guru Yogi ("Holiness is just a quality of life") during his final days in Britain prior to retirement to "a life of utter silence in Kashmir."

And the brought-down, left-behind Mrs. Lennon? Well, she was driven to Bangor by Neil in his pale blue Jag and Jane Asher joined her for the trip at the last moment so everything was fine and the tension was over.

Fishing For Good Music?

Now Available At:
MONTGOMERY WARD DEPARTMENT STORES

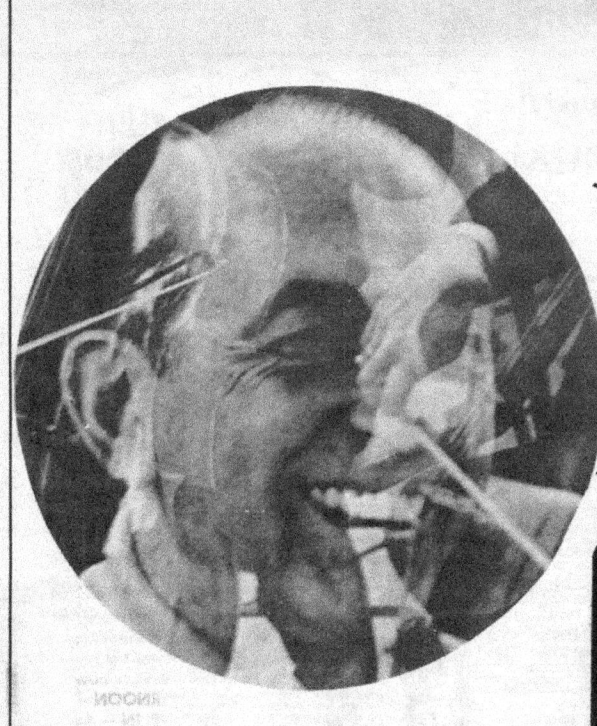

Sounds For Right Now

This Very Moment

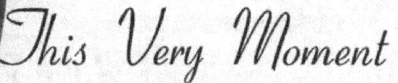

KRLA ARCHIVES

KRLA Line-Up NEW SEASON

Dave Hull 6-9 am
Casey Kasem 9-12 noon
Johnny Hayes 12-3 pm
Reb Foster 3-6 pm
Bob Dayton 6-9 pm
Jim Wood 9-12 midnight
Bill Slater 12-6 am

THE GOLDEN BEAR
306 OCEAN AVENUE (HWY 101)   HUNTINGTON BEACH

Present

"The Vanilla Fudge"
Sept. 12 Through Sept. 17

* * *

Coming Sept. 19 Thru Sept. 24

BIG BROTHER AND THE HOLDING COMPANY

Reservations   PHONE 536-9600
                         536-9102

ICE HOUSE GLENDALE
234 So. Brand Ave. Reservations: 245-5043

Sept. 12-24
Tim Morgan
and
Bud Sharp

One Week Only
Standells
and
Ted Anderson

ICE HOUSE PASADENA
24 No. Mentor — Reservations: 681-9492

Aug. 26-Sept. 24
Bud Dashiell
(formerly of Bud & Travis)
and
Carol Hedin
and
Aeriel Landscape
(Forth & Main)

"A Tribute To A Frustrated Actor"
By Casey Kasem

One of the entertainment industry's best known "behind-the-scenes" men is dead — but Brian Epstein was not the typical "unknown guiding force." His name was as familiar to the world as those of his four major discoveries — John Lennon, Paul McCartney, George Harrison, and Ringo Starr. Perhaps known primarily for his s h r e w d business ability, 32-year-old Brian was colorful, talented man himself.

Not satisfied that he had made himself a millionaire in five years or less, he often described himself as a "... frustrated actor..." and vowed one day to return to the stage and prove his ability.

But time was short then, . . . and now no longer. Brian Epstein can no longer "prove himself to the world . . . and the world has been cheated.

Presenting In Concert
By Pen

Take a look at the partial list of KRLA concerts. Already we have presented "Herman's Hermits," "The Who," "The Sundowners" and "The Strawberry Alarm Clock" at the Anaheim Convention Center on September 8th.

Then there was "KRLA presents San Francisco at the Hollywood Bowl" with "The Jefferson Airplane," "Big Brother and the Holding Company" and "The Grateful Dead."

New Look For News

KRLA, in a pioneering effort, has developed a unique newscast schedule which is expected to bring about a nationwide revolution in local radio news broadcasting. Discarding the traditional music-and-news station practice of depositing hourly five-minute reports, KRLA has expanded its in-depth capabilities with quarter-hour news broadcasts at quarterly intervals . . . 3 o'clock, 6 o'clock, 9 and 12 o'clock reports on a 24-hour basis.

Wood To KRLA

Disc Jockey Jim Wood has joined Los Angeles pop music outlet KRLA.

FUN & FOLK MUSIC
LEDBETTER'S
1621 Westwood Blvd.
Los Angeles
GR. 8-2747

PROUDLY PRESENTS

THE DILLARDS

STEVE MARTIN
Sept. 12-24

NOW HAPPENING EVERY NITE
1—PACIFIC OCEAN
2—DEARLY BELOVED
3—THE JOINT EFFORT
4—POP CORN BLIZZARD
5—THE ABSTRACTS
6—MUSTARD GREENS
7—OCTOBER COUNTRY
8—SIOUX UPRISING
9—SOMEBODY'S CHILDREN
10—THE PLASTIC FORCE

9039 SUNSET

GAZZARRI'S #1 ON-THE-STRIP
CR 3-6606
OL 7-2113
GAZZARRI'S #2 LA CIENEGA
319 N. LACIENEGA

MORE HAPPENINGS
MON. — Dance Contest
$500 Grand Prize
TUES. — Talent Nite
WED. — Fashion Show
SUN. AFTERNOON
GROOVE IN — 4 P.M.

Did You Say,
"Where's the Action"?
What's This . . .
Chopped Liver! ! !

KRLA ARCHIVES

JIMI STUNS Monterey Festival crowd.

... AND THEN burns his guitar.

Hendrix Experience Devastate Continent; Can They Do It Here?

Only one short year after it began, the Jimi Hendrix Experience has left Europe in an emotional shambles after one stunning concert upon another. The only thing that could be more stunning about Hendrix is if he didn't make it big in the United States, his native country.

Just last September, Hendrix was an unknown singer-guitarist playing at Greenwich Village's Cafe Wha? Chas Chandler, at that time a member of the Animals, dropped into the club and became immediately enthusiastic about Hendrix. Things happened fast after that. Chas persuaded Jimi to come to England where they auditioned musicians for the other 2/3 of what was to become the Jimi Hendrix Experience.

With drummer Mitch Mitchell and bassest-guitarist Noel Redding, the group opened at the Olympia in Paris before a standing-room-only crowd. The Hendrix performance, both vocal and visual, completely devastated the French. From there the Experience broke record after record on the concert trail through Europe. Just eight days after the Beach Boys had broken the house record at the Tivoli, Stockholm, by playing to 7,000 fans at two shows, Hendrix came in to destroy that record by playing to 14,500 people for two shows.

SRO Crowds

There was standing-room-only at the Sports Arena in Copenhagen, where only the Rolling Stones had chalked up an SRO crowd. At the Seville Theatre in London, they were the first act ever to sell out both shows.

With this kind of success on the continent and in Britain, Jimi returned to the States this summer to take another crack at American audiences. Judging from the raves he received at the Monterey Pop Festival and on tour with the Monkees and the Mamas and the Papas, the U.S. has finally discovered Jimi Hendrix.

That first big hit, however, has eluded him. A single, "Purple Haze," did well in some cities, and his first album, "Are You Experienced?" has received quite a lot of national attention. Success in the States, then, is probably just a matter of time.

Army Man

Jimi might have been a career army man—he enlisted in the 101 Airborne Division when he was 16—except for a back injury suffered during a parachute jump which ended his military days. For the next five years, Jimi toured the States from coast to coast as lead guitarist backing up many top rock and rhythm and blues singers. Using the pseudonym Jimmy James, he played with the Blue Flames in New York for six months before his stint at the Cafe Wha? in the Village.

Jimi's personal musical tastes are quite wide ranging. He especially likes the blues, jazzman Roland Kirk, harpsichord and a-tonal music. To suit his distinctive tastes, Jimi is compelled to write almost all of his material; of the 12 tracts in "Are You Experienced?" 11 of them were written by him.

Among Hendrix's two sidemen, Mitch Mitchell has the most entertainment experience, having begun acting and dancing at the age of three. The high point of his career before meeting Hendrix was a world-wide tour with Georgie Fame and the Blue Flames. Mitch was on the verge of producing his own records with a band when he was tabbed for the Experience.

Noel Redding was a professional guitar player at 17 when he performed with the Modern Jazz Group. At the Animals audition, Noel met Hendrix, whose first question was "Can you play bass?" Before he could open his guitar case, he was a member of the Experience, doubling from guitar to bass, an instrument he hadn't played before.

America hasn't really begun to appreciate Jimi Hendrix; when it does it's in for an Experience.

Temptations Keep Rolling On

A few years ago Paul Williams of the Temptations expressed his ultimate ambition: to play the Copa in New York. Last month the famous Motown group did just that and startled the blase nightclub goers with outstanding soul music and amazing stage presentation. In fact, the Temptations broke all existing house records for the Copa. The long-famous nightclub had never seen anything like it before.

This success did not come overnight. The Temptations have paid their dues to the music industry many times over perfecting their individual style in club and concert dates throughout the country.

To fully appreciate the Temptations they must be seen. They move across the stage with the masculine assurance of born winners. One of the members takes the lead—all are actually lead singers . . . a very rare thing—and separates himself from the others. He sings while the others come in on the harmony, all the while working out the intricate choreography of a corps de ballet.

Fill-Ins

It all began quite a few years ago when five fellows who usually restricted their harmonizing to friends' parties heard that a local theater needed a "fill-in" vocal group for a rock and roll show. The quintet adopted by "voice vote" the name they use today and turned professional in exchange for fifteen dollars each.

The original group has undergone one change since those rather lean days: Elbrige Bryant was drafted into the Armed Forces and David Ruffin was set to replace him. That new addition seemed to have worked a lucky charm because his first group record, "The Way You Do The Things You Do" hit the top of the record charts.

Separately the Temptations are all interesting fellows. Melvin Franklin, who is usually considered the leader of the group is admittedly friendly and outgoing. He is also an avid reader of Marvel Comics and thinks Tarzan is something else.

Possibly the opposite of Melvin would be Eddie James Kenricks, who is shy and makes a point of being alone when he is in what he calls an "evil" temper.

Otis Miles, a native born Texan, moved to Detroit when he was only eight months old. His closest friend is Melvin Franklin and the two have been like brothers. Outside the group's career, Otis' main ambition is to one day produce records for other groups.

Add to that David Ruffin and Paul Williams, the ex-football player turned singer, and you have the Temptations.

Cool Chic

Although they give the impression of "cool chic" on stage, that feeling is gone when they are alone. They are what Southerners call "homely." They are warm, friendly and altogether engaging. All the "with it" professionalism which is so striking on stage is gone, and in its place is an eagerness and a tremendous enthusiasm.

"We'd crawl to get a job, if we had to," they have said, while reminiscing about the days when they took odd jobs to make carfare for a distant club date that usually barely covered their weekend expenses.

The days when the boys had to struggle for carfare are over, but the drive for perfection is still there.

BEATLE HISTORY PART II
BENEATH ALL THEIR HAIR!

By Jacoba Atlas

The fans knew it all along—the amazing talent that lay under that long hair—and the fans were just waiting to be taken along to the best in pop music which the Beatles would offer them.

There were no giant steps really, no valleys cut without bridges for the fans to cross. George didn't suddenly produce the complete Indian Sound, but exposed his audience to it gradually—first with "Norwegian Wood," and later with "Love You Too" and "I Want to Tell You." John and Paul didn't abandon melody for the mathematics of electronic music, but instead interspersed melody with electronics producing "Strawberry Fields Forever," "She Said, She Said," and of course, "Tomorrow Never Knows."

Paul himself stated, "we can make a bridge, you see, between us and Indian music or us and electronic music, and therefore we can take people with us . . . There is no sense in not taking people with you."

New Maturity

Their lyrics revealed new maturity as in the worn-out love affair depicted in "For No One." "She wakes up, she makes up, she takes her time and doesn't feel she has to hurry, she no longer needs you." Or in the ironic tale of "Eleanor Rigby" "wearing the face that she keeps in a jar by the door—who it is for?"—who indeed.

Love songs were in profusion in *Revolver*; the joyous "Good Day Sunshine," with its honky-tonk piano, the hopeful "Got To Get You Into My Life" and the amazingly beautiful, if sentimental, "Here, There and Everywhere."

But *Revolver* did not just reveal new maturity in the themes of love, but also in such social themes as alienation. If "Taxman" was a special case of social satire, one would certainly be hard pressed to find a person who does not relate to George's feelings of inadequacy expressed in "I Want to Tell You" which deals with the 20th century problem of the inability of people to communicate. The new classic "Tomorrow Never Knows" urged everyone to turn off their minds and float down stream and to intricate electronic sounds thousands did just that.

Separate Careers

This new maturity in songs obviously reflected a growing personal maturity. The world had watched, as it seldom gets the chance, the public education of four young men going from precocious adolescence to intelligent adulthood. All but Paul married, and their tastes ran the gamit from the French playwright Alfred Jarry—a particular favorite of Paul's—to the study of the ancient tribe of the Celts by John.

They branched out into separate endeavors: John to acting, Paul to scoring a film and making his own home movies, George to India to pursue more fully his interest in the Eastern culture, and Ringo to devoting more of his time to his all-important family.

A rather long period without group production led to speculation that the Beatles were breaking-up. From London came disquieting reports and Paul stated that he was "no longer one of the mop-tops." But with their latest album, *St. Pepper's Lonely Hearts Club Band* their future together again seems solidified.

St. Pepper is the progression of *Revolver* following John's desire to make every album better than the last one. Using the theme of a performance, we are given twelve unique songs each with a special and different theme.

Intricate Electronics

Electronics plays a far greater part than ever before, and a full orchestra is used on one number. The Indian influence is carried over to such a non-Harrison song as "Lovely Rita."

From the loneliness of "Eleanor Rigby" we have the haunting declaration "She's Leaving Home" using a similar background as "Rigby" plus some fine and unusual counter-point singing by the Beatles.

"Fixing A Hole" denotes the worth of being alone with one's thoughts—the pleasures of a wandering mind, shades of "Tomorrow Never Knows." "Within You, Without You" expresses similar sentiments as in *Revolver's* "Love You Too."

Cynical Humor

One of the major differences in the types of songs recorded is the lack of love songs on the *St. Pepper* album. For "Got To Get You Into My Life" we have the satirical "Lovely Rita" and for "Here, There and Everywhere" we are given the cynically humorous "When I'm Sixty-Four;" but no real ballads are included.

However, perhaps the most important song on *St. Pepper* both due to its extreme length, almost five minutes, and in the eyes of the BBC who banned the song, is 'A Day In The Life;' a strange tale of a dream employing a forty-one piece orchestra plus electronics. John sings the lead with Paul adding the controversial bridge.

There can be no doubt now that the Beatles have emerged from just being 'bloody phenomena' to brilliant composers and important artists. The fairy-tale image of the clever one, the sweet one, the quiet one, and the sad one have almost completely disappeared, as well they should. The Beatles have much more to give the fans now then just loveable objects at which to scream; and their audience has appreciated that fact. The Beatles are reflectors of an age—as all true artists are—singing of the conflicts and emotions that involve all of us today.

The fairy-tale has ended and with luck we shall all live happily ever after listening for many years to come to four individuals.

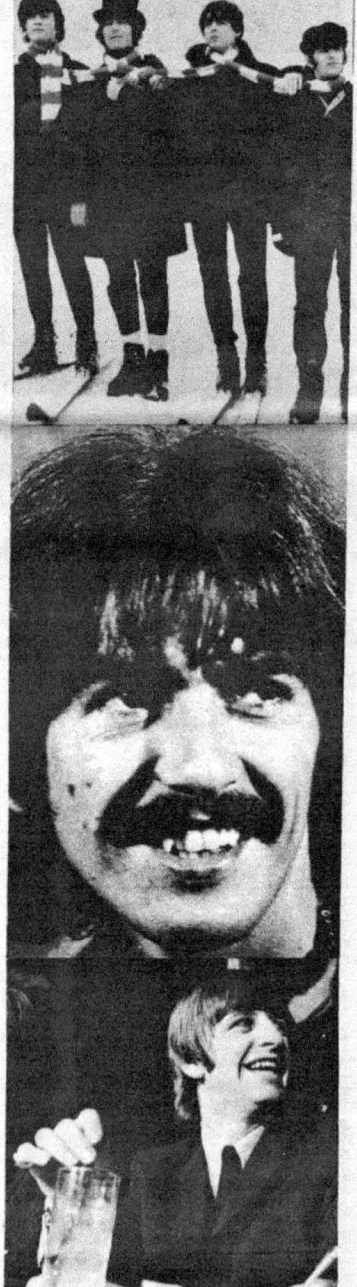

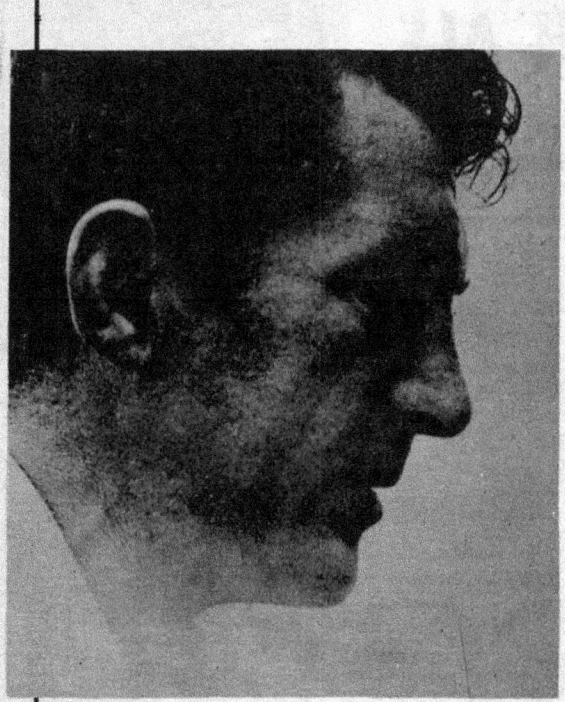

Welcome To Dean's World

A You-Name-It-I'll-Sing-It Kind Of Guy

AVAILABLE AT

'They Helped Turn The Whole Pop Music Scene Around'

'The Byrds Are Still Happening And Very, Very Valuable'

AVAILABLE AT

*In Memory Of
Brian Epstein*

Simon And Garfunkel... On Stage

BEAT Photos: Ed Caraeff

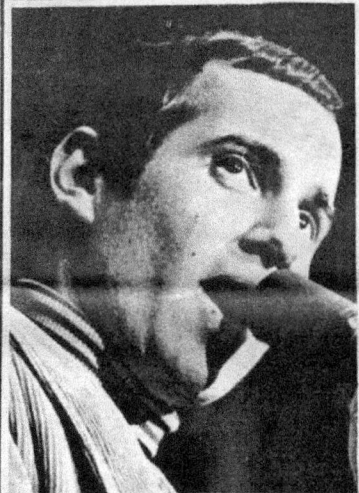

The BEAT Goes To The Movies
'COOL HAND LUKE'

"Iron bars do not a prison make" could well sum up the message in the Warner Bros.-7 Arts production, "Cool Hand Luke." Paul Newman, in the title role, portrays a prisoner on a chain gang trapped in body but not in mind.

Luke is the free spirit, the true rebel who finds society and its confinement impossible whether on the street or on the chain gang. He is a rebel against anything or anyone who seeks to curtail his personal freedom.

The film is a brutal one with violence bordering on the sadistic liberally portrayed throughout the film. Life on a Southern chain gang is one of senseless cruelty and meaningless regimentation. Director Stuart Rosenberg (winner of TV's Emmy award) has sought to create the mood and climate of life inside a chain gang.

In many ways he has succeeded. This area of our state penal codes is rarely explored and therefore to discuss the degree of realism achieved in "Cool Hand Luke" is difficult.

However, this film is not a social comment on the evils of the chain gang. It is the story of one man's desire and will to be free. Luke simply will not stay under, he escapes and he's brought back. He escapes again, and he's brought back and unbelievably brutalized. And still again he escapes. In the process he becomes a legend and an inspiration to the other men in the camp who live vicariously through the rebellion of Luke.

The performances are excellent. Newman seems perfectly suited to his role as Luke, although for the first half of the film he does appear somewhat one-dimensional. Supporting him in interesting roles are George Kennedy, J. D. Cannon and Jo Van Fleet.

It is beautifully filmed on location. Conrad Hall, cinematographer, has captured the closeness, the heat and the underlying violence of the chain gang with his camera.

Unfortunately the final impact of the picture is somewhat marred by a superfilous ending montage of still photographs of Cool Hand Luke, supposedly underscoring Luke's ultimate triumph, but actually only serving to under-rate the audience's intelligence.

However, this film is definitely interesting to watch and fascinating to figure out. It is commenting on almost every human emotion and trait known.

LUKE (Paul Newman) keeps a wary eye out for the Bossman.

KRLA ARCHIVES

THE BEAT — Page 18 — September 23, 1967

Beat Poster Shop

 (B)    (M)

 (N)    (O)

 (P)    (Q)

Send To: BEAT POSTER SHOP, 9121 Sunset Blvd., Los Angeles, Calif. 90069
PLEASE SEND ME THE FOLLOWING POSTERS (LIST BY LETTER) _____
I ENCLOSE $1.75 plus .25 Handling for each*.
Name _____
Address _____
City _____ State _____ Zip Code _____
*California Residents Please Include 5% Sales Tax

AVAILABLE IN THESE PATTERNS:
A. Hearts and Flowers
B. Psychedelic Buttons and Designs
C. Psychedelic Alphabets and Designs
D. Psychedelic Phreaquies

Mail To: BEAT PUBLICATIONS
9121 Sunset Blvd., Los Angeles, Calif. 90069

Circle Sheet Desired   A   B   C   D
Send me _____ sheets Mod-Bod stick-on
(4 psychedelic sheets available at $1 each)
Name _____
Address _____
City _____ State _____
California residents add 5% sales tax.
Stick on everything, waterproof, reuseable.

SPECIAL OFFER TO BEAT READERS!!

AUTHENTIC **MONKEESHADES** by DEBS
- 5 Groovy Colors: rose, yellow, blue, grey, green
- Heavy Mod Golden Chain
- Just Like the MONKEES Wear On Their Swingin' TV Show
- MONKEESHADES are the Wildest!!

ONLY $2 PLUS .25 HANDLING CHARGE
Send to: MONKEESHADES, 9121 Sunset Blvd., Los Angeles, California 90069
PLEASE SEND ME THE MONKEESHADES AS INDICATED. I ENCLOSE $2.00 FOR EACH PR.
COLOR _____ NO. PAIRS _____ TOTAL AMOUNT ENCLOSED _____
Name _____
Address _____
City _____ State _____ Zip Code _____
California Residents Please Include 5% Sales Tax

24 ORIGINAL HAPPENING HITS

As Advertised Nationally on Radio & TV

- **I Think We're Alone Now:** Tommy James & The Shondells
- **Kind Of A Drag:** The Buckinghams
- **Cherry Cherry:** Neil Diamond
- **Turn Down Day:** The Cyrkle
- **Jenny Take A Ride:** Mitch Ryder & Detroit Wheels
- **My Little Red Book:** Love
- **Wooly Bully:** Sam The Sham
- **But It's Alright:** J.J. Jackson
- **Little Girl:** Syndicate Of Sound
- **See You In September:** The Tempos
- **Daddy's Home:** Shep & The Limelighters
- **Why Do Fools Fall In Love:** Frankie Lyman
- **Western Union:** Five Americans
- **Sunny:** Bobby Hebb
- **Daydream:** Lovin' Spoonful
- **Good Lovin':** Young Rascals
- **I Got You Babe:** Sonny & Cher
- **Pushin' Too Hard:** The Seeds
- **Land Of 1000 Dances:** Wilson Pickett
- **Younger Girl:** The Critters
- **I Who Have Nothing:** Terry Knight & The Pack
- **Bermuda:** Four Seasons
- **Gee:** The Crows
- **Maybe:** The Chantels

$1.95 BEAUTIFUL FOUR COLOR JACKET
$4.00 FOR 2 ALBUMS
PLUS 50¢ MAILING (INCLUDES MAILING)

24 Happening Hits
9125 Sunset Blvd.
Los Angeles, California 90069
I enclose $ _____ for _____ albums.
NAME: _____
ADDRESS: _____
CITY: _____ STATE: _____
California Residents Please Include 5% Sales Tax

SPEC-TRIM SUNGLASSES

UNIQUE SHADOW BOX FRAMES
MOD RECESSED LENSES
TWO-COLOR FRAMES
$4 EACH*

*California Residents please add 5% sales tax

AVAILABLE IN:
Blue and White   White and Pink
Purple and White Red and White
Yellow and Black Red and Black
Designate Frame Color

SEND TO:
BEAT PUBLICATIONS
9121 Sunset Blvd.
Hollywood, Calif. 90069

DEBS

Portable Radio — Phonograph
- 2 Speed Record Player
- 7 Transistor Radio
- 3" Speaker

90 Day Unconditional Parts Guarantee
$19.95—California Residents Add 5% Sales Tax ($1)

Send To:
BEAT PHONOGRAPH
9121 Sunset Blvd.
Los Angeles, Calif. 90069

TURNING ON

SPANKY AND OUR GANG (Mercury) *Sunday Will Never Be The Same, Distance, Jet Plane* and nine other tracks. This is totally different from anything else today. Spanky and Our Gang harmonize beautifully and this record contains some of the cleverest arrangements to be found anywhere. The album includes their hit *Sunday Will Never Be The Same* but its primary interest lies with the new original material and adaptations. *Trouble* from Meredith Willson's *Music Man* is great; it combines marvelous humor with the proper amount of irony for today. In *5 Definitions of Love* the group gives an almost ominous quality to this semi-madrigal about the Webster Dictionary definitions. Perhaps the best cut on the album is *Brother Can You Spare a Dime* in which Spanky sings solo. Her voice seems to be a combination of Gracie Slick from the Airplane and Barbra Streisand.

COUNTRY MY WAY (Reprise) Nancy Sinatra. *Jackson, Lonely Again, End of the World* plus nine other tracks. Nancy sounds as good on this album as she ever does. It is well produced and contains a fine choice of songs. If you are a Nancy Sinatra fan this album will be of interest, otherwise it really doesn't have much to offer. She sings the ballads extremely well, especially *End of the World* and her producer Lee Hazelwood joins her for *Oh Lonesome Me* and their hit *Jackson*.

HELL'S ANGELS ON WHEELS (Smash) Original sound track album. This soundtrack which includes a vocal by the Poor was written by Stu Philips. Although this album backs up the movie "Hell's Angels On Wheels," the music is not terribly exciting. It seems rather tame for the subject, and no really interesting musical styles are used. You have heard this album before many times.

SILVER THROAT (Warner Bros.) Bill Cosby Sings. *Little Ole Man, I Got a Woman, Baby, What You Want Me to Do* plus nine other tracks. Bill Cosby is probably one of the most talented men around. A fine comic and a sensitive dramatic actor, there seems little this man couldn't do if he put his mind to it. Unfortunately in singing, Cosby may have met his Waterloo. The material is excellent, running from standard blues songs to funny campy songs, however, although Cosby is fine singing the comic *Little Ole Man*, he is out of his element singing *Big Boss Man* or *Bright Lights, Big City*. Although the album cover reads soul, there is not much soul in evidence. The arrangements are excellent and the harmonica player is almost worth the whole album, but Cosby, as wonderful as he is, should stick to something other than singing. However, the record will undoubtedly be a big hit.

RICHOCHET (Liberty) The Nitty Gritty Dirt Band. *Happy Fat Annie, Call Again, Truly Right* and nine other tracks. This is an interesting group which you will either really like or not at all. They are reminiscent of the 20's but not to the extent of the New Vaudeville Band. Fine musicians, their arrangements are intricate and unusual.

A Psychedelic Art Gallery In Your Home!

THE BIG RED COLORING BOOK

Paint 'Em Yourself!   *Ten Posters*

Each $1.50

These ten, big, all-different posters by psychedelic artist John Powers were made for you to color in just the way you want. You can frame them, hang them on your walls, beautify your room!

BEAT Publications, 9121 Sunset Blvd., Los Angeles, California 90069
Please send me _____ Big Red Coloring Books. I enclose $1.50 plus $.25 for handling*
Name _____
Address _____
City _____ State _____ Zip Code _____
*California Residents please include 5% Sales Tax

September 23, 1967 — THE BEAT

CLASSIFIED

please send me **BEAT**

26 issues only

$3 per year

Mail to: **BEAT Publications**
9121 Sunset Blvd.
Los Angeles, California 90069

☐ New Subscription
☐ Renewal (please enclose mailing label from your last BEAT)
I want BEAT for ☐ 1 year at $3.00 or ☐ 2 years at $5.00
I enclose ☐ cash ☐ check ☐ money order
Outside U.S.—$9 per year

* Please print your name and address.

Name_____

Street_____

City_____

State_____ Zip_____

THE GRAVEN IMAGE LIVE!
Dedicated to RON and BROWN EYES: one stadium co-chairman "Save the Grass Committee" Chicago and Y'zoo
DELAWARE
Join THE MUSEUM Fan Club. Send an S.A.E. to MUSEUM Fan Club, N. K. Jones, 258 So. Oaklnd, Villa Park, Ill. 60181
Hire THE MUSEUM Curator—Bill Kushner
Jagger Grooves!! So true, so true
Joey Robb Happy 20th Karan (San Jose Robbs Fan Club)
Welcome to the world JASON STARKEY
superjohnan'georgealisticespaulala-ringo
Peter Noone, you little devil, I love you
A big birthday message! HAPPY BIRTHDAY, MOLLY—"roinuJ"
BRIAN EPSTEIN IN MEMORIAM
Catch the rain!
Bobby—sunshine, flowers and happiness is our *future* Love, Joy
Freedom Seekers: join PROJECT HILL
Stevie: remember the Warwick? Frodo lives. Love, Dianne
Happy Birthday Craig Robb! Love Carol
Cindy and Gary Loving Hics
THE WORLD WELCOMES YOU, JASON STARKEY!
Leo is Luv for Nancy
THE GROWIN' CONCERN played at George and Martha's last night.
THE COMMON MARKET loves their dog!!!
Happy Birthday to Holgar Emanuel Johnson . . . Us
Happy birthday to L.L.J. Love Sara
I LOVE JAMES PAUL McCARTNEY SARA JANE JOHNSON
Davy Jones is Slumgut
We like Tom Murphy's legs!
Monkees are only Status Seekers
BEATEFUL AMERICA FOREVER
johnpaulgeorgeringo yeahyeahyeah
Monkee fans hang from trees
We all luv ya, Jon-Jon of the **BUCKINGHAMS**
Happy birthday Freddy Weller
Happiness is Don and the Goodtime—Buzzy!

Happy birthday Papa John, Love, Michelle
Beatles? Four delightfully talented gentlemen, who wear their success well!!
I LOVE PAUL
Hey Dan—Remember Lake Tahoe and THE VELVET CHAIN? Please call soon, ok. Sue
Tufty is a FLICKted
Haight not Hate
Happy belated birthday, Ringo LOVE and PEACE
Happy birthday Beve, John N, John H
Reach Cosmic Awareness without drugs—help save mankind from destruction. Write for free booklet, "Cosmic Awareness Speaks," Servants of Awareness, Box 115E, Olympia, Washington
Sleep Learning, self-hypnosis. Details, strange, free catalogue. Nutosuggestion, Box 24-BT, Olympia, Washington
Clyde the Dragon has Cool
Kipper's Back John Bless Her Kandy
I love you, Judy Carne — John Lindsey
BEATLES—FLOWERS MONKEES—WEEDS
I love Midniters and Beatles
John - Perry - Jim - Pil and Tim Create Eigin Marble Power
Happy Birthmark madlennon m'luv
Happy Birthday, Don — *luv* Barbara
Rob Turner plus Chris Hill
David Littlejohn, I love you . . . Lori Burdon
Ann, Gayle, Sharon, Cheryl—four girls who can and will explode!!
Kevin, thanks for the two wonderful weeks, and I'll be back next summer for sure! Love, Sharon
"The Explosive exploration goes on!!
Jackie and Sue, from west Phily, remember David Crockett from Atlantic City
I had a dream about Mark
Raiders—come back! San Jose
McCartney is all man! Nancy
Claire Repella: Happy Birthday! from the phantom hedgehog
I love the lead guitarist of the flipside — J. S.
John Lennon, did you mean what you said in London? I did. C.
Deuce is wilde whip!!
Neal Ford's fanatics groove

Monkees are "Roobish" Beatles Rule
Monkees: masterminded by money minded for mini-minded!
BEATLES RULE
Ralph Plumber is bitchen
Blue persuaders
Dave Clark says Rich McWilliams of The Museum swings
Poet Bruce E. Really likes Judy B. How about that
"A NEW THING" Soul it! Art Maeda, Mike Shirai, Randy Yoshimoto, Bill Ohno, Nic and Al Fred. Long Beach fans.
KRLA'S NEW POLICY STINKS
Brenda—Our time will come, I'll love you always—Bryan
Psychedelic Love
Petunia Love Thumper
HAPPINESS IS THE ASSOCIATION
Wibbage Charges—groovey
Soul for Sale call king of Soul MANARD luv Carroll
David Crosby Happy late Birthday I'm sorry I forgot, Glenda Stephanie . . .
Congratulations to Wm. and Maureen Shears!!
Wake up Mely, somebody loves you. Can't it be like it was? That somebody is me! Bonnie
Wanted: Brian Bucher's draft notice—will gladly take his place, *if* Uncle Sam wants him. Lyn Bastien
P. S. Badly is going places — but where.
Tell the world nice guy Charlie is in Hartford—Brenda
Mike: Texas made ripples but England still rules the waves.
Happy birthday Diane — Luv El
Sonny and Cher are quixotically independent
The Museum is Chicago's greatest group
Chris of "The Museum" is the greatest
TOAD IS OUTASITE!!!!
Happy birthday Mama CASS
SUNSHINE COMPANY REIGHN
To Tony Foley Happy 15th Birthday September 18th
Rolling Stone Posters 2½ ft by 3 ft. $1.75 postpaid Seper Co. 5273 Tendilla, Woodland Hills, California
Frank Converse is Boss! Signed The Blue Coronet

NATIONAL TOP 25 SINGLES

1. ODE TO BILLIE JOE .... Bobby Gentry
2. REFLECTIONS .... The Supremes
3. BABY, I LOVE YOU .... Aretha Franklin
4. THE LETTER .... Box Tops
5. ALL YOU NEED IS LOVE .... The Beatles
6. COME BACK WHEN YOU GROW UP ... Bobby Vee
7. APPLE, PEACHES, PUMPKIN PIE
   .... Jay & The Techniques
8. YOU'RE MY EVERYTHING .... The Temptations
9. LIGHT MY FIRE .... The Doors
10. COLD SWEAT .... James Brown
11. PLEASANT VALLEY SUNDAY ...... The Monkees
12. WORDS .... The Monkees
13. THANK THE LORD FOR THE NIGHT TIME
    .... Neil Diamond
14. SAN FRANCISCAN NIGHTS .... Eric Burdon
14. FAKIN' IT .... Simon & Garfunkel
16. THERE IS A MOUNTAIN .... Donovan
17. FUNKY BROADWAY .... Wilson Pickett
18. TESTIFY .... The Parliaments
19. YOU KNOW WHAT I MEAN .... The Turtles
20. SILENCE IS GOLDEN .... The Tremeloes
21. I HAD A DREAM .... Paul Revere
23. 12:30 .... Mamas & Papas
22. HIGHER & HIGHER .... Jackie Wilson
24. HEROES AND VILLAINS .... Beach Boys
25. THE WORLD WE KNEW .... Frank Sinatra

As Compiled by Cashbox Magazine

Beat is no longer accepting anything but PERSONAL MESSAGES in the classified section. Only messages (including Happy Birthdays) will be run. We will print names but not addresses or phone numbers. Rates are cheap! Only 10 cents per word.

Rates are cheap! Only 10 cents per word.
And remember, BEAT has a new address:

**Classified
BEAT Publications
9121 Sunset Blvd.
Los Angeles 90069**

Deadline for next issue: Sept. 12

KRLA ARCHIVES

Acapulco, here you come!

Look for this display in your market. It could mean an Acapulco vacation for you and a friend. There'll be plenty of winners in our Acapulco Sweepstakes. The prizes—a week for two at one of Acapulco's swingingest hotels. And the two-way trip on Western Airlines. There's nothing to do. Just enter. Go to your market and find out the details. So, get ready for Acapulco!

KRLA ARCHIVES

BEATLES SET FOR WORLD-WIDE TV

25¢

KRLA *Edition* BEAT

OCTOBER 7, 1967

UPI Photo

ANIMAL CAUGHT AT HIPPIE WEDDING

KRLA BEAT

Volume 3, Number 15   October 7, 1967

BEATLES SET FOR WORLD TELEVISION

By Tony Barrow

LONDON — The Beatles have postponed their Odyssey To India in order to complete an hour-long color television special. They will not leave for the Orient before the first week in October.

The boys expect to return to England a few weeks before Christmas after a period of meditation studies under Maharishi Mahesh Yogi.

The theme song for the special, "Magical Mystery Tour," has already been written by John and Paul, and they are currently composing at least four other songs for the show.

Reports indicate that the music will be released either as a series of singles or as an EP disc and not on a full-length LP.

The Beatles are anxious that the special be screened during the Christmas period on a world-wide basis.

The Magical Mystery Tour is a replacement for a previously planned special which was to center around the "Sgt. Pepper" album. There is a possibility that some of the "Sgt. Pepper" material will be included in sequences of the "Mystery Tour."

BEATLES postpone Indian trip

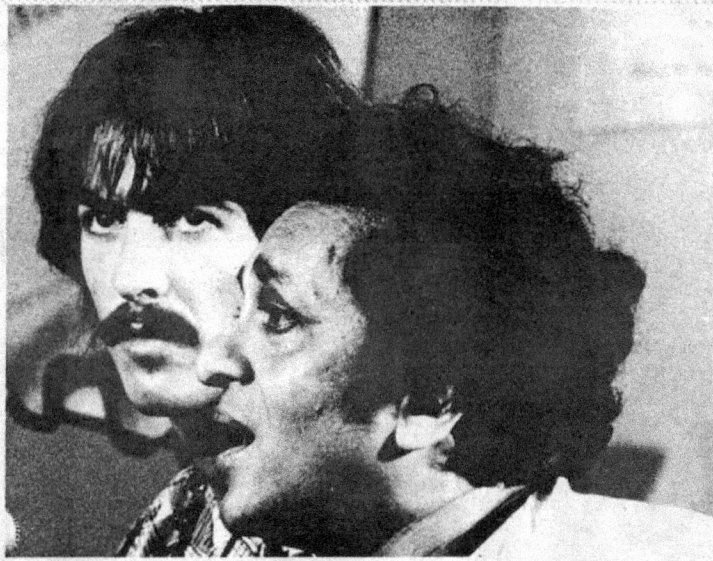

GEORGE HARRISON DRESSES rather like a hippie but says that "they're hypocrites."

Beatle George States Hippies 'Hypocrites'

LONDON — George Harrison's recent trip to the hippie homeland of Haight-Ashbury has left the Beatle with a surprising and unexpected bitter taste. In an interview shortly after his journey to San Francisco, George described many of the Hippies he met as hypocrites who were too hung up on LSD and other drugs to really be hip.

George revealed that he was continually being offered LSD and STP during his short stay in Haight, but refused to take any of it.

"LSD isn't the answer. It doesn't give you anything," he said. "It enables you to see a lot of possibilities that you might never have noticed before, but it isn't the answer."

George described the true hippie as one who knows what's going on and doesn't need LSD or other drugs.

"There was the bit where people were so out of their minds trying to shove STP on me and acid, but I didn't want to know about it. I want to get high and you can't get high on LSD."

Harrison added that he could, and would rather, get high from the practice of yoga and meditation, which he has taken up along with the other Beatles.

In an unusual disclosure, George said he had never deliberately taken acid, but one day before LSD became the subject of everyday conversation someone slipped the drug in the Beatles coffee. "I'm not embarrassed. It makes no difference because I didn't actually go out and try to get some."

Haight-Ashbury is a lot like the Bowery, George said, largely because of the great number of beggars who inhabit the hippie haven.

"These people are hypocrites," George said. "They are making fun of tourists and all that, and at the same time, they are holding their hands out begging off them. That's what I don't like."

'SMOTHERS BROS.' UPSET CENSORS

Once again the Smothers Bros. are deep in controversy. CBS censors have objected to folk singer Pete Seegers' song called "Waist Deep in the Big Muddy." Seeger was set to sing this song on the opening night show aired in September.

CBS agreed to let the folk singer record the song and then after viewing the tape, the station's censors would determine its merits. CBS ruled that the song might be "politically controversial" and anti-Vietnam.

Black Listed

Pete Seeger has been unofficially "blacklisted" (a word which the networks deny exists) for the past 16 years. However, a network spokesman said the ban had nothing to do with the singer only the songs.

"The feeling was it was not the artist, but the content of the song that might open up an equal time situation, as a partisan statement." He went on to add that the material might be considered politically controversial, something the network seeks to avoid in entertainment programs.

Although neither the Vietnam conflict nor the Johnson administration is mentioned in the tune, the network spokesman said they felt "it was anti-Vietnam and bitterly anti-administration."

Minus Mud

Seeger was shown on the program, minus his "Big Muddy" song. In its place, the singer offered "Where Have All The Flowers Gone" which is also an anti-war song, but apparently CBS did not find this one to be controversial.

Last season, the Smothers Bros. show received quite a bit of notoriety as the most controversial show on the air, and the two brothers were continually getting into debates with the network over the content of their show.

Tom and Dick Smothers, often called "the naughty nice boys," have fought with the network censors since their variety show first came on the air last season.

"Every show is compromises and deletions," a disgusted Tommy once told The BEAT. "I was never aware that freedom of expression and personal opinions are really limited."

TOMMY & DICKIE SMOTHERS are back fighting network censors

Rascals Top Belafonte

HONOLULU—It was reported that Harry Belafonte grossed $86,000 in six performances. The last weekend was played to standing room only crowds.

However, Doolittle announced that he did not make any clear profit due to transportation and rent costs.

This gave promoter James Doolittle his highest grossing act except for the Young Rascals who managed to pull in $70,000 for only two performances.

KRLA ARCHIVES

across the BOARD

THEN: 15 YEARS AGO the Everly Brothers were singing with their mother and father on live radio. "Grand Ole Opery" presented the Everly Family singing country favorites.

ZAL YANOVSKY ecstatic over his new contract with Buddah records. Buddah will present Zally's first solo after leaving the Lovin' Spoonful.

NOW: EVERLY BROTHERS sing with their parents for the first time in 15 years. The event took place on the Mike Douglas Show. The appearance of Margaret and Ike Everly came as a complete surprise to their sons. Also pictured are Mike Douglas and Totie Fields.

LONG HAIR on rock and roll singers has long been popular. But this is something new. Smokey Roberts of THE PARADE as he appears in makeup for Twentieth Century Fox's multimillion dollar epic, "Planet of the Apes" (above). A much more natural Smokey (left) as he really is.

PEOPLE ARE TALKING ABOUT *Bobbie Gentry* making it all the way to number one just going to show that occasionally something different will sell . . . "Reflections" being a smash despite the fact that it sounds the same as their others . . . how good it is that "Heroes And Villians" is a hit because what would *Brian Wilson* do after spending all that time and money if it wasn't . . . how fantastic it is that *Neil Diamond* can come up with hit after hit when he gets no publicity to speak of.

. . . The fact that food sells, just ask *Jay and the Techniques* . . . the *Association* being around a long, long time because if they cease to make it as singers they can turn into writers . . . the bets being taken on how many times "Groovin' " will be a hit . . . whether or not *Peter, Paul and Mary* are switching bags . . why the *Mitchell Trio* doesn't release "Cindy's Cryin' " . . . whatever happened to that big announcement *Tommy James* was supposed to make . . . *Lewis* and *Clark* getting some very clever publicity from their record company.

. . . *Bill Cosby* turning singer being fair play since so many singers feel compelled to turn actors . . . how big *Jimi Hendrix* is going to be . . . people allegedly paying up to $100 to get a good table for *Dean Martin's* Vegas' stint . . . why *Simon and Garfunkel* refuse to give out interviews . . . the fact that if *George Harrison* hadn't pulled out a guitar and started singing no one would have recognized him since he looked just like

another hippie . . . how many unknown groups exist in the United States alone and what it takes to make it big . . . what's happening to *Frankie Valli's* "I Make A Fool Of Myself" . . . how long *Elvis Presley* is going to be around and judging from how long he's already been here another ten years would be an accurate guess.

. . . Why *Tom Jones* hasn't turned into the super-star he should have . . . whether the *Stones* have won or lost . . . *Spanky and Our Gang* making sure that every minute counts . . . why all the national magazines are spending so much time on the hippies . . . what's become of *Brian Jones* . . . the *Young Rascals* being very big in Hawaii . . . how long it's been for *Bobby Vee* . . . whatever happened to *Bobby Rydell* . . . ditto for *Freddy Cannon* . . . *Van Morrison* being one person who has become better off by going solo.

. . . The *Harpers* being right about "Anything Goes" . . . *Herman's* visit to the museum not taking of as fast and far as they thought it would . . . even Sir not being able to help *Lulu* make it big Stateside and wondering why . . .

Beat Publications, Inc.

Executive Editor .... Cecil I. Tuck
Publisher .... Gayle Tuck
Editor .... Louise Criscione
Assistant Editor .... Greg Kieselmann
Staff Writers
Jacoba Atlas   Bobby Farrow
Ron Koslow   Shirley Poston
Contributing Writers
Tony Barrow   Sue Barry
Lawrence Charles   Eden
Bob Levinson   Jamie McCluskey, III
Photographers
Ed Caraeff
Howard L. Bingham   Jerry Haas
Advertising
Sam Chase   Dick Stricklin
Business Manager .... Judy Felice
Subscriptions .... Diane Clatworthy
Distribution
Miller Freeman Publications
500 Howard Street, San Francisco, Calif. The BEAT is published bi-weekly by BEAT Publications, Inc., editorial and advertising offices at 9121 Sunset Blvd., Los Angeles, California 90069. U.S. bureaus in Hollywood, San Francisco, New York, Chicago and Nashville; overseas correspondents in London, Liverpool and Manchester, England. Sale price 25 cents. Subscription price: U.S. and sessions $5 per year; Canada and foreign rates, $9 per year. Second class postage prepaid at Los Angeles, California.

KRLA ARCHIVES

AROUND the WORLD

THE BATTLE IS ON: Sinatra vs. the Sands Hotel (Howard Hughes?)

SINATRA EXITS LAS VEGAS WITH FISTS AND TEETH

Sinatra's exit from the Las Vegas nightclub The Sands was marked with a fist fight, two lost teeth, and heated words.

It climaxed an uproarious weekend long tirade by the singer against the hotel's managements, employees and security forces, guests said.

Blow Struck

The blow was struck by Sands vice president, Carl Cohen, who reportedly struck the performer after Sinatra had unleashed a stream of abuse at the hotel's owner in a local restaurant.

Almost immediately, the singer announced his new allegiance to The Caesar's Palace with a three year contract.

This culminated a week long battle with The Sands that began by Sinatra bowing out of an engagement with what was reported as being a "sore throat." Speculation at that time, however, noted that the singer was negotiating to defect to Caesars Palace because Howard Hughes wouldn't buy his Cal-Neva Lodge on the north shore of Lake Tahoe.

Sinatra at one time had held a small interest in The Sands Hotel, his steady Las Vegas place of engagement for the last 16 years, but sold off his share after he was found guilty of associating with an underworld figure.

Sand Pile

One guest reported Sinatra as saying, "I built this hotel from a sand pile and before I'm through that's what it will be again."

Sinatra's new allegiance has led to speculation that the singers close friends, such as Sammy Davis Jr., and Dean Martin would also make the switch from The Sands to Caesars Palace.

Rawls In Wrong Show Business

Lou Rawls' tune, "Show Business" has come up for a plagiarism suit. Irving Berlin Music Company has complained to Capitol's legal department charging that the Rawls song has come too close to the original Berlin tune.

Objection was to several similarities in the lyrics, the most pointed being a variation of the "There's No Business Like . . ." line, according to Capitol's attorney Bob Carp.

Capitol has agreed to the demands, and has made plans to delete the line from the album "That's Lou."

Berlin is reported satisfied with Capitol's decision.

THERE MAY BE 'no business like show business' but for Lou Rawls it should read no business in Berlin's 'Show Business.'

PAUL NEWMAN

Paul, Shirley Stars Of Year

Shirley MacLaine and Paul Newman have been selected as 'Stars of the Year" by the National Association of Theatre Owners. President Sherrill C. Corwin reported that the awards will be presented on October 20, the closing day of the Association's four-day conference in Florida.

Corwin also announced that NATO will present its first Walt Disney award at the banquet. This honor will be conferred on "the individual who has made the greatest contribution to the integrity, excellence and imagery of the motion picture industry."

Entertainers Aid Humphrey

Frank Sinatra is donating his performing services and those of his daughter Nancy, Dean Martin, Milton Berle, and the Fifth Dimension to Vice President Hubert Humphrey's Citizens for Johnson-Humphrey Committee of the Minnesota Farmer Labor Party "Evening of Stars" benefit show to raise campaign funds.

This show will not cost the FLP a penny other than transportation for those performers coming from parts other than California. Those performers who are coming from California will travel with Sinatra in his own jet plane sans cost.

Seating capacity will be around 10,000 at tickets scaled from $5 to $100. It has been reported that other than a short speech by Vice President Humphrey at the close of the show there will be no politics discussed.

British Leader Sues 'Move' For Postcard

LONDON—British Prime Minister Harold Wilson has sued a pop music group called "The Move" as a result of a satirical postcard put out by the singers. The card, which Wilson says libels him, shows him sitting nude on a bed.

Walt Disney Is Honored

WASHINGTON, D.C. — The Senate passed by voice vote a bill authorizing the striking of a gold medal honoring Walt Disney. The legislation now goes to the House for approval.

The measure, sponsored by Senator George Murphy, Republican from California, sets aside $3,000 for this medal and authorizes the making of up to 100,000 bronze replicas which will be paid for by the Disney endowed California Institute of the Arts.

Long Hair OK In NY Schools

TRENTON, N.J. — The New York State Board of Education has ruled that local school boards can't tell students how long they can wear their hair.

Earlier in the year, a former Education Commissioner upheld the expulsion of Francis Pelletreau, a 15-year-old freshman, from New Milford High School for refusing to cut his Beatle-style hair.

In its unanimous decision, the state school board ordered the high school to reinstate Pelletreau for the fall term.

SEAN CONNERY

New Image For Connery

Sean Connery is finally making a break with his James Bond image. The actor has stated that he will no longer play the super-spy in movies, and has just signed to play opposite French actress Brigitte Bardot in a film called "Shalako."

The director will be Edward Dmytrk, and will open on September 10, 1968. The film will be made for ABC subsidiary, Palomar and Pictures.

KRLA ARCHIVES

BEATLES' MAGIC MYSTERY TOUR

By Tony Barrow

There was a little bit of private and personal nostalgia for The Beatles when they set off in their chartered bus to begin shooting "Magical Mystery Tour," their created, self-scripted, self-directed and self-produced color TV special.

The bus, a grand looking yellow and blue vehicle with luminous posters glaring out from its sides and rear, departed from Allsopplace, a little side street close to London's famous Baker-street, Tussaud's Waxworks and the Planetarium. Allsop1place is, by tradition, the departure point for groups setting out on one-nightstand pop tours. It must be all of four years since The Beatles traveled the roads and motorways of Britain in a bus—but way back in the early part of 1963 when they went out on concert tours with stars like Tommy Roe, Chris Montez and Roy Orbision, it was at the Allsop-place that the whole show assembled on the first morning.

The Beatles have been thinking about the "Magical Mystery Tour" project for the best part of five months. As far back as April 25 they began recording the title number for the show. It was their first session since the completition of the last "Sgt. Pepper" album track.

Beatles TV Special

"Magical Mystery Tour" will contain at least three new Beatle compositions apart from the title song. One of the others may well be George Harrison's "Blue Jay Way" a piece written in Los Angeles a few weeks ago when George made his August trip to California for Ravi Shankar's Hollywood Bowl concert.

The entire hour-long TV special will be completed no later than the first week of October. The Beatles have set themselves this deadline in order to leave for India prior to John's 27th birthday on October 9. They will be in the East for two months returning to London shortly before Christmas—the time when "Magical Mystery Tour" is likely to have its first screening on British television.

Flower Wedding

Jimi Hendix wrote "The Burning of the Midnight Lamp" in flight between New York and Los Angeles . . . Mike Jagger and Keith Ricard have written a 16-minute track for The Stones' next album . . . Englebert Humperdinck (Number One in the U.S. with "The Last Waltz") is to star in "Robinson Crusoe," the London Palladium's four-month pantomime production opening December 19 . . . Expect U.S. release of two new singles by The Bee Gees in quick succession . . . "London's First Wedding of the Flower Children"—that's how the press described the Caxton Hall register office marriage of Eric Burdon and model Angie King on Thursday, September 7 . . . Pre-Monkee singles out in U.K. from Micky Dolenz "Huff Pull" and Davy Jones ("Theme for a New Love").

Every teen mag in the world carries 'gossip' and 'scoop' stories about the Beatles. So does this page of The Beat. The difference is that only the true facts appear here. Far too many magazines rely upon building up and then knocking down their own fictitious Beatle rumors—which makes for a lot of sensational copy-selling headlines but leaves the reader confused by such a made mass of unreliable stories!

Keith West, star of the London-based group called Tomorrow, has had fantastic chart success in the U.K. and all thru Europe with his self-penned "Excerpt From a Teen-age Opera." West hopes to promote this and the follow-up via a brief visit to America at the of October.

"Davy and I often giggle about them", said Australian songstress Lynne Randell when required to comment on newspaper romance stories linking her with the name of Davy Jones. She went on: "I'm honestly surprised Day is still such a nice, straight-forward person. He's so friendly he immediately puts people at ease. The first time we met I felt I'd known him for ages."

Ringo Solo

Their own London recording studio to be built and furnished for the Beatles . . . Ringo Starr has said many times that he is interested in the idea of making a solo movie appearance if the right screen-play is presented to him. Most interesting offer yet is under his consideration right now . . . "Gettin' Hungry" by Brian Wilson and Mike Love out in U.K. via Capitol label.

John Lennon's younger fans cannot attend public showings of "How I Won The War" in U.K. because movie has an "X" certificate barring all under-sixteens. So Official Fan Club, trying to find a loophole in the law, wants to organize private screenings for holder of membership cards regardless of their age.

"Top of the Pops" TV girl Samantha Juste away from program because of illness for an extra two weeks after her return from California . . . Prime Minister Harold Wilson has, in effect, given the Move more national newspaper publicity than any PRO could have mustered — by suing the group for alleged libel over a postcard which showed a drawing of Wilson in the nude!

Mothers Appearance

For only U.K. concert appearance of Mothers of Invention — on September 23 at London's Royal Albert Hall—top ticket price less than 4 dollars and lowest around 75 cents. In Melody Maker 1967 Pop Poll award for Musician of the Year to Cream's Eric Clapton, Single of the Year to Procol Harum's "A Whiter Shade of Pale", Album of the Year to "Sgt. Pepper's Lonely Hearts Club Band" . . . Offspring of Paul McCartney's cat Thisby named Jesus, Joseph and Mary.

SHOUTS FROM GENE

By Gene Cornish

Back again!! To talk about the trials, treasure, trappings and tribulations of Rascal-ing!

Did ya hear? We're making a movie—to be produced by our manager, Sid Bernstein. We start shooting April 1—and we end up in Hawaii about a month later . . . Eddie's out right now buying stars for our dressing room doors!

We're almost off to England by the time you read this: October 4-17. We'll be visiting the Beatles and performing—live and on British TV. Dino, the Edwardian of the group, is getting out all his Carnaby Street gear and using words like "Bird" and eating fish 'n chips every chance he gets . . . watch out, England, ready or not here we come!

My parents were with us on our last Hawaiian tour—Eddie's too. We had a great time on the "Island of Flowers"—and we're heading back very soon! (Eddie and Felix might even buy land there!)

Get set! Our newest 45 rpm is "How Can I Be Sure"—sung by Eddie, and "I'm Happy Now"—written by yours truly. We're hopin' for another million-Gold-Record-seller, just like "Groovin'!"

We're all excited—not only about the English tour—but being in Australia on January 20, 1968! And then our World-Wide Peace Tour, starting in February. We want to perform behind the Iron Curtain and bring the "New York Sound" to Russia!

Someone asked me what the Rascals do when they're not performing or traveling—Dino is a painter, sculptor and aspiring actor. He's designed many of our single and album covers, and the layout of our official program. Felix writes poetry and short stories—and reads everything! Eddie is a family man—just bought his mother and father a new home in Lincoln Park, New Jersey. And I'm producing a R 'n R group named the "Brass Buttons"—and trying to furnish an apartment—a year's work in itself!

We were traveling with the Byrds on our last tour—and we're all good friends now—they're great guys!

The newest things—and watch for 'um—are Rascals Official Programs (I mentioned that Dino designed it)—it's available at our concerts—and has some really groovy shots of we four! (There's one photograph we wanted to print, but couldn't—for some reason or other Eddie didn't want to be seen on a bear rug . . .)

"HOW CAN I BE SURE" for Ed Sullivan's 20th Anniversary Show.

HELP! STOP! BAD BREATH BODY ODORS

Now a new and effective aid in controlling offensive odors due to eating strong foods, excessive smoking or drinking, by taking a pleasant tasting chlorophyll tablet. 90% of all mouth and body odors originate in the stomach — don't rely on toothpaste, gum or mouth wash alone — be safe — be sure — don't offend. Order today.

100 day supply $3.00 — 200 day supply $5.00

Send check or money order to
Stops Vitamin Products
P. O. Box 6325
Hillcrest Station
Bakersfield, California 93306

10-day money back guarantee.

THE SEPER COMPANY
5273 Tendilla, Dept. T.O
Woodland Hills, Calif.

Hippie Shoulder Strap Bag - $2.00 P.P.

KRLA ARCHIVES

ON THE BEAT BY LOUISE CRISCIONE

The Association did not cop out! They opened at the prestige-packed Cocoanut Grove in Los Angeles and did *not* alter their stage act to include numerous show tunes aimed at making the adult crowd feel snug. Naturally, some of the older members of the press saw fit to give them mixed reviews for not including lots of "standards" in their act—but who cares? We thought it was fantastic!

Both the Supremes and the Four Tops bowed to the prestige of the room when they played the Grove by cutting down on their pop tunes and way up on the Broadway show tunes and standards. But the Association ought to get some sort of medal for probably being the *only* pop act to ever play a famous adult night club and NOT COP OUT!

Next Pop Festival

Some great news — Sid Bernstein, Rascals' manager, will be presenting the New York International Pop Festival during the latter part of June, 1968. All four of the Young Rascals will be sitting on the Board of Directors and reportedly Paul McCartney will again be active in the Festival preparations.

THE ASSOCIATION

Many of the mistakes at Monterey's Pop Festival will be corrected for New York. The biggest one being the whereabouts of the proceeds. Some of the entertainers who volunteered their services for Monterey were a bit upset by the fact that no one seemed to know exactly where the money would be going. However, this time the New York International Pop Festival will announce *beforehand* exactly which worthy cause will receive the money.

Sonny & Cher Square?

Times have really changed. Sonny and Cher, once thought of as the king and queen of the hippies, are now thought of by the hippies as total squares! The biggest reason being the denunciation of the use of drugs by Sonny. "You can turn yourself on by concentration," says Sonny, Who did so with the result being a solo album entitled "Innerviews."

"I'm afraid of what drugs' influence is on kids," admitted Sonny. "So I sat down and did it (the album) without them. It's not necessary to find new plateaus in music with artificial, external influences."

The Lewis and Clarke Expedition received a nice piece of pie by being signed to sing the title song for "TheTiger Makes Out" starring Eli Wallach and Anne Jackson. The group had previously composed and sang "Foul Owl On The Prowl" for the movie, "In The Heat Of The Night," starring Sidney Poitier.

Things are changing fast and furiously around the Motown stable. First it was the Supremes who received the new billing, Diana Ross and the Supremes. Now it's Martha who receives her dues . . . from now on it will be Martha Reeves and the Vandellas.

Teddy Neeley, who just never was able to snare a big hit record, may get his big break now. He's gone to New York to try out for the male lead in the upcoming Broadway musical, "East Of Eden," which is set to open in January, 1968.

Teddy To Solo

However, if Teddy doesn't get it he won't starve. He's set for a two-week engagement at the Cocoanut Grove in February. He'll be singing solo—no more Teddy Neeley Five.

Van Morrison, once the lead singer for Them, is shedding no tears over his decision to go solo—especially with "Brown Eyed Girl" such a smash. "In a group," says Van, "you first have to discuss it. Alone, if I dig it, I do it." One thing he's set to do is play the Whisky A Go Go on Sunset's Strip on October 9, 10 and 11.

Nice break for the Philly man, Bobby Rydell—he's been chosen to replace Michael Callan in "That Certain Girl," the musical now playing at the Thunderbird Hotel in Las Vegas.

QUESTION OF THE WEEK: Doesn't Don Ho own *all* of Hawaii by now?

SONNY & CHER

WITHOUT EPSTEIN TO GUIDE THEM, speculation is running high on Beatles' future.

BRIAN EPSTEIN'S DEATH IS RULED ACCIDENTAL OVERDOSE

By Tony Barrow

The news of Brian Epstein's tragic death led to an immediate storm of speculation about the future of his artists and his various pop empires—including the parent company NEMS Enterprises, Nempoeror Artists and Nemperor Music in New York, the Seville Theatre in London's West End and his assorted interests in music publishing, film making and tour promotion.

The truth is that whilst nobody —least of all his artists—believes that Brian can be replaced by any one new person, the general functioning of his corporations will continue with the minimum of change.

It is possible to rule out the idea that Brian's management of The Beatles, Cilla Black, Gerry Marsden and so forth might pass to outside parties. The Epstein family, including Brian's 31-year-old brother Clive who has become Chairman of NEMS Enterprises, continue to hold shares in the company. With those held by the Beatles the holding represents a substantial controlling interest which will not be influenced by external bids, British or American.

Quiet Funeral

So far as the artists are concerned, fresh personal managers will not be appointed. The Beatles, for example, will continue to seek the advice and support of all the various experts who have worked for and with them over the years. People like recording manager George Martin.

On the night of Brian's death a new series of 16 Sunday concerts at the Seville Theatre opened with Jimi Hendrix at the top of the bill. The series is continuing without a break—apart from the cancellation of the second performance on the opening night as a mark of respect to the Epstein family.

The Beatles did not attend Brian Epstein's Liverpool burial. At the time they stated their specific reason. The Epstein family wished to keep the funeral quiet and private and the Beatles were specifically requested to stay away so that those wishes could be carried out. On the other hand they spent most of the previous day visiting Mrs. Queenie Epstein, Brian's recently widowed mother, to offer sympathies and condolences.

At the inquest hearing Westminster Cororner Gavin Thruston recorded a verdict of accidental death caused by "an incautious self overdose" of the sleeping duo Carbrital.

Drug Build-Up

There was no evidence that the prescribed dose had been exceeded but there was the suggestion that there had been a gradual and untimely poisonous build-up of the drug's components within Epstein's body.

The Coroner stated: "The post mortem shows the cause of death was carbrital poisoning, the Pathologist, Dr. Tonal Teare, failed to find any drug other than this in his body in any way despite careful analysis. No alcohol was found but there was a trace of a mild tranquilizer. Any question of heroin or morphine or amphetamine can be completely excluded in this case. But his blood showed that he had been taking carbrital over a considerable period of time. His death was caused by a small fatal dose of this and not by a massive dose. He might have become careless or less cautious in taking sleeping capsules. Piecing together all the evidence we have a picture of a man who was sensitive, inclined to be anxious and who had a lot of trouble with sleeping."

Concrete Work

The Beatles' decision to postpone their projected September trip to India for transcendental meditation studies under Marharishi Mahesh Yogi was a clear indication of the group's unanimous desire to get some concrete work done before taking their two-month break. The result is that a full-scale TV Special — "Magical Mystery Tour" a number of new recordings and other immediate projects will be finished within the next week or so. This, in turn, means that at least one new single will be available for releases in Britain and America in either October or November while The Beatles are in India. They'll be home again early in December for further recording sessions scheduled to take place this side of Christmas.

"The Standel Sound"

"The Nitty Gritty Dirt Band"

Professional musicians throughout the world choose the "Standel Sound," the accepted standard for professional musicians who demand professional performance.
(Dept. 9)

A. P.A. Speaker Column Amplifier
B. P.A. Master Control with Reverb
C. Imperial Line Amplifier — Solid State, Dual Channel

Standel
Solid State Music Systems
4918 DOUBLE DRIVE • EL MONTE, CALIF. 91731

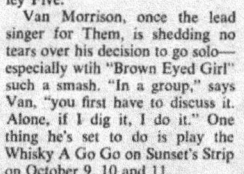
ART INSTITUTE OF PITTSBURGH
57th Yr. Coed. & 24 mo. Diploma Course. Commercial Art, Fashion Art, Interior Design, Begin. & Adv. Vet Appd. Dorm facilities. College referrals for degrees. Free illus. brochure.
Earl B. Wheeler, Director
635 Smithfield St.
Pittsburgh, Pa. 15222

Pet Makes Return To Childhood Job

By Bob Bovino

It's unbelievably hot at Warner Brothers studios on the set of "Finian's Rainbow" but Petula Clark is total cool as she explains her first major American motion picture as an adult actress.

"First of all there's marvelous music. Then, of course, the story. Well, it's really sort of a fairy tale but it's a fairy tale that suddenly comes down to earth. Let me start right from the beginning—Finian is kind of a mad Irishman, a dreamer, typical Irishmen. He drinks a little too much and believes in leprechauns, Irish fairies, and I'm his daughter. We leave Ireland and we go to the United States. You see, he has to leave Ireland, Finian, because he stole a pot of gold from a leprechaun.

Magic Place

"He thinks that Fort Knox is a magic place where gold multiplies and he believes that if he buries his gold in the ground near Fort Knox it will multiply.

"Well, I go along with him, now this is all very fairy like but we finish up in a place called Rainbow Valley in Missatucky, a mythical place in the deep south of America and we run into the racial problems and I get so mad at things that I see going on there that in a fit of Irish temper I wish the Senator black. And I happen to be standing over the pot of gold which is buried in the ground and my wish comes true!

"That's when the picture becomes very involved and very serious but it's a mixture of many, many things and it's very difficult for me to describe. It's a unique story and I think this will be a very extraordinary film."

Veteran Actress

Pet is far from a stranger to motion pictures, having already made 25. "Yes, I have made 25 pictures, that is to say you'll find my name on the cast list! In some of them I have very small roles. I started as a child actress and they kept me a child for a very long time because I was under contract to a film company in England and I was more valuable to the company as a child artist than as an adolescent artist. In fact," laughed Pet, "they used to bind my bosom in so that I would look younger and they made me wear pigtails and little white socks and all that stuff. I hated it of course.

"So, I made most of my pictures as a child artist. I made one or two which were all right. I made one picture with Alec Guiness and one with Peter Ustinov and some of them were good and some of them were pretty bad.

"I really like to look upon 'Finian's Rainbow' as my first movie because that's just how I feel about making it. I feel that nervous about it and I think it's that important. So, I'd rather forget the other 25 pictures if you don't mind."

It's more than difficult to keep two separate careers going at the same time and, therefore, an artist is often forced to choose between one or the other. Pet was first an actress, then a singer and now she's gone back to acting. Will she be forced to make the decision?

Going Together

" 'Finian's Rainbow' is a musical. So really I suppose I was chosen for 'Finian' because I can sing and so far my two careers are going together. I act, of course, in the film. Maybe I'll be able to tell you something about it next year because I've been offered a very dramatic part in a very hard, tough film—definitely not a family entertainment, a kind of a Julie Christie part and I haven't accepted it yet. But that would be something entirely new and quite separate from my singing career. I don't know if I can act, quite honestly, so for the moment I'm sticking to my singing really because I love it and I would hate to give it up."

Change Of Mind?

Those of you who still cling to the idea that making a movie is sheer glamor will certainly have to change your minds when you discover how Pet spends her days on the set.

"Well, I get up at the crack of dawn, at least that's what it feels like. I'm not used to getting up so early in the morning, I usually get up about 5:30 in the morning, sort of stagger into my clothes and somehow manage to drive to the studio without an accident so far, touch on wood, and I scoot along

PETULA DOES A BIT of the Irish jig with Fred Astaire while Tommy Steele looks on.

Does Petula find it difficult to act? "Yes, particularly in films because it's such an unnatural thing. You find yourself in unnatural surroundings and trying to be natural in unnatural circumstances is quite difficult. Although the part of Sharon in 'Finian's Rainbow' is sort of like me, I think, therefore I can really throw myself in a scene and I finish up doing it well without having to try because I just become me. I don't find playing Sharon too difficult. If I had to play Juliet I might find that difficult."

at a frantic speed and put on make-up, etc. The days are pretty long because of light. Francis likes to use natural light, he's our director, and that's what's making the picture so pretty because it's all done in natural light.

"But it also makes it quite difficult, we're shooting out of doors most of the time, and it's very hot. Usually when I get home there's something for me to do, I get home around seven, scrape my make-up off, take a shower and plunge into whatever else there is to be done. Then we have dinner with the children, our two little girls, (they're here with us because we wouldn't think of being away from them for so long) and then I sort of throw myself into bed."

Hard To Say

And how does Pet feel about settling down permanently in America? "It's a bit difficult to say because we don't have a home here. We live in other people's homes and so we rent houses or live in hotels and I don't think you can judge from that. I really only come to America when I have work to do so so far it's a bit difficult to say. Perhaps some day we will live here and have a home here.

"I would suppose that in things like comfort, home comforts and things like that, America would be superior to England and France in many ways but I don't know, I'm European. I think there will probably be more and more people like me in the future. One is either European or American — you know what I mean? I love being here, I'm not putting it down at all but it would be, I think, very difficult for me to really settle in America and know that it was forever."

It's not too terribly difficult to see how Pat remains so petite. Immediately following the wind-up of "Finian's Rainbow," she has scheduled a two week tour of Canada, a two month stay in London for a television series and concert dates and then it's back to America for a TV special, possibly another movie, Las Vegas, Lake Tahoe and perhaps even another concert tour sandwiched in there somewhere.

"FINIAN'S RAINBOW" is a fairy tale down to earth," says Pet.

"I DON'T FIND playing Sharon too difficult," admits Miss Clark.

"I'M EUROPEAN"

KRLA ARCHIVES

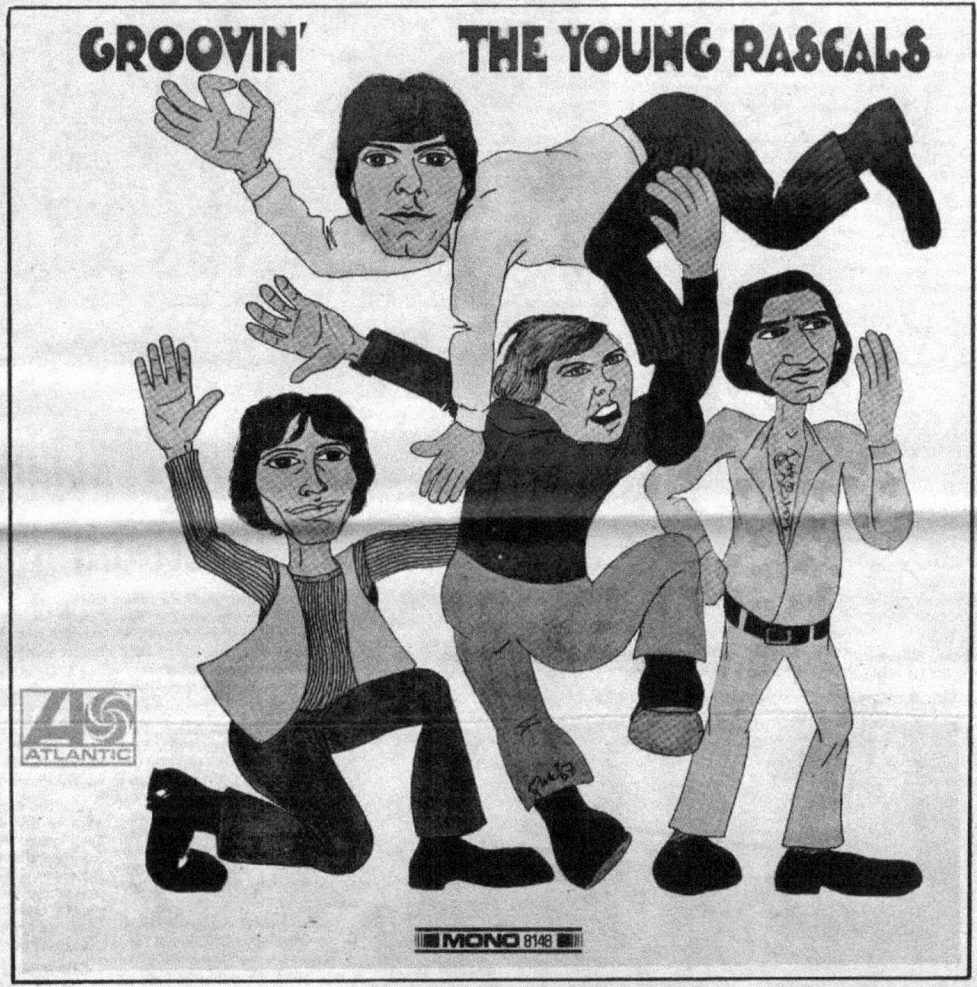

GROOVY!

GROOVIN' THE YOUNG RASCALS

ATLANTIC RECORDS 8148/SD 8148

A GIRL LIKE YOU · FIND SOMEBODY · I'M SO HAPPY NOW · SUENO
HOW CAN I BE SURE · GROOVIN' · IF YOU KNEW · I DON'T LOVE YOU ANYMORE
YOU BETTER RUN · A PLACE IN THE SUN · IT'S LOVE

Available in Mono & Stereo

Write for FREE catalog to ATLANTIC RECORDS 1841 Broadway New York, N.Y. 10023

KRLA ARCHIVES

Don Ho Admits He's
The Guy Who Stole Liquor

DON HO: "If they don't like what I'm doing, I adjust to what they like."

"I'm just the guy who stole the liquor" laughs Hawaiian entertainer Don Ho. And what liquor it is too.

Ho is just about the biggest success Hawaii ever dreamed of. Playing to sellout crowds in his own Island night club, breaking records at Los Angeles' famed Cocoanut Grove, landing a new contract with Singer Sewing Company for television specials, this 37 year old singer is rapidly becoming a phenomena.

His appeal seems to be universal. From the teen-ager who watched him on "Malibu U" to Jacqueline Kennedy who invited him to a party at her home, Ho captures the audience with his infectious warmth.

Ho is a far cry from what many people expect from a Hawaiian performer, indeed Ho only sings "Hawaiian Love Song" when sorely pressed by the audience. His style is more cosmopolitan than that, ranging from rock and roll to the Bossa Nova. His philosophy is to have a good time.

"It simply amazes me. It makes me happy to see so many people having a good time. I enjoy making people happy."

Ho is under no illusion about his talent as a straight singer, "I am not a singer, but an entertainer with an ability to read the mood of the audience."

He comes on strong. Stripped to the waist, showing off his powerful, football build, or dressed solely in white, Ho uses every bit of his appeal to entertain the audience. Ranging from sweet music, to bawdy humor Ho is totally in command of his material.

An islander of Chinese-Portuguese-German-Dutch ancestry Don grew up on the other side of the mountains from Honolulu in Kaneoke, where his parents ran a cocktail lounge called Honeys. Don won an athletic scholarship to Springfield College, Mass. But after one year, Ho returned to the islands to study at the University of Hawaii where he majored in sociology.

After five years in the air force, Don resigned his commission to return to the family business, which by this time was far from thriving. In order to keep customers from walking out, Don started singing and encouraged the patrons to sing too. Within weeks business picked up.

Today Ho has no worries about business. Earning at least $500,000 a year has helped to give a little security to Ho's life. Don owns a record company, real estate as far east as Salt Lake City all in addition to two supper clubs other than Honeys. Don has managed a deal with Restaurateur Trader Vic to have an island chain called Trader Ho's.

But entertaining is still Don's main concern.

"I love what I'm doing and all the people who come to see us. It overwhelms me when I think of it; the different kinds of people. They determine my mood. If they don't like what I'm doing, I adjust to what they like. You might call it a controlled impromptu night of fun. That's my music and my dream; to make music and make people happy and be around Hawaii for a long time.

"I want people to know that when they come to see me it's as if they are in my living room. I want them to be happy."

"I AM NOT A SINGER, but an entertaineer with an ability to read audiences' mood."

Jay and Techniques Make Dream Reality

Many a rock musician has dreamed of putting together the best talent available and forming a group that would blow everybody's mind, but it's rare when someone actually goes out and accomplishes it.

The place was Allentown, Pa., and the time was late 1965. The best musicians in town gathered together hoping to have a great act, and that's just what they got. The group became Jay and the Techniques, and their hit, "Apples, Peaches, Pumpkin Pie," has placed them among the top rock groups on the East Coast, if not the nation.

The seven-man outfit is headed by Jay Proctor, a 26-year-old vocalist who has been associated with music almost from the word go.

"My mother used to sing in a choir and always took me with her to the group's performances," Jay remembers. "And, too, there was much encouragement from my father."

Jay knew for sure that he was in for a musical career after forming a group with several friends in the late '50's. "We soon after appeared on a show sponsored by the local boys' club and did a thing called "Handbone." Then a man heard the group sing, liked us and had us cut a record. As a result of this we got to sing once in a while on local radio station."

After that Jay worked with other groups in the Pennsylvania area until he helped start the Techniques with Karl Landis.

Besides Jay, the others in the group are Landis, 19; Chuck Crowl, 19; George Lloyd, 25; Ronnie Goosley, 18; Dante Dancho, 19; and John Walsh, 19. All live in or around Allentown.

Ronnie, like Jay, thinks he must have been born with music in his blood. "It just comes naturally to me," he says. He started with the group when he was in 10th grade, and admits "That's where I gained my knowledge of showmanship."

John had something else in mind when he first decided to join the Techniques. "We all got together one night with a bunch of guitars and drums and trumpets and saxophones and tried to form a symphony orchestra. That didn't sound too good so we started a rock group instead."

George, who was born in Georgia, credits his mother with stimulating his interest in music. "My mother could sing very well. She just had a natural talent for it."

Dante, whose favorite foods are apples, peaches and pumpkin pie, credits his guitar-playing father for his prowess on lead guitar.

Chuck remembers his funniest incident as occurring when he drove 1,000 miles to a concert and had his car break down less than a mile away from his destination.

Karl, a rhythm and blues fan, keeps up the beat for the Techniques. Of his start he remembers, "I bought a set of drums and practiced up a storm until I met some guys in a group and begged them to let me play since they had no drummer and needed one. I got in the group but we eventually broke up due to a lot of fighting."

KRLA ARCHIVES

Doors An Individualist Group Unified Despite Diversity

By Mike Masterson

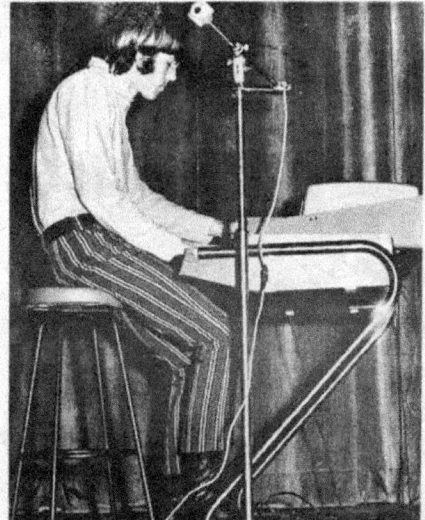

When you open the Doors, you find strange and different things within, as mind-blowing as "Light My Fire," as deep as "The End," as beautiful as "The Crystal Ship."

Paradoxically, The Doors are both communistic and anarchic, they are hippie and anti-hippie their individual tastes range from classical to rock to jazz to flaminco guitar.

"We're a communistic group in the sense that it's a communal brotherhood institution," according to organist Ray Manzarek. "Not meaning communistic having anything to do with politics, but having to do with the word commune, and being a brotherhood. It's a very small Cosa Nostra brotherhood the four of us exist in."

At the same time they're anarchic according to Robbie: "We're pretty unorganized, rather than having a nice, tightly run thing. The group has no leader as such, and if any one of us was to leave the group there would be no group left."

Hippie or Anti-Hippie

As a result of the strain of violence that runs through much of their music, the Doors have been accused of being anti-peace and anti-hippie. Not so, says vocalist Jim Morrison.

"They (hippies and the Doors' music) are connected somehow, they go hand in hand I've always been attracted to ideas about revolt and chaos, about activity that appears to have no meaning. But we're connected to the hippies somehow."

For a group like the Doors, who have a unique sound if there ever was one, there is an obvious interest in who, if anybody, has influenced them. No ready answer is forthcoming, however, since no individual member has anywhere near the same tastes as the other. Maybe this diversity is what actually stamps the Doors as an individualist group among the mass of groups.

Barry and Bach

Morrison cites Elvis Presley, Chuck Barry, Jerry Lee Lewis and Little Richard as the only singers "who ever turned me on," Chicago blues, Stravinsky, and Bach have been Manzarek's guiding lights. Drummer John Densmore considers himself mostly in the jazz vein, while Robbie believes Flaminco music has been the main influence on his guitar work.

The Doors' compositions are also fair ground for a discussion of influences. One New York music critic has said that their music is a strange combination of the ancient Greek playwright Sophecles and the Irish novelist James Joyce.

"Our album (Light My Fire) is heavily influenced by some of the older writers," aditted Robbie. "Especially Shakespeare, Sophecles and the old Egyptian writers. I wouldn't say the whole album was so. I'd say 'The End' is a little like Joyce, but not really."

Jazz Tradition

Another aspect of the Doors' music is improvisation, which is especially evident in the single, "Light My Fire" is really exciting because it's the first time I've heard improvisation in rock that was more than just what the Yardbirds call a rave-up," said Manzarek. "In a way I'm surprised that some of the jazz people haven't picked up on it and realized it's improvisation in the classical jazz tradition."

The eclectic sound of the Doors has been expanded even further on their second album, "Strange Days", which Krieger candidly predicted will be "the album of the year." The four are particularly excited about a 12½-minute tract in it called "When the Music is Over," described by Morrison as "a kind of modern serial."

An Expansion

"Musically, it's an expansion of the four of us. We've added maybe a harpsichord and use of the studio effects and stuff like that, but it's still totally performed by the four of us," Jim added.

For Robbie, "It's more than an expansion; it's a logical progression to follow. It's what you'd expect the second album to do. It's the next step up from the first album."

This logical progression may lead to even more unusual things in the future, something Manzarek calls the electronic theatre.

"I don't know when, it's going to take a couple of albums but be almost a radio play."

Great look, great feel—that's the whole idea behind our new Bare/Foot/Gear *sockless* shoes! Come try some on. They're *leather* sneakers—tough, supple, secret-process steerhide that feels great and outwears canvas two to three times. So forget socks, but remember Bare/Foot/Gear.

Forget socks.

ORIGINAL SOCKLESS SHOES

BARE FOOT GEAR

©1967, WILLIE LOMAN & SONS, INC.

Asheville NC, Bell's Col. Corner; Austin Tex., Reynolds-Pineland; Dallas, Clyde Campbell's; Dayton O, Metropolitan Co.; Des Moines, Reichardt's; Downey Ca, The Gaslite; Greenwich Conn, Outdoor Trader; Jersey City, Zampella's; Long Beach, Kanady's; LA, Zeidler & Zeidler; Memphis, Alfred's; Norman Okla, Harold's; Portland Ore, Lipman-Wolfe; San Diego, Lion's; Santa Ana, Bullock's; Santa Cruz, New Englander; Sausalito, Johnson & Gray; Stamford Conn, Lou Konspore; Tulsa Okla, Orbach's; Worchester Mass, Ware-Pratt.
For information, write Bare/Foot/Gear, 512 Veteran, LA Ca 90024

KRLA ARCHIVES

Herman and the Hermits off in a BLAZE of glory...

AVAILABLE AT

AVAILABLE AT

Wander through the garden fence with PROCOL HARUM

KRLA ARCHIVES

KRLA's New Season

KRLA's "New Season" has started—bringing in a whole new line-up of personalities... and three brand new dee-jays — Bob Dayton, Jim Wood and Rhett Walker. The "old favorites" are still here though... you've just got to find them. Look for Dave Hull early in the mornings (5 a.m.-9 a.m.). Following the old "Hullaballooer" you'll find Rhett Walker, a young New Zealander (9 a.m.-12 noon). At 12 noon an old friend, Johnny Hayes and another at 3 p.m., Reb Foster. The Eastern sea-board sends us the next new-comers. New York's Bob Dayton can be heard from 6 p.m.-9 p.m. and Philadelphia's Jim Wood hits the airwaves at 9 p.m. Following Jim at 1 a.m.—the all-new Bill Slater Show—KRLA's guaranteed sleep substitute.

Weekends are new at KRLA too—especially for Casey Kasem. Casey's now on Saturdays and Sundays only—9-1 p.m. and 6-12 noon respectively. He's finally going to have time to do what he set out to do 17 years ago—to be an actor. The breaks are coming at last and, given a couple of years, he just might be an overnight success after all.

Look for many new and exciting features beginning only at KRLA... concerts featuring the Jefferson Airplane and Donovan... broadcasts and shows from the Cheeta in Santa Monica... and more. And keep watching those movie pages for you-know-who.

A SWITCH—Flower Power Pays Off! An Officer giving Gypsy Boots his autograph! P.S. Officer is one of the "Lovable" Keystone Kops, Frank Walrus.

"Happenings"
By Casey Kasem

Look for the release of a brand new, exciting motorcycle picture November 1st. The working title thus far is "The Glory Stompers." The title might change between now and then, but the stars won't. It stars Chris Noel, Dennis Hopper, Jody McRae, Lindsey Crosby and many other bright new-comers to the motion picture screen. Oh yes, two of those new-comers are KRLA's Dave Hull and myself.

The story-line of the movie concerns that conflict between two motorcycle groups, "The Black Souls" (bad guys) and "The Glory Stompers" (good guys). You guessed it—I'm a "bad guy." Near misses of three moving cars, three stationary cars and a plate glass window in a butcher shop taught me a fast, sincere respect for the true motorcycle devotee... believe me!

More happenings next week... Casey.

THE ASSOCIATION has just finished a successful run at the famous nightclub The Cocoanut Grove. Although this nightclub caters to adults, the Association did not leave their usual sound behind them. Unlike The Supremes and The Four Tops who included many show tunes and other non-rock numbers in their act, The Association sang the hits that made them famous in their own style.

BEST DOCUMENTARY HONOR

KRLA special assignments editor Lew Irwin received certificate of excellence Special Award from Associated Press broadcast executive Robert Eunson. The station was lauded for its "Language of Rock" series which dealt with the suggestive lyrics of today's music. A second KRLA documentary entitled "Down The Up Staircase," exploring the growing use of marijuana and LSD, was named the best radio documentary of 1966.

KRLA has signed disc jockey Rhett Walker for a daily 9 a.m. to 12 noon stanza on that station, according to program director Reb Foster. Walker resigned a post as program director of MOL in Seattle to join KRLA.

NOW HAPPENING EVERY NITE
1—NEW GENERATION
2—PACIFIC OCEAN
3—ABSTRACTS
4—POP CORN BLIZZARD
5—MUSTARD GREENS
6—OCTOBER COUNTRY
7—DEARLY BELOVED

GAZZARRI'S #1 ON-THE-STRIP
CR 3-6606
OL 7-2113
GAZZARRI'S #2 LA CIENEGA
9039 SUNSET
319 N. LACIENEGA

MORE HAPPENINGS
MON. — Dance Contest to select Miss Hollywood A-Go-Go of 1968
$500 Grand Prize
TUES. — Talent Nite
WED. — Fashion Show
SUN. AFTERNOON GROOVE IN — 4 P.M.
Did You Say, "Where's the Action"? What's This... Chopped Liver?!!

THE GOLDEN BEAR
306 OCEAN AVENUE (HWY 101) HUNTINGTON BEACH

Present
Starting
Sept. 19 thru 24th

"BIG BROTHER & THE HOLDING CO."

Plus

BIG MAMA THORNTON

Reservations Phone 536-9600 / 536-9102

KRLA ARCHIVES

Buffalo Springfield Sound Off

If there is one common factor unifying all of today's better rock groups, it would have to be their enthusiasm and their involvement with pop music. For the serious pop group, the one with true creative ability, concerts, recording sessions and after hours clubs are not part of their jobs, but more importantly part of their lives. This is especially true with the Buffalo Springfield, a talented group with many outspoken ideas about how pop concerts, and festivals should be held.

"We would like to play ball parks, if they can be done right. The ideal place to hold a concert is outside where the amplifiers can be turned up as loud as they should be and not hurt anyone's ears.

"But the ball park concert would have to be changed from the way it is now. There wouldn't be any regimentation, and the kids could come up around the stage or dance on the grass, if they wanted to. There would still be seats but people would be able to move about freely.

Audience Connection

"The whole thing about concerts is that you have to groove with the audience. There has to be a connection between the audience and the group that's playing. Of course that can be gotten anywhere, if the audience is willing to really listen, and the group is good enough.

"This can be obtained in a club too, all you need is an air of relaxation up in San Francisco is kind of that. The Fillmore used to be, but they've gotten too hipped out on themselves. They sort of say 'I dare you, turn me on'."

Although the Springfield played at the Monterey Pop Festival and genuinely thought its concert was fantastic, the general impression from the resulting festival was a little less than satisfied.

Original Idea

"The original idea was so great. A three-day blow out with pop artists and folk singers and anybody who wanted to perform. Like the Newport Folk Festival without any pressure, just people playing together with an audience listening. But that idea got sort of lost. There was all sorts of pressure at Monterey that shouldn't have been there.

"Then too there was too much emphasis on San Francisco and the groups from there. Some were excellent, but most of those S.F. groups that played were pretty bad.

"Also everyone seemed to be trying to make it into a love-in. And love-ins should be spontaneous, they can't be planned. You can have a love-in anywhere, in your own home if you want it, and that's the way it's going. There was too much catering to the love generation.

Falseness

"There was a falseness about Monterey that shouldn't have been there."

Unlike many groups the Springfield find it more difficult to reproduce their concert sound in the recording studio than the other way around.

"One of the problems is with the sound that we want.

"We do all our own music. Very rarely we will ask somebody to come in and play something for us, but only if we can't figure any other way of doing it.

Sounds of Horns

"We can't play horns, but we have found a way of making the fuzz tone guitar sound like a horn with over dubbing. We're all learning how to play new things every session too. Because if we can't be turned up as loud as it can be in concert. And so we have to search and find ways of getting around this problem without losing

ONE THING FOR WHICH the Buffalo Springfield are well known is their ability to pose!

only ones playing on our albums and records.

Two of the Springfield had been introduced to pop music through folk singing in New York. But like many other folk singers they eventually turned to rock.

"It's more of an involvement in the physical. It feels good to play hard and to feel that amplifier in back of you working like an instrument in its own right.

"It's just more fun, you can get totally blown over."

In Los Angeles the group is almost as well known for its habit of playing improvisations in after hour clubs with anyone who wants to play as they are for their single hits. The Springfield has been known to groove until the early hours of the morning with absolutely no regimentation or structure to what they are playing.

"This is great in a club, but it doesn't belong in a concert situation. In a concert people come to hear one group at a time and that's all. Perhaps it should be different, and everyone could play together. But concert producers don't seem to want to break down the structure of the concert.

The Springfield's new album is almost ready and will be out in the early part of October if not sooner. They are also scheduled to appear on the new television series, Mannix, and are planning a tour of the East coast cities.

THE GANG—Oz, Malcolm, Nigel and Miss Spanky

Spanky And Our Gang—Instant Insanity

If eccentricity is any sort of requirement for pop singers, then Spanky & Our Gang have definitely won first place among the musical masses.

Spanky, a 24 year old brunette and leader of the Gang, can never be accused of being a carbon copy of anyone. Who else would wear an Army surplus jacket, bell-bottomed jeans, D.A.R. button and glasses without lenses?

Enter Nigel

Then there's Nigel, straight from the country-western bag by the way of a few folk clubs, who finds lots of country and western in the Beatles and slips some into Spanky & Oour Gang "whenever they let me."

Or Malcolm, the only sane note in this symphony of insanity. He's just back from a State Department tour of Viet Nam, shaking his head about a variety of unknown thoughts. He met Spanky when they both sang with the New Wine Singers not too long ago.

Ah, but don't forget Oz, as in the Wizard Of, with a last name as in Beethoven, Oz Bach.

Mustached profusely, Oz Bach alternates between English, German and any other language that fits his fancy at the moment. He relates (in English hopefully) a bizarre story about him and Nigel meeting Spanky in a chicken coop during a hurricane in Miami, though the chicken coop turns out to actually be a home (reconverted) that Spanky was renting at the time and the hurricane one of many that storm the Florida coast each year.

Then there's the family, literally the Gang, that follows each other around the country, one performance to another—people with exotic names like Ruby Tuesday and Johnny Indian.

"We don't communicate with the waitress types," says Spanky "so we prefer to rent a place and someone cooks and it's one big happy family."

Trends?

At which point, Oz took it upon himself to discuss musical trends, or mainly, is rock 'n' roll in danger of getting too far above the audience it is intended for?

"I don't think it's getting too good necessarily," he said, "it gets refined sometimes until it's no longer interesting, but there is always a new thing, like Indian music or soul music.

"There's a great lack of good singers today — both good solo singers and singers in groups."

And with that, Spanky and her Gang took off in a blaze of wild color—presumedly to make every minute count.

KRLA ARCHIVES

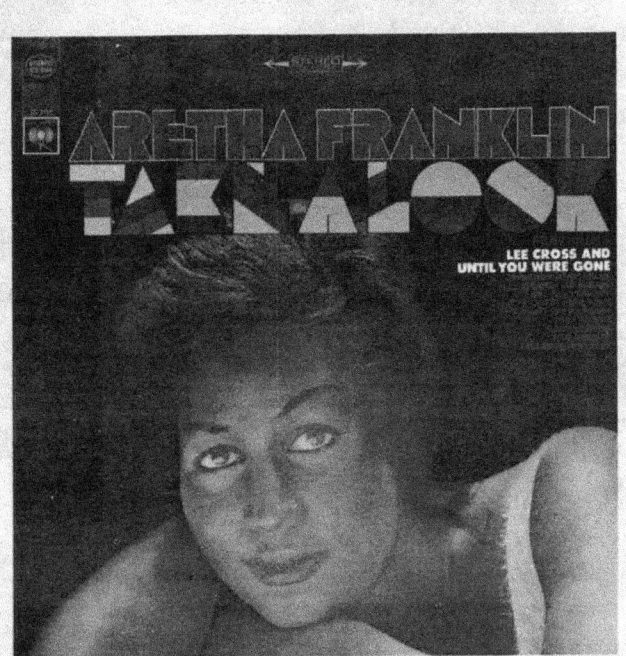

TAKE A LOOK HAVE A LISTEN

The Next Best Thing to Being There

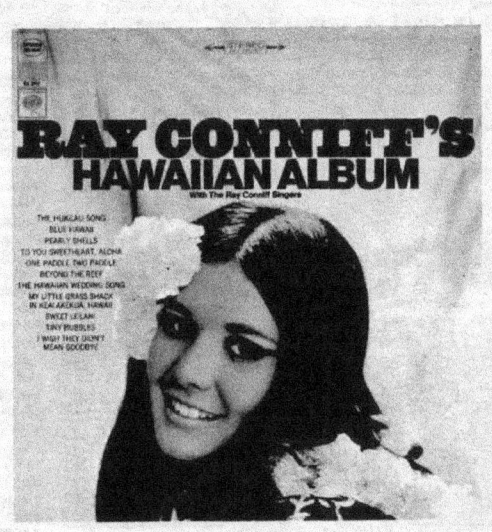

Now Available At:
MONTGOMERY WARD
DEPARTMENT STORES

BEE GEES GET STUNG BY UNITED STATES

The Bee Gees, that British-Australian group which sound startlingly like the Beatles, have been making a tour of the United States getting acquainted with the American press. This is what happened when they hooked up with a BEAT reporter:

Q. What are your impressions of the U.S.? Are they similar to those of Eric Burdon?

A. Maurice Gibb — Well our impressions so far are very similar to what Eric said. It is really a different place.

Vince Melouney — It's really beautiful. We've found it very advancing, and it's so different from England, different from Australia or any other place in the world. England is very old and they want to keep it traditional, and that's beautiful in its own way, but it's beautiful here because it's so advanced.

Drugs?

Q. What is your opinion of drugs?

A. Vince—So many people are taking drugs, it's ridiculous. It's growing every day. You must remember that many years ago alcohol was forbidden to be drunk, and it became legal, you know. Alcohol is terrible, really nobody can say it does you any good. But some drugs can't harm you. Yet they let the drunkards get way with it; they can roam the streets and do anything, but as soon as a guy takes a pill or has a smoke, they're right down on him. We don't smoke because we don't believe in it. The thing is, maybe once you're on to it, maybe you can't get off it. We don't need it. Why should we use it?

Q. What about the rumor that one of the recordings on your album was actually done by the Beatles?

A. Maurice—That song we did on that album was written quite a while ago, and we just did it for the album. I can't think of why people would even think that the Beatles would sing on the album.

Colin Peterson — I don't even know the Beatles, and it would be difficult if they sang on one of our records. I'm sure I'd get to meet them. Everyone feels the need to start a controversy about this or that. But this one is far from true.

Concerts?

Q. Are you going to continue to make personal appearances?

A. Colin—I don't think we're in any position to stop tours. They'll never be obsolete; a group will always have to work live. In my opinion it won't be long before the Beatles start working again on stage, because if you have worked to an audience for so long I don't think you can sort of creep behind the scenes and just record. You feel as if you are missing so much —the kids.

Q. Where is pop music going?

A. Vince—No one can predict where anything is going. You must take it as it comes. We don't follow any trends; we make our own trends. Your music must be advanced because you're working on ideas all the time. The only thing I can say is that music will get more and more advanced, and the kids will go along with it.

Q. What do you think of psychedelic music?

A. Maurice — Different trends come in every year, and the psychedelic thing is just a trend. In England it's there, but then again it's not; it's not a big trend. The move in England is psychedelic, but it can't last if you have to rely on all this mad lighting and stupid things like that—smashing instruments—to go over well, forget it as far as I'm concerned. If you're good enough, and you write good material, and you've got a good stage act, and musically you're reasonably good, you'll last, you'll keep going. But if you depend on trends, forget it.

The Image?

Colin—If a group classes itself as psychedelic when they go on stage and they use lighting effects and everything it's hard to create an image, because what is the image? The image is the actual lighting and everything, which is very hard to remember. I think a group can be more successful if they just rely on themselves, and they can create an image among themselves.

Q. What are you doing to further communication with fans?

A. Maurice — We have to do something different each time; we don't want all our records to sound the same. Like with "To Love Somebody," we've gotten far away from this Beatle kick which everyone thinks we're on. It's sort of a soul ballad, and it's just nothing like "New York Mining Disaster." This is one thing we wanted to get across, and no one can accuse us of copying the Beatles.

(R to L) Barry, Robin, Vince, Maurice, Colin

"It's More Dangerous To Be An American Indian Under 18 Than To Be In VietNam"—Buffy

Buffy Sainte-Marie is one of the most unique performers around. Possessing an almost incredible voice which ranges from the deep blues tones to the pure soprano, there is no singing style in which she cannot excel. Add to this her ability to write beautiful and poignant songs and you have just a fragment of Buffy's accomplishments.

She is a writer who refuses to be categorized. Her "Universal Soldier" is a protest song; but another of her compositions is "Until It's Time For You to Go" which has no clear protest message. This diversification is what makes life and work interesting to Buffy.

"I don't think that it's possible to fit me into any of the categories of music. I particularly don't worry about it. I realize that it's a problem for people writing about music to be able to say she's a country and western singer, although some people think of me as a country and western singer, or some people will say I'm a blues singer and think that I shouldn't sing anything else.

"When people ask me how I want to be introduced, I say just say I'm a singer-composer."

A Sponge

Her ideas for songs come from every imaginable source.

"I write whatever I happen to be thinking about, which is one thing at one moment and something else the next. Or something at all, which is most of the time. Most of the time I'm like a sponge and I'm slurping in instead of giving out. And I find that it's very important not to get worried when I'm not actively creating, because what I am doing is absorbing."

Although many people tend to lump all "folk" singers together into one bag, Buffy is unlike anyone else. She does not consider herself a protestor, yet many people call her exactly that. Actually her life is very related to what might be called "protest" because Buffy is a full-blooded Cree Indian. This gives her an added strong feeling for the injustices that have been thrust upon the American Indian.

Buffy feels her responsibility to her race very strongly, and at each concert she includes songs written about the mistreatment of the Indians and their courage in the face of great odds. However, Buffy is a realist and she does not hold the illusion that her songs are changing social conditions.

Informing People

"My point in trying to inform the people is exactly that. I am trying to inform the people. I can't make the average American man do anything to help the Indians. All I can do is inform him.

"He still goes to the polls. All I can do is prevent this leperous part of American history from being covered up any more. I'm just trying to let some sunlight in.

"I'm talking to students mainly. And these students are going to become lawyers and teachers, and voters and parents and at least they'll know.

"Some things are being done. From the Office of Economic Opportunity there are some very good programs now and then coming into being. Some are very successful and others are not successful.

"I think the way to help Indians is not to weigh yourself down with Indian jewelry and tie a scarf around your head and walk around zonked out of your mind calling Buffy Sainte-Marie 'soul sister,' That's not where it's at.

Good Americans

"I think the way to help the Indians is by being the greatest kind of white man he can be. He doesn't have to become an Indian too. It sounds dumb but I wish we had some good Americans in America.

"I don't really think we have very many for whom reality has come very close to the values that he himself holds. I'm not saying that you should be true to anything that I have in mind, but at least be true to something, or else you walk around dizzy all day."

The problem of the Indians is similar to the Negro cause, but not identical.

"The Indians aren't looking for respect, the Indians aren't really worried about discrimination so much. The biggest problem that the Indians face is starvation.

Now in the past two years more American Indian children have died of 'natural causes,' measles, mumps, starvation than all of the men who have died in Viet Nam so far. That's a fact. It is more dangerous to be an American Indian under the age of 18 than it is to be in the front lines in Viet Nam."

No Clear Answers

"Percentage wise more Indians die. Indians die like flies."

Buffy sees no quick solution to their problems, but she is not sitting idly by waiting for someone else to come up with the answer.

"It's a very complex problem. The Indians can solve it themselves but between the state of panic that exists from whether you are going to be booted off your land tomorrow and the state of complete disgust that exists.

"When a kid in the 5th grade is so disgusted with the school system which is full of lies which doesn't even recognize that he exists. When he drops out of school in the 5th grade, I'm not going to tell him to go back.

"I'm working on my own reserve to encourage the 4 teachers who teach the 400 children. I'm trying to get these teachers to allow them to speak Cree and I'm trying to get these teachers to learn to speak Cree.

Seventeen Magazine

"I mean here's this pretty young school teacher who stands up in front of the class and tells these kids who to be. No they can never be her.

"I tried to be her. I tried to be like the cover of Seventeen Magazine. I tried to do it for years. I cut my hair, I bleached it, I used the shade of powder that they told me to use, I used the ridiculous pink lipstick and I looked awful.

"But it never occured to me that there was anything within myself that was worth developing.

Buffy Sainte-Marie is one of the fortunate people in the world. She has finally realized what she had in herself that was worth developing. She is aware of herself and her abilities and her limitations. Buffy is now trying to help others to realize their own particular potential.

KRLA ARCHIVES

The Secret Recipe

AVAILABLE AT

AVAILABLE AT

Life Is A Dream

KRLA ARCHIVES

The Sounds of Today

KRLA ARCHIVES

Five Turtles On The Line

By Mike Masterson

It's not often that one is able to get the Turtles to sit still enough to give out an interview—it's even less frequent that an opportunity is given to the individual members to speak out on any subject they choose. But it happens.

Howard Kaylan (official or unofficial leader of the group, depending upon w h o m you ask) wasted not a second in picking out his topic and plunging directly into it. "Groups will come and groups will go and no group really expects to stay on top of things forever.

Keep Changing

"In our own instance, we feel we would like to keep changing our music, not only to fit the times but also to fit where our heads are now. We couldn't record a song like (It Ain't Me Babe) now and seriously get into it. Not that it's a bad song by any means; it's just that we want to say other things now. We did a little bit of the protest thing with 'Let Me Be' and we went into happy music with 'You Baby' and now we're doing exactly what we want to do and we've finally gotten to the point where the songs we're recording are really what we want to say.

"Songs that are coming to us from outside sources are done in very close association with the writers who are writing for us. So by the time our songs and albums are released they are really what we want to say; we don't say anything we don't mean.

"We're not trying to preach any morals except 'here we are,' and if people see us and dig us then we're really happy. A super group is just a group that's made it, that's lasted, that people when they hear the name say 'oh yeah, I know them, I know that guy and that guy and they've got the tambourine man with the glasses and the drummer who sits back there' and they know us."

Trip To Canada

John Barbata was about to burst with all the news of the latest Turtle adventures. "A lot of interesting things have happened. We've acquired our own plane, a DC3, and we've really gotten to the point where we enjoy the traveling part of the tour. I don't know, everyday something seems to happen. On our last tour we were at Expo '67 and it's really a truly unbelievable place.

"As far as our shows, I think it was a different experience playing for a lot of people from all over the world. Most of the people have heard of us, a few hadn't, and I think we got down what they wanted. The response was very warm, you could tell they were there to appreciate what you were going to lay down for them.

"Well, the whole place had a very exciting atmosphere, you find you don't get to a place too often where there are so many different environments, where there're so many different ways of life in one area.

"Following that we went to Alaska, which few groups get to do, and I think it's a great experience. A lot of people have some misconceptions about Alaska. It's not so different there, except that its more isolated and the people really get into different things. The people are very warm and friendly and they don't have all the uptightness that seems to surround people in the average continental U.S. city."

Musical Progression

Al Nichol took the floor next and immediately began talking about creating new sounds. "I've been interested in creating new sounds for a long time now because people get tired of the same old things. As music progresses, certain ideas progress and well other groups have shown us, other people have come up with very unique things.

"As far as our music is concerned, we try to incorporate as many new ideas with each song so that we can come up with a new sound for that particular idea and a new way of communicating. And if you communicate to people in a new and interesting way they're going to pick up on it and remember it.

"We have several instruments in our sound that haven't been used too much before. I think that new sounds and weird instruments that you can do musical things on are going to make a great difference in this next year as to whether a group or song or idea becomes commercial and is picked up by a lot of people."

Biggest Break

Jim Pons has been asked the question so many times that he automatically tells you about joining the Turtles. "Well, first of all it's a very fortunate break to make a transition from a group like the Leaves to a group like the Turtles. I call it my biggest break because it really was. The Leaves were a success as far as I was concerned. It was very, very local, we were just concerned with playing our own parties. But I thank God that I had the insight to accept the good chance when it came along. I was struggling with the old group, I was friends with everyone, and we had a good thing but I could see that the Turtles was a better thing to do."

There are quite a few things on Mark Volman's mind but it's not hard to find out that his wife and baby are uppermost. "She understands the line of work I'm in exceptionally well. She's very happy for us. I'm doing my best to keep her out of the publicity as much as possible. I'm married and there's no hang-ups about it. We're both very happy.

"A few of us went to see the Bob Dylan movie, 'Don't Look Back,' and where he was then and where he is now. Bob Dylan is a poet and a philosopher, a very good one. He was the changing point in my life, he added and abetted my thinking up until about a year ago.

"The movie is very good, I enjoyed it. It's a tremendous insight into Bob Dylan as a person rather than just a musician. He's really freaky."

GRASS ROOTS SPEAKING OUT—
We Want to Say Something to People

By Eden

". . . We were a group before we got the name, and we were working with Sloan and Barri before that. The old Grass Roots were a studio group—we had the sound and they thought we had a new place to go, so we moved into that position." Warren Entner, Grass Root speaking.

It had been a relatively quiet day before the Grass Roots came into the office, but all that was changed immediately upon their arrival. Having just flown in from San Francisco, the boys had come to us straight f r o m the airport. Four well-mannered, polite, well-dressed young men walked in the door and immediately I thought something was wrong. They were just too *straight*.

Point One

At least they had long hair — that was one point in their favor —so I figured that they couldn't be all bad, and we began our interview. I was in for a surprise that day—I discovered the Grass Roots to be very intelligent, well-educated, q u i t e talented young men . . . who also just happened to be very hip, but didn't have to *pretend* to impress everyone with it.

I don't want to mislead you by telling you that at least three-fourths of this group are nuts, but let me give you an example. After one member made a funny remark at which we all cracked up, I asked if they could repeat a few of their ha-ha's for me in harmony. My tape recorder is now the proud and sole possessor of the Grass Roots singing "ha, ha, ha" in harmony (key of L Minor).

A few minutes later, Creed asked me if I had a cigarette. Since I don't smoke, I didn't have one and poor Creed was about to have a nicotine fit until the inspiration hit him to go downstairs into the parking lot and bum a cigarette off of a stranger. In fact, he and his newly-found benefactor got on so well, that Creed wound up hitching a ride down to the little market a couple of blocks away, and in a few moments, he came bounding back into the office offering to share some of his Black Cherry Cola and M&M's with us.

Order of Names

". . . this is the team of Entner-Bratton . . . Bratton-Entner. It should have my name first—see, it was Bratton and Entner: Brent, but I wanted Ent-Bratton but that didn't sound right. Besides, in alphabetic order I should get my name first anyway!" "Okay!" The team of Warren Entner and Creed Bratton discussing the order of their names on lead sheets; they are the two Grass Roots responsible for writing much of their material. Warren explained: "On the next album it's split — we write half, and Sloan-Barri write half. The single ("Live For Today") was from Italy; it was written over there and the head of Dunhill brought it back and we did it."

In a rare serious moment, all four of the Roots stopped to analyze what has been happening in the music world around them and decided that the greatest innovation in recent years has been the Beatles. "I think they changed the whole thing; they said something," remarked Warren. Rickey Coonce, drummer for the group, agreed with him, adding that "They brought rock and roll out of its little bag of gold outfits and they made it all on its own again. It's just a form of music now and it's recognized as such."

Untouchable

Creed left his Cherry Cola for a moment to add his own thoughts to the discussion: "They (the Beatles) left the three-chord pattern and now they're doing some fantastically creative things—very Baroque — and they're obviously still untouchable. Creatively, we feel—we're not trying to be conceited—but we feel that once we are exposed, we'll try to go along this vein too, because we want to say something to people."

Warren, too, nodded his head in agreement, and continued for Creed: "I think we've developed some sort of a style; we know what we can do and what we can't do, and we're trying to elaborate on the bag we're in now. There's a long way to go in it, lyrically." "Musically," explained Creed, "were acoustical, electric, very hard-rock with a folk influence, I think. Now, we're growing with the music, so obviously we'll change."

There is one ambition which Creed has hopes of accomplishing one day soon: "It would be very nice to have a song come out and to express in one song a whole mood—like a mood that just the music alone fits so perfectly with the words that everyone has to listen to it. I'd just like to leave an impact on everyone with our name and what we said related to it."

Expressions

Rob Grill, bass player and sometimes—lead singer for the group lead the discussion for a while when we discussed the kinds of things which can be accomplished with music: "You can let people know what you have to say with music and it expresses a lot of your personality. If you have an influence on people with your music—if it goes over—then you have a good feeling of expressing yourself to everyone."

KRLA ARCHIVES

Beat Poster Shop

(N)

Send To: BEAT POSTER SHOP, 9121 Sunset Blvd., Los Angeles, Calif. 90069
PLEASE SEND ME THE FOLLOWING POSTERS (LIST BY LETTER)_____
I ENCLOSE $1.75 plus .25 Handling for each*.

Name_____
Address_____
City_____State_____Zip Code_____
* California Residents Please Include 5% Sales Tax

AVAILABLE IN THESE PATTERNS:
A. Hearts and Flowers   C. Psychedelic Alphabets and Designs
B. Psychedelic Buttons and Designs   D. Psychedelic Phreaquies

Mail To: BEAT PUBLICATIONS
9121 Sunset Blvd., Los Angeles, Calif. 90069

Circle Sheet Desired   A   B   C   D
Send me_____sheets Mod-Bod stick-ons
(4 psychedelic sheets available at $1 each)

Name_____
Address_____
City_____State_____
California residents please add 5% sales tax.
Stick on everything, waterproof, reuseable.

SPECIAL OFFER TO BEAT READERS!!

AUTHENTIC MONKEESHADES by DEBS

• 5 Groovy Colors...rose, yellow, blue, grey, green
• Heavy Mod Golden Chain
• Just Like the MONKEES Wear On Their Swingin' TV Show
• MONKEESHADES are the Wildest!

Send to: MONKEESHADES, 9121 Sunset Blvd., Los Angeles, Calif. 90069
PLEASE SEND ME THE MONKEESHADES AS INDICATED. I ENCLOSE $2.00 FOR EACH PR.
COLOR_____NO. PAIRS_____TOTAL AMOUNT ENCLOSED_____
Name_____
Address_____
City_____State_____Zip Code_____
California Residents Please Include 5% Sales Tax

---

24 ORIGINAL HAPPENING HITS

As Advertised Nationally on Radio & TV

I Think We're Alone Now: Tommy James & The Shondells
Kind Of A Drag: The Buckinghams
Cherry Cherry: Neil Diamond
Turn Down Day: The Cyrkle
Jenny Take A Ride: Mitch Ryder & Detroit Wheels
My Little Red Book: Love
Wooly Bully: Sam The Sham
But It's Alright: J.J. Jackson
Little Girl: Syndicate Of Sound
See You In September: The Tempos
Daddy's Home: Shep & The Limelighters
Why Do Fools Fall In Love: Frankie Lyman
Western Union: Five Americans
Sunny: Bobby Hebb
Daydream: Lovin' Spoonful
Good Lovin': Young Rascals
I Got You Babe: Sonny & Cher
Pushin' Too Hard: The Seeds
Land Of 1000 Dances: Wilson Pickett
Younger Girl: The Critters
I Who Have Nothing: Terry Knight & The Pack
Bermuda: Four Seasons
Gee: The Crows
Maybe: The Chantels

$1.95   BEAUTIFUL FOUR COLOR JACKET
$4.00 FOR 2 ALBUMS
PLUS 50¢ MAILING   (INCLUDES MAILING)

24 Happening Hits
9121 Sunset Blvd.
Los Angeles, California 90069
I enclose $_____for_____albums.
NAME_____
ADDRESS_____
CITY_____STATE_____
California Residents Please Include 5% Sales Tax

SPEC-TRIM SUNGLASSES

UNIQUE SHADOW BOX FRAMES
MOD RECESSED LENSES
TWO-COLOR FRAMES
$4 EACH*

*California Residents please add 5% sales tax

AVAILABLE IN:
Blue and White   White and Pink
Purple and White Red and White
Yellow and Black Red and Black
Designate Frame Color

SEND TO:
BEAT PUBLICATIONS
9121 Sunset Blvd.
Hollywood, Calif. 90069

DEBS

Portable Radio — Phonograph

2 Speed Record Player
7 Transistor Radio
3" Speaker

90 Day Unconditional Parts Guarantee
$19.95 — California Residents Add 5% Sales Tax ($1)

Send To:
BEAT PHONOGRAPH
9121 Sunset Blvd.
Los Angeles, Calif. 90069

TURNING ON

SMILEY SMILE (Brother Records) The Beach Boys. *Heroes and Villains, Wind Chimes, Gettin' Hungry* plus eight other tracks. This long awaited album definitely proves that the Beach Boys have left surfing music far behind them. Continuing in the vein of *Good Vibrations* (included in the album) and *Heroes and Villains* this album includes some beautiful and intricate harmony and electronic manipulation of sound. The cut called *Wind Chimes* is especially impressive with the voices of the Beach Boys blending to become the sound of the wind through the trees. Included is an excellent instrumental cut *Fall Breaks and Back to Winter* and a comic song *She's Goin' Bald*. The album requires careful listening to appreciate all its subleties. There is very little here that will remind anyone of traditional pop music sounds. If the Beach Boys can continue to explore new sounds and techniques with the freshness of *Smiley Smile* they will definitely fulfill all the faith that so many people have shown them.

COME BACK WHEN YOU GROW UP (Liberty) Bobby Vee with the Strangers. *Come Back When You Grow Up, Before You Go, I May Be Back* plus nine other tracks. This album, which includes Bobby Vee's newest big hit, is not very interesting. Although he is attempting to make the transition from the sound of the fifties to the sound of today, his material is not original nor is it new. His style sounds repetitious and the cuts, which might fare better singly, die as an album.

GENTLE ON MY MIND (Capitol) Glen Campbell. *Catch The Wind, The World I Used To Know, You're My World* plus seven other tracks. Glen Campbell on his album includes some of the best material of other writers and singers. Although he does well with them, he does not over-shadow the original interpretation, nor does he add enough to his interpretation to make this album uniquely his own. His best cut is *Gentle On My Mind*, but he does not seem to be able to catch the simplicity of Donovan's *Catch The Wind*. When singing more complex songs such as Jimmie Rodger's *It's Over* or Rod McKuen's *The World I Used To Know* Campbell fares much better. Another fault lies with the arrangements which are over orchestrated for some of the more simple tunes which Campbell is singing.

THE BYRD HITS (Columbia) The Byrds. *Mr. Tambourine Man, Turn! Turn!, Chimes of Freedom, Eight Miles High* and seven other tracks. Remember when the world centered around England and the sounds that were coming out of that small island? America who for so long had ruled the world as the leading exponent of pop music suddenly found itself replaced by the "Limeys." But during that time, one group did emerge in America to help to revolutionize the pop scene and to pave the way for the so-called psychedelic music of today. That important group was, of course, the Byrds whose unique song styling and intricate musical arrangements caused a whole new area of sound to be explored.

A Psychedelic Art Gallery In Your Home!

THE BIG RED COLORING BOOK

Paint 'Em Yourself!   *Ten Posters*   *Each 17"x11"*   *Just $1.50*

These ten, big, all different posters by psychedelic artist John Powers were made for you to color in just the way you want. You can frame them, hang them on your walls, beautify your room!

BEAT Publications, 9121 Sunset Blvd., Los Angeles, California 90069

Please send me_____Big Red Coloring Books. I enclose $1.50 plus $.25 for handling*
Name_____
Address_____
City_____State_____Zip Code_____
*California Residents please include 5% Sales Tax.

KRLA ARCHIVES

please send me
BEAT
26 issues only
$3 per year

Mail to: **BEAT Publications**
9121 Sunset Blvd.
Los Angeles, California 90069

☐ New Subscription
☐ Renewal (please enclose mailing label from your last BEAT)

I want BEAT for ☐ 1 year at $3.00 or ☐ 2 years at $5.00
I enclose ☐ cash ☐ check ☐ money order
Outside U.S.—$9 per year

* Please print your name and address.

Name_____
Street_____
City_____
State_____ Zip_____

NATIONAL TOP 25 SINGLES

1. THE LETTER .... Box Tops
2. ODE TO BILLIE JOE .... Bobbie Gentry
3. COME BACK WHEN YOU GROW UP ...... Bobby Vee
4. APPLE, PEACHES, PUMPKIN PIE ... Jay & The Techniques
5. REFLECTIONS .... Supremes
6. NEVER MY LOVE .... Association
7. YOU'RE MY EVERYTHING .... The Temptations
8. SAN FRANCISCAN NIGHTS .... Eric Burdon
9. THERE IS A MOUNTAIN .... Donovan
10. COLD SWEAT .... James Brown
11. FUNKY BROADWAY .... Wilson Pickett
12. HIGHER AND HIGHER .... Jackie Wilson
13. YOU KNOW WHAT I MEAN ...... Turtles
14. I HAD A DREAM .... Paul Revere
15. 12:30 .... Mamas and Papas
16. I DIG ROCK AND ROLL MUSIC .. Peter, Paul and Mary
17. BROWN EYED GIRL .... Van Morrison
18. DANDELION .... Rolling Stones
19. BABY I LOVE YOU .... Aretha Franklin
20. GETTIN' TOGETHER .... Tommy James
21. MUSEUM .... Herman's Hermits
22. MAKING EVERY MINUTE COUNT .... Spanky and Our Gang
23. I MAKE A FOOL OF MYSELF ..... Frankie Valli
24. ALL YOU NEED IS LOVE .... Beatles
25. GIVE ME A LITTLE SIGN .... Brenton Wood

As Compiled by Cashbox Magazine

CLASSIFIED

LINDA MARDER I love you! RAY.

Happy Belated Birthday Clair LaCross.

Anne—To the grooviest pen pal in England—Becky.

TEDDY BEARS RULE

Mark Lindsay—love from an unknown girl—Barbara.

HAPPY BIRTHDAY CASS Marge Peabody

Happy Belated Birthday PAPA JOHN.

PRAY FOR BRIAN.

Pete Laughner is really Louie Motherball in disguise.

SKY — Memories of your yellow lamp . . .

To all groovy Berry tour guides luv ya Donna Townsley (Doug, Randy, Terry, Andy and Bill).

Happy Birthday, Big John. Love Sally.

Congratulations, Papa Ringo

"Love is all you Need — The Beatles are Love".

The soul of Brian Epstein lives on.

THE ASSOCIATION ELECTRIFIES!!

SKY—thanks for May 1st.

TBT Lives thru Herman.

Hollies Love Peace.

"Harry" McCartney is all love!!

Greg, thanks for an outasite sumer! Love, Debbie

Calalina girls only.

The world is dim, the light dies. Darkness enters—hate exits.

John Lennon lives . . . everyone else just IS.

I love George

Matt Willimas Stinks! Garb shall overcome! Labsang Rampa live—Tad.

MIKE: REVELATIONS FOR FAITHFUL OR REQUIEM FOR FOUR?

REPLACE MIKE.

Happy LATE Birthday MICHAEL PHILIP JAGGER!! I love you—Cyndi.

Sadstde so far luv. Down with Mr. Kite Please, Pandora.

Phony—Thanks Black Eyes. Red

GOD BLESS BRIAN EPSTEIN.

Alan Staller. Where are you? Sue.

BEATLES!!!!

Bill Koepke—I love you very, very much—Sheryll.

I love you, P.F.C. Gary M. Lewis, Marie.

Joan Swarts — How are you? Steve and Jim.

SKY SAXON has soul!

Whoever's writing these things about us Monkee fans "We aren't reading". Paula Taylor.

Gail love GREGG

BEATLES GO MONKEES BLOW

Happiness is . . . PAUL McCARTNEY.

"GROTESQUE MOMMIESK"

Warblers love Spocks.

Join up! The LNNAF Rebellion wants you!

Jeff Hawks . . . Hope your birthday was the Happiest!!! Love, Sandy

Birthday Flowers to Bernie and "Butchie"

Monti Rock III is cute.

STRAWBERRY FIELDS ARE BLIGHTED

Love to Brian Epstein. May he find bliss soon.

Lenny "I be loving you, it'll all be there when my dreams come true". Marion.

Mory Loves Toneys.

Shawn loves Lynne.

DAVY'S WHERE IT'S AT.

Happy belated 20th Birthday Barry Gibb—Kathy.

SGT. PEPPERS LONELY HEARTS CLUB BAND IS LOVE.

Lead Seed—where is the entrance way to play? Crystal.

Andrejsgulbis Stinks.

DAVY WELCOME HOME! we missed you! Love, Linda.

REACH COSMIC AWARENESS without drugs—help save mankind from destruction. Write for free booklet, "Cosmic Awareness Speaks," SERVANTS OF AWARENESS, Box 115E, Olympia, Washington.

SLEEP LEARNING, self-hypnosis. Details, strange catalog free! Nutosuggestion, Box 24-BT, Olympia, Washington.

THE WHO blew minds as well as amps at the Anaheim Convention Center!

REMEMBER KIMBA 4-EVER!

Rolling Stones Posters 2½ ft. by 3 ft. $1.75 postpaid. Seper Co., 5273 Tendilla, Woodland Hills, California.

Cleveland needs a Hollie-day!

HAPPY BIRTHDAY TO HOLLIE BERNIE CALBERT.

Happy Birthday George Donaldson, Lis, Jenny.

Mark Sasaki I'll always love you.

LOVE, LIFE AND LENNON.

Hard Times remember auburn Washington and the girls who love you, Shelley, Kim and Kathy.

Rudy—congratulations on Blew mind! I'm coming to San Francisco. Hope to see you, Shelley.

TO THE ONE (OR ONES) WHO SENT THE BEAUTIFUL BEADS AND QUOTATION IN OLDE ENGLISH. THANKS AND LOVE, MARK LINDSAY.

Les Thompson grooves.

PAUL McCARTNEY you crazy little boy—I love you!!! Lorelle.

Beatles fans grew up four years ago. The Monkees and their fans are still hoping.

Giant Beatle rally coming—Feb. 10th, 1968.

LOVE YOUR BROTHERHOOD.

Ted Bluechel is a PIGment of your imagination.

Ted Bluechel eats PIG newtons.

Ted Bluechel—Good Eternity.

Russ Giguere's mustache tickles.

Brian will love Tiann forever.

Butch has a dirty mind.

Bill Hudson of THE NEW YORKERS is the greatest—Theresa Mayovsky.

JOHN LENNON'S LIKE A PICTURE, HE'S WORTH 10,000 WORDS. Happy Birthday! allmyloving!!! Paula.

to little lester tanaka who's fourth period is mr. abes' drafting class, i love you.

Spider-man swings! R.F.O. Carol.

Bob Dylan and Queen Shaz. What about Project Hill? Eh . . . ?

Happy October Birthdays—Gaye Napoleon, Floyd, John and Wolfgang—marcianne.

DON AND THE GOOD-TIMES—SO GOOD!

Where have the Byrds flown? Joe Edmondson.

To the Wibbage Chargers, Radio 99 of Philadelphia—CHARGE! Hyski — I love you! Luv, Lin

Jerry Larson, We love you!!!

To Elizabeth Rhodes from Bryophyta

Beat is no longer accepting anything but PERSONAL MESSAGES in the classified section. Only messages (including Happy Birthdays) will be run. We will print names but not addresses or phone numbers. Rates are cheap! Only 10 cents per word.

Rates are cheap! Only 10 cents per word.
And remember, BEAT has a new address:

Classified
BEAT Publications
9121 Sunset Blvd.
Los Angeles 90069

Deadline for next issue: Sept. 26

KRLA ARCHIVES

KRLA ARCHIVES

Stones Denied U.S. Work Permits

KRLA Edition BEAT

25¢

OCTOBER 21, 1967

Mamas And Papas Leave Pop For 'Adventure'

KRLA BEAT

Volume 3, Number 16 — October 21, 1967

Beatles' Yogi In U.S. To Spread The Word

LOS ANGELES—Indian Mystic Maharishi Mehesh Yogi was in Los Angeles for the second time in as many years to deliver talks on the benefits of meditation and to organize academies for the teaching of transcendental meditation.

This year was very different for the Indian visitor. Whereas last year his press conference was held in a private home with all reporters kindly asked to remove their shoes, this year's conference was held at the very proper Los Angeles Press Club before a dozen reporters and various cameramen.

Beatle Interest

The main reason for the gained notoriety is the interest the Beatles have shown in the Maharishi's philosophy.

"The Beatles came backstage after one of my lectures," he explained, "and they said to me, 'even from an early age we have been seeking a highly spiritual experience. We tried drugs but that didn't work.'

"You have come to the right place,' I said.

"They are such practical and intelligent young boys, it did not take more than two days for them to discover that transcendental meditation is the answer.

"'We'll do anything you say,' they told me."

It was by the Marahishi's suggestion that the Beatles decided to open an academy for his International Meditation Society in London. They also plan to get together for two or three months in India this October to pursue this way of life.

Questions

During the two days in Wales the Beatles were asked a good many questions by the Maharishi.

"One of them took a badge out of his pocket. I asked, 'What is this?'. He said it was a Ban the Bomb badge. He said there was an organization that wanted to put an end to bombs.

"I told him, 'Be careful, you have a great responsibility, don't go into the abstract idealisms. If you want to ban the bomb you must show a bigger bomb.'

"Then they said the government is awful. I told them, 'As young men, be careful. Whatever party is elected must be supported'."

The Marahishi has yet to hear any of the Beatles music, but he believes that he will eventually, maybe when they join him in India.

The Beatles are not the only pop singers and performers to show an interest in his philosophy. The Rolling Stones, Donovan, some of the Doors and television actor Efrem Zimbalist Jr. have also sought out his counsel.

MAHARISHI: "Don't go into abstract idealism."

MAMAS AND PAPAS leaving to re-find those lost good vibrations.

MAMAS, PAPAS QUIT POP

BEVERLY HILLS — At the swank Beverly Wilshire Hotel the four Mamas and Papas rectified the statement Ed Sullivan made on his September 17 television show.

"We're leaving the country," announced Michelle, though it came as no real surprise since all the city's radio stations (not to mention Sullivan) had already jumped the gun. "We've already stopped recording at this point and we're going to Europe for an indefinite period of time."

Disenchantment

And the reason behind this move is disenchantment with the musical product they've been turning out. "It seems as though we're grinding it out, re-creating the things we've done before. We don't have time to work as creative artists; we're without good vibrations, so we're going on an adventure somewhere," John revealed.

"We're going as a group. We sail from New York to Liverpool, then on to London where we may do a concert and perhaps we'll do concerts in Switzerland and Germany. It's the end of a musical era for us," added Cass.

At the mention of Liverpool and London, the question as to whether the Mamas and Papas will visit with the Beatles was raised.

Beatle Visit?

And, quite logically, it was Mama Cass who answered: "We'd like to spend time with the Beatles but that is not our primary objective."

Nor is their objective in going to Europe a monetary one. "No one ever leaves America to make money," stated Cass. Well then, asked a network reporter, how much money has the group already made? "It's hard to tell," replied Cass. "We've made a bit of money but we're not millionaires by any stretch of the imagination."

"We make $20,000 a night for *(Continued on Page 4)*

No More U.S. Stone Tours

NEW YORK—U.S. Immigration has barred further touring of the United States by the Rolling Stones. The Immigration department based their decision on the recent arrests of Mick Jagger and Keith Richard in London on narcotics charges.

Unless this decision is reversed, this will mean the end of all personal appearances for the Stones in the United States.

HARRISON FINDS HELP IN HOUSE

By Tony Barrow

George Harrison's contribution to the soundtrack of the Beatles' self-directed hour-long television show "Magical Mystery Tour" is a new song which he wrote while he was in California at the beginning of August!

Entitled "Blue Jay Way" the composition relates directly to the location of the hideaway home George rented for himself and his friends during their eight-day visit.

Here's how the song came about. With Pattie, road manager Neil Aspinall and the Beatles' close friend Magic Alex, George arrived at Blue Jay Way on the afternoon of Tuesday, August 1. The long polar jet flight from London had left most of the party ready for some rest. But George decided to stay up for a while and Neil joined him. They telephoned a good friend of theirs inviting him to come over for the evening. Detailed instructions for reaching Blue Jay Way had to be relayed over the telephone. It was this call which proved to be George's inspiration for the new song. He sat down behind a mini-organ and went to work while they waited for their friend to arrive.

Hypnotic Song

"Blue Jay Way" is a slow number with an almost hypnotic atmosphere about it. On the whole it is less complex and more commercial than George's "Sgt. Pepper" piece "Within You, Without You."

Incidentally it was in America, almost four months earlier, that Paul started work on the television show's title song "Magic Mystery Tour." Within days of his return home (after being with Jane Asher in Denver for her 21st birthday party) the Beatles recorded the first track for "Magical Mystery Tour." Since then the general construction of that number has been modified and addi- *(Continued on Page 7)*

KRLA ARCHIVES

Letters to the Editor

TOUGH ON JOHNNY RIVERS?

Dear BEAT:

I buy your magazine every time it's for sale and as a whole I think it's wonderful. In the People Are Talking column you have said a few things that just don't set too well.

I am a very big fan of Johnny Rivers and in my opinion I think he's the greatest thing that has happened since Elvis. Only, *once* have I read any sort of complimentary statement about him. This was on his great success as a businessman.

So you say "Now that the Miracles have a new record out, Johnny Rivers has a follow-up to 'Tracks Of My Tears'." Well, since Motown artists are considered "Soul Singers" how many artists can cut the same record and come up with a smash hit? One that has kept climbing and has hit the number one spot on the West Coast? Not many, even you have to admit that.

Johnny Rivers is a very, very versatile man. His list of achievements are out of sight. A top recording artist: pop, folk, ballads, country and western. A top record producer and song writer, and a great businessman. I imagine there are quite a few other things he's successful at that the public never hears about. I think he will go on to greater heights in the years to come.

Maybe you can call him a "copy cat" well, from the sales of his last two hits someone else besides myself liked them even though they were "old Motown Records."

Johnny Rivers seems like the type of man who does what he wants to do when he wants to do it. I guess your opinions really haven't made a dent.

Why don't you say something nice about him. For instance his charity work or better yet his trip to Viet Nam to entertain our troops. He does have good qualities and it wouldn't kill you to mention a few of these.

A Johnny Rivers' Fan—Jan Talpai

Scratching The Surface

Dear BEAT:

I have read your publication for some time, as a matter of fact I am a subscriber. I realize the scope of your newspaper and how important the teeny-boppers are to your revenue. However, I believe it would be wise and profitable to further try to appeal to the would-be hippies. Lately you have printed some interesting articles on what's really happening but as yet you have not really done more than scratch the surface. I submit that you consider discontinuing Shirley You Jest and The Adventures of Robin Boyd columns. This alone would give you one whole page on which you could begin a serious poetry section and make perhaps some comment on other art forms—films, books, paintings, etc.

The Forum and your excellent coverage of music are to be complimented.

In closing I would like to add that I think most of your young readers would be intrigued by a hippier approach, and that you consider that many of your readers are growing up and if you are to keep their attention you must grow with them.

I hope I said something that will be worthy of your consideration. I also suggest a poetry column. I am sure that many of your readers would welcome a chance to submit their writing, too.

—Tom Lyon

A Phenomenon

Dear BEAT:

I have noticed a rather strange phenomenon which may or may not be interesting to your readers: it is all the pop singers (men) who have kids have sons and no daughters! To name a few: John Lennon, Ringo Starr, Bill Wyman, Lenny Davidson, Rick Huxley, Mike Nesmith, Mike Smith (ex-Raider) etc.

—Hillary Parkes

The Smell Of Flower Power

Dear BEAT:

It was about time that the BEAT had an article about the fabulous Supremes! I know the Supremes are hard to get interviews from, but they have a right to be choosy about whom they let interview them. But I'm glad you at least covered the Cocoanut Grove appearance with pictures and about their performance, even though you didn't get an interview with them. The Supremes deserve a lot more credit and publicity than they get.

The rest of your BEAT about the psychedelic and flower poster groups *stunk*. No paper or magazine should write about groups whose members have been picked up on dope charges (Rolling Stones) or groups whose members take LSD (Beatles). You're not helping the teen-agers who read this paper by writing articles about groups connected with the psychedelic and hippie movement. Some teen-agers idolize such groups as the Rolling Stones, Beatles and Seeds. When they read or hear these groups taking dope they think it is all right for them too.

The psychedelic movement is truly repulsive. The hippies are only proving what ugly, stupid, sobs they are protesting against society with all their love-ins and terrible clothes. What do you feel about the morals of these hippies and psychedelic groups? I hope you stop writing about these psychedelic groups and start writing articles on the decent groups in show business, such as: The Righteous Brothers, Smokey Robinson and the Miracles, The Temptations, The 5th Dimension, the Four Tops, Mel Carter, Marvin Gaye and Tami Turell, Petula Clark and Brenda Holloway. I am not a Negro, but I do enjoy mostly Motown sounds and other good singing groups. Groups from Motown should be given a lot of credit, for they produce hit after hit and are an asset to the singing business.

A Supremes fan

Censorship Asinine

Dear BEAT:

I just want to say that whoever wrote "Hey Mom and Dad has it Really Changed?" is a genius.

I think that censoring songs is one of the most asinine things anyone could do. I know that when I hear "A Day in the Life" by the Beatles, I don't hop in the car and go buy some pot or LSD. That song happens to be one of my favorite cuts from the album and the new album is one of the Beatles' best.

—Nancy Hoffner

FORUM the

The opinions and ideas expressed in the Letters to the Editor or The Forum sections of our paper are not necessarily the opinions of The BEAT. However, we do feel that this is a free country in which each individual is entitled to hold and express his/her opinions and beliefs. Unfortunately, a limited amount of space prevents us from printing every letter submitted to The BEAT. Consequently, we are forced to print only a general cross-section of the mail we receive.

The Editor

Untitled

History repeats itself.
You are part of the repitition that produces change.
Only your change, this generation's, is different.
It is the first of an awakening, yet it scars and cripples.
You speak of peace and end of war.
You create; your songs sing of peace for children, peace
    in which they can laugh and play in freedom.
You are free; what have you done with your time?
These children will include your children.
Change your vision.
Because of the manner of your change, some of your children will
    not only live in peace, they will live in a comparable oblivion.
I have seen their faces; their eyes seem to be your scars, holding
    only the vacant and the oblivious.
Some will be oblivious; unaware.
What if they will be unaware to freedom?
What if they will be unaware to peace?

Jenny Reif

KRLA ARCHIVES

REDDING NO. 1 IN WORLD POLL

Otis Redding has been named by Great Britain's Melody Maker magazine as the top male vocalist.

JOIN NOW...YOU'LL FIND CONTENTMENT IN POSSESSION!

An 8x10 shiny portrait of "The Mendelsohn Quintette Club of Boston" autographed...

A newsletter from Irving Mendelsohn. A resume of notes-happenings-comments sent to you monthly... or by-monthly or every three weeks, or... well you'll always get it when Irving feels like writing.

PLUS: Free admission to "The Mendelsohn Quintette Club's" annual extravaganza at the General Hospital Therapy Center... FREE ADMISSION to all their personal appearances at parking lots, super markets, medical centers, bank robberies, etc. etc. MORE AND MORE BENEFITS TOO NUMEROUS TO MENTION! It costs only 25¢... just 25¢ AND... your card may have the lucky number. Hurry... Hurry... Fill in and mail this coupon now!

COUPON

Enclosed is my 25¢. I yearn to become a member of "THE MENDELSOHN QUINTETTE CLUB OF BOSTON" FAN CLUB.

Name _____
Address _____
City _____ State _____

JAMES B. LANSING SOUND, INC.
3249 CASITAS AVE., LOS ANGELES, CALIFORNIA 90039
BEAT-F

SUNSHINE CO. DIRT BAND IN MOVIE DEBUT

LOS ANGELES—The Sunshine Company and The Nitty Gritty Dirt Band will both make their motion picture debuts in the film, "For Singles Only," to star Milton Berle and John Saxon. The Columbia Pictures feature is due for release in December.

The Sunshine Company, currently riding high on the charts with "Happy," and the Dirt Band and have been dividing their time between playing local clubs and recording film tracks in the afternoons.

The Sunshine Company will do the title song, while the Dirt Band are due to slice two other songs for the score.

Beat Publications, Inc.

Executive Editor .... Cecil L. Tuck
Publisher .... Gayle Tuck
Editor .... Louise Criscione
Assistant Editor .... Jacoba Atlas

Staff Writers
Bobby Bovino   Ron Koslow
Tony Leigh   Shirley Poston

Contributing Writers
Tony Barrow   Sue Barry
Eden   Bob Levinson
Jamie McClusky III   Mike Masterson

Photographers
Ed Caraeff   Jerry Hess

National Sales Representative
Sam Chase Assoc., Inc.
527 Madison Avenue
New York, New York
(212) PL. 5-1688

Advertising Director .... Dick Stricklin
Business Manager .... Judy Felice
Subscriptions .... Diane Clatworthy

Distribution
Miller Freeman Publications
500 Howard Street, San Francisco, Calif.

The BEAT is published bi-weekly by BEAT Publications, Inc., editorial and advertising offices at 9121 Sunset Blvd., Los Angeles, California 90069. U.S. bureaus in Hollywood, San Francisco, New York, Chicago and Nashville; overseas correspondents in London, Liverpool and Manchester, England. Sale price 25 cents. Subscription price: U.S. and possessions $5 per year; Canada and foreign rates, $9 per year. Second class postage prepaid at Los Angeles, California.

Williams In N.Y. Museum?

HOLLYWOOD — Mason Williams, one of the writers for "The Smothers Brothers Comedy Hour," just may find himself hanging in the Museum of Modern Art in New York — or rather his *Bus Book* is being considered for the Museum.

In all fairness, we must admit that Mason's *Bus Book* is really not a book at all but a life-size picture of a Greyhound Bus! It was recently featured in the poster art issue of *Life Magazine* and stands a mere 35' by 8'.

Mason has already written six other books — "Next to the Windows," "Bicyclists Dismount," "Tosadnesday," "The Royal Road Test," "The Night I Lost My Baby — a Las Vegas Vignette" and "Boneless Roast." Before all that, Mason used to drop by the BEAT offices and drink a lot of our coffee!

Elvis—Strong Arm Or Not?

MEMPHIS — Elvis Presley either has a strong arm or he doesn't — it's all a matter of which story you choose to believe.

Elvis' story goes something like this: Troy Ivy, a former yardman at Presley's Graceland mansion, showed up "drunk, belligerent, arrogant, cursing loudly and took a swing at me." At which point, Elvis says he flattened Ivy with a single blow.

Ivy, however, says that just isn't so. His story is that he was leaning up against his car when Presley "dressed in a red suit came roaring down the drive in a red car."

Ivy went on to say that Presley asked him if he were trying to kill his father (Vernon Presley) and then hit him twice. But, says Ivy, neither of Presley's blows were hard enough to knock him down.

Memphis police have taken down both stories and are currently attempting to make up their minds as to which one is fact and which is fiction.

ART INSTITUTE OF PITTSBURGH
57th Yr. Coed. & 24 mo. Diploma Course. Commercial Art, Fashion Art, Interior Design, Begin. & Adv. Vet Assoc. Dorm facilities. College referrals for degrees. Free illus. brochure.
Earl B. Wheeler, Director
635 Smithfield St.
Pittsburgh, Pa. 15222

AIRPLANE MANAGER COLLIDE

SAN FRANCISCO—The Jefferson Airplane and promoter Matthew Katz are in the process of suing each other. Katz claims they signed an enforceable contract with him in 1965 for his services as the group's "personal manager." The Airplane, on the other hand, have stated that Katz was not licensed as an artists' manager, had not rendered an accounting nor opened his books for inspection, and therefore the alleged contract is not binding.

The question now goes before the State Labor Commissioner by ruling of the California Court of Appeals. The Appellate Court's decision was based on the Artists' Managers Act which states: Since the clear object of the act is to prevent improper persons from becoming artists' managers and to regulate such activity for the protection of the public, a contract between an unlicensed artist's manager and an artist is void."

Bobbie Gentry Slated For TV

LOS ANGELES—Bobbie Gentry has been signed to guest-star on NBC-HV's Bob Hope Show which will air on November 8.

The guest shot is the sixth network TV appearance the Capitol singing star has been slated for since her record "Ode to Billie Joe" was released two months ago.

Her first appearance was on the Smothers Brothers Show. Upcoming appearances include the Carol Burnett Show and Perry Como Special.

In addition Bobbie will do two Ed Sullivan shows — including the Sullivan Christmas Special. For the Christmas show Bobbie will pen a special Yuletide song which will be introduced that evening.

"The Standel Sound"

"The Nitty Gritty Dirt Band"

Professional musicians throughout the world choose the "Standel Sound," the accepted standard for professional musicians who demand professional performance.   Dept. B

A. P.A. Speaker Column Amplifier
B. P.A. Master Control with Reverb
C. Imperial Line Amplifier — Solid State, Dual Channel

Standel
Solid State Music Systems
4918 DOUBLE DRIVE • EL MONTE, CALIF. 91731

KRLA ARCHIVES

Mama's & Papa's Leaving All Behind

(Continued from Page 1)
our performances, our albums bring us an excellent income, but we're beginning to feel phony as artists," continued John. And this, apparently, is where the real problem lies.

They can't work under the pressure enforced upon those fortunate (unfortunate?) enough to be successful in the entertainment business. They feel they were much more creative when they were less successful and consequently decided in the middle of a recording session to shove it all aside for awhile "to rejuvenate our foursome."

They're searching for something and if they find it John believes "our music will change drastically, the whole style, the whole approach will be more personal."

The point was raised that since the group is leaving "to find something," perhaps they are disenchanted with the current "scene," and perhaps they feel it is dying.

"As long as we're alive, as long as we can perpetuate our group, we don't care what dies," answered Cass. "It may sound selfish but that's the way it is."

Incense And Candles

Now that the Beatles have gone toward transcendentalism, are the Mamas and Papas heading in that direction as well? "We've always been very spiritual," remarked Cass. "We always feel vibrations." "But," laughed John, "we're taking a lot of incense and candles with us!"

Their fourth album will not be finished; to date they've only cut three tracks and all of those will be scrapped. They'll set up residence in either Greece or Spain and will return to America and the record business when, and if, they find what it is they're looking for.

No Shock

The group's announcement came as a shock to no one connected with the music business. In fact, The BEAT predicted way back in December, 1966 that in 1967 the Mamas and Papas would vanish from the scene.

It was not a hard prophecy to make. The group has never liked nor conformed to the rigid time schedules demanded of a successful entertainer. They have never hidden the fact that work is *not* their favorite occupation in the world.

How long will they stay away, whether or not they will decide to permanently disband or whether they will ever find what they're looking for "remains to be seen."

It's been a great two years for Mama and Papa fans — perhaps there will be more.

SHOUTS FROM GENE

by Gene Cornish

Hey! Hi! How are ya? As for me, I'm still whirling — we just finished a concert at the Singer Bowl (out in Flushing, New York) and the crowds of beautiful fans really had us running and hopping — we barely left the stadium with our shirts on! You should have seen us — like something out of an old-time movie! Good show, though, and lots of fun to do. That concert was our last New York appearance for '67.

It's been *some* two days — the night before the Singer Bowl gig we were guests of Ravi Shankar at his Lincoln Center concert here in New York. It was a fantastic experience — one I won't forget for a long time!

Felix, who fools around with every kind of musical instrument around today, has just bought a sitar! I just read where Shankar spent many, many years studying the sitar with a guru or teacher in India . . . I'll be curious to hear Felix's first number!

Eddie went to the concert wearing some of the clothes he bought out on the West Coast — lots of wild scarves and beads — and crazy candles for his apartment. We loved the Coast and Hawaii — I've just started to get into photography — and I took some great shots of the hippies in San Francisco! I've also been groovin' around Central Park — when I get the chance — and I'm finding out that people really love to find out they're on camera! I can't wait to focus on England — and then on our *Worldwide Peace Tour* I *know* I'll be able to get some great photos . . . and later I'll be on the other end of the lens — when we make that movie about ourselves next April!

Oh — I'm buying my parents (they're originally from Rochester, New York; come to think of it — so am I!) a new home. They're really great — what a ball we had together in Hawaii!

Our fourth album is coming out soon — we've never done anything like it before. I can't believe how excited the four of us are — one of the reasons is that we've composed and arranged every single song in the album . . . And that's pretty satisfying!

The other day a fan asked me what some of my favorite sports are — sports I like to play. Well — I once wanted to be a professional baseball player — but I'm glad the foursome I'm playing with now put a halt to that — but I still love and do play baseball. Any chance I get! I'm also an avid swimmer, sometime surfer and basketball player! Actually, I dig all sports — and would like to be able to participate in them all some day!

I just looked over to the other side of the recording studio (I'm writing to you during a session break at Atlantic) and I see that Eddie is about to pick up my favorite guitar and try to play it like a cello. I guess that calls for a sign-out and some fast action! Talk to you again very soon. Love, Gene . . .

Hippie Shoulder Strap Bag - $2.00 P.P.

Sock-makers hate us.

Forget socks. We did, and came up with Bare/Foot/Gear *sockless* shoes. They're *leather* sneakers—top-grain steerhide—tough, supple, secret-process steerhide that feels great and outwears canvas two to three times. Forget socks, and get the feel of a good idea: Bare/Foot/Gear. We have it for you now.

BARE FOOT GEAR

KRLA ARCHIVES

ZALMAN YANOVSKY
AS LONG AS YOU'RE HERE
BUDDAH 12

Produced by Jack Nitzsche
A Product of Koppelman-Rubin Assoc., Inc.
Personal Management R. J. Cavallo

Exclusively on
BUDDAH RECORDS
1650 Broadway, N.Y.C.

KRLA ARCHIVES

FAREWELL TO THE GOLDEN ERA OF
The MAMAS And PAPAS

Now Available At:

KRLA ARCHIVES

ON THE BEAT
BY LOUISE CRISCIONE

Bill Cosby has reportedly dropped his plans to film "Busman's Holiday." Instead the Cosby-Campbell-Silver Corporation will shoot "God Save the Mark" which Cosby says is "fuller" and besides—there will be a chance for romance in this one!

Encouraged by the tremendous success of his first album as a singer, Cos plans to cut another one as well as a show tune album—I swear. The old Cos is really getting 'em from all sides, and isn't it great?

The Peanut Butter Conspiracy has always been sort of a tell-it-like-it-is group but I really had to laugh when John Merrill gave his reason for cancelling a club engagement. Said John: "Everything was going along smoothly until this nut told us that our single had to be cut immediately. We're not loafers. We were going to try to sandwich the gig in but the bread wasn't too good anyway. Besides, we don't want to spread ourselves too thin." Amen.

Don Ho Cancelled

Due to the strike against the ABC-TV network, Don Ho's appearance on the "Hollywood Palace" had to be cancelled. But it doesn't mean time off for Don, who instead of taping "Palace" will now record a new album for Reprise. That's during the day—at night he's appearing at Melodyland Theatre in Anaheim, California. No wonder he's so successful—he works all the time!

Ken Kragen and Ken Fritz, managers of the Smothers Brothers, have finally taken on a folk/rock group, the First Edition. The group consists of four ex-members of the New Christy Minstrels and now that Kragen and Fritz have taken them on just about the only way they can go is up.

Smothers Busy

As for the Smothers boys, Mercury Records is ready to launch their newest album, "The Smothers Comedy Brothers Hour," with the largest single promotion in the history of the company.

Have some Association dates for you—October 17, Appalachian State University, Boone, North Carolina; October 18, Dan Cannon Auditorium, St. Leo, Florida; Oct. 19, University of Chattanooga, Tenn.; Oct. 20, University of South Florida, Tampa, Florida; Oct. 21, Tennessee Polytechnic Institute, Cookeville, Tenn.; Oct. 26, Southern Oregon College; Ashland, Oregon; Oct. 27, University of Idaho, Moscow, Idaho; Oct. 28, Oregon State University, Corvallis, Oregon; Oct. 30, Oregon Tech Institute, Klamath Falls, Oregon; Oct. 31, Chico State College, Chico, Calif.

QUICK ONES: Donovan was a smash at his Hollywood Bowl show . . . a lot of bets are being taken that the Sunshine Company will be another Mamas and Papas . . . how long will the Stones stay at the top without work permits? . . . the way that their record is descending the national charts, a certain group should be glad they ever got into the paper in the first place . . . Bob Gaudio and Jacqueline Sussan supposedly have written a little song for "Valley Of The Dolls" . . . you have to hand it to Bobbie Gentry, she has the whole nation talking about what Billy Joe threw off the bridge—the joke is, even Bobby doesn't know!

Neil Diamond has discovered a group called the Penny Candy and is busy attempting to make them go. The group (five boys and three girls) will be cutting Diamond material under the watchful eye of Mr. Diamond. "No recording contract has been signed," revealed Neil. "I'm going to cut a couple of singles on my things and see where we go from there. But I envision no difficulty in going the way I want to go with this project."

QUESTION OF THE WEEK: What's happened to Herman? And if you think I mean success-wise, you've missed the whole point.

POP IDOLS TAKE-OVER GOVERNMENT

By Tony Barrow

The production company which made the volatile Paul Jones/Jean Shrimpton movie "Privilege" is following up with a second screenplay which depicts the political

HELPFUL HOUSE

(Continued from Page 1)

tional lyrics were worked out by John and Paul before the final version of the composition was put on tape.

20 Hrs. of Film

All filming for "Magical Mystery Tour" has now been completed after five days of location shooting in Devon and Cornwall, the production crew moved into an almost deserted old Royal Air Force base just outside the tiny historic village of West Malling in the county of Kent. A couple of giant aircraft hangars served as ideas substitutes for film studio soundstages. Here all the indoor sequences were filmed to link up wtih the material put together during the Beatles' five-day bus ride around Southwest England.

The most difficult part of the whole operation is the editing of the finished product. The Beatles have been viewing over and over again more than 20 hours of color film, deciding which pieces to use and which to discard. The final task for the foursome prior to their departure for India will be the writing and recording of incidental music for the soundtrack, a job which cannot start until the edited film is ready in its finished form.

At press time the indications are that the Beatles will leave for India on or about October 24 but if everything does not go according to schedule Paul and, perhaps the others will postpone their trip for the third time to cope with last-minute details of the "Magical Mystery Tour."

Amongst the many special scenes filmed for inclusion in "Magical Mystery Tour" are an army recruiting office sketch involving guest star Victor Spinetti in the role of a sergeant, a Soho strip club sequence in which Striptease girl Jan Carlson is seen working alongside guest group the Vonzo Dog Doo Dah Band, a swimming pool segment involving veteran comedian Nat Jackldy plus a dozen bikiniclad teenyboppers John (heavily disguised with paint-and a restaurant scene in which ed moustanche and sleeked-back hair!) plays a waiter.

power which could be exerted by top pop people. Scheduled to go into production next month (November) the new John Heyman picture is to be called "Seventeen Plus." The story—about teenage voters managing to replace existing political parties with a government dominated by their pop idols—has been written by famous stage and screen author Wolf Mankowitz.

Procol Harum has been invited to star in "Seventeen Plus!" It is almost certain that they will accept—agreeing not only to come be the centerpiece of the film but also to write the full soundtrack score.

Prior to commencing his current month-long concert tour of America, Donovan recorded two special compositions which he will be heard singing in the movie "Poor Cow" which stars Terence Stamp and Carol White.

The Bee Gees, currently climbing the U.K. Top 10 with "Massachusetts," have almost finished their second LP album. It is to be issued in Britain via Polydor and America via Atco this side of Christmas under the program title "Horizontal." Following fan club protest demonstrations in London secretary Julie Barrett received an official letter from 10 Downing Street, London home of Prime Minister Harold Wilson. The letter confirmed the Home Office instruction that Australian Bee Gees Vince Melouney and Colin Peterson must leave Britain because their six-month visitor's permits have expired. But it added that the pair would be given a further extension and would not be required to quit the country before the end of November. Meantime, the group's personal manager, Robert Stigwood, is seeking further legal advice in new attemps to gain permanent U.K. residence for the Commonealth visitors.

The New York arrival of the Rolling Stones a couple of weeks ago was void of all the usual publicity trappings. The group shrank back into the privacy of their suites at the Warwick Hotel, huddling in a series of concentrated meetings with business manager Allen Klien.

A few days later in London the story one had been expecting for quite some time broke in the national newspapers. Andrew Oldham had ceased to be the group's recording manager. Oldham had already relinquished the formal title of Personal Manager, a position he held until Klein came on the scene last year.

The Beatles' delayed departure date to India has allowed John Lennon to accept an invitation to attend the World Premiere of his film "How I Won the War" on October 18 at London's Pavillion Theatre in Piccadilly Circus.

John, Paul and George are very strict vegetarians, refusing to eat any dish containing meat or meat products. Ringo often joins them in their specialist diet if the group is having a meal together.

Faux Pas

A New Zealand newspaper headlined its full-page story about mystic Mararishi Mahesh Yogi with the words "Seer Slugs Beatles." The report began: "The Beatles are mugs. Or that's what many New Zealanders are thinking. The Hindu mystic who has them entralled with his 'secret of happiness' is the same man who was laughed at when he toured here in 1962." Later the newspaper says: "New Zealanders couldn't get out fast enough when he lectured in the Wellington Town Hall in March 1961. Without genius Epstein to watch over them, the Beatles appear to have made their worst faux pas since . . . who was it said 'we are more popular than Jesus Christ?' And if a week's income was the price for a session of meditation, it could have been an expensive faux pas at that."

WARREN ENTNER, Bob Quill, Creed Bratton, Rick Coontz.

KRLA ARCHIVES

BILL COSBY CALLS THE SHOTS

"They're not lost. No man is really lost who is searching. Most people are aware of what's going on; they just want a better life for themselves. I don't think the grown-ups have shown where they're so hip — the way the world is set up today . . ."

By Eden

We all go through changes . . . millions of them; every day of our lives. We change, the world around us changes, and everything in that world is part of a circular pattern of change and development.

Bill Cosby is human like the rest of us and he, too, has his share of changes. There was a time in Philadelphia when Cosby attended classes at Temple University as a Physical Education major, but that has changed. Now he remembers his days of books and basketball in funny sketches he shares with the world.

Most Romantic

Once there was a time when Cosby made his first appearance on TV, and earned for himself the reputation of "most promising young comedian." That has changed. Now he *is* one of the very best of comedians and his promise was fulfilled.

Once there was a tense first night — the beginning of a brand new TV series, the beginning of a brand new life. Cosby became an actor. He also became a Pioneer in the Vast White Wasteland of TV, and blazed a trail across that wilderness. Twice there were official recognitions, and Cosby earned two Emmys!

Time has moved and things have changed; they always do. Today Cosby has a nickname — Silver Throat, and he is gaining increasing acceptance as a singer. That's one more trail he had to clear out in the forest; one more hurdle he had to jump.

Once he was an easy-going man of seeming relaxation; today he is a successful bundle of nervous energy that never stops or takes a rest. Five days a week he films "I Spy," and sometimes on the weekends he films a TV special. There are recording sessions, benefit performances, personal appearances, guest shots on top TV variety shows, and a thousand and three other activities which claim him and his time.

Using It

He is an older man now, but that stands to reason. He, too, is a subject of time. In his case, however, he *uses* time to his advantage, and learns and grows in mind and stature with every passing day. He uses much of his precious time to think; thoughts of so many things. Thoughts of today's younger generation, for example, and the state of the world.

"I see them as I'm driving down Sunset; I see them when I go into the Whisky; I see them when I go into Wallich's Music City. Most of them are very well-mannered — 'Mr. Cosby this, Mr. Cosby that' — they're not as out-of-line as some grown-ups I've met who say, 'Hey Bill, so forth and so on' — and the grown-ups are *drunk*, you dig? I also was brought up in my early show business days in Greenwich village, where folk music was the thing.

Clothes Do Not . . .

"The girls wore long hair and they wore the black stockings then, and they all looked *very, very* hip; and as soon as you began to discuss things like *life* with any of them — they didn't know where they were, or who they were, or what was going on. It was just the clothing that made them look so hip.

"So I think I have a pretty good idea of where most of them are; they're *not* lost. *No* man is really lost who is searching. Most people are aware of what's going on; they just want a better life for themselves. And certainly I don't think the grown-ups have shown where *they're* so hip, the way the world is set up today where we have an extended war.

"Now, if you say, 'What are your thoughts on Viet Nam?' My main thought is this: *who* digs a war? *Nobody* — really; nobody digs to have a war. Nobody really digs killing another man. But, if somebody says — 'Now, let's get the war over with.' My wife and I have discussed this many times. My wife says: 'Well, listen — we have so much strength, how come we're fooling around?' And I say, yeah — but you can't have the same thing like we had at Hiroshima, where we dropped the bomb and we *still* have people scarred and messed up. But, by the same token, we can't let the cats run over us.

To The Dead?

"If we pull out — if we just say, 'Okay everybody . . . forget it! We were wrong, *zank!*' Then, what happens to the *thousands* of young American boys that *died* over there in that soil? Every cat that died happened in vain, or was a *mistake*. So, we're *sorry!* So I think it's almost impossible that, one — we can go in there and drop a huge bomb and just burn everybody up, because as weird as it may seem . . . it isn't just *humane!* And, you can't pull out because you've lost thousands and thousands of people over there. What are their families going to think?

"So, with this total *mess-up* with this particular war — and I *do* believe that there will be many, many more; I don't think America and Russia will ever come toe-to-toe — I think what they'll do is just go around and mess up all those other little countries that can't help themselves. And this is one way that they can satisfy each other's ego, because by this time they're *too* big. Now, we have a third party which never figured out in my philosophy, which is Red China. I don't know yet what to do about them or what they're going to do; but they certainly are a threat. Which may push Russia and America *together!*

Depressing Situation

"It's a difficult situation; it's a *depressing* situation to get up every morning and think about. The young men of the world have got to think about, 'Am I gonna get drafted and go into this war?' And, as soon as they pick up a rifle, they're sent out there and the bullets are flying. And there's no time for you to stand around and say, 'Am I *right?*' It's self-preservation; you've got to protect yourself."

A man of many changes; a mind that skips from one thing to the next with the speed of lightning, changing and even formulating his own ideas in mid-air. These have been just a few of his many ideas.

KRLA ARCHIVES

Two Great Albums:

LN 24199/BN 26199*

LN 24304/BN 26304*

An Unusual New Single:
KRIS KRISTOFFERSON
"Golden Idol" 5-10225

EPIC RECORDS

*Stereo

®"EPIC", Marca Reg. T.M. PRINTED IN U.S.A.

KRLA ARCHIVES

A SINGER NAMED SMOTHERS?

When Dickie first told me that he wanted to do an album by himself, my first reaction was to beat him up. Look what happens—you bring a kid along, teach him the ropes, lend him your Flexi Flyer, give him your best baseball trading cards, never complain even if Mom did always like him best, and the first thing you know he gets out on his own!

When you listen to this album I think you'll understand why I am confident that Dickie, in spite of having a name only a mother can love, can't help but be a great singing star as well as my best straight man and brother.

Tom Smothers

Now Available At:
MONTGOMERY WARD
DEPARTMENT STORES

Take A Trip To Mexico
Via A
Kaleidoscope Of Sound

Available At . . .

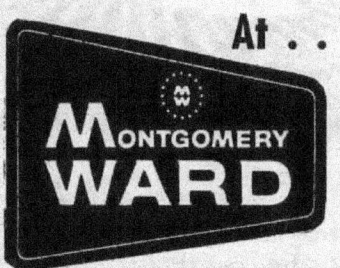

KRLA ARCHIVES

KRLA...A Second Concert Series

By Bob Dayton

KRLA's concert series' successes are being heralded from city to city. And, even though the present series is still in progress, we've already been bombarded with inquiries for advance information about KRLA's Second Concert Series beginning in November.

Never to leave our listeners unanswered, I've been called upon "to cop out." November 4th, "KRLA PRESENT THE SUPREMES, SANDY BEVIN, AND HUGH MASAKELA" at the UCLA Poly Pavilion. November 17th, "KRLA PRESENTS JUDY COLLINS" at the Santa Monica Civic Auditorium, and December 2nd "KRLA PRESENT JOAN BAEZ" at the UCLA Poly Pavilion.

KRLA PRESENTS... JUDY COLLINS November 17th

ICE HOUSE GLENDALE
234 So. Brand Ave. Reservations: 245-5043

Oct. 3rd thru 8th
THE GOOD TIME SINGERS of the ANDY WILLIAMS SHOW...

THE SECOND HELPING
Viva Record Artists
"Don't You Remember the Good Times"

Oct. 10th thru 15th
HEARTS AND FLOWERS
with their hit
"ROCK AND ROLL GYPSIES"
and
The Stourbridge Lione

ICE HOUSE PASADENA
24 No. Mentor — Reservations: 681-9942

Oct. 3rd thru 15th
- CASEY ANDERSON
- STEVE MARTIN
- WALT CONLEY

NOW HAPPENING EVERY NITE
1 — PACIFIC OCEAN
2 — OCTOBER COUNTRY
3 — POP CORN BLIZZARD
4 — ENEMIES
5 — HUMAN EXPRESSION
6 — ABSTRACTS

WED., OCT. 11th La Cienega
"Jimmy O'Neal Presents"
DEAN HOLLY

GAZZARRI'S #1 ON-THE-STRIP
9039 SUNSET
CR 3-6606
OL 7-2113

GAZZARRI'S #2 LA CIENEGA
319 N. LACIENEGA

MORE HAPPENINGS
MON. — Dance Contest to select Miss Hollywood A-Go-Go of 1968
$500 Grand Prize
TUES. — Talent Nite
WED. — Fashion Show
SUN. AFTERNOON GROOVE IN — 4 P.M.
Did You Say, "Where's the Action"? What's This... Chopped Liver?!!

Would you believe... THE BEAT?

ASH GROVE
NOW! Bessie Griffin & GOSPEL PEARLS
with Delores Addison
CLIFTON CHENIER
GREATEST OF THE CAJUN BANDS
Oct. 13-22
8162 Melrose Ave. — OL 3-2070

THE GOLDEN BEAR
306 OCEAN AVENUE (HWY 101) HUNTINGTON BEACH

PRESENTS
NOW THRU OCT. 8th

Mike Bloomfield's "ELECTRIC FLAG"

Reservations PHONE 536-9600
536-9102

CAROUSEL THEATRE
West Covina
ON STAGE   IN PERSON

Oct. 17-22 • 1 Week Only
Bobby Darin
special guest stars
Little Richard Revue

Oct. 24-29 • 1 Week Only
THE SOUL SOUNDS OF The Righteous Brothers

SEATS NOW at box office, by mail and at all ticket agencies.
Phone (213) 966-4571

GARY BERWIN'S ANNUAL ARTIST'S and MODEL'S BALL IN COSTUME

OCT. 29 8 PM
CENTURY PLAZA HOTEL — GRAND BALLROOM
$6.00 PER PERSON

NO ADMITTANCE WITHOUT A COSTUME!!
AWARDS... ENTERTAINMENT... REFRESHMENTS
Reservations Limited to Persons Associated With the Entertainment Industry

The Artist's and Model's Ball is Produced By
LONDON PRODUCTIONS INC.
9000 Sunset Blvd., L.A. 90069

Tickets and Information 278-4488

PRODUCER: Gary Berwin; EXECUTIVE/PRODUCERS: Harvey Fierstein & Jordan Wank

KRLA ARCHIVES

OVER 500 WINNERS
BEAT MAGAZINE
PROUDLY PRESENTS
THE GREAT RACE

FIRST PRIZE—CORDLESS TAPE RECORDER
2nd Prize—Portable Radio/Phonograph
100 3rd Prizes—1 Year BEAT Subscription or Renewal
200 4th Prizes—Popular Record Albums
200 5th Prizes—Beautiful Red and Silver BEAT Pens

Starring all BEAT REPRESENTATIVES

Featuring 500 Prizes including first prize of a TAPE RECORDER, second prize of a portable record player and radio, runner up prizes of top selling albums, free subscriptions or renewals to THE BEAT + Beautiful Beat Pens.

WATCH AS BEAT REPRESENTATIVES throughout the country compete for the most subscriptions.

THRILL AS YOU watch YOUR list get longer and longer.

QUAKE WITH ANTICIPATION as the contest draws to a close.

Send in subscription blanks NOW through NOVEMBER 30. Contest ends at midnight on Nov. 30th.

Don't miss out on the biggest spectacle of the year!
If you are not now a BEAT REPRESENTATIVE don't miss out—just fill out this form and send it to:

BEAT REPRESENTATIVES
9121 Sunset Blvd.
Los Angeles, California

Yes! I want to be a BEAT Representative and enter the Great Race.

Name_____
Address_____
City_____ State_____ Zip____

If you are not a current subscriber, your own subscription can count as your first order sold.

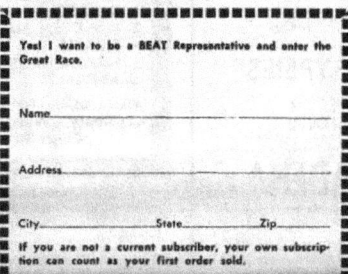

CLASSIFIED

Bonzo McGinly DIGS Dottie O'Donnell.

John, you have a groovy voice —call again. Luv, Kathy.

Happy Birthday Genie KRYCL

BETH ABRAMS write us or else??? Barbara and Andi.

FLOWERS CAN'T GROW WITHOUT SEEDS!!

Joankireallygoveeonyauabiem

Amelia Rusty forever, Merry Christmas Colleen Steve

JOHN I'm glad we're groovin' together — Julie

Bruce . . . my psychedelic baby . . . Kathy.

"To my Brother Tom Meeks." You're the greatest brother anyone could have, and I love you very, very much. Margie.

To the BEAUTIFUL BEATLES: You made me so happy — I'm so glad you came into my life! Love, Sylvia.

Rick McWilliams — WOW

Fang — Happy Birthday Evie J The MUSEUM are outasite!

HAPPY BIRTHDAY Muzzie —Thede

Thede and Nancy say Hi DICK

Nancy Kay — Have a HAPPY RING

THORINSHIELD GROOVES! REACH COSMIC AWARENESS without drugs—help save mankind from destriction. Write for free booklet. "Cosmic Awareness Speaks," SERVANTS OF AWARENESS, Box 115E, Olympia, Washington.

Ralph Scale, even though you walk through glass doors we still love you. Love from Chicago, Betty and Marianne

Ralph Lynn, Hope your head is better now. Marianne and Betty from Chicago

SLEEP LEARNING, self-hypnosis. Details, strange catalog free! Nutosuggestion, Box 24-BT, Olympia, Washington.

Rolling Stones Posters 2½ ft. by 3 ft. $1.75 postpaid. Seper Co., 5273 Tendilla, Woodland Hills, California.

Happy Birthday Jeri—ABCD

Ralph Scala is — always will be. Love You, Ralph Terry Kirkams, my heart's yours.

Ernie and Frank, Rolling Stones Rule! Turn-On, Lyv, Carla

BEATLES People rule! MONKEE people drool!

Seattle misses the Liverpool Five

Steve Laine — Love

Carlos — Remember HE can't erase! Don't let HIM down. Lorraine

Rise with the sound of the MIDNIGHT RAIDERS — Janesville, Wisconsin

Lennon walks on water

Hi, Schocker!

Rick, to know you is to love you — Barb

Enjoy L.A. Elise? Barb

HAPPY LIVES

WBZ loves you

Mike Mattson, I luv you, you fool! Luv, Pat Sorensen

The CYMBOLS of TIME

HAPPY BIRTHDAY, MIKE MATTSON! Luv, Pat Sorensen

"Thank God for 27 Years of Lennon. *Rabbi Birfmark,* Luv. VISH!"

California will always be Dreamin' about *their* Mamas and Papas!

CHERRYCHILDREN LOVE DAVY JONES!!!

TO JOHN: Haddiegrombletoyouhaddiegrimbletoyou Haddiegrimblemerry happyhappybirthday meto THE CHICAGO TRIBE Chrisheyman, Karensturans, Ettacampbell, Suemellor, Judylindquist, Evklaus, Darlenegromall

In loving memory of JAMES BYRON DEAN who in the frantic search for his meaning, lost his life twelve years ago. Dean Young.

We're convinced. No further word.

Rovin' kind rule!

Joe Coniglio deserves a hand!

Lonnie Graves — "outasite"

BEWARE TAHOE — forgrits in runaway shall return!!

Jackbobjoejayveydickielonnieccbbtom OUTASITE

Danna Bradford is as beautiful as Petula Clark!

. . . attention, King John Henderson! Be kind to the Queen and Larry . . .

Happy borthday Phillip Edward Volk from Pat

Jimi Hendrix is

the GROTESQUE MOMMIES Smell Nice

Happy birthday Joe Romero!!

Happy Birthday Russ Giguere — Gloria

Mary Lindsay: There is a huge tin letter waiting for you at Sunset address, Edie.

Where have the Byrds flown? Joe Edmondson.

To the Wibbage Chargers, Radio 99 of Philadelphia—CHARGE! Hyski — I love you! Luv, Lin

Jerry Larson, We love you!!!

To Elizabeth Rhodes from Bryophyta

DAVY'S WHERE IT'S AT.

MOVING?

Writing about a subscription?
Be sure to fill out this form

For FASTEST service on address change, missing copies, etc., attach old mailing label in first space below. Otherwise please print clearly your address as we now have it.

OLD ADDRESS (Attach old label here if available)
NAME
ADDRESS
CITY
STATE   ZIP CODE

NAME
ADDRESS
CITY   STATE   ZIP CODE

MAIL TO: BEAT PUBLICATIONS
Circulation Dept.
9121 Sunset Blvd., Los Angeles, Calif. 90069

Please allow 3 weeks for change to take effect.

KRLA ARCHIVES

The Association: Coping With Success

James McClusky III

The school of contemporary popular music s h o u l d be very proud of itself; among its many other accomplishments it has produced one of the finest groups of talented and creative musicians in the world. A group whose members have all succeeded in graduating with h o n o r s in Talent, Creativity, and Perseverance.

It has been a long time since the lean days before their first hit record, "Along Comes Mary" — two years to be exact. In that time the Association has made the long jump from local coffee houses to the internationally known nightclub — The Cocoanut Grove. The Association had graduated from obscurity to the Big Time. They had really made it.

After the show I found myself interviewing them once again. They hadn't changed radically over the last two years; just grown up and matured a bit.

"We've changed *some*," Ted agreed. "We've gone on to *new* goals, that's all. We just strive for different things we haven't done, different e x p r e s s i o n s, different sounds, different jobs. Everything just keeps going further and further in."

Personal Change

Jim felt that c h a n g e s in the group had been more of a personal thing. "Probably our individual tastes have altered a slight bit, thus creating a different set of *collective* tastes. But, I don't think our goals have altered, really; I think we're all still striving to achieve the same level of perfection in our music and in our show. We're just sockin' *it to it* and trying to do it!"

Ted suddenly rushed over to proudly show his brand new wrist watch off. It was a special Big Wrist Watch with h a n d s that move. Ted hadn't changed. He was still the tall, blue-eyed, handsome young men that parents described as "All-American," girls described as "darling," and the rest of the Association describes as a "lousy lover!" He was still the irrepressible "Pig Man" of the Association; success hadn't altered that a bit.

What about this success? Putting the question to the slow-talking, deep-thinking, largest moving component of the Association machine, Terry replied: "To me it means that we thought something — we laid it down — and they liked it. It means more than just being a good singer, or being a good performer; it means a lot more.

"I feel pleased as a writer . . . I feel pleased as a one-sixth member of the group . . . I don't particularly feel successful as either. I don't think I could do that for another two or three years. If in two or three years I could have a big catalogue of music that I had written or collaborated with other people on — then I could say, 'Well, I've been successful;' rather than just accidentally stumbling onto a passing think like a lot of people have. It could all be a big accident as far as I'm concerned."

Strange Word

"Success is sort of a strange word," Russ added s e r i o u s l y. "There's nothing I think of as success. I believe there are a lot of doors that haven't been walked through, that a lot of people say are closed. I believe that all doors are open — and all you have to do is walk through them. My goal is to walk through as many doors as possible."

Clothed in a striped slip-over shirt and levis, Russ dropped his slim, blond frame into a nearby chair and settled down for a moment. He has quieted down — a little — over the last two years; but he is still the eternal little boy who goes through life opening locked doors and climbing through closed windows. Sort of an *Allen in Wonderland*, a bundle of nervous and inquisitive energy; that's Russell Giguere.

The one new member of the Association — Larry R a m o s — seated himself, cross-legged, on a cushion on the floor nearby. He, too, had some ideas about success. "It represents many things to me. Success means a garage full of beautiful, exotic cars that my own personal talent has paid for. Success means happiness in my home life with my children and my wife. I feel very successful *right now* — as a family man, I've gotten everything I want from my family; in my business I'm in now I feel successful because I'm doing what I want to do.

Bad Taste

"I can be *more* successful — I hope! — later on, and happier, perhaps." He went on to explain that one of the heights of success for him would be to become a successful song writer. He does a great deal of song writing now, although the group has yet to use any of his material he claims that they all suffer from bad taste. "I say a single message, because I have really nothing to beef about or to protest about, because I'm a simple person. I just enjoy and get as much out of life as possible.

Being of a minority group, I don't feel the world owes me a living. I feel that I owe *myself* a living, and I owe my family a living. I think a person who is successful is a person who is happy with his work."

Larry describes himself as a "simple man," but he is only simply delightful. Just as intelligent as the other Associates, he is sort of an elfin minstrel who is singing his way home.

Brian Cole . . . *B r a n k*; the Ramble-On Philosopher and Part-Time Psychologist of the group, paused momentarily to pass comment on success. "The Grove is just a place I happened to stop on my way to wherever I'm going. And success is sometimes defined by two different sets of people, or two different definitions. Success in the big living, breathing, game world — financial success; that's making it, doing whatever you're doing. There's that definition of success, and then there's success meaning your own personal success which is personal happiness. That's how I define it; if you're happy within yourself, then you're successful within yourself. I don't know many p e o p l e who ever achieved any perfection in either one."

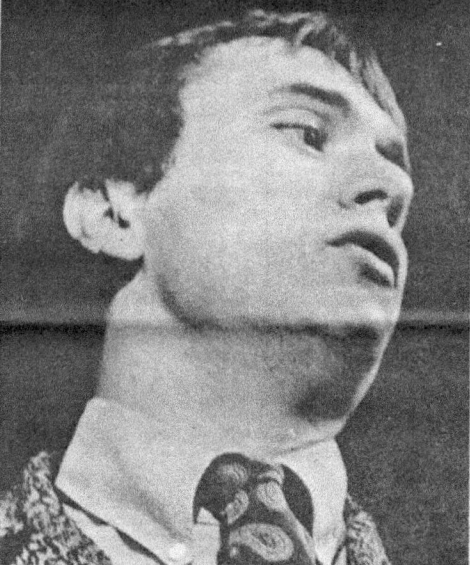

Graduation is always a sentimental thing; an almost-sad thing; a nostalgic time of remembering so many things; good and bad. Like a very young Russ Guiguere with his many buttons and unusual expressions, his effervescent personality and never-ending energy.

Like Brian Cole — the sometimes-cynic who can be so gentle; the tousle-haired thinker who often makes others think he is psychotic. The slightly-strange young man who will be one of the best friends you ever had — if you let him.

Like Jim Yester — blue-eyed, cute, and deceptively normal. He's actually subversively intelligent and just as zany as the rest of them (although rumor has it that he s o m e t i m e s verges on the "straight" side!)

Like Terry Kirkman — the coffee shop philosopher who can frequently be found wandering through Music City in the heart of Hollywood, along with all the other civilians. Tall, talented, and tenaciously perceptive — this Associated song-writer gives himself away with his sincere gentle smile.

Like Ted Bluechel — the beat-looking Pig Man in town! And, Larry Ramos — the uncomplicated musical complication which completes the Association.

Happy Graduation, Associates.

KRLA ARCHIVES

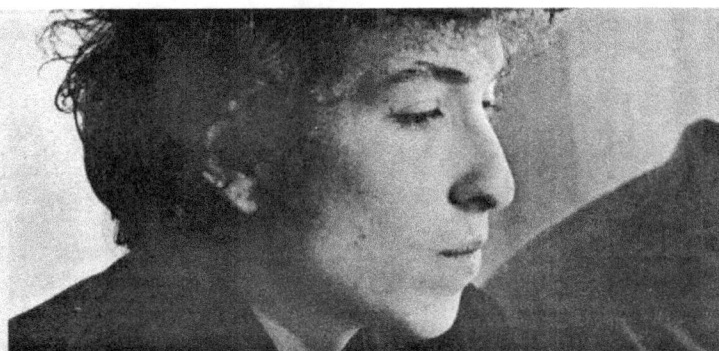

Who Believes Dylan?

By Mike Masterson

What have we here?

There he stands, and who can believe in him? Black corduroy cap, green corduroy shirt, blue corduroy pants.

Old tattered guitar, whooping harmonica and shrieking little voice that sounds as if it were drifting over the walls of a tuberculosis sanitarium or like the howl of a dog with his leg caught in barbed wire.

He's been compared to Salinger's Holden Caulfield in his cockiness. He's been called the Patrick Henry of the folk revolution and the king of rock and roll.

Who is the most influential American writer-performer to emerge in a decade according to Variety? It is Bob Dylan.

He is a 25 year old folk singer who looks more like he is seventeen and whose personal appearance resembles something out of another world.

Sour Milk

Dylan has a long, nervous face covered with the skin color of sour milk; a seemingly untameable mane of curly brown hair which stands up in a bramble of countless tangles; and dark-circled porcelain pussy-cat eyes usually hidden by dark prescription sunglasses.

But the way Dylan presents himself isn't what has made him the most celebrated contemporary composer in music for the sixties.

The pacesetting troubadour began in 1962 by becoming the civil right's movements' bony prophet-post-minstrel of protest.

Musical spokesman of the civil rights marches was his beginning and from there he became one of the most controversial subjects among college students.

Dylan the protestor can be quite forceful in bringing across what he wants to bring across. He also can be vague, repetitive and confusing. Baez said in a 1964 New Yorker magazine article: "Bobby is expressing what I, and many other young people feel—what we want to say. Most of the 'protest' songs about the bomb and race prejudice and conformity are stupid. They have no beauty. Bobby's songs are powerful as poetry and powerful as music."

In one song, *Masters of War*, the villains are the people who profit from the manufacture of war weapons.

College Drop-Out

However, the former scholarship winner to the University of Minnesota and later dropout after three months, always seems too restless, idealistic and angry but still skeptical of neatly defined causes.

He always seems in a hurry. He never seems to be able to catch his breath. Dylan calls an autobiopraphical sketch of himself "Life on a stolen minute."

Pete Seeger, one of the elders of American folk music, says Dylan may become the country's most creative balladeer—if he doesn't explode. Folklorist Alan Lomax says Dylan really is a poet, not a folk singer and that if the former native of Hibbings, Minnesota is given time, he'll go down as a great poet of this time—unless he kills himself.

Among his rapidity, Dylan seems to create his own depression and hence shows tremendous insight of American's despairing poverty problems.

There is one side to Dylan—and that is reality. Dylan is quite real in his use of images or factual incidents.

But Dylan has his followers and his critics. The former feel he has a superb ear for speech rhythm, a generally astute sense of selective detail, and a natural storyteller's command of narrative pacing. They admit, though, his songs sound as if they were being created out of steel history rather than carefully written in an air of tranquility.

His doubters or non-followers often remark that he is just jumbling words and really has no message. They often say that his songs make very little logical sense, but surprisingly always make very good poetic sense.

Folk/Rock

In 1965, Dylan made the big switch: from folk to rock. The new sound was and is justly called folk/rock. In other words, from the Spanish guitar and Holner harmonica to a clamor of topical folk music gushing through the electronic means of instruments went Dylan.

A folk music magazine, *Sing Out*, called the new sound and its innovator, "a freak and a parody." At the 1965 Newport Folk Festival Dylan was booed off the stage.

But where he lost the folk purists he acquired a larger band of followers and financially the change was paying off.

From a select group, Dylan turned commercial. His first attempt didn't quite make it in the charts or with the public, but his second attempt, "Like a Rolling Stone" did. And from here on, Dylan has it made.

So from Minnesota's vast farm land where he ran away from home seven times and only once wasn't caught, Bob Dylan has developed into a multi-millionaire. From the distinction of folk singer and folk writer, his present style now has been labeled "folk rock"—a blend of serious, poetic lyrics and rock and roll music.

Dylan no longer resembles a cross between a choir boy and a beatnik. He still dons a mop of tousled hair but he no longer carries that cherubic look. He has long rid of his Huck Finn corduroy cap. His voice remains not to be pretty and he still composes new songs faster than you can remember them. But Dylan now has other interests besides recording his thoughts and impressions musically.

He is working on a book for MacMillan called *Tarantualla*.

And he is reaping in the royalties from his songs which have been recorded in more than 200 other versions.

From Stan Getz to Lawrence Welk—from Marlene Dietrich to little Stevie Wonder.

Genius Is Insulting

About his songs, Dylan admits that they are not great, for they are not meant to be great. Dylan says "I don't think anytime I touch something it will then be destined for greatness. Genius is a terrible word, a word they think will make me like them. A genius is a very insulting thing to say. Even Einstein wasn't a genius. He was a foreign mathematician.

Dylan says he will never decay. "Decay is something which has for instance, looking at your leg and seeing it covered with creepy brown cancer. Decay turns me off. I'll die first before I'll decay."

Dylan has one principle as a poet and a musician. "I define nothing," he says. "Not beauty, not patriotism. I take everything as it is, without prior rules about what it should be."

You might well ask what is next for Dylan? Will he start a new movement with his new musical innovations?

You can't tell. Dylan is such an unpredictable character, you can't really know what to expect from him.

So where do you find the answer?

In the wind, my friend, in the wind.

VIKKI CARR – THE ALMOST ATHLETE

Vikki Carr is probably one of the most straight-forward performers in existence. It's true that she changed her name from Florencia Biscenta de Casillas Martinez Cardona to simply Vikki Carr but it's equally true that during the course of her club act she inevitably reveals her given name to the audience—every last syllable of it!

She's a Mexican-American and proud of it. Born in El Paso, Texas and raised in the San Gabriel Valley of Southern California, Vikki's early days seemed to point to the fact that she would end up as the first female to ever make it on the Rosemead High School football team!

Fourth 'Man'

She became the fourth "man" on her brothers' teams, developed a good arm for propelling a football on a thirty-yard pass and became highly proficient in baseball, bolling, basketball and golf.

However, she did have one point which saved her from the life of a complete athlete—she loved to entertain. Consequently, she sang with the capella choir in high school as well as a pop group called the Crystalettes.

Showmanship, stage presence and finesse were acquired due to the Latin custom of not dating. Vikki was extremely active in planning many of her school's dances but could not attend them unless she was singing with the band there. It didn't take too long before Vikki's popularity increased sufficiently to warrant her increased weekend bookings until she graduated from high school.

Mexican-Irish Band

She then received the opportunity to audition for the soloist's spotlight with the Peppe Callahan Mexican-Irish Band; an opportunity which she took and soon after found herself and the Band opening at the Chi-Chi in Palm Springs. From there it was Reno, Las Vegas, Lake Tahoe, Hawaii and finally the change from Florencia Biscenta de Casillas Martinez Cardona to Vikki Carr.

Back in Los Angeles Vikki cut her first demo record, eagerly took it around to the record companies, quickly won a long-term contract as is characteristic of Liberty Records.

From that point on, Vikki has been running to the top clubs in the nation, television specials, guest spots on the top variety shows and now a single, "It Must Be Him," which is bounding up the pop charts at an amazing rate of speed.

In the future you can expect to see Vikki make her movie debut and perhaps do a television series of her own. And then, of course, there are Broadway musicals.

But through it all, Florencia Bisenta de Casillas Martinez Cardona remains essentially the same —the girl with the big voice who loves to entertain (and throw 30-yard passes).

VIKKI CARR—from 30 yard passes to "It Must Be Him."

KRLA ARCHIVES

SEEDS = FUTURE

AVAILABLE AT

Thrifty CUT RATE DRUG STORES

KRLA ARCHIVES

NOW THE ALBUM YOU'VE BEEN WAITING FOR!

BEE GEE'S 1st

AVAILABLE AT

Vanilla Fudge is HAPPENING now ARE YOU?

AVAILABLE AT

KRLA ARCHIVES

TOUGH LESSON FOR BOBBY VEE

By Tony Leigh

Anybody over 17 who has listened to pop music since the days when it was referred to only as rock and roll will remember a baby-faced singer named Bobby Vee. A soft-spoken young man with an infectious personality, Bobby scored with successive hits like "Rubber Ball," "More Than I Can Say," "Take Good Care of My Baby," "Run to Him," and "The Night Has a Thousand Eyes." Then came what Bobby himself calls a "cold period," when the hits simply didn't come. But now, more mature, more handsome now that the baby look has left his face, more sure of his music and himself, Bobby is back on the charts with an enormous hit, "Come Back When You Grow Up."

This new single has brought Bobby back into the limelight of the profession he has called his own since he was 16. But the two years absence of Bobby was well spent, giving the young singer new dimensions and new perspectives.

"Well, hopefully, I've matured vocally, I think I understand music now more than I did. I understand a little more the meaning of a song, how to interpret the song, rather than just singing it.

"I've been studying drama for the last three years off and on between tours. I've also been studying dancing and voice. My drama class is taught by actress Agnes Moorhead. We do scenes in class and try to perfect them in class with criticism from anybody who wants to offer any.

Serious Actor

"I would like very much to get into acting. Either in television or in motion pictures. And I would like to start doing summer stock too, maybe next year.

"Well, it's been kind of a draught in the past few years and with the success of this record, 'Come Back When You Grow Up" and we have an album with the same title which has just been released, I hope things will start rolling again.

"I would like to get into clubs, I've played a few young adults' clubs this past summer and they were a lot of fun. And I found that the young adults, the ages from about 20 to the early 30s remember and are familiar with most of my songs of the past so it's kind of warm, it makes it nice.

"I first started listening to rock and roll at the time of its inception, and there has been a lot of changes since then. People used to say rock and roll would die. For example, Chuck Berry, if he was considered rock and roll, then rock and roll has died.

Big Arrangements

"But everything has just graduated, progresively gotten better, I would think.

"And of course, when I started out in the early 60s, we were at the point where violins and big arrangements were being used. And then in 1964 when the Beatles started getting a hold on the pop scene it went back to the groups and gradually it has been built up with the bigger arrangements again.

"It's not any better or worse than it used to be, just different, just something new. I think that anything different is welcome in this business. We need new things as an incentive. It stimulates business when somebody can come out with an original sound.

"Even the psychedelic thing, I'm not flipped over the psychedelic movement per se, but I think it has opened a lot of doors for creative people.

Good Material

"One of the most difficult aspects of performing is being able to find good material. In fact, not too long ago I sat down in the office and listened to about 100 songs that had been sent in from people across the country and publishers, and I didn't use any of them. They were all just terrible.

"So it's really hard to find songs. I have a lot of friends who write, and I've used a lot of their songs, and I have some good friends at publishing companies that bring me songs a lot.

"This current record, 'Come Back When You Grow Up,' was given to me by a disc jockey in Oklahoma City, Dale Weeba, who is now in Detroit, but he heard the song, thought it would be good for me, flew to Los Angeles with it, and we cut the song and it was just one of those things. So I can thank him for it.

No Sinatra

"I would consider myself more of a ballad singer than anything else. As for my nightclub act, when I do clubs, I'm not the kind of singer to go in and do the Sinatra kind of thing. It's not right for me to do that kind of thing. I want to stay as current as possible. And there are enough top 40 songs that are really good songs. If they are arranged right, they sound like standards and the older generation appreciates this.

"The first time I hear a song I look for a hook; anything that I can remember when the song ends. The first thing that comes to mind. If you can remember the song when it has finished after only one hearing, you know there is something there.

"I started out quite young. I was 16 when I cut my first record, so I guess I missed out on a lot of things. But I shouldn't say that, because so many other things came my way that I had a ball.

"I like, when I'm singing, to look out at the people and see them smiling and enjoying themselves. It gives me the feeling that they are accepting me and my music and having a good time.

Difficult Business

"I've learned a lot of things from being in this business from

BOBBY VEE and producer Dallas Smith during recording session.

such an early age. For one thing, I've discovered how hard it is to get a hit record.

"As I said, I started out when I was 16 years old, the first record I cut was released in our home town area of Fargo, North Dakota, and it went to number one. Liberty bought the rights to it and put it out nationally and it went up to 75 in the nation, which was very good.

"Every record I put out after that gradually went a little bit higher until "Devil or Angel" in 1961, which was a top five record.

"So I really didn't appreciate how much work people have to go through to get a hit record until I went through a cold spell starting in 1964, and the top ten records weren't coming as they had in the past. You really appreciate how much there is to coming up with a hit record, how really hard it is."

The BEAT Goes To The Movies

'POINT BLANK'

Point Blank has everything Hollywood could want in a movie: suspense, fine color photography, good performances, and a plot without any social significance. It also has to its credit an endless stream of senseless violence and sadism straight out of television.

The Hero, Lee Marvin, is double-crossed by his wayward wife and best friend while they are stealing a large sum of money from an unnamed Underworld Syndicate. The plot centers around Marvin's attempts to get back his share of the stolen loot. In the process countless people meet with mayhem and murder. But again, in the finest moral traditions of Hollywood, our hero only commits the mayhem, he leaves the murders to the other hoods. After all, Marvin must go free in the end, and murders, as everyone knows, can't go un-avenged.

The picture is beautifully made, with fantastic shots of Alcatraz and some of the more interesting parts of Los Angeles. Director Boorman also makes fine use of an excellent supporting cast, including Angie Dickinson and Lloyd Bochner and uses them to dress up his excuse for a film with compelling performances. Boorman also uses some very interesting cross-editing in flash-backs that distract the picture slightly from its sadistic and senseless plot.

The picture, to be sure, is entertaining, and if blood and guts is your idea of a film, you'll love *Point Blank*. It is slick, colorful and fast moving, a veritable 2 hours of unredeemed vicious brutality expertly disguised by the excellence and professionalism of both the cast and crew.

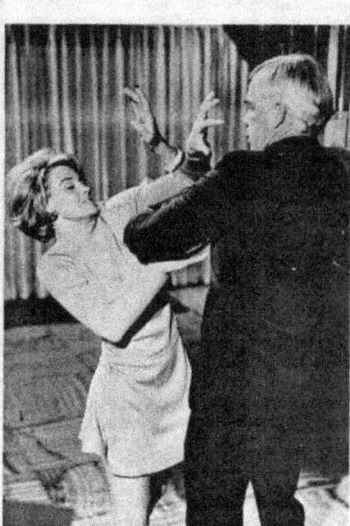

ANGIE TRIES HARD but is no match for Lee.

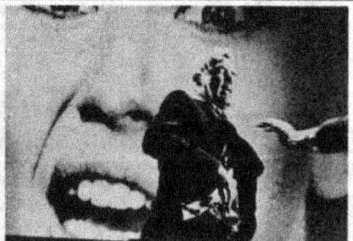

A BIT TOO MUCH violence??

NATIONAL TOP 25 SINGLES

1. The Letter .... Box Tops
2. Never My Love .... Association
3. Come Back When You Grow Up .... Bobby Vee
4. Ode to Billie Joe .... Bobbie Gentry
5. Apple, Peaches, Pumpkin Pie .... Jay and The Techniques
6. Higher and Higher .... Jackie Wilson
7. Dandelion .... Rolling Stones
8. Brown Eyed Girl .... Van Morrison
9. Give Me a Little Sign .... Brenton Wood
10. To Sir With Love .... Lulu
11. I Dig Rock And Roll Music .... Peter, Paul and Mary
12. Little Ole Man .... Bill Cosby
13. Gettin' Together .... Tommy James
14. How Can I Be Sure .... Young Rascals
15. Reflections .... Supremes
16. Hey Baby, They're Playing Our Song ...... Buckinghams
17. I Had a Dream .... Paul Revere
18. People Are Strange .... Doors
19. There is a Mountain .... Donovan
20. You Know What I Mean .... Turtles
21. Expressway to Your Heart .... Soul Survivors
22. Natural Woman .... Aretha Franklin
23. Groovin' .... Booker T
24. What Now My Love .... Mitch Rider

As compiled by Cashbox

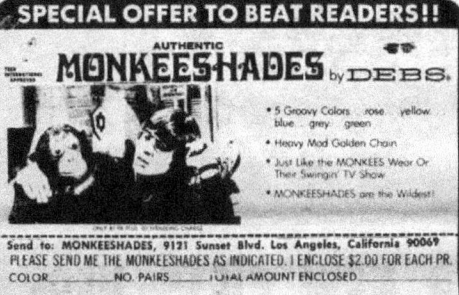

SPECIAL OFFER TO BEAT READERS!!
MONKEESHADES by DEBS

- 5 Groovy Colors: rose, yellow, blue, grey, green
- Heavy Mod Golden Chain
- Just Like the MONKEES Wear On Their Swingin' TV Show
- MONKEESHADES are the Wildest!

Send to: MONKEESHADES, 9121 Sunset Blvd. Los Angeles, California 90069
PLEASE SEND ME THE MONKEESHADES AS INDICATED. I ENCLOSE $2.00 FOR EACH PR.
COLOR .... NO. PAIRS .... TOTAL AMOUNT ENCLOSED ....
Name ....
Address ....
City .... State .... Zip Code ....
California Residents Please Include 5% Sales Tax

A Psychedelic Art Gallery In Your Home!

THE BIG RED COLORING BOOK

Paint 'Em Yourself! — *Ten Posters*

These ten, big, all-different posters by psychedelic artist John Powers were made for you to color in just the way you want. You can frame them, hang them on your walls, beautify your room!

BEAT Publications, 9121 Sunset Blvd., Los Angeles, California 90069
Please send me .... Big Red Coloring Books. I enclose $1.50 plus $.25 for handling.
Name ....
Address ....
City .... State .... *California residents please include 5% Sales Tax.*

SPEC-TRIM SUNGLASSES

UNIQUE SHADOW BOX FRAMES
MOD RECESSED LENSES
TWO-COLOR FRAMES

$4 Each
Calif. residents please add 5% sales tax
AVAILABLE IN:
Blue and White   White and Pink
Purple and White   Red and White
Yellow and Black   Red and Black
Designate Frame Color

SEND TO:
BEAT PUBLICATIONS
9125 Sunset Blvd.
Los Angeles, Calif. 90069

DEBS

SPECIAL ISSUES STILL AVAILABLE
☐ Monterey Pop Festival souvenir Issue
☐ History of the Hippies
25 cents each plus 10 cents for mailing and handling.

SEND TO:
BEAT PUBLICATIONS
Los Angeles, Calif. 90069
9125 Sunset Blvd.

Name: ....
Address: ....
City: .... State: ....
Calif. Residents include 5% sales tax

24 ORIGINAL HAPPENING HITS
As Advertised Nationally on Radio & TV

I Think We're Alone Now: Tommy James & The Shondells
Kind Of A Drag: The Buckinghams
Cherry Cherry: Neil Diamond
Turn Down Day: The Cyrkle
Jenny Take A Ride: Mitch Ryder & Detroit Wheels
My Little Red Book: Love
Wooly Bully: Sam The Sham
But It's Alright: J.J. Jackson
Little Girl: Syndicate Of Sound
See You In September: The Tempos
Daddy's Home: Shep & The Limelighters
Why Do Fools Fall In Love: Frankie Lyman
Western Union: Five Americans
Sunny: Bobby Hebb
Daydream: Lovin' Spoonful
Good Lovin': Young Rascals
I Got You Babe: Sonny & Cher
Pushin' Too Hard: The Seeds
Land Of 1000 Dances: Wilson Pickett
Younger Girl: The Critters
I Who Have Nothing: Terry Knight & The Pack
Bermuda: Four Seasons
Gee: The Crows
Maybe: The Chantels

$1.95 BEAUTIFUL FOUR COLOR JACKET
$4.00 FOR 2 ALBUMS (INCLUDES MAILING)
PLUS 50c MAILING

24 Happening Hits
9121 Sunset Blvd.
Los Angeles, California 90069
I enclose $ .... for .... albums
NAME ....
ADDRESS ....
CITY .... STATE ....
California Residents Please Include 5% Sales Tax

TURNING ON

THORINSHIELD (Philips) Thorinshield, *Life is a Dream, Here Today, Collage of Attitudes* plus eight other tracks. This an interesting first offering by a new group called Thorinshield (they got their name from the Tolkien books). Unfortunately the group seems to just miss. They can't quite figure out what style of music they want to sing. They seem to ride the fence between the conventional sounds of a Gary Lewis and the Playboys and the unusual sounds of a group like the Bee Gees. Consequently their music seems rather disconnected. Musically the songs are excellent, but vocally they leave a great deal to be desired. The arrangements use many intricate over-lappings of sounds and instruments, but the voices can't seem to measure up to the music. One song that points up this contradiction is *Prelude to a Postlude* which is so beautiful in places that it only serves to heighten the overall disappointment.

MARY IN THE MORNING (Capitol) Al Martino, *Mary in the Morning, Love Letters in the Sand, Love Me Tender* plus eight other tracks. Martino is a fine ballader. He lacks the sophistication of Frank Sinatra or Tony Bennett but he does ooze sincerity. With big orchestrated arrangements this album offers very pleasant listening.

THE EVERLY BROTHERS SING (Warner Bros.) Everly Brothers *Bowling Green, Whiter Shade of Pale, It's All Over* plus nine other tracks. The Everly Brothers are so talented it's amazing. Changing with the times and the moods of music, they sound better than ever on this album. There is none of the nonsense of *Wake Up Little Susie*, they have rightly replaced that sound with new sophistication and subtleties. They have two excellent, sure voices which blend together like finely tuned instruments. One particularly effective song is *Talking to the Flowers*. The Everly Brothers also do a beautiful job singing Procal Barum's *A Whiter Shade of Pale*, at last you can understand all the lyrics.

THE JIM KWESKIN JUG BAND DOING THEIR THINGS IN THE GARDEN OF JOY (Reprise) Jim Weskin Jug Band. *If You're a Viper, Ella Speed, My Old Man*, plus nine other tracks. This is excellent jug band music, but its strange sound will either really appeal to you, or not at all. They all have fine voices, especially the female singer who seems to be doing most of the vocals, and they play their music beautifully. It's an easy, lazy, down home sound which is totally different from most popular sounds today.

BEATLE POSTERS

Available in black light, hand screened poster. Pink, green, orange added to make a groovy image.

Cost is only $1.00 plus 25c handling. Get your order in to The BEAT now!

California residents include 5% sales tax.

October 21, 1967 THE BEAT

BE A BEAT SANTA THIS YEAR!

Please your friends with a BEAT SUBSCRIPTION For CHRISTMAS at these Special Holiday Rates

FIRST 1-YEAR GIFT $3.00
EACH ADDITIONAL GIFT $1.00

Foreign Subscriptions $9.00 Per Year

Mail to: BEAT GIFT SUBSCRIPTIONS
9121 Sunset Blvd., L.A. 90069

Dear BEAT,
   Enter my subscription as my first gift subscription at $3.00.
   Renew my subscription as my first gift subscription at $3.00.
   Please send the BEAT for one year to my friends listed below.

My Name _____
Address _____
City _____ State _____ Zip Code _____
Enclosed is $ _____ for _____ gift subscriptions.
I understand that you will send all gift cards to me so that I may give them to my friends and that their first BEAT will be delivered the week of Christmas.

RENEW BEAT GIFTS HERE

NAME _____
ADDRESS _____
CITY _____ STATE _____ ZIP _____

NAME _____
ADDRESS _____
CITY _____ STATE _____ ZIP _____

NAME _____
ADDRESS _____
CITY _____ STATE _____ ZIP _____

ENTER NEW GIFTS HERE

NAME _____
ADDRESS _____
CITY _____ STATE _____ ZIP _____

NAME _____
ADDRESS _____
CITY _____ STATE _____ ZIP _____

NAME _____
ADDRESS _____
CITY _____ STATE _____ ZIP _____

KRLA ARCHIVES

Acapulco, here you come!

Look for this display in your market. It could mean an Acapulco vacation for you and a friend. There'll be plenty of winners in our Acapulco Sweepstakes. The prizes—a week for two at one of Acapulco's swingingest hotels. And the two-way trip on Western Airlines. There's nothing to do. Just enter. Go to your market and find out the details. So, get ready for Acapulco!

KRLA ARCHIVES

GEORGE AND JOHN DISCUSS RELIGION

KRLA Edition BEAT

25¢

NOVEMBER 4, 1967

RINGO SIGNED FOR ROLE IN 'CANDY'

MAMA CASS DISCOVERS SOMETHING ROTTEN IN STATE OF ENGLAND

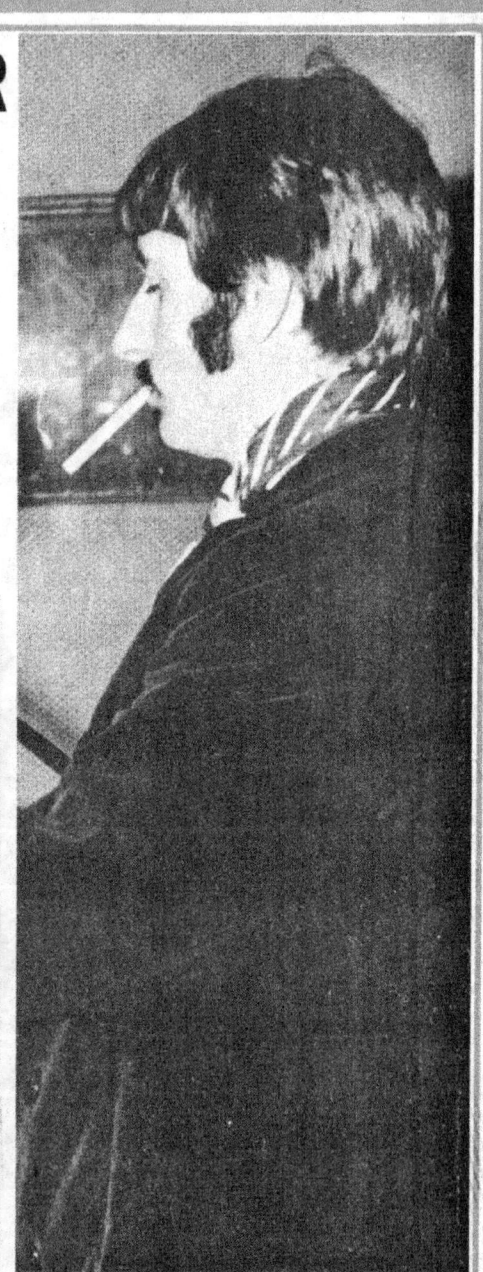

KRLA BEAT

Volume 3, Number 17   November 4, 1967

BIG MAMA ARRESTED BY SCOTLAND YARD

By Tony Barrow

SOUTHAMPTON—When the liner France docked at Southampton on Thursday, October 5, Mama Cass Elliot was involved in a series of fantastic quayside incidents which culminated in her arrest by Scotland Yard Special Branch Officers.

Cass spent that night in a West London Police cell before appearing in the Magistrates Court on a charge of larceny. The charge related to the disappearance of two keys and a pair of blankets from Kensington's Embassy Hotel at the end of February.

Arrest

Of the Southampton arrest manager Lou Adler said "We'd just come off the liner when a little man in a grey suit said he had a warrent and led Cass away. Six uniformed policemen joined him. We managed to get Cass into our car but the doors were ripped open. They pulled and we pulled. They pulled harder and Cass was taken into a police vehicle."

The rest of the Mamas and Papas, plus Lou Adler and Scott Mackenzie, waited outside Southampton city police headquarters in two Rolls Royce limousines until they were given the news that Cass was to be moved to London for the night on a Metropolitan Police warrant alleging larceny.

In court Friday afternoon Cass was cleared when the prosecution offered no evidence in the case.

Magistrate Seymour Collins told Mama Cass: "You leave this court without a stain on your character." Outside the court the rest of the group and a bunch of friends cheered the freed Mama, bouncing her up and down on the sidewalk. Later she told a reporter: "Your London police are wonderful but I don't think much of your jails. There just weren't enough blankets last night in my cell. Believe me, one blanket doesn't go far around this chick!"

Unpaid Bills

The charges regarding the theft of keys and hotel blankets related to a suite of apartments occupied by Cass and one or two other people towards the end of February. Apparently Cass left the hotel unaware that her friends had not returned the keys and, indeed, had left a portion of the bill unpaid.

Before leaving London to head for the vacation isle of Majorca with the rest of the group, Mama Michelle revealed that she and Papa John are expecting a baby next February. The group also discussed a fresh long-term recording contract with the Dunhill label but confirmed that there may be a considerable delay between the current "Farewell to the First Golden Era" release and the completion of a further album.

(Continued on Page 4)

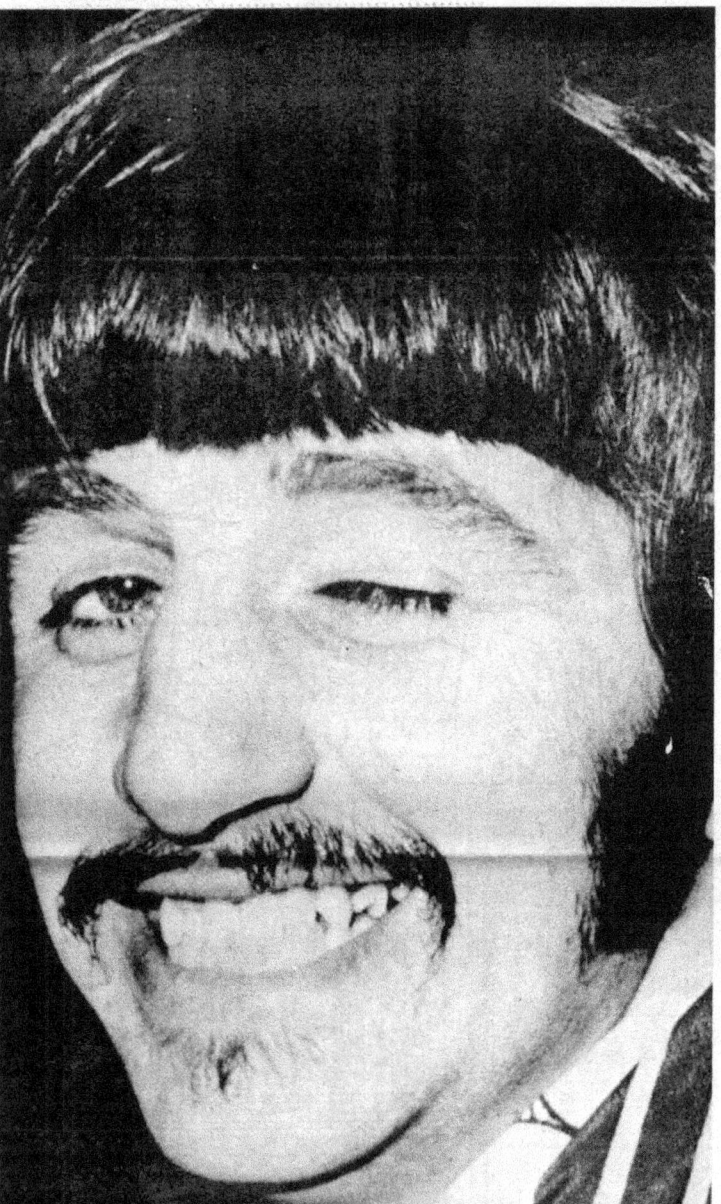

Controversy Explodes In Pvt. Gripweed Disc

LONDON — A storm of controversy blew up in London this week over the release via the United Artists label of a single called "How I Won The War" featuring Musketteer Gripweed and the Third Troup. Since John Lennon plays the part of Private Gripweed in the film, many fans of the Beatles assumed that this record contained instrumental and/or vocal contributions by John.

In fact the single is an orchestral recording of composers Ken Thorne's movie title theme. Above the music snatches of soundtrack dialogue and battle noises are to be heard. Amongst the voices is that of John Lennon but no more than five or ten seconds of his speaking is included. Neither John or the other Beatles are involved in the composition work. They do not sing or play any of the music on the record or on the film soundtrack. The second side of the single is Ken Thorne's "Aftermath," a piece which is not in any way connected with "How I Won the War." Again on this side the label credits the performance to "Musketteer Gripweed and the Third Troup."

The Beatles' U.K. Fan Club secretary Freda Kelly stated: "In fairness to fans in Britain and abroad we are making it clear that this record is nothing more than a souvenir of the film theme. We are not slamming the record or suggesting that it should not be issued. But we don't want a whole army of fans complaining on the groups that they expected to hear more of John on it. The fans are aware that John plays Gripweed. Therefore the name Gripweed on the label of the record has led to confusion all around."

Ringo Lands Role In 'Candy'

By Tony Barrow

LONDON—Just over a year ago John Lennon accepted his first solo screen role, playing Private Gripweed of the Third Troop of the Fourth Muskateers in the Dick Lester picture "How I Won The War." At that time Ringo admitted that he'd be willing to consider following in his fellow Beatle's footsteps if and when he was presented with a suitable film script.

Candy Role

A month ago (October 7 issue of The BEAT) I indicated that the most interesting solo movie appearance yet received for Ringo was under consideration in London. Now the big news has broken—Ringo Starr has been signed to play alongside Richard Burton, Marlon Brando and a number of other important screen names in "Candy" which is based upon the sex-stacked satirical novel by Terry Southern and Mason Hoffenberg. "Candy," first published as long ago as 1958, is banned in many countries and the book is still unobtainable via normal retail sources in London.

Ringo will appear in the cameo role of Emmanuel, the Mexican gardener boy employed by Candy Christian's father to mow the lawn each Saturday.

Apart from the currently uncast title role, all the parts in "Candy" are little more than brief guest appearances, characters who move briskly in and out of Candy's teenage life.

Indian Trip

Ringo's acceptance of the part will cut short his visit to India. There is still no certain departure date for the Beatles' much-postponed trip to the East as the guests and pupils of Maharishi Mahesh Yogi but, in any event, Ringo will be unable to spend more than a few November weeks studying Transcendental Meditation with the others. After that he will be due to spend between two and three pre-Christmas weeks shooting his "Candy" sequences. It is most unlikely that Ringo would be called upon to visit Hollywood or any other part of America in connection with the making of this picture.

In London, Ringo told me: "This is exactly the type of part I have been hoping somebody would offer me. It's a part with a lot of scope for turning Emmanuel into an interesting screen personsonality. It's also a very small part which is all I want to consider at the moment.

(Continued on Page 4)

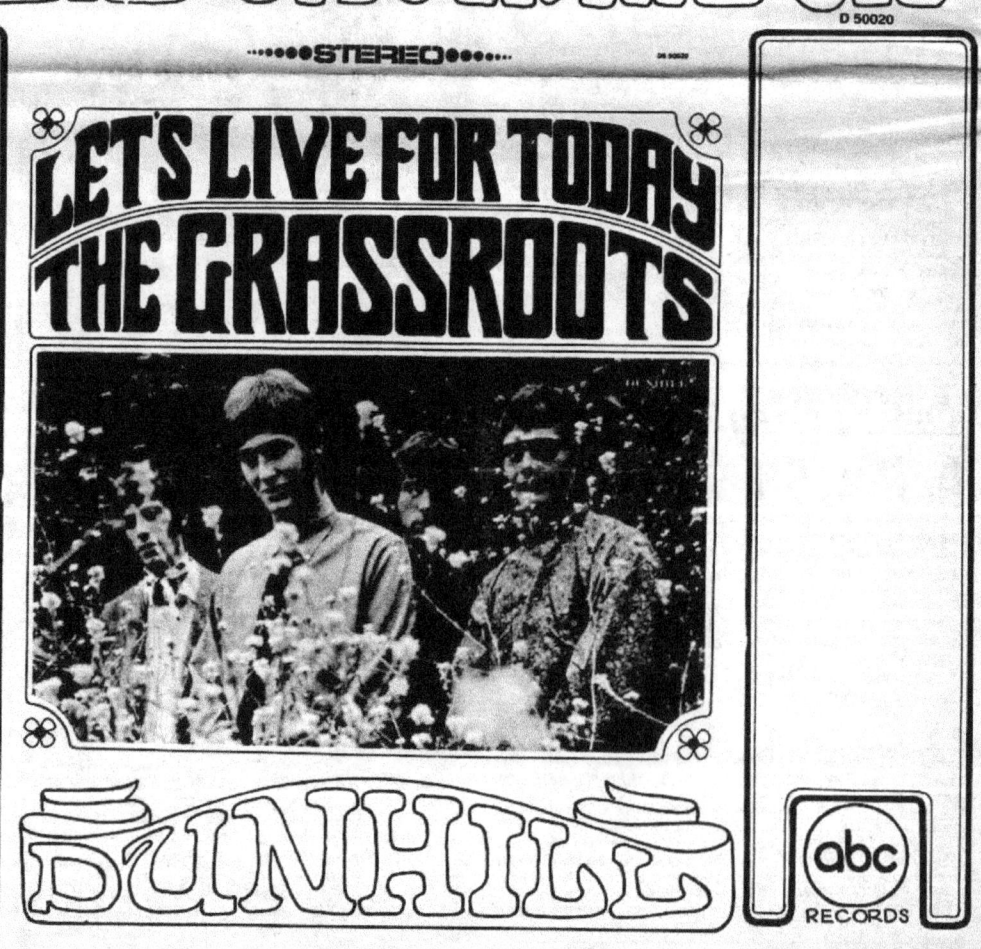

KRLA ARCHIVES

AROUND the WORLD

DONOVAN ON TOUR

LOS ANGELES — Donovan launched a coast-to-coast concert tour with his appearance September 22 at the Cow Palace in San Francisco. Referring to the concert, *Variety* said that Donovan "initiated a whole new style of pop concerts. Such is the balladeer's personal charisma that one might have heard a petal fall during his songs."

Donovan's long awaited American tour will continue through the middle of November.

Richard Pryor Fired By Hotel

LAS VEGAS — Popular comedian, Richard Pryor, was fired by the Aladdin Hotel here because of alleged obscenities during his 17-day engagement at the club.

Dick Kanellis sacked Pryor after taping the comedian's show during which Pryor allegedly used obscene language after having already been warned four times against such conduct.

Kanellis revealed that because of the tape the American Guild of Variety Artists will not attempt to penalize the hotel since Pryor's contract reportedly calls for the comedian to perform "as directed by the operator."

This, unfortunately, marks the third time Pryor has been in "hot" water . . . the two previous mistakes by the entertainer went the legal route.

NOTHING BUT WORK

Talk about tired! The Glories have the corner on that market for a while and for good reason. Over a three day period the girls played no less than seventeen shows as a result of a dual booking.

The Glories had been booked into Trude Heller's in New York, when their manager had a call from the Apollo Theatre also in New York asking him if the girls could replace James and Bobby Purify for one week. They said yes and ran back and forth between the two engagements.

But that was not all, during the middle of the double run, the girls were scheduled to play a one-nighter in New Jersey.

PITNEY TOUR BIG SUCCESS

Gene Pitney has just concluded his most successful American tour since first undertaking the annual 30-day trek five years ago. According to the William Morris agency, the Gene Pitney Show grossed over $200,000, a record for 27 playing dates.

At the close of the tour, Pitney, who has always played a key role in getting up the talent for his tours, said that in the future he intends to focus an increasing share of attention on the college circuit. His next American tour, probably to take place in the spring, will encompass the college type of audience almost exclusively.

Beach Boys Tape Stint

HONOLULU — The Beach Boys' "Summer Spectacular" shows in Honolulu have been recorded for later release on their own label, Brother Records.

HOLLIES ON TV

NEW YORK — The Hollies are scheduled to make one of their infrequent visits to the United States in the middle of November.

The group will make a number of television appearances and are slated for a possible national tour. During their U.S. visit which will coincide with the release of their new album, they will appear on the Smothers Brothers CBS-Television show on November 17. Other network television appearances are being lined up for the group.

SAM & DAVE TO EUROPE

DETROIT — Sam and Dave, popular exponents of the "Memphis Sound" have embarked on a one month tour of England and Europe, their second visit this year.

The duo of Samuel Moore and David Prater will be accompanied by their full orchestra.

Hippie Shoulder Strap Bag - $2.00 P.P.
PSYCHEDELIC POSTERS BUMPER STICKERS BUTTONS FREE LIST
THE SEPER COMPANY
5273 Tendilla, Dept. T.O
Woodland Hills, Calif.

ART INSTITUTE OF PITTSBURGH
57th Yr. Coed. & 24 mo. Diploma Course, Commercial Art, Fashion Art, Interior Design, Begin. & Adv. Vet Appd. Dorm facilities. College referrals for degrees. Free illus. brochure.
Earl B. Wheeler, Director
635 Smithfield St.
Pittsburgh, Pa. 15222

PEOPLE ARE TALKING ABOUT the trouble big *Mama Cass* had in England and the fact that she's no doubt saying "why me?" . . . the *Smothers Brothers* dropping into the Luvy Duv shop on the Sunset Strip, causing the shop's owner to bounce around yelling at the top of his lungs, "I'm a success!" . . . why the *Rolling Stones* split with *Andrew Oldham* and why Andy never returned those photos

. . . how well *Zal Yanowsky* will make it as a solo act . . . the fact that the "Smothers Brothers Comedy Hour" is probably the only show which would allow the *Association* to sing "Requiem for the Masses" . . . how *Bobbie Gentry's* album could get so high on the charts when all the cuts sound like "Billie Joe" and deciding it's only because Billie is such a popular guy—despite his bridge antics

. . . the mock funeral in the Haight being a little over-done by the news media since hippies reportedly constitute only 1% of the nation's population . . . how happy Atlantic is that *Aretha* just can't lose . . . the fact that *Vicki Carr* could probably make a hit out of our National Anthem . . . why *Dusty Springfield* doesn't come Stateside and at least make some television appearances

. . . whether or not *James and Bobby Purify* really exist and if they do where they are . . . the votes being cast on how long the *Monkees* will remain a top group . . . what *Frank* thinks about *Mia* flying off to India . . . the fact that there really is a 103rd Street in Watts . . . whether or not *Gene Dozier* is serious about "A Hunk Of Funk" and hoping that he's kidding about the title

. . . *Bobby Vinton's* new one sounding just like his old ones but becoming a hit anyway . . . why, with a voice like his, *Englebert Humperdinck* would want a name like that . . . the *Cowsills* proving that family business is big business . . . the fact that *Rod McKuen* is tempting fate quite a bit by resuming his work so soon after being bedded with hepitius . . . why *Florence* really left the *Supremes* —opps, sorry about that, Diana Ross and the Supremes

. . . why entertainers adopt gim-

micks when it's been proven that they're the most fickle things in the world—not to mention the most boring . . . *Miriam Makeba* being back again and sounding good . . . *Bob Lind's* new album being excellent and wondering why more of his material is not recorded by other artists . . . the *Cake* and which bag is theirs . . . the absence of the San Francisco groups on the pop charts and wondering if it is an indication of things to come—or go . . . the *Beatles* turning down a million dollar offer from Sid Bernstein to play Shea Stadium because they can't reproduce their 1967 sound on stage

. . . Rascal *Felix Cavaliere* buying some property in Hawaii and *Don Ho* buying Hawaii . . . the evil mind which decided *Lesley Gore* should record "Brink Of Disaster" . . . *Brenda Holloway* getting a hit record — finally . . . whether or not *Stevie Wonder* is still strolling around the University with Diana Ross' sister . . . the *Sunshine Company* may be a poor man's *Mamas and Papas* but they're doing all right and it's hard to knock success

. . . the fact that the *Who* cannot possibly see for miles—not with all that smoke from their exploding equipment . . . when the girl look is going to be "out" for the boys . . . which pop group contains four very big-headed members?

Beat Publications, Inc.

Executive Editor	Cecil J. Tuck
Publisher	Gayle Tuck
Editor	Louise Criscione
Assistant Editor	Jacoba Atlas

Staff Writers
Bobby Bovino — Ron Koslow
Tony Leigh — Shirley Poston

Contributing Writers
Tony Barrow — Sue Barry
Eden — Bob Levinson
Jamie McClusky III — Mike Masterson

Photographers
Ed Caraeff — Jerry Hass

National Sales Representative
Sam Chase Assoc., Inc.
527 Madison Avenue
New York, New York
(212) PL. 5-1688

Advertising Director	Dick Stricklin
Business Manager	Judy Felice
Subscriptions	Diane Clatworthy

Distribution
Miller Freeman Publications
500 Howard Street, San Francisco, Calif.
The BEAT is published bi-weekly by BEAT Publications, Inc., editorial and advertising offices at 9121 Sunset Blvd., Los Angeles, California 90069. U.S. bureaus in Hollywood, San Francisco, New York, Chicago and Nashville; overseas correspondents in London, Liverpool and Manchester, England. Sale price 25 cents. Subscription price: U.S. and possessions $5 per year; Canada and foreign rates, $9 per year. Second class postage prepaid at Los Angeles, California.

KRLA ARCHIVES

RINGO SIGNS FOR 'CANDY'

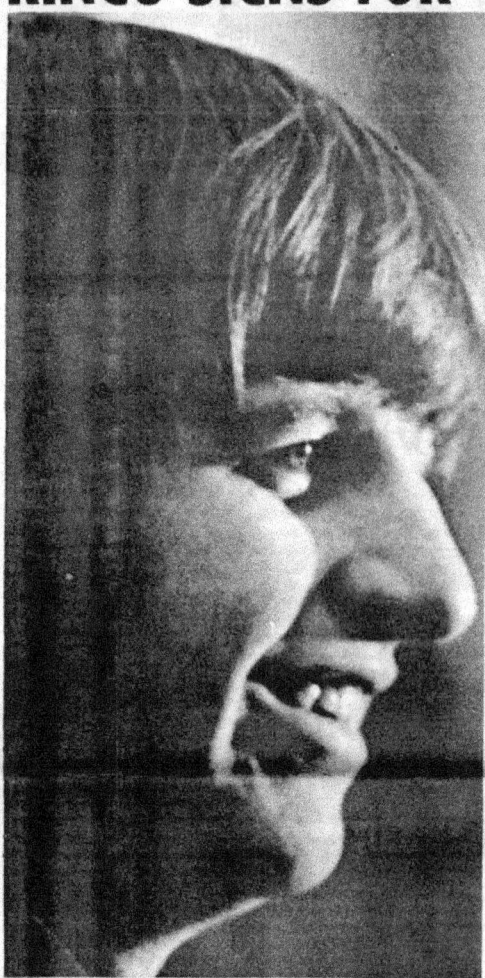

WILL RINGO STARR be forced to look like this again for "Candy?"

(Continued from Page 1)

"Apart from anything else I don't want to be away from the Beatles for too long. The timing is fine because the others will be having a break in November and December so I am not holding up any group work by taking the part. I wouldn't want a bigger film role. I have no idea whether I'm even capable of tackling a really big part.

"This is a major production with a lot of big people in it and a lot of big money behind it. I'll just be one of various names taking part. John didn't have a very large part in 'How I Won The War.' My part in 'Candy' is not as big but that doesn't mean it is anything less than an important step for me to take. I'm looking forward to this very much indeed.

Straight Acting

"In the new year the Beatles will be getting together another film. That's another reason why I wouldn't accept any solo work which would get me too involved over a long period. The 'Candy' part is a straight acting role. There's no question of turning Emmanuel into a drummer or anything like that and neither I nor the other Beatles will be involved in any soundtrack music."

The news of Ringo's signing for "Candy" came almost upon the eve of the London premiere of "How I Won The War" at the West End's London Pavilion Theatre. A record-splintering number of pop personalities attended the star-studded premiere with United Artists announcing a virtual 100 per cent acceptance level for invitations sent out to recording and other celebrities. Apart from the Beatles, the list of attending stars included members of the Rolling Stones, the Who, Procol Harum and a score of other groups plus Cilla Black, Sandie Shaw, Anita Harris, Marianne Faithfull and numerous movie stars.

MAMA CASS

(Continued from Page 1)

Meantime, after playing a concert date at the Paris Olympia, The Mamas and Papas are scheduled to co-star with Scott Mackenzie in a special stage show at London's 7,000-seater Royal Albert Hall Wednesday, November 1. At this time it is not clear whether the group will be prepared to undertake a limited number of other er concert engagements in the U.K. before Michelle's pregnancy reaches an advanced stage. There is talk of at least one North of England show date in Manchester and the possibility of promotional TV appearances to coincide with the next U.K. single.

MAMA CASS AND two missing blankets and a set of keys!!!

Why Not Give

THE BEAT

For Christmas?

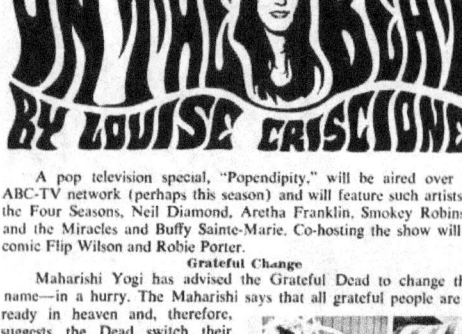
by Louise Criscione

A pop television special, "Popendipity," will be aired over the ABC-TV network (perhaps this season) and will feature such artists as the Four Seasons, Neil Diamond, Aretha Franklin, Smokey Robinson and the Miracles and Buffy Sainte-Marie. Co-hosting the show will be comic Flip Wilson and Robie Porter.

Grateful Change

Maharishi Yogi has advised the Grateful Dead to change their name—in a hurry. The Maharishi says that all grateful people are already in heaven and, therefore, suggests the Dead switch their name to the Eternal Lives. So far, the Dead are remaining non-committal.

Micky Curtis, one of Japan's hottest entertainers, has come to the conclusion that he has reached a dead-end artistically (having made over 90 movies) in Japan and as a consequence is setting out (with his six-mon combo) for Europe and the United States.

"At present, I feel there are much too few Japanese acts going overseas," says Micky. "A good part of the reason is that they are afraid of the unknown." Micky, apparently, is not.

In sort of a trans-Pacific deal, American rock singer Teddy Neeley is heading for Japan to make his acting debut in Steve Parker's "Tomorrow We Sing." Teddy recently broke with his group, formerly called the Teddy Neeley Five.

GRATEFUL DEAD

It was almost a feather in Merv Griffin's cap. The television personality had received permission from the Russian government to tape his television show there. But the word out of Russia now is that they're much too busy with the preparations for the Soviet's 50th anniversary celebration, so Griffin will have to wait until next April—maybe.

Canada's top pop group, the Lords of London, are keeping their fingers crossed that their latest Canadian hit, "Cornflakes and Ice Cream," will be a smash in the United States so that they can come over and tour. The hit song was written by talented 16 year old Greg Fitzpatrick.

Procol Contract

A&M Records (Herb Albert's label) has announced the signing of the Procol Harum to a long term recording contract. The group is currently touring Stateside, primarily on the strength of their "Whiter Shade Of Pale."

Well, they had a funeral in Haight Ashbury to proclaim the "death of the hippies." Seems as though the hippies do not like their present image at all. "We need a new image," said the hippies. "We wish to be known as free men." Currently, Haight Street is being overrun by teenyboppers, college students and motorcycle gangs. Violence is on the upswing and the police are kept busy day and night making dope raids.

However, all is not dreary—at least not according to San Francisco police chief, Tom Cahill, who believes that the hippie situation is getting a lot better and his own police officers are gatherng about them a clearer understanding of some of the hippies' problems.

If Reprise Records has anything to say about it, the First Edition will be one of the hottest groups in the nation before long. They're currently playing the Unicorn in Boston for two weeks and then on November 8th they open at The Bitter End in New York for ten days and then on to The Chateau in Denver for two weeks.

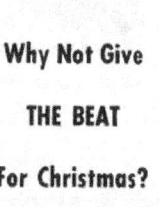

MGM is certainly sinking a lot of money into the Cowsills. Last night they held a cocktail, dinner and show party at the posh Century Plaza Hotel in Los Angeles. The swank Beverly Hills Room was packed with people from Elke Sommer on down the line. Quite an affair—and who knows, the Cowsills just may make it really big. At least they have a novel idea. No one else has their mother singing with them!

THE COWSILLS

QUESTION OF THE WEEK: How have the Box Tops managed to stay on top of the record charts for so long when hardly anyone has so much as a photo of the group?

KRLA ARCHIVES

CHUCK BERRY
The Miller Band

KRLA ARCHIVES

The Conspirators In The Incense And Peppermint Plot Reveal Themselves As...

THE STRAWBERRY ALARM CLOCK

AVAILABLE AT **Thrifty** CUT RATE DRUG STORES

KRLA ARCHIVES

Harrison & Lennon Discuss Religion

By Tony Barrow

Before departing for India and the beginning of a two to three month meditation study course under the guidance of Maharishi Mahesh Yogi, Beatles John Lennon and George Harrison talked at length about the value and meaning of Transcendental Meditation.

After appearing with David Frost in the television discussion show, "The Frost Program," John commented: "If just one in every thousand viewers who watched the program was encouraged to look into Transcendental Meditation then it was well worth doing. We want to get the message across to as many people as possible that meditation can help everyone. Not just a special few, or brainy people or cranks but everyone."

The following is an abbreviated transcript of the views and explanations given in London by John and George before they left for India:

JOHN: Through meditation I've learned how to tap energy that I've had in me all the time. Before I could only reach this extra energy on good days when things were going well. With meditation I find that if it's not too good a day I can still get the same amount of energy going for me. It means I am more used to myself and to others. Put it another way—the worst days I had without meditation were much worse than the bad days I have now, days when it's difficult to get going.

Latent Energy

GEORGE: The energy is latent within everybody. It's there anyway. Meditation is a natural process of being able to contact that energy each day and give yourself a little more. You're able to do whatever you normally do with a little bit more happiness, maybe.

Each individual's life sort of pulsates in a certain rhythm. They give you a word or a sound which pulsates with that rhythm. The idea is to transcend to the most subtle level of thought, to replace your ordinary thought with the word or sound. Finally you lose even that and you're at a level of pure consciousness.

GUESS HAS BEATLES AT OVER $70 MIL.

LONDON — An "uneducated guess" by Northern Songs executive, Dick James, points to the fact that the Beatles during the past five years have earned from $70 to $86 million dollars!

James made the statement while accepting an award for the Beatles' "Sgt. Pepper" album and although admitting that his guess "may be a conservative one" he pointed up the fact that he did not have sufficient information to make a truly accurate estimate on the group's earnings during the last five years.

James' calculation was made on the basis of the around-$14 million figure which the Beatles have earned for their songs. Of course, added to that would be their earnings from films, records, artists' fees and fees from the endorsement of goods. All of which may add up to as much as $114 million!

GEORGE HARRISON AND JOHN LENNON DISCUSS TRANSCENDENTAL MEDITATION WITH TV HOST, DAVID FROST (left).

JOHN: You sit there and let your mind go. You introduce the word, the sound, the vibration to take over from your thoughts. You don't will thoughts away.

GEORGE: When your mind is a complete blank it's beyond all previous experience. That level is timeless, spaceless. You can be there for five minutes or much longer. You don't actually know how long when you come out of it and back to the everyday, the gross level of thinking.

JOHN: It's like sleeping. You don't know you've been sleeping until you're awake again. It seems as though no time has gone at all.

GEORGE: You can't really tell anybody exactly what it is. The teaching of Transcendental Meditation is all based on the individual. If you want to do it you get instruction. That leads to some sort of experience. Upon that experience you're taught the next part, you're told how you can go on from there to the next stage.

Impossible Description

JOHN: It's like asking someone to say what chocolate tastes like. It's impossible to describe.

GEORGE: Or to tell somebody how it is to be drunk. They've got to be drunk themselves before they know what it is.

JOHN: You don't feel you have more actual knowledge — or at least I don't — but you feel more energetic. You come out of it and it's just a sort of "let's get going" feeling about whatever work you've got to tackle.

GEORGE: It takes a lot of practice to arrive at a point where you can remain in that frame of mind, that attitude to life, permanently. I've had definite proof after only 6 or 7 weeks that this is something that really works. It'll take a long time to arrive at a state where I can hold the level of pure consciousness and bring it back with me into everyday levels of activity and thinking. That's the eventual aim.

Gold Cloth

JOHN: One of the Maharishi's analogies is that it's like dipping a cloth in and out of gold. If you leave it in it gets soggy. If you leave it out the sun will fade it. So you keep dipping it in and bringing it out and, eventually, there's the same amount of gold in the cloth whether it's in or out. So you don't meditate ALL the time but you DO meditate regularly if you want to get anywhere with it. Twenty minutes a day—something like that.

GEORGE: Drugs don't really get to the true you, the real self. The way to approach the real you is through meditation or some form of Yoga. We're not saying that this particular form — Transcendental Meditation—is the only answer. Yoga incorporates lots of different techniques but the whole point is that each soul is potentially divine and Yoga is a technique of manifesting it to arrive at that point which is divine.

JOHN: Meditation doesn't actually change you, make you different in any way. It's just something beneficial which you can add to yourself, add to your routine. When you add to your religion you don't change your religion. Whatever you are—you carry on.

If you ask any of the Maharishi's people to give you a few laws for living by they'd be virtually the same as Christianity. Chritsianity is the answer as much as this is.

GEORGE: Christianity as I was taught it was a demand that I should believe in Jesus and in God but they didn't actually show me any way of experiencing God or Jesus.

Directly Related

JOHN: The bit about "The Kingdom Of Heaven Is Within You" seems to relate directly to meditation. Have a peep inside. Find out. I still am a Christian but had I been taught meditation at 15, well now I'd be pretty groovy.

GEORGE: The word God means all sorts of things to me. The first concept I had of a man in the sky, well, I kicked that one a few years ago but I'm coming back to that now because, yes, it's a man in the sky as well if you like, it's just every aspect of creation, all a part of God.

JOHN: I think of God as a big piece of energy, like electricity, a big powerhouse.

GEORGE: Or the energy which runs through everything and makes everything one.

JOHN: Everything you read about, all the religions, are all the same basically. It's just a matter of people opening their minds up. I don't know how divine or superhuman Maharishi is. He was probably born quite ordinary but he's working at it.

In Order

GEORGE: If everybody took up meditation it would help them to sort out their own problems, put their houses in order, if you like. People cause all the world's problems. So if people fix up their personal problems that's it, we're well on the way aren't we. It's up to each individual, every person, to make his own move.

JOHN: The main thing is it's simple. All you've got to do is to be interested. If you don't believe in meditation and you're cynical about it there's still no reason why you shouldn't try to find out what you're so cynical about. And the only way to find out is to learn about meditation and give it a try. Then you'll have the right to condemn or otherwise.

"The Standel Sound"

"The Grass Roots"

Progressive musicians throughout the world choose the "Standel Sound," the accepted standard for professional musicians who demand professional performance.

A. P.A. Speaker Column Amplifier
B. P.A. Master Control with Reverb
C. Imperial Line Amplifier — Solid State, Dual Channel

Standel
Solid State Music Systems
4918 DOUBLE DRIVE • EL MONTE, CALIF. 91731

KRLA ARCHIVES

Rascals Cancel British Visit

By Tony Barrow

Unknown in the U.K., American songstress Gigi Balon receives substantial billing when she takes over from top chart girl Anita Harris for the final 38 shows on a six-week series of one-nighters starring Englebert Humperdinck. The tour opens in Slough on October 26 and Miss Galon takes over from Miss Harris at Exeter on November 12.

Anita Harris, currently filming "Follow That Nurse," was insured for three million dollars when the movie company released her for mid-production on New York TV appearances on the Ed Sullivan and Joey Bishop show this month. Anita's next single is likely to couple a pair of film songs — Lionel Bart's titlepiece from "Danger Route" plus the song "Comes the Night" from the Dirk Bogarde picture "Mr. Sebastian."

The Young Rascals cancelled their October U.K. concert tour for Promoter Tito Burns at the eleventh hour because of Eddie Brigatti's illness. New York promoter Sid Bernstein flew into London on the eve of the tour with Rascal Felix Cavaliere to explain the group's problem and help set up a 1968 U.K. tour for the Young Rascals. While in our capital Bernstein made the latest of his prolific and predictably impressive offers for the Beatles to play new Shea Stadium dates in New York. For one appearance at the 60,000 seater venue Bernstein told the London press he was prepared to pay The Beatles no less than one million dollars.

Complexity

The Beatles, unmoved by financial spectacles of this sort, conveyed to Bernstein their long-standing policy statement to the effect that they will not consider future stage appearances until and unless they can devise some acceptable new method of presenting their contemporary music in the context of a stage concert. At the moment, their music growing more and more complex as their uses of such wide variety of additional instruments expands, there seems little hope that material like "All You Need Is Love," "Baby, You're a Rich Man" or any of the "Sgt. Pepper" tracks could be presented on stage with any degree of authenticity by a four-man group.

One of the most expensive pop publicity campaigns ever mounted in Britain is launching the sound of David McWilliams as "something new in and on the air today." An almost life size photograph of David's face was spread across the front and back cover of Britain's top-selling music weekly *New Musical Express*. Inside the same issue a further whole page quoted some of the singers first favorable press reviews. The record which goes with all this unprecedented ballyhoo is "Harlem Lady" and "The Days of Pearly Spencer" issued by the Major Minor disc label.

U.S. Tours

Three-week U.S. promotional visit for Procol Harum will keep the group on your side of the Atlantic throughout the first part of November. The Who tour American colleges between November 15 and December 3 ... John Philips' "Like An Old Time Movie" is on the top deck of new U.K singles by Scott Mackenzie ... Self-penned "Little Miss Love" likely next single for Jimi Hendrix Experience ... Songstress Cilla Black, to be seen as David Warner's co-star in the movie "Work" ... Is A Four-Letter Word" which will be premiered early in 1968, begins her own series of nine hour-long BBC Television Spectaculars in January.

Emperor Rosko, hosting pre-recorded Saturday lunchtime record show each week for BBC's new Radio 1 pop channel, building a name for himself as one of the wildest deejays in Europe ... Arriving at Leed General Infirmary for closed-circuit radio programme broadcast to hospital patients deejay Jimmy Saville dressed up as the World's First Hip Surgeon, wore upmteen beads and bells over a white operating theatre robe!

Following upon October 22 Ed Sullivan appearance "To Sir With Love" songstress Lulu booked for December 3 "Red Skelton Show." With her U.S. popularity leaping little Lulu has turned down Christmas season London pantomime offer to accept further American dates.

Pre-Christmas album by the Hollies will be called "Butterfly" and will include 12 original compositions by the group ... Lightning two-day visit to London for Petula Clark so that she can record a new Tony Hatch-Jackie Trent number for her next single before returning to "Finian's Rainbow" filming work ... Second gold disc handed to balladeer Englebert Humperdinck, who has sold more than one million copies of "The Last Waltz" in U.K. His first goldie was the single "Release Me."

National Theatre in London plans to stage as an experimental production Adrienne Kennedy's adaptation of John Lennon's "In His Own Write" book early 1968 ... Seeker Judith Durham has second solo single out in U.K. at the beginning of November. It will feature her self-penned number "Again and Again."

Rush-release in U.K. for "World," the latest Gibb Brothers' composition recorded by the Bee Gees ... Scott Walker in the recording studios to work on much-delayed first solo single ... Tom Jones opens for 4-week stint at New York Copacabana February 12.

Beat'e Denial

Official Beat-le denial number 1: The Beatles have no intention of changing their group name. Forget the rumors that they have even considered the idea of switching to "Sgt. Pepper's Lonely Hearts Club Band."

Official Beat-le denial number 2: The cover of the Beatles' "Sgt. Pepper" album is not intended to represent the funeral of the group. Forget the rumors that those flowers at the front were to depict the group's burial prior to a change of name.

Then there was the true story of a New York editor who received a batch of precious brand-new photographs of the Beatles taken a few days earlier in London. Editor looked through the pix and air-mailed them back to London with a note that read: "Must have recent photographs. These are so old they show John and Paul without moustaches."

THE FACT IS, YOU REALLY HAVEN'T BEEN TURNED ON UNTIL YOU'VE BEEN TURNED ON BY **THE BAROQUES**

CHESS RECORDS

"Tomorrow's Sound Today"

CHESS LP/LPS 1516

KRLA ARCHIVES

KRLA ARCHIVES

IT'S VERY SIMPLY STREISAND

Now Available At:

KRLA ARCHIVES

PENTACLE RECORDS

PRESENTS

"THE THINKING ANIMAL"
b/w
"THE NEW WING"
Rec. #P-101

Underground from Canada

Representation: Pete Manuele
P.O. Box 349
Hollywood, Calif.

REB FOSTER IN LONDON

By Bob Dayton

Is the Maharishi a genuine, sincere individual or a get-rich charlatan? The Beatles, Mick Jagger of the Rolling Stones, Mia (Sinatra) Farrow and other top artists have placed their faith in him —while the American Press and a great majority of the underground newspapers have disclaimed both he and his precepts.

KRLA's Reb Foster decided to find out the truth by going to London and directly contacting those people who know it. Reb will be speaking with members of the Transcendental Institute, many of the artists who follow the Maharishi and many of those who don't. In addition to this, Reb will be conducting special interviews with European underground press representatives, ex-pirate ship disc-jockeys now employed by the BBC and more. All to be heard exclusively on KRLA, LISTEN.

OCTOBER 20-21-22

"MIKE BLOOMFIELD'S ELECTRIC FLAG"
An American Music Band

Plus

"CLEAR LIGHT"

COMING OCTOBER 27-28-29

The Soul Crusade of
"THE MANDALA"

"ODE TO THE GREAT PUMPKIN BALL"

PRIZES FOR THE FREAKIEST COSTUME
- Honda Motorcycle, One Way Ticket to Haight Ashbury...
- One Year Supply of ZIG ZAG Papers
(Great to clean glasses or roll your hair with)

TWO BIG SHOWS
8:30   11:00

BY THE SEA

1 NAVY STREET
P.O.P.
STA. MONICA
392-4501

CHEETAH

3rd Annual Miss GAZARRI'S Dance Contest

LA CIENEGA	9039 SUNSET	NOW HAPPENING
SHINDIG'S		1—THE PACIFIC OCEAN
JIMMY O'NEIL		2—OCTOBER COUNTRY
presents	CR 3-6606	3—POP CORN BLIZZARD
DEAN HAWLEY	OL 7-2113	Monday Night's Dance Contest
SUNDAY	#2 LA CIENEGA	to Select Miss Holywood
JIMMY'S TALENT NIGHT	319 N. LACIENEGA	A Go-Go of 1968 $500 Grand Prize

DOUG WESTON'S
Troubadour

Singer Composer
ROD McKUEN
plus
Comedian
VAUGHN MEADER

CR. 6-6168
9081 Santa Monica Blvd.
at Doheny
★ HOOTENANNY EVERY MONDAY NITE ★

KRLA ARCHIVES

OVER 500 WINNERS
BEAT PUBLICATIONS
PROUDLY PRESENTS
THE GREAT RACE

FIRST PRIZE—CORDLESS TAPE RECORDER
2nd Prize—Portable Radio/Phonograph
100 3rd Prizes—1 Year BEAT Subscription or Renewal
200 4th Prizes—Popular Record Albums
200 5th Prizes—Beautiful Red and Silver BEAT Pens

Starring all BEAT REPRESENTATIVES

Featuring 500 Prizes including first prize of a TAPE RECORDER, second prize of a portable record player and radio, runner up prizes of top selling albums, free subscriptions or renewals to THE BEAT + Beautiful Beat Pens.

WATCH AS BEAT REPRESENTATIVES throughout the country compete for the most subscriptions.

THRILL AS YOU watch YOUR list get longer and longer.

QUAKE WITH ANTICIPATION as the contest draws to a close.

Send in subscription blanks NOW through NOVEMBER 30. Contest ends at midnight on Nov. 30th.

Don't miss out on the biggest spectacle of the year!
If you are not now a BEAT REPRESENTATIVE don't miss out—just fill out this form and send it to:

BEAT REPRESENTATIVES
9121 Sunset Blvd.
Los Angeles, California

Yes! I want to be a BEAT Representative and enter the Great Race.

Name_____

Address_____

City_____ State_____ Zip_____

If you are not a current subscriber, your own subscription can count as your first order sold.

CLASSIFIED

Attention ALL BEATLE FANS write to Mary Kraciuneak, 3930 North 20th Street, Milwaukee, Wisconsin 53206 if you want 'em back for tour. Jane

Happy Birthday Jan Savage—Baltimore—

Savage Birthday—Baltimore—Best to Jan Savage

Happy Birthday Rick Joslin

What does "BOENZEE CREYQUE" mean? And what is that mind bending instrument Rusty plays?

SONNY AND CHER: Your flowers in the spring will never die. Happy A III, Love, Jena

Helen Hood Hoe Holt Ho? Happy Birthday from K. Dog

John and Janet Mean business

JOHN LENNON is all man—luv on your 27th. Toni

Happy Birthday Russ Giguere

Hey Joe turns HOOKE on

Toad wears glasses

Isaac loves

Bill Hudson—Happy 18th Birthday—I love you—Theresa Mayousky

Happy Anniversary Sonny and Cher

Mark Lindsay—You rule Chicago!

KIRSTEN BARKER, what's become of you? Write Robbie in Houston.

Happy 27th Birthday John Lennon!!

Paula Tayor—I figured Monkee fans couldn't read! Beatles rule your mini mind.!'

I love PAUL

Four of a Kind is Dead. Not responsible for blunders and debts incurred.

FAFCONJMH

i love life; you bob. understand? Meredith

P.J.?

Pick up on the MOTHERS

Thank you, Columbia Guard, Cathy

COLIN PETERSON IS DARLING!

Chris—straight hair rules!

HAPPY BIRTHDAY TO RICK IN VIETNAM FROM MARI-LYNN WITH LOVE.

The Society Psychs-out . . . Stevi

Ace . . . Groovey!!!

George Harrison is his own (what a!) man!

Decode: 191-20524; (2202) 6185191415, 16514-1611219. Yes? John Lindsey

A world without Beatles is a world without love.

Beatles Great, Monkees Hurt

Monkees — psychedelicperfectiongroovy. Micky-George C.—groovey

Everyone please give "What Now My Love" a chance.

HAPPY BIRTHDAY SKIP. H.! LOVE LINDA J.

Happy birthday Nancy —luv Rick

KEITH MOON says Happy Birthday Nan.

WHO ARE!

Deep in his soul Brian Epstein has happiness.

Monkee fans over twelve have problems.

The ASSOCIATION is 1940's style soppy.

. . . PEACE . . .

October 9th is the day.

Rick Parcells and Herman forever!

Coach Poteet of the Somerville Panthers is groovy during football practice.

ART . . .

Doors Posters 2½ ft. by 3 ft. $1.75 postpaid. Seper Co., 5273 Tendilla, Woodland Hills, Calif.

WOW! George Harrison is so George Harrison!

To my very special kind of honey, Mark Lindsay. I truly understand you — soon we'll meet and hold each other "tighter" maybe then there won't be an "unknown girl." Me Thanks.

HOBBITS OF THE WORLD . . . UNITE.

Happy birthday Ken — a friend.

Mr. Ward is high.

Turp: Hi! — Luv "Fluke"

FRODO BAGGINS LIVES . . .

C. Treantatalo: Happy birthday—sincerely Anne S.

Tune in to Tolkein.
Ravi Shanker is ALL.

Happy belated birthday to John Lennon.

THE ALPACAS FROM NORTH CAROLINA IS WHAT'S HAPPENING. WOW!

Ray Kubal I LOVE YOU PAM.

Dave Sharkey isn't a duck!

MOVING?

Writing about a subscription?
Be sure to fill out this form

For FASTEST service on address change, missing copies, etc., attach old mailing label in first space below. Otherwise please print clearly your address as we now have it.

OLD ADDRESS (Attach old label here if available)

NAME_____
ADDRESS_____
CITY_____
STATE_____ ZIP CODE_____

NAME_____
ADDRESS_____
CITY_____ STATE_____ ZIP CODE_____

MAIL TO: BEAT PUBLICATIONS
Circulation Dept.
9121 Sunset Blvd., Los Angeles, Calif. 90069

Please allow 3 weeks for change to take effect.

KRLA ARCHIVES

EVERY MOTHER'S SON MIND EXPANDING

By Tony Leigh

No one should want to stay the same; change is one of the most important parts of life. Being able to grow with new experiences and learning to recognize what is worthwhile and what is not is one of the fundamental parts of living. Every Mother's Son has found this to be especially true during this past summer.

Being rather restricted in travel during the year because four of the five "Sons" attend college in and around New York, they found this summer an eye opening experience. Starting in California and attending the Monterey Pop Festival, the group traveled throughout the United States and assimilated all the experiences to which they were exposed.

Denny Larden, lead singer and lead guitarist, puts it this way, "There hasn't been any character re-arrangement. But because of school we were restricted to one area. This past summer we were able to travel and experience new things and come in contact with new people."

New Appearance

One outward manifestation of change has been in their appearances.

"We're much more colorful now. Working with the British groups has influenced the way we dress," stated Denny.

"Wearing more theatrical clothes makes me feel more like I'm in show business, rather than just coming on stage in street clothes," added Bruce Milner, organist for the group.

Lary Larden, who is now a graduate student at Columbia University in New York City insisted that he always liked crazy clothes.

"I like wearing clothes that express what I feel. Chicago really influenced my dressing a lot. But this clothes thing shouldn't be over emphasized. Sure we've changed the way we look a bit, but basically there has been no fundamental change, only natural growth. Traveling extensively has just given us all more things to relate to."

Although when their first record "Come Down To My Boat," became a national hit, the record company billed them as "straight" and the anti-thesis of the psychedelic sound, this is no longer true. It is not that they have become "hippie." What they have been able to do is take what they want from where they want and make it into their own thing. Interpret what others are doing and when applicable make it their own.

Complicated Outlook

Going to college has given them a somewhat more complicated outlook on what is happening. As usually happens for students with a liberal arts b a c k g r o u n d, one thought jumps to several thousand others, and statements without contradictions are hard to come by.

"Psychedelic music is a misnomer; there is really no such thing, or very little of it. I mean if you define psychedelic the way McLuhan does (The Medium is the  Massage) then it means a sound which is totally random without any pattern," stated Lary.

"It's also totally sensual. You feel it rather than just hear it. But so many groups are called psychedelic that really aren't. The Airplane for example, they are not random musicians, they have patterns."

But a cross discussion with all five "Sons" proved to conclude that the term psychedelic is too relative to discuss in only one sense. Therefore what might seem psychedelic to one person might not to another, and that McLuhan was only one opinion. This honest and thoughtful exchange of opinions seems an important part of their personal and professional relationship.

Like many pop singers today, Every Mother's Son got their start singing folk. But like other "folk singers" they too turned to pop.

"Pop music is folk music in that it says something; it has a message. It's meant to be listened to," offered Lary.

Bruce was a bit more emphatic, "Folk music just came to a dead end, it was finished."

Lary continued, "It's really logical. Folk is just an expression of the times, now rock has become contemporary folk. Rock says what folk used to say."

Common Bond

Although all the "Sons" have many interests, they found a common bond in music.

Schuyler Larson who plays bass is studying at the Academy of Aeronautics at LaGuardia Airport, in New York. This may seem quite far removed from music, but not so for Schuyler.

"I love music, it's a part of me. I want to prove to myself that I can make it in music before I settle down and do something else. But music is in me, and for a while at least, I have to follow through with it."

Denny states, "I enjoy making music. It's great having the kids laughing and enjoying themselves, and you with them. There's joy in our music."

Christopher Augustine, drummer, and the oldest member of the group, came back to drumming after years of being an actor.

"I would give up music for acting, but when I left drumming I found that I wanted to go back to it. Drumming gave me something.

"I want to be as big as we can get. It's important to me, and then I will concentrate on acting."

While the others are studying at colleges during the year Chris is constantly studying acting in New York. That is when he is not actually in rehearsal or performing. Chris has studied at the American Academy of Dramatic Arts, one of the finest acting schools in the country and has performed with the New York Shakespeare Festival Company.

Every Mother's Son is composed of five very individual young men. Some people looking at what they were before last summer, seeing the sweat shirts and college look replaced by Indian beads and Cosack shirts, might feel that they have just coped out to trends and fads. But this is not true, clothes don't make the man, and costumes don't make the group.

Every Mother's Son is made up of five people who think and evaluate what is happening today. Any changes are for the better and have been thought out clearly before being made. With their talent and inquisitive minds, they should prove to be as successful as they want to be.

BRENTON WOOD — SUCCESS SIGN

Jacoba Atlas

Growing up in the poorer section of Los Angeles is not one of the easiest things that can happen to a child. Breaking the cycle of poverty is even more difficult. Yet that is exactly what Brenton Wood has done. One of eleven children, he spent his childhood selling coke bottles, catching fish to sell to restaurants and dreaming the dreams that eventually freed him from the Ghetto.

Music was the magical key for Brenton, music and a determination to become somebody. A realist with both feet surely on the ground, Wood is able to draw on his background for the stimulus that he needs today as a singer-composer.

"Music has always been with me, since I was a little boy. People used to tell me that I would beat on things and just hum tunes till one day when I was about nine years old, I saw a piano on the stage of the gymnasium where we used to play basketball.

"This guy was just playing the piano and it sounded so interesting to me, that I said, 'hey I want to do that.' Well, it took me about eight years to learn to play the piano, but I finally learnt.

"Since I play solely by ear, I can't play classical, really only R&B and other things that I've heard and really liked. I just pick things up, since I can't read music."

No Obstacle

It has been a long road for Brenton since the day when he first saw that piano and wanted to play. Since his family was on welfare, money for a piano was certainly out of the question. But that did not prove too great an obstacle for Brenton.

"I started in high school. I used to bug this lady about her piano. I used to go and play this piano all day, from noon till night. When everybody else was out playing, I was over there beating that piano. I knew they were wondering when I was going to go home.

"One day this lady saw an advertisement in the paper about this record company that wanted talent, so she gave me the number and I called them. It was Hooven and Winn who are now my producers.

"Anyway they told me to come over with my material.. I brought about 100 things on tape and they picked out about 75 to record, and we've been working on them ever since. My manager, Hal Winn helps me with the words in my songs because although I don't deal with big words, I want to get a fair meaning across. He just helps me interpret myself better."

Expressing Feelings

Brenton writes all his own material, and wrote both his hits, "Oogam Boogam" and now "Gimme a Little Sign." Writing and expressing his feelings through his songs is a very important part of life for Brenton.

"Every singer is trying to tell the public something. He is trying to show people how he feels. The songs that I have recorded so far are dreams that I have had in the past. They are the way I picture things to be, in my own mind.

"You have to have a story to tell in a song, and to be able to explain it sincerely, I want to do all my songs this way. My songs aren't really way out, they are something that I've felt inside."

Although by anyone's standards Brenton Wood is a success he maintains that he still has a long way to go. Paying dues to the music industry is something that Brenton takes for granted, he is no something for nothing guy. He learn how to take care of himself and work for the things he wanted.

Fantastic Plans

"I would like to help people who are helping themselves. I worked at selling papers, catching fish and selling them to restaurants, anything to make some money. But today the kids just want things to be given to them for nothing. I see my nephews and nieces just sitting around refusing to do anything for themselves.

"I had to get out of the system. I didn't like the way my mother was having it. I wanted more than that.

"I would like to have things settled, I would like to be able to do things business wise. It really would be a disaster to come up with something after all the changes I've been through.

KRLA ARCHIVES

SYMBOLIZING THE "DEATH OF THE HIPPIES" the flower children of Haight Ashbury in San Francisco hold a funeral procession and carry a "dead" hippie on a slab, followed by a symbolic 25-foot casket and a sign proclaiming "the brotherhood of free men is born."

open your mind
and discover

CLEAR LIGHT

Now Available At:
**MONTGOMERY WARD
DEPARTMENT STORES**

KRLA ARCHIVES

DON HO PLAYS IT WITH COOL

ANAHEIM — Muumuu-clad women and aloha-shirted men thronged to Melodyland Theatre last night to witness the return of Hawaii's number one son, Don Ho, and his talented Aliis.

They say that if you once catch a Ho performance you automatically become a life-long fan. It's not far from the truth. Hawaii's version of Cool has the most amazing ability to judge an audience and then proceed to play directly to them.

Missing Challenge

His opening night at Melodyland contained an audience ranging in age from six to sixty. It meant that Ho had to watch himself, making sure that his jokes did not send irate parents scurrying out the exits with their tender offspring clutched firmly by the ear. Missing was the typical Ho challenge to the girls to come on stage and make him miss a word of a song.

His repertoire is by no means "typically Hawaiian" but rather one which manages quite effectively to bridge the gap between "What Now My Love" and "Pearly Shells."

There were no lulls in the almost-two-hour show what with Ho's constant ad libbing, the marvelous talent of the Aliis (his back-up musicians or "my boys" as he prefers to call them) as well as a number of other exceptional performers which came along with the price of admission.

People arriving 15 minutes after the show began found themselves with their seats mysteriously occupied. Ho saw to that. "Before we go any further," he announced after his first number, "all you people who are sitting in the back come on up and find a seat in the expensive section. If you all move at once they can't do anything about it."

Ho says that he is not a singer —I suppose one could effectively argue that point—but without question he *is* one thing . . . a master of the elusive art of personal contact with the audience, inviting them on stage, spending the majority of the intermission on stage signing autographs and coaxing the audience to sing along.

Even with the house lights down, Ho read his audience brilliantly and instead of inviting the co-eds on stage he called the servicemen, the anniversary couples and the children. The servicemen and anniversary couples received the typical Ho teasing and the audience roared. The children were beautiful and the audience thundered its approval as Don sat a tiny girl on his lap and gathered the rest of the children around to sing "Tiny Bubbles."

If Hawaii ever sires a President, don't be surprised if it's Don Ho. As a matter of fact he even admits that he'd make a few changes. "I'd move the White House to Hawaii, paint it brown and call it the Brown House! I was going to call it the Ho House, but . . ." Another thing Ho would do if elected is lower the drinking age. "If an 18 year old boy is old enough to fight and die for his country, he's old enough to suck 'em up for his country. Girls should be able to drink at 18 too—we don't want the young boys going into bars and drinking with the old ladies!"

When "Born Free" wrapped up the show, there was none of the familiar garbage of an army of security guards hustling the "star" off stage to protect him from his adoring fans. Fact is—there was not a guard in sight. The Aliis ambled off stage and headed toward the dressing rooms in the midst of the departing crowds. However, Don remained on stage to sign programs and speak to anyone who cared to come up. There was no pushing, no shoving, no button-tearing. Just a couple of hours worth of "good times."

If you ever want to see a thoroughly entertaining show, sing a little, laugh a lot and applaud like crazy—catch the Don Ho show. Makes you feel good. And for those of you Island-bound, you can catch Don at Duke Kahanamoku's in Honolulu.—L. Criscone

FOUR TOPS—LESSON IN BEING PROFESSIONALLY PROFESSIONAL

By Jamie McCluskey III

On top of the record charts with insistent consistency are the four talented men from Motown, collectively known as the Four Tops. Levi Stubbs, Jr., Lawrence Payton, Renaldo "Obie" Benson, and Abdul Carib Fakir ("Duke")—a dynamic quartet that never stops reaching out for success.

After thirteen years together, the Tops have reached a pinnacle of success, recently playing the Cocoanut Grove in Los Angeles, one of the top night clubs in the country. Onstage — whether they are at the Grove or one of the many discotheques around the nation—they are total professionals, never missing a note or a cue.

Humanly Distinct

Off-stage, they are just as human and individually distinct as the rest of us; perhaps a little more so in their case. Lead singer, Levi Stubbs, is a quiet, brooding sort of individual. Until he loosens up, and then he lets you have it with both guns. He is outspoken, decisive, opinionated, and a man of his convictions (some people call that "stubborn," but with Levi it's just a matter of being true to himself).

Actually, Levi is quite a gentleman, but like many "men of convictions," he must always be in control of every situation. And so he usually is. The one thing he would like most to be able to control is the extent to which his talents reach the public. For Levi, success is "reaching as many people as possible and making them happy."

Inhibited

Quite obviously then, one of his greatest sources of aggravation is being inhibited in this area; prevented from reaching a majority of the people; "not being able to perform before *all* audiences. Being put in one bag and not being allowed to sing everything. Being typed as only a *rock and roll* singer or only a pop singer instead of being considered a *total* performer. I want to be able to sing *everything* for *everyone*."

While Levi is frequently the "serious" member of the group, his exact opposite can be found in fellow Top, Obie Benson. Obie is without a doubt the *smilingest* individual in the world! He is a happy-go-lucky sort of sunshine-fellow whose favorite sport is simply "making people happy, baby,' cause that's where it's at!"

Of course, even Obie can be serious at times. For example, when he is discussing his idea of a performer's responsibility to do the best possible job onstage. Not only to give an audience their money's worth . . . but, much more. If they paid four dollars to get in, then I think a performer ought to give them *eight* dollars worth of entertainment!"

Devilish Gleem

Lawrence Payton is the group's arranger and generally works closely with the band or orchestra backing them up. Although he, too, can be a quiet individual, there is a very definitely devilish gleem in his eyes which give away his strong Practical Joker tendencies.

He admits to having pulled some pretty funny tricks on his fellow Tops as well as some of the other Motown recording artists, including breaking up a show the Miracles were giving by running onstage in wigs and skirts! "Sometimes we have a very nutty sense of humor," he explains, "sometimes we have a very dry humor—according to how we feel. Sometimes we feel differently . . . but, we definitely have a sense of humor! Even onstage we have a sense of humor—at times, the audience doesn't even know what we're doing!"

Because the Four Tops have been able to weather the frequent storms of the often-fickle world of pop music, they can look back at the past decade in the business from an excellent vantage point.

"Over the past decade, the changes made in music—which I think is a great change—is the way that rock music has become a great part of this American music," Duke explained. "Plus," he continued: "the music itself has turned around to good music; if you really take rock music structurally—by chords, and so forth— you'll find that there is some very good, very beautiful, very difficult music in rock music.

Musical Structure

"The only thing that keeps it from being a standard-type thing is the beat that it carries—which is the rock beat. But music itself has turned out to be really fantastic structurally. I look at it for the music itself, and some of it is very intricate and very interesting."

Currently, the Four Tops have returned to the tops of both of the national charts, in both singles and album sales. Two of their latest LPs—"Reach Out" and "The Four Tops Greatest Hits"—are both riding high, and their latest single— "You Keep Running Away"—is rapidly running in the same successful direction. All of which leads one to believe that the Four Tops will very probably never touch bottom.

KRLA ARCHIVES

HAPPENINGS KEEP HAPPENING

Nothing happens overnight. The sudden hit records, the immediate popularity only results from years of hard work and consistent discipline.

In 1966 a group "burst" on the scene. Called the Happenings, they bounded up to number one on the charts with their recording of "See You In September." Since then they have repeated their initial success with records such as "Go Away Little Girl," "I Got Rhythm," and "My Mammy." But, although it looked like an overnight success, nothing could be farther from the truth.

Beginning almost four years ago under the unsuccessful name, the Four Graduates, Ralph De Vito, Bob Miranda, Tom Giuliano and Dave Libert worked constantly to find a sound which would give them the exposure they needed. Working in part-time jobs that ranged from selling to hairdressing, they sought to perfect their performances.

Polished Reformers

Meeting with The Tokens proved to be a lucky "happening." Producing their first hit record and all subsequent records, The Tokens guided the Happenings to the top of the charts.

Although all of the Happenings play musical instruments they do not accompany themselves when they perform with the exception of Dave who plays the organ. Theirs is not the typical rock act, but moreover a nightclub performance, and Bob, Ralph, Tom and Dave found playing their own music a hinderence rather than a help.

On stage the Happenings do impersonations and comedy. They have hired a drummer and a guitarist to travel with them and provide the necessary music, leaving the group free to be more expressive in their performance.

Traveling is one of the main concerns of the Happenings. Although San Remo Song Festival in Italy was their first trip abroad, the Happenings have a grueling schedule of one nighters, and college concerts around the country. In the year since they have become the Happenings they have covered almost every state in the nation, doing the college circuit as well as personal appearances in clubs.

Antiques & Drums

All of the Happenings pursue very different interests in their free time. Tom has become interested in antiques after purchasing an antique chandelier in Spain. It started him off in antiques and is now a frequent visitor of New York's Third Avenue, long famous for unusual art objects.

Bob, has become involved in painting as well as composing. His first painting was based on his own musical composition, "Girl On A Swing."

Dave who also composes has devoted his free time to mastering as many musical instruments as possible. Dave had formal training in musical theory and harmony along with the piano and organ. He is now teaching himself the violin, the trumpet and the drums.

Ralph is interested in photography and the theatre. During the Happenings' stage act, it is Ralph who achieves the comic relief but this does not exclude him from wishing to be a famous dramatic actor. The clown who wants to play Hamlet.

Except for Dave who lives in New York City, all of the Happenings remain in their home town of Paterson, New Jersey. They remain extremely close to their families, and enjoy the small percentage of free time that they have to lead "normal" lives in one place. With their present hit "Why Do Fools Fall In Love" already zooming the charts free time will be even more difficult to find.

'FAR FROM THE MADDING GROUP'

"Far From the Madding Crowd" is a visually beautiful movie. Filmed entirely on location in what the English call "Hardy Country" the film is populated with real faces and authentic period costumes and sets. However, this eye to history is all the film has to offer.

Although the film lasts just under three hours, it seems twice as long. The story is rather complicated. Based on the 1874 novel by Thomas Hardy, it tells of the trials of one Bathsheba Everdene, played with one emotion by Julie Christie. The three men in her life are Gabriel Oak, the farmer who stays by her side through all her other adventures, portrayed by Alan Bates; Sergeant Troy, the rake who sweeps Bathsheba off her feet and marries her, played by Terrance Stamp, and finally Boldwood, the wealthy landowner who kills for her, played by Peter Finch.

Unfortunately, none of these people are given anything to do other than stand around and look romantic. Burdened with beautiful cinematography that doesn't fit what the story is trying to say, and encumbered with a rambling script that is far too ambitious for the limitations of this film; everyone looks ridiculous.

Julie Christie manages only to smile continually, or utter distraughtly at lease 100 times, "I can't promise." The three men, portrayed by excellent actors, are given little to do, with the exception of Terrance Stamp as Troy. Mr. Stamp plays his role with a bravado that fits an 1850 melodrama but not a 1967 interpretation.

The fault must lie with the director, John Schesinger and screenwriter, Frederick Raphael. Both of these men are extremely talented, having combined their creative abilities in such tight and precise films as "Darling" and "Billy Liar." However, this time disregarding all they knew about telling a story without superfluous shots and unnecessary action, they instead produced a rambling movie that negates people and refuses to deal with honest emotions.

Schlesinger has unfortunately felt that he had to make a choice between characters and beautiful shots and chose the latter. 180 degree angle shots, blurred backgrounds, color fade-outs bursting into the next shot are all marvelous tricks of both the cinematographer and the editor, but they should not be used indiscriminately to subvert the narrative of the film. At least half of the shots made no sense to the action of the movie.

Granted the story is a melodrama—it was written in the heyday of the flowery love story — but Schlesinger has added smulzth on top of melodrama. Using ridiculous gimmicks such as a folk song that comes out of nowhere to re-tell the story of Sergeant Troy which the audience has just spent the last two hours observing was unforgivable. Then, too, Raphael, who was able to give such insight into his characters in "Two for the Road," seemed unable to pick through the fripperies of the novel and come to terms with the basic human emotions that surely were to be found. Raphael produced a screenplay that was too enamored with the sweep of the novel to be valid.

To be sure, people will flock to see "Madding Crowd." It is perhaps worth it. Most people will never be able to travel to Dorset in England, and certainly none of us will ever be able to return to the middle 1800s which the film so faithfully and beautifully re-creates. But as a film it dies; without valid characters, with superfluous distracting shots, and unforgivable melodrama, "Madding Crowd" emerges as a pitifully empty film.

BATHSHEBA is escorted to the Circus by Boldwood (Peter Finch).

GABRIEL OAK (Alan Bates) shows Bathsheba (Julie Christie) how to play the flute.

TROY (Terence Stamp) awakens his new bride.

KRLA ARCHIVES

EVERYBODY WINS!
IN YOUNG AMERICA RECORD CLUB'S
CARNABY STREET
100,000 PRIZES
SWEEPEROO!
NOTHING TO BUY – NO OBLIGATION!

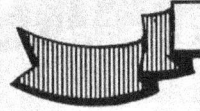

Round-trip for two to LONDON'S CARNABY STREET
Round-trip with your best friend to Carnaby Street. Fly Pan Am jet to London — and "live it up" for two out-of-sight weeks on Carnaby Street — all expenses paid. Get a fab Carnaby Street wardrobe plus mad mad money!

- 5 Raleigh Motor Bikes
- 20 TV Sets
- 20 Stereo Phonograph Players
- 10 Tape Recorders
- 10 Hair Dryers
- 10 Fun Fur Parkas
- 50 Transistor Radios

EVERYBODY CAN WIN FREE KODACOLOR FILM PRIZE
Next time you shoot a roll of film, develop it with our "Picture Pal" service and get another roll of film free! No limit!

- 30 Weekend Luggage Pieces • 40 Theatrical Make-Up Mirrors • 200 Beauty Boutique Sets
- 1,000 Paper (Pow!) Dresses • 2,000 Mod-Bods (Groovy Designs!) • 10,000 wall-size Posters

Claim your prize today. Mail "Carnaby Street" Sweeperoo Ticket (or facsimile) below... and turn-on to a groovy way to save $ $ $ on LPs, Singles and Tapes, too (AT DISCOUNTS UP TO 75%!)

Look at the loot!... EVERYBODY WINS in Young America Record Club's Carnaby Street Sweeperoo! Right now there's over 100,000 groovy prizes to be won at Prize Headquarters — and there's one for you. To claim your prize, fill out and mail your Carnaby Street Sweeperoo Ticket today!

But that's not all! By joining Young America Record Club, you can buy all the LPs, all the singles, all the tapes you want — any star, any label, no exceptions! — AT BIG, BIG DISCOUNTS (25%, 33⅓%, 50%, up to 75%)! Just look at the prices — top-hit LPs sell for as little as $1.77 — even as low as 94¢! And...

FLASH — there's never $1.00 extra charge for stereo — stereo and mono LPs are the same price!

What's more, unlike other record clubs, you don't have to buy a minimum number of records — you buy all the records you want or nothing! And there's no long wait; your records are shipped same day ordered.

LOOK AT THE "EXTRAS" YOU GET!
Reports on your favorite stars... the end records... special groovy news about you, the member... Lucky Record purchases... Surprise Birthday Gifts... Free products (cosmetics, beauty aids, etc.) from famous manufacturers... Lucky Date with favorite 'teen stars... pen pals and lots more!

As a member, you order latest releases any day — anytime! — even before hits are in stock in your home town! At the same time you'll also receive regular bulletins of the hits being played most by the disc jockeys, on the juke boxes, from the "Top-of-the-Charts". Yes, all the latest and newest releases — the break-outs — are yours when you want them — at the Club's low, low prices with just a small charge for handling and mailing.

It's What's Happening!...
so join the gang!... join Young America Record Club! Membership dues are only $2.00, good for a full year of fun and big dollar savings. You'll save as much as $25.00 a year alone on the LPs, singles and tapes you want — the "sounds" you're going to buy anyway. Not to mention the prize you win in the Carnaby Street Sweeperoo!

DON'T DELAY! FILL out the Sweeperoo Ticket (or facsimile) now — and be sure to enclose your membership dues if you want to save money on LPs, singles and tapes where the action is!

THE ONLY RECORD CLUB IN THE WORLD WITH ALL YOUR FAVORITE STARS!

Young Rascals, Turtles, Jefferson Airplane, Music Explosion, The Association, Happenings, Every Mother's Son, Simon and Garfunkel, The Animals, Herb Alpert, Blues Magoos, The Beach Boys, Johnny Mathis, Ventures, Peter, Paul and Mary, Righteous Brothers, Five Americans, Moby Grape, The Love Generation, Lettermen, Tony Bennett, Englebert Humperdinck, Dave Clark Five, Jack Jones, Fifth Estate, Ed Ames, Scott McKenzie, Aretha Franklin, Temptations, Bill Cosby, The Monkees, The Yardbirds, Rolling Stones, Herman's Hermits, Four Tops, Paul Revere, The Bee Gees, Dionne Warwick, Johnny Rivers, Lovin' Spoonful, Petula Clark, Harpers Bizarre, Supremes, Stevie Wonder, Elvis Presley, Sonny and Cher, Frank Sinatra, Nancy Sinatra, Mamas and Papas, Dean Martin, Bob Dylan, Nancy Wilson, Buckinghams, Connie Francis, Brenda Lee
MANY MORE

COMPARE YOUNG AMERICA RECORD CLUB WITH OTHER "SQUARE" CLUBS!			
DOES THE CLUB...	CLUB "A"	CLUB "B"	YOUNG AMERICA RECORD CLUB
Bring your favorite 'teen stars?	Some	Some	ALL 'teen stars
Obligate you to buy records?	YES—12	YES—10	NONE
Bill you for records you didn't order?	Possibly	Possibly	NEVER
Ship records right away?	5-6 wks	5-6 wks	Same day ordered
Discount your records?	NO	NO	25% – 33⅓% – 50% – 75%
Offer tapes and singles	NO	NO	YES
Offer all labels?	NO	NO	ALL LABELS
Do you get all new records as soon as released?	NO	NO	YES – all of them
Offer 'teen activities?	NO	NO	YES – fun galore!
Offer "lucky purchase" records— bring you free products, etc.?	NO	NO	YES – So join today!

SWEEPEROO RULES:
1. Just fill out coupon (or facsimile) and mail. Names to be drawn at random by independent organization.
2. Everybody wins a prize. No purchase required.
3. Drawing for prizes to be made May 31, 1968.
4. Sweepstakes void in States where prohibited by law.
5. Employees of Young America Record Club, members of their families and their agency not eligible for prizes.

© Young America Record Club 1967

★ SWEEPEROO TICKET ★
c/o BEAT, Box 23, Planetarium Sta., New York, N.Y. 10024

YES—tell me the prize I've won in the Sweeperoo.

YES—enroll me as a member of Young America Record Club. I enclose my $2.00 membership fee in ( ) check ( ) money order ( ) cash. I understand I need buy nothing and no records will be sent to me unless ordered.

YES—send free monthly newsletter. Gives me advice, inside information on 'teen stars, recordings, plus fashions, news about members.

☐ NO—I don't want to belong. Tell me what prize I've won.

YES—give my name to manufacturers for free products.

YES—surprise me with a gift on my birthday.

YES—I like the idea of Lucky Records which win a prize... of Free membership in Pen Pals International... of the Miss 'Teen and Mr. 'Teen contests to be staged by Young America Record Club.

YES—I want to participate in all the fun and activities of the Club being lined up for 'teens.

PRINT NAME ....
ADDRESS ....
CITY .... STATE .... ZIP ....
My birthday is .... MONTH DAY YEAR

KRLA ARCHIVES

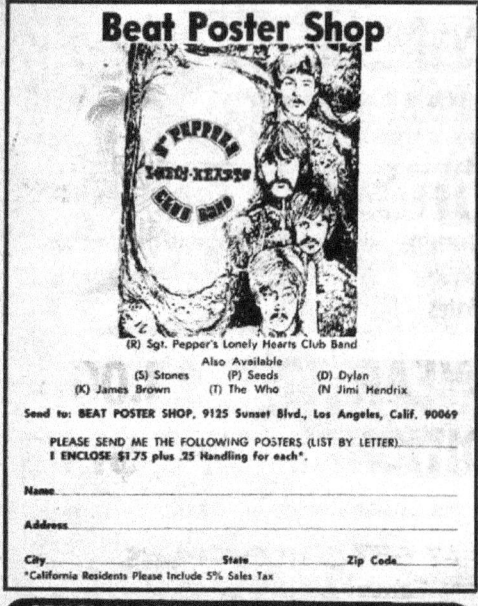

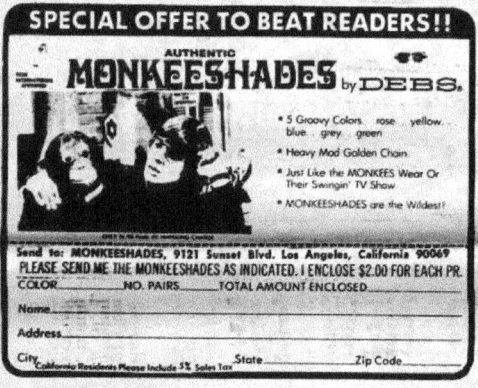

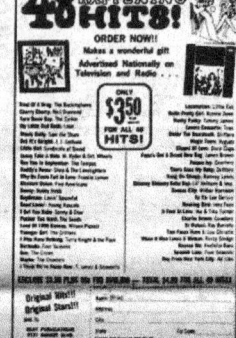

TURNING ON

ALIZA KASHI (Jubilee) *Aliva Kashi. Born Free, A Man and a Woman, My Cup Runneth Over* plus nine other tracks. Miss Kashi is an Israeli singer who may be familiar to people through her continuous appearances on the Merv Griffin Show. She has a good voice, but is not spectacular. She doesn't have the individuality of a Streisand, nor the power of a Lannie Kazan. She is good, but nothing outstanding. Perhaps in person Miss Kashi fares better, for on the album much of her potential seemed lost. She is not helped by a rather dated arrangement of material that concentrates too much on the back-up singers and not enough on Miss Kashi. She does offer a rather unusual rendition of *Bill Bailey Won't You Please Come Home* — singing the familiar tune in rather unfamiliar Yiddish.

PANDEMONIUM SHADOW SHOW (RCA) Nilsson. *Ten Little Indians, 1941, She's Leaving Home* plus nine other tracks. Nilsson, who wrote the better portion of songs on this album, is extremely talented. Writing unusual words dealing with unique subjects, Nilsson manages in this, his first album for RCA, to come up with something new that is always interesting. Produced by Rick Jerrard, who was mainly responsible for Jefferson Airplane's *Surrealistic Pillow, Shadow Show* is fantastically put together with varying arrangements and unique sounds. Except for an opening dialogue there are no gimmicks used, just interesting songs, well sung. One particularly good offering is *Cuddly Toy*, and a strange tale of abandonment called *1941*. *Cuddly Toy* is particularly interesting because of its double meaning; ask someone familiar with motorcycle gangs what a "Choo-Choo" train is. This album is definitely one to be listened to over and over again, for many musical subtleties will be lost the first time you hear it.

CHUCK BERRY LIVE AT THE FILLMORE (Mercury) Chuck Berry. *C. C. Rider, Feelin' It, Flying Home, Johnny B. Good* plus eight other tracks. Live this album is! And great! Backed up by the Steve Miller Blues Band, who are a whole thing in themselves, this album, recorded at Bill Grahams' Fillmore Auditorium is fantastic. There will never be anyone like Berry, and in this album he is able to do what he wants without an ear to top 40 sales potential. Berry is much more soulful than he ever was in his singles, and relates the blues with special feeling. Listen to *Everyday I Have the Blues*, what can be said? The Steve Miller Blues Band matches and heightens Berry's style with their own own special blend of rock and blues. To everyone's credit they are allowed to play a good many solos which are fantastic. Don't miss this album, it shows what talent can produce.

BEATLE POSTERS

Available in black light, hand screened poster. Pink, green, orange added to make a groovy image.

Cost is only $1.00 plus 25c handling. Get your order in to The BEAT now!

California residents include 5% sales tax.

KRLA ARCHIVES

BE A BEAT SANTA THIS YEAR!

Please your friends with a BEAT SUBSCRIPTION For CHRISTMAS at these Special Holiday Rates

FIRST 1-YEAR GIFT $3.00
EACH ADDITIONAL GIFT $1.00

Foreign Subscriptions $9.00 Per Year

Mail to: BEAT GIFT SUBSCRIPTIONS
9121 Sunset Blvd., L.A 90069

Dear BEAT,
Enter my subscription as my first gift subscription at $3.00.
Renew my subscription as my first gift subscription at $3.00.
Please send the BEAT for one year to my friends listed below.

My Name_____
Address_____
City_____ State_____ Zip Code_____
Enclosed is $_____ for _____ gift subscriptions.

I understand that you will send all gift cards to me so that I may give them to my friends and that their first BEAT will be delivered the week of Christmas.

RENEW BEAT GIFTS HERE

NAME_____
ADDRESS_____
CITY_____ STATE_____ ZIP_____

NAME_____
ADDRESS_____
CITY_____ STATE_____ ZIP_____

NAME_____
ADDRESS_____
CITY_____ STATE_____ ZIP_____

ENTER NEW GIFTS HERE

NAME_____
ADDRESS_____
CITY_____ STATE_____ ZIP_____

NAME_____
ADDRESS_____
CITY_____ STATE_____ ZIP_____

NAME_____
ADDRESS_____
CITY_____ STATE_____ ZIP_____

KRLA ARCHIVES

Acapulco, here you come!

Look for this display in your market. It could mean an Acapulco vacation for you and a friend. There'll be plenty of winners in our Acapulco Sweepstakes. The prizes—a week for two at one of Acapulco's swingingest hotels. And the two-way trip on Western Airlines. There's nothing to do. Just enter. Go to your market and find out the details. So, get ready for Acapulco!

KRLA ARCHIVES

KRLA BEAT

Volume 3, Number 18   December 2, 1967

Facts Behind Rumored Beatle/Stone Merger

Here are the real facts behind all the merger stories you've been hearing in the past couple of weeks regarding possible joint ventures involving the Beatles and the Rolling Stones.

At the outset, let me emphasize that nothing has been settled, nothing has been signed, nothing has been agreed. The simple truth is that Mick Jagger has had a few wholly informal chats with his close friend, Paul McCartney. In the course of conversation both parties realized that they had a common aim—to acquire and operate a private recording studio. From this, and from nothing more, grew a frantic storm of speculation suggesting that everything was much further advanced, that the two groups would be setting up a joint talent center for record production and the launching of new names.

'Leaked' News

The rumors were given substance via the new Saturday television show, "Good Evening," hosted by Jonathan ("Everyone's Gone To The Moon") King. King claimed to have unearthed evidence that McCartney/Jagger discussions were about to be resolved and a Beatles/Stones merger was all-but-finished. The London-based Sunday newspapers picked up his "leaked" story and gave it front page headlines.

As this issue of The BEAT goes to press, the subject is still open for further discussion between the Beatles and the Rolling Stones. It is true that Mick and Paul are equally capable of handling record production for other artists. It is true that the construction of a recording studio, financed and furnished by the two groups, makes economical and practical sense. At present each group spends a great deal of money renting studios in or around London to make their records. Then they sell the finished product under longterm contract to rival record companies.

Interesting Theory

The theory of a joint corporation is an interesting one so long as we appreciate that this project would be an additional activity in no way replacing nor making obsolete the various professional, music and business relationships which already surround each group.

Obviously, a production unit backed by such important people would be influential. On the other hand, we cannot expect to see any merger bringing together the Stones and the Beatles on one nine-man record since existing longterm recording contracts would prohibit this.

—Tony Barrow

Conviction For Jones; An Appeal Is Pending

While Rolling Stones' Mick Jagger and Keith Richard were busy huddling with their business manager, Allan Klein in New York, two major legal actions affecting the group and its future were going ahead in London.

The first involved Brian Jones, accused of possessing marijuana and allowing other people to smoke it in his apartment in Courtfield Road, South Kensington, May 10th of this year.

Manager's Suit

The second involved Andrew Oldham and Eric Easton, former joint managers of the group. Easton sought an interim high court order freezing the payment of record and other royalties pending the hearing of an action in which he will claim that Oldham owes him a substantial back payment representing his share of the group's earnings during the 1963-1966 period.

Convicted at London Sessions Court, Rolling Stone Brian Jones was sentenced to nine months imprisonment. The court heard evidence that Drug Squad officers had found enough cannabis or cannabis resin at Jones' apartment to make ten cigarettes.

Passing sentence the judge said: "I have given your case anxious and careful consideration. These offenses to which you have pleaded guilty are very serious indeed."

Appeal Pending

Jones spent 24 hours in prison before being released on bail pending an appeal court hearing. He was allowed to leave the jail on the condition that he place himself under medical care. It is possible that the appeal will not be heard until the early part of this month.

Mystery Surrounds The Mamas & Papas' Future

LONDON—First there is a Mamas and Papas, then there is not a Mamas and Papas, and then there is! Confusion piled high upon confusion! We've had conflicting reports, contradictory quotes, concert cancellations.

As the November 4th issue of The BEAT went into print my front-page story was accurate and up-to-date. Days later the entire situation had changed.

Here is a retrospective date-by-date rundown on the whole fantastic affair...

Announcement

October 4: London promoter Tito Burns announced Royal Albert Hall November 1 concert to co-star Mamas & Papas and Scott McKenzie.

October 5: Group plus Scott McKenzie and manager, Lou Adler, sailed into Southampton aboard the liner France. Mama Cass arrested on the quayside.

October 6: At West London Magistrates Court, Mama Cass cleared ("without a stain on your character") of charges relating to the disappearance of blankets and keys late last February from Kensington's Embassy Hotel.

October 11: Tito Burns re-scheduled Royal Albert Hall "Evening With The Mamas and Papas and Scott McKenzie" for October 30. Top-priced seats at $3.50 began to sell in substantial numbers. Cheapest tickets priced at only 50 cents! Burns confident of 7,000 sell-out.

Cancellation

October 14: Group cancelled Royal Albert Hall appearance. Also projected Paris Olympia concert. Group admitted that Majorca vacation plans had been scrapped.

October 15: Mama Cass indicated to London press the probability of a total break-up in the group and left the impression that she, at any rate, would not be remaining a part of the Mamas and Papas.

October 17: Unconfirmed London reports declared that Cass and Denny had left for America while John and Michelle were vacationing in Germany.

October 18: Yesterday's reports shattered by the surprise appearance of Mama Cass amongst the celebrity audience at the World Premiere of the Michael Crawford/John Lennon movie, "How I Won The War," at London's Pavilion Theatre in Piccadilly Circus. "But I'm flying back to the States in the next 24 hours," Cass admitted.

Peace Of Mind

October 19: Manager, Lou Adler, did his best to clarify the situation by declaring that the group had decided to take a break for an indefinite period. They had pulled out of the London concert "to get started on their holiday right away." This was not in protest of police action in making Mama Cass spend a night in jail but was "simply to help them restore their peace of mind."

October 20: Promoter, Tito Burns, expressed his fury at the cancellation of the Royal Albert Hall date saying he was disgusted by such an "unethical and unprofessional" act. He was quoted as adding: "If this is all they think of their British fans they don't deserve to have any. It is quite diabolical."

Clear Fact

From all this chaos one clear fact emerges: the Mamas and Papas are unanimous about their future. They seem to agree that a segment of their group career is at an end. What they are yet to decide is whether or not available new musical directions are out of the question. Certainly they have individual ambitions for solo projects and it is doubtful whether they will find a way of doing each of their personal things within the framework of a group called the Mamas and Papas.

Lou Adler has expressed his confidence that the Mamas and Paas will be together again in the recording studio and he believes he can persuade them to undertake personal appearances. He is cautious about the timing of these future activities.

I imagine any London promoter would be more than cautious about setting any further U.K. concert dates for the group without advance evidence that other appearances are not the subject of last-minute cancellation.

Meanwhile, "Twelve Thirty," the current U.K. single by the Mamas and Papas has failed to climb into our National Top 50. It is my personal opinion that the sympathy drawn by Cass Elliott over her arrest has been more than cancelled out by the group's refusal to stay in London for that heavily publicized and eagerly awaited Royal Albert Hall show. It all added up to bad publicity relations whatever unrevealed behind-the-scenes motive the group's members may have had for going away from London in opposite directions.

—Tony Barrow

MAMA CASS LEAVING impression that it's all over

KRLA ARCHIVES

BEACH BOY FAN SPEAKS UP

Dear BEAT:
I am a devoted fan of the Beach Boys with plenty to say. I think it's about time the Beach Boys get the recognition they deserve. The Beach Boys rule. Allow me to explain why.

Along in about 1961 4 young Californians recorded "Surfin'." Later they recorded more surf songs and then some hot rod songs (Little Duece Coupe, 409, Shut Down). They had started a new type of music. They had made their dent in pop music before the Beatles had. During the early days of the Beach Boys people mostly heard "Beach Boys Rule" or "Surfers Rule."

In 1963 when the Beatles stepped foot on U.S. soil they conquered America. The Beach Boys had already conquered American and had been on the top of the charts for 2½ years. The Beatles' popularity did not stop the Beach Boys from making and selling records.

In 1966 the Monkees came about. They took over America after the Beatles had been on top for 2½ years. What was to happen to the Beach Boys? Were they to die? NO! The Beach Boys were the first American groups to ever be grooved over as much as the Beatles in England. They took over the British throne. Did this surprise the Beach Boys' fans? No, but it sure surprised a lot of people. The Beach Boys conquered Britain before the Monkees even had time to think about Britain. What can be attributed to the Beach Boys long success? The most contributing factor is probably Brian Wilson, in my opinion the pop genius of our time. Brian puts himself into every song. Brian is John Lennon, Andrew Oldham, Sir Arthur Sullivan, Hamlet, Murph the Surf, Gypsy Boots, Sydney Carton, Huck Finn, also Napoleon. He is a genius.

Beach Boy Carl Wilson has recently been acquitted of a charge of evading the draft. I'm not going to keep on writing. The fab Beach Boys have left 15 albums (including their wildly accepted Pet Sounds) and 20 singles behind them. They are not ready to stop. They will always be so great that all their fans will always be able to say "The Beach Boys Rule."

Jim Maufair

TEEN-AGERS
By Marlene Myhre

Someday teen-agers will be looked upon as something other than just "those crazy kids." We can't help it if we don't like the things grownups like. I really don't think we should,

We have our own little world. A world of laughter, rock and roll, London, and the boy down the street. It seems as though adults are always trying to turn in our world for us.

So what if we like boys with long hair, mini skirts, psychedelic guitars, and all the rest. It's what we like. We're not saying that everyone has to like them. We don't like everything that our parents or other adults do. Everybody has to go their own way and I think that this age is the most delicate, 13-17, whether we will go with the crowd or be individuals.

Just because there are hippies and teen-agers who get thrown in jail, don't blame it on the whole group. Can't you think of their disposition. Can't you see they might have that feeling of insecurity. If you think of it, YOU might be just the one to help.

So please, parents, don't try to take our little world away from us. We'll come out soon, just be patient. We are still your sons and daughters, no matter how we act. Just hold on to our hand and wait.

A SECRET

Dear BEAT:
The BEAT is the only true tradespaper on the stand amongst all the other muckraker teen magazines. This is my second year of subscribing and I wanted to tell you what a great paper you have. I also have a question to ask. Who writes the column "In" People Are Talking About? It's one of my favorite features. I also have a fe contributions to make to it:

Please are talking about going barefoot in the park; how many Pleasant Valley Sunday's there are in America; what Big Brother is Holding; why; the Monkees going dramatic and deciding that with their personalities it's going to be hard to do;

Linda West

The name of the person who writes "In" People is the best-kept and only secret in our office! The Editor.

NICE GOING

Dear BEAT:
I want to congratulate you and your staff on your fine paper.

My brothers and I are managers of bands in Spokane and Seattle, Washington. I've seen the Beatles and the Beach Boys and I met groups like Don and the Goodtime, Paul Revere and the Raiders etc.

While I was on leave this August, I saw some of the groups that you've written about. Now I want to tell you about them. The Fifth Dimension and the Vanilla Fudge had the crowd clapping during some of their songs. When the Vanilla Fudge did "You Keep Me Hanging On" the crowd yelled wild approval.

The New Yorkers was the group that really impressed everyone. The group dresses, acts and sounds like the Beatles. They played several cuts off of the Sgt. Pepper LP that sounded so close to the Beatles that it was hard to believe. The boys age from 16 to the baby 14, and they consist of 3 brothers and a friend.

The service keeps me from being with bands and the people that make up the "pop" music world. In the 3 short years that I have had a hand I've found out that the people in the music world are the nicest in the world. Thanks to your paper I can at least keep up on "What's Happening."

Larry Ehachatt

Beat Publications, Inc.

Executive Editor .... Cecil I. Tuck
Publisher .... Gayle Tuck
Editor .... Louise Criscione
Assistant Editor .... Jacoba Atlas

Staff Writers
Bobby Bovino   Ron Koslow
Tony Leigh   Shirley Poston

Contribution Writers
Tony Barrow   Sue Barry
Eden   Bob Levinson
Jamie McClusky III   Mike Masterson

Photographers
Ed Caraeff   Jerry Hoss

National Sales Representative
Sam Chase Assoc., Inc.
527 Madison Avenue
New York, New York
(212) PL 5-1688

Advertising Director .... Dick Stricklin
Business Manager .... Judy Felice
Subscriptions .... Diane Clatworthy

Distribution
Miller Freeman Publications
500 Howard Street, San Francisco, Calif.

The BEAT is published bi-weekly by BEAT Publications, Inc., editorial and advertising offices at 9121 Sunset Blvd., Los Angeles, California 90069. U.S. bureaus in Hollywood, San Francisco, New York, Chicago and Nashville; overseas correspondents in London, Liverpool and Manchester, England. Sale price 25 cents. Subscription price: U.S. and possessions $5 per year; Canada and foreign rates, $9 per year. Second class postage prepaid at Los Angeles, California.

FORUM

The opinions and ideas expressed in the Letters to the Editor or The Forum sections of our paper are not necessarily the opinions of The BEAT. However, we do feel that this is a free country in which each individual is entitled to hold and express his/her opinions and beliefs. Unfortunately, a limited amount of space prevents us from printing every letter submitted to The BEAT. Consequently, we are forced to print only a general cross-section of the mail we receive.
The Editor

The Right To Rebel?
by Ken Woo

On October 6, 1967, about 300 members of the John Marshall High School student body took part in a student strike in protest of the cancellation of the Sunshine Company because of their long hair from a student body activity card holder's assembly.

The night before a Los Angeles radio station received a tip that the demonstration was planned for the following day, and one of their deejays began broadcasting the proposal over the airways. That same night Lance Ito, Student Body president, sent out a statement saying that he and other members of the school's student leadership were working to avert the intended strike. However, Ito did not promise that their efforts would be successful.

As it turned out, Ito proved unable to call a cancellation of the demonstration. Friday saw 300 students participating in the strike. However, as this number only represented a small portion of the total number of students at John Marshall, one demonstrator misguidedly pulled the fire alarm bell, thus creating havoc and confusion as teachers and students poured into the halls.

As I am one of the members of the Leadership class, I feel that I must write this article showing both sides of the incident. Many garbled and misinterpreted reports have been filtering out of the school, and many of the press media were banned from the general area during the strike.

Starting from the student's standpoint, I heard rumors of the strike about a week ago when the Principal, Mr. William Ruess, talked to our class about his own support of the school's policy on long hair. Evidently his lecture upset many students, giving rise to the decision to strike.

Mr. Ruess told the class that the reason he would not permit the Sunshine Company to perform was because their long hair was in violation of the good grooming policies of the school.

I myself feel this reasoning to be false, for the group's members are not part of the student body at John Marshall High School, and therefore should not be bound by the school's grooming regulations.

However, from the Administration's point of view, I feel that many parents might have been angered had the Principal permitted the group to entertain. This is excluding what the Principal's Association and the Board of Education might have said or done in connection with the assembly.

A Principal has many responsibilities that he must assume, and I think, from the administrative point of view he made a wise decision.

In writing this article, I must take an impartial view, but if you have any opinion or remarks, whether you are a student, parent, or businessman, we would appreciate any ideas or comments that you would care to send in, please write in care of this publication.

COLORS
By Mark Backlund

Green Yellow Red Blue
Do I see them the same as you
Or do each of us see a different color scheme
Through different eyes and different means
If you could break through the dimension that holds our world
And see a mass of new colors, some distinct, some swirled
And after you're been there a time
Wouldn't it be wonderful to find
To get there you don't need to get high out of line
All you have to do is open your mind.

KRLA ARCHIVES

SHOUTS FROM GENE

By Gene Cornish

Hello! I'd like to start off with a few recommendations: Watch out for "The Donuts," an up-and-coming group in the New York area—managed by Frank Scinlaro and Lenny Borgone, The Rascals' former road manager. We wish Lenny and Frank and the group the best of luck!

A place to be seen: "The Scene," an exciting, not-to-be-believed discotheque in Manhattan. "The Brass Buttons," a group I'm producing, will be back there in November.

Homebody

These days I'm furnishing a new home I recently bought for my parents in Long Island. I'm aiming for a different atmosphere, a different age of history in each room. (I guess I'm really a homebody after all!)

But *most* of my time these days is spent at Atlantic's recording studio—we're still perfecting our fourth album (not titled yet). The album encompasses every genre of music—and many of The Rascals' friends are going to appear in the songs—and a Salvation Army Band we met one day last week.

Felix and Sid Bernstein (The Rascals' fine manager) just returned from England—where Felix visited George Harrison—and talked about philosophy and the experience of sitar-playing and learning. More about that journey later....

Third Million?

Our latest 45 rpm—"How Can I Be Sure"—is heading up the charts. By the time you read this (our fingers are crossed!) we expect it'll be another Gold Record million-seller (our third after "Good Lovin' " and "Groovin' ").

You'll be able to 'hang' The Rascals soon—we'll be available in poster-form soon—in stores and through our fan club....

Speaking of The Rascals' fan club—if you'd like to join, write for information to us at Box 380, Planetarium Station, New York, N.Y. 10024. Let us know your feelings—about things you like and things that bug you!

Talk to you again soon—for now—Love, Gene.

'BILLIE JOE' SCORES TWICE

HOLLYWOOD — Bobbie Gentry has been awarded another Gold Record for the album entitled "Ode to Billie Joe." The single by the same name was certified a million seller in September.

This album attained the certification last week, having surpassed the $1 million sales mark.

Miss Gentry last week returned to her home state of Mississippi to pose for Life Magazine photographers.

ART INSTITUTE OF PITTSBURGH
57th Yr. Coed, & 24 mo. Diploma Course, Commercial Art, Fashion Art, Interior Design, Begin. & Adv. Vet Appd. Dorm facilities. College referrals for detrees. Free Illus. brochure.
Earl B. Wheeler, Director
635 Smithfield St.
Pittsburgh, Pa. 15222

Elvis Presley Holds Auction

MEMPHIS—Elvis Presley is set to depart with some of his property. It seems that Elvis has decided to quit the cattle business and raise horses instead.

Therefore, an auction is being held at Presley's "Circle G" ranch near Horn Lake, Mississippi.

Among the items that will go to the highest bidder are five house trailers which have been used by Elvis' guests, farm implements and equipment, television sets, a coffee bar and matching chairs, desks and lounges. Also up for sale is a five-horsepower cart which was built especially for Elvis and valued at $12,000.

Biggest Deal Ever
Don Ho Signs New Contract

HONOLULU—One of the largest nightclub salary deals ever set has been drawn up between Don Ho and Duke Kahanamoku's nightclub. The deal calls for Ho to earn $2½ million straight salary plus a percentage of the profits during the next five years.

The contract calls for Don to headline at Duke's for 20 weeks each year for the next five, with the dates more or less at his option between concert, nightclub and television appearances on the mainland and in Europe.

Don, currently headlining at Duke's along with the talented Aliis, also owns various nightclubs in the islands and his contract does not preclude his working in his own spots once his 20 weeks a year at Duke's are fulfilled.

And that, brother, *is* a big thing.

PEOPLE ARE TALKING ABOUT *Lulu* making it to number one in the nation with "To Sir With Love" and wondering how much the movie helped.... "Pata Pata" just going to prove that you don't have to know what the words mean to dig a song and what that does to McLendon's theory ... whether or not *Jerry Quarry* will make it as an entertainer ... how that schooner fit into a member of a pop group's decision to leave

... who thought up the cover for the *Doors'* latest album ... what's going to happen to any artist produced by the combined forces of *Lennon/McCartney* and *Jagger/Richard* ... who the *Hombres* are ... how big *Nilsson* is going to be ... *Rod McKuen* being so talented it's almost a sin ... the *Cowsills* being surprisingly good and even drawing *Rock Hudson* out to see them at the Century Plaza Hotel

... *Glen Campbell's* "By The Time I Get To Phoenix" being his best ever ... the fact that *Bill Cosby* came very close to having the top single in the country with "Little Ole Man" and what a coup that would have been ... why someone doesn't put a top 40 variety show on one of the networks ... *Them* still being around ... whether or not there will ever be another *Mamas and Papas* album and deciding that there won't

... *Jay and the Techniques* being on the scene for a long time because they hit a great middle of the road between soul and pop ... what's going to happen with *Jimi Hendrix* ... why the *Checkmates* haven't come up with a hit record lately ... whether or not *Dionne Warwick* will ever record another single which is not written by the *Bacharach/David* team and coming to the conclusion that tossing a winning team aside is more than foolish

... some radio stations refusing to play *Stark Naked & The Car Thieves* records because they didn't like the group's name—if you can believe it ... *Pat Boone* busily covering *Glen Campbell's* "By The Time I Get To Phoenix" ... *Frank Sinatra* cutting a single from "The

Cool Ones" and wondering what that means ... why *Noel Harrison* doesn't stick to acting ... how long it will be this time for the *Bono's* to get "Chastity" released after its's finished shooting

... the fact that two front-page "news" stories were nothing but set-ups for publicity ... the *Spoonful* doing all right without *Zollie* but how's Zollie doing without the Spoonful? *Peaches and Herb* taking up where *Mickey and Sylvia* left off ... *Boby Vee, Bobbie Gentry* and the *Box Tops* being the only artists with million sellers on the national charts

... *Sunshine Company* coming a long way from the *4 Seasons'* concert in Santa Monica ... why *Tommy James* and the *Shondells* don't know that it's spelled "Kahuna" not "Kahoona" and deciding that they really don't care as long as their records keep becoming hits ... the member of the *Strawberry Alarm Clock* who drinks Ginger Beer and leaves the bottle on our table ... how long the *Beach Boys'* "Wild Honey" is going to bubble under

... *Tony Bennett* giving it a nice try but failing to nab a bullet ... what's so great about an old time movie ... the expose' of a new publication gave to the Monterey Pop Festival and the people who organized it—complete with figures ... *Spanky and Our Gang* being one of the best new groups going ... whatever happened to *James Brown's* planned retirement ... why *Stevie Wonder* keeps wondering ... the fact that, other than *Herb Alpert, Bill Cosby* has more singles and albums on the national charts than any other artist ... the *Soul Survivors* making it all the way into the top ten without any publicity to speak of ... how ironic it is that a small-time group feels compelled to rent a limousine when they hit town but a group as big as the *Association* is still not above taking a bus ... who are the birds in Britain ... how badly the critics panned "How I Won The War" and how disappointed *John Lennon* fans are going to be if they think he has a large part in the film ...

KRLA ARCHIVES

KRLA ARCHIVES

ON THE BEAT BY LOUISE CRISCIONE

Anyone who believes that the Beatles are no longer big business is in for quite a shock. "Magical Mystery Tour," the one-hour television special written and directed by the Beatles, is not even ready for screenings yet, but is already attracting huge offers from companies all over the world.

All three major American networks are competing for the special and rumor has it that the winner may have to bid a nifty one million dollars to cinch the deal!

Forty offers for the special have already been received from eleven European countries as well as Japan, Australia, South Africa and Mexico.

Coming Up Stones?

Although the Rolling Stones were denied U.S. work permits last month, the talk now is that the group will resolve their difficulties with U.S. Immigration officials and will be able to r e s u m e touring Stateside. At least, the Immigration office has requested the court records of the recent drug cases in England involving Stones' Mick Jagger and Keith Richard.

The Lovin' Spoonful have decided to drop their "goodtime" sound and try something a little different. First record out under their new sound is "She's Still a Mystery to Me" and from sales figures it looks as though the Spoonful have made a wise decision.

KEITH RICHARD

Love-In at Woburn

If you can believe it — hippies took over the stately home of the Duke of Bedford in England for a love-in. But no one is thinking beautiful thoughts because of it. Fact is, some of the artists who performed, including Eric Burdon & the Animals and the Move, are claiming that they haven't been paid. At any rate, it is highly likely that the fantastic grounds of Woburn Abbey have seen their first and last love-in.

WE'VE HEARD EVERYTHING NOW DEPARTMENT: Group Therapy, a new group on the New York circuit, is departing this month for a history-making expedition to the North Pole! Honest. And the reason for the trip? To provide an opportunity to penetrate the last frontier of pop music sources as yet untouched by today's writers and producers — naturally. The expedition will cost an estimated $20,000 and will include, among other things, the musical culture of the Angakoks, a little-known Polar Eskimo tribe believed to have a centuries old musical tradition.

QUICK ONES: The Sunshine Company is going the commercial route by doing the vocal background in a new television commercial for Clairol — lots of money in commercials . . . . you should hear the reasons given for the cancellation of the Mamas and Papas Albert Hall concert — they range from a protest move against the arrest of Mama Cass all the way to illness . . . Petula Clark, probably the busiest female entertainer in the business, will star in her own special to be aired over NBC-TV on April 12 — sponsor of the show is, of course, Chrysler . . . Gregg Morris, r e g u l a r on "Mission Impossible," has been signed by ABC-Paramount Records and is set to cut an album . . . . the Jefferson Airplane have been signed for the "Perry Como Holiday Special" to be aired November 30 over NBC . . . A lot of people are wondering whether or not Arlo Guthrie, Woodie's son, will take over where his father left off.

Managed to dig up a few group concert dates for you . . . FOUR SEASONS: November 23, Convention Hall, Philadelphia; Dec. 1, Ontario, Canada; Dec. 2, Eastman Theatre, Rochester, New York; December 3, Seton Hall, South Orange, New Jersey. MOMS MABLEY: November 19, St. Louis, Missouri; Nov. 22, Chicago, Illinois; Nov. 26, Birmingham, Alabama.

FOUR SEASONS

SPANKY & OUR GANG: Nov. 22, Cobo Hall, Detroit, Michigan; Nov. 26, Masonic Temple, Davenport, Iowa; Dec. 1, Nassau, Long Island, New York; Dec. 17, Ed Sullivan Show; Dec. 18-31, Holiday House, Monroeville, Pa.

Jerry Quarry Set To Sing

LOS ANGELES—Jerry Quarry, heavyweight title contender, has signed a personal management contract with the Attarack Corporation.

The good-looking Jerry is set to cut his first single within the next ten days. One side will feature Jerry and the flip side will feature his sister, Dianna, joining him.

Plans are also being made for Jerry and his sister to appear in Las Vegas. The BEAT first spotted Jerry entertaining at the Don Ho Show at Melodyland Theatre when Don called Jerry up out of the audience to sing a couple of songs. It was obvious then that the potential was there but Jerry will need quite a bit of polish.

JOIN THE JBL MOVEMENT

NO LUXURY SO GRATIFYING OR INEXPENSIVE!

Don't be an uninvited...a social outcast . . . Don a "MENDELSOHN QUINTETTE CLUB OF BOSTON" T-Shirt . . . AND ELEVATE YOUR SOCIAL POSITION!!
THE PRICE ONLY $1.25. A TRULY GRAND OFFER!
They come Small, Medium and Large. . . . get one for yourself . . . get matchmates . . . get one for your Mother . . . YOU'LL FEEL SECURE IN YOUR "MENDELSOHN QUINTETTE CLUB OF BOSTON" high-neck, top quality T-SHIRT!
GUITAR PLAYERS LOVE 'EM . . . BASS PLAYERS LOVE 'EM . . . GREEN BERETS LOVE 'EM . . . SURFERS LOVE 'EM . . .
YOU CAN'T AFFORD NOT TO OWN ONE!
Fill in and mail the coupon below.

COUPON
Enclosed is $____ please send me (__) "MENDELSOHN QUINTETTE CLUB OF BOSTON" T-SHIRTS.
Size_____ Name_____ Address_____ State_____
JAMES B. LANSING SOUND INC.
3249 CASITAS AVE., LOS ANGELES, CALIFORNIA 90039

WHAT'S UP DOC?

Dear Doc:
Some of my friends have tried marijuana and each one has had such different effects. It doesn't turn all of the on at all. Is there something wrong with them?
Observer

Dear Observer:
One of the reactions of marijuana (pot or grass) is the variability in its effects on people. The effect of smoking it depends a great deal on the environment and the feelings of the person at the time. Also the effect depends upon the purity of the material used. It hardly seems worthwhile at this point to ponder the effects when being caught with pot is a felony, i.e., the same as an assault with a deadly weapon or similar crime! Besides, you can let yourself be turned on by a lot of things besides drugs.

Dear Doc:
What do you think about having my ears pierced? I am a 15-year-old girl and it seems that all of my friends have had it done. One of them even offered to do it for me free.
Old-Fashioned

Dear Old-Fashioned:
The decision to have your ears pierced must be weighed carefully by the possibility of the complications of infection and ugly scar formation. The complications are quite rare and are certainly less apt to occur when done by a competent doctor in his office. Save your baby-sitting money!

(Do you have a problem you'd like Dr. Bolter, M.D. to answer? If so, please send it to What's Up Doc? Beat Publications, 9121 Sunset Blvd., Los Angeles, California 90069.)

A NEW DEVELOPMENT— AN ELECTRIC SITAR

Eleven years ago a pixieish Indian named Ravi Shankar hit these shores. His sole objective in coming here was to make the western world aware of traditional Indian music, and his most important piece of luggage was a primitive Indian instrument which hasn't changed an iota in seven centuries—the Sitar. He was 15 years old when he began studying the Sitar, and now, at 47, he just barely feels he has mastered the instrument.

Two years ago the "raga rock," the label pop vendors attached to the traditional Indian sound, caught on. The interest was directly sparked by the union of Shankar and Beatle George Harrison, who had heard the sound and became so enthralled that he immediately purchased a sitar and hired a coach. Harrison introduced the sitar sound in an elementary passage in "Norwegian Wood," a Beatle number which came out in December of 1965. Since then recording groups have been clamoring for the sound, and Shankar has been elevated to a position of "top celebrity."

Vincent Bell, one of America's top recording guitarists, recognized the importance of the new sound, took up the Sitar, mastered its technique with incredible speed, and introduced it on recordings, firmly establishing the "Sitar Sound" on the pop music scene.

The demand for the sound increased even more and Bell came up with a concept for an ELECTRIC SITAR, an instrument which would produce the Sitar sound, and be within the playing range of any guitarist. He approached Nathan I. Daniel, president of Danelectro Corporation. After years of research, Danelectro introduced the "World's First Electric Sitar."

A real understanding of the strides of Danelectro with its development of the Electric Sitar cannot be achieved without a more involved understanding of the primitive Indian instrument. The Sitar, is roughly the equivalent to the European lute or chitarrone. Its teakwood neck supports as many as 19 strings (six playing strings, four melody and two rhythm, and thirteen sympathetic or resonating strings), bristles with tuning pegs which correspond to each of the strings, and dried gourds at either end which amplify the sound. Shankar has noted that "the tuning is never 100 per cent perfect. One difficulty is the 13 resonating strings; they cannot resonate properly unless perfectly tuned, and we don't live in a perfect world."

With this new instrument every serious musician will be able to play the popular instrument. Vincent Bell, states, "Many of the top recording groups have lauded the new flexibility in sound made possibly by the Electric Sitar, it represents a significant contribution to the contemporary music scene."

THE SEPER COMPANY
5273 Tendilla, Dept. T.O.
Woodland Hills, Calif.
SM. PEACE SYMBOL — NECK STRAP $1.25 P.P.

KRLA ARCHIVES

LULU sings
To Sir With Love

On EPIC RECORDS

AVAILABLE AT

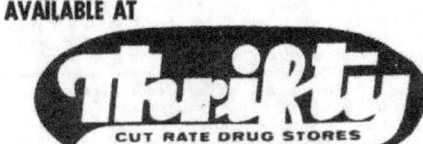

KRLA ARCHIVES

Is There No Stopping The Cowsills?

By Kimmi Kobashigawa

The Cowsills would have to be considered one of the most unique pop groups in the country if for no other reason than the fact that their *mother* sings with them. Mrs. Cowsill—and that is the *real* last name of this singing family—is a performing member of the group, and is in the words of her oldest son, and lead singer, Bill—"a mini-Mom."

There are seven children in the Cowsill family, and six of them are male. The seventh is a beautiful, dark-haired little girl of eight who has somehow remained a very feminine, non-tomboy type despite the many young men surrounding her.

No Pre-Meditation

We asked Susan's oldest brother, Bill, how the family began singing together as a professional group, and he explained: "This would have to go back many, many years when we weren't even aware of it. Nothing was pre-meditated—that is, we didn't say, 'Well, let's have a group and let's everybody start playing instruments.' Everything just kind of fell into place.

"Of course, when we *noticed* it, then we started trying to work toward the goal we're working for now. But, up until then it was just good fun in the house, and we decided to take it out of the living room and into the world. As far as music goes, nobody has had any formal training at all—everybody is self-taught.

"I started the guitar when I was about six years old and Bob picked it up after me, then Barry—who now plays bass—played drums with us for a year before John took over the drums; now John plays drums and Barry plays bass! But, Barry also plays drums and guitar and John can also play bass. Bob plays guitar and organ, and I play drums, bass, and guitar. So, we switch around every now and then; it's kind of fun."

Beside The Pool

Bill is twenty years old, tall and slender, and possessed of an absolutely disarming smile and two of the smilingest blue-green eyes. We spoke to the Cowsills as they lounged beside the pool at the hotel in which they were staying; sitting next to Bill was "Mom" Cowsill who explained just how she became a participating member of the group.

"My husband spent 20 years in the Service, and I said 'Good-bye' so many times in my life—you know, 'Good-bye-to-father-as-he-goes-over-seas.' The boys have asked me for quite a while now if I would sing with them, and pretty soon I noticed that *they* were leaving and I was *still* saying 'Good-bye!' I *like* my family, so instead of 'Good-bye it became 'Hello!' and here I am! To coin a phrase, 'if you can't beat them, *join* them."

Ten Sullivans

The group has already appeared on the Johnny Carson show and have just signed to appear on *ten* Ed Sullivan shows, which is a pretty phenomenal achievement for a group of brothers and sisters—and one Mini-Mom!—who began singing in their living room just for fun.

Also in the works right now are long-range plans involving either a movie or a TV series which would feature the entire Cowsill family. By the way, two of the brothers act as Road Managers for the group, and Mr. Cowsill, Sr. is the manager. And that's *really* "keeping it in the family!"

Most of the younger Cowsills enjoy popular music and include the Beatles and the Association among their favorites. Mrs. Cowsill admits that she has an *appreciation* for the kind of music her children are listening to—"I know it must be good, because *they're* good!"—but prefers to listen to folk music when she is at home.

Conglomerate Rock

Although all of the members of the group have their own particular favorites in the music industry, they haven't set out to copy any of them. In so far as the influence of other artists' styles on the style of the Cowsills is concerned, Bill explained: "We term our sound 'Conglomerate Rock' because everything you hear influences you. Directly, or indirectly—even Beethoven was influenced by, say, Bach. But, you take what you hear—rearrange a few things—*not* steal it or copy it—and you use it and it becomes uniquely *you*—*if* you use it in the right way. Concepts are known—you take this concept and improve upon it, modify it, and you use it as *you* would use it and it becomes *yours*."

All seven of the junior Cowsills are in school, Bob and Bill being the only two in college. While the group is on tour, a tutor is along to continue the studies of the other five who range in age from seven to sixteen.

Bob and Bill are also the songwriters of the group, and wrote all but one of the tunes on their first album. Eventually, Bill hopes to go into record producing and other areas of the business.

Dick smiles out at the world beneath a deep tan and light brown hair. Although he doesn't perform onstage, he does act as sound engineer, with the help of his father, and works on lighting and staging. Younger brother, Paul, is the official Stage Manager, and in the words of his older brother, Dick, "he does a *great* job."

On Probation

Cherubic eight year old Susan agrees in a slightly husky little-girl voice that she would enjoy remaining in the entertainment business, but is kind of thinking about becoming a nurse, instead. Her older brothers tease her about being on "probation" for several months with the group until they could decide whether or not she would work out as a permanent member. The final decision was left up to the audiences for which the group performed on the cross country tour they have just completed, and the decision was unanimous: Susan *stays!*

John has dark brown hair and a slightly mischievous look about him, but he is actually a very serious young man. He is looking forward to becoming a songwriter in the near future, and like his older brother, Bill, is very much interested in eventually producing records.

Barry agrees with John in his appreciation of the Beatles music, but agrees even more strongly with Bill in his love for rhythm and blues—real "soul" music.

In their live act, the Cowsills like to include a wide variety of music—ranging from Country and Western to Rhythm and Blues, sometimes going as far back as 1933 and Maurice Chevalier if it is requested. "We try to please everyone, and it all depends who we're playing for. We try to make everyone in our audience feel important and as though we're playing *their* kind of music," explained Bill.

Practical Jokers

Mr. Cowsill, Sr. admits that his family is definitely a fun-loving group of practical poke-prone people: "Just getting up in the morning some days constitutes a practical joke! Just meeting one another. It's a very continuous operation—we call it *fun!*"

And, what about the current "hippy movement," Mr. Cowsill? "Wouldn't miss it! It's very interesting, and a necessity if for nothing else than to prove that it *won't* last! They need that time to freak-out and find out and evaluate themselves and people a r o u n d them. Some just go with it, some are very serious—but we won't knock it."

The Cowsills are a very large, very warm, very close-knit family who have taken their personal warmth and joy as a family out of their Rhode Island, Connecticut living room and shared it with families in other living rooms across the nation. And if anyone should ever ask you just what a Cowsill is anyway—you can tell them it's something very nice!

KRLA ARCHIVES

Van Morrison: 'I Can't Mix, — My Problem'

Van Morrison is hunting for himself.

Van is 22, Irish, former lead singer of Them, writer behind such hits as "Gloria," "Mystic Eyes," "Brown Eyed Girl," and his latest single, "Ro Ro Rosey," and a very mysterious young man.

If you had to use one word to describe Van it would probably be uncommunicative. He seldom talks and reveiwers have often criticized him for not communicating with his audience.

This is true. He doesn't really communicate with people in general much, but he knows this.

"Sometimes I think I may just be an underground thing, but if that's the way it has to be, that's it. I'm not really too commercial because I don't come across. I can't mix, you see that's my problem. You have to be able to mix if you want to be in show business. That's why I say I may be an underground thing."

That quote alone is a sign of a new Van Morrison—the one that is now searching for himself.

A year ago he would not have said anything like that, for he was unaware of himself, the people around him or the world at large. It's almost as though he didn't exist a year ago.

It all began several years ago with the formation in Belfast, Ireland of the group called Them.

There are various stories about how and when the group was formed and exactly who was in it at what time. But one thing is certain. By the time they got started on their string of international hits including "Gloria," "Baby, Please Don't Go," "Here Comes The Night" and "Mystic Eyes," Van was the lead singer and song writer.

But about the time they were getting out hit after hit it all began to fall apart for Van.

"Everything just got out of proportion. In the beginning the thing was great 'cause everybody dug it. There was no motive behind anything you did. You just did it because you wanted to do it and you enjoyed doing it. That's the way the thing started, but it got twisted somewhere along the way and everybody involved in it got twisted as well, including me.

"It became a trial, a sort of endurance test like the Indians used to make people walk while they hit them with sticks. It was no longer people making music and grooving together. It became a whole conscious business trip. It became sick. There was no point in caring about anything 'cause there was nothing to care about."

A year ago Them made their first visit to America—they never got over here during the peak of their success—and this trip and the months following might be called the end for the old Van Morrison.

The trip was really a bit of a waste. They had trouble proving they were the real Them, though they were. Them at that time consisted of Van, Alan Henderson, Jim Armstrong, Ray Elliott and David Harvey.

They played a lot of gigs—mostly on the West Coast, earned a little money, spent most of it, quarreled among themselves and with their management.

When their visas expired they returned home broke, disgusted, disappointed and discouraged. The second big break for Them had not materialized.

Then Van took a step that anyone knowing him could not imagine him ever doing—he went out on his own, as a solo singer.

As lead singer, Van had had four other guys standing between him and the world. He didn't have to talk or communicate, because the other guys, much to their chagrin, would cover for him.

But then Van stepped out on his own and it looked like he would be forced to stand alone. Then Bert Burns, who produced several of Them's records, stepped in and brought Van to Bang Records and once again Van was protected from having to communicate.

VAN MORRISON: "I think I may be an underground thing."

Burns, Van's manager and producer, now stands between Van and the world, with the added help of Van's three man back-up group, who also add to the buffer zone between Van and the world.

And so Van Morrison is born again. He's coming outside of himself and the private world he's dwelt in for so long, but very gradually. He's aware of people around him more. He looks at his audience and you get the impression that for the first time he is aware they are there, watching and listening to him. His handshake is no longer like a five day old dead fish—it has life in it, as does Van.

He's being born after 22 years of supposed nothingness and it's confusing to him. He claims he has no home, but is looking for one, just as he is looking for himself.

He's been compared to Dylan, but that doesn't bother him, "because I know I'm me. I don't know who that is, but it must be somebody or I wouldn't be doing it, otherwise I couldn't do it. It's got to be leading up to something.

"Right now I just want to do my thing and groove with it."

What is his thing? What does he want to do?

"I want to turn people on."

—Carol Deck

Candymen Busy Spreading Their Candypower

What do Roy Orbison, Bobby Goldsboro, Billy Joe Royal and Sandy Posey have in common?—The Candymen. They were Roy Orbison's back-up group and Bobby Goldsboro was once their guitarist. They backed up Billy Joe Royal's "Down On The Boon Docks" and wrote Sandy Posey's last single.

Since they decided less than a year ago to try to make a name on their own, they've become known in Europe, Great Britain, Australia, almost everywhere for their extraordinary live performances, their musical ability, their professionalism, originality, and quality. Alan Dale, of Cashbox, called them "tight as any he's ever seen."

Razor-Sharp Carbons

The Candymen, five young Southerners between the ages of twenty and twenty-three, first attracted attention with their razor-sharp copies of recording hits by other artists which they performed at every personal appearance convincing many fans that the copies outshone the originals. The group has since concentrated on original material, for the most part written by the five Candymen, with no specialization by any of them in music or lyrics.

John Rainey Adkins, lead guitar, was the first Candyman on the scene. Playing with Bobby Goldsboro, after attending high school and college with the star, John gained valuable experience. While continuing to perform he spotted Billy Gilmore (bass) playing in a club and they teamed up. John had seen Bob Nix playing drums in Jacksonville, Florida, when he was there and added Bob to the group. Singer Rodney Justo was next added to the group to replace Bobby Goldsboro who had gone on to other things.

Dean "Ox" Daughtry was the last to join the Candymen. For several years, he had been playing club dates in his native Dothan, Alabama, as well as being the regular pianist and organist with a country band on WTVY. John, also a native of Dothan, had been a fan of Dean's for a long time and when the group found the need for a pianist and organist, Dean was tagged for the job. This completed the group and the Candymen were on their way.

Regarding their beginning repertoire, the Candymen explain that Southern groups ordinarily just don't play original material, and that copying other artists' hits is standard routine. It just happens that the Candymen were better at it than anyone else. Now that the group has attracted widespread interest, the emphasis is on original material and their performances of these songs at the Scene have shown them to surpass even the Candymen's own previous imitations.

Light Group

As far as organized choreography and costumes the Candymen turn thumbs down. Although they're described by critics as one of the tightest groups working today, the boys feel they must each do exactly as they feel in order to release their inhibitions and sincerely feel the music they perform. There's no "one-to-three kick" routine about the Candymen and the clothes they wear are just that, and not the regulation uniforms worn by most performers. Individual expression is the keynote of the Candymen.

Although the Candymen are only now reaching sensational proportions in the United States, they have toured professionally throughout many foreign countries. Their biggest thrill was meeting The Beatles in London's "Bag of Nails" club. The Beatles had heard an unreleased record by the Candymen recorded in England, and offered their congratulations and strong endorsement.

Watch and listen for the Candypower of the Candymen!

KRLA ARCHIVES

THE **Box Tops** are

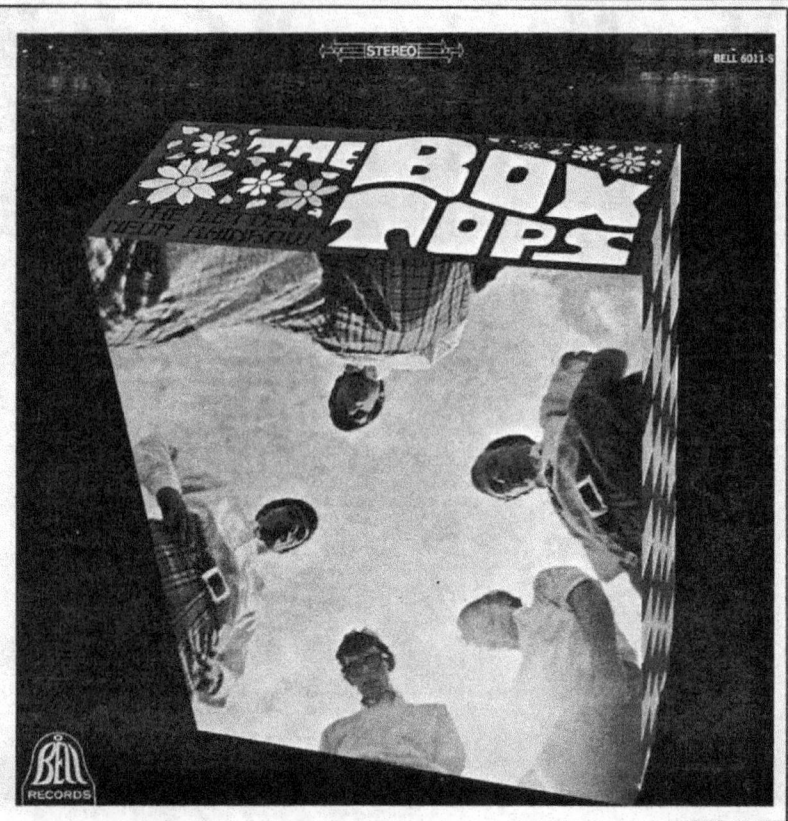

Now Available At:
MONTGOMERY WARD DEPARTMENT STORES

the mixed bag of **RICHIE HAVENS**

Available At....

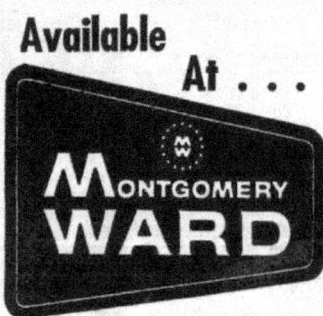

Why Not Put Out A Smile?

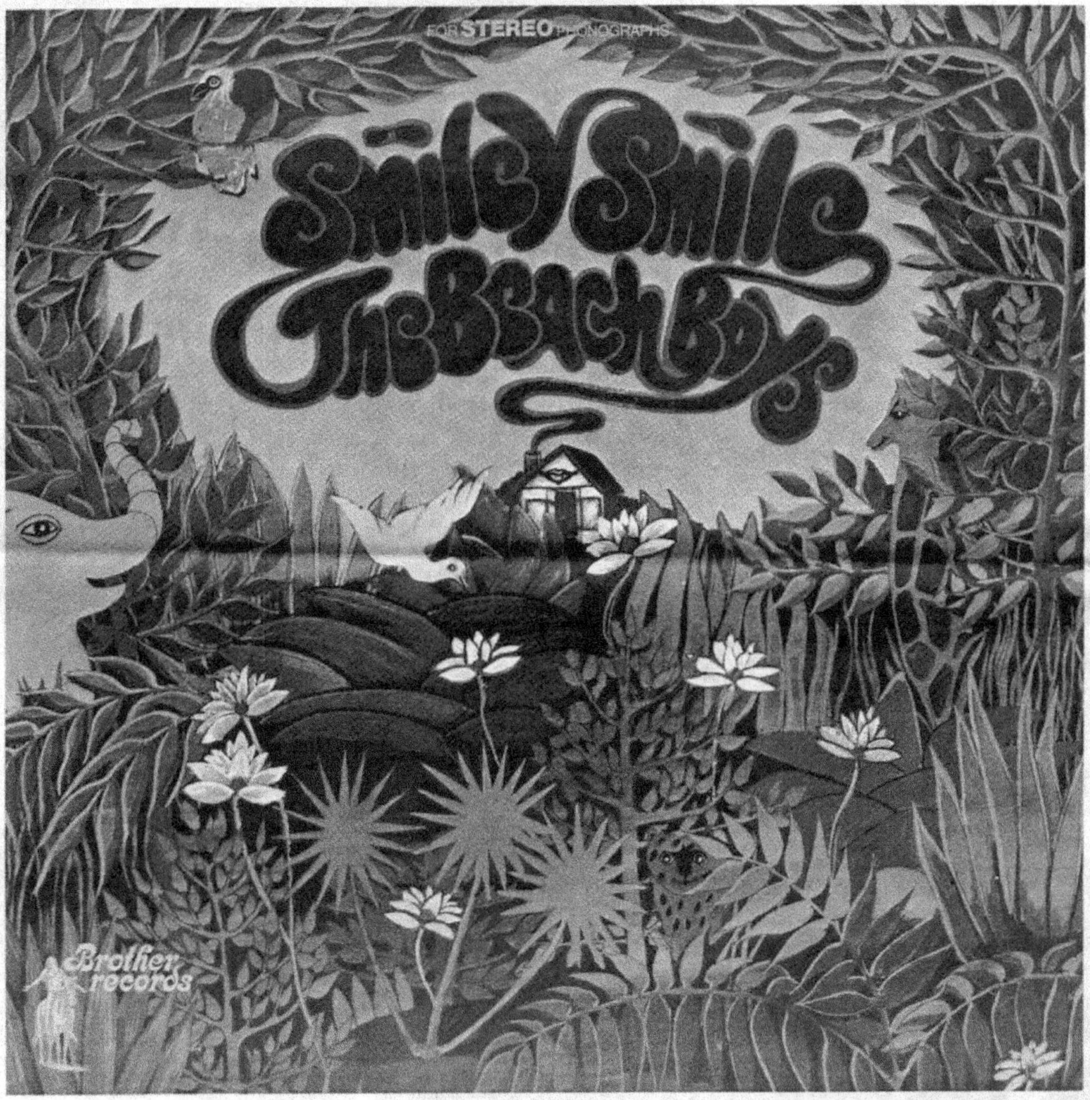

The Beach Boys Have

Now Available At:

KRLA ARCHIVES

'Understanding Is Very Important' — Steve Wonder

By Eden

"I started out when I was about nine-and-a-half or ten years old, and my first 'engagement' was on my *front porch!* My first professional performance was at the Apollo Theatre in New York on the Motor Town Review. Marvin Gaye and Marv Johnson were on the show . . . and the Supremes—when they first started out with 'Let Me Go The Right Way.' And the Miracles were starring the show."

Self-Assured

Such was the beginning of a simply "Wonder-ful" career of a talented lad named Stevie. Currently hitting the top spot on record charts across the country with his latest release, "I'm Wondering," Stevie Wonder is a highly talented, self-assured entertainer, with a maturity far beyond his seventeen years.

"I think any entertainer should treat his public kindly," he explained in a rare serious mood, "and, I believe they should find time to talk to the fans; because, after all—it's the *public* that makes you or *breaks* you . . .

"It would be impossible for me to say that a certain kind of music is actually *absurd*—because, there is *somebody* that will buy it, even if it's only one person! For instance, I could say—'I don't like this kind of music because it hasn't got *feeling*.' Well, this might be feeling to them. *Soul* doesn't belong to one minority group. *Anyone* can have soul; it depends on what you call soul. Soul is actually just *feeling*—if you *do* put feeling in a song. . . .

Popularity

"Well, being popular—I don't say: 'I'm *Stevie Wonder*, baby, get away from me 'cause I'm *out of sight!*' This isn't the way I feel. There's no reason for anyone to feel this way. As far as adjusting to success, I didn't really have to, because I knew it couldn't be just ice cream and cake all the way.

"I like hard work—like, writing; actually, after I *did* fail and come back down (briefly after "Fingertips")—I had a chance to write more, and this is what I really dig. I came up with 'Uptight,' and I'm very thankful to God because I came up with the basic idea for it myself.

Conceit?

"As far as adjusting—I was very *thankful* I wasn't — and I've *never* been and I never will be conceited, because I don't see any reason for it. . .

"I want anyone that likes me to like me for *what* I am—not *who* I am. At least, I want them—after it's all over with—to know me like this; know that I'm not conceited, know that I have nothing to hide. . .

"I love to know people; and, to know people is to just get right in there. *Not* to be nosey—but, to be able to *really talk* to them. Communications are so out-of-sight! Being able to communicate is the most fantastic thing in the world.

Takes Awhile

"Actually, when people are being phony, it takes you a while to get the hang of it—but, you can't stay on a cloud all the time. It's outofsight to know when someone comes down, so you can *really* know them. . .

"*Understanding* is *very* important; if we—and I mean *all* people today!—understood each other . . . the situation in the United States, the situation in Viet Nam . . . all of it would be so much easier to get to. And, being together, or, understanding is really *leveling* with somebody.

"For instance, I was in Detroit during the riots, and I heard many different opinions about how ignorant the people were for doing this, and so forth. But, actually—all of this probably could have been solved a long time ago if understanding really had been put forth —understanding by the people who *are able* to get along with people.

"The people who *meet* people; for instance, I meet a lot of people, and I think it's up to me to set an image for my people—a very *good* image for my people. Music has done a great amount of it—music is *out-of-sight*. What could someone do without a song? I couldn't!"

Very Fortunate

"Many people think that *any* handicap is a *hang-up*, without actually thinking that God takes away one thing but gives you another one that's even more fantastic. I think I'm very fortunate—I'm very *happy* to be blind, because I can really *observe* people by themselves.

"Sometimes you might meet someone and they might *look* very bad, and this causes you to dislike them because you *expect* them to look good—not looking at their *heart* and their *feelings*. And this is very important; I find a lot of people judge a book by its cover, not really knowing the person. Time is precious, but p e o p l e shouldn't jump to conclusions."

All of these are the thoughts of a seventeen year old young man, who's insight and maturity carry him far beyond his own years, or the years of others.

STEVIE going to the top

From The Sixpence To A Strawberry Alarm Clock

By Jamie McCluskey III

The Strawberry Alarm Clock is a group of timely significance in the pop world. Their music runs the full range from jazz and hard rock to raga-classical rock . . . and back again. Their first hit, "Incense and Peppermints" was just in time to awaken a vast pop audience to their unique song stylings and now they are well on their way to becoming a permanent, all-time favorite establishment in the music industry.

Leader of the group, Mark Weitz, spoke of the good things he sees happening around him in the pop music today. "The main thing I'm interested in right now is that they're mixing the sound of a big philharmonic orchestra into rock and roll and making a more sophisticated sound out of it. It's getting to be more of a complicated thing than most people realize."

Jazz Into Rock

George Bunnell, bass guitarist for the group, explained that: "Jazz is being oriented into rock and roll a lot. I noticed that most of *our* original material is coming out jazz—and we don't write it to be jazz, it just comes out jazz and we play it. We hope this kind of music comes over well."

The Alarm Clock as it is today was formed as a group about six or seven months ago, and was a composite of two different groups. The name of the group—which was not Strawberry Alarm Clock —had to be changed shortly afterwards as another group managed to get a record released before them using their name.

Big Mistake

Lee agrees now that it was actually for the best. The boys were just getting ready to release their own record at the time. "We would have released this record under this name (The Six Pence)—which probably would have been a big mistake!—and we had to change our name to release the record, because they wanted it out immediately.

"We were sitting in Mark's bedroom trying to think of a name, and the 'Strawberry' thing kept coming back. We hit 'Strawberry Alarm Clock'—it was n o t h i n g planned, it just happened."

Mark continued the explanation: "Usually when they ask us what the name means, we explain that— 365 days of the year for the rest of your life, you'll be waking up to an alarm clock. So, you might as well name something after it! Or, it could mean an 'awakening' of a new type of music. And, the word 'strawberry' more or less signifies the love-type new generation thing happening, and it all fits together in one thing."

One of the main contributions of Randy Seol, drummer for the group, is his insistence on originality in the material which they use. "As I got into the group about five months ago, they weren't doing too much original material, except for the current release which they had just put out—'Incense and Peppermints.' I stressed it very hard, and they realized it too in playing personal appearances, that original material was apt to make a hit group, and you just have to do it that way.

Talented Musicians

"All the guys in the group are really talented musicians—this is one reason I really dug getting into the group—and, once we started really working on it, the original material came very easily. And, the style came to be more different as far as the things we're trying to put over."

The boys are currently beginning work on a new album which they hope to complete sometime around Christmas, and all selections will be original. Also, on this LP, *all* of the members of the group will be writing.

George, having already written about four songs on the first album, explained: "When I write, I don't really write for the people—at least *then* I didn't. I wrote for myself—I wrote to satisfy myself with what I liked. At that time, I heard of guys who were writing commercially and just what the people wanted, and I couldn't see it. Then, when 'Incense and Peppermints' made it, I was surprised and decided to start writing commercially. Now I'm writing commercially for what the people want, and not really what I want. But, I feel like I gained something out of the stuff I wrote for myself."

Emotion Expressions

Ed, also writing for the group, added: "I feel that writing music, you can accomplish your emotional expression—if it's violent, it turns to chaos, or whatever; or if it's smooth—you can write to fit the way you feel."

Randy looked back over the past few months and did a little philosophizing: "At first, when the group was working day and night after the first release to try to win out when we couldn't get all the air play we wanted, we were working constantly; there was no money in it at all—we were *paying* to play! We figured that this was something that we had to do—and it *did* pay off in the last.

"But, when you work with six guys with six different personalities—then say that 'All Men Are Equal,' but man, it doesn't work that way! They're all equal, but I think that they each have the same amount of faults and the same amount of good things, but they're completely different subjects. So, you have many, many arguments and when there is work involved and there's no money—and really, there's no comfort in any way, except for when we got to play somewhere.

"When we play, we never have any disputes; but, it's when we're practicing and working all day and night and week—especially with no money at first, we had *so* many arguments. But, I think this is with any group. When money comes in, your conditions are better to live under. You can work just as hard if the tension has gone down like 98%, but better."

Teeter-Totter

Mark tried to sum this problem up: "I think that every group—no matter *who* it is—has their own stress. You know that you're on a teeter-totter type thing, and that you have to stay in the middle, because if one of the ends gets too heavy—you get into too many arguments."

KRLA ARCHIVES

Serving Up Soul
SAM AND DAVE
WILSON PICKETT

AVAILABLE AT

A Full Spoon Of
Sky Saxon's Seeds
MAKES EVERYTHING BETTER

AVAILABLE AT

KRLA ARCHIVES

ALL THE WAY with KRLA and Steve Allen "Unpredictable" Gypsy Boots to WALK-RUN-HOP-STAND ON HIS HEAD again this year in the famous HOLLYWOOD XMAS PARADE OF STARS.

GYPSY BOOTS and John Phillips of Mamas and Papas at Monterey Pop Festival. Holding the album, **Gypsy Boots — Unpredictable**, is Johnny Martin, of Bakersfield. Look for Gypsy Boots to appear in some wild scenes in "Mondo Hollywood."

"R.H.W. I"

Name a d.j. at KRLA who has two degrees in music, has studied at the Sorbonne in Paris, is a professional concert pianist, vocalist, sporadic player of drums and guitar . . . and comes into the station sporting a "new Image" DAILY. The ONLY d.j. who could fit that description is KRLA's new, affable personality heard 9 a.m.-12 Noon — Rhett Hamilton Walker I. Semi-bearded (today at least), strawberry-blonded (as reported yesterday), Australian-born (let's see him change that), R.H.W. I has all of the forementioned listed talents and more. A man of varied interests — he likes all types of music with the exception of opera. However, he does have one constant and consuming interest — PEOPLE. His favorite day on KRLA is Sundays — "cause that's the day the studio is jam packed full of people." Future plans for RHW I include more high school, college and special event appearances and a return to television.

MAHARISHI — FAKE OR GENUINE?

KRLA'S REB FOSTER has just returned from England. In an effort to learn more about the celebrated Transcendentalist, the MAHARISHI, Reb spoke with his representatives, Brian Southcomb and Matthew West. The following information was the outcome of their meetings. The Beatles first met the Maharishi when they attended one of his lectures given in the ballroom of the London Hilton Hotel. Mick Jagger and Marianne Faithful first met their teacher while in Amsterdam. All were interested in this master's concept of thought as taught by his international Meditation Society. The concept of Transcendentalism was explained by the Maharishi's representatives simply as "self-knowledge" — the art of getting into your own mind and unlocking parts of the brain that most people don't have access to even though they possess this unknown self. It is a learned process — and naturally as a student learns more about himself — he will learn more about others. Before the Maharishi became a teacher of Transcendentalism he was an established physicist. Rumors have spread about his supposed amount of wealth — but these are untrue — he owns only a robe, a goatskin rug and an exploring, creative mind.

KRLA ARCHIVES

OVER 500 WINNERS
BEAT PUBLICATIONS
PROUDLY PRESENTS
THE GREAT RACE

FIRST PRIZE—CORDLESS TAPE RECORDER
2nd Prize—Portable Radio/Phonograph
100 3rd Prizes—1 Year BEAT Subscription or Renewal
200 4th Prizes—Popular Record Albums
200 5th Prizes—Beautiful Red and Silver BEAT Pens

Starring all BEAT REPRESENTATIVES

Featuring 500 Prizes including first prize of a TAPE RECORDER, second prize of a portable record player and radio, runner up prizes of top selling albums, free subscriptions or renewals to THE BEAT + Beautiful Beat Pens.

WATCH AS BEAT REPRESENTATIVES throughout the country compete for the most subscriptions.

THRILL AS YOU watch YOUR list get longer and longer.
QUAKE WITH ANTICIPATION as the contest draws to a close.
Send in subscription blanks NOW through NOVEMBER 30. Contest ends at midnight on Nov. 30th.

Don't miss out on the biggest spectacle of the year!
If you are not now a BEAT REPRESENTATIVE don't miss out—just fill out this form and send it to:

BEAT REPRESENTATIVES
9121 Sunset Blvd.
Los Angeles, California

Yes! I want to be a BEAT Representative and enter the Great Race.

Name

Address

City _____ State _____ Zip ____

If you are not a current subscriber, your own subscription can count as your first order sold.

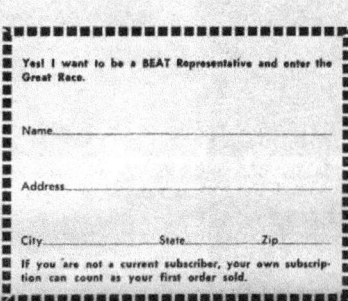

CLASSIFIED

"Massachusetts" Bee Gees forever! Rich Kolon

The Circuit will turn on again!

Donovan—I hope loves come right through them all with you. Princess Jan

Happy Birthdays Ron, Neil, and Buck

Sandy Gillespie wants to be famous

So do I—Venita Smythe

The Note have you ever venus flytraps is catching on.

Petroilli is crazy!!

"MR. MAN" Strictly a LYRIC Bag...

MONKEES

What's Left lives on...

Princess Anita should be a Queen Bee—Lovesy Eugene

Pete: Thanks for the wonderful memories of our summer and special weekend. I'll never forget you. D.

Steve, cherish is the word...

November 24—Happy Birthday Jim Yester

Monkees: overage Mouseketter

Happiness is ... Mark Lindsay. Rose

Happy birthday Frank, Pat, Mother and Father Aldridge. From Lonabergers

Happy birthday Eddie of the Rascals. Love always, Charlotte

Happy Birthday Peter Noone—Chris

Jim is Groovy!

Cindy, Marge, Linda from Chicago; Ralph Scala IS! ditto: Emil Theilhelm, Geoff Daking, Ronnie Gilbert, Mike Esposito.

SCALA POWER

Happy Birthday Phil Volk. Come to tour San Jose. Jackie

Paula Taylor—"You said it!!"— Marie

Happy Birhtday Chispy!

The Merry-Go-Round will be big. Get their first album and see for yourself. Nancy Carpenter

THE BEE GEES WILL BE BIG.

HAPPY BIRTHDAY, CHARLIE CO—Catherine

Mike: Falsely untruthful cowardly knave doesn't injure noble knack. Carol

JAN SAVAGE — happy birthday!

RUSS GIGUERE!

Lost . . . Smokestack Lightnin'

QUEUE—a message of grok to you through your owner from MAD TARANTULA through her owner, Madeline. DUMB RED FERRARI!

PETE PORTER, WHOO—99 and the MAGIC CIRCLE rule FLORIDA!

DON HO is outside and RUDY is groovy.

Ride With The Sound of THE MIDNIGHT RAIDERS — Janesville, Wisconsin . . .

Kathy—I'd kind of like to talk to lyou. Steve

Darling George Harrison, remember *proteins!*

THE BLUES MAGOOS ARE HERE!

HAPPY BIRTHDAY, CHARLIE COE

HAPPY BIRTHDAY JOE CORRERO, JR.

ross — please call. johnspeed. love, jane

John Lennon is the Great Pumpkin — Love from Norman Flicka

HAPPY LATE BIRTHDAY, HERMAN! Love "Choni"

I know the Jacks! Do you!???

"This is OUR Song," Petula Clark — Happy Birthday, Pet (you're our NUMBER ONE gal)! Two ADORING and ETERNAL fans, Patty and Debbie.

Carl is beautiful

So-called hippies make me sick

the one and only original BROTHERHOOD is in Annadale, Virginia

P. J. Proby! I'm with you!

Phil really means love. Happy birthday Phil Volk. Love, Carolyne.

"RAVI RULES!!!"
Barbs H., I love you. Bill

P.M. have a *savage* birthday! the *Sky's* the limit. M.S.

LITE MY FIRE posters—4 colors 33"x42", $2.00 P.P. Seper Co. 5273 Tendilla, Woodland Hills, California 91364.

Donna—Weren't the Monkee concert and old town groovy? Holly

"Joy, Love ya always, Skippy"

Beatles are everybody, Monkees are nobody

Welcome Kimberlyn Marion Locklin

Happy Birthday to Bill

Beatles Rule Forever

The YARDBIRDS Rule

Chris Klein is bitchin'

All Fords groove too

THE BEAT will accept only personal messages in the classified section. We will print names but not addresses or phone numbers.

Rates are cheap! Only 10 cents per word.

Your deadline for the next issue is: Nov. 14.

MOVING?

Writing about a subscription?
Be sure to fill out this form

For FASTEST service on address change, missing copies, etc., attach old mailing label in first space below. Otherwise please print clearly your address as we now have it.

OLD ADDRESS (Attach old label here if available)
NAME
ADDRESS
CITY
STATE ZIP CODE

NAME
ADDRESS
CITY STATE ZIP CODE

MAIL TO: BEAT PUBLICATIONS
Circulation Dept.
9121 Sunset Blvd., Los Angeles, Calif. 90069

Please allow 3 weeks for change to take effect.

KRLA ARCHIVES

The Sunshine Company Believe In Responsibility To Public

By Anna Maria Alonzo

One of the "happiest" pop groups in the world today is the Sunshine Company, still elated over the success of their first record—"Happy"—and even more thrilled over their second consecutive hit, "Back On The Street Again." The talented quintet has already established itself firmly in the pop world, and can be very happy about the bright future glowing ahead of them.

Mamas And Papas

In the short time since the public was first introduced to the Sunshine Company, there have already been numerous comparisons made between them and the Mamas and Papas. Maury Manseau, the "leader" of the group, acknowledged these comments, adding: "I think the comparison is valid only in the fact that both of us are vocal groups. But, then — it's not really that either, because we do our own instrumentals all the time, and they have a band behind them. It's a great compliment! But, I think we've got our own thing, and it's different."

Doug "Red" Mark came out from behind his dark glasses long enough to assure us that he is, indeed, quite happy with the success the group has been enjoying, adding pointedly: "Success means a lot to me — I don't play on *skid row* any more! That plus the fact that now the whole world, not just the people in the neighborhood, can hear us and what we're trying to put across; and I think we'll do it."

"Success To Me"

The man behind the beat — Merle Bregante — smiled beneath his heavy golden fringe and explained that he used to play on skid row along with Red; he seemed quite content with the improvement. "Success to me is helping my parents and being able to do something I've always wanted to do," he explained in a rare serious mood.

Tall, slender, and very talented, Larry Sims leaned forward with an earnest expression as he explained: "I think we have a responsibility to our public, as far as treating them like they are the ones who make us — we really don't make ourselves. We give them what they want to buy, maybe, but it takes *them*, so we have to give them what they want."

This was readily agreed upon by the other members of the group, all of whom take their particular relationships to and with the public very seriously. One way in which this concern is manifested is n the quality and type of performance which they offer the public.

Reproduce Sound

All five members of the group insist upon re-creating onstage the sound which the public has been hearing on their records as nearly as it is possible for them to do so. And, when they return to the recording studio to record their next album, Maury insists that they will personally play every instrument which is heard on the record themselves. Honesty and sincerity in their music and their personal relationships with the public is of the utmost concern to each of them.

Larry has been playing guitar since he as 12 years old, and the other sunny members of the group regard him as one of the best—and with good reason. A serious individual until he lights up with a little-boy sort of grin, Larry sat back for a moment to discuss what he considers to be some of the best aspects of contemporary music.

"The big groups, the top name groups—the Beatles, the Mamas and Papas, The Association—they're setting the standards of the songs now, I believe, so everybody is trying to come up to *their* standards. So, they're riting *better* songs, the quality of songs is getting a lot better. And, I've noticed a definite change in engineering. The quality of the sound in records is so much better these days, and I'm very glad that everything is progressing like that."

First "Live"

One subject which is bound to set the Sunshine Company to babbling is that of the Joey Bishop Show on which they recently appeared. Maury, want to tell us about it? "Were we pleased with the Joey Bishop Show?! Let me tell you about the Joey Bishop Show! You know what they always say about rock and roll groups *live* —and this was the first one we did live; this is our one pride—the vocal thing. We can do it *live*—a lot of groups can't. They make beautiful records, but they can't do it live.

"And, at the Joey Bishop Show —I was *never* more scared! I knew that 50,000,000 people were out there and when I go out there, I mean to tell you that if you were to have asked anything more than my name, I would have *cried!*"

All of the members in the group immediately agreed that the show had been a success and they were quite proud of the achievement. They were also unanimous in their praise for Joey himself. Larry acted as spokesman for the group as he proclaimed: "I'd like to say that Joey Bishop is a very fine person."

"And he *cares*," added Maury.

Judging from Joey's reaction to the group, the feeling was quite mutual.

Definition Of 'Hippies'

We switched to a topic which has been discussed around the country incessantly recently—that of the hippies. But, instead of trying to condemn or condone them once and for all, we attempted to *define* them, to find out just what a hippy really is.

Maury led the discussion: "I would like the term 'hippy' to mean—to me—somebody who is at the utmost, all the time, very sensually and very spiritually aware of everything that's going on around him, in both those mediums.

"But, it's been commercialized and it's been overdone and no one knows what it means any more. I would like it to be that—somebody who's very hip to the things that are going around."

Larry—again very serious—joined the conversation, commenting thoughtfully: "I would just like to say that a hippy is a beatnik who turns on; it's just a new stage of beatnik. They brought in the drug scene and they had to change the name a little, that's all; next year it'll be another name. I think it's wrong to label people like that."

Red chimed in, explaining: "I think the most guilty group is the middle aged group; they think of a hippy as a dirty, filthy person that's always dropping some kind of narcotic, or whatever. Now, I'm 25—I've got medium-long hair, and I've got a beard, and people think: 'Oh God, a hippy!' That's not true—I'm married and I've got two kids; I support them and I'm doing a darned good job of it, so I don't consider myself that sort of thing."

Maury explained that they are hoping to write the majority of the songs on their upcoming album, with the exception of one song written by Steve Gillette which they will include.

DIONNE — LEARNING TO TAKE HER TIME

By Eden

Dionne Warwick has been acclaimed by fans and critics the world over as one of the greatest and most distinctive song stylists in the music industry today. Her unique and sensitive manner of treating the material which she sings has endeared her to hundreds of thousands of music lovers all around the globe.

And yet, strangely enough, Dionne was not exactly over-anxious to become a singer when the opportunity presented itself originally. "It began about eight years ago; I was in college, and during semester breaks and summer vacation I was doing background work. Bachrach and David wrote three very groovy tunes for the Drifters and asked my group to do background for it. . .

"We did and—I don't know, they called me 'loud-mouth Dionne!'—I guess I must have been singing a little bit too loud back there or something, and they kind of wanted to hear a little more of it.

Teaching School

"They asked if I would be interested in doing demos for them; I said 'sure,' and started doing demos and more background work with my group for them. One thing led to another and they kept badgering me—'why don't you record?!'—and I kept saying, 'Hey— I want to *teach!* That's why I won't record; I'm making good money doing what I'm doing and it's a gas to go to school and *really* do what you want to do, and then sing if you *want* to!' And that's exactly the way I felt about it and they went along with it for two years.

"But, they didn't think I was using my talents the right way and they kept badgering me till the point that I *did* record! It was a Thanksgiving semester break, and I recorded and then went back to school. In May, I got a telegram saying, 'You've got a hit record—Come home!' and that was it . . . and, here I am!"

No Regrets

She sat back for a moment, thinking about all that had happened in the interim, then, smiling, explained: "I can't say that I have any regrets—it's been a fantastic thing that has been happening with me. It's enlightening me, as far as being with all the people is concerned, and traveling quite a bit. Quite a bit? Wow! *All my life*, it seems!! I don't regret it one bit—in fact, I enjoy it one hundred per cent!"

Over the past few years, Dionne has made the transition from a talented school girl who sang background on her school vacations to earn a little extra money to an international star. Being in the public eye, she is continually subjected to the uncomfortable and often distasteful intrusions on her jealously-guarded privacy, something which she abhors; and yet, she handles these intrusions like a *lady* —a rare quality in this business.

"People who enjoy you—who like you—have a tendency to naturally want to know about you, and that does involve personal kind of things that go on in your life. But I do think that, if they *really* dig you, that there are certain things they *wouldn't* want to know about you. That's your life and that's the way it should be lived.

Right To Privacy

"I think it's not fair to really invade *all* of the privacy that's afforded you. After the door closes, it's none of your business what I'm doing! I don't understand it and I don't like it—I *really* don't!"

Dionne is an extremely intelligent young woman, and carefully thinks through everything she does and says. She is also very concerned about the kind of influence which she can have an members of her audience simply by virtue of her position as an entertainer.

Dionne feels very strongly about the *kind* of message which is involved in the lyrics of contemporary music, and is quite concerned about the kind of influence and effect these lyrics can have on some of its listeners.

"The people who enjoy listening to Dionne Warwick would never get a message other than something that's true or something that has a good foundation for saying. I couldn't *think* of saying—'Why not pop a pill into you,' or, 'there's evil around the corner,' or, 'let's take a trip!'—you know, it's so *dumb!* Because *you* do it, don't expect to turn the *whole world* on! Whatever *they* want to do is their privilege.

"I think performers should be a little more careful—e s p e c i a l l y when kids are involved, because these kids are really listening and leaning on you for their advice of today. And, if this is what we're doing to the minds of these poor kids, I'd rather stop recording altogether and let qualified instructors in schools take over!

No Rush

"Because, really—a lot of people are patterning their lives a f t e r what's happening on radio. That 45 record? A lot of kids today are living by it—and it's sad, because there's not enough *good* things h a p p e n i n g, recording-wise, for them to live by."

Eventually, Dionne wants to enter every possible phase of the entertainment industry, encompassing Broadway plays and musicals, motion pictures, television, records.

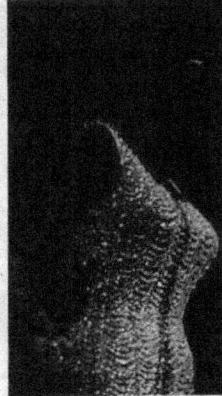

"**DON'T** expect to turn the world on"

PHIL OCHS

OUTSIDE OF A SMALL CIRCLE OF FRIENDS... there really are no words to be wrung from an adman's skills to decorate the art of a poet who dyes his mind in music and makes it sing and dance to the meter of humanity's joys and follies. PHIL OCHS is a poet who has stretched his art beyond the accepted limitations of the industry of recorded sound. There are few words now...nor next week. Nor ever. PHIL OCHS (and what and who and why he is) is all there in the album; even the word "album" is inadequate. What PHIL OCHS has created is a movie without pictures. See it in the nearest drive-in (which is your own mind).

Look outside the window—there's a woman being grabbed.
They dragged her to the bushes and now she's being stabbed.
Maybe we should call the cops and try to stop the pain.
But Monopoly is so much fun—I'd hate to blow the game...

Riding down the highway, yes my back is getting stiff.
Thirteen cars have piled up—they're hanging on a cliff
Maybe we should pull them back with our towing-chain
But we gotta move and we might get sued and it looks like it's gonna rain...

Sweating in the ghetto with the colored and the poor
The rats have joined the babies who are sleeping on the floor
Now wouldn't it be a riot if they really blew their tops—
But they got too much already and besides we got the cops...

There's a dirty paper, using sex to make a sale
The Supreme Court was so upset they sent him off to jail.
Maybe we should help the fiend and take away his fine
But we're busy reading Playboy and the Sunday New York Times...

Smoking marijuana is more fun than drinking beer
But a friend of ours was captured and they gave him thirty years.
Maybe we should raise our voices, ask somebody why—
But demonstrations are a drag, besides we're much too high...

But outside of the small circle of friends is a large rhomboid embracing most of the people of the world who are waiting for friendship, praying to belong, aching for comfort. PHIL OCHS' album "PLEASURES OF THE HARBOR" is like the coming of a Dawn—it is not an Answer, but it offers the opportunity of an Awakening.

The album "PLEASURES OF THE HARBOR" (and the songs within its tracks; "Outside of a Small Circle of Friends" is one) is tossed into the rhomboid in the hope that a few more minds may be spun inside the small circle of friends and, thus, the circle may be enlarged.

PHIL OCHS

KRLA ARCHIVES

CATCH A STONE PONEY
AND TAKE YOUR MIND FOR A RIDE

AVAILABLE AT YOUR

REVERE INTERVIEWS LINDSAY — AND VICE VERSA

By Chari Wine

You'll have to agree that there could be no two people who are closer than "Uncle" Paul Revere and Mark Lindsay. The two super-talented young men have known one another for many years and have a friendship that goes beyond the boundaries normally set up for friends.

Because they are so close, it seemed logical that no two people could be as familiar with each of their individual personalities as the two of them would be, so we asked them if they would agree to do an in-depth, serious interview with each other. Both Paul and Mark thought it an excellent idea and agreed immediately, promising to do the first "straight" interview of their careers together for us.

Need we explain that *seriousness* was never so far away? There was *no way* we were going to get these two lovable clowns to settle down and be serious, so instead we let them take over entirely and the hilarious results, which are not to be believed, are printed below. By the way—Uncle Paul has promised that we *will* get that "serious" interview someday very soon.

MARK: I'm sitting here in the beautiful penthouse apartment of Mark Lindsay, and interviewing Paul Revere—that illustrious and lovable, amicible and dynamic leader of Paul Revere and the Raiders. Tell me, Mr. Revere . . .
PAUL: Yes . . .

MARK: How long have you been in the business?
PAUL: What business?
MARK: The rock and roll business.
PAUL: I can't remember when I wasn't in the rock and roll business.
MARK: If someone would come to you and say, "Gosh Paul —I'd like to be a musician or have a successful rock and roll band; how would I go about it?" What would you tell them?
PAUL: I'd say. "Sign here, kid!"
MARK: You'd sign them up?
PAUL: You bet! *And then* I'd listen to them.
MARK: Does that help them?
PAUL: No, it helps *me!* Just in case they're good, *I'm* fixed! I would advise them—seriously—as a father and a *good* "Uncle Paul"; No! *Forget it!* I don't need the competition—I have to be practical!
MARK: Oh.
PAUL: Now, if I were to advise them on the level of a musician, I would *still* advise them against it, because . . . well, actually, the *same* reason! No matter how you look at it . . .
MARK: . . . you don't need the competition . . .
PAUL: . . . don't need them; there's already too many bands! And, when you figure out the percentage of groups that make it, that's like setting your goals out to be an ambassador for Montreal, Canada; the chances of your winding up there would be rare!
MARK: What about the groups that explode into the Top Ten overnight?

PAUL: Those are in the category of the same groups that explode into the lower 300 the next week. The ones that make it overnight—I haven't seen one stay there yet.
MARK: What about Elvis Presley?
PAUL: Well, he was pickin' and grinnin' quite a while before he made it overnight.
MARK: Just testing your memory, Paul.
PAUL: Now, there's a guy who worked hard too—Rudy Valee!
MARK: Rudy Valee? I think he was a little before my time!
PAUL: Oh, well, that was when *I* was a kid—I remember him.
MARK: Then, you must be older than your admitted 58 years.
PAUL: Yeah, a little, but you know—you *cheat* a little when you get *that* old!
MARK: O.K. Paul—everybody knows how shrewd you are, how cunning and how keen your brain is . . .
PAUL: That's a fallacy—I'm a *bobo!*
MARK: Getting into the more *human* part of you: the warm, tender . . .
PAUL: . . . you mean, like the *pancreas?*
MARK: Not quite that far; I wanted to get at the *heart!* Now, everybody knows that you're a happily married man . . .
PAUL: . . . Certainly!
MARK: And, everybody knows that if you're married, by golly!— sometimes there's kids. It just kind of happens.
PAUL: That *is* apt to happen! It seems to run hand-in-hand.
MARK: *A lot* of married people have children . . .
PAUL: . . . I've noticed!
MARK: I was just going to try and bring out the warm, human side of you, instead of the stingy old codger that your publicity department has built you up to be.
PAUL: *Why* did they do that to me, Uncle Mark?
MARK: I don't know.
PAUL: Why did they make me out to be just a . . . maybe it's because I'm not *pretty!* So, they thought I should be shrewd!
MARK: Well, now, I wouldn't say you're not pretty . . .
PAUL: *I* think I'm a *gas!*
MARK: I mean, you and Phyllis Diller have a lot in comon.
PAUL: That's what . . . I *know!*
MARK: And, I think she's a gas too, Old Phil.
PAUL: She *is;* we don't know what *type* of gas she's made of yet, but she *is* a gas!
MARK: But, instead of just a cunning, shrewd, businessman, tycoon, codger, old fink . . . I wanted to paint you as a kindhearted, lovable, sweet, affable, affectionate old man!
PAUL: What colors would you use in this painting?
MARK: Probably orange and gray.
PAUL: Why orange and gray —if I may reverse this interview?
MARK: Better than green and purple!
Well, been nice talking to you

Uncle Paul, and we'll see you soon.
PAUL: I'll go along with that.

• • •

PAUL: Hi gang, this is only Uncle Paul speaking to you, and I'm going to speak to Mr. Mark Allen Lindsay, for it is that he needs to be interviewed seriously for the first time in his life by me. And, it's very diffcult for us to talk to each other on a *serious* note.
MARK: That's right!
BOTH: Hmmmmmm! (a serious note).
PAUL: That's a pretty serious note to start out with. I was wondering, do you . . .
MARK: Sometimes!
PAUL: Well, how often?
MARK: Well, a couple times a day.
PAUL: You're *kidding!*
MARK: Nope.
PAUL: Well, enough of *that*. Ho do you react to the fact that reaction is hard to react to?
MARK: Well, I keep moving, because I can't pay my rent, you see—that's why I keep moving so often. A lot of people say, 'Why do I see you in a different house in a different magazine every month?' and I say, 'Well, that's 'cause I'm poor and I just keep moving around.'
PAUL: Well, you keep getting good magazine coverage out of it.
MARK: That's right.
BOTH: Hmmmmmm! (a serious note).
PAUL: You seem to have a problem with cars.
MARK: No, I don't have a problem at all; I *love* cars.
PAUL: That's your problem! What are you going to do with all these cars? Have you ever thought to be practical about these cars?
MARK: Well, actually, right now I only have three cars.
PAUL: That's all I have. Do you have a *practical* one?
MARK: I have a little one, a big one, and a fast one. And that's all the cars a guy needs nowadays. But, I think I'm going to sell the fast one because next year they're coming out with a *faster* one! The little one's practical — I've got a Mini Cooper named Emmy. He's *yeller* . . . but he's fast! He's also practical 'cause he's got two seats. My big car's got *six* seats—which is better than four, but not quite as good as two . . . unless you happen to be driving backwards, then it's kind of a drag.
PAUL: Why?
MARK: Because you get headaches.
PAUL: Yeah.

The interview went on for some time, but it never did quite get around to being serious, All in good fun, though, and Uncle Paul has promised us that just as soon as he and all the Raiders get back from Memphis where they are currently recording their first rhythm and blues LP, he will set down and do a real-live-honest-to-goodness serious interview with Mark and Allen.

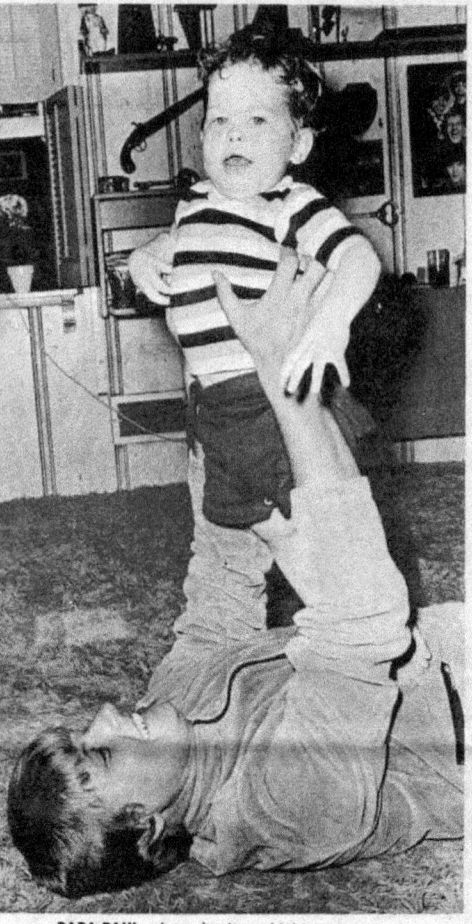

PAPA PAUL enjoys playtime with his young son

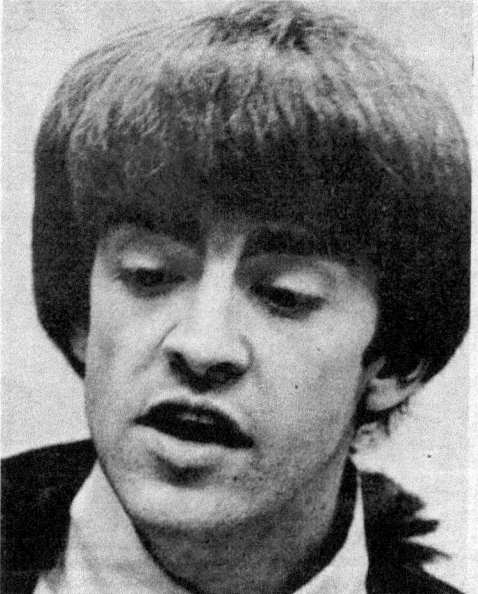

MARK LINDSAY: "No, I don't have a problem at all!"

KRLA ARCHIVES

THE BEAT — December 2, 1967

BEATLE POSTERS

Available in black light, hand screened poster. Pink, green, orange added to make a groovy image.

Cost is only $1.00 plus 25¢ handling. Get your order in to The BEAT now! California residents include 5% sales tax.

Name..

Address.....................................

City................State............Zip..........

A Groovy Christmas Gift to be enjoyed the year round. A giant (22" x 28") Calendar Poster in black, white and red.

PLEASE SEND ME THE CALENDAR POSTER
I ENCLOSE $1.75 plus .25 Handling fo each.*

NAME..
Address.....................................
City................State............Zip Code..........
*California Residents Please Include 5% Sales Tax

SPEC-TRIM SUNGLASSES

UNIQUE SHADOW BOX FRAMES
MOD RECESSED LENSES
TWO-COLOR FRAMES
$4 Each*

*Calif. residents please add 5% sales tax

AVAILABLE IN:
Blue and White   White and Pink
Purple and White Red and White
Yellow and Black Red and Black
Designate Frame Color

SEND TO:
BEAT PUBLICATIONS
9121 Sunset Blvd.
Los Angeles, Calif. 90069

DEBS

---

48 GROOVY HAPPENING HITS!

ORDER NOW!! Makes a wonderful gift. Advertised Nationally on Television and Radio

ONLY $3.50 FOR ALL 48 HITS!

SPECIAL ISSUES STILL AVAILABLE

☐ Monterey Pop Festival souvenir Issue

☐ History of the Hippies

25 cents each plus 10 cents for mailing and handling.

SEND TO:
BEAT PUBLICATIONS
9121 Sunset Blvd.
Los Angeles, Calif. 90069

Name:........................
Address:.....................
City:............State........
*Calif. Residents include 5% sales tax

BUY BEAT For Christmas

NOW......
PSYCH-A-DELIC STROBE LIGHTS
for the home

Min-A-Strobe
by Tower
$24.95

For the grooviest parties, excellent Christmas gift
Professional models available from **$99.95**
Complete line of light show supplies
Send check or money order

TOWER ELECTRONICS

15233 Ventura Boulevard
Union Bank Plaza, Suite 916
Sherman Oaks, California 91403

Beat Poster Shop

(Y) Maharishi
Also Available
(R) Sgt. Pepper   (S) Stones   (P) Seeds   (D) Dylan
(K) James Brown   (T) The Who   (N) Jimi Hendrix

Send to: BEAT POSTER SHOP, 9121 Sunset Blvd., Los Angeles, Calif. 90069

PLEASE SEND ME THE FOLLOWING POSTERS (LIST BY LETTER)..........
I ENCLOSE $1.75 plus .25 Handling for each*.

Name..
Address.......................................
City................State............Zip Code..........
*California Residents Please Include 5% Sales Tax

KRLA ARCHIVES

NOW AVAILABLE AT YOUR

Have A Heart To Heart Talk With The Doctor

KRLA ARCHIVES

LOVE, FROM ANDY WILLIAMS

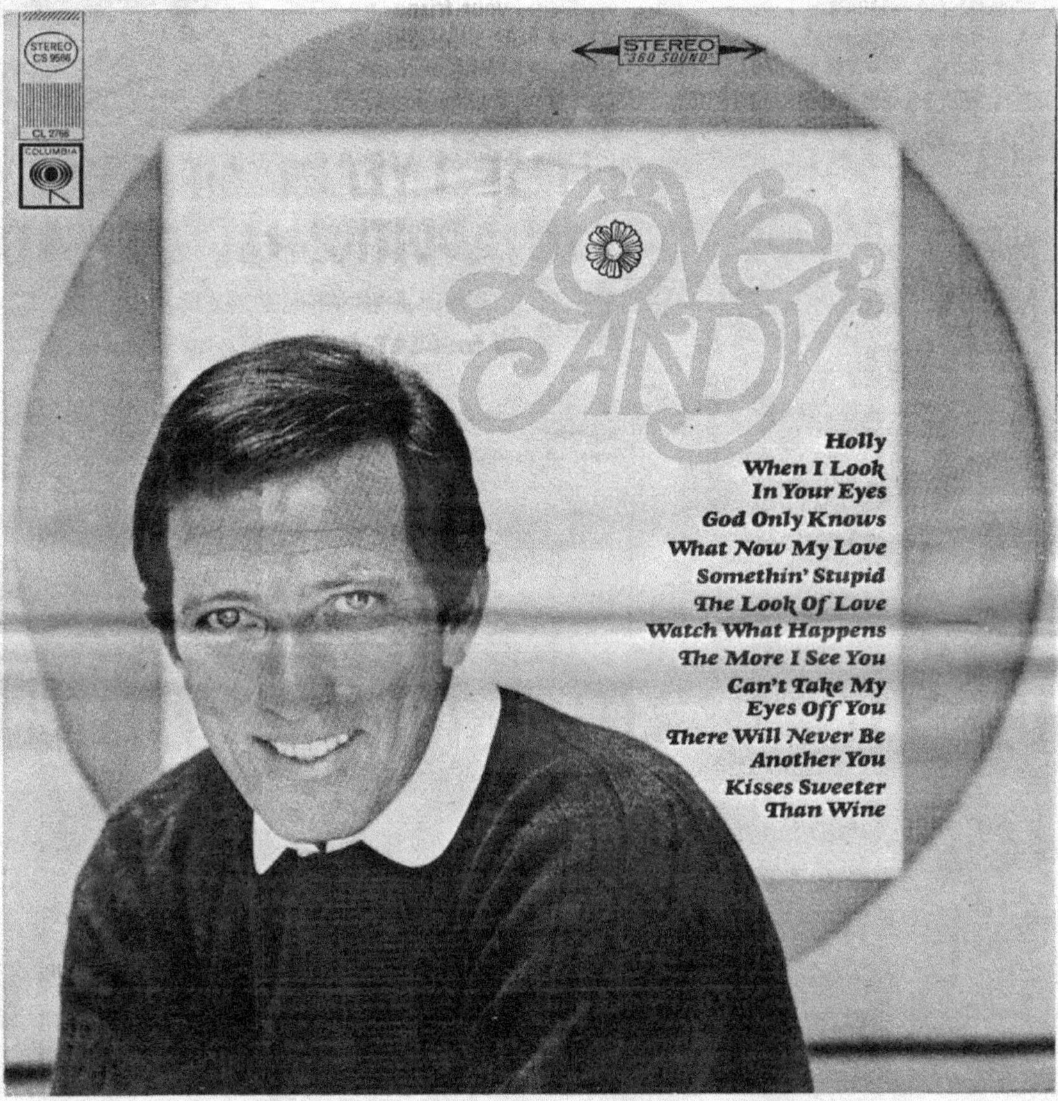

Holly
When I Look In Your Eyes
God Only Knows
What Now My Love
Somethin' Stupid
The Look Of Love
Watch What Happens
The More I See You
Can't Take My Eyes Off You
There Will Never Be Another You
Kisses Sweeter Than Wine

Now Available At:

KRLA ARCHIVES

BE A BEAT SANTA THIS YEAR!

Please your friends with a BEAT SUBSCRIPTION For CHRISTMAS at these Special Holiday Rates

FIRST 1-YEAR GIFT $3.00
EACH ADDITIONAL GIFT $1.00

Foreign Subscriptions $9.00 Per Year

Mail to: BEAT GIFT SUBSCRIPTIONS
9121 Sunset Blvd., L.A 90069

Dear BEAT,
☐ Enter my subscription as my first gift subscription at $3.00.
☐ Please send the BEAT for one year to my friends listed below.

My Name_____
Address_____
City_____ State_____ Zip Code_____
Enclosed is $_____ for_____ gift subscriptions.
I understand that you will send all gift cards to me so that I may give them to my friends and that their first BEAT will be delivered the week of Christmas.

ENTER BEAT GIFTS HERE

NAME_____
ADDRESS_____
CITY_____ STATE_____ ZIP_____

NAME_____
ADDRESS_____
CITY_____ STATE_____ ZIP_____

NAME_____
ADDRESS_____
CITY_____ STATE_____ ZIP_____

ENTER NEW GIFTS HERE

NAME_____
ADDRESS_____
CITY_____ STATE_____ ZIP_____

NAME_____
ADDRESS_____
CITY_____ STATE_____ ZIP_____

NAME_____
ADDRESS_____
CITY_____ STATE_____ ZIP_____

RETURN THIS ENTIRE FORM WITH YOUR CHECK OR MONEY ORDER

KRLA ARCHIVES

Acapulco, here you come!

Look for this display in your market. It could mean an Acapulco vacation for you and a friend. There'll be plenty of winners in our Acapulco Sweepstakes. The prizes—a week for two at one of Acapulco's swingingest hotels. And the two-way trip on Western Airlines. There's nothing to do. Just enter. Go to your market and find out the details. So, get ready for Acapulco!

KRLA ARCHIVES

SEASON'S GREETINGS FROM THE BEAT 25¢

KRLA *Edition* BEAT

DECEMBER 30, 1967

KRLA ARCHIVES

KRLA BEAT

Merry Christmas

Volume 3, Number 19   December 30, 1967

Brotherhood. Have a Christmas Cool.
CANNED HEAT

Peace on Earth, Goodwill to Men.
LINDA RONSTADT OF THE STONE PONEYS

A Groovy Chickasaw Christmas y'all.
BOBBIE GENTRY

To the readers of The BEAT we wish you a Merry Christmas and a Happy New Year.
SONNY AND CHER

My very best to all BEAT readers at this Christmas time and in the New Year. Have a Happy.
JACK JONES

To all our fans and friends, our best wishes for Happy Holidays and a very prosperous New Year.
DAVY, MICKY, PETER AND MIKE THE MONKEES

Season's Greetings from the Springfield Again.
BUFFALO SPRINGFIELD

... God Bless Us Every One ...
NILSSON

For all of you, I hope Santa's bag is like mine — sincere soul wishes for a groovy '68 ... may it be great.
BRENTON WOOD

We wish love to the world and peace to all mankind. Christmas is a time of reflection brought about by the observance of a beautiful tradition. May this tradition bring you and yours much joy and a wonderful New Year.
SUNSHINE COMPANY

Santa has a new bag, fun timey music. Hope your holidays are full of Good Old-Fashioned fun.
NITTY GRITTY DIRT BAND

Happy Hollie-days.
THE HOLLIES

Wishing all the BEAT readers a White Christmas.
HARPER'S BIZARRE

Peace and love to be shared throughout the world. Join us in keeping the Christmas spirit always.
HAPPINESS THE RASCALS— FELIX, EDDY, GENE, DINO

I gave my daughter more toys last Christmas than I received throughout my whole childhood. Merry Christmas.
BILL COSBY

Wishing all the BEAT readers the Merriest Christmas and the Happiest New Year,
PETULA CLARK

We wish you all a Merry Christmas and hope that the New Year brings peace to all mankind.
PETER, PAUL AND MARY

Merry Christmas and a Happy New Year to all our Soul Brothers and sisters.
SUPREMES, 4 TOPS, TEMPTATIONS

Peace.
THE BEATLES

I wish all of the BEAT readers could be here with me in Hawaii. Christmas here is unlike Christmas anywhere else in the world. Maybe with more airline service the cost will be less, and I will be able to see all of you at Duke's. Mele Kalikimaka.
DON HO

Merry Christmas to all the BEAT readers.
TOM AND DICK SMOTHERS

A beautiful Christmas to all the Beautiful People who read the BEAT.
KENNY O'DELL

Merry Christmas and Happy New Year from Charles Westhover.
DEL SHANNON: CHARLES WESTHOVER

Have a wonderful Christmas and all the best in the New Year.
NANCY SINATRA

FROM THE BEAT

KRLA ARCHIVES

LOVIN' SPOONFUL — ARE THEY IN OR OUT?

To anyone with an open mind:

I don't know how the BEAT feels about the Lovin' Spoonful now that they have been declared "out" by the majority of the music lovers, but I can't help but see them as one of the most talented and versatile groups in the world of music today. Not only do their albums display the fine intermingling of folk-traditional, blues, rock, electronics, country and instrumental sounds, but they have the invisible quality of making a person feel happy inside. In this world of war and flowers when one doesn't know where to turn, happiness is all that we have in common. And in the lives of the young today, this seems to be a major concern.

The older set who used to enjoy listening to the melodic hums of the Lovin' Spoonful, and dance to their liveliness seems to have dropped them after the incident in Greenrich Village. Talking with Frity Richmond (of Jim Kweskin Jug Band) I learned that the majority of their fans are now between 12 and 16 years of age (the Screamie Age). I would like him and the others who think that is so to know that I wasn't even that age when they first came out, nor were 90% of the people I write to or know who like them.

The Lovin' Spoonful lack the psychedelic lights and musical effects, and lyrics that can be twisted into double meanings produced by many of the top groups today, but they convey important messages of love and happiness, and I'm proud to be a part of them.

Love 'n' Spoonfuls of Joy and Peace,
Linna Dunlap

A NEW POET TIM BUCKLEY

Dear Beat,

I know you get a good deal of mail pertaining to new groups that various people throughout the country feel are talented. Because of the amount of people recording and performing much of the commentary on the various groups becomes lost in over-used adjectives. However, during the last week in November I was able to see an astonishing young man named Tim Buckley perform at the Troubador Cafe in Los Angeles.

Tim Buckley is a truly remarkable performer and writer. Although he was on stage for more than forty-five minutes he only sang about five or six songs. Each one was his own composition and each one was more moving than the last.

Buckley has been wrongly compared to both Bob Bylan and Donovan. This comparison comes mainly from people who don't know what to do with an individual when he appears, except to try to pigeon-hole him into previous categories. However, this is a great disservice to Buckley. This 19 year old is his own singer/writer. His style is totally his own. His voice is excellent musically, and almost unbelievable in range and dramatic ability.

His latest album is now out on Electra, called "Hello-Goodbye". You won't be sorry if you buy it; it is new, exciting and beautifully moving. If he plays a club or concert date in your city, try to see him, for Buckley in person is an incredible experience.

Thank you, Marty Schaffer

Beat Publications, Inc.

Executive Editor .... Cecil I. Tuck
Publisher .... Gayle Tuck
Editor .... Louise Criscione
Assistant Editor .... Jacoba Atlas

Staff Writers
Bobby Bovino   Ron Koslow
Tony Leigh   Shirley Poston

Contributing Writers
Tony Barrow   Sue Barry
Eden   Bob Levinson
Jamie McClusky III   Mike Masterson

Photographers
Ed Caraeff   Jerry Hass

National Advertising Representative
Sam Chase Assor., Inc.
527 Madison Avenue
New York, New York 10022
(212) PL. 5-1668

Advertising Director .... Dick Stricklin
Business Manager .... Judy Felice
Subscriptions .... Diane Clatworthy

Distribution
Miller Freeman Publications
500 Howard Street, San Francisco, Calif.

The BEAT is published bi-weekly by BEAT Publications, Inc., editorial and advertising offices at 9000 Sunset, Suite 1000, L.A., California 90069. U.S. bureaus in Hollywood, San Francisco, New York, Chicago and Nashville; overseas correspondents in London, Liverpool and Manchester, England. Sale price 25 cents. Subscription price: U.S. and possessions $5 per year; Canada and foreign rates, $9 per year. Second class postage prepaid at Los Angeles, California.

Improving Concerts

Dear Beat,

One of the things that has always bothered me about the larger concerts is the restrictive attitude of the people who give them. I know this is due in part to the locations picked for the concerts, but I feel this too should be changed. Good examples of this would be the recent Donovan Concert Tour of the States. While in San Francisco, Donovan played the Cow Palace, a large, drafty place not at all conductive to Donovan's type of music.

Why is it not possible to book large acts into more intimate stages? Places w h e r e kids can move about if they feel like it, and come closer to the stage. The regimentation at most indoor and some outdoor concerts is terrible. I realize there is a great deal of money involved, and the promoters want to get in the most people for the least amount of concert dates played in one city, but I do feel that the artists themselves should insist upon better performing areas. I know their followers would appreciate the improvement.

Christy Hellman

REMEMBER?

Dear Beat,

I'm writing about the split of one of the greatest groups ever — the Kingston Trio. Their breaking up brings an end to a three man team who had become almost a legend. Their recording performances proved them completely deserving of their fame; but records can't even begin to hint at the impact that seeing the Trio live carries. They're absolutely fantastic! It's hard to believe they could ever be happy being off stage and away from the people, because their music seems so much a part of them. Much credit is due Dean Reilly, their bass player, and his unforgettable chicken suit. The Kingston Trio are fantastically sincere, warm, and sensitive friends, husbands, fathers, writers, and performers. A long, rich and peaceful life to John, Nick and Bob. They deserve it.

A friend

the FORUM

The opinions and ideas expressed in the Letters to the Editor or The Forum sections of our paper are not necessarily the opinions of The BEAT. However, we do feel that this is a free country in which each individual is entitled to hold and express his/her opinions and beliefs. Unfortunately, a limited amount of space prevents us from printing every letter submitted to The BEAT. Consequently, we are forced to print only a general cross-section of the mail we receive.

The Editor

The Breeze

Beneath the mammoth, shady trees
There stirs a whisper of a breeze.
A stillness reigns,
A silence golden,
And peaceful are the leaves.

I hear the distant beat of drums.
Leaping terror goes and comes
I fear the mighty guns.

Between the hardy, dark-lit trees
There runs a fun-filled laughing breeze,
Changing things
Within its path,
Disturbing now the leaves.

Crouching shapes against the ground,
The silence holds but one thin sound,
The fall of leaves upon the ground.

Around and through the quaking trees
Crashes a thundering, biting breeze,
Hating all;
Attaching all,
And fearful are the leaves.

Napalm sears the weary trees,
And untold men are severed free
To live and die in agony.

Beneath the mammoth, shady trees
Stirs the whisper of a breeze.
A stillness reigns,
A silence golden,
and peaceful are the leaves.

Joan Morley

HERE I AM holding one of my BEATS. Behind me is the Saigon River. Around my neck is a horseshoe that a guy from Greenwich Village gave to me. **DON RUIZ**

AROUND the WORLD

U.S. Tour For Rawls

Lou Rawls and the Fifth Dimension have been set to play a 10-date concert tour produced by Dick Clark Productions.

The tour which will begin in March of 1968 will include dates at the Coliseum in Memphis, the Civic Arena in Cleveland, the Memorial Coliseum in Atlanta, and the Gardens in Cincinnati.

BEATLES' RELEASE

A new Beatles' Album has been released this Christmas. This is the surprise outcome of talks which have taken place in London between Capitol Records executive Voyle Gilmore and the Beatles. Gilmore met with the group to discuss the American presentation format for the six new recordings featured on the soundtrack of the Beatles upcoming color television film "Magical Mystery Tour."

One side of the new album features the six soundtrack numbers, while the other cintains five tracks that have previously been released as singles. Side two includes "Penny Lane," "Strawberry Fields Forever," and "All You Need Is Love."

Capitol is using all the cartoons and photographs from the original U.K. book but the American version will have much larger pages. However, there will be no extra charge for the "book" and the album will sell at regular album prices.

RAIDERS TO HOST TV SHOW

Paul Revere and Mark Lindsay have been signed to co-host a new weekly series on ABC-TV called, "Happening '68". The debut date for this Dick Clark production will be January 6, 1968 from 1:30-2 p.m.

Paul Revere and Mark Lindsay have previously worked for Dick Clark Production on "Where the Action Is" and have toured the country on many of Clark's concert tours.

SUPREMES SET NEW RECORDS

Diana Ross and the Supremes grossed a record $109,498 at two concert appearances in California. One at the Oakland Coliseum drew a capacity crowd of 14,000 people. A second concert at Pauley Pavilion at UCLA drew another capacity crowd of 13,000 people.

Previous records at these two concert houses were set by Lawrence Welk at Oakland and Harry Belafonte at UCLA.

The Supremes plan to continue concert dates throughout the United States with dates set for Cincinatti, Ohio and Columbus, Ohio next March.

Busy Future for Bill Cosby

LOS ANGELES — Bill Cosby and his production company Campbell, Siver, Cosby Corporation will be extremely busy in the months to come. A "Bill Cosby Special" for NBC will be aired in March of 1968, and the actor/comedian has already been set for two additional specials in 1969 and 1970.

Cosby himself is planning a feature film during his hiatus from filming "I Spy." The feature will be called "God Save the Mark."

Radio has not been left out of Cosby's plans either. The star will tape five different comedy caricatures in five-minute stripped episodes that will be syndicated to Top 40 formated stations across the country.

PEOPLE ARE TALKING ABOUT the Strawberry Alarm Clock making it all the way to number one in the nation and proving just how wrong you can be . . . how many people are going to record "Can't Take My Eyes Off You" . . . ditto for "Windy" . . . why the Young Rascals would go all the way to Puerto Rico to film four minutes of "It's Wonderful" and why Felix wants to buy a farm in Connecticut . . . now that we have "Chattanooga Choo Choo" on the charts, when's someone going to cut "Singing In The Rain."
. . . who are the Union Gap?
. . . the interesting fact that only "Open Letter To My Teenage Son" and not one of its "answer" records is making any sort of progress on the charts at all . . . why haven't the Yardbirds had a big hit in many months.

. . . why all the little notes concerning Sally Field and Davy Jones are now being circulated . . . how amazing Bill Cosby really is . . . when Smokey Robinson and the Miracles are going to miss . . . the significance of "I Am A Walrus" . . . when short hair and suits are going to be "in" again.
. . . who had "Beautiful People" first . . . what's really going on with the Mamas and Papas . . . when Neil Diamond is going to make that movie . . . the fact that Peter, Paul and Mary may never go out . . . Russ Giguere having another decoration for his bathroom wall now that the Association has another Gold Record . . . what's become of Fabian and Dion and people like that . . . whether or not the Small Faces are serious about Itchycoo Park . . . how Bobbie Gentry is going to do at the San Remo Song Festival.
. . . the Lettermen making it back on the record charts . . . when Motown is going to get some new dance steps for their artists . . . the fact that Kenny O'Dell of "Beautiful People" wrote "Next Plane To London" for the Rose Garden . . . whether or not Lulu will enjoy continued top 40 success . . . how ironic it is that Marvin Gaye and Tammi Turrell have found their biggest musical success by becoming a team . . . the amazing fact that every time people began to think Johnny Rivers has had it he comes up with another hit record.

. . . why the 4 Seasons are not as hot on the West Coast as they are on the East Coast having something to do with the fact that you can count on one hand the number of times they've performed out West . . . why old Simon and Garfunkel compositions were used in "The Graduate" instead of the new ones . . . what happened to Bobbie Gentry's follow-up to "Ode To Billie Joe."

. . . why certain entertainers become swell-headed and others never do . . . why we haven't heard from Herman in a long time . . . how nice it is that Gladys Knight and the Pips finally have a top 10 record on the national charts.

LULU AND A BEE GEE

LULU SAYS she and Maurice have no marriage plans.

"To Sir, With Love" songstress, petite 19-year-old Glasgow girl, Lulu, is in love with a Bee Gee! Her steady date is bass guitarist Maurice Gibb, one of the group's two 17-year-old twins.

Too Young

"I am very fond of him," she admitted in London—adding that she wasn't planning marriage because "we're both too young for that."

And from Maurice came: "I'm equally fond of her. We met at the BBC Television show, "Top Of The Pops," and for the last few weeks we've been seeing each other nearly every night. It's true that were both a bit young for marriage so I don't want to give the impression that there's anything serious between us."

For her recent birthday, Maurice gave Lulu one of his own rings but he is emphatic that there was no special significance about the gift. When Lulu snatched a brief holiday in the South of France, Maurice flew out there from London to join her.

Second Bee Gee

This is the second romance story to involve the Bee Gees within a couple of weeks. When they were passengers on a Hastings to London train which crashed near Hither Green, South London (in November) it was revealed that Robin Gibb, Maurice's twin brother, had been dating telephonist/receptionist Mollie Hullis, 20-year-old employee at the London headquarters of NEMS Enterprises.

The Late Brian Epstein

On behalf of the Beatles and relatives of the late Brian Epstein, I have been asked to thank the thousands of people who write letters of sympathy and condolence after Brian's death at the end of August.

The Epstein family have been particularly impressed to know that so many total strangers wished to sympathize with them in their bereavement. It would be impossible to reply individually to so many letters and all those who have written either to the Beatles, Brian's family or to me are asked to accept this acknowledgment of their kindness.

Tony Barrow
London, December 1967

ON THE BEAT BY LOUISE CRISCIONE

If we're not careful, Bill Cosby and Don Ho will own the entire entertainment industry. Cos is currently talking deals with both ABC and CBS, while the Campbell-Silver-Cosby Corporation is busy winding up filming on "Picasso Summer," the movie starring Albert Finney. For Ho's part, Don Ho Enterprises will open a booking office in Sydney, Australia. The Ho organization already has 55 acts under contract and is busy booking talent into clubs throughout Hawaii and the Pacific.

Cowsills' Deal

Just off a smash record and with a ten-show deal with Ed Sullivan tucked securely under their collective arms, the Cowsills have now come up with another laurel. MGM has signed the family to sing the title song for the movie, "The Impossible Years," starring David Niven.

Donovan has gone way over to the anti-drug side, saying: "I am now publicizing the banning of all drugs so that the dawning generations may be allowed to blossom without the stain of the false-god drug."

The Singer Company is ready to launch a nationwide talent search to uncover gifted teens. The finalists will star in a television special around Labor Day, 1968. The contest will concentrate on the 13 to 19 age bracket and eliminations will determine the top male, female and group vocalists as well as instrumentalists. Three winners will be selected by stations in the top 40 markets and nine finalists will appear on the TV special. Prizes for the winners will include a recording contract, cars, musical instruments and hi-fi equipment. The Singer Company has recently been getting into the music field by sponsoring television specials starring such entertainers as Tony Bennett, Herb Alpert and an up-coming Don Ho special.

Association Gold

Congratulations to the Association . . . they've just been awarded another Gold Record. The RIAA has certified "Never My Love" a million-seller and J. K. Mike Maitland, president of Warner Bros./7 Arts Records had nothing but praise for the group when he received the Gold Record news: "It is extremely gratifying to see the courage of our convictions become a reality as it has with our initial belief in the Association and their subsequent success."

It looks as if everyone is now coming out with the short films to go along with their new single releases. The Beatles have done it, the Young Rascals just did it in Puerto Rico and now Eric Burdon is doing it in Monterey, California. The completed film will be distributed to key TV stations in the U.S., Canada and Europe and will, of course, be the visual interpretation of the new Burdon single, "Monterey."

France may never be the same. Don Ho and the Allis are set to invade the country next summer for a headlining two weeks at the Olympic Theatre. Following that, Ho and the Allis will headline a benefit in Nice with the proceeds going to the French Red Cross.

Tommy Boyce and Bobby Hart, the team first nationally recognized for their work with the Monkees, have been signed by Columbia Pictures to sing the title song for the Dean Martin movie, "The Ambushers," set for release this month.

Raider Concerts

You Raider fans will be interested in knowing that the group is set to play concerts at White Auditorium, Bryan, Texas on January 5th; Municipal Auditorium, Beaumont, Texas on January 6th; and Municipal Auditorium, Atlanta, Georgia on January 7th.

DID YOU KNOW . . . Bill Cosby is Warner Bros./7 Arts top record seller since 1963 with record sales "close to seven million, for a gross of over $30,000,000."

Before I sign off, I'd like to take an opportunity to wish all of you a very Merry Christmas and the best New Year ever. And a huge "thank you" to all BEAT readers and music people who helped to make the last year so very groovy.

50,000 GIFTS FOR OUR BEAT READERS

THE BEAT tried to think of some concrete way of thanking our readers for being so loyal all through 1968. Consequently, we managed to get our hands on 50,000 collector's items—the shelved album cover from the second Buffalo Springfield album!

"Buffalo Springfield Again" is the group's second album. It was originally to have been 'Buffalo Springfield Stampede." However, the Springfield decided to delete the "Stampede" album for several reasons: they felt the new cover was groovier and, most important, the content represents their greatest sound to date. The group is constantly changing their material, and therefore, they felt the earlier material was dated.

Now the "Buffalso Springfield Stampede" cover has become a real collector's item with their thousands of fans attempting to get their hands on one of the covers.

All you have to do to receive a "Stampede" cover is to send a stamped, self-addressed business envelope to: BEAT Publications, 9000 Sunset Blvd., Suite 1000, Los Angeles, Calif. 90069 and the first 50,000 of you will receive free of charge a "Stampede" cover. Remember—you must include a stamped, self-addressed envelope.

Merry Christmas from The BEAT and the Buffalo Springfield.

Christmas Is A Happening...

Thanks To

THE BEATLES

JIMI HENDRIX

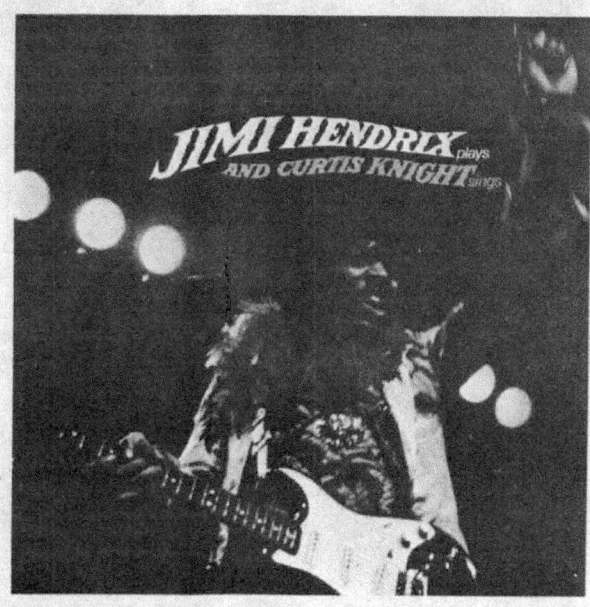

THE BEACH BOYS

and Capitol Records

AVAILABLE AT

KRLA ARCHIVES

KRLA ARCHIVES

U.K. POP NEWS ROUND-UP

Bee Gees Set For U.S. In January

By Tony Barrow

Contrary to press reports in America and Britain, I understand that the Bee Gees will not be undertaking a full-length concert tour of the U.S.A. and Canada before next summer. On the other hand, they will play an isolated pair of performances in the Los Angeles area early in the new year — probably during the final week of January.

This is the exclusive information given to me in London by the group's manager, Robert Stigwood, as this issue of The BEAT goes to press.

Commenting upon a press story that the Bee Gees were scheduled to appear in two concerts at the New Forum Stadium, Los Angeles, on Saturday, January 27, 1968, Robert Stigwood told me: "I cannot confirm the venue or the precise date but I can say that the only two shows the Bee Gees will give during their late January trip to America will be in Los Angeles. Otherwise, the purpose of the visit is several television appearances — including one for the Smothers Brothers program. Our American concerts will be booked through General Artists Corporation who will be setting up a full series of coast-to-coast concerts for one of the summer months."

When the group returns home to Britain in February, preparatory work for their first feature film will begin. Zany actor/comedian Spike Milligan is in line for the job of screenplay writer for the movie which is to be called, "Lord Kitchener's Little Drummer Boys." Shooting on location in Kenya will take place in March or April.

Bee Gees In Special

In the meantime, the Bee Gees are to be the only pop attraction in an unusual Television Special to be networked throughout the U.K. on the evening of December 24th. The group is writing special Christmas material for the special-plus new arrangements of traditional Christmas carols and seasonal songs.

Tom Jones, currently climbing the U.K. charts with "I'm Coming Home," is to give a one-man concert performance at the Hollywood Bowl on April 17, 1968. He will come into L.A. direct from Las Vegas where he will have completed a month-long cabaret season at the Flamingo.

The Hollywood Bowl appearance is to be filmed and is likely to be shown on television on both sides of the Atlantic. Tom's agent, Colin Berlin, will finalize arrangements during his pre-Christmas trip to America. I understand that he may arrange a limited series of other stage shows for the star to follow immediately after the Bowl date.

Foundations Latest

The Foundations are the latest group to make the Number One spot in Britain. With their recording of "Baby Now That I've Found You," they took over the pop peak position form "Massachusetts" by the Bee Gees.

The Foundations are a truly international unite, their eight members hailing from London, Jamaica, Ceylon and Trinidad. The group includes 38-year-old Mike Elliott and Pat Burke (30) who are Jamaican saxmen, 18-year-old organist Tony Gomez from Ceylon, Trinidad's Coem Curtis, a 27-year-old boxer-turned-singer, trombone player Eris Allendale (31) from Dominica, 27-year-old Londoner Allan Warner on lead guitar with fellow Londoners Peter Macbeth (24) on bass guitar and Tim Harris (19) on drums.

The emergence of this octet as a headlinemaking act is of particular significance for several reasons — the line-up mixes white and Negro musicians who are out to achieve a replica of the American soul sound in Britain and, with eight people involved, this is the largest group (or the smallest band!) on the U. K. pop scene.

Eric Allendale appears to be the unit's main spokesman, although he declares that the Foundations do not have a leader: "Everybody has his say although I do most of the arranging. We're a very easygoing group."

Success has come so fast that the Foundations have still to work out several December club and more than 120 dollars! New bookings are now putting the group in the thousand-dollars-a-date class.

Their next single, "Back On Our Feet Again," is by Tony Macauley and John McLeod who gave them the chart-topping "Baby" composition. Both records are to be the subject of heavy promotion in America and the Foundations plan brief trips to your side of the Atlantic for TV and radio dates aimed at helping repeat in America their initial U.K. chart-topping success.

New Stone LP

"Her Santanic Majesty Requests And Requires," the new LP by the Rolling Stones, has simultaneous release on both sides of the Atlantic this month. If the Stones were out to rival the unprecedented album cover splendour of "Sgt. Pepper" I can only say that they have succeeded!

The new release contains ten lengthy tracks, the entire album being self-composed and self-produced by the group. The titles are "Sing This Song Altogether," "Citadel," "In Another Land," "2000 Men," "Sing This Song Altogether And See What Happens" (which is a continuation of the first track to form a recording which lasts for a total of twelve minutes!), "She's A Rainbow," "The Lantern," The Lady, The Lillies And The Lake," "200 Light Years From Home" and "On With The Show." "In Another Land" is an original Bill Wyman specialty, while all the other numbers are Jagger/Richard compositions.

Color film clips of "Hello, Goodbye" for worldwide television screening were made on the stage of the Saville Theatre in London's West End. For the occasion The Beatles wore a fantastic selection of gear including collarless Cardin-style suits worn four years ago when the group was undertaking its earliest bill-topping concert tours of the U.K. and the equally familiar but more colorful "Sgt. Pepper" band uniforms which the group introduced less than six months ago via the cover of the LP.

Dancing Girls

With them on the Saville stage were six dancing girls pleasingly and sparingly attired in grass skirts and bikinitype tops. The filming of the series of three film segments took the whole of one day with Paul McCartney acting as director.

Final concerts in the 1967 series of Sunday shows at London's Saville Theatre included appearances by Joe Tex and his band, Gladys Knight and the Pips, Motown songstress Chris Clark, Eddie Floyd, Felice Taype and Sounds Inc. . . . In Decca's London studios Brenda Lee recorded material for a new single . . . for the first time in the history of British pop charts all top twenty places occupied by British talent. Lower down in the Top 30 the only Americans holding chart places are Felice Taylor, Stevie Wonder, The Box Tops, The Four Tops and Gene Pitney . . . Jim Proby now settling in Britain "on a long-term basis" with cabaret and club bookings being made for him well ahead into 1958 . . . after early 1968 concerts in Japan the Yardbirds will make yet another lengthy tour of America in March and April . . . Bobby Vee was over here to promote his newie, "Beautiful People" . . . Latest by the Seekers on a U.K. single is Kim Fowley's "Emerald City" . . . London's Carnaby Street, the capital's teen-fashion center, magnificently bright this Christmas season with spectacular illuminations. The big turn-on ceremony was attended by Faye Dunaway, deejay Simon Dee and The Bee Gees. Street was closed to traffic and groups layed for dancing . . . although it was a "B-side" record title in Britain Lulu sang "To Sir With Love" in the 1967 Royal Variety Show. Press reports acclaimed her appearance as the highlight of the show.

THE BEE GEES COMING STATESIDE in January for "The Smothers Brothers Show"

☛ NOW YOU MAY GET J. B. LANSING'S NEWEST RELEASE...THE EXPLOSIVE, UNCENSORED STORY OF "THE MENDELSOHN QUINTETTE CLUB OF BOSTON", AS NARRATED BY IRVING MENDELSOHN!

A JBL ORIGINAL

You've cherished their records ..."Meet me at the Liberty Bell Sarah, cause you're a ding-a-ling" . . . "The Boulder Colorado Rock" . . . "These Socks" . . . and many more. You've thronged to their stand-up and sit-down concerts...you've traveled miles to their appearances at corner stone layings, super market galas, quilting bee hops, AND NOW you can read the true, little-known facts about your beloved quintette club. You won't be happy until you've read it . . . so get it now!

MAILED FREE!!!
On receipt of 25¢ for handling.

Fill in and mail this coupon.

COUPON
Enclosed is 25¢ for handling charges. Please send me the story of "THE MENDELSOHN QUINTETTE CLUB OF BOSTON"

Name
Address
City   State

JAMES B. LANSING SOUND INC.
3249 CASITAS AVE. LOS ANGELES, CALIFORNIA 90039

THE SEPER COMPANY
5273 Tendilla, Dept. T.O
Woodland Hills, Calif.

SM. PEACE SYMBOL — NECK STRAP $1.25 P.P.

KRLA ARCHIVES

Some Love From Cher

Including Cher's Current Smash Hit
YOU BETTER SIT DOWN KIDS

Available At...

on Imperial Records

KRLA ARCHIVES

THE ROLLING STONES HAVE DONE IT

Their Satanic Majesties Request

Now Available At:

KRLA ARCHIVES

A Groovy Christmas Gift To Be Enjoyed The Year Round!

I enclose $1.75 plus 25 cents handling for each*.

A BEAT Calendar Poster

in black, white and red

NAME_____

ADDRESS_____

CITY_____ STATE_____ ZIP CODE_____

*California residents please include 5% sales tax.

KRLA ARCHIVES

KRLA PRESENTS PHIL OCHS IN CONCERT

Would You Believe—THIS?

You can make it a hit: You decide

MERRY CHRISTMAS

THE GOLDEN BEAR
306 OCEAN AVENUE (HWY 101)   HUNTINGTON BEACH

Presents
December 16-17
The Byrds

December 26 – Jan. 7
(nightly)
Ian and Sylvia

Reservations   PHONE 536-9600
536-9102

HAPPY NEW YEAR

Ash Grove
Oct. 13-22

NOW!   DEC. 15-23
NITTY GRITTY DIRT BAND

DEC. 25-31
THE
CHAMBERS BROTHERS

8162 Melrose Ave.   OL 3-2070

SUNSET STRIP	9039 SUNSET	NOW HAPPENING LA CIENEGA
1—ABSTRACTS		
2—BURNSIDE		1—THE THIRD EYE
3—POP CORN BLIZZARDS		2—THE WEST WINDS
SUNDAY AFTERNOON LOVE IN – 4 P.M.	GAZZARRI'S #1 ON-THE-STRIP CR 3-6606 OL 7-2113	3. CHURCHILL DOWNS
MON. DANCE CONTEST Grand Prize $500 Finals Mon. & Tues. Jan. 1st & 2nd	GAZZARRI'S #2 LA CIENEGA	
	319 N. LACIENEGA	

Holiday happenings at the Troubador
ONE WEEK ONLY
DEC. 12-17
Jim Kweskin Jug Band
Plus song — with
Bob Lind

DOUG WESTON'S
Troubadour
CR. 6-6168
9081 Santa Monica Blvd.
at Doheny

Dec. 19-26
CANNED HEAT
BLUES BAND
Dec. 27-31
BUTTERFIELD
BLUES BAND
—●—
Jan. 5-6
HOYT AXTON

★ HOOTENANNY EVERY MONDAY NITE ★

KRLA ARCHIVES

HOLLIES: 'THE STONES ARE LOSING POPULARITY NOW'

By Eden

The Hollies have been, for several years, one of the top groups in Great Britain. They have also been one of the most influential groups across the Pond, earning the respect and admiration of most of their pop colleagues. Apart from their many musical interests, the Hollies are also very much involved in helping other people and are especially interested in charities.

Donation

While they were in Los Angeles on a promotional tour during November, the Hollies appeared on the Joey Bishop Show. Another guest on the program was actor Ross Martin, who has a charity of his own which the boys became interested in after hearing him speak of it. So interested, in fact, that on national television, Graham Nash informed Joey Bishop that the group had decided to donate their entire wages for that evening's performance to Ross's charity. They also invited Joey to come to England and appear on a charity program with them. Graham explained further:

"Ross Martin had been on the show several bars before talking about the charity for asthmatic kids. He has a hospital somewhere, tucked away, that has about 135 beds in it for the kids. He was just generally talking about the very good work these people are doing for very little money.

"We felt very good about it, because we're on this scene in England. We have a major special to do at the Albert Hall which is our show and we're just trying to sort out some nice people to come on the show with us, and do the whole thing for charity. It should fetch a lot of money for charity.

"We invited Joey to come across and star in *our* show. The date isn't fixed yet; it's very free, except that we want to do it—we've approached the Albert Hall . . . " "We approached the Albert Hall in a taxi, actually," interrupted Bobby . . . and it's all just generally getting it together now.

"It will benefit *all* charities, but it's mainly for the kids. The bulk of the money will go to an orphanage that we found in England, called The Hollies. It's been in existance for about 50 years."

At heart, the Hollies are very definitely cut-ups. Although all five of them are very intelligent, they are also very witty and are constantly pulling verbal cut-ups. For example, when I began speaking to them about the British musical invasion of three years ago, Graham interrupted to inform me: "It started with William the Conqueror, you know."

"Yeah, 1066" added Alan Clarke. "He had a group, of course," continued Graham matter-of-factly. "It was called Willie and the Conquerors."

British "Inversion?"

"Bill Conq we called him for short," explained Alan. "And then it got related to just conquing," Graham went on, taking a sip of coffee. "Now then, about the British inversion", Graham looked at me inquiringly.

After a brief explanation of my original question (which I'd long since forgotten!), Graham (the eternal spokesman for everyone!) explained: "I think the scene with the British inversion was that it was very fresh. It wasn't particularly any better than the music that was already coming from here, except that we did it in a way that we meant it. It was very raw and very crude, but it was meant—you dig?

"And, it got over this fantastic freshness, and that's what—I guess —knocked people for six." Bobby took over the conversation here for a moment. "I think mainly the British groups are more nonconformist than the American groups. I think, essentially, American people, really. They all really like to conform, they all like to follow one another.

"Whereas, I think the English people think that they have different things going, their own individualities."

Alan managed, finally, to get a word or so in as well: "I think it's nice to see pop music, or rock and roll, as you want to call it, being accepted amongst all age groups. And also, a lot of audiences are quietening down now, and listening to the music—which is nicer!"

"I have a theory about that, actually," Graham chimed in again. "In 1964-65, when the Stones really sort of were so raw, and spade-sounding, they demanded everybody's attention; and people like the Stones dragged everybody out of the mud of the Bill Haley and that scene, and they'd done their job. That's their job—that's why I think the Stones are losing popularity now.

"Their era's past, you dig, and it's up to the other people now to carry on from where the Stones left off, but with a different type of music. It's a lot softer and gentler now. But, the Stones and people dragged them all out of the mud, to set them on the bank, for the rest of the world to play to."

SHOUTS FROM GENE

By Gene Cornish

Hi! We've been doing a lot of concerts lately and getting chances to say hello to fans we haven't had a chance to meet with yet — Painters Mill Music Fair, Baltimore; Colby College, Iona College and St. John's University. And we'll be heading California-way this month. On December 18th, we'll be performing in West Covina and on December 20th, at Anaheim. We just learned that we'll also be doing the "Red Skelton Show" while we're on the coast. One of our favorite comedians of all time!

Last At Old Garden

While all this is going on we'll be staying at the Century Plaza Hotel in Los Angeles . . . then back home for the Madison Square Garden Concert on December 23rd. Our concert will probably be the last musical event at the Old Garden — the new Madison Square Garden is scheduled to open on the site of Pennsylvania Station sometime early next year . . .

Our newest single, "It's Wonderful," is due out shortly (maybe some radio stations have broken it already) — we're practically finished with the album. And here's that bit of information I've been promising you about this LP: the title is "Once Upon A Dream" and the entire album is one continuous theme, a combination of western and eastern sounds, ranging from country-western to raga . . . Dino has designed the cover — a sculpture-photograph of Rascals' memories and favorite things . .

Show With Lesley

Oh, we just completed taping the "Leslie Uggams Show" with Robert Morse, Noel Harrison and beautiful Leslie . . . it should be aired sometime in February or March . . .

That new home on Long Island that I bought and am furnishing for my mother and father is coming along just fine. I'm at the point where I'm handling the details — like delivering piles of firewood for the fireplaces!

One thing I've been concentrating a lot on these days is listening to the Beatles' latest — and I have to say it again — I can do nothing but appreciate what they do.

Rascal Friends

Also been digging some old movies — I can't see enough of Laurel and Hardy and Lloyd and Chaplin. They've got the best form of comedy — slapstick. My own acting ambitions head that way also — when we make that feature length film next year, I'm going to explore those ambitions . . . and practice pure comedy.

Keep writing — I love your letters — Chow for awhile . . . be talking to you again very, very soon . . . Love, Gene.

MOVING?

Writing about a subscription?
Be sure to fill out this form

For FASTEST service on address change, missing copies, etc., attach old mailing label in first space below. Otherwise please print clearly your address as we now have it.

OLD ADDRESS (Attach old label here if available)

NAME
ADDRESS
CITY
STATE   ZIP CODE

NAME
ADDRESS
CITY   STATE   ZIP CODE

MAIL TO: BEAT PUBLICATIONS
Circulation Dept.
9000 Sunset Blvd., Suite 1000,
Los Angeles, Cal. 90069

Please allow 3 weeks for change to take effect.

KRLA ARCHIVES

Linda Leading Stone Poneys To Gold Water

By Tony Leigh

There is a new type of singing group at the forefront of the pop music industry—the group that is led by a female singer of remarkable range and power. Using this innovation, the Jefferson Airplane and Big Brother and the Holding Company have been able to create new and moving sounds. Now another group has been added to their ranks, a new group with the talent and musical ability worthy of everyone's attention: The Stone Poneys.

The Stone Poneys have as their lead singer Linda Maria Ronstadt, an extremely interesting and attractive 21 year old Arizonian. Linda's interest in music dates back to her childhood when she sang locally with her brother and sister.

Although music was always foremost in her mind, and for her future it was generally agreed that she would be a singer, Linda made a slight detour to the University of Arizona. It didn't take long for her to realize that formal study held little interest for her.

"I started out taking a lot of classes, and then one by one I would just drop them, until I realized that it was a waste of my time and everyone else's for me to be there."

By this time one of her friends from Arizona, Bob Kimmel had gone to Los Angeles to pursue his own hopes of a musical career. Linda decided that L.A. was the place she should be too, and joined Bob in that city. These two then met up with Ken Edwards, a native Californian and formed what is now the Stone Poneys.

Although with the hit record, "Different Drum," Linda has been receiving most of the attention, she is adament that there will be no split in the group.

No Solos

"I wouldn't want to sing on my own. I don't think I could be comfortable on stage unless I knew that I was sharing the stage with my friends. I guess," she added candidly, "I need the security a group gives me."

One of Linda's most engaging qualities is her honesty and openness. There is nothing phoney or pretentious about this girl: she is warm, friendly and eager to exchange honest and unaffected ideas with everyone.

Honesty and the ability to convey love are two of the qualities Linda hopes comes across in their music. Although Linda has her own distinct styling and vocal range she is a great admirer of the mood created by both Janis Joplin and Grace Slick.

"They have the ability to communicate love, and move everyone musically. That's something really wonderful, and I hope that we can do that with our music too."

Linda lives in the somewhat rural community outside Los Angeles called Topanga Canyon. This area is rather woodsy and has garnered the local reputation of being a haven for home loving, family hippies. In the Canyon, Linda is surrounded by all sorts of animals, who she adores, and strange, but interesting people.

One benefit of living in the Canyon is one's ability to get closer to nature.

Lose Senses

"The trouble with living in the city is that you lose many of your senses, they just become numb from not being used. We depend on mechanisms and machines for doing so much for us that we don't know how to cope with things ourselves. We can't react openly to everything around us. That's one of the reasons I live away from the city; I don't want to become numb to the world."

Another unusual part of Linda's character is her close relationship with her mother. Although for all practical purposes Linda has left home, and lives totally on her own, she maintains a warm and open relationship with her family. For their part, her mother and father display unusual tolerance and enjoyment of their daughter and her somewhat strange friends.

LINDA, PONEYS' lead singer: "I wouldn't want to sing on my own."

Dusty Springfield Has

THE LOOK OF LOVE

DO YOU?

AVAILABLE AT

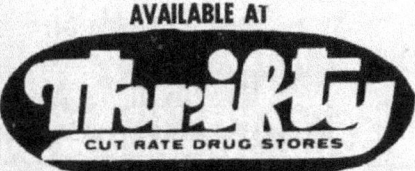
CUT RATE DRUG STORES

PHILIPS

KRLA ARCHIVES

TOMMY JAMES & the SHONDELLS NO ONE HIT WONDERS

By Jamie McCluskey III

When Tommy James and the Shondells arrived on the pop scene many people called the group a "one-hit wonder", and indeed — with the success of their first hit, "Hanky Panky," the group became almost an inside *joke* in the entertainment industry.

People "in the business" cried out that the record was a fluke, a "throw-back" to the early, undeveveloped days of rock and roll (you should pardon the expression!) and people simply laughed.

Once again, however, the joke was on them and today—Tommy James and the Shondells can sit back—in their Gold Record-lined rooms! — and laugh. They have had several hits in a row and show every indication of becoming something more than just a "one-hit wonder".

Even the success hasn't erased Tommy's sense of humor, or his honesty. He candidly admitted that, "There's no doubt about it— our first two or three records and 'Hanky Panky' were about as *bad* as you can get! I guess the first two were in pretty much the same *rank*, nothing as bad as 'Hanky Panky'."

Constant Sound

This has changed now; Tommy agrees that his first three records, hits though they were, were not any great "sensations—but fortunately, that changed along about the fourth record. "I Think We're Alone Now" is the record Tommy credits with the beginning of the change in direction which his group has taken, and is quite pleased with the "groovey" sort of bag which he feels they are currently getting into. "The general sound is pretty constant throughout most of our records," he explained, "even though we may go from bag to bag."

There is actually a story behind "Hanky Panky", and one which even Tommy admits will almost justify the criticisms of the pop journalists. He explained that, 'Hanky Panky' was recorded five years ago. "I was fifteen years old and it was a high school group called The Shondells. It was released and it really *bombed* — because it was really *bad!*

"But, a disc jockey in Pittsburgh picked it up just last summer, just four years later. He picked it up out of a *record cemetery* somewhere and started playing it. Four weeks later it was Number One in the nation. Very strange!"

Changes

At least Tommy is very concerned now with the kind of things which are going on in popular music, and he took a moment to evaluate the current trends.

"The whole pop market is changing—we're in kind of a transition period right now between what people *thought* they liked, and what they *really* like. And, I think what people *thought* they liked was the old English sound, with a touch of harmony. I think now we're definitely going over into a rhythm and blues bag. The whole general outlook on music is much more open-minded now and is accepting a lot now that *wasn't* accepted a year ago. They're getting into some really good things now and there are a lot of good records out now which I don't think would have made it a year ago."

Looking to the future, Tommy feels that: "You can't go much farther than to have hit records—commercially, that is. And, I wouldn't want to get hung-up in any type of artistry other than commercial music. But, eventually I'm going to be producing and I also will start my own record company which I should have within two years."

Although the first hit record for Tommy and his group came about almost by accident, he knows that it takes a lot more than "accidents" now to keep a pop group on top today. "I think it takes a sincere desire and interest in what you're doing, because 'where there's a will there's a way'. And, I've always found that whenever I was looking for a new single or a song, I'd always find one because I'd always break my back looking for it. Any business or anything that you take sincerely and treat it with the same respect, so to speak, that you treat your bread and butter—because that's what it boils down to. But, even more so—a personal dedication. Anybody who feels this was has *got* to succeed sooner or later."

Hugh Masekela Is Alive

So Is His Trumpet

Give 'em Both

A Listen

Now Available At:
MONTGOMERY WARD DEPARTMENT STORES

KRLA ARCHIVES

"I-FEEL-LIKE-I'M-FIXIN'-TO-DIE"
Country Joe and The Fish

A FINE KETTLE OF FISH

Now Available At:

KRLA ARCHIVES

BEATLE POSTERS

Available in black light, hand screened poster. Pink, green, orange added to make a groovy image.

Cost is only $1.00 plus 25c handling. Get your order in to The BEAT now!

California residents include 5% sales tax.

Name..

Address..

City..................State..............Zip..........

CLASSIFIED

SCORPIO INDIANS Rule!!

TOAD RULES you fools! Diane and Bonnie.

Ralph Scala, Happy 20th Birthday, December 12th. Mariaane and Betty.

JIM PILSTER — Happy 21st! Love, Ellen.

Happy Birthday Neil Young; Navaho Ro.

I WHO HAVE NOTHING, love you, want you and need you.

Good Luck SCOUNDRELS of YORK!

Happy Birthday Robin Racoon!

Joey, 6-27-67 David found me!! Please write soon. luv, Sini

The SOUTHE is Rising

Happy belated Birthday to Bruce Kunkel of the NITTY GRITTY DIRT BAND.

Hurry back to Philly. Luv, Pat Greenhagen.

sgtpepperslonelyheartsclubband

Mark Lindsay: Thank you for making life so beautiful. Rose.

Peggy—Davy Jones is nice.

SEEDS, SEEDS, SEEDS.

Happy Birthday again Ralph Scala.

Happy Birthday, Hooke. Love, Laura.

LITE MY FIRE posters — 4 colors 33" x 42", $2.00 P.P. Seper Co. 5273 Tendilla, Woodland Hills, California 91364.

MARK LINDSAY—The Orange Letter Affair wants you at the Sunset address.

Bill Cowsill, Happy 20th, You're the greatest! B. J. Gallo

REACH COSMIC AWARENESS without drugs—help save mankind from destruction. Write for free booklet, "Cosmic Awareness Speaks," SERVANTS OF AWARENESS, Box 115E, Olympia, Washington.

SLEEP LEARNING, self hypnosis. Details, strange catalog free! Nutosuggestion, Box 24BT, Olympia, Washington.

Peggy Brooks is bitchin'. R.P.G.

LEFT BANKE RULE.

WILD POSTERS, far-out bumper strips, buttons! Crazy Labels, Box 21-M, Olympia, Washington.

THE BEAT will accept only personal messages in the classified section. We will print names but not addresses or phone numbers.

Rates are cheap! Only 10 cents per word.

Your deadline for the next issue is: Dec. 19.

SPEC-TRIM SUNGLASSES

UNIQUE SHADOW BOX FRAMES
MOD RECESSED LENSES
TWO-COLOR FRAMES

$4 Each*
*Calif. residents please add 5% sales tax

AVAILABLE IN:
Blue and White   White and Pink
Purple and White Red and White
Yellow and Black Red and Black
Designate Frame Color

SEND TO:
BEAT PUBLICATIONS
9000 Sunset, Suite 1000
Los Angeles, Calif. 90069

DEBS

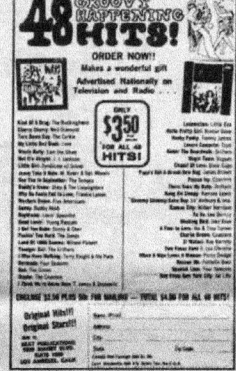

48 GROOVY HAPPENING HITS!

ORDER NOW!

$3.50 FOR ALL 48 HITS!

SPECIAL ISSUES STILL AVAILABLE

☐ Monterey Pop Festival souvenir issue

☐ History of the Hippies

25 cents each plus 10 cents for mailing and handling.

SEND TO:
BEAT PUBLICATIONS
9000 Sunset, Suite 1000
Los Angeles, Calif. 90069

Name:_____

Address:_____

City:_____State:____
*Calif. Residents include 5% sales tax

BUY BEAT For Christmas

TURNING ON

AFTER BATHING AT BAXTER'S (RCA) Jefferson Airplane. *Ballade of You Me and Poohneil, The War is Over, Saturday Afternoon,* plus nine other tracks. This third offering from the Airplane returns in part to the sound that brought them to the forefront of the San Francisco groups and turned them into a world recognized musical influence. This album is less "produced" than was *Surrealistic Pillow*. When listening, one feels that there is more Airplane and less RCA. The musical effects plus over-dubbed voices work perfectly on *A Package of Value*. It is one of the few times that what is meant to sound like actual studio recording banter plays as such. Listen to the screaching of "no man is an island" and the reply of "penninsula" . . . Gracie's laughter. With an unusual amount of vocal and musical integration from within the group, the Airplane emerges as a more complete unit, with less emphasis on one performer within the whole. The words to their music are also quite exceptional. This album is proof positive (as if any more proof were needed) that the Airplane is an important force in music—all music—today.

PLEASURES OF THE HARBOR (A&M) Phil Ochs. *Pleasures of the Harbor, The Party The Crucifixion* plus five other tracks. Phil Ochs is one of those amazing singer/writers who came to prominence singing protest songs and have now turned to contemporary poetry. Bob Dylan is, of course, the prime example of this. But listen to this album, Ochs is not far behind. Beginning with an incredible song entitled *The Party* Ochs paints a verbal picture of today's society and its gatherings . . . the hostess, the guests, the heroes of our time. "To the winners go the hangers on." His *Pleasures of the Harbor* is almost cinematic in its vivid images. The Sailor, the girl, the lonliness, . . . the song is fantastic. But, by far, Ochs most important work to date is the 12 minute *The Crucifixion*. This is an ncredible indictment of the world and its hungers. The song deals with every man whose innocence and intellect has ever been sacrificed to the masses. "A blinding revelation is served upon his plate, that beneath the greatest love is a hurricane of hate, and God help the critic of the day." The only fault with this work is the over orchestration which tries its best to drown out the powerful lyrics of Ochs song.

BY THE TIME I GET TO PHOENIX (Capitol) Glen Campbell. *Homeward Bound, Bad Seed, Tomorrow Never Comes* plus nine other tracks. In this album Campbell is trying to get somewhat away from the pure country and western bag that he was in formerly. With songs like Paul Simon's *Homeward Bound* and *By The Time I Get To Phoenix* he may be able to do so. However, this new trend is not consistent on the album, and in the final analysis it does emerge as a country and western offering.

BUFFALO SPRINGFIELD AGAIN (ATCO) Buffalo Springfield. *Mr. Soul, Rock and Roll Woman, Sad Memory* plus either other tracks. The Buffalo Springfield is one of the most important groups to come out of Los Angeles. Cutting their teeth in local nightclubs, they now emerge a complete and important rock group. One of the most amazing things about the Springfield is their ability to project their sound in recordings. The music is beautiful, the words meaningful and the harmony and arrangements intricate and musical. This is definitely one group that has not received the acclaim that is due them.

Beat Poster Shop

(Y) Maharishi

Also Available

(R) Sgt. Pepper (S) Stones (P) Seeds (D) Dylan
(K) James Brown (T) The Who (N) Jimi Hendrix

Send to: BEAT POSTER SHOP, 9000 Sunset, Suite 1000, Los Angeles, Cal. 90069

PLEASE SEND ME THE FOLLOWING POSTERS (LIST BY LETTER)_____
I ENCLOSE $1.75 plus .25 Handling for each*.

Name_____

Address_____

City_____State_____Zip Code_____
*California Residents Please Include 5% Sales Tax

Want To Fly?

Why Not Take A Jefferson Airplane?

AVAILABLE AT

KRLA ARCHIVES

Now Available At:
MONTGOMERY WARD DEPARTMENT STORES

KRLA ARCHIVES

BE A BEAT SANTA THIS YEAR!

Please your friends with a BEAT SUBSCRIPTION For CHRISTMAS at these Special Holiday Rates

FIRST 1-YEAR GIFT $3.00
EACH ADDITIONAL GIFT $1.00

Foreign Subscriptions $9.00 Per Year

Mail to: BEAT GIFT SUBSCRIPTIONS
9000 Sunset, Suite 1000, L.A., Calif. 90069

Dear BEAT,
☐ Enter my subscription as my first gift subscription at $3.00.
☐ Please send the BEAT for one year to my friends listed below.

My Name _____
Address _____
City _____ State _____ Zip Code _____
Enclosed is $ _____ for _____ gift subscriptions.
I understand that you will send all gift cards to me so that I may give them to my friends and that their first BEAT will be delivered the week of Christmas.

ENTER BEAT GIFTS HERE

NAME _____
ADDRESS _____
CITY _____ STATE _____ ZIP _____

NAME _____
ADDRESS _____
CITY _____ STATE _____ ZIP _____

NAME _____
ADDRESS _____
CITY _____ STATE _____ ZIP _____

ENTER NEW GIFTS HERE

NAME _____
ADDRESS _____
CITY _____ STATE _____ ZIP _____

NAME _____
ADDRESS _____
CITY _____ STATE _____ ZIP _____

NAME _____
ADDRESS _____
CITY _____ STATE _____ ZIP _____

RETURN THIS ENTIRE FORM WITH YOUR CHECK OR MONEY ORDER

KRLA ARCHIVES

DAVY JONES SUES FORMER MANAGER

KRLA *Edition* **BEAT**

JANUARY 13, 1968

25¢

KRLA BEAT

Volume 3, Number 20   January 13, 1968

MONKEE DAVY JONES SUING EX-MANAGER

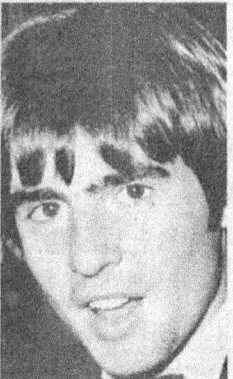

LOS ANGELES—Davy Jones, the tiniest Monkee, is having a bit of a legal problem. In a declaratory relief damage suit against his former manager, Al Cohen, Davy is asking in excess of $150,000.

In his suit, Davy alleges that the contract he signed with Cohen is not valid because Davy was a minor when the contract was signed.

He is, therefore, asking for an accounting of all the money stemming from Davy's merchandising over the past year. The action is being brought in Los Angeles Superior Court.

Davy, along with his fellow Monkees, is currently enjoying a hiatus from their popular television show "The Monkees." The season's filming was completed just before Christmas.

PET SET FOR 'CHIPS'

HOLLYWOOD—The announcement has been made—Petula Clark has been signed to star along with Peter O'Toole in the MGM musical version of "Goodbye Mr. Chips."

Filming begins in April with Peter O'Toole playing Mr. Chips and Pet set to act as Mrs. Chips.

Ever since MGM leaked the news that they would be making the film, a giant guessing-game as to who the stars would be have been running rampant. Originally, it was thought that Richard Burton would play Chips and Lee Remick his wife. Still later, Rex Harrison's name was mentioned.

But now it's all settled . . . Peter O'Toole and Petula Clark have been victorious.

Acting is really not anything new to Petula who, as a child and adolescent actress, made a total of 25 motion pictures. However, she recently completed "Finian's Rainbow" and says "I like to look upon that one as my first movie because that's just how I felt about making it."

Although she is very much of a veteran in movies, she still admits that she finds it difficult to act "because it's such an unnatural thing. You find yourself in unnatural surroundings and trying to be natural in unnatural circumstances is quite difficult."

CONGRATULATIONS FROM DAD TO NANCY—Make no mistake about it — Nancy Sinatra is a big star. Proving the point is the famous Mr. Nielsen and his equally famous television rating system.

Nancy's special on the NBC network, "Movin' With Nancy" grabbed a neat 31.8 rating while the combined forces of "National Geographic Special" and "Lucy Show" received a rating of 15.

Pin another laurel in Miss Sinatra's cap — she's moving!

KRLA ARCHIVES

CONGRATULATIONS TO THE ASSOCIATION . . . the top pop group! See On The Beat for details.

ON THE BEAT
By Louise Criscione

A huge congratulations to the fabulous Association for copping the Bill Gavin Award as the best Pop-Rock Artist . . . also, congratulations are in order to the runner-up in that category—the Beatles! Honest!

As expected Frank Sinatra won as the top Non-Rock Artist with Herb Alpert and the Tijuana Brass coming in as number two. Winner for the top Rhythm and Blues Artist was Aretha Franklin with the Temptations coming in as runner-ups.

Laugh Time

Laugh of the week comes to us courtesy of Governor Nelson Rockefeller. Mr. Rockefeller wants a copy of Mason Williams' album, "Cinderella Rockefella." You may have heard Mason singing the title song with Nancy Ames a few weeks ago on the "Smothers Brothers Show."

It seems that Jimi Hendrix is on two record labels at once . . . and neither one of them is too overjoyed with the situation! Consequently, attorneys for both Warner Bros./7 Arts Records and Capitol Records are attempting to discover which label legally has Hendrix under contract. Meanwhile, both labels have out albums by Hendrix . . . "Jimi Hendrix Experience" on the Warner Brothers label and "Get That Feeling" on Capitol.

Beatle Deal

The Beatles new record company, Apple, has just signed a deal with Terry Melcher Music to publish Melcher's songs in England. For his part, Terry is planning to start his own label, Equinox, Stateside in 1968 along with a new publishing firm, Egg.

QUICK ONES: Roy Orbison just did all right for himself in Canada—brought in just under $90,000 for nine dates. Needless to say, Roy is planning a return visit to his friends up North . . . John Davidson has been set to play the Plaza Hotel in New York beginning April 17 . . . Bobbie Gentry will co-star with Bobby Darin on "Kraft Music Hall Special" to be aired over NBC-TV sometime this month . . . if the East is not meeting the West, at least the East is teaming up with the East. A Japanese Tea House, The Mikazuki, in Honolulu will now feature a floorshow consisting of Chinese poetry and Chinese folk dancing!

Lopez Honor

Trini Lopez had one more honor accorded him by his native state of Texas when he was presented the keys to the city of El Paso.

Trini is one artist who manages to always be busy. He'll guest on a "Carol Burnett Show" on January 15 and then push off for a tour of South Africa beginning on January 25 and winding up on February 25.

Continuing in their policy to keep it all in the family, it has been announced that two of the Cowsill family, Bill and Bob, will now produce all the Cowsill records. The group's first hit, "The Rain, The Park And Other Things," was produced by Artie Kornfield.

Million For Stones

The Rolling Stones received a Gold Record for their latest album, "Their Satanic Majesties Request," before the album was even released! This marks the eighth consecutive Gold Record by the Stones for album sales of more than one million dollars. Quite an achievement.

Wayne Newton has signed a two-year contract with the Frontier Hotel in Las Vegas which calls for Wayne to work a total of eighteen weeks. His first appearance will be on August 18th.

David Janssen, television's ever-popular "Fugitive," has just been signed to co-star with Tony Quinn and Sir Laurence Olivier in the movie, "The Shoes Of The Fisherman."

Those of you who may think Charlie Brown is not a popular fella will be interested in knowing that he topped the television rating again this year . . . just like he did the first time he was aired. Must show something . . .

Now limited in England
Unavailable anywhere in this country

Beatle Monthly Book — Issue 1-56 $2.00 an issue (8 for $10.00)

Rolling Stone Monthly Book — Issue 1-30 $2.00 an issue (8 for $10.00)

Charlie Watts Book, "Ode to a High Flying Bird," $5.00
Beatle Photo Album Christmas Special 1966 $3.00

ALL DIRECT FROM ENGLAND

Pictorial album of Beatle Help movie $3.00
Send cash, check, money order to:
Mala Bo
P.O. Box 2151
Hollywood 28, Calif.

State which issue or what book.
California residents add 5% sales tax on books

Beat Publications, Inc.

Executive Editor .... Cecil I. Tuck
Publisher .... Gayle Tuck
Editor .... Louise Criscione
Assistant Editor .... Jacoba Atlas

Staff Writers
Bobby Bovino   Ron Koslow
Tony Leigh   Shirley Poston

Contributing Writers
Tony Barrow   Sue Barry
Eden   Bob Levinson
Jamie McClusky III   Mike Masterson

Photographers
Ed Caraeff   Jerry Hass

National Advertising Representative
Sam Chase Assoc., Inc.
527 Madison Avenue
New York, New York 10022
(212) PL. 5-1668

Advertising Director .... Dick Stricklin
Business Manager .... Judy Felice
Subscriptions .... Diane Clatworthy

Distribution
Miller Freeman Publications
500 Howard Street, San Francisco, Calif.
The BEAT is published bi-weekly by BEAT Publications, Inc., editorial and advertising offices at 9000 Sunset, Suite 1000, L.A., California 90069. U.S. bureaus in Hollywood, San Francisco, New York, Chicago and Nashville; overseas correspondents in London, Liverpool and Manchester, England. Sale price 25 cents. Subscription price: U.S. and possessions $5 per year; Canada and foreign rates, $9 per year. Second class postage prepaid at Los Angeles, California.

KRLA ARCHIVES

AROUND the WORLD

BRIAN JONES WINS APPEAL

LONDON — "You cannot go boasting about saying you have been let off. If you commit another offense of any sort you will be brought back and punished afresh for this offense. You know the sort of sentence that you will get..."

With these words of warning Lord Parker, the Lord Chief Justice of England, set aside the nine-month jail sentence passed two months earlier on Rolling Stone Brian Jones.

The appeal was heard in London before three High Court judges who decided to substitute a fine of one thousand pounds (more than 3,000 dollars) for the prison sentence.

Although he was not involved in the Appeal, Mick Jagger attended the hearing. He heard Defense Counsel (James Comyn, Q.C.) say that while people in the public eye must accept their responsibilities it followed that "their humiliation is all the greater." Medical opinion agreed that Brian Jones had "been brought to his senses which his colleagues were standing trial."

TRINI SETS CLUB DATES

LOS ANGELES—Trini Lopez has been signed for three top night club engagements in 1968, reports his manager, Bullets Durgom.

Trini is set for a two-week date at the Waldorf Astoria in Manhattan beginning May 31, followed by another two-weeks at the Latin Casino, Cherry Hills, New Jersey, beginning June 17. The third engagement will be at Harrah's Club in Reno, starting on August 29.

THE FOUR TOPS, one of Motown's most popular recording artists, are shown receiving the Variety Club Award from Harold Salkind, Chief Barker for the Variety Club of Philadelphia, during a dinner honoring Ralph W. Pries, International President of Variety Club International. The Four Tops are (left to right) Levi Stubbs, Renaldo Benson, Abdul Fakir and Lawrence Payton. The Four Tops returned to Detroit following the dinner to rehearse for their engagement at the Copacabana in New York.

AL MARTINO SET FOR MUSICAL TV SPECIAL

HOLLYWOOD — Al Martino, who makes his third headlining engagement in as many seasons at London's famed Talk Of The Town in April, will be moonlighting during most of his three-week stand by starring in his own musical special for Granada-TV.

Martino, who created the special, will also serve as executive producer. Arrangements have also been finalized for Capitol Records to release an album version of the show.

PEOPLE ARE TALKING ABOUT what a nice honor it was for the Beach Boys to get invited by the French Government to perform at the UNICEF affair with all proceeds (estimated $500,000) going to help underprivileged children all over the world... the fact that 18-year-old Michael Lloyd arranged and produced "October Country" but had his name left off the record.

... group changes in the Nitty Gritty Dirt Band ... whether or not the rumor that the Doors are breaking up will prove true or false ... the fact that if the Monkees are losing popularity it certainly can't be proven by the record charts ... the Young Rascals finishing up their fourth album at Columbia recording studios in Hollywood.

... the Association beating out all the other group's for the annual Bill Gavin Awards and how sweet that is ... what the story is behind Mama Cass supposedly asking a very well-known record producer to produce her as a single artist ... whether or not Vikki Carr will stay as musically popular as she should and deciding that if all's fair she should be the biggest female vocalist in the nation.

... how many pop people the Rolling Stones have managed to reveal on the cover of "Satanic Majesties Request" and the fact that the four Beatles are the easiest to spot ... why Marianne Faithful ended up as the first artist on Mother Earth Records ... whether or not Bobby Hart and Tommy Boyce will make it big as singers.

... the Canned Heat really being excellent ... the Lettermen coming back on the charts in a big way ... how sick the Motown artists make the psychedelic groups look when it comes to style, polish and showmanship ... how many people think the Foundations are an American group ... Herman's every-few-months tour of the United States falling way off and wondering why.

... Jerry Moss with his moustache being mistaken for one of the Tijuana Brass ... why the Stone Poneys cancelled out of their scheduled benefit appearance ... the speculation that the group scene will die in 1968 ... the person who thinks up the titles to Joe Tex songs being very imaginative ... who the Epic Splendor are.

... whether or not the Stones will ever regain the popularity they once enjoyed ... what happens at one of the Bowl football games when a press agent is for one side and his client is sitting on the opposition's bench ... the walls that keep getting knocked out ... all that good penny candy ... why we haven't heard any hit noise out of Mitch Ryder for quite awhile ... how many groups are being offered television series like "The Monkees" being equal to the amount of those turning the others down.

... who will answer Ed Ames ... who are the Lemon Pipers ... the fact that the Four Tops' engagement at a showplace like the Copacabana was long, long overdue ... who thought up the Electric Prunes' album jacket ... the fact that Bill Wyman's solo record is not exactly bounding up the national charts.

KRLA ARCHIVES

U.K. Pop News Round-Up
Rolling Stones Form Record Company

By Tony Barrow

Barry Gibb, tall, lean, good-looking leader of The Bee Gees was married in secret! ("Hiss! Boo!").

Barry Gibb, tall, lean, good-looking leader of The Bee Gees has parted from his wife! ("Hurray! Hurrah!")

It's just like an old-time movie isn't it? And what thrills and spills for the excited teenybopper! First her heart is torn apart by the mighty grief of learning that her fave rave Bee Gee is married. Then, suspense upon suspense, another secret leaks through to dry her tears and feed the aching marrow of her mind — he's married but he's parted from his wife!

Secrets Out

In London, Barry has admitted all the secrets at once. Questioned about his marriage he revealed that he had kept it quiet "because I did not want it to spoil my image."

His wife is the former Maureen Bates, a 19-year-old blonde from Birmingham. The marriage took place in Sydney, Australia, in the late summer of 1966, a few months before Barry and rest of the Gibb family left for London.

Said Barry: "I suppose the fans will think I have deceived them but I wanted to keep my private life private. The marriage lasted just over a year. I think we were too young to make a proper go of it. There is no chance of us getting together again. We have not decided about a divorce."

It is unlikely that Barry and Maureen would find it easy to secure a formal divorce for themselves for another couple of years. Meanwhile Barry has left Maureen in occupation of the West End apartment which manager Robert Stigwood passed to the couple some months ago when he was moving into a new house.

The Question

So where does all this leave the precious image of Bee Gee Barry? I doubt if it has been tarnished. Neither marriage nor honesty has done the career of the Beatles much harm over the past five years, Barry!

New Vaudeville Band's Mick Wilshire married Hollywood chick Therese Helguin at Holborn Registry Office, London, December 10.

For two years Scott Walker managed to conceal his florishing romance with 21year-old Danish girl Mette Teglbjaerb from fans and all but the closest of friends. Scott and Mette got to know each other when the Walker Brothers played Copenhagen dates in 1965. The twosome has been steady ever since. "She organizes my life for me," admits Scott but he gives no hint of any wedding plans. Another exceptionally well-preserved secret?

Traffic Loss

Traffic, the highly successful new unit formed by Stevie Winwood when he broke away from the Spencer Davis Group, has lost one of its key members, writer Dave Mason. Having made a huge U.K. chart headlines with three consecutive best-selling 1967 singles — "Paper Sun," "Hole In My Shoe" and "Here We Go Round The Mulberry Bush" — Traffic rates as one of the most important new groups on the current scene.

Apart from composing "Hole In My Shoe," Mason was lead vocalbuster. At present Traffic is having an extended vacation due to come to an end around January 18. After that we shall know for sure whether or not Stevie Winwood intends to appoint a replacement for Mason. Early indications are that Mason will not be replaced and Traffic will operate in the future as a trio.

Stone Company

The Rolling Stones have named their new record company Mother Earth. It will be a London-based international operation which will have Mick Jagger and other members of the quintet acting as producers of new chart-aimed record talent.

Mother Earth will have its own administrative and studio staff but physical manufacture and distribution of the product will be handled by London's vast Decca organization via which the Rolling Stones issue their own records.

First releases on the Mother Earth label are expected in February or March and Marianne Faithfull is the record company's first major signing. Mick Jagger has already supervised a series of fresh sessions with Marianne and there is no reason why a single from the songstress should not be among the very first Mother Earth releases.

Heard Around

SCENE AND HEARD . . . Songstress Sandie Shaw spending the first week of the New Year in hospital following her collapse during London Talk Of The Town cabaret season . . . John Lennon and George Harrison flew to Paris to see the Beach Boys and Ravi Shankar in a massive UNICEF charity shindig . . . Second pre-Christmas UNICEF concert starred Petula Clark and Paul Jones . . . Promotional visit to America for Simon Dupree and the Big Sound who just made big news on our side of the Atlantic with their first-ever Top Ten smash, "Kites" . . . February 12 is probable opening date for Lulu at Talk Of The Town, the top West End of London cabaret revue where Diana Ross and the Supremes are about to appear . . . March and/or April cabaret bookings for Dusty Springfield should include appearances in Los Angeles. During the same visit Dusty will guest on Jonathan Winters' television show . . . Otis Redding was scheduled to tour Britain with Carla Thomas in April. News of Redding's death was received with deep regret in London music circles. Said George Harrison: "It's a bitter tragedy. He will be missed by a great many admirers. He was top in his field." . . . Major concerts for the Tremeloes set in Montevideo, Sao Paulo, Rio and Hawaii following uopn the group's February weeks in New York, Chicago, San Francisco and Los Angeles.

"Apple is a co-ordinating project incorporating some activities now looked after by our management firm, NEMS, and other companies"—Paul McCartney.

Apple is a creative concept, a nucleus of ideas, a potential network of international business organizations and the most fantastic new boutique London's West End has ever seen. Apple is the collective brainwave of the Beatles, an all-embracing name they're using to describe their 1968 movement into the world of non-musical big business.

First Mention

The first public mention of the name Apple was on the "Sgt. Pepper" album cover. More recently the Beatles' TV film soundtrack recordings from "Magical Mystery Tour" have been released under an "Apple Presents . . ." headline. And on Thursday, December 7th Apple became a visible and concrete fact in the form of a shop at 94 Baker Street, London W. 1. The shop, beautiful from floor to ceiling, is stacked high with the widest possible range of goods from electronic gadgets (most of them invented and/or built by the Beatles' brainy buddy, electronic genius Alex Mardes, whom they call "Magic Alex"), clothing for men, women and tiny hip kiddies, ornaments and a hundred other items. At Apple you can buy the carpet off the floor or the paintings off the walls if they take your fancy.

The decor for the Apple shop is the work of Dutch couple, Simon and Marijke (say it Simone and Maracca) who have set up their own design organization called The Fool. Marijke and her friend Josie ave created most of the more beautiful gear worn by Beatle wives over the past year. For sale at Apple they have combined fantasy with economy so that you can buy a velvet cape for less than 20 dollars while you watch snow white clouds of light float over a brilliant sky-blue ceiling.

A Beginning

The highly colorful Baker Street boutique is just a beginning. The future possibilities for Apple enterprises seem to be limitless. In a nutshell, Apple means that the Beatles have decided to put great chunks of their fortune to work in ways which are personally dear to them rather than letting wise old men of money handle their gilt-edged investments for them. Shops, manufactured goods, discotheque clubs . . . Apple might eventually build on a worldwide scale. Rumors that the Beatles plan a vast network of clubs coast-to-coast across America have been grossly exaggerated by one or two entertainment papers but behind these blown-up stories lie a hard core of theoretical if not practical fact — and that hard core can be traced to the heart of the Apple itself!

Twenty-four year old, Dec Cluskey, last unmarried member of the famous harmony trio, The Bachelors, has admitted he'll have a wife before the New Year is very old. She is pretty blonde-haired dancing girl, Sandra Williams, 22, of Essex.

Sandie became the Irish Bachelor's steady date during the summer of 1966 when she was dancing in a season-long stage production in Blackpool with the Bachelors and Cilla Black toping the bill. Before that Sandie's name had been linked romantically with that of Liverpool singer, Billy J. Kramer, who was her constant escort following a series of one-nighter concerts which starred the Everly Brothers and Kramer.

Proposal

According to Sandie, her fiance proposed over dinner one night in a crowded restaurant "to stop me laughing at somebody over the other side of the room!"

The other Bachelors are Dec's brother Con Cluskey and John Stokes who are both married and have children.

There are few surprises among this year's winners in the *New Musical Express* Pop Poll. Elvis Presley and Tom Jones head the Male Singer sections, the Beatles, the Beach Boys and the Rolling Stones are the most popular Vocal Groups, Lulu and Dusty Springfield claim top places in the Female Singer department while poll voters judge the Bee Gees and Engelbert Humperdinck as the most promising new chart names of the year. Top singles are "A Whiter Shade of Pale" by Procol Harum and "All You Need Is Love" by the Beatles.

Monkee End?

"The Tail End Of Monkeemania?" asked the bald, blunt headline in *Disc And Music Echo* last week. Down the page the story continued: "At the BBC there is talk of ending the current Monkees series. Their records are no more sure of reaching number one than anyone elses. The early promise as their young socks galloped into 1967 seems to have petered out." Meanwhile "Daydream Believer" climbed very quietly from 21 to 18 in that week's *Disc And Music Echo* chart list.

Quote from Graham Nash of the Hollies: "All the nice people have moved down to Mexico. All the real Flower People have moved out of Haight Ashbury."

ROLLING STONES form Mother Earth Records and sign Marianne Faithfull as artist.

THE SEPER COMPANY
5273 Tendilla, Dept. T.O.
Woodland Hills, Calif.

SM. PEACE SYMBOL — NECK STRAP $1.25 P.P.

KRLA ARCHIVES

PICTURES IN THE NEWS

THE EVERLY BROTHERS, who opened San Francisco's FESTIVAL OF STARS at the Playboy Club, take time out to entertain Viet Nam veterans at Oak Knolls Naval Hospital. The boys took their music into the amputee wards and visited with the wounded.

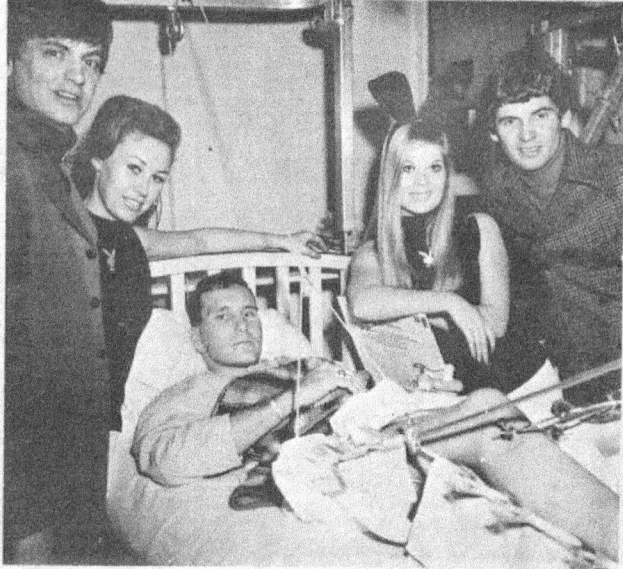

DON AND PHIL, and San Francisco Bunnies Sandee and Connie with Viet Nam casualty Cpt. Edward C. Burke, of Santa Ana, California.

TOKYO ... TRINI LOPEZ was welcomed American style ... at the Tokyo International Airport upon his arrival for a 15-day tour of Japan and the Far East. The advance ticket sales indicate SRO crowds from Tokyo to Manila and Sydney.

JERRY MOSS, President of A & M Records, and his partner, Herb Alpert, present Sergio Mendes with a Gold Record for sales of over one million copies on the album, "Herb Alpert Presents Sergio Mendes and Brasil '66. The album was produced by Alpert and arranged by Sergio Mendes.

KRLA ARCHIVES

IN MEMORIAM

The Bar-Kays

Jimmy King

Phalon Jones

Ronnie Caldwell

Carl Cunningham

KRLA ARCHIVES

IN MEMORY OF
OTIS REDDING

KRLA ARCHIVES

SPANKY AND OUR GANG: AN EXCEPTION

Young people may go out of their way to look and act differently, protest, and dress unusually with the end result that they look alike and sound alike. Spanky and Our Gang never bothered to get special props or wild costumes only because they are different . . . naturally. Their sound is different, their material is good . . . in short, Spanky and Our Gang are truly something new in the pop field.

Their repertoire covers every kind of music from Jugband tunes (Coney Island Washboard) to the Country-Western bag (Steel Rail Blues) to the folk-rock (Come and Open Your Eyes), with stops at musical comedy (Trouble in River City), from contemporary folk music (Suzanne) and modern pop (Lazy Day).

Time brings changes and in this case there is no exception. The group has made many changes, trying to discover where they want to go musically. They started as a trio, added lead guitar and vocal, Malcolm Hale and percussionist, John Seiter alias the "Chief," who also sings. Geoffrey Myers, who completes the present quintet, plays bass guitar and sings.

Friends

The group was close friends before getting together. Spanky has a blues-dixieland background and also sang with the New Wine Singers, Nigel toured the Country-Western circuit. Malcolm's background is classical and folk guitar; he also toured Viet Nam for the State Department. Geoff is the songwriter of the group; and the "chief's" background is from everywhere. All were former artists.

After the success of their first single, "Sunday Will Never Be The Same" the group was not happy doing the same material over and over again only because it was successful. They wanted to branch out in all musical directions, and because of this they have just recently announced the singing of their new independent producers, Stuart Scharf and Bob Dorough.

The group declared, "We do not want to be put into any one musical bag. We want to sing songs we dig." Mercury Records backed them to the hilt.

Spanky and Our Gang spend most of their time playing college campuses across the nation. They do a great deal of television including Ed Sullivan, Hollywood Palace, The John Davidson Special, The Tonight Show and many others. From the reaction of their record sales and personal appearances, they have lived up to everyone's expectations including Robert Shelton of the New York Times who wrote: "Spanky and Our Gang as they call themselves, are so refreshing an act and so versatile musically that the pop music scene is undoubtedly going to do some changing of format to keep up. Whatever the sources of its inspiration, the group is creative and original in its own right. Spanky and Our Gang seems likely to paint a mustache on the face of our pop music."

GLEN CAMPBELL ON HIS WAY

. . . the seventh son of a seventh son . . . born in Delight, Arkansas . . . from the time he was a small boy, music was his life . . . first love was guitar . . . then he discovered his voice . . . it turned out to be pleasing . . . but Delight, Arkansas is no place for a boy with talent . . . not if he wants to use it to entertain a lot of people . . . he was young . . . and headed west . . . to make his name known . . . he did it . . . slowly . . . first as a musician . . . creative guitarists are needed in the music hills of Hollywood . . . Glen became known as the best . . . then it was time to sing . . . and he did . . . first for anyone that would listen . . . then for several small record companies . . . then for the people at a big record company . . . they liked him . . . gave him a contract . . . happiness is a recording contract . . . now the boy from Delight could delight a lot of people . . . overnight success is rarely ever that . . . it took a while for Glen, too . . .

KRLA ARCHIVES

Who said the best things in life are free? If it's good it's worth what you have to pay for it. Whether in money, blood or heart—you pay. And these days, the going price on dreams is high. Jerry Butler has paid it. And listeners who have followed the balladeer down the years have heard him wrench the last ounce of soul from every love story he has told.

Now Available At:

KRLA ARCHIVES

HERB ALPERT'S NINTH

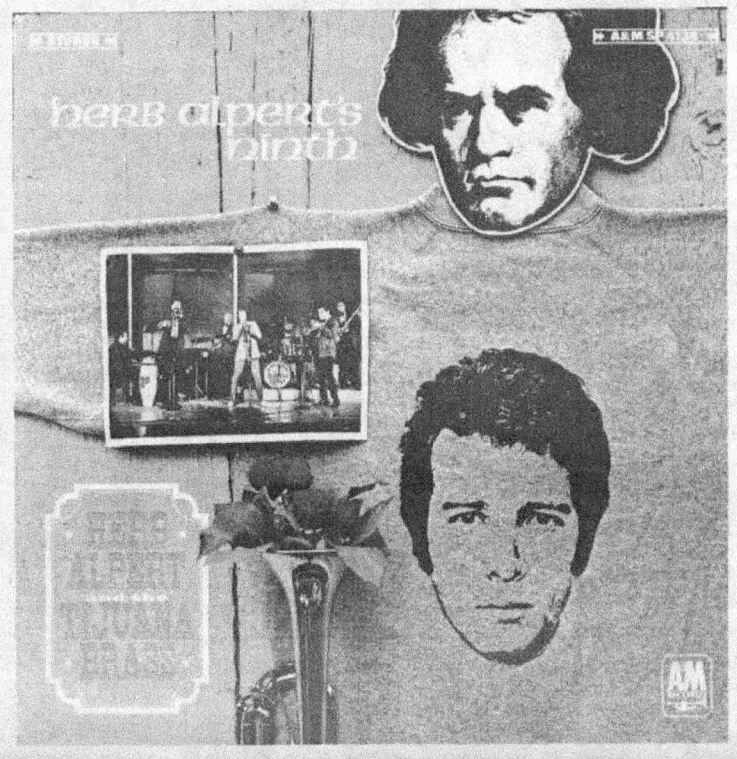

BEETHOVEN AS HE'S NEVER BEEN HEARD BEFORE

Now Available At:
MONTGOMERY WARD DEPARTMENT STORES

A SHOW STOPPER

AVAILABLE AT

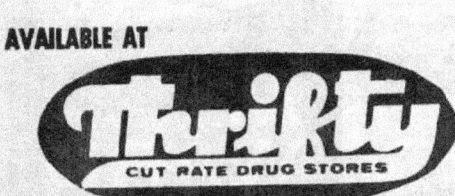

KRLA ARCHIVES

TROUBADOR REVIEW
CANNED HEAT

Tony Leigh

Canned Heat, a blues oriented group that bases itself in the Los Angeles area, opened at the Troubador to an enthusiastic audience. The response from the crowd was well earned. Combining the best of the funky blues sound with the electronic sound of pop music, Canned Heat created an impact that was solidly felt.

The group which has been popular in the city for many months now has changed drummers since their first album was released. The change has been more than beneficial. The new drummer named Fito de la Parra is completely fantastic and the equal of any of the best jazz drummers around. Adding more than just a driving beat to Canned Heat's music, de la Parra creates a whole sound of his own which totally integrates itself into the three other instruments being used. His solo which had the audience literally screaming from their seats was masterful.

The lead singer is, of course, Bob "The Bear" Hite. Large, friendly, and totally into the sound of the Blues, Hite is able to make the audience feel a part of what is going on on stage. There is no introspective playing with Canned Heat. Although there is super communication between musicians on stage, and they give the impression that they would rather be playing together as a group than do anything else, the audience is also brought into this feeling.

Playing the bass guitar was Larry Taylor. With Taylor it became a whole new instrument. On his solo he did things with that instrument that no one has really ever done before. Along with Al Wilson, also on guitar and Henry Vestine on guitar and a kind of harmonica, the sound was totally fantastic.

This group is completely able to play the finest solos and yet they are a totally integrated group which functions best as a unit. Any chance you get to see Canned Heat don't pass it up. Their sound and their personal magentism when playing could not possibly be recaptured on records. They need to be seen and heard in person; there is really nothing like Canned Heat.

LARRY "THE MOLE" TAYLOR

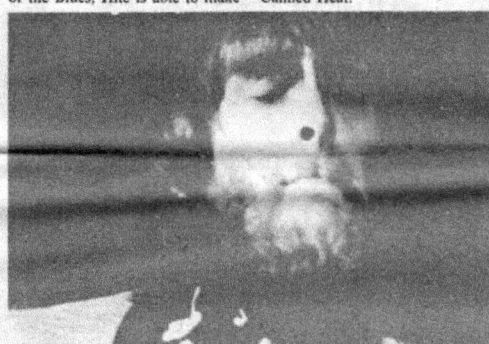
HENRY "SUNFLOWER" VESTINE

CANNED HEAT—(L. to R.) Bob "The Bear" Hite, Larry "The Mole" Taylor, Henry "Sunflower" Vestine, Al "Blind Owl" Wilson. Missing is new drummer Fito de la Parra.

NOW! **DEC. 25-31**
ASH GROVE
THE CHAMBERS BROTHERS
Oct. 13-22
8162 Melrose Ave. — OL 3-2070

AL "BLIND OWL" WILSON

5 DAYS ONLY
DEC. 27-31
BUTTERFIELD BLUES BAND
plus
THE SONGS OF LISA KINDRED

DOUG WESTON'S
Troubadour
CR. 6-6168
9081 Santa Monica Blvd.
at Doheny
★ HOOTENANNY EVERY MONDAY NITE ★

Jan. 5-7
HOYT AXTON
Jan. 23-Feb. 4
IAN AND SYLVIA
Jan. 9-21
ARLO GUTHRIE

LA CIENEGA	9039 SUNSET	NOW HAPPENING
1—EDDIE JAMES AND THE PACIFIC OCEAN	GAZZARRI'S #1 ON-THE-STRIP CR 3-6606 OL 7-2113 GAZZARRI'S #2 LA CIENEGA	1—THE JOINT EXTANT
2—ABSTRACTS		2—THE THIRD EYE
3—CHURCHILL DOWNS		
4—BURNSIDE	319 N. LACIENEGA	

KRLA ARCHIVES

What's Making Cos Succeed?

As little as three years ago, no one would have bet a nickel that a young comedian named Bill Cosby, who was born in Philadelphia, went to Temple University and majored in physical education would ever become Warner Brothers/7 Arts top selling record artist. Today no one is foolhardy enough to bet that Cos will not do anything he sets out to do.

To date, Bill's records have grossed a neat $30 million for the record company . . . he has been awarded two Emmys for his work in "I Spy" . . . has advanced the cause of Negro performers trying to break into steady starring spots on television . . . has broken concert records . . . is part of a corporation (Silver - Campbell - Cosby) currently busy producing its first full length motion picture . . . his first effort at commerical singing, "Little Ole Man," although no match for the vocal abilities of Frank Sinatra (or Elvis Presley, for that matter) stands an excellent chance of becoming a million-seller . . . he will soon be heard five times a week on his own radio show aired over 600 stations across the country . . . will star in his first movie as soon as he gets some time off from the ever-popular "I Spy."

Why Cosby?

So, what's making this Bill Cosby succeed where so many others have failed? His personality, intelligence, quick wit, luck, talent? A lot of all of these things, probably. But much more than that, what sets Bill apart, what makes him the performing giant he is, is his unique ability to be identifiable. Bill's humor is commonplace. It's a water bottle in the icebox, a football game in the street, a stick-shift drive on the hills of San Francisco, a tonsilectomy. Things that everyone—old or young, hip or unhip, male or female—can identify with, remember and enjoy. That's what makes Cos so special. He's immediately identifiable — to everyone past the age of seven.

Basic Truth

If you've ever seen Cosby on stage, you know this is his basic truth. His audience runs the gamut from diamond-ringed, blue-haired matrons to the long-haired, mini-skirted, I-am-utterly-cools... from tuxedoed over-35's to college football heroes. They're all there and they're all laughing at the wonderfulness that is Bill Cosby.

But it works two ways—they give and he gives back. Cosby needs his audience and is honest enough to admit it: "You cannot perform without an audience; I cannot perform without an audience. I can go on and say some stories, but I wouldn't know where, exactly, to go without an audience That's how heavily I lean on them."

No Insults

If an audience is cold (which is rarely the case with a Cosby audience) Bill does not insult them as so many comedians do when the laughs fail to come. He merely cuts his show. Without ever telling them they're a dead audience, he simply goes faster and leaves the stage earlier.

Although apparently with the world in his hip pocket, the young comedian-actor-singer does not expect to stay in the entertainment business more than another five years. Instead he intends to go back to his real love—young people. Bill Cosby wants to become a school teacher!

And not a teacher in a high class snob school, but a junior high school teacher. "I want to teach junior high school," says Cosby in all earnestness, "very lower, lower class level, because these kids need help. The teachers who teach in that area need a boost and I think that an entertainer giving up the stagelights and so on to come in and teach, without really wanting to wield a giant stick—a guy who just wants to come in there and do his job, do it quietly without sounding on everybody— I think it would give them a boost, give the students a boost, and perhaps lend an answer to some of the problems that exist in that area."

Part of Cos

That, then, is part of Bill Cosby —the man who successfully made it all the way from a lower class section of Philadelphia all the way up to a high class section of Los Angeles . . . and fully intends to end it teaching a junior high school class in a slum.

KENNY O'DELL: WRITER PRODUCER, SINGER

By Tony Leigh

"It's more difficult to produce your own record, but it's also a good deal more rewarding", stated 23-year-old Kenny O'Dell. "It takes more time, more energy and you have to rely on your own resources, without the concert help of other people. I do respect the opinions of the musicians on the set, but in the final analysis the decision is mine."

The decisions have proved to be the right ones, for O'Dell's single "The Beautiful People" is well up in the charts. His reputation as a writer was also solidified; the song has been covered by another popular singer.

"It's always flattering when somebody else records your music, but naturally, I think, you want to do it first. In this case, I think the cover has hurt us both, because the public has been split between the two offerings, and neither is going quite as far as it might otherwise have gone."

Reluctant Singer

Although Kenny would rather record the songs himself, conversely he is a rather reluctant pop singer. "I would rather stay behind the scenes and supervise other groups. Writing is my first interest, and making personal appearances, while I understand the necessity for them, becomes difficult when it cuts into my writing time. That has to comes first with me.

"I have played a lot of club dates, in lounges and things like that, but it was mainly to support myself while other things were developing for me. I like singing for people, but I don't really see my future in that area.

"I try to be honest when I sing. I remember when I was younger seeing a very popular 'teen idol' lip syncing for thousands of teenagers. I really think that is all wrong, you should try to reproduce the sound you make in the recording studio, and not fake it to an audience."

Lives in Vegas

Besides having a hit of his own, Kenny also wrote the single "Last Train to London" which has been recorded by the Rose Garden. But contrary to popular opinion, the song was not written for the Garden, but was originally written for Kenny himself.

"I like their recording of it, and I'm glad that it's so successful. But interestingly, it's quite different from the way I recorded it, the sound I had in mind." The sound he had in mind is about his new album "Beautiful People."

Kenny lives in Las Vegas, which he calls home, and plans to stay there. His lastest single and his new album were both recorded there.

KRLA ARCHIVES

Johnny Crawford Rides Again

By Tammy Hitchcock

Johnny Crawford, former Mousketeer, former child star of TV's the Rifleman, is presently embarking upon a singing career. His new record is called "Angelica" a very pretty, melodious tune that has been widely played. However, singing, and the pop scene are not Johnny's main interests; they still lie with acting and with a rather dangerous but fascinating sport.

"It's hard to say which I like better, between acting and singing. I like them both, and they're both so completely different. I guess I like acting a little bit more, because it's more involved. It's harder, and it takes longer than cutting a record."

One of Johnny's main interests is in Rodeos, and not as an observer, as these pictures indicate. "On my weekends I go to Rodeos. I do calf-roping and steer wrestling. I guess it just came naturally for me, because I've always had an interest on horses and horse sports."

"I did a couple of appearances at major Rodeos and working on the Rifleman brought me in contact with a good many professional cowboys. I became interested in the sport and took up calf-roping."

Good Horse

"In calf-roping you have to depend on your horse a great deal. No matter how good a cowboy is, he can't do it alone. You have to have a horse that can get to the calf without taking up too much time. Calves run awfully fast, some of them seem to fly."

"The first burst of speed is important for a horse, so you have to have one that doesn't get nervous while the calf takes its head start."

"After you get the calf, you have to have a good stop; and then he has to be able to keep the rope tight for you. So you can see you need a lot of help from your horse."

"The horse I have right now, I've raised since he was a colt. And I trained him myself, although I had a lot of advise and help from others on this count. Actually I think I learned as much from the horse as I taught him."

Working from the time he was five was an interesting experience, one that Johnny does not regret in the least.

"I think it was very good for me. I enjoyed it tremendously because most of the time I was working I was on a western series which couldn't have been better."

Adult Communication

It associated with mostly adults too, so it gave me a chance to talk to them, and communicate with them. A chance that not too many kids get today.

"I know I missed playing with other children my own age, but I think there were compensating factors."

Although Johnny has fond memories of the Rifleman series, he is not looking forward to doing another.

"Every actor gets tired of doing the same role over and over again. Especially after he's freelanced and had the opportunity to play many roles. Whenever I get to feeling that I was fed up with it though, I would sit down and count my blessings, think about how lucky I was to have it at all."

For the last two years Johnny has been in the army. He just got out this last Christmas. Fortunately in the army he was able to work in a field in which he was familiar. He was able to direct and produce training films for recruits. This activity took him all over the country, where he could observe all phases of the army. It also will help him in his career if he later decides to go into motion picture production.

Johnny Crawford has grown up, the child actor is there no longer. He is presently working on his future as an adult actor, singer and perhaps, future Rodeo champion.

THE AMERICAN BREED

AMERICAN BREED: BACK TO THE HARD ROCK SOUND

By Jacoba Atlas

Creating a sound that is totally hard rock and commercial is something that a good many groups strive for, and only a few manage to accomplish. Somehow, the driving beat that formed the basis for rock and roll in its infancy has alluded many of today's groups. Then, too, many other contemporary groups have abandoned that original sound in favor of more complex and intricate sounds, in many cases borrowing from India and the 12-tone scale developed by such 'classical' composers as Cage and Stockhausen. However, the American Breed, in the best traditions of their name, have remained faithful to the sound of America: the rock/blues sound that created rock and roll in the first place.

Originating in Chicago, this young, four man group has created a sensation in the mid-west that is finally spreading to the rest of the country. With hits like "Step Out of Your Mind" and now "Bend Me, Shape Me" the rest of the country is turning on to the sound of The American Breed.

Although there has been a good deal of discussion about what could be called "The Chicago Sound" the American Breed denies that there really is one particular sound to the city.

Gary Loizzo, who sings lead and plays lead guitar, states the "Pop music sound is too fickle to be really classified in one way. You just can't call all music coming from Chicago the "Chicago Sound."

Live Audiences

The group made their name performing for live audiences, first in their native city, and then throughout the mid-west. They describe their type of music as happy music.

"We try to create a sound that is happy and care-free", explained Gary, "we want people to be happy when they hear our music."

"That's one of the reasons, unlike other groups, we like to have everyone dancing to our music. Not just listening. I guess when you put a lot of work into a song, you want everyone to concentrate on it, and really hear it, but personally, even then, I would rather have them dancing," added Lee Graziano, who provides the driving beat that typifies the American Breeds' sound.

Charles Colabert, better known as Chuck backs this up by saying "we want to get everyone involved in what we are doing. That involvement from the audience is a result of how Gary works with them."

Participation

"I try to get them to participate. Usually I just start by having them clap with us, or something like that. We start with a number that will help that, something they know and like immediately like 'Land of 1000 Dances'," explained Gary.

Along with guitarist Alan Ciner, all four of the American Breed believe that it's essential to produce the same sound in person that they do in the recording studio. Although in sessions they can add a few instruments here and there when needed, they compensate for that loss when performing in person. There are no tricks with this band.

The American Breed is certain to have hit after hit. Their sound is the thing that has sold records since the beginning of the rock era. It is slick, interesting, moving, with a terrific beat. As long as there are people who dance and 'dig rock and roll,' there will be a need and an audience for the American Breed.

KRLA ARCHIVES

JAY and the TECHNIQUES SERVING THEIR TIME

Jay and the Techniques, riding high on the charts with their latest single, "Keep The Ball Rollin'," recently completed a week-long tour during which they entertained U.S. servicemen waiting to be sent to Viet Nam.

Throughout their visit to Army and Marine personnel at Fort Rucker in Alabama, Fort Bragg and Cherry Point Marine Base in North Carolina, and Fort Eustis and Quantico Marine Base in Virginia, they performed to capacity crowds, ate with the troops in mess halls and even accompanied the servicemen to the drill fields.

The seven-member group donated its services because, as their manager, Gene Kaye put it, "Several of the fellows who are currently 1-A draft status and know that in the future they may be called up felt that until they are asked to serve this is just one more way of serving their country."

And, said 26-year-old leader Jay: "In this era of draft card burnings I've never felt so honored as I did by performing before our country's fighting men.

Accompanying Jay on the tour were the other Techniques, Karl Llandis, 19; Chuck Crowl, 19; George Lloyd, 25; Ronnie Goosly, 18; Dante Danchow, 19, and John Walsh, 19. All of them are from the Allentown, Pa., area.

The outfit dazzled the servicemen with their fancy routines and repertoire of R&B songs, including their first national hit, "Apples, Peaches, Pumpkin Pie," and their latest, "Keep the Ball Rollin'."

"They just did a beautiful job," exclaimed Spec/5 Nick George, Professional Entertainment Director for Special Forces at Fort Eustis. "They had a way of handling themselves both on and off-stage that was just perfect."

Among the momentoes presented to Jay and the Techniques in appreciation of their efforts were a sterling silver serving tray and a letter of commendation from Col. S. M. Coggins, Assistant Chief of Staff at Fort Eustis. It reads:

"On behalf of the Commanding General, I would like to express the appreciation of the Command for your appearance at this installation on 15 October 1967.

"The enthusiastic response from the audience of United States Army soldiers and their dependents, generated by you and your All-Star cast, represented a significant contribution to service morale and welfare.

"Thank you for your voluntary contribution of time and talent and best wishes for continued success."

CAMELOT

The mythical legend of Camelot is one of the most beautiful love stories ever told; it is also one of the most idealistic political stories ever told. Alfred, Lord Tennyson immortalized it in his Idylls of the King, and countless others including T. E. White who wrote "The Once and Future King" have sought to re-create the legend in all its splendor.

Six years ago, Alan J. Lerner and Frederick Lowe took the T. E. White version of the legend and created the Broadway musical "Camelot." This year, Warner-Bros-7 Arts have taken that musical and turned it into a film under the direction of Joshua Logan.

This film is as disappointing as the material on which it is based is rewarding. It is difficult to say where the film has gone wrong, for certainly most people will find it thoroughly moving entertainment. Understandibly too, for the story itself is one of great passion, heart and humor. But these innate virtues only serve to make the overall picture more disappointing.

It is not so much that "Camelot" is a bad film, only that it could have been a great one, and unfortunately it does not even come close. Certainly the performances are excellent, were it not for the beauty and majesty of Vanessa Redgrave as Guenevere and the commanding performance of Richard Harris as King Arthur the entire film would have been hopeless. Their scenes together, especially in the second half are worth the entire film. Their performance of "What Do The Simple Folk Do" brings new and heartbreaking meaning to the familiar song. Both sing extremely well, and although Miss Redgrave does not have the polished voice of a professional singer her interpretation of the lyrics more than makes up for her lack of range.

Franco Nero, a newcomer to the screen, plays Lancelot du Luc, the young Frenchman who travels to the Court to aid the Round Table and only succeeds to bring about its downfall. He has one of those faces that will either appeal to you very much or not at all, but he does well with what he is given to do, and his love for Guenevere and hers for du Luc seems quite credible.

Unfortunately "Camelot," which was filmed in 70mm panivision contains no sweeping shots of England, no feeling for the country over which Arthur ruled. This is sadly due in part to the fact that the entire production except for the final battle scenes was shot at the Warner Bros-7 Arts studios in Burbank. But it is also due to back-lot sets, ridiculously false outdoor scenes, and a sparsely populated supporting cast.

Nevertheless, one should see the film, for it is not typical musical fare. The story is basically a tragedy and this in itself helps to raise the film above the mundane. The film is entertaining, it is moving, but it is also sadly disappointing. "Camelot" does not live up to the promise that it gives, nor does it live up to the overwhelming possibilities.

KRLA ARCHIVES

KRLA ARCHIVES

TURNING ON

SONG CYCLE (Warner Bros-7 Arts) Van Dyke Parks. *Vine Street, The All Golden, Pot Pourri* plus eight other tracks. "She made perfume in the bathtub" in a house on Vine Street in Los Angeles. This is an interesting album that somehow doesn't quite come off. It is, exactly as the name implies a song cycle: a continues song which conveys a solidified image and point of view. Van Dyke Parks is quite young, and perhaps his youth is one factor in the album's inability to really focus on something solid. This does not mean that the album is not worth hearing; on the contrary this is an important and different offering that deserves close attention. Creating an image of L.A. in the first cycle, Parks conjurs up visions of "hollywood where age is losing hold." This album has more of the flavor of an American pop opera, words and melody that work against the orchestration all blending into one another. One curious aspect of this album is that the whole thing slightly smacks of a massive put-on. "Won't you widows walk and wall amoung the willows . . . do-si-do." There is a marvelous song about Laurel Canyon which is just off the Sunset Strip and has become a sort of area known for its 'hippie homes'. "What's up in the Canyon will eventually come down." Is this album an evaluation of America and life as we do or don't know it, or is it really something very different? Listen and see if you can decide.

MOVING WITH NANCY (Reprise) Nancy Sinatra. *Got To Get Out of This Town, Up, Up and Away,* and *Friday's Child* plus eight other tracks. This is another slick offering from Nancy. As with all her other albums, this one is well produced and well performed, if you like this Sinatra's sound. There can be no disputing the fact that Nancy is rather slight on actual talent, but she compensates admirably for this lack by surrounding herself with talented people and knowing what is right for her and what isn't. The record is pleasing, sometimes moving, and always enjoyable. Nancy knows what sounds good, what has taste, and she conveys it with sincerity.

I FEEL LIKE I'M FIXING TO DIE (Vanguard) Country Joe and the Fish. *Janis, Magoo, Song* plus seven other tracks. *Janis,* is of course a lovely ballad dedicated to Janis Joplin of Big Brother and the Holding Company "into my mind the sound of her voice . . . we once were there." *Thought Dream* begins with an opening statement that sounds like a cross between Elmer Gantry and a circus barker. But the words are not light, it pleads, as a sort of chorus comes into the background "don't drop that H bomb on me, drop it on yourself, don't drop that H bomb on me." Then the whole thing blends into a sort of melodic offering conjuring up images of "scented air of summer nights" that slowly grows into foul smells. Incredible. The album is at once harsh, tender, loving, slightly brutal and always fascinating.

A giant (22"x28") Calendar Poster in black, white and red.

PLEASE SEND ME THE CALENDAR POSTER
I ENCLOSE $1.75 plus .25 Handling fo each.*

NAME_____
Address_____
City_____ State_____ Zip Code_____
*California Residents Please Include 5% Sales Tax

BEAT SHOWCASE

CELEBRATION

The Celebration, whose solid rock beat is on the Challenge label, are starting to move upwards.

The five-man group, consists of bearded Phil Parker on drums, Flip Arellano on trumpet, Steve King on sax and flute, Gary Bovine on lead guitar, and Eddie Beyer on organ.

They have already been set for appearances on the syndicated Woody Woodbury and Pat Boone television shows. Joey Bishop has been negotiating with them to make their network debut on his program.

They have also been set for a guest appearance on "Romp", a forthcoming ABC-TV young people's special, which they will tape during the week of Feb. 7. Pepsi Cola will sponsor.

GOOD & PLENTY: Living in a World of Make Believe

Beat Poster Shop

(Y) Maharishi
Also Available
(K) James Brown (S) Stones (P) Seeds (D) Dylan
(T) The Who (N) Jimi Hendrix

Send to: BEAT POSTER SHOP, 9000 Sunset, Suite 1000, Los Angeles, Cal. 90069

PLEASE SEND ME THE FOLLOWING POSTERS (LIST BY LETTER)
I ENCLOSE $1.75 plus .25 Handling for each*.

Name_____
Address_____
City_____ State_____ Zip Code_____
*California Residents Please Include 5% Sales Tax

UNIQUE SHADOW BOX FRAMES
MOD RECESSED LENSES
TWO-COLOR FRAMES
$4 Each*
*Calif. residents please add 5% sales tax
AVAILABLE IN:
Blue and White   White and Pink
Purple and White Red and White
Yellow and Black Red and Black
Designate Frame Color
SEND TO:
BEAT PUBLICATIONS
9000 Sunset, Suite 1000
Los Angeles, Calif. 90069

DEBS

KRLA ARCHIVES

FLOWER LADY
By Phil Ochs

Millionaires and paupers walk the hungry street
Rich and poor companions of the restless beat
Strangers in a foreign land strike a match with a tremblin' hand
Learned too much to ever understand.
Lovers quarrel, snarl away their happiness
Kisses crumble in a web of loneliness
It's written by the poison pen, voices break before they bend
The door is slammed, it's over once again
But nobody's buying flowers from the flower lady.
Poets agonize they cannot find the words
And the stone stares at the sculptor, asks are you absurd
The painter paints his brushes black, through the canvas runs a crack
Portrait of the pain never answers back
But nobody's buying flowers from the flower lady.
Soldiers disillusioned come home from the war
Sarcastic students tell them not to fight no more
And they argue through the night, black is black and white is white
Walk away both knowing they are right
But nobody's buying flowers from the flower lady.
Smoke dreams of escaping souls are drifting by
Dull the pain of living as they slowly die
Smiles change into a sneer, washed away by whiskey tears
In the quicksand of their minds they disappear
Still nobody's buying flowers from the flower lady.
Feeble aged people almost to their knees
Complain about the present using memories
Never found their pot of gold, wrinkled hands pound weary holes
Each line screams out you're old, you're old, you're old
But nobody's buying flowers from the flower lady.
And the flower lady hobbles home without a sale
Tattered shreds of petals leave a fading trail
Not a pause to hold a rose, even she no longer knows
The lamp goes out, the evening now is closed
And nobody's buying flowers from the flower lady.

THE PARTY
By Phil Ochs

The fire breathing rebels arrive at the party early
Their khaki coats are hung in closet near the fur
Asking hand outs from the ladies while they criticized the lords
Boasting of the murder of the very hands that pour
And the victims learn to giggle for at least they are not bored
And my shoulders had to shrug as I crawled beneath the rug and retuned my piano.
The hostess is enormous, she fills the room with perfume
She meets the guests and smothers them with greetings
And she asks how are you and she offers them a drink
The countess of the social grace who never seems to blink
And she promises to talk to you if you promise not to think
And my shoulders had to shrug as I crawled beneath the rug and retuned my piano.
The beauty of the hour is blazing in the present
She surrounds herself with those who would surrender
Floating in her flattery she's a trophy prize caressed
Protected by a pretty face sometimes cursed sometimes blessed
And she's staring down their desires while they're staring down her dress
And my shoulders had to shrug as I crawled beneath the rug and retuned my piano.
The egoes shine like lightbulbs so bright you cannot see them
Blind each other blinder than a sandbox
All the fury of an argument holding back their yawns
A challenge shakes the chandeliers the selffish swords are drawn
To the loser go the hangups, to the victor go the hangers on
And my shoulders had to shrug as I crawled beneath the rug and retuned my piano.
They travel to the table, the host is served for supper
And they pass each other down for salt and pepper
And the conversation sparkles as their wits are dipped in wine
Dinosaurs on a diet on each other they will dine
Then they pick their teeth and they squelch a belch saying
Darling you tasted divine
And my shoulders had to shrug as I crawled beneath the rug and retuned my piano.
Wallflower is waiting, she hides behind composure
She'd love to dance and prays that no one askes her
Then she steals a glance at lovers while her fingers tease her hair
She marvels at the confidence of those who hide their fears
Then her eyes are closed as she rides away with a foreign legionaire
And my shoulders had to shrug as I crawled beneath the rug and retuned my piano.
Romeo is reeling, counting notches on his thighbone
And my shoulders had to shrug as I crawled beneath the rug and retuned my piano.
The party must be over, even the losers are leaving
But just one doubt is nagging at my caustic mind
So I snuck up close behind me and I gave myself a kiss
And I led myself to the mirror to expose what I had missed
There I saw a laughing maniac who was writing songs like this
And my shoulders had to shrug as I crawled beneath the rug and retuned my piano.

THE EXTRAORDINARY MIND OF PHIL OCHS
By Jacoba Atlas

Phil Ochs, has packed concert houses from New York's famed Carnegie Hall to the Santa Monica Civic auditorium, has sung at Civil Rights Marches in Washington, and student rallies in Berkeley, has been called everything from a Saint to a charlatan, from a revolutionary to a nihilist, and is, in actuality, totally his own man.

As a protest song writer he is on a par with the best. His first two albums "I Ain't A Marching Anymore" and "All the News That's Fit To Sing" include topical and political satires and indictment. His latest album, "The Pleasures of the Harbor" seems at first to be a departure from his old style, but, according to Ochs himself, it is not.

"I never wrote them (protest songs) for a purpose. I write everything as it moves me to write. The only question is if a song artistically successful, not is it politically successful.

"But over the years it has turned out that some people have been affected poltically by these songs. As I go around to do concerts I met people who come backstage and say that they have changed their minds because of the Peace movement or civil rights because of a song.

"I'm happy when it happens, but I've never intended that.

Lyrical Songs

"With my new album, it's just that I had this lyrical stretch of writing and I wanted to put them together in a package and orchestrate them in a fairly classical manner.

"I like the use of orchestration in this album. I think it varies from song to song as to how effective orchestration can be. It's a matter of getting the right arrangements. The kind of chord structures that I use lend themselves to other instruments.

"But I still come on stage with a guitar and my voice. The good thing about 'Harbor' Album is that I didn't change my style at all. The arrangements were written around what I normally do, so even with the complexities of the 'Cruxifixion's' arrangement, I can still do a stage performance that sounds the same.

Kennedy & Christ

"That song covers a lot of ground sociologically and politically, and historically. On the Kennedy level, when he gets killed in the song, the arrangement starts to go into dissonents and go into all these things that I think really reflects the world of chaos which is what happened. But the song isn't just about Kennedy, it's also about Christ and hero slaying. It covers all martyrs.

Film Concept

"People have likened the song 'Pleasures of the Habor' to a movie, and although that wasn't really the intent, it did happen. Actually, before I ever thought about doing an orchestrated album. I walked around talking about 'Pleasures of the Harbor' as a film. Then when we got to making a record of it, it was scored like a movie. That's one of the concepts of the album.

"The album has a few concepts. It is an attempt to create a total sound experience. It's not designed as a pop album; I wanted to reach all age groups. I don't think the songs are much different from the last album, they are just extended from it, the next period of the writer, you might say.

"I had these songs over a year before I recorded them. I wanted to do a classical album, but not a straight classical album. I wanted to relieve it with humor and other musical instruments like a honky-tonk piano and dixieland.

"I knew the 'Crucifixion' would be the last cut because it is the heaviest number, and I also knew I wanted a surreal arrangement of it. I also wanted the album to be very movie conscious, because I consider this more and more a movie age.

"Part of the inspiration for the album came from a movie. An old John Ford film called 'The Long Voyage Home' based on plays by Eugene O'Neill with John Wayne. I saw this movie when I was a kid, and it stuck in my memory for a long time. And I had the melody for 'Harbor' in my head, and all of a sudden that scene with Thomas Mitchell carrying back John Wayne to the ship came into my head, and they came together in that way. So the album was inspired by a movie.

"The album reaches its climax with the 'Crucifixion'. The cuts gather strength because of where they are placed. I would have been disastrous to put 'Harbor' next to 'I've Had Her.' It's a very sequential album.

Total Experience

"In the future I want to make movies. Movies are the art form of today, actually, a cross between movies and music. Those are the two main art forms of this generation. Films are this because they're a perfect marriage of art and science. It's the urge to create the total experience.

"Too little is being done with films, it's a very frustrating form. Kids sit around on college campuses and high school too where kids are getting into films, and they realize the ridiculousness of the movie situation.

"They have this mass subconscious feeling that what is on the screen is much lower than what could be on the screen.

"'Bonnie and Clyde' was a certain break through because it was done against all the rules. There is nothing stronger than an idea whose time has come, and Warren Beatty had that thing going for him.

"Another breakthrough is the 'Battle of Algeries', I think all young people should *demand* to see this film, because it is one of the all time great films. Much better than 'Bonnie and Clyde' but outside of New York it just isn't playing.

End of Folk

"What happened to folk music was that it reached its saturation point. It was aired and commercialized out of existance. That's what's happening to pop music today. The standards are definitely dropping in pop music from what they were in 1965 when the Beatles, Stones and Dylan were doing those fantastic things, and they were new.

"Now none of the new people are anywhere near that quality, all the groups who have made it this year and last, well there is no value to any of them.

"I think one of the most important records has been Procol Harum's 'Whiter Shade of Pale' because it combined classical with R and B. I'm hoping the new trend in pop music will be towards classical.

"A similar thing happened to pop music in the 1950's with Elvis and the rest. Then from about 1958 to 1961 it was commercialized out of existance with the Dick Clark syndrome, you know, Fabian and Frankie Avalon. Buying and selling the market the way they did.

"Then folk happened, and it got commercialized into the Beatles things which was a big jump in quality. Then with the Beatles up to about 1965, now this double revolution is being bought out and sold by groups that are making records now. It's all a cycle.

"We're going through bad times now, but people will demand better music, and the bad will be weeded out. I never really worry about music in that sense it seems to have a life force of its own."

So does Phil Ochs.

KRLA ARCHIVES

LSO-1147 STEREO

The NEW Broadway Cast Recording
DAVID MERRICK presents
PEARL BAILEY

RCA VICTOR
DYNAGROOVE
RECORDING

featuring
CAB CALLOWAY

Book by
MICHAEL STEWART

Music and Lyrics by
JERRY HERMAN

Based on the Original Play by Thornton Wilder

Scenery Designed by OLIVER SMITH · Costumes by FREDDY WITTOP · Lighting by JEAN ROSENTHAL · Dance and Incidental Music Arrangements by PETER HOWARD · Musical Direction by SAUL SCHECHTMAN · Orchestrations by PHILIP J. LANG

Re-Staged by LUCIA VICTOR
Dance Assistant JACK CRAIG

Original Production Directed and Choreographed by
GOWER CHAMPION

A DAVID MERRICK and CHAMPION-FIVE INC. PRODUCTION
Produced for Records by George R. Marek and Andy Wiswell

PEARL BAILEY'S DOLLY IS SUPERB!

AVAILABLE AT

KRLA ARCHIVES

CLASSIFIED

REACH COSMIC AWARENESS without drugs—help save mankind from destruction. Write for free booklet, "Cosmic Awareness Speaks." SERVANTS OF AWARENESS, Box 115E, Olympia, Washington.

SLEEP LEARNING, self hypnosis. Details, strange catalog free! Nutosuggestion, Box 24 BT, Lympia, Washington.

WILD POSTERS, far-out bumper stickers, buttons! Crazy Labels, Box 21-M, Olympia, Washington.

Sarah of Compton: Gee thanks loads . . . NEIL of Santa Monica! 1967

"DOCTOR" SMITH STINKS —Jeff Dumas

Happy birthday darlin' Davy. Love, Sherry

The PAGE V ARE ALIVE, and more!

The SOUTHE is Rising

RON HENLEY: Belated Happy Birthday

Dave Ellis: Every girl in school likes you. Your daughter

Ralph Magoo is beautiful.

The Blue Maggos are!

Monkees Fan Club, Pennsylvania Chapter, write: 260 East Avon Road, Parkside, Pennsylvania 19015

Free: Liverpool Five Club, 8135 Rectr Drive, St. Louis, Missouri 63134

Merry Christmas, BEATLES

Out-a-site Liverpool Five

Is Korny Orvil real? Dudley

my "DEAN" let it all hang out! Luv you—Char

Mr. Cape—Marty

Happy Birthday KURT NOLTE—love, ME

Happy New Year to Don Wayne, Joey Paige, Everly Brothers, Redondo Beach Fans

HAPPY BIRTHDAY TO JIM MORRISON OF THE DOORS FROM KAREN

MARK LINDSAY is the greatest thing that ever happened to Denver!

The groovy BUCKINGHAMS were a smash at the Cheetah, Chicago.

Put some warmth into your life: try CANNED HEAT

Melody I luv you—Eddie

Joe is a Honey Chicky Baby Doll. Love always, Me

THE BEAT will accept only personal messages in the classified section. We will print names but not addresses or phone numbers.

Rates are cheap! Only 10 cents per word.

Your deadline for the next issue is: Jan. 13, 1968.

---

please send me BEAT

26 issues only

$3 per year

Mail to: BEAT Publications
9000 Sunset Blvd.
Los Angeles, California 90069

☐ New Subscription
☐ Renewal (please enclose mailing label from your last BEAT)
I want BEAT for ☐ 1 year at $3.00 or ☐ 2 years at $5.00
I enclose ☐ cash ☐ check ☐ money order
Outside U.S.—$9 per year

* Please print your name and address.

Name_____
Street_____
City_____
State_____ Zip_____

The 'Controversial?' Daisy Chain

The Daisy Chain is an unusual group who is making quite a name for themselves in the Los Angeles area. By playing such clubs as the Cheetah, and the private, star studded club The Daisy (no connection to the group) these four girls are attracting a good deal of attention

A few people consider the Daisy Chain controversial, perhaps you can tell why by looking at them. What you can't see is that they come on stage wearing long robes and no shoes. But the girls insist that they are not doing this to attract attention. "We wear the clothes that we want to wear. We didn't decide to dress the way we do because we wanted to attract attention," stated lead guitarist Shele Lee.

"Actually we started out not wearing any make-up on our faces, and then we started wearing just one little flower, and from there the whole thing evolved," added Sherry Scott, organist.

The girls realize that they face a tough time convincing people that they have something to say—or sing. Girl groups have never been noted for reaching the top ladder of success in this country.

"I think to a certain extent, girls resent us. They come to dances to get to meet boys and then these girls come on stage and they see us as competition. Which is really too bad. Actually, we have come up against quite a bit of hostility," explained Shele.

"When we played the Daisy club in LA the response was a bit better because I think, the girls who were there were professionals themselves, so they understand our situation," she added.

The group which also includes Dee Dee Lea on drums, and Rosemary Lane on base guitar, states that they like doing concerts better than anything else.

"It's great being able to play for a live audience, and get the response from them."

They insist that they want to be judged not on their musical merits dress. The proof is in the listening . . .

COUNTRY JOE AND THE FISH, one of the most popular groups to come out of the music scene in San Francisco. The new album, "Feel Like I'm Fixing to Die," is already rising on the charts.

KRLA ARCHIVES

KRLA ARCHIVES

SKYROCKETING RECORDING COSTS

25¢

KRLA BEAT

Edition

JANUARY 27, 1968

BEE GEES ASSET TO POUND

KRLA BEAT

Volume 3, Number 21   January 27, 1968

The Smothers Last Season?

This may be the last season for the Smothers Brothers on CBS-TV. According to Tom and Dick Smothers, they are completely at odds with the network over the problem of censorship.

"Lots of people say they will quit when things get tough with a network and then nothing happens," said brother Tommy, "but we are really serious about this. Trouble is that they want us to do a program that pleases everybody, but we don't and can't work that way. We hold too many strong beliefs on certain matters."

The Smothers boys have an ultimatum for the network. "Unless the entire approach to censorship is changed, then this will be our last series. We think the company will come around, but one of the things they will have to do is to allocate us our own program practices official," Tommy admitted.

When their current show first hit the nation, their "social comment" was rather hidden behind a barrage of comics, but now the two brothers can't seem to get through a show without taking a swip at President Johnson or the war in Vietnam.

The fate of the Smothers Brothers and the CBS network remains to be seen and the question of the hour has to be: just how much will CBS lose if Tommy and Dick Smothers depart?

BEATLE RINGO STARR and his wife, Maureen, make a colorful departure from the Rome airport. Ringo had just finished several weeks of filming on "Candy" in which he plays the role of a Mexican gardener.

WILL THIS BE the last season for Tom and Dick Smothers?

THE HIGH COST OF RECORDING

The high cost of recording keeps getting higher all the time. Experimentation, electronics, overdubbing all require hours in the studio; hours that mean staggering costs for both the record company and the producer.

The Beatles are of course famous for this. One estimate for the time spent on "Sgt. Pepper's Lonely Hearts Club Band" reaches as high as 900 hours. The Fifth Dimension's new LP cost close to $40,000 while the Association's album ran as high as $80,000.

One independent producer blames this trend on the Beatles themselves. Now other groups want to follow suit and spend hours in the actual recording studio rehearsing. A recording studio rental usually runs about $60 an hour.

One label, who is slightly fed up with the whole situation has sought to limit the time a new group can spend on one album. It has been suggested that the Jefferson Airplane had completed their third album when they found out how much time the Beatles spent on "Magical Mystery Tour," and the Airplane promptly went back to the studio to over dub, add layers of sound and echo into tracks.

Another problem with these new groups who know nothing about the old three-hour recording schedules, is that they tie up the sound studios for weeks at a time. Capitol for instance will open its studios on Saturday on a regular basis instead of a special week-end schedule as they had previously done.

One other factor that tends to raise the cost of recording is the fact that most groups obtain their sound through trial and error. One sound will lead to another and so consequently they have to hear themselves on playback, and this makes rehearsing in an auditorium useless. They need the taping equipment to hear if their concepts are valid.

With all these drawbacks the companies are still signing the San Francisco groups and other urban groups whose sound is intricate and complicated. Just recently Capitol signed the Steve Miller Blues Band and The Quick Silver Messenger Service. If the records sell, and sell well, the company is able to recoup the high cost of recording; however, if one album that has taken week after week to record fails, the record company runs into deficit spending.

WAS IT WORTH IT?

KRLA ARCHIVES

LETTERS TO THE EDITOR

TIPS FROM STARS

Dear BEAT:

As you probably know, the Beatles have a new album out featuring such hits as "Penny Lane," "Hello Goodbye," "All You Need Is Love" and "Strawberry Fields." Plus some new songs such as "Flying" and "Blue Jay Way." I hope you cover this album as well as "Sgt. Pepper."

I really dig your paper but what about something on Cream, Five Americans, Yardbirds, Beach Boys, Donovan and the Turtles? As you probably know, many of your readers play instruments (I play lead guitar for a group called the Blue Society, in which I've penned all our songs). Well, anyway, how about a column on tips from the stars on how to play guitar, drums, etc.

Raymond Tasffe

By Bread Alone

Dear BEAT:

I've been subscribing to the BEAT for the past two years and when my current subscription runs out I think I'll subscribe again. You have the only teen publication which is in the least bit interesting. I don't think anybody really cares what their favorite likes to eat for breakfast. Instead we care about what they think... musically, politically, and personally. Which is what you write about.

My only complaint (and it's a big one) is that you don't write enough. Lately, half of your pages are filled with ads! Please go back to how you used to be..., a lot of stroies and hardly any advertisements.

Thank you for taking the time to read this.

Mark Perina

It's not by bread alone that the BEAT prospers, you know Mark!
The Editor

Never Enough

Dear BEAT:

I enjoy your magazine very much and read it as often as I can. Please have more information on the Beatles. I don't care what anybody says—they are not "out." If they were "out," then there would not still be so much controversy going on about them. I think that they're a great group—they always have been and, in my opinion, always will be.

Donna Martin

Beat Publications, Inc.

Executive Editor .... Cecil J. Tuck
Publisher .... Gayle Tuck
Editor .... Louise Criscione
Assistant Editor .... Jacoba Atlas

Staff Writers
Bobby Bovino   Ron Koslow
Tony Leigh   Shirley Poston

Contributing Writers
Tony Barrow   Sue Barry
Eden   Bob Levinson
Jamie McClusky III   Mike Masterson

Photographers
Ed Caraeff   Jerry Hess

National Advertising Representative
Sam Chase Assoc., Inc.
527 Madison Avenue
New York, New York 10022
(212) PL 5-1668

Advertising Director ..... Dick Stricklin
Business Manager .... Judy Felice
Subscriptions .... Diane Clatworthy

Distribution
Miller Freeman Publications
500 Howard Street, San Francisco, Calif. The BEAT is published bi-weekly by BEAT Publications, Inc., editorial and advertising offices at 9000 Sunset, Suite 1000, L.A., California 90069. U.S. bureaus in Hollywood, San Francisco, New York, Chicago and Nashville; overseas correspondents in London, Liverpool and Manchester, England. Sale price 25 cents. Subscription price: U.S. and possessions $5 per year; Canada and foreign rates, $9 per year. Second class postage prepaid at Los Angeles, California.

OR

DOES IT MATTER

Dear BEAT:

I am a 16 year old BEAT reader and pop music lover who has only one complain—I am sick and tired and completely fed-up with the filthly-looking groups.

Please tell me why they think that long, straggly, filthy dirty hair and equally filthy skin is attractive to female? I am one female who thinks it is sickening. And I am not alone.

Water is free and no person is so poor that he cannot wash himself and his hair and his clothes.

No wonder the adults, or the establishment if you prefer, think we teenagers are nuts to like people like that. We are!!

I say let's go back to clean-looking groups. Keep long hair if you like, only please learn to wash it.

Mary Kirby

FORUM

The opinions and ideas expressed in the Letters to the Editor or The Forum sections of our paper are not necessarily the opinions of The BEAT. However, we do feel that this is a free country in which each individual is entitled to hold and express his/her opinions and beliefs. Unfortunately, a limited amount of space prevents us from printing every letter submitted to The BEAT. Consequently, we are forced to print only a general cross-section of the mail we receive.

The Editor

REMNANT MAN MAKE YOUR STAND

Now, prancing words pirouette pass his mental armor
From an unfamiliar familiar face lashin';
 lashin' out in shotgun fashion.
Remnant man make your stand.
Remnant man do you have a plan?
Now, flashing light on the dormant monster that hides in the caves
 of the mind.
A monster that when aroused at the tender walls it mauls.
Remnant man make your stand.
Remnant man have you done what you can?
Now, beads of sweat break the calm facade releasing broken
 words with repeated syllables.
Lips now quiver and hands dance, he holds his stance.
Remnant man make your stand.
Remnant man do you have feet of sand?
Now, scraps of verbiage fail to mend the functionless
 mental shield.
Penetra'ed by thoughts it crashes to the dust echoing defeat
 and retreat.
Remnant man make your stand.
Remnant man why give up your land?
Now, a twist of the lip strips the man of the words that were
 his plan.
Engulfed by agony he runs away, a little more chipped away.
Remnant man make your stand.
Remnant man have you done all you can?
Remnant man make your stand.
Remnant man can I len you a hand?

—Gerald Santos

THE YOUNG LION

The young lion taught me to live
The young lion taught me to love
The young lion strayed from here
Leaving behind what seemed to be
All he had ever known.
He preached of all the hate of men
Of their worthless beatings and plunders
Of the sweet earth that gave them life
Only to be ripped and torn apart in heartless revenge.
He preached of all the wondrous lands
That lie beyond the horizon
He said one day when all war ceased
That all mankind would live in peace
Together in these heavens.
The young lion could not understand
The dreadful destruction of man
And all too soon he found it true
That in the cold and cruel world
There was no place for him.
The young lion escaped with disillusion
"There must be greater heights to reach —
There must be greater depths to fall to"
He cried out in pain and went alone
To seek, to conquer the unknown.
The young lion all afire
Once more gives all he has
Like spirals of flame his voice trails on
And all ablaze it echoes on —
But the young lion is gone.

—Eileen Stewart

KRLA ARCHIVES

AROUND the WORLD

SIGN SANDPIPERS FOR SAN REMO

LOS ANGELES — The Sandpipers have been asked to appear for the first time at the international San Remo Song Festival in San Remo, Italy on February 1, 2 and 3.

The Sandpipers will perform "Cuando M'Innamoro" at the festival. The group (Mike Piano, Jim Brady and Richard Shoff) met in 1956 when they were all singing with the Mitchell Boys Choir.

The biggest hit to date was the phenomenally successful "Guantanamera." Both the single and the album by the same name were on the Italian record charts and the album has achieved well over one million sales around the world.

DONOVAN: A NEW STYLE

LONDON — Donovan has come a long way from "Mellow Yellow." In the dedication of his new album, "A Gift From A Flower To A Garden," Donovan has urged all young people to stop the use of drugs.

"I call upon every youth to stop the use of all drugs and banish them into the dark and dismal places. For they are crippling our blessed growth."

Donovan, who has just completed a two month tour of the United States, began a whole new style of pop concerts by causing the overflow audiences to sit in silence and listen to what he was saying rather than jump up and down and scream . . . and miss the whole point.

Presley Car In Australia

SYDNEY—Elvis Presley's Gold Car seems to get around much more than the singer/actor himself! The custom built Cadillac, which has been on tour throughout the United States, was shipped to Australia for a visit to all this country's major cities.

Viewers' donations are to be given to the National Benevolent Society. Elvis, who has long been noted for giving very generously to charities, has had the car filled with hundreds of toys and stuffed animals as a personal gift to various children's orphanages in Australia.

The Gold Car is really something to see. It's painted with forty coats of translucent diamond dust paint, features a portable television, record player, two telephones and a stereo tape machine.

Tentative plans are also being discussed to exhibit the car in other foreign countries, again with all the money raised going to charity.

THE SANDPIPERS are set for San Remo Festival.

Bizarre Set For Special

HOLLYWOOD — Harper's Bizarre, the group who rose to national fame last year with such hits as "Chattanooga Choo Choo," has been set as the first group for the ABC-TV music special, "Romp."

"Romp" is an hour-long color special which is scheduled for airing in April. The Harper's Bizarre were chosen for the special because the producers consider them to be the first group in the world that has adapted the sounds of yesterday's standards to the Top 40 pop sounds of today. For example, "Chattanooga Choo Choo" was a smash hit in the 1940's . . . and 1967!

The Bizarre will tape their part of the special in Nassau. David Winters is director, Al Burton is the show's producer and Burt Rosen is the executive producer.

PEOPLE ARE TALKING ABOUT a certain duo attempting to bow out gracefully . . . a member of a top pop group acting so high-hat with the members of another top and more talented group and wondering what he's going to do when his pretty balloon bursts . . . what highly successful comedian sent the strangest Christmas message and trying to decide if it was a joke or what

. . . "Darlin' " not sounding at all like the Beach Boys . . . the criticism following the debut of the Beatles' television special and wondering why the Beatles insisted upon doing it all themselves . . . Lulu making it number two in a row . . . the question being who will figure it out—not who will answer . . . whatever happened to Tom Jones' plans to play all the big U.S. night clubs —in fact, wondering what's happened to Tom Jones

. . . the Buckinghams coming back time after time . . . who are the Human Beinz and who flunked spelling . . . why we haven't seen the Dave Clark Five in months . . . now that the Lettermen are back on the charts, what about the Four Preps . . . what's happening with the Jefferson Airplane . . . how many of these publicity-stunt "arrests" we are going to be blessed with—especially now that the press is wise to the gimmick

. . . the one sure thing that success means to the Association is plenty of travel . . . the Young Rascals groovin' at the Troubador when they were last in Los Angeles—also the Whiskey . . . who put the anchor on "Itchycoo Park" . . . how many follow-ups the Stone Poneys can hope to achieve . . . what a surprise John Fred & His Playboy Band were to everyone — themselves included . . . what this year is going to bring

. . . whether or not there will be a Pop Festival in 1968 and if there is, how successful or disasterous it is going to be . . . when the Supremes are going to get their next number one . . . how sweet it is to have Bob Dylan back and working again . . . Country Joe and the Fish bombing out something terrible at the Blue Law

. . . Lulu bagging the number one spot on the Billboard list of 1967's top records . . . the secret behind getting an album way up in the charts but failing to ever register with a single . . . Arlo Guthrie doing all right for himself . . . whether or not "Incense And Peppermints" are ever going to fall off the record charts

. . . how the Dave Clark Five will do the second time around . . . those in the 'know' predicting that this is the last season for the Monkees on television . . . when Aretha Franklin is going to miss . . . whether or not Nancy Sinatra will now star in her own major motion picture.

KRLA ARCHIVES

BEATLES IN TV CONTROVERSY

By Tony Barrow

A violent storm of controversy surrounded the London unveiling of "Magical Mystery Tour," the Beatles' first self-made TV movie. When the show was screened by the BBC on December 26, the switchboard at the TV company's London headquarters was jammed with calls from baffled viewers who didn't understand what "Magical Mystery Tour" was all about.

General reactions were unexpectedly varied and amongst the press critics opinion was sharply divided.

In *The Sunday Times*, Hunter Davies described the film as "excellent entertainment, funny, clever and very professional looking." He went on: "They went into it all with their eyes closed to all the traditions, ignorant of all the ridiculous conventions which have ham-strung almost every British film director who ever wanted to make a film exactly as he wanted."

Too Chaotic

In the *Daily Mirror*, Mary Malone's view was that "it was chaotic." She wrote: "Too Toot Tootsie John, Paul, George and Ringo as film makers. It's hello—and goodbye."

In the *Sun*, Richard Last called it "a bore based on the proposition that improvisation and random selection are a valid substitute for organized art."

In the *New Musical Express*, Norrie Drummond hailed it as "a most entertaining film" with "extremely clever" sequences for the musical numbers. He went on: "They break many of the rules which established directors stick to but this only seems to add to the delightful, free and easy atmosphere."

The rest of the musical trade press was just as enthusiastic as the *New Musical Express*, "Ringo emerges in this hour-long fairytale as a delightful comedian with a real touch of brilliance" decided Penny Balentine in *Disc and Music Echo*.

Record Mirror reviewer Derek Bokwood wrote that "there was comedy, pathos and some beautiful fantasy scenes—all held together by the multi-colored magical mystery bus."

Must Be Color

It is worth nothing here that the more favorable press reviews of the show were written by critics who saw "Magical Mystery Tour" in color. Inevitably special color effects play a major part in the show's fantasy sequences.

In television and newspaper interviews the following day, Paul McCartney attempted to clarify the situation. "The show was made up of a lot of different scenes we like the look of" he said. "If people were looking for a plot they were bound to be disappointed. We used the excuse of a Mystery Tour to string together all the bits of Magic. We thought people would understand. We thought the title itself was explanation enough.

The trouble is if people don't understand they say 'A lot of rubbish' and switch off. We will make another film. We learned a lot and making another film will be a challenge."

By the end of December two and a half million copies of the Beatles' "Magical Mystery Tour" record and book package had been sold in Britain and America. The cartoon version of the "Magical Mystery Tour" story in the book which accompanies the album differs from the TV movie version in various minor ways. For one thing the scenes are in a different sequence and the book includes a couple of scenes which had to be excluded from the film to bring the screening time down to fit a one-hour program schedule. The main deletion is the "What a Marvelous Lunch!" segment including "Happy Nat's Happy Dream."

Despite the mixed reaction to the initial screening, "Magical Mystery Tour" had a repeat BBC showing in color on January 5 throughout the U.K.

My own feeling is that some viewers were looking for too much reality in a film which relied upon the magic of fantasy, the mystery of unfamiliar happenings. Maybe some folk were a little afraid of the unfamiliar. At any rate "Magical Mystery Tour" is being accepted all over the world as an important and successful experiment in TV moviemaking. And where experiments are concerned you'll always encounter opposition.

ON THE BEAT
By Louise Criscione

The Vanilla Fudge did a very nice thing this Christmas. They played a benefit concert for cerebral palsy victims. The group played to a capacity audience of 3000 in the Action House on Long Island and commented after the performance that it was a "good show for a good cause."

The Fudge's second album, "The Beat Goes On," should be released right about now and according to their manager "is another experiment by the Vanilla Fudge to expand the musical possibilities of a four-piece group." A complete understatement since the album spans four centuries of musical styles!

Bob Dylan is back! After a year's absence, the singer/composer has recorded a new album in Nashville and all selections are new. The cover features three Indians with Dylan in the middle. "Blonde On Blonde," was Dylan's last new-material album and that was released in May of 1966.

It appears that we have another Simon in the music business. Paul Simon's younger brother, Eddie, has been signed to an MGM recording contract. Perhaps you caught Eddie (along with Paul) on a recent Kraft Music Hall.

The recording team of Peaches and Herb, who have had several hits in a row, has changed members. The original Peaches, Francine Day, has been replaced by Marlene Mack.

There were no heated arguments involved . . . Francine just decided that the exhausting schedule of the duo was too much for her. She says she would much rather stay closer to home (Washington, D.C.) and concentrate on a career of her own. The new Peaches was formerly lead singer for a group called the Joytones.

The Young Rascals did all right for themselves at Madison Square Garden. They grossed $65,000 and drew 16,000 fans for the show. The concert marked the first time that the Rascals were backed with a full orchestra. Another first was the appearance of Rascal Eddie's brother, David, who is also a guest singer on the Rascals latest album, "Once Upon A Dream."

It's interesting to note that Aretha Franklin, the "over-night" favorite female singer of 1967, spent five long years making records that never quite happened. Then in 1967 she signed with Atlantic Records and has had four solid single hits in a year — "I Never Loved A Man," "Respect," "Baby, I Love You" and "Chair of Fools." An overnight star Aretha is not . . . the top female vocalist of 1967 she definitely is!

KRLA ARCHIVES

PICTURES IN THE NEWS

GEORGE HARRISON is the last Beatle to attempt a solo venture. He will write the entire score for an English movie, "Wonder Wall." The film will have its London premiere in the late Spring or early Summer.

IT'S ALWAYS NICE to see at least one pop star admit that he is a married man when so many try to hide the fact. Mitch Ryder is one artist who doesn't. To prove it here's a photo of Mitch at home in Detroit with his family (wife Sue, daughter Dawn, Jenny the spaniel and Puff the cat). Mitch receives some helpful hints from his daughter when it comes to his new songs. "If Dawn doesn't like a song she puts her hands over her face and sits down in the corner!"

THE BEE GEES are now officially recognized as a major financial asset to Britain. When the two Australian members of the group, Vince Melouney and Colin Peterson, were recently threatened with deportation after their working permits had expired, dozens of fans arrived by helicopters in the grounds of the Prime Minister's home in the Scilly Isles. They carried signs saying "don't deport the Bee Gees — they are important dollar earners." Mr. Wilson ordered an immediate inquiry and after discovering that the group is replacing the Beatles as Britain's big dollar earning attraction he instructed Home Secretary Roy Jenkins to rescind the deportation order.

KRLA ARCHIVES

Herman Nabs Choice Role

By Tony Barrow

Peter (Herman) Noone is due to fly into Los Angeles within the next few weeks to begin work on a 90-minute TV spectacular which NBC-TV is expected to screen on December 25, 1968.

He will play the title part in a new Walt Disney TV production of "Pinocchio" and there will be at least five new numbers for him to sing in the show.

World Premiere

The world premiere of the "Mrs. Brown You've Got A Lovely Daughter" is scheduled to take place at New York's Radio City at Easter and Herman's Hermits will be Guests of Honor. Agent Danny Betesh had postponed the group's preposed April concert tour of America since Herman will now be spending so much time on the West Coast in the early part of this year.

An unconfirmed London rumor suggests that the part of Pinocchio was first intended for Davy Jones but it is not clear whether or not the Monkee turned down an offer before Herman was approached and signed.

When Herman's Hermits crossed the Atlantic for Christmas and New Year TV engagements in America, the group's drummer, Barry Whitman, was accompanied by his bride, Dale, whom he had married ten days before Christmas in Swinton.

Strong Lyrics

Scott Walker has a huge hit in Britain this month with his solo single, "Jacky." At first it looked as though the record would not get valuable deejay airspace because of its strong lyrics which have been variously described as "earthy," "sophisticated" and "vulgar."

In May, Scott will play a three week cabaret starring season at London's famous Talk Of The Town nighterie.

Because of a suspected appendicitis, Scott was rushed into the London Clinic at Christmas but he discharged himself because an operation would have prevented his end-of-December departure for a concert tour of Japan.

When they flew out of London, bound for Tokyo, both Scott and Gary Walker were searched by Hethrow Airport customs officials. Gary claims the search was for drugs but he confirmed: 'Of course we didn't have anything for them!"

The Grapefruit

A group which has Terry Melcher for record producer and the Beatles for backers begins life with a decided advantage! The outfit involved is a new London-based quartet called Grapefruit, formed in part from former members of the Castaways (the backing unit which works behind Tony Rivers).

Grapefruit is managed by Terry Doran, Liverpudlian Managing Director of Apple Publishing, the new music company operated and financed by the Beatles. It was John Lennon who suggested the group's name. "Grapefruit sounds nice," he declared, "it goes nicely with apple!"

So, Grapefruit went into the recording studio and cut a single called "Dear Delilah," the com-

(Continued on Page 13)

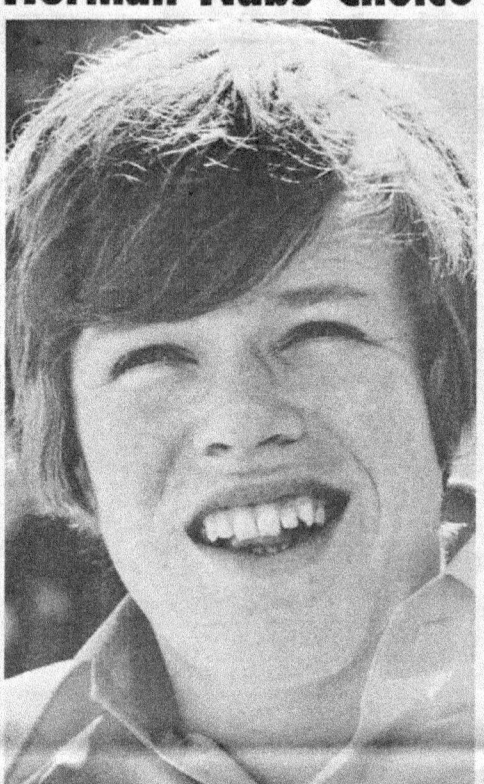
HERMAN set to play Pinocchio

RUMOR HAS IT DAVY JONES was originally intended for part.

SCOTT WALKER will play Talk of the Town in May.

TERRY MELCHER shares a table with Cass & group with Beatles.

PET CLARK—combining business with pleasure.

KRLA ARCHIVES

U.K. Pop Scene Revisited

By Tony Barrow

Almost five years ago, in January 1963, the Beatles hit the top of the U.K. pop charts for the first time with a record called "Please, Please Me." It looks as though the group will celebrate its fifth anniversary while not just one but two releases — the "Hello, Goodbye" single and the special "Magical Mystery Tour" package — bustle about the Number One spot in busy self-rivalry!

Monkee Arrival

Almost one year ago, in the early weeks of 1967, the Monkees arrived on the British scene. An advance sample of their work, the single "Last Train To Clarksville," had been issued on our side of the Atlantic but without extraordinary results. It was not until their weekly TV series took to the BBC screens that Britain became engulfed in the full fury, the raucous raging, of Monkeemania. The Monkees became the world's most important pop attraction of 1967 in a matter of weeks.

The teenybopper magazines helped to create and sustain Monkeemania. Many of those same publications had been caught on the hop when the Beatles broke big. This time they found there was plenty of pre-produced picture and story material coming out of Hollywood so it was used across front pages and center spreads in one of the biggest voluntary publicity campaigns ever offered to a pop group by Britain's teen-market press!

Everyone expects the chart-topping lifespan of the Monkees to be brief. Most experts gave Monkeemania a year to burn itself out. Twelve months ago this week the BBC transmitted the first episode of the group's series. "Daydream Believer," an extremely catchy little ditty sung by Davy who is by far the most popular Monkee, is the group's slowest chart-climber of the year. I expect to see the Monkees get into the 1968 Top 20 lists but I think the peak of their extraordinary international popularity is past. At the end of June they drew about 50,000 people at their Wembley concert appearances. By the summer of '68 I doubt if they will be capable of drawing half that number of patrons for a London performance.

Jealousy

The massive success of the Monkees led to a lot of jealousy in the pop business. Group's who will never manage to do Monkee-scale things gripped about a situation where a Hollywood-built TV-machine could gain such a strong hold on the charts in such a short time. Without entering into yet another fruitless argument about how much or how little true musical talent the Monkees possess I must put on record at the end of this Monkeemaniac Year my admiration for any team which can generate pop excitement so vastly, so colorfully and so convincingly!

Apart from the Monkees no new American group made great impact upon the 1967 British pop scene. We had the Box Tops up near the top for a spell with "The Letter" but I'd say this was a hit song and not a hit group; there's no indication that the average fan wants to know anything about the Box Tops as people!

Yes, we had spasdomic chart appearances by the Beach Boys and the Mamas and Papas but not one of America's new outfits made a big breakthrough. This confirms the continuing difference between the pop tastes of record collectors in Britain and America. No more than a handful of British fans have heard about the Cowsills, Strawberry Alarm Clock, Spanky and Our Gang, the Buckinghams and the Doors, although I see all these among the current U.S. Top 40 list!

Unfair To Motown

My last couple of paragraphs may sound unfair to Motown. The stars of Detroit's talent-stacked Tamla Motown organization have continued to shine brightly throughout Britain. In fact, Tamla record successes in 1967 have been greater than ever with substantial hits coming the way of Stevie Wonder, Gladys Knight, the Temptations and Marvin Gaye as well as the established favorites such as the Four Tops and the Supremes.

Conventional sweet-corn love ballads have enjoyed amazing success during the past 12 months. A whole army of male balladeers led by Engelbert Humperdinck and Tom Jones — have scored hit after hit, their record sales usually approaching if not passing those of top groups like the Beatles! Firm faves have included Vince Hill, Val Doonican, comedian Harry Secombe and Ken Dodd and comparative "veteran" Frankie Vaughan who thought he'd left his Top 20 days behind him but found immense success with "There Must Be A Way." With this list we can bracket America's Scott McKenzie whose sudden brief-lived fame was not limited to Flower Power Followers despite the sentiments of "San Francisco."

And Matt Monro?

There is one very important singer of ballads missing from my list — Matt Monro. Perhaps his lack of U.K. chart appearances is connected with his absence from the country for so much of 1967.

DAVY JONES holds his ears as the giant Monkee canon of success goes off!

In any event I'm sure he'll be back in the Top 10 as soon as he finds the right piece of material and the opportunity to expose it before British audiences.

Lulu Takes Over

Little Lulu took over the girlie scene on an international scale. She went zooming up our charts with "Boat That I Row" and "Let's Pretend" but she did even better in America where she went to number one and sold two million copies of "To Sir With Love." Her emergence as the most successful female vocalist of the year tended to overshadow existing top girls like Dusty Springfield and Cilla Black.

Mind you Sandie Shaw didn't do too badly. She won the Eurovision Song Contest for Britain by singing "Puppet On A String" so many times on telly, radio and (it seemed) just about any other available medium of communication that millions were hypnotized into believing this to be the most magnificent record of the century! Songstress Anita Harris had one great big hit ("Just Loving You") and so did stylish American cabaret star Vikki Carr ("It Must Be Him") but neither managed to find equally strong follow-up discs.

Less Of Sinatra

We heard much less of Nancy Sinatra this year but we welcomed the refreshingly folksy presentation of Bobbie Gentry who sounds as though she has a highly promising pop future on both sides of the Atlantic.

Three powerful new British groups came into the headlines last Spring. First there was Traffic, a new quartet built by Stevie Winwood who had just left the Spencer Davis Group. Then came Procol Harum, built (in part) from a previously unsuccessful unit known as the Paramounts. Finally there was the Bee Gees, claimed as the most significant new musical talent of 1967.

All these groups have consolidated their initial triumphs by issuing further smash-hit records during the year and all look set for equally great things in America. The success of the Foundations and the Dubliners has been national rather than international. In the case of the Foundations I'd say there was a fair chance of more widespread fortune ahead.

Beat Goes On

Two or even three years ago we were all predicting the immediate end of the Beat Boom, the professional death of every beat group in earshot. Yet here we are at the end of 1967 and the best of the groups are still notching up new hits with just about everything they record. Of the earliest gang I'm thinking of the Beatles, the Rolling Stones and the Hollies. Then there are slightly more recent additions such as Dave Dee's quintet, the Who, Cream and the Kinks. They've all done excellent business throughout 1967. Then we had a surprise surge of interest in the Dave Clark Five who climbed as high as number two with "Everybody Knows," the most popular single they've produced in three years!

Although they've put a stop to touring and concert performances in general, the Beatles have been prolific and progressive in 1967. No, they didn't get around to their much-postponed third film but the records they produced kept them in their own very special talent class a few hundred miles above all rivals! The way they tackled "Magical Mystery Tour" might turn out to be an unintentional pointer towards the future. Instead of just making a record, the Beatles created visual entertainment to accompany the sound. There was a color television show and a color book with photographs and cartoon drawings. Surely in a few years from now when new visual dimensions are added to record-playing equipment we shall see the equivalent of a "Magical Mystery Tour" show while we listen to our LP record albums!

Concerts 'Out'

In the meantime 1967 has been a slackening of interest in pop stage shows. British fans have stopped going to one-night-stand concerts. That, in a nutshell, is the fact which emerges at the end of a year when fewer concert tours took to the road and even fewer came anywhere near showing a profit! They say that since the Beatles stopped theatre appearances only Tom Jones and Engelburt Humperdinck are capable of filling theatres for one-nighter concerts outside London.

One of the biggest pop controversies of the year centered around the (metaphorical) sinking of Britain's pirate radio ships, the network of Top 40 stations bobbing up and down around the coast, never much more nor any less than three miles from the water's edge, safely beyond territorial limits yet close enough to transmit clearly to a maximum number of homes.

During the previous couple of years stations like Radio London and Radio Caroline had taught millions of listeners what commercial radio was and is all about. For the first time in Britain you could hear a 24-hour daily serving records, punctuated only by commercials, jingles and chummy deejay voices. The BBC had never been like this!

Only One Pirate

The Marine Offences Bill became law last summer and, since the early part of August, only Radio Caroline has defied the Government and stayed on the air. But there's Radio One, the BBC-operated channel which uses most of the better ex-pirate deejays and even bought its station identification jingles from the same Texas firm which supplied Radio London!

When Radio One had been on the air a week I refused to believe that its policy of mixing "live" studio performances with records could ever be totally successful. Despite the steady improvement in general program presentation, I still believe that the BBC must persuade the Musicians' Union to relax the current regulations which limit the amount of records broadcast each day and demand that the rest of the airtime be filled with "live" material.

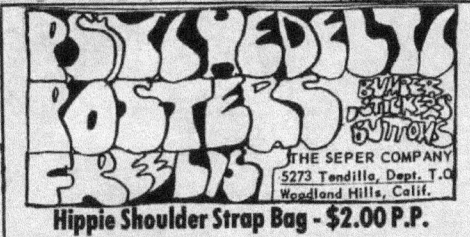

THE SEPER COMPANY
5273 Tendilla, Dept. T.O
Woodland Hills, Calif.

Hippie Shoulder Strap Bag - $2.00 P.P.

KRLA ARCHIVES

An Underground Artist Surfaces

by Jacoba Atlas

Nilsson is a new singer-composer who is wholly unique. It is totally superfluous to compare him to anyone else on the pop scene today, for he fits into no one else's niche. His first major album for RCA called "Pandemonium Shadow Show" has been reviewed by critics across the United States with unanimous acclaim. Nilsson's individual singing style and writing ability has put him into the forefront of the creative, unique popular music field.

Nilsson's songs have been described by one major national magazine as 'vignettes.' This is somewhat of a clue to the type of material he writes. "Songs are vignettes, they are slices of life. My idea of a song is that it's like a book or a movie only you only have two or three minutes to convey the idea.

"I write from personal experience, personal contact. It's like you experience A and B and then come up with C. Basically they must start from one person, in this case the song writer and go to another person, the listener.

Although such people as the Monkees (Cuddley Toy) and Jack Jones (Without Her) have recorded his songs, Nilsson, who dislikes his first name and avoids using it, prefers to record them himself.

Personal Songs

"I feel much easier. I guess it's just the songwriter instinct. The songwriter basically knows how he wants a song sung, and very few people are capable of transcribing someone elses thoughts in the same way he thought it. So therefore I would rather record them myself.

Although music controls most of his time now, Nilsson just recently entered into the pop music field. "I started writing professionally about 4 years ago. Prior to that my writing consisted mainly of making up neat little songs in the car a cappela.

"I can write music, but it takes me all day. I prefer to use tape, because it's so much simpler. As far as learning music, well, its better to break the rules after you've learned them, and it's very helpful to be able physically to write music, but it doesn't help you to be able to write a song really."

Composite Sound

The direction of pop music is being shaped by many people today, and although Nilsson is not as well known as other writers/singers, his impact is being felt on the pop music scene and will continue to be felt with even more force. As for himself Nilsson is more than enthusiastic about the future of pop music.

"Pop music is of course a combination of all the prior input. Today's music is marvelous in that it offers so many varied sounds.

"Where it's going is a little more difficult to say. It would seem if indeed the 60's are reflecting the mood of the twenties then we are in for another 30's or 40's sound, although not necessarily an exact copy of the big band sound. But music today is more expanded. The sitar sound has led to that, and that sound is giving way to a more encompassing sound, something even more potpourri.

Nilsson is working in close collaboration with two of the most talented men in the record field. Rick Jarrard who produced the Jefferson Airplane's Surrealistic Pillow and the engineer on that album, Dick Bogert. Along with his arranger Nilsson feels that these two men are most responsible for the excellence of his sound.

"The arranger specially has to interpret the song the way the composer wants. He has to be able to communicate that to the listener.

"Rick Jarrard has a marvelous ear. He has the ability to listen to a sound and relate it to someone else, and that ability is priceless in the record field. It's the listening ability that counts: listening, evaluation and judgment.

"The engineer is responsible for getting that sound to come across right. Without the engineer you wouldn't acquire the sound that fits the song."

One of Nilsson's most talked about songs is *You Can't Do That* a conglomeration of Beatle songs all put together.

"One time I was just toying with my guitar and I struck this chord and it seemed to lend itself to a million different songs. I noticed how many Beatle songs could be played with this one chord, so I ran down to Wallach's Music City on Sunset at about midnight right before it closed, and bought the Beatle songbook, and finished the song that night."

George Harrison

The response has been so complimentary that when Beatle George Harrison visited Los Angeles, in August, Nilsson was invited to Blue Jay Way.

"Meeting George Harrison was a great day in my life. He was extremely aware of everything, a gentleman. He made sure everyone's glass was full, listened to all the conversations. He was so alive and seemed happy. It's incredible to think that someone could be a Beatle and still be sane. To go through *all that* and still be normal.

"Harrison was also very complimentary to my work and took back my album to give to the other Beatles."

His new album is now in the works and should be released sometime in March. It's called *Nilsson's Aerial Ballet* named perhaps after his grandparent's European circus act of over sixty years ago. It will be another immediate success among those who know and appreciate new and unique musical talent. His first album, was a critical success, and an underground success, hopefully with his second album, the rest of the public will be turned on to the fantastic talent of Nilsson.

JANIS: JOAN OF ARC AND BENGAL TIGER

By Ron Koslow

When Janis Joplin of Big Brother and the Holding Company sings, and screams, and moans and does her "thing," she is the most incredible female in the history of the human race. She is a cross between Bessie Smith, Joan of Arc and a Bengal tiger. A very, very beautiful animal who all at once makes you want to laugh and cry and shriek with terror.

The S.F. group's first L.A. appearance at the Whisky A Go Go permanently altered the emotional atmosphere of the city — we won't be the same until Janis and her "boys" come back to us.

A word to the wise — don't judge them by their album. It's a loser (technically) and does not do justice to the excitement of their sound. You must see them in person and when they come to your town let nothing stop you, rest assured it will be a formidable experience in your life.

All of their material is great, but their real "monsters" are "Down On Me" an upbeat number that really rattles your brain and "Ball And Chain" which will make you cry.

Big Brother and the Holding Company has yet to achieve national acclaim or even a Top 40 record, but just wait. And you won't have to wait too long.

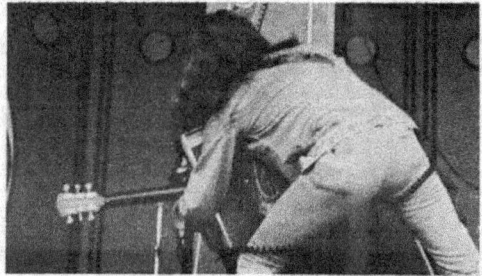

KRLA ARCHIVES

TURTLES TRAUMA

By Steve Rose

If THE TURTLES had a Merry Christmas and a Happy New Year it was in spite of a series of improbable and frustrating incidents. The group recently completed a tour which took them to major cities across the United States. During the jaunt, their equipment, all of it, was stolen — twice. Include five incidents of lost baggage, two incidents of lost Turtles, one incident of lost management, and twenty-five incidents of loss of mind. Add to the happening one missed plane, one grounded plane, one crippled plane. Season with lost travelers' checks, a mis-repaired rental car, and it equals the First group nervous breakdown in pop music history.

The culmination of all this mis-fortune occurred in Emporia, Kansas, which is not included on the list of major cities. In the middle of the concert, with three-thousands eager and paying fans, a ham-radio operator in Kansas City began broadcasting through the Turtles' P.A. system. He began the conversation by declaring loudly that he was really lucky to have gotten this particular frequency. He also made mention of the weather, his five month old baby girl named Sheilah, and his re-built '56 Ford. Howard and Mark politely listened to the dialogue and began making some pointed and unprintable remarks. Finally, order was restored and the concert went merrily along toward its conclusion.

The Turtles are normally a happy, easygoing unpretentious, and generally contented group of guys. They have changed almost radically since this last tour. Johnny Barbata is more cautious now, Howard Kaylan talks in his sleep to an unidentified P.A., Al Nichol carries 300 pounds of equipment on his back, Jim Pons expects to miss his next breakfast by three minutes, and Mark Volman cries in the morning.

In a more serious vein, The Turtles have made some very significant changes in both their music and their personal lives. On January 3rd, they go into the White Whale Studios to cut a new album which will contain all their own material. They will also be producing themselves and arranging the material. They will enter the studio with a barrage of new instruments including several Indian instruments, an electric sitar, one large bagpipe, and an assortment of home-made percussion instruments. Personally, The Turtles are definitely settling down in grand style. John Barbata just purchased a 4½ acre Malibu beach pad, Howard has acquired a house in Laurel Canyon, Al Nichol bought an estate in Woodland Hills, and Jim Pons is still sleeping in the street. Actually, Jim is now looking for a home for himself and his new bride.

If the houses don't burn down and the group doesn't get lost or misplaced on the way to the studio, 1968 should be the most fabulous year yet for THE TURTLES.

Harpers Bizarre Easy, Fun Sound

Harper's Bizarre has a unique sound which they refuse to compromise for the demands of the top 10 charts. Achieving a large amount of popularity with their first single "59th Street Bridge," the group has gone on to a double hit, both rock and roll and easy listening with "Chattanooga Choo Choo."

Born in Santa Cruz, California, the group is extremely close knit. All want to stay in the pop music field and all take their music seriously. They have been known to practice as much as 10 hours a day.

The group consists of five very talented young men. Ed James, lead guitarist, is a fairly retiring person who finds parties and personal appearances equally terrifying and likeable. He went to college for a while and insists that one day he is going back. A surfer, Ed somehow sympathizes most with people who seem to go it alone.

Dick Scoppettone, lead singer and rhythm guitarist, is also the song writer of the group. He began in the music business with his friend Dick Yount when they were a duo singing folk songs. He feels he is somewhat of a misplaced person in the music field, "because I'm the type who usually becomes a normal lawyer or doctor."

Ted Templeman who plays rhythm guitar and is lead singer along with Scap Scoppettone claims that the hippie movement is over. "It will leave nothing but a pleasant memory." His advice to beginners is "learn to listen. One hit doesn't make a record."

Dick Yount collects comic books written before 1940 and thinks that his idea of a movie is anything with Peter Sellers. He would like to end up living in Switzerland.

John Peterson provides the beat to the group. Once he thought of only being a session man, backing up other people's groups, but an audition with the Harper's Bizarre brought him back into the front lines.

They all describe their music as "fun loving, easy listening." Both their sound and their famous name has prompted both Harper's Bizarre and Vogue magazine, two pinacles of fashion, to do a picture layout on the group.

KRLA ARCHIVES

TWO BEE GEES SOUND OFF

By Mike Masterson

LOS ANGELES—Two of the Bee Gees, brothers Robin and Barry Gibb arrived in Los Angeles on their way to Australia. They were in town to discuss plans for their only U.S. concert appearance on January 27th in this city, along with a guest appearance on the Smothers Brothers Show. Although three Bee Gees were missing, the two brothers managed to stir up quite a bit of controversy between them.

Regarding the tendency of people to compare the Bee Gees to the Beatles, Barry stated emphatically, "that's all rubbish really. We never pretended to be anything but the Bee Gees. We're the Bee Gees and not the Beatles. It gets tiring to hear people say you're the next Beatles or something. Like with actors, they're always saying so and so is the next so and so.

"Why can't you just be you? If you can't do it on your own name, then you're just wasting time. We don't want to be the next Beatles. We just want to be the Bee Gees. If we can't do that then it's no good going on."

Devaluation

Although the devaluation of the pound has hit the small island very hard, the Bee Gees aren't affected by squeeze. "It doesn't really effect us, because a good deal of our money is earned outside of England. It will and has effected the average Britain, the middle class. They will have to pay more for the normal things like food. Weekly wages mean less."

"It will also effect American artists being booked into Britain because they will have to work for less, unless they were booked before the devaluation, then they're formr wage was guaranteed," added Robin.

Their decision to play only in Los Angeles in the month of January stems from their manager. "Our manager thinks we should limit our appearances here. I think this is not to overexpose ourselves. We have been very lucky that the Americans have accepted our records and the fastest way to spoil this would be to come into America and work all over the country for about six weeks. Then they'd say 'oh yes, we've seen them, we're not interested.'

"We're coming back this summer to play every major city in the U.S., so this time we are limiting ourselves to playing only Los Angeles."

New Movie

The Bee Gees are set to star in their first collective movie to be called *Lord Kitchner's Little Drummer Boys*. It is a self-proclaimed mad, mad movie. "It takes place in Narobi during the Boer War. We get sort of shipped out from London to the war. We try to get out of the army, actually we desert the army at the front. Then we run into the enemy, but we don't know its the enemy. We're trying to make this film as farsical as possible.

"There will be songs in it, but we don't know how yet. We want everything to be authentic, so you really couldn't use electric guitars and still be in keeping with the time."

Unlike many pop artists, the Bee Gees are unafraid of disputing the quality of the new offerings from the Beatles and the Stones.

"I listened to the Stones album last week for the first time over at a friends' flat. I loved the cover, but I disagree with the songs, not with what they say, but with the noises and the sound effects.

"I don't know why they put belching noises on the end of tracks or coughs, or snorings. These things mean a lot to the Stones, but not to anyone else. I think that it is time this group and a lot of other groups realized this.

"The groups will lose their audiences because with all those noises, the kids won't go for it. That's why the early and middle Beatles were much more popular than they are now.

"*I Am The Walrus* is alright except for the part that goes 'you've been a naughty girl, you let your knickers down'. The lyrics are nonsensical and very suggestive. I don't think the Beatles have to do this, because their music is good enough without it.

"A lot of groups are putting things into their songs about sex and drugs because they want their records to be banned. They think it will help them sell. But that's not true now, I can't understand what the lyric to 'Walrus' is all about."

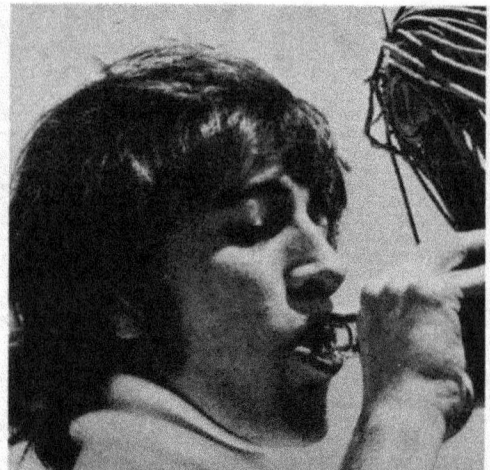

ROBIN GIBB

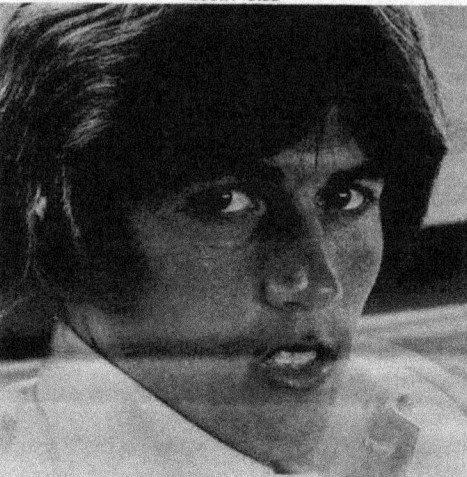

BARRY GIBB

BEE GEES

"'I Am the Walrus' lyrics are nonsensical and suggestive. The Stones are adding noises that mean nothing to anyone but themselves."

MOVING?

Writing about a subscription?
Be sure to fill out this form

KRLA ARCHIVES

BEE GEES TIE UP TRANSATLANTIC LINES

LONDON — Vince Melouney of the Bee Gees pop group snatched some sleep today after American fans kept him awake all night because Los Angeles radio station KRLA broadcast his telephone number.

"The first I knew about it was when a KRLA disc jockey Bob Dayton called me to say he had just given my number out over the air during his show," said Melouney whose home is in the Kensington district of London.

"After that the calls came in non-stop. I didn't get a wink of sleep all night. I'm told the international exchange out there was blocked by kids wanting my number."

KRLA presents the Bee Gees in concert January 27, 1968 at the Anaheim Convention Center.

CASEY KASEM IN "THE GLORY STOMPERS"

MOUTH (CASEY KASEM) (left) and Monk (Lindsay Crosby) members of the "Black Souls" a renegade motorcycle gang do some fancy riding on their "choppers."

The Glory Stompers is a great new motorcycle flick. Starring Dennis Hopper, Jody McCrea, Cris Noel, Jock Mahoney and last but certainly far from least, CASEY KASEM.

Filmed in colorscope, this is another American International picture, dealing with the thrill seeking renegade motorcycle gang called the "Black Souls." Don't miss it!

THE GOLDEN BEAR
306 OCEAN AVENUE (HWY 101) HUNTINGTON BEACH

Presents

Jan. 9 thru 14th

Bola Sete

Starting Jan. 16 thru 21st

Big Brother
AND THE HOLDING CO.

Reservations   PHONE 536-9600
                      536-9102

GUESS WHO?

LA CIENEGA	9039 SUNSET	NOW HAPPENING
1—EDDIE JAMES AND THE PACIFIC OCEAN	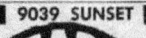  GAZZARRI'S #1 ON-THE-STRIP CR 3-6606 OL 7-2113 GAZZARRI'S #2 LA CIENEGA 319 N. LACIENEGA	Sunday Afternoon GROOVE-IN — 4 P.M. Monday Nite Dance Concert to select Miss Sunset Strip A-Go-Go $500 prize. Wednesday Audition & Talent Night Dancing 17 & Over Cocktails 21 & Over
2—CHURCHILL DOWNS		
3—ABSTRACTS		
4—JOINT EFFORT		
5—BURNSIDE		

KRLA ARCHIVES

WAILING WITH CANNED HEAT

Tony Leigh

Canned Heat plays the Blues. Not the Blues of the 1920's and 30's, but an extension of that sound, that era, brought up to date to render it meaingful for today. It's still the same funky sound, the expression of soul, of hard times, of loneliness, but it is now tempered with the electronic advancements brought about by pop music.

Henry Vestime who plays guitar states, about this union, "I always wanted to play the Blues. I've played with rock groups around the city and that wasn't what I wanted. Finally I came together with Canned Heat, and now I'm doing exactly what I want."

All of the Canned Heat feels exactly the same way. They are all playing what they want, when they want. It is not a job, but a labor of love. They have something that means a great deal to them, and they want to convey that feeling to everyone else.

Solos

The group is totally unique in every way, but one trait when performing especially stands out as different. All four musicians take solos.

Lead singer, Bob Hite, explains, "We all agreed to the solos. It gives everyone a chance to do his thing, and not get lost in the group."

This is particularly important for Larry Taylor who plays bass guitar. "With an instrument like the bass guitar, you just never really get to do any heavy playing. You just back up the group, but with the solos you are able to do what you want, and play the way you want to."

Canned Heat has recently changed drummers. The new drummer comes from Mexico City, where he first became familiar with Canned Heat through their former drummer Frank Cook. Fito de la Parra has had no trouble taking Cook's place.

"I had played the Blues in Mexico, American Blues. When I started playing with Canned Heat everything just clicked. I had no problems at all," stated de la Parra.

More Complete

The rest of the group is even more enthusiastic about the change.

"For the first time we are really a complete group. I can just relax and sing and not worry about the rhythm being carried," added Bob Hite.

This change has even been more beneficial to Larry Taylor whose bass guitar held the rhythm sections together when they felt the drumming wasn't strong enough.

"Now I can just concentrate on playing, and play the way I want to. I'm getting back to playing in my old way, it's much better."

Even with this change in drummers which has been helpful in solidifying the groups sound, they feel Canned Heat has ever really come across in records. Their first album simply titled *Canned Heat* was somewhat of a disappointment for the group. The next one, to be released later this month, is hopefully much closer to their live sound.

Bob Hite explains, "The thing with recording in the studio is you have nothing to stimulate you. There is no audience to give you something when they're really with you, it just makes you so much better. You have to find it in yourself, without any help.

"With a studio, you keep doing things over and over again, and then you keep getting more up tight as the sounds just don't come. But with an audience, they can get you over that feeling, and help you to your sound.

"Unlike a lot of groups, we don't take very much time in the studio to record. We rehearse just about everyday, and so we can cut five or six tracks in one day. If things are right. But without a live audience, it just gets that much more difficult."

Bogie

"The new album is called *Bogie With Canned Heat*. This time we've been able to get closer to what we want. We have trouble with our sound in the recording studio, ideally we should record live, but then you have trouble with volume and that thing. Our producer has helped us on this one, to get the sound we want.

"Al Wilson does our arranging. On *Bogie* I wrote all of the songs.

"What Wilson will do is work out all our parts and then we take it from there. It's not static, not just Wilson," added de la Parra.

Bob Hite has always had a life long ambition to be a disc jockey, and finally, in part this is coming true. Along with Henry Vestine, Hite has a Monday night program on a Los Angeles FM station.

"We wanted to lay some really good music on Los Angeles. Nobody else is really doing that. A couple of guys will play one or two good things a night, but that's really all."

Old Blues

"Henry and I have been collecting old records for years. Between us we have thousands. I started collecting when I was about four. We find them everywhere, but some of the old ones, cut before we were born are impossible to find. I refuse to devulge my sources."

Although Canned Heat started in the smaller clubs of Los Angeles, the group is split as to the kind of place they like to play. De la Parra states, "I like the smaller clubs where everyone is together."

Hite disagrees, "I'd rather play concerts; colleges I suppose. The trouble with clubs is that you're there every night. It gets to be like a job, you could be typing."

"Clubs have almost the same audiences every night, you can't really feel a change from night to night. It would be different if you could just play one or two nights in one place," adds Larry Taylor.

"But clubs are good because people really listen to what you have to say. They're not dancing.

"I'd prefer people not to dance when we're really playing something great. I want them to listen," added Vestine.

People *have* been listening to Canned Heat. This February they have been invited to play a benefit for old Blues singers at, of all places, The Electric Circus in New York, or as Bob calls it "The original Plastic City." But they are very enthusiastic about being able to contribute to the welfare of the men who helped create the sound they play today. The people whose records Henry and Bob play on their radio show.

Now from a sold out stint at the Ash Grove and Troubador in Los Angeles, Canned Heat is going on a national tour taking them to Denver, Boston, New York and Chicago. They are confident that wherever they play the people will dig "what we're putting down." Their confidence will be well justified. They love the Blues, it's their music, they know how to play it for today and no audience has any choice but to respond in kind.

From l. to r.: Larry Taylor, Bob Hite and Al Wilson. Missing is guitarist Henry Vestine and drummer Fito de la Perra.

Union Gap Sweeps Country

The Union Gap is a new group with one record to their credit, but what a record. It is climbing so high on the national and local charts that it's almost incredible. "Woman Woman" has established the Union Gap as a top selling group.

Formed in January of last year the group originates from San Diego, California. They have named themselves after the historic town of Union Gap, Washington. True to their name they garb themselves in Union Civil War uniforms.

The group is comprised of "General" Gary Puckett, vocals, guitar; "Sergeant" Dwight Bement, tenor sax; "Corporal" Kerry Chatter, bass guitar; "Private" Gary (Mutha) Withem, wodwinds, piano; and "Private" Paul Wheatbread, drums.

In addition to being the groups leader, Puckett is also their songwriter, with over 30 songs to his credit so far. Bement who was a former music major at San Diego State College, made his debut playing with a school assembly while attending the fifth grade. Chatter, who was born in Canada, hopes one day to be considered "the best composer-arranger around." And Gary Withem was a music teacher before joining the group. Wheatbread who plays the drums claims to love fast cars and motorcycles almost as much as he loves making music.

The Union Gap prior to their colossal success with "Woman Woman" attracted a good size following in their native California where they played college concerts and club dates from Northern California to the south.

KRLA ARCHIVES

SCENE AND HEARD IN BRITAIN

(Continued from Page 6)
position of the group's own bass guitarist 20-year-old Scotsman George Alexander. John and Paul looked in at the session and said a lot of helpful things. "Dear Delilah" is set for a January release in Britain.

How did the celebrated Terry Melcher come into the story? Melcher has just signed a two-way transatlantic publishing deal with his namesake Terry Doran. While in London, he heard tapes of the first Grapefruit sessions and (obviously) liked what he heard.

During her six-week London visit Petula Clark tried to combine business with pleasure — seeing friends and working in numerous television appearances. Her plans for 1968 include summer filming with Peter O'Toole in "Goodbye Mr. Chips," plus her first-ever appearance in a Western picture.

In an interview with Dennis Hall of the London Sunday Express, Pet claimed: "Money and security are not the driving forces for me. I work because I enjoy it."

SCENE AND HEARD . . . Old misunderstandings having been sorted out, his father Freddie Lennon now a longtern houseguest of John Lennon . . . Reg Presley of The Troggs discovered a Nottingham group called the Nerve, signed them to a management agreement and produced their first single called "Magic Spectacles" . . . After eight years BBC Television's "Juke Box Jury" show is off the air for good. For the final program, panel members included Lulu wearing a ringlets wig . . . American 12-inch album version of The Beatles' "Magical Mystery Tour" selling in Britain for just under six dollars — an expensive imported souvenir! . . . Simon and Garfunkel play London's Royal Albert Hall (March 7) as one of seven U.K. concert dates promoted by Tito Burns . . . This month the Small Faces co-star in Australian dates with the Who and John Walker . . . Promotional visit to Britain for Sonny and Cher expected once they finish shooting "Chastity" . . . the Scaffold have a stage act lasting 150 minutes!

Title of mid-January U.K. single by the Bee Gees is "Words" and "Sinking Ships" on the second side . . . New Vaudeville Band expect to earn nearly 100,000 dollars in America during four-week springtime visit . . . Circus Alpha Centouri concert promotion syndicate brought in Country Joe and the Fish for Christmas shindig at London's Roundhouse and plans extensive concert appearances in Britain for Big Brother and the Holding Company, Jefferson Airplane and Peanut Butter Conspiracy . . . Top U.K. deejay Tony Blackburn out with his own vocal disc called "So Much Love" . . . Ten-year-old movie "Smiley" which starred a 9-year-old Colin Petersen shown on BBC-TV color channel at Christmas but Bee Gee drummer Colin wasn't around to watch — he'd flown home to Australia for a family holiday in Brisbane!

Manfred Mann group (who scored heavily with "Just Like A Woman" here some time ago) have made Bob Dylan's "The Amazing Quinn" the top deck of their January single . . . New Englebert Humperdinck single is "Am I That East To Forget" . . . Beach Boys Mike and Bruce were personal guests of the Beatles at "Magical Mystery Tour" London party . . . Peter Frampton, 17-year-old singer with the Herd, being tipped as the most promising 1969 pop scene sex symbol . . . Cowsills due to begin short promotional visit to London February 7 . . . Press controversy stimulated rather than diminished interest of overseas TV networks in the Beatles' "Magical Mystery Tour" film.

SONNY & CHER are expected in England on promo tour.

SIMON AND GARFUNKEL will play London's Royal Albert Hall on March 7.

ENGLEBERT HUMPERDINCK continues to do well all over!   COWSILLS ARRIVE IN London on February 7 for a short visit.

KRLA ARCHIVES

TOP 100 OF 1967

No.	Title	Artist	Wks. on Top 10
1	Ode To Billie Joe	Bobbie Gentry	8
2	Windy	Association	8
3	I'm A Believer	Monkees	9
4	Happy Together	Turtles	9
5	Groovin'	Young Rascals	9
6	To Sir With Love	Lulu	8
7	Light My Fire	Doors	8
8	Daydream Believer	Monkees	8
9	Never My Love	Association	6
10	Something Stupid	Nancy/Frank	7
11	Georgy Girl	Seekers	7
12	The Letter	Box Tops	8
13	Hello/Walrus	Beatles	6
14	Snoopy-Red Baron	Royal Guards	5
15	All You Need	Beatles	6
16	Ruby Tuesday	Sones	6
17	Rain, Park, Other Things	Cowsills	6
18	Good Thing	Paul Revere	6
19	Little Bit Of Me	Monkees	6
20	Respect	Aretha Franklin	7
21	Whiter Shade Of Pale	Procol Harum	7
22	Incense And Peppermints	Strawberry Alarm Clock	7
23	I Say A Little Prayer	Dionne Warwick	5
24	Penny Lane/Strawberry Fields	Beatles	5
25	She'd Rather Be With Me	Turtles	6
26	Love Is Here	Supremes	6
27	Need Your Lovin'	Johnny Rivers	6
28	Love Me Forever	Bobby Vinton	6
29	Reflections	Supremes	7
30	Can't Take My Eyes Off Of You	Frankie Valli	7
31	Pleasant Valley Sunday	Monkees	7
32	The Happening	Supremes	6
33	Dedicated To Love	Mamas and Papas	6
34	Kind Of Hush	Herman's Hermits	5
35	Through The Grapevine	Gladys Knight	5
36	San Francisco	Scott McKenzie	5
37	Kind Of A Drag	Buckinghams	5
38	In And Out Of Love	Supremes	5
39	Tell It Like It Is	A. Neville	6
40	I Was Made To Love Her	Stevie Wonder	6
41	Sweet Soul Music	A. Conley	6
42	Precious Love	Marvin and Tammi	6
43	How Can I Be Sure	Young Rascals	6
44	Sit Down Kids	Cher	4
45	Somebody To Love	Jefferson Airplane	4
46	It Must Be Him	Vikki Carr	4
47	This Is My Song	Pet Clark	5
48	Words Of Love	Mama Cass	5
49	Expressway To Your Heart	Soul Survivors	5
50	White Rabbit	Jefferson Airplane	5
51	Ain't Got Nothing	Blues Megoos	5
52	Baby I Love You	Aretha Franklin	5
53	You're My Everything	Temptations	5
54	Girl Like You	Young Rascals	5
55	Don't Sleep In The Subway	Pet Clark	4
56	Bernadette	4 Tops	6
57	Little Bit Of Soul	Musical Explosion	4
58	Release Me	E. Humperdinck	4
59	Dandelion	Rolling Stones	4
60	Think We're Alone Now	Tommy Janes	4
61	Western Union	5 Americans	4
62	You've Got What It Takes	Buffalo Springfield	4
63	For What It's Worth	Dave Clark Five	4
64	Mercy, Mercy	Buckinghams	4
65	Little Ole Man	Bill Cosby	3
66	Him Or Me	Paul Revere	3
67	I Can See For Miles	The Who	3
68	Second That Emotion	Miracles	4
69	Don't You Care	Buckinghams	4
70	You Know What I Mean	Turtles	5
71	I Got Rhythm	Happenings	5
72	Gimme Some Lovin'	Spencer Davis	3
73	Massachusetts	Bee Gees	3
74	Open Letter	Victor Lundberg	3
75	Live For Today	Grass Roots	3
76	Be Home Soon	Lovin' Spoonful	4
77	Creeque Alley	Mamas and Papas	3
78	C'Mon Marianne	4 Seasons	3
79	Shadows Of Love	4 Tops	3
80	98.6	Keith	3
81	Sock It To Me	M. Ryder	3
82	Sunday Will Never Be The Same	Spanky and Our Gang	3
83	Come Back When You Grow Up	Bobbie Vee	3
84	Natural Woman	Aretha Franklin	3
85	To Love Somebody	Bee Gees	3
86	I Dig Rock And Roll Music	Peter, Paul and Mary	3
87	Nashville Cats	Lovin' Spoonful	3
88	Beat Goes On	Sonny and Cher	3
89	Track In My Tears	Johnny Rivers	3
90	Up, Up And Away	5th Dimension	3
91	59th Street Bridge	Harpers Bizarre	2
92	Close Your Eyes	Peaches and Herb	3
93	I'm A Man	Spencer Davis	3
94	Keep The Ball Rolling	Jay and Techniques	2
95	Get On Up	Esquires	2
96	Twelve Thirty	Mamas and Papas	2
98	Mirage	4 Seasons	2
97	Tell It To The Rain	Tommy James	2
99	Boogaloo Down Broadway	Johnny C	2
100	Heroes And Villians	Beach Boys	2

Reprinted by permission of Tempo Newsletter. Listing is based on radio station listings, airplay and national sales reports during the year 1967 (some records include factors from late 1966).

Rating is on a week-to-week basis, and positions are determined by the number of weeks in the top 10, weeks at #1 or highest position.

KRLA ARCHIVES

THE SWEET SOUND OF CREAM

By Sue Barry

The name is simply Cream, not Fresh Cream as so many people seem to think, the latter being the name of the group's album. But it's understandable why the term fresh is so often added to the name of this English group for their sound can truly be described as fresh and exciting.

Cream represents a new wave of English performers. No longer is it possible to get on the American charts simply because one is British. In this age of "homegrown" groups talent and lots of it is essential.

But then, Cream could hardly miss. Being composed of Eric Clapton, voted in 1966 best guitarist by members of other groups, Jack Bruce an ex-Manfred, and Ginger Baker whom Charlie Watts considers the best drummer in the world, it is only natural that good things happen when these three play together.

Cream is not a new group. In fact, their album, Fresh Cream, is just now enjoying popularity here in America and it was issued in England in December of 1966!

What of this fresh Cream sound?

Jack Bruce put it very nicely in explaining how the name Cream was decided upon. He said, "We chose our name simply because we thought our sound was thick and rich-like cream."

But in discussing their sound it is almost necessary to put it into two classifications — Cream on record and Cream live.

Cream on record and notably their album Fresh Cream, since they as of yet have not issued a single in the United States, is a beautiful thing to listen too. It confirms the validity of the name Cream. The album is a collection of songs that exhibit a perfect blend of rich, full harmony, so much so that the listener often feels as if he is being submerged into a thick bowl of cream. If it sounds unbelievable take a listen and see for yourself.

But Cream "live" is something else. Gone is the rich, full harmony that is exhibited on Fresh Cream. Instead Jack Bruce, Eric Clapton and Ginger Baker combine to produce one of the most excitingly electric sounds ever heard. This is where the great talents of the three seem to come to a head. While on record their mellow harmony and strong melody is particularly evident, on stage their expert craftmanship is undeniable.

Jack Bruce, whose strong forceful voice carries vocal lead in most songs, plays his bass guitar as a bass has never been played before. He gives the impression that he is trying to play lead guitar. It is most impressive.

On stage Eric Clapton is unmatched. His superb work with the guitar is such that he and the instrument seem one and the same. Eric, who feels there is more satisfaction in teaching oneself to play guitar than in taking lessons has said, "When I was sixteen I tried to learn guitar by copying off discs. But soon I found there was more to it than that." He aptly proves this point when he plays — and he plays fantastically!

Ginger Baker, the third member of Cream is a fierce, though expert drummer. An impressive figure himself at 6 ft. 1 in. with curly red hair, he plays a very fine set of drums. To watch him play fifteen minutes of a drum solo from "Toad" is enough to diminish the doubts of anyone who doesn't believe he is one of the best drummers in the world.

Cream writes their own material with Jack Bruce taking most of the honors. He says of the songs he writes: "When I write a song, I build up word pictures — hoping people who hear it will do the same." In this respect he has been successful.

Right now Cream is more or less an underground group with has not yet enjoyed the great success that it deserves. Perhaps with more exposure Cream will win the appreciation of all America. Let's hope so. Cream is an experience no one deserves to miss.

WAIT UNTIL DARK

It all started with *The Perils of Pauline*. It progressed to the thirties with Dorothy McGuire in *Spiral Staircase*, to the forties and Joan Fontaine in *Rebecca*, to the fifties with Grace Kelly in *Dial M for Murder*. The lady in distress has always held a certain amount of charm for the movie going public. Now with the suspense thriller, *Wait Until Dark* (Warner Bros.-7 Arts), Audrey Hepburn brings that special brand of horror fully to life for the sixties.

Wait Until Dark is an excellent movie, combining all the best Hollywood can muster for their films. It will entertain you, shock you, and fascinate you. Supported by Alan Arkin (Russians Are Coming, Russians Are Coming) and Richard Crenna (Sand Pebbles), Audrey Hepburn gives one of the finest performances of her outstanding career.

The story tends to be a little trite and contrived, but that won't bother anyone a bit. The acting and the direction are perfect. Terrance Young (best known for his James Bond films) has created a modern day horror story that for those who aren't familiar with the early days of Alfred Hitchcock stands second to none.

Wait Until Dark is guaranteed to make you scream with fright. It's great fun to see a movie that just entertains while scarring you silly. Don't miss it.

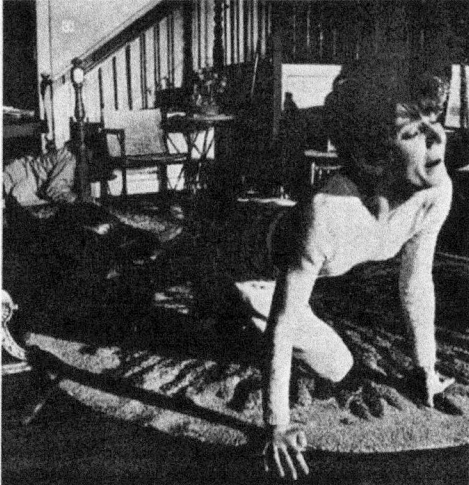

KRLA ARCHIVES

KRLA ARCHIVES

BEAT SHOWCASE

HARK!

A WORTHWHILE CAUSE! A WORTHWHILE CAUSE!

JOIN THE JBL CAUSE!

IRVING MENDELSOHN SWINGS

LOYAL FANS OF "THE MENDELSOHN QUINTETTE CLUB OF BOSTON" HELP BRING JOY TO ONE AND ALL...MAKE YOUR FELLOW MAN HAPPY...LET THE WORLD KNOW THAT "IRVING MENDELSOHN SWINGS"!!! Get your bumper sticker and button now! Friends will gather around you... Strangers will rush to greet you... Cars will stop behind you at red lights. HANDSOMELY ILLUSTRATED... CHEAPEST ON EARTH!

ONLY 25¢ FOR BOTH!

No Deposit...no references ...just send your money along with this coupon.

COUPON
Enclosed is 25¢. Please send me my "IRVING MENDELSOHN SWINGS" bumper sticker and button.

Name _____
Address _____
City _____ State _____
Postal Zone _____

JAMES B. LANSING SOUND INC.
3049 CASITAS AVE., LOS ANGELES, CALIFORNIA 90039
(BEAT-G)

OCTOBER COUNTRY

The October Country is a new folk rock group that came to West Coast attention through their appearances at Gazzarri's, a discotheque located on Los Angeles' famed Sunset Strip. Their first single is called appropriately enough "October Country."

The group consists of six performers: Joe De Fransa (vocals and guitar), Carole De Fransa (vocals, guitar), Bruce Wayen (bass), Bob Wian (piano, organ, guitar), Marty Earle (guitar, clarinet) and Gerry Pasternack (drums, piano).

SPEC-TRIM SUNGLASSES

UNIQUE SHADOW BOX FRAMES
MOD RECESSED LENSES
TWO-COLOR FRAMES
$4 Each*

*Calif. residents please add 5% sales tax
AVAILABLE IN:
Blue and White   White and Pink
Purple and White   Red and White
Yellow and Black   Red and Black
Designate Frame Color

SEND TO:
BEAT PUBLICATIONS
9000 Sunset, Suite 1000
Los Angeles, Calif. 90069

DEBS

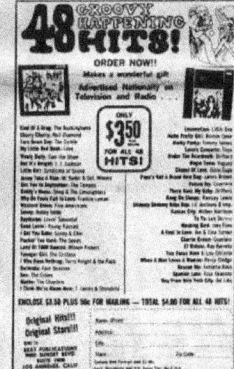

48 GROOVY HAPPENING HITS!

ORDER NOW!!
Makes a wonderful gift
Advertised Nationally on Television and Radio

ONLY $3.50 FOR ALL 48 HITS!

Original Hits!!!
Original Stars!!!

BEAT PUBLICATIONS
9000 SUNSET BLVD
SUITE 1000
LOS ANGELES, CALIF.

ENCLOSE $3.50 PLUS 50¢ FOR MAILING — TOTAL $4.00 FOR ALL 48 HITS!

Beat Poster Shop

Giant 22x28
Love Poster
in Full Color

(L) Love
(ty) Maharishi (s) Stones (r) Jimi Hendrix (i) Dylan (t) The Who (o) Country Joe (w) Strawberry Alarm Clock

Send to: BEAT POSTER SHOP, 9000 Sunset, Suite 1000, Los Angeles, Cal. 90069

PLEASE SEND ME THE FOLLOWING POSTERS (LIST BY LETTER) _____
I ENCLOSE $1.75 plus .25 Handling for each*.

Name _____
Address _____
City _____ State _____ Zip Code _____
*California Residents Please Include 5% Sales Tax

A GIFT FROM A FLOWER TO A GARDEN (Epic) Donovan. This double offering from Donovan is most beautiful. It is a self-acclaimed tribute to life and an affirmation of living. In his opening poem, *Oh, What a Dawn Youth is Rising To*, Donovan states, "I wish only to enhance and beautify the days of youth." That is exactly what these albums do. In the first, Donovan stays with the style of singing that was evident on *Mellow Yellow* and *Sunshine Superman*. Singing *Wear Your Love Like Heaven* and *Oh Gosh* the songs are pleasant but not quite up to his former standards. The only exception to that is *Sun*, "sun, the earth is turning and love is the access." But on the second record, Donovan is at his most poetic and beautiful. It is gentle, timeless, and very reminiscent of the olde English folksongs that were popular a few years ago. It has the same quality as *Legend of a Girl Child Linda*, and *Guinevere*. The songs really have very little to do with the twentieth century. Conjuring up the sounds of spring, of crickets, of waves beating against a shore, of a baby crying, Donovan creates a mood that is totally his own. Using rather obscure phrases to describe things people never see, the whole record has the aura of sound out of time. The background is simple, usually just a single guitar, with a bit of background sound effects added. There is a lullabye as lovely as anything ever written, *Song of the Naturalist's Wife*, and a tale of a gypsy straight out of the 18th century. If Donovan before *Sunshine Superman* appealed to you, you'll love this album. It is a slightly difficult one to accept, because it goes so completely away from what is presently done by anyone. But do listen, its beautiful.

PENNY'S ARCHADE (Buddah) Penny Nichols. This is a young California girl whose impact on the record world will be felt very shortly. She sings with a pleasant untrained voice, that has the kind of quality of early Baez. Her songs are her own. Singing about love, and the sea, and other rather ephmeral things, Penny creates the same feeling as her predecessors, Mimi Farina, Judy Collins and Joan Baez. She now lives in Los Angeles, after spending much of her time in San Francisco and other parts of the Bay Area. She has become a rather important underground singer/writer at the moment. This is her first album, and although it is far from perfect, the promise of a fine artist is more than evident. "Springtime games of winds and rains have washed away the meaning of Today." In the notes about the album it states that the songs have no continuity because Penny herself, like most people today have no continuity. What she does have is talent and tenderness.

A giant (22"x28") Calendar Poster in black, white and red.

PLEASE SEND ME THE CALENDAR POSTER
I ENCLOSE $1.75 plus .25 Handling for each.*

NAME _____
Address _____
City _____ State _____ Zip Code _____
*California Residents Please Include 5% Sales Tax

KRLA ARCHIVES

THE DOORS BY THE DOORS

JAZZ IS DYING
By Robby Krieger

"The first music I head that I liked was 'Peter and the Wolf'. I accidentally sat on it and broke the record. (I was about seven) then I listened to rock and roll — I listened to the radio a lot — Fats Domino, Elvis, The Platters.

"I started surfing at 14 . . . there was a lot of classical music in my house . . . my father liked march music . . . there was a piano at home. I studied trumpet at ten, but nothing came off it.

"Then I started playing blues on the piano — no lessons though — when I was 17, I started playing guitar. I didn't get my own until I was 18 . . . it was a Mexican flamenco guitar. I took flamenco lessons for a few months. I switched around from folk to flamenco to blues to rock and roll.

"Records got me into the blues. Some of the newer rock and roll such as Butterfield. If it hadn't been for Butterfield going electric I probably wouldn't have gone into rock and roll.

"I didn't play on rock and roll, I wanted to learn jazz; I got to know some people doing rock and roll and with jazz and I thought I could make m o n e y playing music.

"In rock and roll, you can realize anything that you can in jazz or anything. There's no limitation other than the beat. You have more freedom than you do in anything except jazz — which is dying — as far as making money is concerned.

"In the Doors we have both musicians and poets and both know of each other's art so we can effect a synthesis. In the case of Buckley or Dylan you have one man's ideas, here, we use everyone's ideas. Most groups today aren't groups. In a true group all the members create the arrangement among themselves."

ROCK & ROLL WITH CREEPS
By John Densmore

"I've been playing for six years. I don't really have too much to say about all of this. I took piano lessons when I was ten. They tried to get me to play Bach; they tried for two years. When I was in junior high I got my first set of drums. I played symphonic music in high school. I used to play sessions in Compton and Topanga Canyon (in Los Angeles County). Since last year it's been rock and roll with these creeps."

We're Like America
By Ray Manzarek

"I grew up in Chicago and left when I was 21 for Los Angeles. My parents gave me piano lessons when I was nine or ten. I hated it for the first four years — until I learned how to do it — then it became fun; which was about the same time I first heard Negro music. I was about 12 or 13, playing baseball in a playground; someone had a radio turned into a Negro station. From then on I was hooked. I used to listen to Al Benson and Big Bill Hill — they were disc jockeys in Chicago. From then on all the music I listened to was on the radio. My piano playing changed; I became influenced by jazz. I learned how to play that stride piano with my left hand and I knew that was it: stuff with a beat — jazz, blues, rock.

"At school I was primarily interested in film. It seemed to combine by interests in drama, visual art, music and the profit motive.

"Before I left Chicago, I was interested in theatre. These days, I think we want our theatre, our entertainment, to be larger than life. I think the total environmental thing will come in. Probably cinerama will develop further.

"I think the Doors is a representative American group. America is a melting pot and so are we. Our influences spring from a myriad of sources whch we have amalgamated, blending divergent styles into our own thing. We're like the country itself, America must seen to be a ridiculous hodge-podge to an outsides. It's like the Doors. We come from different areas, different musical areas. We're put together with a lot of sweat, a lot of fighting. All the things people say about America can be said about the Doors.

"All of us have the freedom to explore and improvise within the framework. Jim is an improviser with words."

Revolt: Road To Freedom
By Jim Morrison

"You could say it's an accident that I was ideally suited for the work I am doing. It's the feeling of a bow string being pulled back for 23 years and suddenly being let go.

"I am primarily an American; second a Californian; third a Los Angeles resident. I've always been attracted to ideas that were about revolt against authority. When you make your peace with authority, you become an authority. I like ideas about the breaking away or overthrowing of established order. I am interested in anything about revolt, disorder, chaos. Especially activity that seems to have no meaning. It seems to me to be the road toward freedom — external revolt is a way to bring about internal freedom. R a t h e r than start inside I start outside, reach the mental though the physical.

"I am a Sagitarian if astrology has anything to do with it. The Centaur, the Archer, The Hunter. But the main thing is that we are the Doors.

"We are from the West. The whole thing should be like an invitation to the West. The sunset, the night, the sea, this is the end.

"Anything that would promote that image would be useful. The world we suggest should be of a new wild west; a sensuous evil world. Strange haunting, the path of the sun, you know?

"On our albums we all cented about the end of the zodiac. The Pacific Ocean, violence and peace, the way between the yound and old."

KRLA ARCHIVES

please send me BEAT

26 issues only $3 per year

Mail to: **BEAT Publications**
9000 Sunset Blvd.
Los Angeles, California 90069

☐ New Subscription

I want BEAT for ☐ 1 year at $3.00 or ☐ 2 years at $5.00
I enclose ☐ cash ☐ check ☐ money order
Outside U.S.—$9 per year

* Please print your name and address.

Name
Street
City
State   Zip

CLASSIFIED

REACH COSMIC AWARENESS without drugs—help save mankind from destruction. Write for free booklet "Cosmic Awareness Speaks," SerVANTS OF AWARENESS, Box 115E, Olympia, Washington.

SLEEP LEANING, self hypnosis. Details, strange catalog free! Nutosuggestion, Box 24 BT, Olympia, Washington.

WILD POSTERS, far out bumper stickers, buttons! Crazy Labels, Box 21-M, Olympia, Washington.

INDIAN LOVE BELL AND ENGRAVED BRASS BELL FROM INDIA. STRUNG ON RAWHIDE NECK STRAP. TWINKLE AS YOU WALK. $2 P.P. Speer Company, 5237 Tendilla, Woodland Hills, Calif. 91364

The UNION GAP will be number 1 in 1968.

Paul Wheatbread. Happy Birthday! Penny

In Washington, D.C., THE THYME BEGINS are a happening thing!

Chicago loves the Blues Magoos.

Happiness is knowing Ralph Scala.

Peggy Brooks is bitchin'. RPG

BUBBLE GUM SYNDROME are coming!

Happiness is the greatest guy in the world. David Jones

The YARDBIRDS have a heart full of soul.

Happy Birthday JIM MAY from your green friends.

LEFT BANKE RULE.

Happy Birthday, Hooke. Love Laura

"Hello/Goodbye" and "I Am The Walrus" Rule! I love James PUMP McCartney. Lurelle

Beatles rule everyone.

PAUL IS LIFE!

Happy Birthday Stephen John!

To JoElla, Love Brett

Does anybody have an Association fan club?

Bill Cowsil, Happy 20th. You're the greatest. B. J. GALLO

Listen to Donovan.

MARK LINDSAY—The Orange Letter Affair wants you at the Sunset Address.

Dylan lives!

THE MONTGOMERY LANE GANG rides tonight. Watch out Babes.

Happy Birthday to Jeff Ray!

Mark Hudson and the New Yorkers, love forever!!! Tracy and Kim

George Harrison: Transcendentally terrific!

Neal Ford and Baby John have soul

Doors Posters 2½ ft. by 3 ft. $1.75 postpaid. Seper Co., 5273 Tendilla, Woodland Hills, Calif.

Due to popular demand THE BEAT is returning to its policy of accepting all forms of classified advertising. Included will be For Sale, items to Trade, Fan Clubs, etc., priced at 20¢ per word. Personal messages will be only 10¢ per word. Include money with your message.
Deadline for next issue will be January 17, 1968.

Live Sound Of The Grateful Dead

By Tony Leigh

One of the most influential groups to emerge from the musically prolific city of San Francisco is the Grateful Dead. Universally recognized as the leading exponent of that city's sound, the Dead are taking over where the Airplane left off. Proving that is the fact that *After Bathing At Baxter's*, the Airplane's latest recording, is dying on the record stands, whereas the Grateful Dead's second album is being impatiently awaited.

The Dead's sound can be best described as the new blues. With raunchy chords and funky sounds, they grip their live audiences with a burst of sound that patrons of San Francisco's famed Fillmore Auditorium maintain cannot be duplicated on records.

Led by Jerry Garcia, who commands an almost religious respect among his copious followers, the Dead come on with hard, hoarse, screeching sounds that are almost unbelievable. Garcia himself admits, "I don't believe the live sound, the live excitement can be recorded."

Besides Garcia, who was born in Mazatlan, Mexico, there is Phil Leash on bass. Leash recounts his life: "born in a jail cell, the last of a line of at least three generations of horse thieves. Thereafter, history took over leaving me bewigged, lathered and ready for the axe."

Ron McKernan, better known to everyone as Pigpen was born in San Bruno, California. Before joining the Dead, Pigpen was the leader of an all-organ blues band. He earned his nickname while still in high school. "I began singing at 16. I wasn't in school, I was just goofin'. I've always been singing along with records, my dad was a disc jockey, and it's been what I wanted to do." One noted San Francisco jazz/pop critic has called Pigpen "one of the major bluesmen in America."

Bill Sommers, who is their drummer played in about ten bands until the Dead finally asked him to join them. Bill has a background in football at Stanford.

Their rhythm guitarist is one of the youngest guitarists ever to play with the Dead. Bob Weir was only 18 when he began playing with the group. Weir is also a fine artist whose rather interesting interpretation of Pigpen is being worn on thousands of tee-shirts across the city.

The group is extremely together. Working and living together has brought the group so close that it is almost impossible to tell where one mind stops and the others start. This closeness, this ability to become one being, is perhaps the greatest asset any group in pop music today can have. Through the closeness of sound and mind, they can make their individual achievements heighten considerably as a group.

They are at their best in front of an audience. They have fun while on stage, and it is evident that this is where they want to be. Garcia explains, "Audiences are where it's at. We get into a thing by ourselves, but if there's a few people listening it makes a big difference."

Phil Leash perhaps sums up the Deads sound best when he states, "you just do what you do and we all kind of fell together. We orbit around a common center. It is impossible to define but it has something to do with making good music of any kind. That's the Grateful Dead."

THE VANILLA FUDGE, top 20 in album sales for many weeks, but somehow this English group can't break into the single charts. From l. to r., Carmine Appici, Vince Martell, Mark Stein, Tim Bogert.

KRLA ARCHIVES

KRLA ARCHIVES

KRLA BEAT

Volume 3, Number 22   February 10, 1968

TWO BEE GEES COLLAPSE IN PLANE

LONDON—Two of the Bee Gees, Barry and Robin Gibb, collapsed in a London-bound plane on their way home from a brief visit to relatives in Australia and had to be taken off the plane at Istanbul to receive medical attention.

Barry and Robin were accompanied by their manager, Robert Stigwood, who said: "They collapsed from sheer strain. We went to Australia for a holiday visiting Los Angeles en route. But for the entire time they were away from London they were being pursued by fans and they must have done a hundred and one interviews. The pressure was tremendous. On the plane soon after we left Sydney it was apparent that Barry was quite ill and Robin was little better. Their international fame has come about comparatively suddenly and I suppose they weren't geared for such pressures."

What price success?

A MONKEE UPSET

Peter Tork Surrounded By Mystery

LONDON—Two of the Monkees (but especially Peter Tork) caused quite a commotion here. After taking a brief ski holiday in Switzerland, Davy Jones returned to London and prolonged his stay on our side of the Atlantic by taking up temporary residence in a quiet but centrally positioned West End apartment.

Tork Flys Out

Meanwhile, a bearded Peter Tork flew out of London's Heathrow Airport with quite a mystery trailing behind him. Leaving with Peter were a tall, long-haired blonde and tiny baby boy. On the passenger list for their Los Angeles flight his companion was named as "Mary Harvey" which did little to clarify the situation. The baby was named as Justin.

Banner Heads

The press made much of their departure with the *Daily Mirror* headline announcing "A Monkee, A Mystery Girl, And A Baby Fly Out."

During his ten days in our capital, Peter Tork had not made any attempt to keep the girl and the baby in hiding. They accompanied him when he visited the EMI recording studios to watch Beatle George Harrison engaged upon the recording of his "Wonderwall" movie soundtrack music. When Peter gave his strictly limited number of London press interviews they waited outside in a conspicuously grand Rolls Royce. The hotel at which the trio stayed allegedly knew nothing of a "Miss Harvey" but reportedly confirmed that "Mr. Tork took a suite here with his wife and baby."

Slow Mover

The Monkees current U.K. single, "Daydream Believer," has been moving slowly but surely up our charts and is at number five as I write. After two weeks in the shops, their "Pices Aquarius, Capricorn & Jones, Ltd." album has climbed to ninth place on the LP charts.

—Tony Barrow

PETER TORK causes British to ponder the mystery

DAVY JONES has taken up temporary residence in London

KRLA ARCHIVES

LETTERS TO THE EDITOR

MORE PEOPLE ARE TALKING

Dear BEAT:

I have a "People Are Talking About" item that should be interesting to a number of Beatle and Rolling Stones' fans. So, here goes: People are talking about the Beatles appearing on the new Rolling Stones album cover and wondering how many people will be able to spot them on their own."

Keven Boone

NEW YORK POP FESTIVAL

Dear BEAT:

My friend and I are planning on going to the New York International Pop Festival. Would you please tell me where to write and get tickets, and also when it will be?

Thank you.

Christie O'Brien

I'm afraid you're as much in the dark as the rest of us, Christie. Since the first announcement was made of the Festival to be held in New York during the summer, there has not been another official word uttered. Rumor has it the whole idea has been shelved, but no one really knows for sure . . . or, at least, no one is talking.

The Editor

Neglecting A Diamond

Dear BEAT:

I received my first issue of your paper yesterday, having not read it before, and was very much impressed with it. However, this is not why I am writing.

This year I attended a "Where The Action Is" show and one of the stars of it was Neil Diamond. Up until then, I was just an admirer of his records. But I was very stunned at his showmanship and his friendliness and perhaps that is why I like him and his work now.

The thing that bothers me is that the magazines and newspapers across the nation fail to recognize him. Why? I can't answer that and I don't think you can either. All I know is that he deserves to have his name written in big, bold letters! I hope you realize that too.

His album, "Just For You," is remarkable. How many times do you find an album in which you like every song on it? He has a great voice —listen to "Shilo" or "Red, Red Wine" for proof—and remarkable ability as a writer.

He is not only a singer and writer but also an actor. Try "Mannix" for proof!

I don't want to go an and on about him but, please, on behalf of all us kids back in Toledo try to write a few stories on him!

Sharon Saam

Beginning Of End

Dear BEAT:

I want to commend you on the fine job that you and your staff have done since I subscribed to the BEAT this past year.

I saw by the old handwriting on the Teen Publication that the Monkees are losing favor among the teens which is quite understandable because what group stays on top for long nowadays. Which seems a shame because there are some good groups which never get there no matter how hard they try. They are passed by and aren't given the recognition they deserve and a manufactured group is taken to the heart of every self respecting teenybopper. Now that the Monkees music is improving they are beginning to go. Such though is the fate of any self respecting pop group.

As for me (one of the oldest teenagers in my state at 26) I will still dig the groups new and old: The Beatles of Rubber Soul and after, The Rolling Stones of Their Satanic Majesties Request, The Byrds of Younger Than Yesterday, The Beach Boys of Pet Sounds and Smiley Smile, Johnny Rivers of Rewind, Marianne Faithful of Faithful Forever, Monkees of albums 3 and 4, and on into the sunset.

I hope you continue your album reviews and keep up the people are talking column. You must have an inside track on this because it usually happens.

Sincerely,

JAMES P. DIXON

Beat Publications, Inc.

Executive Editor .... Cecil I. Tuck
Publisher .... Gayle Tuck
Editor .... Louise Criscione
Assistant Editor .... Jacoba Atlas

Staff Writers
Bobby Bovino   Ron Koslow
Tony Leigh   Shirley Poston

Contributing Writers
Tony Barrow   Sue Barry
Eden   Bob Levinson
Jamie McClusky III   Mike Masterson

Photographers
Ed Caraeff   Jerry Hass

National Advertising Representative
Sam Chase Assoc., Inc.
527 Madison Avenue
New York, New York 10022
(212) PL. 5-1668

Advertising Director .... Dick Stricklin
Business Manager .... Judy Felice
Subscriptions .... Diane Clatworthy

Distribution
Miller Freeman Publications
500 Howard Street, San Francisco, Calif.

The BEAT is published bi-weekly by BEAT Publications, Inc., editorial and advertising offices at 9000 Sunset, Suite 1000, L.A., California 90069. U.S. bureaus in Hollywood, San Francisco, New York, Chicago and Nashville; overseas correspondents in London, Liverpool and Manchester, England. Sale price 25 cents. Subscription price: U.S. and possessions $5 per year; Canada and foreign rates, $9 per year. Second class postage prepaid at Los Angeles, California.

LIP-SYNC CONTROVERSY

Dear BEAT:

A point of curiosity here. In the January 13th issue, you had an article on Kenny O'Dell wherein he stated his disgust for lip synching and stated: "I think that is all wrong, you should try to reproduce the sound you make in the recording studio and not fake it to an audience."

The same day I read it, I found that Kenny O'Dell would be appearing on Dick Clark's "American Bandstand" show. There, as I expected, was Kenny O'Dell lip synching in the typically bad "American Bandstand" tradition.

My question: who told whom that Kenny O'Dell was such an all-out good guy? Your publication is usually pretty accurate about facts, but I think someone goofed here.

Don R. Betzold

Apparently, you don't quite understand lip synching on television. On certain television programs (such as "American Bandstand") there is no orchestra or band or even a guitarist available. Therefore, an artist (whether he despises or blesses lip synching) has no choice but to lip sync his/her record. On other shows (Tonight, Ed Sullivan, Smothers Brothers, etc.) an orchestra is on hand and an artist does not (in fact, in some cases may not) lip sync. Hope that clears up your question.

The Editor

Simple Lyrics Not Always Best

Dear BEAT:

I am a subscriber and I love your newspaper. However, I have opinions concerning several things.

First, I completely and absolutely agree with Donna Markin from January 27, 1968 BEAT. She is completely correct. The BEATLES are, have always been and always will be the greatest group around.

Also, I disagree with Barry Gibb of the Bee Gees. Just because "I Am The Walrus" makes no sense to him, is it a bad song? Does a song have to have "moon in june" lyrics to be good? I like the Bee Gees very much. They are talented and I like their songs. But in my opinion (and I grant him the right of his) he has no right to rank on the Beatles who are a much more established group than the one he is a member of.

Peace,

SHARON

KRLA ARCHIVES

AROUND the WORLD

Miriam Makeba Sets Bookings Thru April

NEW YORK—Miriam Makeba, the "new" star who has been in the music business for years, is so much in demand since "Pata Pata" that she has set her schedule as far ahead as April!

This month alone Miriam is going to Caracas, Venezuela for three days at the Hotel Tamanaca and then back to the United States for dates at White Plains Community Center on February 10; Philadelphia's Academy of Music (11); War Memorial Auditorium, Boston (17); Kleinhan Music Hall, Buffalo, New York (18); Detroit's Cobo Hall (23) and the Columbus, Ohio Music Hall (24).

In March, Miriam returns to Chicago's Mister Kelly's for a two-week stand (18-31), getting in dates beforehand at Symphony Hall in Newark, New Jersey (2); the Hilton Hotel in Washington, D.C. (3) and Harper College in Binghampton, New York (8). The famed Cocoanut Grove in Los Angeles has claimed Miss Makeba's services from April 2 thru April 15.

An astonishing multi-personality of talent, humor, intelligence and great personal courage, Miriam has filled Carnegie Hall, Lincoln Center and the Greek Theatre many times, sung for the late President Kennedy at his birthday celebration in 1962, testified before the United Nations on social injustices, performed for state functions in most of the independent African republics, and has played to packed houses in London, Paris, Amsterdam, Dublin, Bonn, Melbourne and Copenhagen. She sings in eleven languages and dialects . . . Zulu, Swazi, Sotho, Shangaan, Spanish, Hebrew, Portuguese, Yiddish, Indonesian and English.

New Contract For Yarbrough

BURBANK—Warner Brothers/ 7 Arts Records has announced the signing of Glenn Yarbrough to a long-term, exclusive recording contract.

Yarbrough has been with RCA Victor Records for the past six years both as a single artist and as a member of the Limeliters. In addition to being a strong album selling artist, Yarbrough has the enviable reputation of being one of the most successful college concert draws in the entertainment industry.

Recently, Yarbrough has been doing a good deal of television work and upcoming in the very near future is a special on NBC-TV titled "Travels With Charlie" in which Glenn performs original material by Rod McKuen. Meanwhile, Warner Brothers/7 Arts Records is planning an album from this show constructed around a John Steinbeck work with Yarbrough doing the narration.

ALPERT SETS TV SPECIAL

HOLLYWOOD—Herb Alpert is set to have another television special sponsored by the same firm, the Singer Company, which sponsored his other two specials (one in April and one in November of last year).

The new special will air on April 22 on CBS-TV. The initial showing of "Singer Presents Herb Alpert and the Tijuana Brass" gathered the highest Nielsen rating of any hour special in the history of television.

This latest special will be filmed entirely on location and will devote the full hour to Herbie and his Brass.

Zappa Voted Top Musician

NEW YORK — Frank Zappa, leader of the Mothers of Invention, has been voted the "Pop Musician of the Year" in the Fifth Annual International Critics Poll conducted by Jazz & Pop magazine.

In the same survey, the Mothers' "Absolutely Free" album came in a close second to the Beatles' "Sgt. Pepper" LP. The Mothers' new album, "We're Only In It For The Money," has just been released.

Raiders Set Tour Dates

HOLLYWOOD — Paul Revere and the Raiders have been set for 13 tour dates during the months of February and March.

Scheduled dates are: February 9, Charleston, West Va.; Dayton, Ohio (10); Chicago, Ill. (11); Sterling, Ill. (12); Warrensburg, Mo. (13); Cape Giradeau, Mo. (14); Springfield, Ill. (15); Wichita, Kansas (16); Kansas City, Mo. (17); Denver, Colo. (18).

Three dates have been scheduled so far for March—Seattle and Vancouver on March 16 and Spokane on March 17.

PEOPLE ARE TALKING ABOUT the tremendous publicity push a powerful organization is giving a certain group and wondering if the young people will buy it . . . how many listeners Bill Cosby is going to pull in with his nightly radio show and betting it will be a very significant number . . . when Bunky and Jake will hit the music world in a big way — or if they will

. . . the female singing group who have to be a giant put-on because no one could actually look like that . . . the once-top American group who is having all kinds of difficulties in getting a record up the national charts . . . the publicists who think it's "cute" to send out asinine bios getting just what they deserve in print

. . . the fact that Jay and the Techniques have hit the big time — at least big enough to be able to charter their own plane for tours . . . the group who is suffering from an ego hang-up which enables them to forget all about the people who were nice to them on their way up . . . the high cost of recording not showing up much in the finished product

. . . a certain manager of a pop group who cannot seem to keep his mouth closed during group interviews and what a drag that is . . . the older singer who had one hit record about two years ago but keeps reappearing

every few months with a new act as well as new outfits and still manages to lose . . . why the Supremes haven't had a number one record lately . . . how many groups will now do their concerts with a full orchestra.

. . . what really has happened to the plans behind the second International Pop Festival . . . the going price for a new Donovan three-package album . . . the significance of the three Indians . . . the group who has a lead singer who can never be expected to be at a gig on time or to be in condition to perform when he is there . . . the fact that a hit record does not a hit group make and vice versa

. . . how witty Peter Noone can be when he sets his mind to it . . . Del Shannon's "Runaway" getting on the Australian record charts again . . . the group who insists upon taking a cut of everything they can . . . where Dave Dee, etc. came up with "Zabadak" . . . the Scaffold doing business everywhere but in the States and wondering why

. . . why it took Eric Burdon so long to come up with "Monterey" . . . whatever happened to the feature film the Monkees were supposed to make . . . giving an award for the weirdest album title and deciding there would be too many contenders for the prize . . . the group who had their first hit stay in the national top ten for months but can't seem to come up with a follow-up . . . the fact that "Born Free" hardly has a chance to get off the charts before it's back on again and how sweet that is for the publishing company.

KRLA ARCHIVES

SHOUTS FROM GENE

By Gene Cornish

First of all, I'd like to thank everyone everywhere for the beautiful Christmas cards and gifts my family and I received . . . we sincerely wish you all a very Happy New Year . . .

We're certainly looking forward to seeing all our friends in Los Angeles and Hawaii again soon! On January 27th we performed at the Carousel Theatre in West Covina, California and then took off for Hawaii for a giant show at the Honolulu International Center . . . the weather in New York City was about five degrees below zero when we left so you can understand our excitement about the trip to California and Hawaii!

A group to watch for: "The Collection," an up-and-coming rock band that's now playing in clubs around New York . . .

A couple of big hellos: to Dewey of The Buffalo Springfield; to Davy Jones of the Monkees, someone who is really outasite; to Dave Crosby wherever you are; and to Mike Greco, road manager of the Grass Roots and my dear friend for showing me such a wonderful time in LA . . . Also like to mention the groovy time I recently had at New York's The Scene with Bob Cowsill . . .

We're also excited about the release of our latest album, "Once Upon A Dream," which will be on the air and in record stores by the time you read this . . . and congratulations to Davy Brigati, Eddie's brother, for his fine performance of the title song from the album at Madison Square Garden in New York . . .

Oh, here's a little bit of news that I definitely want to get cleared up now and forever . . . contrary to popular rumor, I AM NOT MARRIED and have not been married for the past three months . . . I really wish I knew how that got around and how it all started.

I've been on vacation for the past three months — but, believe me, it hasn't all been glamorous . . . I'm still recovering from a fall I took on Dino's new spiral staircase . . . I have to say that Dino's new duplex is fantastic — but that staircase is *not* included in that description!

I guess that about takes care of the Rascals' most recent happenings . . . but I'll be talking to you again very soon . . . be seeing you soon in person, I hope.

Love,
Gene

WHAT'S UP DOC?

By Arthur Bolter, M.D.

Dear Doc:
I am getting desperate about my skin. My folks say that I will grow out of it, but I hate to go anywhere because I am such a mess and I feel that everybody stares at me.
                                Miserable

Dear Miz:
Acne occurs as the glands in our skin mature. They secrete more oily material and the pores become plugged. Therefore, the aim of treatment is to keep the skin as clean as possible.

Skin problems are so common in young people that they are often belittled. However, there are some things than can be done to alleviate your misery. Let us remember soap and water more often than once in a while for mild cases.

For severe problems, medical science has a lot to offer, so do not be hesitant to consult your physician or even a specialist in skin problems (a dermatologist).

Dear Doc:
My problem may sound silly but it worries me. I've written to Dear Abby, etc., and they tell me to see a doctor, so I thought this was my chance. I'm a freshman in high school and I have varicose veins. I don't even think I spell it right! I hate going through high school with a worry like this. You may think I have just a few but if I did that wouldn't worry me. I have a crossword puzzle of them on my upper legs.
What's your advice?
                                Worried

Dear Worried:
Varicose veins are not a "silly" problem, particularly in a young person. They are the result of a number of different conditions and are more commonly found in older people, usually related to some trouble with circulation. Mild forms can sometimes be covered with make-up or the new "mod body paint." However, you should be sure that what you see are only varicose veins.

Therefore, I would also strongly recommend seeing your family physician so that he can make the proper diagnosis. Neglect of varicosities can lead to complications such as thrombo-phlebitis (inflamation of the veins).

Dear Doc:
My friends think my problem is funny but it is terribly embarrassing to me. I am forever going to the bathroom. I usually go like between every two or three classes for fear that I might have to go during the next class and it's awful asking to be excused. Is it just nerves? What else could it be? (We go to the Clinic: we have no family doctor.)

My second problem is: I have a 22" waist and 34" hips and people say that when I walk I stick my stomach out as well as my derriere giving me a fat, awkward appearance. I'm almost certain I have a slight curvature of the spine. Could this be fixed by wearing a brace only at night or something? I can't swim, so that's no help. Is there any exercise or anything?

Doctor, I'd appreciate any help or advice you could give me. Thank you.
                                Embarrassed

Dear Embarrassed:
What you describe is usually called "urinary frequency" and is commonly associated with nervous excitement. If that is all it is, you could gradually increase the time between trips to the bathroom in order to stretch your bladder. This may take quite awhile, so do not get discouraged.

Concerning problem number two, it sounds like simply poor posture may be the cause of your awkward appearance. If so, exercises could be beneficial and perhaps your P.E. teacher could suggest some suitable ones for you.

Ho Receives Highest Pay

HONOLULU—Don Ho has tucked another first under his belt. The Hawaiian entertainment giant has just signed a new contract with Duke Kahanamoku's night club on Waikiki whereby Ho will play the club on-and-off and earn $10,000 a week for his services.

This makes him the highest paid entertainer in the history of the Islands. The contract is for the next 12 years.

ON THE BEAT BY LOUISE CRISCIONE

The Bee Gees are one group never at a loss for things to occupy their time. They should be in London right now filming a television special, "Cucumber Castle," which is scheduled for a world-wide release in the spring.

Then on February 27th the Bee Gees embark upon a Scandinavian personal appearance tour with extra stops in Paris and Germany before beginning their first British concert tour accompanied by a 60-piece orchestra at London's Royal Albert Hall on March 27.

Their first full-length motion picture, "Lord Kitchener's Valet," should be finished by the time they take off for their American tour in early summer. Other than that the Bee Gees don't have a thing to do!

RASCAL NOTE: The movie the Rascals are planning to make very shortly finally has a script . . . which is a nice start.

Dylan Hits

Bob Dylan's latest album, "John Wesley Harding," is making the people over at Columbia Records very happy. It sold over a quarter-million copies in less than a week! Dylan has already been awarded Gold Records for four of his albums and no one has the slightest doubt that "John Wesley Harding" will make number five for Bob.

Charlie Rich, best known for "Mohair Sam" and "Lonely Weekends," has just been signed to an exclusive recording contract by Epic Records. His first release for the company is due out any day now and is titled "Set Me Free." Hmmm.

Since their personal manager is the head of the Beatles' Apple

Publishing Company, their recording manager is Terry Melcher and their name was suggested by John Lennon, I have this feeling that we'll all be hearing quite a bit about the Grapefruit.

Introducing Grapefruit

So, I thought I might as well be the first to give you a short "who's who" in the group. John Perry is the lead guitarist; Pete Swettenham is the rhythm guitarist; Geoff Swettenham is the drummer; and George Alexander is the bass guitarist. George hails from Glasgow but the other three Grapefruit are London products.

Remember the name . . . with the power behind them, the Grapefruit can go no where but straight up.

Trini Lopez has all of Japan talking. He recently finished a concert tour of the country and managed to do the impossible. Japanese audiences are noted for their rather silent approach to concerts. In fact, when he arrived in Japan, Trini was told not to expect any reaction at all. But, says Trini: "I did my best and they went out of their minds." A literal statement if there ever was one.

Amazing Lopez

What an amazing man Mr. Lopez is . . . if you can believe it, he already has his next year mapped out — down to the final week. "I hope to do only 20 weeks of personal appearances, playing only the top places, such as Las Vegas, New York and the important countries. And 20 weeks a year for pictures — about two a year. Of the other 12 weeks, I would devote six to recording and six to resting and playing golf and tennis."

THE GRAPEFRUIT CANNOT MISS!

KRLA ARCHIVES

PICTURES IN THE NEWS

RAVI SHANKAR, noted Indian musician, has composed the music to a new motion picture called "Chappaqua." Combining the sitar sound with rock and roll, Shankar has contributed immensely to the impact of this important film. The musician-composer is now on a tour of college campuses throughout the U.S.

BRENTON WOOD with three hits in a row to his credit has embarked on a European tour to begin in London, England.

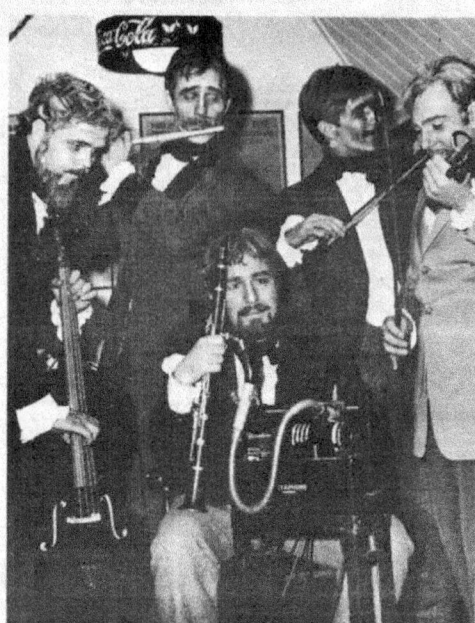

THE MENDELSON QUINTETTE CLUB of Boston may start a new fad. Unable to get back to the studio to cut a new record, the Quintette recorded into a private dictaphone. JBL loudspeakers were used to insure the sound.

THE DOORS NEED YOUR HELP. Their new album which will be released in March contains one side consisting of only one song! Now, your problem is to name that song. Obviously, because this contest is running before the album is released, the name for the song will have to be based on what you already know about the group. Mail your suggestions to Diane Gardiner, 250 North Canon Drive, Beverly Hills, Calif. 90210. The winner will receive one of the first copies of the album, autographed by the Doors, along with a personal note from Jim Morrison. So hurry, become a part of the new Doors' album.

KRLA ARCHIVES

U.K. POP NEWS ROUND-UP
GEORGIE FAME'S BACK WITH 'BONNIE'

By Tony Barrow

A year ago Georgie Fame spent several weeks at London's Saville Theatre as co-star with American folk girl Julie Felix in Brian Epstein's "Fame in '67" production. Around the same time he began a fresh segment of his recording career with a new label, minus his early backing group, The Blue Flames.

As it turned out, 1967 was not a fantastic year for Fame, although a staunch but small army of followers gave him a series of sell-out concerts.

Fame Riding High

Now Georgie Fame is back with a big bang, riding high in not only the U.K. charts but in the best selling lists of more than 15 different countries. The record which has put him back in the spotlight is "The Ballad of Bonnie and Clyde," a Mitch Murray/Peter Callender composition based on the story-line of the trend-setting film but having no direct connection with it.

Selling at the rate of 10,000 copies each day in Britain, the single has qualified for a Silver Disc Award, the first of 1968.

To increase his chances of building "The Ballad of Bonnie and Clyde" into a top worldwide hit, Georgie Fame is setting out on a series of jet-stop promotional trips to territories as far apart as Germany and Australia; also being set up is a short but busy promotional visit to America but precise dates and details were not available as this issue of The BEAT went to press.

Traffic as Trio?

Stevie Winwood's group, Traffic, minus key personality Dave Mason, has decided upon a unique way of agreeing whether or not to stay as a trio. Winwood is not anxious to replace Mason but, to find out just how important his loss is to the group's "live" performance popularity, Traffic has been making a series of out-of-town club, ballroom and university appearances.

Meanwhile the Island record label is to issue Traffic's "No Face, No Name, No Number" track from the "Mr. Fantasy" aubum as a February U.K. single. When this is released Winwood will make a final decision whether to add a new name or keep his outfit as a three-man operation.

Scene and Heard

Ringo Starr becomes the first Beatle to make a solo guest appearance in a TV variety show. He's scheduled to duet with songstress Cilla Black in her new BBC Television series February 6 and has been rehearsing his part in a comedy routine with her for the same program . . . Having vacationed with Marianne Faithfull and her two-year-old son, Nicholas, in the Bahamas, Mick Jagger has been soaking up some more winter sunshine in Rio de Janeiro. I understand that Decca has no plans to issue a single from the Rolling Stones' "Their Satanic Majesties Request" album in Britain and that the group's first post-vacational task in London this month will be the recording of two entirely new Jagger/Richard compositions for rush release . . . "Am I That Easy to Forget" by Engelbert Humperdinck only just issued in

(Continued on Page 7)

FAME cashes in on "Bonnie & Clyde"

JOHN LENNON coming to America?

MICK JAGGER soaking up the sun in Rio de Janeiro

DIANA ROSS and Supremes in London for television

KRLA ARCHIVES

PROCOL HARUM PLAYED TO celebrity-packed audience at the Speakeasy

(Continued from Page 6)

U.K., entered our Top 20 at number 16 and has zoomed into the Top 10 . . . Apologies to Manfred Mann and Bob Dylan — I described the new Manfred single as "The Amazing Quinn" instead of "Mighty Quinn" . . . Former bandleader Vick Lewis, promoter of 1967 London concerts by the Monkees, appointed new Managing Director of Nems Enterprises, the Nempire built up by the late Brian Epstein. Brian's brother Clive Epstein remains as company chairman.

Vacation for Lennon

Lightning six-day vacation in Casablanca, Morocco, for John Lennon and his wife Cynthia when they decided at the last minute to accompany actor Victor Spinetti to North Africa . . . John Lennon's brilliantly painted Rolls Royce (the one the newspapers love to call "psychedelic") shipped to New York for possible touring use by the Beatle in America later in the year. However, he has no immediate plans to cross the Atlantic as the Rolls could be in storage for quite a long time!

During Rome shooting of the movie "Candy," Ringo and Maureen Starr became very friendly with Elizabeth Taylor and Richard Burton . . . Estate Duty Office in London declared an estate of just over one million dollars (gross) left by Brian Epstein who died last August without making a will. But the gross total does not include a yet-to-be-agreed valuation of his major business interests.

Spencer Davis Stateside

Spencer Davis Group will be in America from March 29 to May 5 . . . Liverpudlian screen actress Rita Tushingham met up with George Harrison during the Beatle's recent trip to Bombay. Rita was in India for location work on her new picture "The Guru," George was there to write and record Eastern-influenced segment of his "Wonderwall" movie soundtrack score.

John Lennon's 55-year-old father, Alfred (Freddie) Lennon plans imminent marriage to former Exeter University student, Pauline Jones, 19 . . . Unscheduled stopover for Bee Gees Barry and Robin Gibb in Turkey when they were returning to Britain from Australia at New Year. Both group members collapsed on the aircraft and spent several days under sedation in an Istanbul hospital . . . Two of Britain's top girl singers chose ski holidays — Petula Clark broke her ankle in Switzerland, Cilla Black returned from Austria unhurt but her boyfriend, Bobbie Willis, broke a leg!

Harum at Speakeasy

John Walker failed to return to Britain with Scott and Gary following recent Far East dates. Word is John will settle in America with his wife, Cathy, and start a fresh solo career on your side of the Atlantic . . . Procol Harum played to star-stacked audience at London's Speakeasy discotheque, group's first U.K. date in more than nine months.

Week-long cabaret-starring stint at Cesar's Palace for Lulu broke all club's existing attendance records — that's not the Las Vegas location but a venue advertised as "Britain's most luxurious Casino" at Luton in Bedfordshire, just north of London . . . In January 28th London Palladium TV show Diana Ross and the Supremes co-starred with Tom Jones.

Special for Pet

First February job for Petula Clark following her European visit will be making her own 60-minute NBC-TV spectacular . . . The Dubliners, top Irish folk unit who have been heavily promoted to Top 10 success by Radio Caroline (still a potent if outlawed force in U.K. radio), make their U.S. television debut when they guest in the St. Patrick's Day edition of the "Ed Sullivan Show" in March.

RINGO now friends with the Richard Burtons

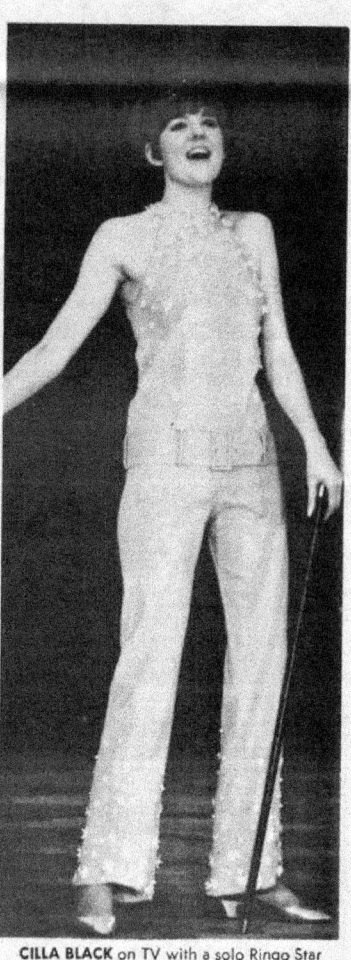

CILLA BLACK on TV with a solo Ringo Star

KRLA ARCHIVES

GET YOURS NOW WHILE THE SUPPLY LASTS!

I enclose $1.75 plus 25 cents handling for each*.

A BEAT Calendar Poster in black, white and red

NAME
ADDRESS
CITY   STATE   ZIP CODE
*California residents please include 5% sales tax.

KRLA ARCHIVES

The Controversy Surrounding 'Judy'

By Rochelle Reed

He's 6'5" tall and would have a difficult time going anywhere in disguise since he can't even find clothes to fit at Hollywood's better mens' shops.

But that doesn't dampen the spirits of John Fred, who along with his Playboy Band cut the surprise song of the new year, "Judy In Disguise."

Written some seven months ago for an album titled "Agnes English," "Judy In Disguise" was never thought of as a single release by either co-author John Fred or his Playboys.

Their Decision

"The record company thought it would be a real good single and it was their decision to put it out — it wasn't ours. We didn't think it was that strong for a single. But it was and we're not complaining!" John says.

"In fact, I'm very surprised at the success of 'Judy,'" he continues. "I'm getting laughed at now by people in the record company. They all said it was going to be the biggest record we ever had—and I'm the first to admit it—I didn't think the record was as good as others we've cut."

Southern Success

John Fred and His Playboy Band have been successful in the South for the past three years and have three albums to their credit. They hadn't made it in the North or West, however, until now.

Very Beatle-ish in flavor, "Judy In Disguise" actually came from "Lucy In The Sky With Diamonds," according to John.

"The first time I heard the record I thought they were saying "Lucy In Disguise" so I just got the idea. I didn't steal anything, really. This song is entirely different. I just got the idea and I brought it to Andrew Barnard (a member of the Playboy band and co-author, with John, of almost all the Playboy songs). Then we just wiggled around with it a little bit.

"We wrote the tune at Andrew's house—he likes to work late at night though I don't really care when we work. I just get ideas that come into my head and I just write them down. I can write any time. It doesn't make any difference. I'm not a mood writer—well, I'm not a mood writer in the sense that I have to get into the mood to get an idea.

Stays Around

"But once I get an idea, I'm lucky enough that I can keep it in my head. I'm not like some people—they have to get to a piano right then. But if the idea's really good—like 'Judy In Disguise' stayed on my mind for three or four days before I brought it to Andrew—the whole song is laid out in my head—everything, even the bridge.

"Usually you have to say, 'Well, I got the first verse, now I have to write a bridge.' This time I wrote the entire song in my head and even the first verse of lyrics."

"Judy In Disguise" has created consternation among disk jockeys and radio station personnel, plus lots of curiosity from listeners, because with John's Southern drawl, it is difficult to determine whether it's "Judy in disguise with glasses . . ." or "Judy in disguise with acid. . ."

"This is the way I feel about it," John says by way of explanation. "If they want to believe that, that's fine, because I've heard so many records like that by the Beatles or Eric Burdon or the Rolling Stones, and everyone gives their own in-

JOHN FRED and His Playboy Band making it happen with a seven month old record.

terpretation to what they are saying—and it's not what they think.

No Misinterpretation

"Honest and truthfully, we did not intend for it to be misinterpreted. In fact, the first time I heard the "acid" version, I thought it was the greatest thing I'd ever heard. I didn't really laugh, I just said 'Well, that's great 'cause I mean I hope it helps to sell the record.'

"It's like the Beatles—they know what a song's about in their minds but there's such a triple meaning behind the tune that they love for you to kind of wiggle around with it like 'Judy In Disguise With Acid.'

"'Judy' is really a simple song. It doesn't have a triple meaning. It's like some songs you can pinpoint — to me, 'Penny Lane' is about a street and a city—it's pretty plain.

"But then you have songs like 'Strawberry Fields Forever' or 'I Am The Walrus.' I can sit here and talk and we can discuss what you think the song is about and I can discuss what I think the song is about and John Lennon can tell you what he thinks the song is about—but really, nobody can say what it's about. NOBODY CAN REALLY SAY.

Who Else?

"I hate to keep going back to the Beatles, but who is there to go back to?"

Looking to the future, however, John Fred, 22, received his bachelor's degree in physical education from Louisiana State University last month. The rest of the Playboys are all either college students or recent graduates.

"'Judy In Disguise' is not basically the sound of the Playboy Band, I'm sorry to say," John explains. "Most people would probably lie and say it is but it's not really us.

"If you ever hear us in person, still tell it's us on record."

you'll know what I mean. We do a little bit of everything from the Beatles to Otis Redding to Wilson Pickett to the Rascals. But you can

And Next?

The question of what is next on the Playboy agenda is bothering John Fred, to put it mildly.

"I'm not going to follow it up with something like 'Snoopy's Little Sister' or 'Judy Has Contact Lenses And Is Back On The Scene Again,'" he insists.

"I might never have another hit record—but I won't follow 'Judy' with something basically the same. I want to try and progress!"

And part of John Fred's path of progression is about to be heard on an upcoming album—he lassoed the entire Dallas Symphony Orchestra for one track.

SOME 'STRAIGHT' ANSWERS FROM THE LEMON PIPERS

In the last six months or so, new American groups have been climbing up the national charts with amazing speed and accuracy. The latest group to accomplish this feat is the five-man union known as the Lemon Pipers. Their hit? "Green Tambourine."

Bill Albaugh, the 19-year-old drummer, likes heights . . . at least one would be forced to make that deduction from the fact that Bill not only likes to fly a plane but also to climb mountains!

However, he lists his hobby as writing "Happy Birthday" on school buildings acrss the country . . . though, that's up to you to believe.

Art Of Playing

R. G. Nave is the 22-year-old who enjoys playing an organ, tambourine, fog horn and toys. When not performing with the group, R. G. indulges in scuba diving and sky diving. R. G.'s accomplishments are succeeded only by 21-year-old Bill Bartlett's "hobbies" of burning holes in his bedspread and smoking spinach. Bill majored in chemistry and mathematics at Syracuse University. Unfortunately he gave that up and is now a senior in fine arts at Miami University.

Steve Walmsley is the 18-year-old bass guitarist for the Lemon Pipers and was born in New Zealand. A poet, he looks deeply into other peoples' minds, feels uncomfortable around adults and says he likes to catch passing freight cars.

Tower Money

Ivan Browne, 20-year-old lead singer and rhythm guitarist, lives in a tower and admits that his best friend is money. Other than the green stuff, he enjoys swordfighting, chemistry, Hershey bars, motorcycles, weird clothes and climbing trees.

Although they obviously love a good joke and straight answers, it is a known fact that they perform all types of music from folk ballads to psychedelic sounds, from blues to country and western music. They write most of their own material and if you're in New York between February 28 and March 11 you can catch the Lemon Pipers at the Bitter End . . . and discover the truth for yourself!

THE LEMON PIPERS and their "Green Tambourine" are pushing up the charts.

KRLA ARCHIVES

Cosby's Back SINGING!

AVAILABLE AT

fever tree is coming

KRLA ARCHIVES

LISTEN TO COSBY
Monday-Friday
8:00
KRLA

COSBY—WHY I TURNED SERIOUS

By Bill Cosby

Whenever the talk gets around to "career," I always get the question: "How come you changed from stand-up comedian to serious actor?" Actually, my start in comedy was as natural as stubbing your toe, but my dramatic work is the result of a carefully thought-out decision.

When I was a kid I always used to pay attention to things that other people didn't even think about. I'd remember funny happenings, just little trivial things, and then tell stories about them later. I found I could make people laugh and I enjoyed doing it because it gave me a sense of security. I thought that if people laughed at what you said, that meant they liked you. Telling funny stories became, for me, a way of making friends.

No Jokes

My comedy routines come from this story-telling knack . . . I never tell jokes. I don't think I could write an out-and-out joke if my life depended on it. Practically all my bits deal with my childhood days back in Philly where the most important thing on the block was how far you could throw a football.

I think what people like most about my stories is that they can identify. I had a man once stop me and say, "Hey, you know that story you tell about street football and how you'd cut behind a car? Well . . . I used to do the same thing in the country but I used a cow!"

The situations I talk about people can find themselves in . . . it makes them glad to know they're not the only ones who have fallen victim to life's little ironies. For example, how many of us have put the ice water bottle back in the refrigerator with just enough water left so we won't have to refill it? Be honest now.

A Happening

That's how I got involved in comedy . . . it just sort of happened. Once I decided it was a way to make a living, the struggle was on. Breaking into show business is one of the hardest . . . longest . . . most discouraging things you can do. If you want to make the old school try, you better have plenty of guts and determination 'cause you'll need all you can muster up.

I was quite satisfied with my work after I got going. Night clubs were good to me . . . and TV suddenly started opening up. It wasn't until "I Spy" came along that I really felt established . . . at least to a certain degree. It was so completely different from anything I had ever done. Story-telling is one thing, but playing a definite character . . . and serious, yet . . . that's something else.

In the beginning I was careful to keep my "Bill Cosby comedian" personality strictly separated from the personality of Alexander Scott, who I play on the show. After awhile, though, I began to realize that Scotty was a man with characteristics and I had to develop them.

Real Person

I also felt that separating my comedy self from my dramatic self was not right. In the end I just relaxed and let things come naturally. As a result Scotty has become a very real person to a lot of very real people who watch "I Spy" every week. He isn't a type . . . you can't see through him and you can't predict what he'll do next. Sometimes he's even hard to understand, but aren't we all?

Now that I've gotten into playing a serious role, I really enjoy it. I must admit I was nervous in the beginning, but the experience has really been great for me. I know it's hard to keep pushing yourself into different areas, but you have to if you want to be around in a few years. In this business, if you stand still, you disappear!

As for the future, who knows? The only limits are the ones you put on yourself. So far I've been lucky enough to avoid them. And if I sound serious about all this, believe me . . . I am.

Bring Back Star Trek

Unique among the nation's college campus population, the students at the California Institute of Technology at Pasadena have shown little interest in protests and demonstrations.

But last week, Cal Tech students joined forces with KRLA, nationally recognized for its humorous promotions involving contemporary social satire, to call for a protest march, replete with live band, picket signs and all the trappings, to voice opposition to the rumored cancellation of NBC-TV's science fiction "Star Trek" series.

Tradition

During the week KRLA took to the air, with tongue deeply buried in cheek, to point out that the half-humanoid character Mr. Spock, in the true American tradition, raised himself from a Vulcan slum to become a national folk hero.

By Saturday night, the appointed time for the march on the NBC-TV studio in Burbank, the ranks of the Cal Tech protestors swelled to over a thousand as sympathetic students from other Los Angeles area colleges and high schools heeded KRLA's call to action.

Decision Pending

The well-managed marchers, escorted by jovial Burbank police and KRLA officials, paraded to the web's lavish facilities where they were met by NBC director of film programs, James Seaborne, who assured all that a decision on "Star Trek" is "still pending."

Caught up in the spirit of the occasion, the NBC brass and corps of press agents even sported, with only the slightest trace of embarrassment, bright yellow badges bearing the call letters of non-network KRLA.

GYPSY BOOTS I love a parade and KRLA.

KRLA ARCHIVES

MARK LINDSAY and Paul Revere with Charlatan Production's Producer-Director **PETER GARDINER.**

Charlatan Productions: Mind Blowing Films For Pop Groups

By Jacoba Atlas

The arena is empty, the fog is rolling in from the coast. Eric Burdon steps into the bleak setting; the soundtrack whistles with the blowing wind. Suddenly, as Burdon looks up the screen bursts with the impact of milling people; it is the Monterey Pop Festival in full swing. Thus begins a five minute film on Eric Burdon's record called *Monterey*.

This film was produced by Charlatan Productions, a small intensely creative organization involved in doing promotion films for rock groups. The word promotion here can be deceptive; it to talk only in terms of contribution to an art form. These films would be more accurate perhaps are only promotional in that they are dealing with a group, with one or two records. But nevertheless they are some of the more interesting and involving film work being done today.

The company consists of three young men, Peter Gardiner, Tom Rounds and Allen Daviau. Alive, talkative, individual fantastically interested in both film and music, they have found the key to conveying the best in the audio medium with the best in the visual medium.

Beatle Influence

Their services are constantly in demand. So far they have completed 15 films, and have recently signed contracts to film 26 for MGM-Verve, and contracts with other various record companies are negotiating. Their competition is growing, but really in number only. Too many other companies are still in what can only be called the Lester-Beatle syndrome. Their idea of a pop music film is to have the groups run about on a field, or pop out from behind in trees and then disappear. None of this is done by Charlatan.

What is done is a fantastic piece of art work that best exemplifies the group and the music. Peter Gardiner who is responsible for the final editing states, "we listen to a record under the most receptive conditions. Then we meet and discuss our ideas. Finally we come to the group and see what they want. "But," he emphasized, "the groups know that although we will listen to their ideas, the final decisions must come from us, otherwise the whole thing will die."

The field is growing rapidly, and record companies are putting their wholehearted support behind this endeavor. Tom Rounds explains, "This whole thing involves what might be called a shotgun approach to music, or maybe a wider approach would be a better choice of words. The companies are realizing that they need a better way to promote records than just relying on top 40 programming. Many times it's difficult to get them to play a new group, or to take a chance with someone who might be doing something different. This reluctance stems from necessity. I know, I used to be a program director in the Bay Area.

Film Oriented

"But anyway, companies are now realizing the necessity to find another way to get the kids to know the records. And film was the logical thing. All the groups want to do features anyway. Everyone is terribly film oriented. If we had tried to do this five or six years ago, the companies and the groups wouldn't have wanted the films. But now, everyone wants them.

"The outlet will be in television, and the market is fantastic there. Everything from Dick Clark to the local shows. Even network specials want them. This doesn't mean that we don't want to see them go into theatres. There is a lot of discussion about putting these out as shorts with films, but nothing definite is set yet."

Peter and Tom met while they were studying at Amherst College. In fact, they worked together on the first pop radio program on FM at the college. It was called King Peter, although it didn't refer to Peter Gardiner. This was way back in 1957, and they even did their own critiques and chart work. Peter was a music major. But after college they went their separate ways for ten years. It was only last year that they got together again.

Special Effects

They began doing special effects, which they still get calls for, the most notable perhaps is for the psychedelic film, *The Trip*. They also do the opening sequence for the Les Crane Show here in LA.

Their approach is to combine music and film into one unit. They have done just that. Peter, because of his background in music is able to integrate the two forms into becoming one. It takes hours of hard work, a five second film sequence can take as long as two hours of intensive work.

"I do the editing with the music in my head constantly. It's very important to edit to the music. Sometimes you want to cut right on the beat, sometimes slide in before or after, but it has to be intentional."

They find that the groups are easy to work with, although sometimes a great deal of tact is necessary. Peter explains, "a lot of the groups think they are born comedians. Then too they have seen the Beatles films and the Monkees and their idea is to run about and have fun. Sometimes it just becomes benefical to let them get that out of their system, and then start shooting.

"We film sort of erratically. Only once have we come out with a film that followed the original script. In fact the idea of a script is sort of away from the way we work. Only the American Breeds' film really followed a pattern."

They have filmed the Cowsills, Jimi Hendrix (a mind blowing film that's incredible), Eric Burdon. In the future they will do Aretha Franklin, The Young Rascals, Cake and many others.

Assaulting Senses

"We see our future in full length productions really. The great thing about today is the kids are oriented to sound and color and lights, and having the senses assaulted with visual and audio images. It's great for us."

To talk about new waves and new trends in pop music is always a little dangerous. This is a here today gone tomorrow industry, but seeing the work of the Charlatans compels one to realize that their ingenuity and creativity will enable them to stay on the top. It is gratifying to see young people, without establishment hangups finally able to come into their own creatively *and* commercially. Charlatan Productions is a whole wonderful thing in themselves.

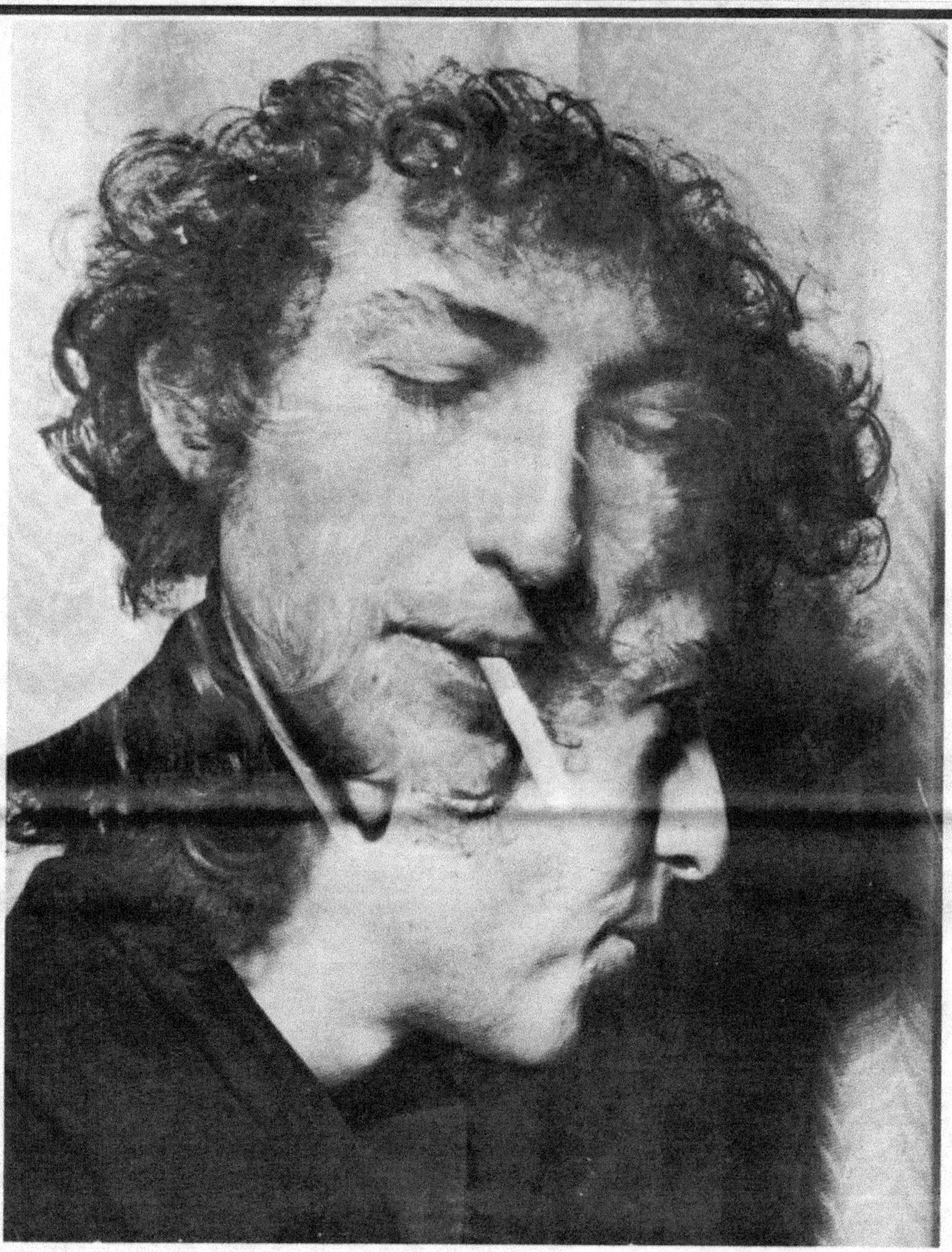

KRLA ARCHIVES

AVAILABLE AT

KRLA ARCHIVES

A PRETTY PICTURE

Now Available At:
MONTGOMERY WARD DEPARTMENT STORES

THE SPREADING CONSPIRACY

KRLA ARCHIVES

"Our Music Is Family Music"

By Tony Leigh

Jay and the Techniques know how to sell a song. Combining good rhythm with interesting catchy words, they have found themselves the proud owners of three hit records in a row. There seems to be nothing these boys can do that is wrong. Their first album did tremendously well, and their second, which is just off the press, is slated to do likewise.

The leader of the seven man group is, of course, Jay Proctor. Articulate, polite, hip, and interesting, he has very individual views on himself, the group, his life, and success as a whole.

"I started out like most Negro entertainers in church. I sang gospel with my mother and my aunt. From there I finally went into singing pop music, and after playing with several groups, all of us finally found each other.

"That meeting was mainly just people knowing people and then other people knowing them. We came together about two years ago, and have been playing ever since."

Jay and the Techniques originate from Allantown, Pennsylvania. They still all live there, in the neighborhoods where they grew up. Jay, who is extremely friendly and down to earth, has found that although success hasn't really had any adverse effects on him, old friends have not remained likewise unchanged.

"A lot of my old friends don't like me anymore. I guess it has something to do with being jealous of my success. Then the other thing that really makes me sad is that people see me and don't say anything. Later they'll tell someone they saw me and they didn't say hello because they thought I wouldn't answer. That's so ridiculous, and it really hurts. Now when I get home, I try to give a large party, and tell everyone I see that I really want to talk to them, and be with my old friends."

Success doesn't really leave much time for staying at home seeing ones friends. The group is usually on tour, or recording in New York. Their producer is Jerry Moss, a man for whom Jay has the upmost respect and trust.

"Jerry picks our material. I have some say, but I trust his taste and his judgment. He is also responsible for the arrangement.

"He's incredible at a recording session. He'll know just what to say to get the guys to do the right thing. He even knows my range better than I do.

"A local DJ in Allantown brought us to Jerry. We had been playing local hops and college dances, and then Jerry started working with us.

"Our stage act contains a lot of soul music, because our own records aren't plentiful enough to sustain an entire evening. But our sound really isn't soul. It's more something for everyone. The kids can dance to it because it has a good beat, it's not so loud older people can't enjoy it, and for the youngsters there's the lyrics. You might say our music is family music.

"I especially enjoy doing concerts. It's great to get the feeling from the audience. Even in a large auditorium you can get that close feeling."

Jay and the Techniques are unique in many respects, none the least of these is the fact that the group consists of two Negro singers, backed up by five white musicians. The pop industry has lately come under much attack for its lack of inter-group integration.

"This was totally accidental. We had no intention of choosing people because of color. They were just the best people we could get for the job. We think we have the best lead guitarist, and it doesn't matter what he is."

Although Jay would be the last person on earth to set himself up as an example to other people, his success has brought him a measure of just that.

"What happens is with parents really. They come up and say that their kids play this or that instrument, and should they concentrate on that only.

"I usually tell them it's really important to just concentrate on music, but after you get a good education. You need that background no matter what you do. If you're really serious about music, well you can do that while you're going to school. And if you can't then just wait until you're out and then there is still plenty of time."

Although Jay left home at a very early age, because he thought he needed that independence; he is back with his parents now. Looking back, Jay doesn't really regard the move for independence as a mistake, but it was attempted at too young age.

"I thought I knew everything there was to know at sixteen, but I really didn't know anything. You're just a kid at sixteen, no matter how smart you think you are."

Jay plans to stay with the group for "as long as they'll have me" and although this article has singled him out to be interviewed, Jay insists, that he is only one of the group.

"There are no stars in this group, certainly not me. We all are together, one unit, and that's the way it will always be. I have no plans to go out on my own."

Totally Unique: Country Joe And The Fish

Country Joe and the Fish is one of the most creative groups to come out of the Bay Area. Their first two albums were immediately recognized as being truly unique. **Feel Like I'm Fixing to Die** is a definite chart climber.

The Fish, as they are collectively called, is a strange animal in the pop field. There seems to be little or no commercialism attached to the group. Playing free concerts whenever asked in parks and arenas, they seem to have little regard for the financial considerations of most groups.

Their latest album includes a marvelous piece of merchandising called the Fish Game. To appreciate what that is all about, one must buy the album. But even without gimmicks like Fish Game, which is truly clever and original, the group is something very worthwhile.

They are planning to travel all over the world this year. One of the places they will stop will be Chicago where, along with Phil Ochs, The Fugs and Allen Ginsberg they will take part in a Youth Festival.

Just recently they have been the subject of a yet to be completed film called **How We Stopped the War**, filmed at a peace demonstration in San Francisco. They hope to be able to show this very soon, but the producer, Dave Peoples, isn't giving any guarantees.

BEAT SHOWCASE

PENNY CANDY is a brand new group breaking out of New York and spreading all across the country. The first unusual thing about Penny Candy is obvious — there are eight group members! They are Patsy Lombardi, Julie Anne Thompson, Mary Jane Mandala, Larry Wurtzel, John Shykun, Russ Rosenfeld, Al Dittrich and Bob Love. Watch out for them — they're destined to make a big sound!

Beat Poster Shop

Giant 22x28 Love Poster in Full Color

(v) Maharishi (s) Stones (r) Jimi Hendrix (i) Dylan (t) The Who (c) Country Joe (w) Strawberry Alarm Clock (L) Love

Send to: BEAT POSTER SHOP, 9000 Sunset, Suite 1000, Los Angeles, Cal. 90069

PLEASE SEND ME THE FOLLOWING POSTERS (LIST BY LETTER) _____
I ENCLOSE $1.75 plus .25 Handling for each*.

Name _____
Address _____
City _____ State _____ Zip Code _____
*California Residents Please Include 5% Sales Tax

SPEC-TRIM SUNGLASSES

UNIQUE SHADOW BOX FRAMES
MOD RECESSED LENSES
TWO-COLOR FRAMES
$4 Each*
*Calif. residents please add 5% sales tax

AVAILABLE IN:
Blue and White — White and Pink
Purple and White — Red and White
Yellow and Black — Red and Black
Designate Frame Color

SEND TO:
BEAT PUBLICATIONS
9000 Sunset, Suite 1000
Los Angeles, Calif. 90069

DEBS

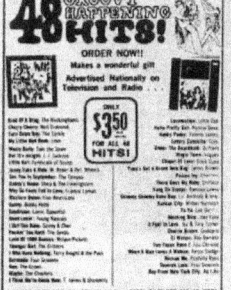

TURNING ON

WILD FLOWERS (Electra) Judy Collins. *Micheal From Mountains, Sisters of Mercy, Sky Fell,* plus seven more. This is one of the most perfect albums ever produced. Combining the simplicity of folk music with the complexity of classical music, Miss Collins conveys a mood that is truly unique. The individual songs are incredible. Singing her own compositions for the first time, Miss Collins also emerges as a fine writer. Again, Miss Collins choose three Leonard Cohen songs (the Canadian poet who wrote *Suzanne* and *Dress Rehearsal Rag*) and two by another young poet named Joni Mitchell.

The album is fully orchestrated by Josuha Rifkin. The arrangements are absolutely flawless. Never before in a folk rock album has the combined efforts of musician and singer been used so well to create a single mood. One of the most important aspects of this album is the fact that all of the components work so well together instead of functioning as separate features as so often happens with orchestrated pop albums. It is the perfect blending of poetry and sound, of mood and harmony, of voice and orchestra.

One beautiful Joni Mitchell song is called *From Both Sides Now,* "I've looked at love from both sides now, but it's love's illusions I recall, I really don't know love at all."

Due to singers ike Miss Collins, the French singer composer Jacques Brel is becoming known in this country too. Here, we have *La Chansons des Vieux Amants* (the Song of Old Lovers), in her last album, *In My Life,* Miss Collins sang M. Brel's *La Colombe* (The Dove). M. Brel wrote the original *If You Go Away* which Rod McKuen has translated into English. (The original in French is called Ne M'Quittez Pas — Don't Leave Me.)

MASS IN F MINOR (Reprise) The Electric Prunes. Nothing the Prunes has ever done in the past will prepare you for this new sound. Written and arranged by David Axelrod, the album is exactly what the title states — a Mass in F Minor. Singing in Latin the familiar phrases "Gloria in excelesis Deo" or "Dona nobis pacem" the Prunes are singing what amounts to a mass. However, the background music is a combination of pop and church music. The album is fantastically interesting, a blending of the modern day sound with the ancient tribute to God. It is the 20th century equivalent to the 18th century Gregorian Chants. This album is rapidly becoming one of the most important underground albums of the day; listen to it. One interesting sideline to the album is the fact that it has been used in actual masses in the San Francisco area.

A giant (22"x28") Calendar Poster in black, white and red.

PLEASE SEND ME THE CALENDAR POSTER
I ENCLOSE $1.75 plus .25 Handling fo each.*

NAME _____
Address _____
City _____ State _____ Zip Code _____
*California Residents Please Include 5% Sales Tax

KRLA ARCHIVES

February 10, 1968   THE BEAT   Page 17

THE BEAT GOES TO THE MOVIES

Blackbeard's Ghost

FORMER UCLA All-American football star, Bob Stiles, portrays an athlete who finds weird things happening to him with the aid of Peter Ustinov in Walt Disney's "Blackbeard's Ghost."

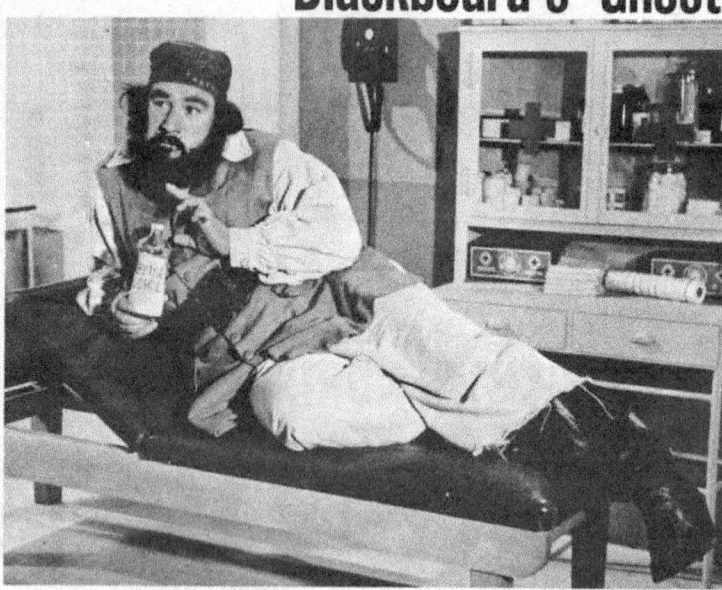

PETER USTINOV, as the spirit of long-dead pirate, Edward Teach, temporarily quenches his taste for rum with rubbing alcohol found in a track team's training room! Must be awfully tasty!!!

The Graduate

"The Graduate" is probably one of the closest examples of American satire that we will ever have. Depicting with humerous clarity the materialism, possessiveness, and emptiness of a great segment of American life, the film makes its point felt without too much immediate sting. The sting comes a few hours later, or the next day when the laughter subsides.

The story centers around a young college student who has returned home after graduation. He is, as the ads indicate and as Benjamin himself states throughout the beginning of the film "a little worried about his future." His parents, who view him as more of a status symbol to be displayed before their friends than as a separate human being, want him to go on to graduate school and chock up more honors for the family. Benjamin isn't really sure what he wants, but he has a definite feeling of dissatisfaction with his parents' life and their wishes.

The summer drifts on, and Benjamin drifts not so slowly into an affair with a friend of his parents, Mrs. Robinson, expertly played by Anne Bancroft. From there, Benjamin goes out with Mrs. Robinson's daughter, Elaine, falls in love with her, and spends the rest of the film trying to secure Elaine for himself.

The film contains an amazing amount of truisms. At one point when Benjamin is drifting in the pool his father asks what the four years of hard work at college were for if not for graduate school. Benjamin without a bit of malice, looks up and says simply "beats me." Not very profound maybe but incredibly true.

Mike Nichols who directed the film, states that the film is partly about the Los Angelesism of the world; meaning that L.A. has a tendency to be more superficial, more materialistic per capita than almost anywhere else. The film points up this tendency beautifully. Also the portrayal of the graduation party composed of Benjamin's parents' friends is a masterpiece. Do parents really sound like that? Just possibly...

The film has beautiful sequences, and is photographed on location in Los Angeles (showing the Strip) and in Berkeley (using both the University of California at Berkeley and USC) as the campuses depicted. The editing is interesting to watch and until the last 15 minutes of the film, it is very swift.

Dustin Hoffman makes his major motion picture debut in the role of the 21 year old graduate. Through most of the film is a victim. Someone who all his life has been used by his parents, and is now trying to find another way. He is quite excellent, if a trifle monotoned.

Elaine is played by Katherine Ross with an honestly rarely seen. When she is viewed walking through Sather Gate at Cal, she really looks like a Berkeley student, not someone's idea of what a Berkeley student looks like. This authenticity runs throughout the film. See it, there's enough of all of us in it to render THE GRADUATE an important personal film.

"BLACKBEARD'S GHOST" is up to Walt Disney's unusually high motion picture standards. The plot centers around the spirit of Edward Teach (Peter Ustinov) who is accidentally brought back to "life" by track coach Steve Walker (Dean Jones). The movie is a fantasy-comedy filmed in color and starring, in addition to Ustinov and Jones, lovely Suzanne Pleshette.

Sounds For Now

JIMI HENDRIX

LOVIN' SPOONFUL

CRYAN' SHAMES

Now Available At:
MONTGOMERY WARD DEPARTMENT STORES

February 10, 1968 — THE BEAT — Page 19

BEAT WINTER SPECIAL
TWO for $4.00

GET A FRIEND TO SUBSCRIBE
PAY ONLY $2.00 EACH

Save $1.00 Each Off the Regular Subscription Price

A Big Savings of $4.50 Off the Newsstand Price

THIS OFFER FOR A LIMITED TIME ONLY

ACT NOW TO SAVE $ $ $

Mail to: BEAT PUBLICATIONS
9000 Sunset Blvd.
Los Angeles, California 90069

☐ NEW SUBSCRIPTION

We want BEAT for ☐ 1 year at $2.00 each ☐ 2 years at $3.50 each

Outside U.S. $9.00 per year each

Please print your name and address

My name is .... My name is ....
City .... City ....
City .... City ....
State .... Zip .... State .... Zip ....

ENCLOSED IS $4.00 for 2 One Year Subscriptions
$7.00 for 2 Two Year Subscriptions
$18.00 for 2 Foreign Subscriptions

Payment is in ☐ cash ☐ check ☐ money order

—CLASSIFIED—

REACH COSMIC AWARENESS without drugs — help save mankind from destruction. Write for free booklet "Cosmic Awareness Speaks", SERVANTS OF AWARENESS, Box 115E, Olympia, Washington.

SLEEP LEARNING, self hypnosis. Details, strange catelog free! Nutosuggestion, Box 24BT, Olympia, Washington.

WILD POSTERS, far out bumper stickers, buttons! Crazy Labels, Box 21-M, Olympic, Washington.

P. J. PROBY I'm with you!

Kathy Carlssen, with love, John Lafhl.

Apple Pappy Yoddlers LIVE!

HAPPY BIRTHDAY — Geoff, Ron, Dave of SATURDAY'S CHILDREN * * luv, Barb.

Tim of Ohio: Thank you for a groovey night at Winterland. Love, Terri.

Happy Birthday Jim Van Allen. Love, Chrissie.

"My Friend" Lemon Drops.

Anthony and Danny, We love you. Love Sue and Bette.

FRARE

BEATLES WE WANT YOU TO COME BACK.

Walrus, say hello to BIMBO for me, hello goodbye. Ken Johnson.

Happy 18th Birthday JOHN KEITH with love, BWAN Fan Club.

Cheryl

Cheryl

Cheryl

Cheryl

Cheryl—why

Did you have

to say no?

luv Don.

Cheryl

Cheryl

WARREN BEATTY IS OUTASITE!

The QUICKERLY FOREST is particular about who they love!

Interstate 405 rule.

ASSOCIATION Chapter Club for L.A. 66 and vicinity, 12927 Bonaparte Ave., L.A., Calf. 90066.

l ove oo Becki-gator.

JIMMY MAY, KENNY COX: Best wishes for Very Happy Birthdays!

Pat + Rich = Luv.

Hello — Julius, Carol.

Congratulations to Sylvan Welli of Nighterawlers on Marriage to Sally Klein.

Where's the BROTHERHOOD?

ERNESTLOPEZISA "FINCA" BUNCHANDDANIELS!

The Emeralds of Society are fab.

Happy Birthday Marie Modin — Davy.

Raiders In Monkees Out.

The CRYAN SHAMES are friendly.

LOVE PEACE PAUL
Neilyounggindianofthespringfieldsiloveyou.

LOVE LIFE PEACE
BRIANMCHUGHANDHISHARMONICAFOREVER.

PAUL McCARTNEY grooves.

Dear Eddie, "The Look of Love" Love ya, always, Sherri.

THE BEAT will accept only personal messages in the classified section. We will print names but not addresses or phone numbers.
We will also accept Fan Club addresses in care of The Beat.
Rates are cheap! Only 10 cents per word.
Your deadline for the next issue is: February 14, 1968.

KRLA ARCHIVES

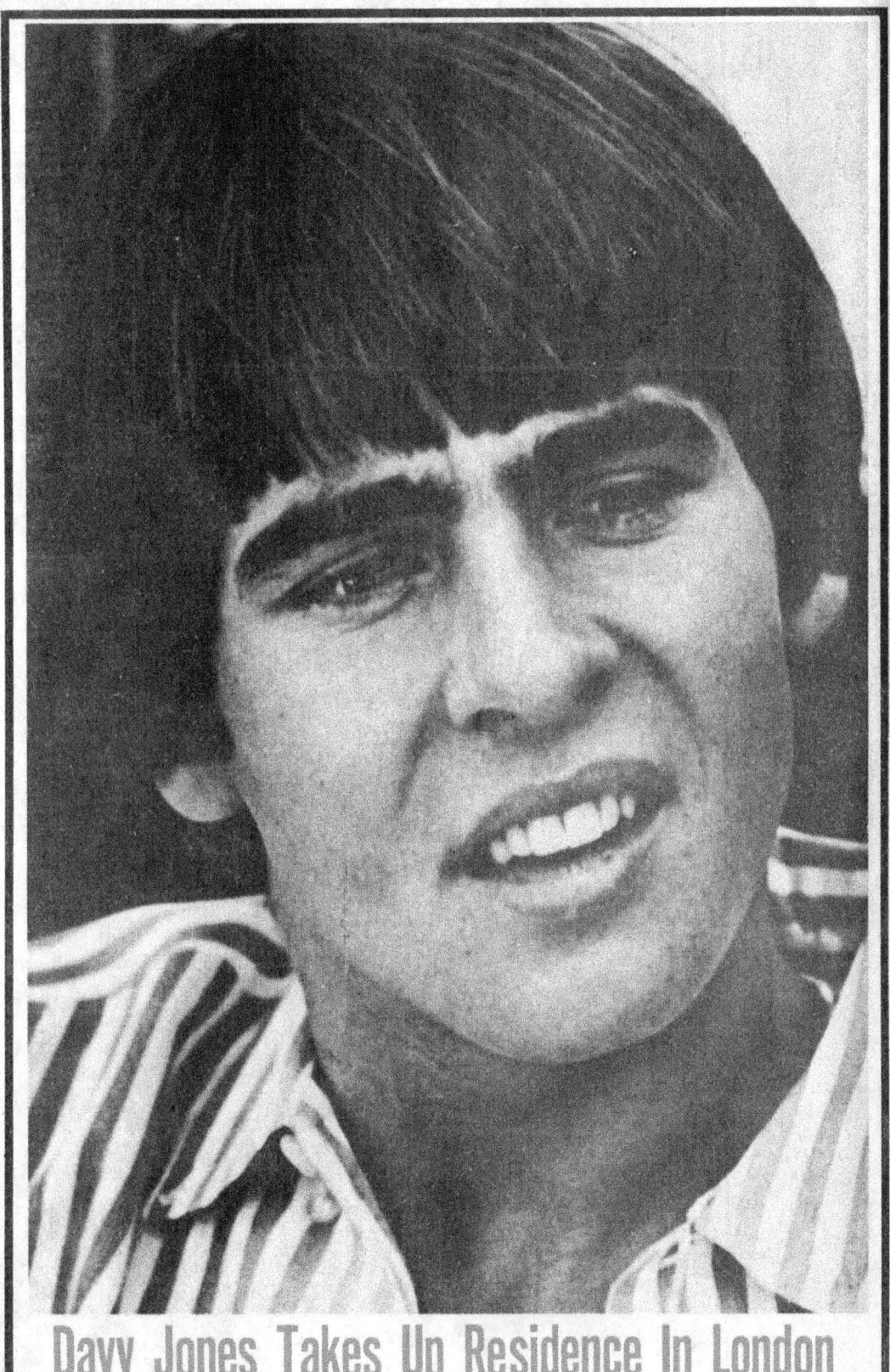

Davy Jones Takes Up Residence In London

KRLA ARCHIVES

SHOOTING IT OUT WITH RASCALS

KRLA BEAT Edition

FEBRUARY 24, 1968

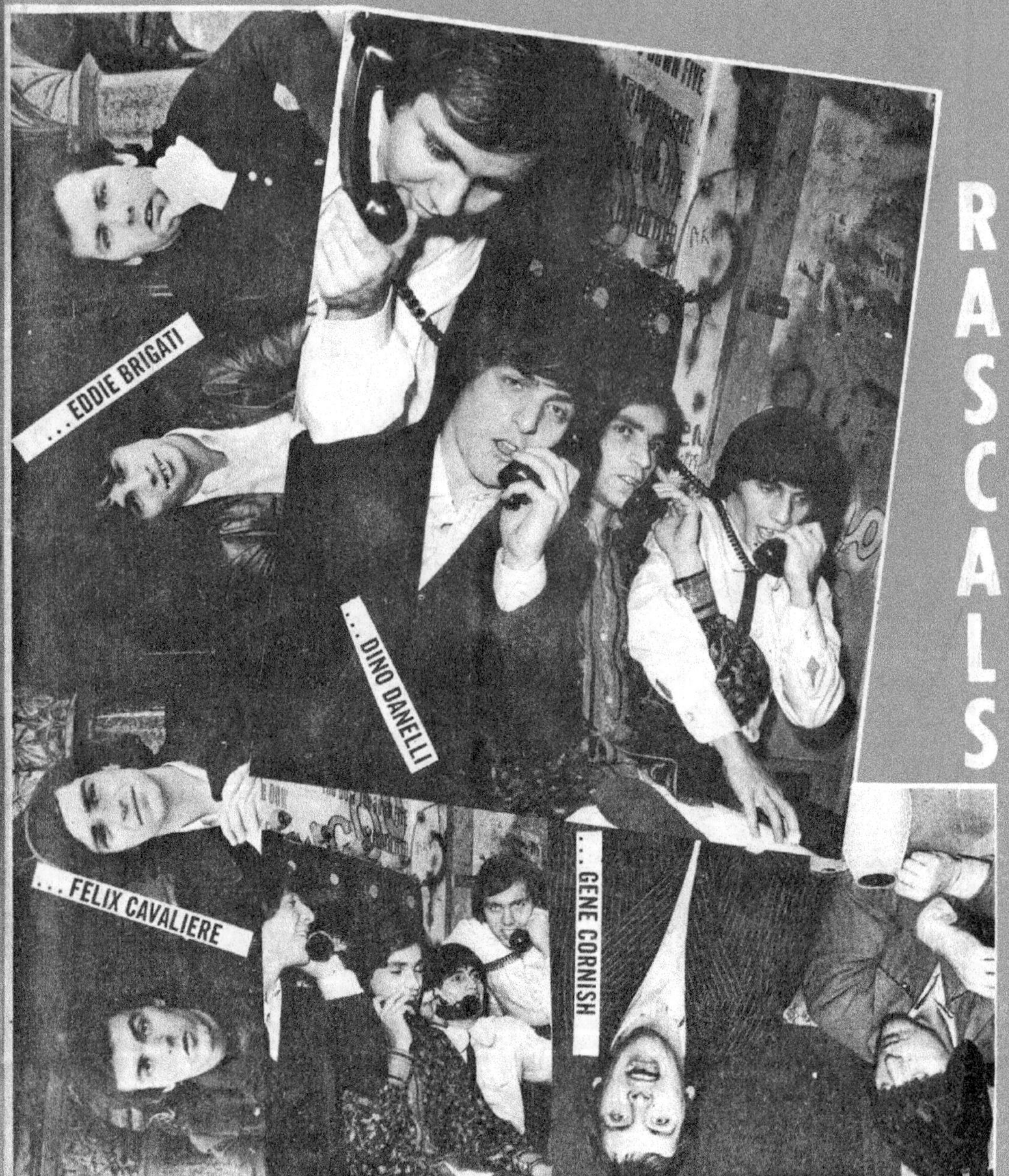

25¢

...EDDIE BRIGATI

...DINO DANELLI

...FELIX CAVALIERE

...GENE CORNISH

RASCALS

KRLA ARCHIVES

KRLA BEAT

Volume 3, Number 23   February 24, 1968

Righteous Brothers Break Team

LOS ANGELES — The great Righteous Brothers, Bobby Hatfield and Bill Medley, announced today that they are breaking up! Each has "different ideas about the future." Bill will concentrate on acting, music publishing and record production.

Bobby has retained the name "Righteous Brothers" and has found a new partner, Jimmy Walker (formerly drummer for the Knickerbockers).

Bill is already set to make his solo debut on March 5 at the Circle Star Theatre in San Carlos, California.

Hatfield's new partner was born in the Bronx, New York and, ironically enough, while he was a member of the Knickerbockers he told reporters that one of his favorite groups was the Righteous Brothers!

The BEAT takes this opportunity to wish both Bill Medley and Bobby Hatfield the best of luck in their independent careers. Both have given greatly to the world of music.

Letters To The Editor

Pleasing All Of The People

Dear BEAT:

"Fabulous BEAT subscriptions?" "Action packed issues?" Thank you dear BEAT for brightening my drab day with your funny jokes. The BEAT has gotten to be about as "fabulous" as a comic book and I haven't seen an "action packed" issue in 12 months.

As soon as you began publishing semi-monthly issues, The BEAT came down in quality and even in quantity. Observe the January 13 issue for example. Out of 19 pages, six are FULL PAGE advertisements. The smaller advertisements add up to about two pages, leaving eight pages, or only about one-half of the paper which has anything readible in it.

My regrets to Louise Criscione and the rest of The BEAT staff. They had a good thing going once upon a time. Too bad a good thing can't last forever. As for renewing my subscription . . . I think the telephone book would provide more interesting reading.

Nancy Peterson

Dear BEAT:

I began buying The BEAT in April of 1965 and I've been subscribing since October of the same year. This is the third time I have renewed my subscription and I just realized something . . . you are never satisfied.

You keep adding new and better articles to the paper. I just want to say, keep up the beautiful work and don't stop. I know I speak for many, many people.

Tim Laughlin

Cleanliness Or Not

Dear BEAT:

My congratulations to Mary Kirby on her comment regarding filthy looking pop groups. Actually, her complaint is an understatement!

The Beach Boys, Everly Brothers, Elvis Presley, TJB, Sandpipers, Trini Lopez, Roy Orbison, Jerry Lee Lewis, etc. all sport "longish" hair; however, they look "professional" and even neat.

Then look at the Canned Heat, the Turtles, Cream and the Doors! As Mary Kirby stated: "no wonder the Establishment is so down on pop groups."

And who started it all? The Stones, who else?

You think I'm anti-pop music, right? Quite the contrary! I dig every artist I've mentioned, only they're giving pop music the bad name it has and not the spectators.

After two years of thoroughly enjoying every issue of BEAT, my subscription shall continue to bring it to my mail box. For my money, The BEAT is to the readers and devotees of pop music what adrenalin is to the heart. I, for one, couldn't do without it.

Satisfied reader

POWER OF SUGGESTION

Dear BEAT:

I think The BEAT is a great newspaper but I have a few complaints to make. First of all, The BEAT isn't as good as it used to be. I remember when there were lots more interesting articles, like the Adventures of Robin Boyd, and many more want ads. Could you please put back some of the good articles?

Also, you don't have enough about the Beatles. I think they're the greatest and always will be. I know I'm not alone in my opinion. I have one more suggestion. Could you maybe put posters in the paper? You have so many good pictures but they're too small!

Thank you for reading this.

Mary Catalano

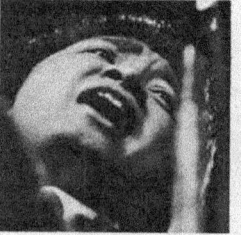

Association

Dear BEAT:

Please publish articles and pictures of my favorite group, the Association, and thank you for all the nice things you have written about them in past issues. I look forward to buying The BEAT at my newsstand when it has something about the Association.

Unsigned

Cryan' Shame

Dear BEAT:

I've waited as long as possible, but I can't stand it any longer. Why don't you ever print anything about the Cryan' Shames? They are Chicagoland's number one group! And you are Chicagoland's most aware newspaper. Why not get together?

At least you could feature "A Scratch In The Sky" in "Turning On." Please do an article on the Shames. I shall be camped on my mailbox waiting for The BEAT . . . and the Cryan' Shames.

Sandi

That Is The Question

Dear BEAT:

How do you expect the beat to go on if the groups aren't looking good? We mean, how do you expect the adults to accept the younger generation if the groups keep getting sloppier? We don't mean all the groups, just some of the ones who don't have any pride in themselves.

We remember the first time we saw the Beatles, they were really looking good. But now when we look at some of the groups we wonder "what is the younger generation coming to," even though we're part of it.

We'd like to end this letter by asking: "Don't you care if the groups aren't look good," because we do and we know we're not alone.

Roberta Shakespeare
Debbie Strickland

Vanilla Fudge

Dear BEAT:

I have recently bought the Vanilla Fudge album and I feel that they deserve an article, especially after their "superb" performance on the "Ed Sullivan Show." Watching them is like watching the Rascals when they first began.

In your January 27th issue, you only devoted 31 words and a fairly small picture to this group . . . and on the last page yet! Big deal! Well, in my opinion, a group of their caliber and unique ability of showmanship should be strongly considered as the subject of one of your future articles.

Terry Witter

Beat Publications, Inc.

Executive Editor .... Cecil I. Tuck
Publisher .... Gayle Tuck
Editor .... Louise Criscione
Assistant Editor .... Jacoba Atlas

Staff Writers
Bobby Bovino   Ron Koslow
Tony Leigh   Shirley Poston

Contributing Writers
Tony Barrow   Sue Barry
Eden   Bob Levinson
Jamie McClusky III   Mike Masterson

Photographers
Ed Caraeff   Jerry Hass

National Advertising Representative
Sam Chase Assoc., Inc.
527 Madison Avenue
New York, New York 10022
(212) PL. 5-1668

Advertising Director .... Dick Stricklin
Business Manager .... Judy Felice
Subscriptions .... Judy Worth

Distribution
Miller Freeman Publications
500 Howard Street, San Francisco, Calif.
The BEAT is published bi-weekly by BEAT Publications, Inc.; editorial and advertising offices at 9000 Sunset, Suite 1000, L.A., California 90069. U.S. bureaus in Hollywood, San Francisco, New York, Chicago and Nashville; overseas correspondents in London, Liverpool and Manchester, England. Sale price 25 cents. Subscription price: U.S. and possessions $5 per year; Canada and foreign rates, $9 per year. Second class postage prepaid at Los Angeles, California.

KRLA ARCHIVES

Miriam Makeba Sings For Watts Boutique

NEW YORK — Miriam Makeba's "Pata Pata" will provide the musical background for a United States Information Agency film on a highly successful African boutique in Watts, California.

Filmed as a three minute news story for the weekly TV program "Washington Correspondent," the story will be televised to audiences in the Congo, Gabon, and the Ivory Coast.

Recently returned from an African concert tour, Miss Makeba said she was glad to cooperate with the U.S.I.A. "in bringing attention to the success and the creatively of my people."

Miss Makeba is a multi-talented singer, composer, comedienne and fashion designer (she has held shows of her own in New York), who has filled Carnegie Hall, Lincoln Center, and the Greek Theatre in Los Angeles.

She has been an outspoken opponent of the social system in her native South Africa, testifying before the United Nations Committee on Apartheid.

She sings in eleven languages and dialects, has appeared at state functions for many independent African republics and played to packed houses in London, Paris, Amsterdam, Stockholm, Copenhagen, Bonn, Melbourne and Dublin.

RYDELL SIGNS WITH REPRISE

Bobby Rydell has been signed to an exclusive contract by Reprise Records. Rydell who has just returned from a six week tour in Australia has been in the recording business for over 10 years.

Initial disc for Reprise is "The Lovin' Tyings." Rydell has recorded such million sellers as "Kissin' Time," "Wild One," "We Got Love" and "Volare"

NABORS WINS

Jim Nabors' recording debut has paid off in a Gold Record! The Record Industry Association of America (RIAA) has certified that "Love Me With All Your Heart" has sold over one million records.

Charlatan Films Two

Charlatan Productions has been signed by Verve-Forecast Records to produce a three minute promotional film based on the recording "People World" by Jim and Jan.

The Production company headed by Peter Gardiner and Tom Rounds has also been set to produce a film for Paul Revere and the Raiders based on the record "Too Much Talk, Not Enough Action." This film will be shot in the ruins of the Guidini Castle in the Hollywood Hills and like "People World" it will be distributed for use on television throughout the United States and Canada.

BOBBY RYDELL just signed to exclusive Reprise contract.

JIM & JEAN, husband and wife team, next for Charlatan.

THREE FOR HERB ALPERT

For a change, Herb Alpert has come up with another award. This time it's from Playboy Magazine. Alpert has won three awards in that magazine Jazz and Pop Poll which was based on ballots cast by their readers.

Alpert was the recipient of the best trumpet award, best instrumental combo for Herb Alpert and the Tijuana Brass and the best small combo album for "S.R.O." by Herb and his brass.

PEOPLE ARE TALKING ABOUT the misinterpretation of a certain song being the big reason that it made it all the way to the top of the charts ... Paul Mauriat being the surprise pop hit of the new year — so far ... the fact that Glen Campbell is finally getting the break he deserves and wondering whether he'll still be doing session work five months from now

... how long a certain female singing artist is going to go on singing the chorus while someone else sings the rest of the song ... how amazing it is that the Classics IV have made it so high in the charts when no one seems to know the first thing about the group ... why Cher has recorded a Miriam Makeba composition and whether or not it will be the hit "Pata Pata" was

... the Young Rascals selling-out a show in a matter of hours, making other groups wonder why they can't sell out a show in a matter of months ... how uptight a member of a group got just because his shining face was not on the calender ... the fact that they never thought they'd see the day when Al Hirt would cover a pop record ... whether or not the Lovin' Spoonful will ever regain the popularity they once enjoyed

... the Strawberry Alarm Clock sounding an awfully lot like the "old" Association on "Tomorrow" and wondering why that would be ... several motion picture studios supposedly auditioning a group's lead singer and wondering why, with his tremendous amount of charm (?), he hasn't already been made a huge star ... whether or not the Grapefruit will be as big as their promoters are counting on them being

... how funny a certain attorney in the music business really is and how very sweet it is of us to say so in print ... the fact that lately Frankie Valli has been getting more hits than his fellow Four Seasons ... Spanky and Our Gang coming off better than a certain heavily-promoted British group in a recent concert and wondering what will happen to summer touring plans if the nation's promoters hear the word

... why the Four Tops chose to record an oldie like "Walk Away Renee" when Motown has never had any trouble getting hits with originals ... whether or not we'll be hearing big things very shortly from the talented Robin Wilson ... who put the anchor on Lulu's "Best Of Both Worlds" and whether or not it's an indication that she won't be the star attraction people thought he'd be

... how "Green Tambourine" got to be number one in the nation ... why the Monkees have been keeping so still lately and whether or not they'll be back with us next season ... Johnny Tillotson giving the charts another try ... the member of a once-top rock group supposedly on his way to Maui to get married ... the fact that the Beatles are reportedly going to have another go at a television special all by themselves — despite what happened with "Magical Mystery Tour" — and wondering why they want to travel that bumpy road again?

KRLA ARCHIVES

Page 4 — THE BEAT — February 24, 1968

THE COWSILLS board plane at Kennedy Airport for their first European tour.

HERMAN'S HERMITS have a release date for "Mrs. Brown" film this spring.

ON THE BEAT
By Louise Criscione

A nice break for a nice guy... Glen Campbell has been set as the summer replacement for "The Smothers Brothers Show." Glen must be a popular man with the Smothers because he'll make his third appearance on their weekly outing on March 3rd.

If all goes as planned, the Association will be making their motion picture debut in their own film (probably for Warner Bros./7 Arts) utilizing the best script, best director, best everything that's available to them. One thing is positively definite... it will NOT be the usual garbage of "singing group makes movie."

Ravi On Broadway

Ravi Shankar has come a long way from India... literally. Shankar will supervise the music for a new Broadway play, "The Guide," opening on February 26.

A bit of information on the Human Beinz, supplied by BEAT reader Dee Perkins of Ohio: First off, says Dee, the unique spelling of "Beinz" came about completely by accident. The record company misspelled the name on the label and the group decided to just keep it that way. The group numbers four: Mel Pachuta, 21, bass guitarist; Mike Talman, 20, drummer; Richard Bellay, 20, lead guitarist and singer; and Joe "Ting" Markulin, 21, rhythm guitarist.

GLEN CAMPBELL

The group hails from Youngstown, Ohio and, of course, have a giant hit with "Nobody But Me."

Accent On Youth

Someone somewhere has decided that youth can help boost Nielsen ratings. Consequently, Joey Heatherton and Frank Sinatra Jr. will take over as the summer replacement for the "Dean Martin Show." Youth will form the basis for the hour-long weekly show with comedy, music and young talent heavily accentuated. Nice — for a change.

Sidney Poitier can now consider himself a success... he's having an album re-released! The album, originally titled "Poitier Meets Plato," features a background jazz score by Fred Katz. The LP was first released in 1964 but the feeling at WB/7 Arts is that now there is a much greater acceptance of this type of product by radio stations. New title will be "Sidney Poitier Journeys Inside The Mind" and, among other things, will have itself a new cover and a major promotion campaign.

Ryder All Over

Mitch Ryder is keeping himself busy with personal appearances these days. The month of March finds Mitch performing at the University of South Carolina (March 6); East Carolina University (March 13); University of North Carolina, Chapel Hill (March 14); Salem Municipal Auditorium, Salem, Virginia (March 15); and Hampden Sydney College, Hampden Sydney, Virginia (March 16).

Beatle George Harrison met up with fellow Liverpudlian, Rita Tushingham, in an unlikely Bombay. Harrison was there recording sitar music for the film "Wonderwall" and Miss Tushingham was there shooting her film, "The Guru." The world's getting smaller.

Nilsson To Europe

Nilsson, a name you're sure to be hearing a lot about in months to come, has been booked for an April tour of England, France and Italy just off the strength of his "Pandemonium Shadow Show" album on RCA. A very talented young man... if he fails to make a really substantial dent in the music business, there is no justice.

Congratulations to Gary Lewis and his wife, Sara Jane Suzuara Lewis, on the birth of their first baby, a daughter (would you believe it... finally a daughter in the Lewis family!!) in Monterey, California. Papa Gary is currently playing exclusively for Uncle Sam.

PROUD PAPA LEWIS

PICTURES IN THE NEWS

MITCH RYDER (left) is shown above being presented with the Heart and Torch symbol of the American Heart Association by William F. Laporte, Chairman of the 1968 Heart Fund campaign. Named "Prince of Hearts," Mitch will serve throughout the year as the Heart Association's representative to America's youth.

DEWEY MARTIN, one fifth of the Buffalo Springfield, and Jane Nelson, the former Miss United States, revealed they were secretly married. Drummer Martin and his bride were married on December 30th at the Little Brown Church in San Fernando Valley, California.

EDDIE KENDRICKS and his fellow Temptations have proven without a doubt that the Motown Sound is as hot as ever. Besides riding high in the charts with "I Wish It Would Rain," they just grossed an impressive $113,450 for three nights of entertaining!

FROM NOW ON THE MONKEES will be flying first class. Along with such groups as the Doors, Jefferson Airplane and the Stones, the Monkees will be listed in the March, 1968 edition of Who's Who in America. Quite an honor.

The Glory Stompers are taking over the town

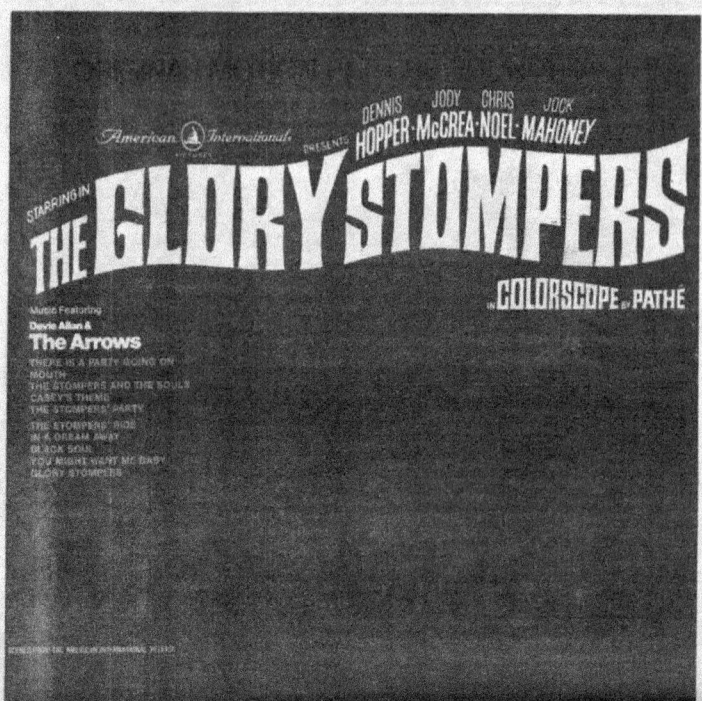

their soundtrack will take over the charts.

Better get yourself ready.

AVAILABLE AT

The Paradoxical Who Out For Trends

Who is the Who?

One question, yet it requires four answers, for the four members of the Who are complete musical entities themselves and only incidentally are they members of one rock group.

Nice Paradox

And yet, each member is indispensable to the group. Pete, Roger, John and Keith all agree that if one member left, the group would split up. So they are fiercely independent and yet totally interdependent, a nice paradox.

But their success is no paradox. In their five years together, they have risen to the position of being England's third most popular (and third highest-paid) group behind the Beatles and Stones. They have been responsible for at least three worldwide trends in that time affecting music, fashion and philosophy at given times.

Stale Performance

Right from the start, they felt that in-person performing had grown stale, that people were entitled to more of a show than they were getting. Coupled with this was the desire to do something meaningful on stage. The answer was their now famous policy of breaking their instruments at each performance.

Since they began it in England, dozens of other groups have picked up on it and tried to outdo each other in destructiveness. Consequently, the Who have abandoned the technique in England, but will still do it on their coming U.S. tour in February.

Interestingly enough, though they invented this form of showmanship, they never were offered the opportunity to do the instrument-breaking scene in "Blow-Up." Antonioni saw them do their thing at the invitation of the group's manager and one year later, hired the Yardbirds to break it up in "Blow-Up." Asked why he didn't hire the Who for his film, Antonioni replied: "What the Who do is too meaningful. I wanted something utterly meaningless, so I couldn't use them."

Mini-Opera

The Who's second attempt at pace-setting was the comic "mini-opera" Peter Townshend wrote called "A Quick One While He's Away." It took up half of one side on their "Happy Jack" album and set the style for longish pieces of music. Also, Townshend's dabbling in the opera format may have produced the impetus for much blending of rock and classical that is currently being attempted (sometimes quite successfully).

When the Who decided that the fashion world needed an injection of excitement, they started and became the symbol of the Mod cult. Townshend had a jacket made out of a Union Jack while other members of the group affected velvet pants, lace shirts, cowboy boots and whatever else happened to strike their fancy.

However, all their previous ground-breaking was just a prelude to their latest creation, an album called "The Who Sell Out."

Complete Show

It is a complete radio show, with twelve songs, spoof commercials of baked beans, deodorant, blemish remover and the Charles Atlas body-building course plus several jingles from the pirate radio station, Radio London.

In short, it is the first record album unified in philosophy, form and content. Unfortunately, some people aren't crazy about the cover which pictures Townshend, Roger Daltrey, John Entshistle and Keith Moon in the four commercials they spoof on the album.

The group's plans right now are centered around going into films. They have been offered (and have turned down) a number of opportunities to do the standard teeny-bopper publicity movie. Instead, they would like to venture into the world of black comedy which they feel better suited to their talents.

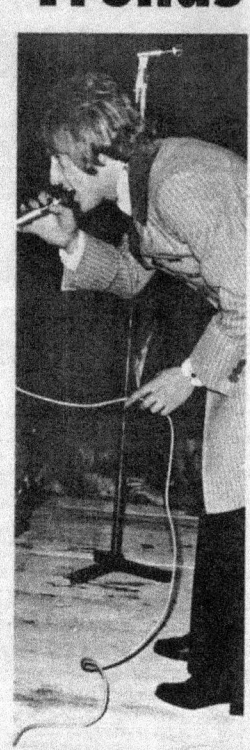

Shooting The Rascals

By Jacoba Atlas

Soundstages even at major motion picture studios tend to be barns. But when you rent one on Sunset Blvd. *down* the street from Columbia Pictures — you're liable to get a real one. A barn, with a few improvements. Like padded ceilings for the sound, and kelogg lights standing around, and a telephone hook up. Other than that, it's cold, drafty and .... empty sort of wierd.

Monday in Los Angeles was unbearably cold for those of us unused to Eastern winters. It was something like 55 degrees out, and ice covered the ground in the morning. By late afternoon it was even colder. The Young Rascals, in town to do the Joey Bishop Show and to film a short promotion film with Charlatan Productions, were scheduled to play this certain barn on Sunset Blvd. They had been filming all day in the Silverlake District, in that freezing cold weather, in the early hours of the morning, and now they were going to film in this barn. And they were about two hours late, according to two of their equipment managers.

These two young men had been waiting for the group with the equipment, in this cold, drafty barn. They had spent the time reading want ads in the Free Press, a local underground newspaper with rather interesting classifieds. They told me, the Young Rascals were due any time now.

About a half an hour later, two other young men arrived, both with Charlatan Production. Both went immediately to work, transforming this cold, drafty barn, into a cold, drafty soundstage. There was a great deal of discussion about where the key lights were going to be hung, and the color of the backdrop, and whether or not this particular soundstage would have any gells (colored transparent paper to put over the lights to change the color of the walls, etc.).

New Drummer

A few minutes later, the two owners of Charlatan Productions, Tom Rounds and Peter Gardiner walked in. They added to the discussion about lights, and as Tom went to set up their sound equipment, Peter walked to the drums, and after a quick question to the equipment managers as to whether Dino would mind his drums being played, the director of the film began to drum. He wasn't bad.

By this time it was so cold, you could barely move. Tom kept saying that as soon as the lights went on the place would warm up, but I had my doubts.

Then, in walked the Rascals, carrying beautifully colored shirts that they were going to change into latter for the actual filming. unbelievably cooperative, they stood in their spots while the shot was lit and relit for better exposure.

Almost immediately, Dino went to his drums and began drumming. I really don't remember it stopping once, except for the actual rehearsal, when he drummed a special song that was to be filmed, Later Felix joined him on the electric organ, and they did a very funny sort of honky-tonk rendition of the Spoonful's "What A Day For A Daydream."

If you've ever watched the filming of anything, you have some idea of how long it takes, even to get to the rehearsal stage. Although this was moving faster than most, possibly due to the youth of all the participants, it was at least two hours before a preliminary take was reached.

Felix told me how the Rascals themselves had shot a film in Puerto Rico. They had filmed the thing in only one day, with amateurs holding the camera. They had used the entire island as their backdrop, and although it had been a fun experience, none of the Rascals was holding out great hopes for the finished product. But after the editing was done, back in New York, they realized they had a good, if not fantastic, film and decided to show it to the world on their visit to the Joey Bishop show.

Hot Sauce

Tacos were brought in now, and it seems that if you're not from the Southwestern part of the United States tacos are a little outside your realm of eating. The hot sauce that usually belongs inside the taco, was left untouched until they had finished eating when one of them realized their mistake.

They were lip syncing this segment of the film, and no one was very happy about it. Eddie said that he only sings aloud with a lip sync when he likes the song, but Felix added, that they all hated to do lip sync. "We'd rather do our songs live, even if they can't sound exactly the way we do on records. It's really cheating if you're lip syncing."

They had been out very early this morning chasing a large beach ball up and down the stairs in the Silverlake district. "It was bitter cold," was the only comment I could get from them.

Peter added that everything went exceptionally well. "The people sort of looked out of their windows and said, 'hey they're filming a movie' and then went back inside. I had given strict instructions to the Rascals that if the police came, everyone was suppose to act super funny. But they never came, and no one else seemed to care either." There's nothing like filming in jaded L.A.

By this time the lights were lit and the barn was warming up. The lights had changed position two or three times, and the Rascals had changed position on "stage" about the same amount. The gells which were to change the color white to pink were ditched when they couldn't be hooked up right. The camera was being moved in mock simulation of an actual take. "A two-shot through Eddie's arm should show Felix," "Come through here for a close-up of Gene," Peter blocked out the takes.

They began filming about three hours after their arrival at the barn. Tom had their song synced on a special tape recorder and the Rascals did an excellent job of pretending to sing. Tomorrow they are going to do something very different in the early hours of the morning when the frost will still be on the ground in the Greek Theatre. That would be the end of shooting for the group, at least on this particular film. The rest would be up to Peter in the editing room.

Someone asked if they wanted to see the Swami that evening. He is connected with the same sort of Meditation thing as the Maharishi Mehese Yogi. That seemed to be a good idea — all the Rascals agreed they wanted to see him.

GET HIP

Date the Modern Way

minimum of 5 dates

total **$5** cost

COMPUTER DATE OF AMERICA

Phone or write for compatability test

273-0323

(24 hours)

9000 Sunset Blvd.
Los Angeles, Calif. 90069

KRLA ARCHIVES

LIGHT SHOWS: ADVENTURE INTO EXPERIMENTAL LIVING

By Jacoba Atlas

There's a revolution happening; happening on all levels of society. From the streets to the museums people are talking about new trends, new ways of looking at themselves and their surroundings, and new ways of relating to what they see.

The impact is being felt from San Francisco to New York, and it isn't missing many cities in between. Rock music in its present form is an expression of this revolution. Poster art, pop art, op art, kenetic paintings and sculpture, experimental and underground films all reflect and shape what is happening in people's minds.

One of the most important and least discussed creative aspects of this revolution is the mixed media happening — the Light Show. Almost everyone now knows what a light show is, in its most simple and basic form. There seems to be a consensus of opinion that light shows are a necessary part of any rock hall, any rock concert. Consequently although most young people have seen *a* light show, most have seen only the worst. The creative, the artistic light shows are few and far between.

It is significant to discuss the relative importance of Light Shows to today's society because of their rightful claim to be "the" new expression of movement. Not that light shows in themselves are new. The Brothers Lumiere in Paris at the turn of the century were working with the components of the present day light shows, and the first color organ (an instrument that translates sound into color) was recorded as far back as 1903. In other words, Andy Warhol with his Velvet Underground, Bill Graham with his Fillmore Auditorium and Chet Helms with his Avalon Ballroom were not the originators of this current phenomenon. However, they were and are the catalysts that made the light show become standard "equipment" for any rock promoter.

Art Form

This popularization and commercialization of the light show has resulted in many difficulties, none the least of which is the fact that amateurs knowing nothing about art, films or the creative process have begun putting the worst of the light shows *everywhere*. However, many people now doing light shows seriously regard this as a "new art", a new endeavor with all the trappings of a valid art form.

One such person is Dan Bruhns, a young, soft spoken Californian, who has come down to Los Angeles to handle the light shows for the Blue Law in Torrance after serving in the same capacity for the Fillmore in San Francisco — a city he still considers home.

But defining what is good in light shows and what is not, is difficult even for one so closely involved in the execution of the event. "I really don't know how to separate the good from the bad. That's really the issue, especially here in Los Angeles, where there is every level of clubs faking it.

"It's not really a matter of the one that I do being better. Someone could come along and do a better effect, but still I would maybe come down on it, for some reason. Maybe it's not topical or it has nothing to do with what is current movement.

"Another aspect with what's wrong with most light shows is the kids who are doing them. A lot of these young kids who step into light shows, well, they know something about what . . . about turning projectors on maybe. And sticking things into them. But do they know anything about art. That's the fundamental issue. It ought to have something to do with art, it ought to have something to do with the contemporary scene.

"One might wonder if Hippies off the street or wherever they come from know anything about art and about current movement, even through they are involved in it. It may take someone with a little wider perspective to come up with any kid of valid statement."

Bill Kerby, a Los Angeles filmmaker who also got his feet wet in the Light Show happening for the Kaleidoscope last year, is equally adamant about the poor effort most people pass off as a Light Show. Approaching the problem of putting on a valid light show with an emphasis on the kinesthetic power of film, he and two other young men, Dave and Tim came up with unbelievably clever, but fantastically expensive ideas.

"One of the main things that we were interested in was the power that film can have. One of the things that we wanted to do was take two cameras and film the same even with both camera with a zoom lens on each. And then, at a given instant, you know, 1-2-3 we'd snap both of them at an exact difference so the image would pow in on one side and pow out on the other. It would have the power to spin you over and make you fall. Now if you could get four or five cameras operating in tandem like this all around you, you could do incredible things.

"I think the light show with colors and so-called psychedelic images is finished. I guess that's beautiful and every light show should have one, but because it means nothing to me, I can only give a kind of cursory appraisal and say 'yea, that's pretty now lets get over to the interesting stuff'.

Liquid Light

"There are so few artists that are really workable with liquid lights. Everybody, of course, thinks they can do it well. But it's really like whipping a dead horse.

"Light Shows besides being sort of cutesy-poo attempts at *decor*, are really an art form.

Bill added, that the reason most places on'y want the colored light sort of light show is financial. "From a production standpoint the advantage is that the machine doesn't cost a lot and it will cover a really huge area. Now with films it costs a million dollars to make the moves, to rent the camera, to buy an arc projector which you need in the circumstances." "Of course," he added, "once you'd done that, you've really got something tangible to work with."

The appeal of light shows is almost universal. The explanation

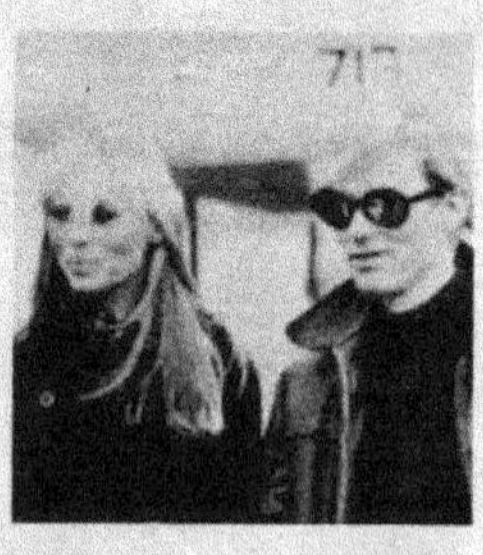

for this is manifold. Judith Bettlehiem, an art history student at UCLA preparing for a master of arts degree with a special interest in the new mixed media art movement stated, unhappily, "As to the appeal, well one of the main things you have to think of first is the appeal of a fad. The fad and everything that has to do with the hippie movement. People think that's where it's at, and this is what the 'real' people are doing."

Dave latter seconded this unfortunate theory by stating, "It's almost like light shows have become obligatory. It doesn't matter about the quality. If you are going to have a rock group then you have to have a light show. That's why there are so many bad ones around."

Dan believes that Marshall McLuhan has helped a great deal to explain the importance of a light show. "Work is being done in the idea of the rock hall as a laboratory. Concepts are being worked out that are being placed in a central position in this media movement that is really happening now.

"Television is beginning to produce some of these efforts. I've seen some commercials that have been photographed in marvelous stop frame style. Things I'd run in the middle of my light show without feeling asthetically embarrassed at all."

"Kids are looking for a new way to relate to what's happening. And media has to do with relating. So a light show has to do with relating, and new music has to do with relating. It's not experimental art anymore, it's experimental living.

Judith added by way of explanation "what happens when you go to a light show. You're an individual and the environment is happening around you. And you have to relate to an environment that's been set up for you. When you walk out of a light show you find yourself in a totally different environment and you're relating to *it* as it's set up around you."

Dan went on, "let me introduce some words to explain this. You step out of a sequential environment which is your everyday environment, and you step into an instantaneous, non-sequential simultaneous environment. You have to relate to music, to other people and to the light show. You're also relating to your own consciousness."

Commercial Problems

One of the problems to do a creative light show comes from the promoters themselves. Either they don't want to spend the money to do the things right, or they become scared by the possible reactions of the community. This is in no way to imply that light shows are subversive, immoral or otherwise detremental to good, clean living. It's just that promoters want to make money, and taking chances has never been a very popular endeavor for them."

Kerby explains, "To do a bad light show is very easy. I suppose they impress 12-year-olds who have never been any better, or who have never closed their eyes and imagined any better. Also they impress chamber of commerce type people. That's why slides and other things like that are used. Always the most available photograph of rock and roll people. And then you do a little work when a fast number comes on and you add some colored water and that's it. Really terrible.

"Also everyone wants what's been done before, no experimentation. If it was good before, stick to it. The mentality of most of the people who open rock shows is like that. The Kaleidoscope was like that, they said they wanted exactly what was up at the Fillmore. And they wanted it everywhere. That whole liquid light thing, it's gone as far as it can go.

"Another thing that's been overworked is the strobe light. When they're all over they don't even work. They cancell each other out. It looks like you're walking into Acme Supermarket where all the flourescent lights are just about to go and you think, my God, the top of my head is going to come off, and I have to get groceries. You have to control it."

Tension Levels

Dan sees the Light Show as part of a much greater whole. 'My own purposes was with tension levels. You have an individual and you subject him to a certain amount of social stress, and if it exceeds a certain level, he freaks out.

"One of the implications of mixed media (McLuhan) is if you re-educate the preceptual structure of at least the kids who are still receptive, you can train them to absorb more tension.

"One of the ways you can introduce that is to hit the person with a lot of visual images, sensory images, sound images. You can just saturate a person's perceptual capacity. One important thing is to have enough going at one time. To put one more item in per time second than a person can absorb."

Kerby, although he agreed in theory with what Bruhns was saying, disagreed in the practical application of that concept. "Who knows what people can take. You are making a light show for maybe 3,000 people. And everybody has a different tolerance stress. I mean, that all sounds really very great, I'm not putting the cat down who said that . . . but I am. Because that's the sort of thing that really sounds great and outasite, like he's got some sort of intellectual basis for what he's doing. That's cool, I suppose. But what he probably means is that he's sticking one more thing in

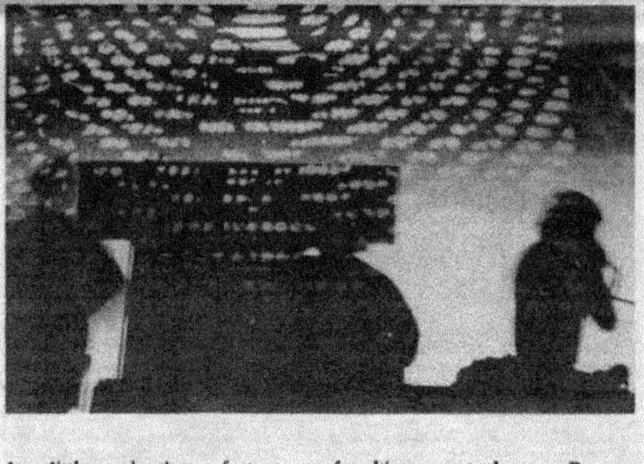

for *his* perceptual span. Because everybody's is different.

"You could put in your room, a television, stereo, an FM radio, two other clock radios and your alarm clock, and put them all on at the same time and a lot of very strange things start to happen. You get shifts of sound and you begin to see things. And you know, would one more radio make any difference, who could say?"

But Dan does see a whole intellectual basis for the light show. He went on to liken it to an Oriental world view and metaphysics. Having to do with becoming a part of your environment on many different levels. Relating and communicating without territorial considerations whether they be a wall or your mind.

Next time you go to a light show look at it critically. What is it creating? What is it bringing to you and *from* you? Colored lights and pretty moving pictures are not enough, are they?

SPICE UP YOUR LIFE
Season with ...

THE TAMS · THE MAMAS & THE PAPAS · THE CANDYMEN · INFLUENCE · abc RECORDS

ABC RECORDS, INC.
NEW YORK/BEVERLY HILLS
DIST. IN CANADA BY SPARTON OF CANADA

EDEN'S CHILDREN ABC/S 624

THE TAMS
A LITTLE MORE SOUL ABC/S 627

CASHMAN, PISTILLI & WEST
BOUND TO HAPPEN ABC/S 629

INFLUENCE ABS/S 630

THE DIRTY BLUES BAND BLUESWAY BL/S 6010

ARTHUR
DREAMS & IMAGES LHI/S 12000*

JESSE JAMES 20th CENTURY FOX 3197*

THE BUBBLE GUM MACHINE SENATE/S 21002*

THE MAMAS & THE PAPAS
SPRINGBOARD DUNHILL D/S 50031

THE GRASS ROOTS
FEELINGS DUNHILL D/S 50027

LADY NELSON & THE LORDS
PICADILLY PICKLE DUNHILL D/S 50028

3's A CROWD
CHRISTOPHER'S MOVIE MATINEE DUNHILL D/S 50030

THE CANDYMEN
BRING YOU CANDYPOWER ABC/S 633

GABOR SZABO
BOB THIELE
LIGHT MY FIRE IMPULSE A/S 9159

INTERNATIONAL SUBMARINE BAND LHI/S 12001*

* Distributed by ABC Records, Inc.

EARNING 'LETTERS'

The Lettermen are one of those groups easily classified as "perennial." Although months go by without a national hit single by the group, sooner or later they always bounce back with a top ten record.

Born in 1962, the group has gone far in all phases of the music business. They've played just about every college and every big club in America, have appeared on all the top television shows and have, throughout their career, managed to do the impossible — appeal to both adults and the young people.

Perhaps it is this which has caused the Lettermen to remain successful for six years. While the young are not sending a Lettermen single up the charts, the adults are packing the nightclubs to see them perform.

Individually, the Lettermen (Tony Butala, Jim Pike and Bob Engemann) had been group vocalists for some time, with Tony singing in a quartet and Jim and Bob singing with trios. Tony met Jim during a shift in one of the vocal groups and the two found that their voices blended extremely well together. Jim had previously met Bobby at Brigham Young University; the three got together in Los Angeles and thus was born the Lettermen.

Contrary to most vocal groups, the Lettermen all have the same range and, therefore, are able to interchange their parts, singing the melody line, top or bottom. They feel another reason for their success is the fact that all do solos which makes for a more interesting show on stage. Throwing in comedy and vocal impressions as well as the ability to play instruments, the Lettermen have managed to surpass the title "group" and move onto the all-encompassing title of "entertainer."

LETTERMEN at recording session

THE THREE who always come back

HENSON CARGILL SKIPS A ROPE

Henson Cargill is his name and 1968 is his year. Or so it would seem if the giant success of "Skip A Rope" is any indication of things to come.

Born in Oklahoma City, Henson's early years gave no warning that he would end up at the top of music charts. He went through grade and high school and then on to Colorado State University for two years. During this time his part-time occupations ran the gamut from truck driver to Deputy Sheriff.

His family background was one of law. His grandfather was the Mayor of Oklahoma City during the 1930's and at one time ran for Governor. His father was a lawyer and, in fact, both his father and grandfather formed a litigation practice that at one time was considered one of the tops in the field.

But for Henson it was a different story. Music was his bag. He lived it and wanted very much to make it big, though his main ambition was to earn enough money to buy a fairly-large ranch.

He began aiming at the music business while in college. He took over a local television show which kept him busy for a year, chalking it up as "musical education." When he felt he was ready he hit the nightclub circuit, covering most of the Western states (Oklahoma, Colorado, Wyoming, Montana, Idaho, Nevada, California, New Mexico, Missouri and Arizona) and improving with experience.

For the country sound in music, there is no better place than Nashville . . . and so off Henson went. He knocked on an awfully lot of doors in the country capitol but no one was interested enough to answer.

Not one to be easily discouraged, Henson made another decision—he'd scrape together enough money to make his own record. He never quite made it, but he did make a tape and came back to Nashville to let some more people listen.

One of the men who listened was Don Law. Law told him the sound was fine but the material was too weak. However, he did arrange a recording session, the fruit of which was four songs. Henson then began re-making the rounds with the finished product.

Monument Records not only bought the master but signed Henson to a contract. The master they purchased? "Skip A Rope." The rest of the story you know.

HENSON CARGILL has 1968 for his year and "Skip A Rope" for his record

KRLA ARCHIVES

February 24, 1968 — THE BEAT — Page 11

Music Industry Steals Show At KRLA's "How I Won The War" Benefit

While the traditional Hollywood motion picture premiere features scores of celluloid celebrities and all the filmtown trappings, the pop music colony stole the show at the Los Angeles premiere of Richard Lester's "How I Won The War" at the Fine Arts Theatre. Los Angeles pop music outlet KRLA sponsored the first night festivities as a benefit for the Los Angeles Free Clinic, Inc., on Sunday (28).

Staging a two-hour live broadcast from the foyer of the theatre, KRLA program director Reb Foster and station disc jockies hosted the cream of the pop music world while thousands of screaming teenagers cheered them on from behind hastily erected police and fire department barricades.

Among the top personalities and groups represented at the KRLA gala for the anti-war film starring John Lennon and Michael Crawford were the Bee Gees, who just the night before had grossed $62 thousand for KRLA in two shows at the Anaheim Convention Center.

AMERICA'S BIGGEST CUSTOM CAR SHOW
THE WESTERNNATIONALS
CUSTOM CAR SHOW AND TEEN MARDIGRAS

ATTENTION BANDS!!! (14-21 years)

★ Enter Larry Tremaine's Battle of the Bands for hundreds of dollars in prizes, free recording time and 3 foot trophies.

ALSO

★ Enter the Wild Go-Go Girl Contest
★ Enter the Miss Teen-A-America Queen Contest or the Mini Skirt Revue

CALL 934-5400

Wild Action Every Day and Night

★ Heavy Top Name Acts All 4 Days
★ 4 Acres of Futuristic, Experimentals, Custom Cars
★ Outlaw Motorcycles, Funny Cars, Dune Buggies, Boats, and Feature Cars
★ George Barris' Movieland Motorcade Featuring "The Expo '67 Car"
★ World Record Holding "Drag Boats"
★ World Land Speed Record Holder Craig Breedlove's "Spirit II"
★ San Francisco Light Show and Free Drag Movies

ALL HAPPENING
GREAT WESTERN EXHIBIT CENTER
SANTA ANA FREEWAY AT ATLANTIC BLVD.

4 BIG DAYS
Feb. 22 — 1 p.m. to midnight
Feb. 23 — 6 p.m. to midnight
Feb. 24 & 25 — Noon to midnight

Call Larry Tremaine NOW at 934-5400
or
National Custom Car Club Assn. at 341-7156

Save 50¢ on General Admission with this ad!

ICE HOUSE GLENDALE
234 So. Brand Blvd.   Reservations 245-5043

Feb. 13-25
TIM MORGAN
hero of Fink Records back with song

with a great new act premiering with a new album

THE COLLAGE

ICE HOUSE PASADENA
24 No. Mentor   Reservations 681-9942

Feb. 13-25
THE FIRESIGN THEATRE

That "Radio Free Oz" gang in a weird comedy spree at The Pasadena Ice House. Featuring Peter Bergman, Philip Austin, Philip Procter and David Ossman. An "in happening" and a comedy bonus act.

STEVE MARTIN & CLABE HANGAN
ALSO PLAYING

MARK LINDSAY of Paul Revere and the Raiders with TV columnist RONA BARRETT.

NOEL HARRISON takes a breather with MICHELLE of the Mamas and Papas and singer SCOTT McKINZIE.

GAZZARRI'S-ON-THE-STRIP
NOW HAPPENING: 9039 SUNSET BLVD.   CR. 3-6606

1. Pacific Ocean
2. Churchill Downs
3. The Joint Effort
4. Adam
5. The Young Dept.

● Every Sunday Afternoon
● Free Groove-In- 4 p.m.
● Every Monday Nite
● Dance Contest - $500 Grand Prize
● Every Wednesday - Audition & Talent Nite
● Dancing 17 & Over — Cocktails 21 & Over

KRLA ARCHIVES

COMING NEXT ISSUE..

ASSOCIATION **ARLO GUTHRIE**

JEFFERSON AIRPLANE **FRANKIE VALLI**

Stateside Visit From The Bee Gees

BEE GEE ROBIN GIBB stands in front of a California palm tree outside of the Beverly Hills Hotel during his Stateside visit.

ROBIN AND BARRY glance over a program in the emptiness of the Anaheim Convention Center. Several days later, when the Bee Gees took to the stage, the auditorium was far from empty!

NEXT ON THE BEE GEES' itinerary was some time off to talk to BEAT reporter, Mike Masterson, in their suite at the hotel.

KRLA ARCHIVES

BONNIE & CLYDE

NOW SHOOTING

ON WAX!

Now Available At:
MONTGOMERY WARD DEPARTMENT STORES

The KING Is Back

With Another Volume

Of Gold Records

The Rose Garden — On Spanning A Quarter Of A Century Together

Take five very talented and young singers ... and some exceptional harmony ... sprinkle in a tune titled "Next Plane To London" and you have all the ingredients needed to create one of the most exciting new vocal groups in the country — The Rose Garden.

It was exactly those elements that skyrocketed the group and its first single record into the Top 10 of every major music survey in the country and, at the same time, established the Rose Garden as one of the most promising quintets to debut in some time.

Youthful Experience

The five (four boys and a girl) not only comprise one of the newest groups on the music scene, but one of the youngest as well. Three of the members are 18 or under, and the oldest is an "ancient" 22. Despite their youth, each of the five has had considerable experience in music and their entertainment careers total to almost a quarter-century.

Although the Rose Garden didn't officially make its debut until late 1967, when "Next Plane To London" was released, the nucleus of the group was formed nearly five years ago when Jim Groshong (leader of the Garden) and John Noreen combined their lead and rhythm guitars to form a singing / instrumental duo. Less than two years later they added a drummer (Bruce Bowdin); then guitarist Bill Fleming and in early 1967, vocalist Diana DeRose.

On The Way

By the Spring of 1967, the group had earned a reputation as one of the better vocal/instrumental quintets in the Los Angeles area. And, it wasn't long before Charlie Greene and Brian Stone, independent producers, approached them with "Next Plane To London." The rest, of course, is history. The Rose Garden recorded the tune; signed with Atco Records and by November, 1967, they were on their way.

Individually, the group lines up with Jim Groshong, leader and founder of the Rose Garden. A native of Santa Monica, California, Jim's entire background was in music and entertainment. His father sang with Freddy Martin's band; his mother was a singer and his great grandfather was also quite an "entertainer" — Lafitte the Pirate.

Jim attended high school in Southern California and then went on to Pierce College and the University of Oregon. In-between the schooling he had his own groups and eventually started the Rose Garden when he got together with John to play some college dates.

Musical Track

Bill Fleming, one of the younger members of the group at 18, was an accomplished pianist at 13, and by the time he was 15 he was also playing trumpet and guitar. Originally, his ambition was to be an attorney but music and the Rose Garden sidetracked him. A native of Hawthorne, California, Bill spends most of his time between engagements at an unusual avocation — kite flying.

Diana DeRose is the only female and only foreign member of the group. Born in Blackpool, England, Diana came to the United States early in 1964 with her mother and lives in California. Shortly after traveling West, the dark-haired guitarist landed several jobs at some of L.A.'s better-known folk/rock clubs. It wasn't long before she was a regular on the late "Hootenany Show;" then after leaving the Hootenany circuit she spent a few years with a group called the Holy Alieance before joining the Rose Garden. Now, along with Jim, Diana supplies the unusual harmony that has become a trademark of the group.

The Mechanic

John Noreen is the co-founder of the Rose Garden. Music and the desire to be part of a successful and creative group, have always been his ambition. The youngest member of the five, John is also the most mechanically-minded. He spends most of his spare time tinkering with engines ... taking them apart and then putting them back together.

Nearly every group has its easy-going member and as far as the Rose Garden is concerned, Bruce is it. Born in Minneapolis, Bruce is usually smiling no matter what happens.

CHAPPAQUA

"Chappaqua" was meant to be a purge. Written, directed and produced by Conrad Rooks, the film served as therapy to keep the former alcoholic addict off liquor and drugs. Hooked at 14 on hard liquor, soaked with drugs at 19, Rooks underwent "cure" after "cure" to no avail. Finally, taking a sleep cure in Switzerland, Rooks realized the futility of addiction. Realizing that he needed help in becoming part of the "straight" world, the 32 year old American began this film as a warning to young people and as a testimony to his own ordeal.

The film is sporatically brilliant. Combining every imaginable style of film from the German Expressionism of the twenties to the modern clear cut documentary, Rooks has created a film that is moving, interesting and in many instances quite devastating.

Black and white and color, combine and flow into one another without separation. Images collide into one another creating a mental state of mind with crystal clarity. The truely incredible part of this film is that the imagery and hallucinations are perfectly understandable.

Rooks was aided in realizing his autobiographical film by such noted actors and personalities as Jean-Louis Barrault (director of Paris Theatre de France-Odeon), Allen Ginsberg, Ornette Coleman and the Fugs. His cameraman was experimental film maker Robert Franks, noted for his "Sins of Jesus" and "Pull My Daisy".

The music was written and directed by Ravi Shankar. Shankar combines rock and classical with the Indian sounds to heighten and reconfirm the subconscious action on the screen.

The picture is a must for anyone interested in films and in the new areas of film technique. It is a truly experimental film, both in execution and in content. Possibly one of its most important functions will be to awaken the moviegoer to the power of underground films.

TRINI LOPEZ re-signed with W7.

48 GROOVY HAPPENING HITS!

ORDER NOW!!
Makes a wonderful gift
Advertised Nationally on Television and Radio...

ONLY $3.50 PLUS MAILING FOR ALL 48 HITS!

Kind Of A Drag: The Buckinghams
Cherry Cherry: Neil Diamond
Turn Down Day: The Cyrkle
My Little Red Book: Love
Wooly Bully: Sam the Sham
But It's Alright: J. J. Jackson
Little Girl: Syndicate of Sound
Jenny Take A Ride: M. Ryder & Det. Wheels
See You In September: The Tempos
Daddy's Home: Shep & The Limelighters
Why Do Fools Fall In Love: Frankie Lyman
Western Union: Five Americans
Sunny: Bobby Hebb
Daydream: Lovin' Spoonful
Good Lovin': Young Rascals
I Got You Babe: Sonny & Cher
Pushin' Too Hard: The Seeds
Land Of 1000 Dances: Wilson Pickett
Younger Girl: The Critters
I Who Have Nothing: Terry Knight & the Pack
Bermuda: Four Seasons
Gee: The Crows
Maybe: The Chantels
I Think We're Alone Now: T. James & Shondells

Locomotion: Little Eva
Hello Pretty Girl: Ronnie Dove
Hanky Panky: Tommy James
Lovers Concerto: Toys
Under The Boardwalk: Drifters
Magic Town: Vogues
Chapel Of Love: Dixie Cups
Papa's Got A Brand New Bag: James Brown
Poison Ivy: Coasters
There Goes My Baby: Drifters
Hang On Sloopy: Ramsey Lewis
Shimmy Shimmy Koko Bop: Lil' Anthony & Imp.
Kansas City: Wilber Harrison
Ya Ya: Lee Dorsey
Mocking Bird: Inez Foxx
A Fool In Love: Ike & Tina Turner
Charlie Brown: Coasters
El Watusi: Ray Barreto
Two Faces Have I: Lou Christie
When A Man Loves A Woman: Percy Sledge
Rescue Me: Fontella Bass
Spanish Lace: Four Seasons
Boy From New York City: Ad Libs

ENCLOSE $3.50 PLUS 50¢ FOR MAILING — TOTAL $4.00 FOR ALL 48 HITS!

Original Hits!!!
Original Stars!!!

SEND TO
BEAT PUBLICATIONS
9000 SUNSET BLVD.
SUITE 1000
LOS ANGELES, CALIF.

Name: (Print)
Address:
City:
State: Zip Code:
Canada And Foreign Add $1.00
Calif. Residents Add 5% Sales Tax. No C.O.D.

TURNING ON

LEONARD COHEN (Columbia) Leonard Cohen. This is the first album for a very talented Canadian poet. Prior to this album, Cohen's reputation rested mainly on his film scoring for "Nobody Waved Goodbye" and recordings of his material by other artists such as Judy Collins and Buffy Sainte-Marie.

Cohen's poetry is outstanding. The Boston Times honored the young Canadian by stating "James Joyce is alive and well in Montreal". Cohen's wording is unbelievably beautiful, dealing with cryptic images that establish complicated meanings. His songs require close attention and careful interpretation.

Dealing with the familiar themes of loneliness, desertion, and communication, Cohen turns universal concepts into personal trials. Conversely, he is also able to make his most obscure and personal poetry have deep meaning for everyone.

Perhaps the most moving cut on the album is "The Stranger Song". Unbelievable. It is impossible to describe the image and mood of this song. Using religious concepts and familiar happenings, Cohen conveys with unusual power the story of misplaced love, "It's true that all the men you knew were dealers/ who said they were through with dealing/ Everytime you gave them shelter."

One of his most poignant songs, which has also been recorded by Judy Collins is "Hey, That's No Way To Say Goodbye." Almost a prelude to "No Way To Say Goodbye" is the preceding cut "So Long, Marianne." Together they create a beautiful image of compassionate love that must end in separation.

Another amazing aspect of this album is the music. Each melody underscores the mood of the words. The almost resigned torment of the melody in "Master Song" emphasing the meaning of Cohen's poetry. "I believe that you heard your master sing/ When I was sick in bed/ I suppose that you told him everything/ That I kept locked in my head."

"Sisters of Mercy" is set to an intricate melody heightening the alegorical meaning of the words "Well they lay down beside me/ I made my confession to them. They touched both my eyes/ And I touched the dew on their hem. If you life is a leaf/ that the seasons tear off and condemn/ They will blind you with love/ That is graceful and green as a steam."

I think it is quite evident from the quotes re-printed here, that Leonard Cohen is an important poet who can only contribute to the growing significance of what is lumped into the general category of pop music. For those who worry about the word being replaced by seer sound, they need only to listen to Cohen's first album to gain heart.

THE GENUINE ARTICLE!

JBL BRINGS BACK THE MENDELSOHN QUINTETTE CLUB OF BOSTON YEA YEA

JUST BACK FROM THEIR TRIUMPHANT TOUR OF BOSTON
HOLLYWOOD PALLADIUM

YES, IT'S YOUR OWN FAVORITES "THE MENDELSOHN QUINTETTE CLUB OF BOSTON", yea yea...

AND... You lucky readers of this ad now have' the opportunity to possess this priceless masterpiece. A possession like this insures love and a happy home. Through the courtesy of J. B. Lansing Sound, Inc., we offer you this poster of your idolized quintette group at an unbelievable price... NOT $5.00... NOT $3.00... NOT $3.50 but just 25¢... that's right ONLY

GIANT SIZE 22"x35" BARGAIN PRICE 25¢

NO ONE ELSE CAN COMPETE WITH THIS OFFER... COMPETITION ASTOUNDED!!
Take advantage of this offer while it lasts... the demand is great.
Fill in and mail this coupon now.

COUPON
Enclosed please find 25¢. Send me the priceless poster of "THE MENDELSOHN QUINTETTE CLUB OF BOSTON".
Name_____
City_____ State_____
JAMES B. LANSING SOUND INC.
3249 CASITAS AVE., LOS ANGELES, CALIFORNIA 90039
(BEAT-D)

Beat Poster Shop

Giant 22x28 Love Poster in Full Color

(v) Marharishi (s) Stones (r) Jimi Hendrix (i) Dylan (t) The Who (o) Country Joe (w) Strawberry Alarm Clock (L) Love

Send to: BEAT POSTER SHOP, 9000 Sunset, Suite 1000, Los Angeles, Cal. 90069

PLEASE SEND ME THE FOLLOWING POSTERS (LIST BY LETTER)_____
I ENCLOSE $1.75 plus .25 Handling for each."

Name_____
Address_____
City_____ State_____ Zip Code_____
*California Residents Please Include 5% Sales Tax

A giant (22"x28") Calendar Poster in black, white and red.

PLEASE SEND ME THE CALENDAR POSTER
I ENCLOSE $1.75 plus .25 Handling fo each."

NAME_____
Address_____
City_____ State_____ Zip Code_____
*California Residents Please Include 5% Sales Tax

KRLA ARCHIVES

Now Available At:
MONTGOMERY WARD DEPARTMENT STORES

AVAILABLE AT

AVAILABLE AT

February 24, 1968 — THE BEAT — Page 19

BEAT WINTER SPECIAL
TWO for $4.00

GET A FRIEND TO SUBSCRIBE
PAY ONLY $2.00 EACH

Now you can send a free Beat Subscription to any serviceman in Viet Nam

(Send his name and address to Beat Publications)

Save $1.00 Each Off the Regular Subscription Price

A Big Savings of $4.50 Off the Newsstand Price

THIS OFFER FOR A LIMITED TIME ONLY

ACT NOW TO SAVE $ $ $

Mail to: BEAT PUBLICATIONS
9000 Sunset Blvd.
Los Angeles, California 90069

☐ NEW SUBSCRIPTION

We want BEAT for ☐ 1 year at $2.00 each ☐ 2 years at $3.50 each

Outside U.S. $9.00 per year each

Please print your name and address

My name is .... My name is ....
City .... City ....
City .... City ....
State .... Zip .... State .... Zip ....

ENCLOSED IS $4.00 for 2 One Year Subscriptions
$7.00 for 2 Two Year Subscriptions
$18.00 for 2 Foreign Subscriptions

Payment is in ☐ cash ☐ check ☐ money order

—CLASSIFIED—

"Organized Confusion" is an experience.

The INTERSTATE 405 grooves.

HEDGE and DONNA we love you!

Welcome back BB, DC5, HH, Missed you. Your turn, Gerry.

Outfitism is better than love.

Free: English Penpals. Write c/o Beat Publications, 9000 Sunset Blvd., Suite 1000. Enclose self-addressed envelope.

The PENNY ARCADE are tops in Cleveland, so is their lead singer ANDY HANGEL.

Carl — Your cilli's getting cold! Pete.

P. J. Proby, I'm with you.

Nick the Barber — I love you. I do, *I do!!*

Jon Jon come home!! Barb

Nut-Nut Tufano forever!!

Genius is spelled GREBB.

San Bernardino Pete: Did you get a ride? Love, Chris.

Original songs. I write rock, folk, soul, country and western, anything, Contact Bill Riche c/o Beat Publications, 9000 Sunset Blvd., Los Angeles, California.

HAPPY BIRTHDAY LINDA! WHO ELSE BUT THE FABULOUS VERNON.

BRAD HARRIS knows the KA

JEFFBECK / ERICCLAPTON / JIMHENDRIX / STEVIEWINWOOD / REALLY / SWING.

WILD POSTERS, for way-out bumper stickers, buttons!—Crazy Labels, Box 21-M, Olympia, Washington.

Maureen I love you — Poop.

Jeff Beck is beautiful, says Mary Hughes.

Pen Pals wanted from everywhere! Anyone from age 16 to 25 please write to Edith Eskridge c/o Beat Publications, 9000 Sunset Blvd., Los Angeles, California.

Aardvark Power.

Bob says Jack and Tom are groovy.

The Smokestack Banana shuts down the Bottles of Goodness.

HAPPY BIRTHDAY GRAHAM NASH — Feb. 2nd.

SLEEP LEARNING self hypnosis. Details, strange catalog free! Nutosuggestion, Box 24 BT, Olympia, Washington.

NAZZ

Lorelle I love James "Pump" McCartney toooo! Mary.

REACH COSMIC AWARENESS without drugs — help save mankind from destruction. Write for free booklet "Cosmic Awareness Speaks". Servant of Awareness, Box 115E, Olympia, Washington.

Association Fan Club C, Adam c/o The Beat, 9000 Sunset Blvd., Suite 1000, Los Angeles, Calif.

Band X.

The Groop is super-fab.

Love The Groop.

The Groop groves.

MAGICAL MYSTERIOUS BEATLES RULE!!!

"Hi, Brad, Ron".

Happiness is sharing, daring and daring to crave its enjoyment.

"Sherwood Ernie" Love you Madly "Raytown Bumps".

"Keep U.N.C.L.E. on so it can turn you on!!! Write in.

Hear Onion Street.

A belated happy birthday to Kenny of For Days and Night.

The obsolete Lampside, now. Bands 14-21 years needed for TV show & Teen Center. Bookings call Larry Tremain 934-5400.

THE BEAT will accept only personal messages in the classified section. We will p r i n t names but not addresses or phone numbers.

We will also accept Fan Club addresses in care of The Beat.

Rates are cheap! Only 10 cents per word.

Your deadline for the next issue is: February 24, 1968.

KRLA ARCHIVES

The Righteous Brothers Call It Quits

KRLA ARCHIVES

Exclusive Interview with Airplane 25¢

KRLA *Edition* **BEAT**

MARCH 9, 1968

Association Laughin' It Up

KRLA BEAT

Volume 3, Number 24 — March 9, 1968

ARE THE BEATLES GOING ON TOUR?

HOLLYWOOD— In the coup of the year, Jerry Perenchio Artists Ltd. has whisked away United States and Canadian bookings of the Beatles from General Artists Corp. GAC had booked all previous Beatle appearances in the U.S. Interestingly enough, Perenchio himself once worked for the giant GAC.

The switch poses one gigantic and obvious question: will there be any more U.S. bookings for the Beatles? The Beatles have said a flat "no" but then why would Perenchio want to secure the Beatles if he doesn't know something that we don't know? Silence seems to be the key word and until someone violates it, neither the Beatle fans nor the press will know for sure if the Beatles are indeed coming back to the U.S.

TOM JONES COMES BACK TO U.S.

NEW YORK — It has finally happened . . . the long-promised arrival of Tom Jones to the U.S. for an extended tour of night spots and television shows has finally come to pass.

Jones, who hasn't had a top five record in quite awhile, opened a two-week engagement at the famed Copacabana in New York. Following the Copa, Tom heads out west for a series of television shows, including "Red Skelton," "The Hollywood Palace" and "Jonathan Winters."

On March 21, Jones opens a month-long stand at the Flamingo Hotel in Las Vegas.

From a Welsh mining town, Jones went off to London where he eventually met with success as a singer. His career zoomed to a peak during the "British invasion" of America and his music charts during 1965-66. Probably best known for "What's New Pussycat," Jones enjoyed tremendous success up until the past year when his absence from American charts and television shows has been marked.

However, with his talent, it's not much of a bet to say that Jones will be back on top within the next three months.

The Beach Boys Haul In $60,000 For Four Days!

LOS ANGELES—Probably the most often repeated question asked concerning the field of pop music is "how much money does a successful group make doing personal appearances?"

The net amount is almost impossible to determine but for a successful group such as the Beach Boys the gross for a five performance "short" tour is $60,000.

Take, for example, the Beach Boys' recent swing through the Northwest. Their opening date at Everett Community College broke all existing records for the small institution and grossed $8,050 from a sell-out house scaled from $2.00-$5.00.

Their date at the Seattle Sports Arena (also scaled $2.00-$5.00) grossed a nice $18,885 despite the area's snow storms. Vancouver's Agradrome (with tickets scaled from $3.00-$5.00) was another complete sell-out, grossing $10,000.

An afternoon date at the Portland Coliseum was the top money, grossing $18,918 with the tickets scaled from $2.50 to $4.50. The Beach Boys final date was at St. Martin's College in Olympia, Washington. The concert (with tickets scaled from $2.50 to $5.00) grossed $8,000.

So there you have it. If you're as popular as the Beach Boys you can gross $60,000 for four days of work. Needless to say, not many pop groups are as popular as the Beach Boys . . . But, then again, if you're as popular as the Beatles, $60,000 is peanuts.

DOUBTS DISPELLED: BOTH 'BROTHERS' SUCCESSFUL

HOLLYWOOD — In the last issue of The BEAT we announced the break up of the Righteous Brothers. If anyone had any serious doubts about the success both Bobby Hatfield and Bill Medley would encounter by going their separate ways, you need doubt no more.

Bill Medley has just opened a solo engagement at the world-famed Cocoanut Grove in Los Angeles . . . to rave reviews.

Bobby Hatfield and his new partner, Jimmy Walker (formerly of the Knickerbockers), have been set for their initial major night club engagement at the same club during the prime "prom season" from May 7 through May 20.

Away from the spotlight, Hatfield has formed his own production company, Righteous Productions, and has singed his first recording act-to the company, Alice and The Wonderland Band. Hatfield's company will produce all single and album recordings by Alice and the Band.

JIMMY WALKER . . . NEWEST 'BROTHER' — BILL MEDLEY SOLO — HATFIELD FORMS OWN PRODUCTION COMPANY

KRLA ARCHIVES

Judge Rules Against Jimi Hendrix In Suit

NEW YORK—U.S. District Court Judge Charles M. Metzner ruled this week against Jimi Hendrix in the singer-guitarist's attempt to have Capitol Records temporarily enjoined from manufacturing or selling the recordings released by Capitol in an album entitled, "Get That Feeling."

Judge Metzner did issue a temporary injunction prohibiting Capitol from further sale of "Get That Feeling" in the album jacket originally used. The original jacket was, in the judge's opinion, possibly confusing to the public.

"Naturally, we're pleased that we shall be able to continue to sell what we feel to be very fine recordings including the talents of a great musician, Jimi Hendrix," said Voyle Gilmore, Capitol Vice President. "We are now in the process of designing a new album cover that will satisfy the requirements of Judge Metzner's opinion."

Presumably undaunted by the decision, Hendrix continues with his cross-country tour which began on February 1 and ends on March 30.

The Scaffold 'Thanks You'

LONDON — It's been a very long time coming but the Scaffold have finally released a single, "Thank U Very Much," which has received air play on American radio stations.

Thus far, the group has been best known for the fact that it includes Mike McGear, otherwise known as Paul McCartney's brother.

"All this attention for Mike doesn't bother us," says John Gorman and Roger McGough (the rest of the Scaffold), "because he has the good looks and youth. We're both not exactly pin-ups and it's natural that people want to talk to Mike rather than us."

A three-way split finds Mike adding the musical element of the group while John handles the comical part and Roger the political aspect of the act.

It remains to be seen which "end" of the act will be responsible for eventual Stateside success.

Yarbrough For 'Charley' Show

HOLLYWOOD — Glenn Yarbrough has been signed to sing the entire background music for "Travels With Charley," an hour-long special set to air on March 17 on NBC-TV. Henry Fonda will narrate the special which deals with John Steinbeck's 10,000 mile trip across the country in a camper with his pet poodle.

Yarbrough, who records for Warner Bros./7 Arts, is currently on a 75-city college concert tour.

On The Beat
By Louise Criscione

The Union Gap have just accomplished what most groups would give anything to do . . . receive a Gold Record for their very first single! The record is, of course, "Woman, Woman" and the RIAA has just certified it a million-seller.

The Union Gap is made up of Gary Puckett (vocals, guitar), Dwight Bement (tenor sax), Kerry Chater (bass guitar), Gary "Mutha" Withem (woodwinds, piano) and Paul Wheatbread (drums). Formed a little over one year ago in San Diego, California, the group named themselves after the town of Union Gap, Washington. Donning Civil War uniforms, their appearance was hard to miss and now, thanks to "Woman, Woman," their name is etched in the field of pop.

Diploma For Hendrix

Apparently there is more than one way to obtain a high school diploma. At least for Jimi Hendrix there is. While in Seattle (his hometown), Jimi paid a visit to Garfield High School to receive an honorary diploma from the institution which he left quite unceremoniously six years ago.

And that wasn't the only honor bestowed on the fire-making Hendrix . . . he was also presented with the key to the city of Seattle!

Things are definitely looking way up for England's Georgie Fame. In addition to having Britain's number one record ("Bonnie And Clyde"), Fame has just been signed to sing the title song for the forthcoming Elizabeth Taylor/Richard Burton movie, "Goforth."

Valli In Town

Frankie Valli in town to do a little promo work on both his solo record ("To Give") and the Four Seasons' latest ("Will You Still Love Me Tomorrow") was kept so busy he hardly had time to eat. And there's no time off in the foreseeable future either. On March 11, the Seasons open at the Latin Casino in New Jersey and then move on to the Music Hall in Cleveland for a concert on March 22. Youngstown, Ohio gets the group on March 23 for a gig at Stambaugh Auditorium.

QUICK ONES: Jerry Lee Lewis is far from vanishing but he has switched from rock to country and western music. Not surprising since that's the bag Lewis grew out of quite a few years ago . . . Dionne Warwick's "I Say A Little Prayer" is a million-seller according to her record company, Scepter Records. However, there will be no Gold

Record for Dionne since Scepter does not belong to the RIAA and, therefore, cannot get their certification . . . Laura Nero ("Wedding Bell Blues") has signed a contract with Columbia Records.

Leonard Nimoy is one entertainer who still believes in getting out and meeting his public. Quite naturally then when his latest album, "Two Sides Of Leonard Nimoy" came out, television's Mr. Spock took off for the record stores and spent innumerable hours signing his album as it went past the cash register! It's nice to know that there is one performer around who doesn't mind rubbing elbows with the plain old record-buyers.

AMERICAN BREED receive gold records for "Bend Me, Shape Me."

KRLA ARCHIVES

More Goodies For Schifrin

HOLLYWOOD — Good things just keep happening for Lalo Schifrin. Schifrin is certainly an Oscar contender for "best original score for a motion picture" with his score for "Cool Hand Luke." He's riding high in the national record charts with his "Mission: Impossible."

And now Schifrin has signed a long term multi-faceted contract with Paramount Pictures! The deal includes an exclusive recording contract with Dot Records and Paramount's publishing firms in addition to a nonexclusive pact for the scoring of at least one motion picture per year.

Schifrin arrived in Hollywood in 1964 and since that time has scored such movies as "The Cincinnati Kid," "The Fox" and "The President's Analyst" for Paramount.

Television programs have not escaped the Schifrin touch either as the talented composer-conductor has scored numerous shows, including several for Wolper Productions.

Schifrin began his musical studies at an early age in his native Argentina.

AL MARTINO: RED CARPET

LAS VEGAS — Al Martino is getting the red carpet and then some rolled out for him when he opens at the Flamingo Hotel this month. It's the first time in Vegas for the singer and in honor of the occasion the hotel is calling it "Al Martino Day" and is working in association with the local Chamber of Commerce for the event.

Deal For Connie

MIAMI BEACH — Remember Connie Francis? Well, obviously the Miami Beach patrons do. The singer has switched her loyalty to the new Hilton Plaza Hotel here (after long being associated with the famed Eden Roc) and has been signed to a three year contract by the Hilton.

The Hassles To Arrive?

NEW YORK — Expect to hear a lot about a new group called the Hassles. Why? Because United Artists Records is about to launch a major national promotion and merchandising drive in connection with the group. Their first album is due out momentarily.

The Hassles include John Edward (Little Jon) Dizek, 19, singer and tambourine shaker; William Joseph Martin (Billy Joe), Joel, 18, lead singer, piano and organ; Phil Marden, 19, bass guitar; Jonathan Craig Small, 20, drums; and Richard McKenner, 21, lead guitar.

Eric Burdon Busy

NEW YORK — As you probably already know, Eric Burdon spends more time here than he does in his native England. This, of course, tends to make his U.S. fans and booking agents most happy . . . with fans being able to see a lot of Eric and the booking agents being able to make a lot of bookings.

Consequently, Eric and the Animals will be appearing at the Los Angeles Whiskey a Go Go until March 3, at which time they head up to Las Vegas for a March 8th appearance at the Convention Center. March 9 finds them at the VIP Club in Tucson; March 12-13 in Dallas; March 15 at New York State University; March 16, Village Theatre in New York City; March 22-23 at the Grande Ballroom, Detroit.

PEOPLE ARE TALKING ABOUT who started the rumor that the Beatles and Stones are considering a joint concert tour of the U.S. . . . the large record company which is about four months too late putting the big push on a group with the shoulder-length hair . . . the confusion over when Herman is due to arrive Stateside and wondering why it all happened

. . . the very talented female singer who only had one hit and then took off and wondering if she can now comeback . . . how many things the Fireballs did before "Bottle Of Wine" . . . the Stones' failure to get 'She's A Rainbow' into the national top ten causing people to wonder if their career has been damaged by their less-than-sparkling publicity

. . . why the Vanilla Fudge moved their album way up in the charts but can't seem to get a single off the ground . . . the First Edition proving that a big promotional campaign can't hurt . . . the fact that Georgie Fame is back all the way with "Bonnie And Clyde" and wondering how many others will be able to cash in on Beatty's brainchild . . . the surprise combination of the year being Jackie Wilson and Count Basie

. . . the Hollies drawing an impressive array of entertainers to their first personal appearance in Los Angeles . . . the Royal Guardsmen being back on the charts with a song which fails to have "Snoopy" in the title and wondering if wonders will never cease

. . . what the Human Beinz' faces look like on their album cover and whether or not it was intentional

. . . the fact that when a rock group picks a name like 1910 Fruitgum Company you know how many group names have already been taken . . . how Bill Cosby can maintain his cool in the face of all those obnoxious autograph demanders and how the autograph demanders can lose their cool in the face of Cosby . . . how much better Harry Belafonte is when he sticks to singing and leaves the hosting behind.

. . . how broad-minded the American record buying public is when they can put the Fireballs, the Mills Brothers and James Brown all on the same record chart . . . how many Grammy Awards pop artists are going to receive this time around . . . the Mamas and Papas on-again, off-again career getting too ridiculous for words . . . why no one can come up with the money to purchase the great master Mike Nesmith cut

. . . whether or not Bobby Rydell will be able to make a top 40 comeback to go along with his new recording contract . . . snow job number 581 coming up on a group which keeps hanging on the fringes but never moving forward . . . Spanky and Our Gang being most impressive in concert . . . the Four Seasons chosing an oldie instead of a new Gaudio composition but probably having themselves a giant hit anyway.

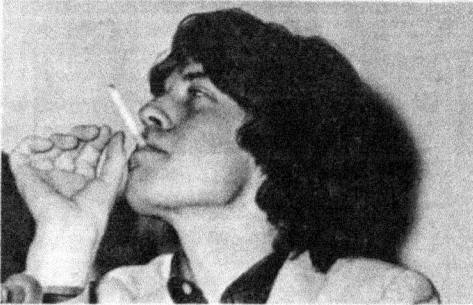

KRLA ARCHIVES

SPICE UP YOUR LIFE
Season with ...

THE TAMS • THE MAMAS & THE PAPAS • THE CANDYMEN • INFLUENCE • abc RECORDS

ABC RECORDS, INC.
NEW YORK/BEVERLY HILLS
DIST. IN CANADA BY SPARTON OF CANADA

EDEN'S CHILDREN — ABC/S 624
THE TAMS — A LITTLE MORE SOUL — ABC/S 627
CASHMAN, PISTILLI & WEST — BOUND TO HAPPEN — ABC/S 629
INFLUENCE — ABS/S 630
THE DIRTY BLUES BAND — BLUESWAY BL/S 6010

ARTHUR — DREAMS & IMAGES — LHI/S 12000 *
JESSE JAMES — 20th CENTURY FOX 3197 *
THE BUBBLE GUM MACHINE — SENATE/S 21002 *
THE MAMAS & THE PAPAS — SPRINGBOARD — DUNHILL D/S 50031
THE GRASS ROOTS — FEELINGS — DUNHILL D/S 50027

LADY NELSON & THE LORDS — PICADILLY PICKLE — DUNHILL D/S 50028
3's A CROWD — CHRISTOPHER'S MOVIE MATINEE — DUNHILL D/S 50030
THE CANDYMEN — BRING YOU CANDYPOWER — ABC/S 633
GABOR SZABO / BOB THIELE — LIGHT MY FIRE — IMPULSE A/S 9159
INTERNATIONAL SUBMARINE BAND — LHI/S 12001 *

* Distributed by ABC Records, Inc.

KRLA ARCHIVES

PICTURES IN THE NEWS

THE HAPPENINGS are one of the busiest groups in the nation as far as personal appearances go. Bookings set for the group include the "Merv Griffin Show" on March 6; Doylestown, Pa. (8); Holyoke, Mass. (9); and Chester, Pa. (15). The Happenings will play the posh Eden Roc in Miami from April 1 through 7.

SOME PEOPLE THOUGHT it would never happen but Glen Campbell is really going to leave his lucrative job as a session musician to work full-time on his own career! Biggest date upcoming is his hosting of the Smothers Brothers' summer replacement TV show.

PET CLARK has come a long, long way from winning her first Grammy. The petite entertainer, who has just finished her first film starring role as an adult, is being sought to play the lead role in the movie version of "Peter Pan."

HERB ALPERT, who is always moving, will go all across the country in his next television special airing on April 22 on the CBS-TV network.

THE ALAN PRICE SET is heading across America on a five week tour in conjunction with a heavy promotional push on their new album, "The Price Is Right." Cities set for the Price invasion are New York, Hollywood, Dallas, Phoenix, Tucson and Detroit.

A QUIET AFTERNOON WITH THE AIRPLANE

By Tony Leigh

It was a weird sort of afternoon. The Airplane were in Los Angeles, holed up at a motel on Franklin Blvd. in Hollywood. Their public relations firm had decided that it was about time the Airplane gave a few interviews to the local press, so three or four editors were called with the news the Airplane would love to talk to them.

It turned out that the problem really wasn't that the Airplane didn't want to talk, it was just that things weren't quite set up that way. It's a fine and lovely style to just follow people around for days and get bits and pieces of information over a period of time, this makes for insights and interesting reading. But when you're limited in time to an hour in one afternoon, you need quiet, cooperation and order.

For better or worse, none of that was present at the motel. What was present was unusual — all six of the Jefferson Airplane together in one room. They had obviously been clued that they were do to about three or four interviews that afternoon and they

were slightly ready for it.

There seemed to be a million people in the room, a tape recorder, and a cameraman who needed shots of the group. And of course, their PR man sitting discussing life and the inability of reporters to ask questions. Spencer talked almost constantly, Jorma and Jack sat reading Crawdaddy, who had just come out with a super-intellectual-aren't-they wonderful review of "After Bathing At Baxters," Marty was getting up and down every few minutes, justifiably bored with the whole thing, and Grace was looking around for some pain pills, anything stronger than aspirin.

Airplane Cooperative

It wasn't that the Airplane didn't want to talk, or to give a real interview, it's just that the whole thing wasn't set up that way. It was more sort of catch as catch can, the feeling that they and you all had better things to do. Amazingly enough, as a whole they were most friendly and cooperative, two adjectives not usually associated with the group.

One point that was discussed almost immediately and was evidenced even in that afternoon, was the extreme egos of every member of the group.

Spencer explained, "you have to be an ego freak to get in front of an audience, to expose yourself, to give them something groovy. Before you can face an audience your ego has to be there. But ego is not necessarily negative."

That is probably the understatement of the year, for the Airplane after recording in this city for seven months, has earned the rather dubious reputation of being six complete walking ego trips. Grace readily admitted that one of their hardest problems is to agree on anything. That was certainly proved when a slight business discussion seemed to pop up out of nowhere, and a debate ensued.

About this time, their PR man got into a discussion with Spencer about jazz musicians and having to leave Los Angeles to make it in New York, and the problems of money. Also there was a strange conversation about only wanting cover stories in national magazines. Spencer thought cover stories should be all they should try for, settling for less when absolutely necessary, but only as a last resort. It seemed that a few months before a major magazine had lived with the group for a couple of weeks, pertaining in copious private and group interviews, being in the center of the Airplane at all times, only to come forth with a few paragraphs of nothing when the magazine was finally released. This, Spencer thought was unforgettable. The PR man tried to explain to him the facts of magazine life, about editorial control over the cover and all that, but Spencer held his ground.

There was a lull in the cross conversation long enough to ask about audiences and dance concerts, Paul explained, "about a half and hour before we go on, we start to warm up and plan what we are going to do on stage, depending on how we feel . . . what feels good tonight.

Vibrations

"It's important to get a response from the audience, especially for the singers, you need the vibrations."

The Airplane caused quite a stir in this city last summer when they played the Hollywood Bowl. It seems that they wanted the audience to be able to dance — a perfectly logical request except that the Bowl is a concert stadium and not a dance auditorium, a fact which the police noticed immediately as they tried to undo the "damage" Marty, Paul and Grace were doing.

"It's important for the audience to dance so that they won't feel inhibited, they have to feel free, and not have cops standing around . . . that's a drag, no one can enjoy themselves."

Then Paul added, "I also like wiggly bodies, they turn one on. The audience is more involved, dancing is like applause it shows they are with you, but unlike applause it goes on all the time."

The importance of light shows was also discussed. The Airplane was, of course, one of the first groups to use a light show and now they almost never perform without one. They brought one of the best light shows to national television when they performed on the Perry Como Show.

"We usually take our own with us, unless the promoter of the concert can guarantee that they have one of their own. It's just that much more added environment. The Head Lights go with us."

There has been a good deal of uncomplimentary talk about the Airplane in their home town of San Francisco. It seems the group that helped to create the San Francisco sound, the group that played one of the first free concerts in the park, the group that speared flower power throughout the world, has lost favor with a good many Bay Area residents. The complaints range from "they are too Hollywood" (whatever that means) to "they sold out" (mainly due to the fact that they rented a fantastic house in the Hollywood Hills for a fantastic price — the very same house the Beatles stayed in when they were in town). But the Airplane could not be bothered with such comments.

"We have to develop. This is where the Airplane is now, if you don't like 'Baxter's' then you don't like the Airplane. You can't say you liked us more when we did 'Pillow' then now, because we have to change. There's nothing we can do about the people who think we've 'sold out' we haven't, that's all. You gain some people and you losse some people with everything that you do."

Then, as an afterthought it was added that some people after each of their three albums have stated that they have "sold out."

The rest of the afternoon, was devoted to pictures taking and private conversations. Grace was hungry and ordered Chicken Delight — the delivery boy was in for a big surprise. Paul and Jack decided they wanted to go see a movie, and the new Italian Western flick, The Good, The Bad and The Ugly seemed like the best possibility. The PR man was saying the reviewer for the Times was due any minute and that he would have some intellectual questions.

It was sort of a wierd afternoon.

JACK

JORMA

PAUL

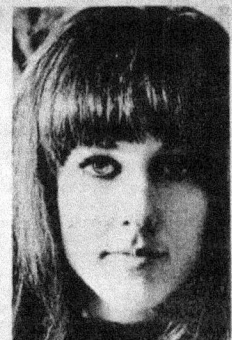

MARTY

GRACE

SPENCER

KRLA ARCHIVES

THE ASSOCIATION display three gold records they just received from Joe Smith, General manager of Warner Bros./7 Arts Records, for their "Along Comes The Association" and "Insight Out" albums as well as their "Never My Love" single.

A 'PARALLEL TWENTY THREE' ON THE DAYS OF THE ASSOCIATION

RUSS GIGUERE

TED BLUECHEL

By Patty Johnson

The past two and a half years have been fast and furious for the talented six known collectively as the Association. In that length of time Brian Cole, Ted Bluechel, Russ Giguere, Jim Yester, Terry Kirkman and recently Larry Ramos have racked up over a thousand shows, roughly a hundred television shows, one book, numerous awards and five gold records.

The last batch of gold records were just presented to the group at a cocktail party held at the Beverly Hills Hotel. It was obvious that the six young entertainers are still as unpretentious and fun-loving as ever when they had a tug-of-war over their new trophies!

One of the songs on their gold-plated "Insight Out" album is "Parallel Twenty-Three." It compaers the past and present in our society . . . a society from which the Association have decided not to drop out. And like that society there are comparisons and parallels to the Association "then" and the Association "now."

On July 1, 1965, six nervous, identically brown-suited musicians made a dubious debut at a place called the Ice House in Glendale, California. One year later they headed out on their first tour . . . a magnificent itinerary of the back of a railroad truck, a platform in the middle of a lake and other such interesting and prestige-laden places.

The past year the Association entourage stopped at such places as Houston's Astrodome, San Francisco's Cow Palace and Los Angeles' Greek Theatre.

But . . . "We have basically the same act and the same format. The show starts and it ends," says the fast-thinking Ted Bluechel. "We try to add as much new material as possible and still leave our favorites."

Summer of 1966 saw the release of their first album, "Along Comes The Association." January 1968 was the month the Association received their gold record for the album, signifiying sales of one million. "It was recorded before I joined the group," admits Larry Ramos, "but it's pretty good anyway!"

"Rennaisance" and "Insight Out" followed in the heels of the first album and their fourth long playing object d'art is due out any day now. Says Ted of the latest: "Ten of the cuts on it are original compositions. And, as any group, we like to grow. We are trying some new things, especially a lot of new vocal concepts on this album."

Unusually enough, during the two and a half years they've been together, there has been only one personnel change in the group. Their former lead guitarist, Gary Alexander, made his exist and was replaced by Larry Ramos, formerly of the Christy Minstrels. "Replaced" is not really the correct word because both of them have contributed to the group in their own individual ways.

That was the past . . . the present is busy and the future is called promising.

BRIAN COLE

LARRY RAMOS

TERRY KIRKMAN

JERRY YESTER

KRLA ARCHIVES

ARLO GUTHRIE TELLING HIS STORY

By Jacoba Atlas

He's slight of build with long hair that hangs almost to his shoulders in curls. At 20, he is an incredible mixture of youth and age, of knowledge and innocence. He is also the master of the put-on. He is Arlo Guthrie, son of the famous Woody Guthrie, the man who reflected a whole generation of people with his interpretation of the Depression, the man who influenced another generation of songwriters with his music.

But Arlo is not simply Woody's son, as the song says, "God bless the child that's got his own." In front of an audience, Arlo is outstanding. No matter how much you may love "Alice's Restaurant" on record, there is nothing like seeing Guthrie sing it live. He has a rapport with the audience that is most unusual in seasoned performers much less a 20-year-old "newcomer."

Arlo's songs are totally unique in music today. They seem to be more of a summation and interpretation of the world and it's hang-ups than anything else. Gone is the protest song, or the questioning song. Arlo is not so much asking why, as he is saying what is. They don't have the tone Dylan's early period of "Blowin' in the Wind", nor are they the poetical outbursts of "Desolation Row". Although Arlo resembles Dylan in voice and appearance he in no way emulates Dylan's style.

Although Arlo's song could be interpreted as political, the troubador refuses to accept this label. "I'm not really politically minded in my songs. The songs are sometimes about politics, have things about politics in them, but the songs aren't political at all. Because they don't say to choose one politic or another."

Another label Guthrie shuns is that of a spokesman. "No one can ever be a spokesman for someone other than himself . . . and I'm a spokesman for myself. In my own life, I'm of course in touch with other people, and mostly people who are my age, people who are doing the things I'm doing. And that want to do the things that I want to do. So in that sense I know a little about what's happening with my kind of people. And since I know about that, I write about it. So I'm not really a spokesman, I'm just doing my thing, telling my story. Which isn't altogether unrealted."

Rock As Folk

Many people have declared that folk music has died. The impetus that brought us the early sound of Dylan, the voice of Joan Baez sans electronic accompaniment, the melodies of Tim Hardin, has given way to the driving sound of rock. But Arlo sees a close connection between the two forms of music.

"Rock is folk music. Well, it's what makes folk song a folk song. It's not a guitar certainly that makes a folk song a folk song, and it's not the way you play it or how it sounds. It's what you say.

"Folk music is things that communicate with people. If I can say that that is folk music, then I can say that rock is folk music. So

folk music didn't really die, it just changed. To assume that it died would be to say that people don't think anymore, that people don't relate to other people anymore.

"To say that Woody didn't use an electric guitar and all this; well, very simply he didn't have it and if he did have it no one would have listened then anyway. Rock at one time wasn't listened to for meaning. And that's why it wasn't folk music. Ever since it became playable, anybody can buy an electric guitar for ten bucks if he want rock became folk oriented.

No Protest

"The songs haven't changed except that the way of getting something done hasn't been to protest anymore. In other words protesting is when you're against something so violently or so that it upsets you so much that you have to so 'no that's not any good' that's a protest. But when you do something else in place of not doing something it ceases to be protest.

"The Hippie thing isn't a protest against anything, they're just doing something else. And the music has changed from being against a lot of things to being for a lot of things. They're just different things. So this is why the protest thing has died, because people happen to be for things instead of against things."

Although many reviewers across the country have criticized a recent concert in New York's Lincoln Center in honor of Woody Guthrie for being a vehicle for seeing Bob Dylan perform after 18 months, Arlo sees it in a much different light. "I don't think it's true. They couldn't have had any good feelings previous to going into the concert. They sound like they wrote (the reviewers) it before they went in. It was an absolutely beautiful concert. There were no ego trips as far as anyone was concerned. It was a very nice thing, indescribable really."

Because most of Arlo's songs deal with society in its present state, there is somewhat of an underlying pessimism implicit in his songs. However, Guthrie himself is an optimist for the most part. A least, however, he doesn't feel society is stagnate.

"Things change whether you're for change or not. I see some change as a natural growth. Whether people are for it or not really doesn't have any significance. What's changing is the kind of society and the kind of world we live in, and that's always changing. It's only that people have to be aware that things are changing and be ready for the changes when they happen. Not to prepare in the way to defend yourself against the changes which seems to be the way with most of today's older people. You know, how to stay the same in a changing world, that's a ridiculous idea. That would be like a tree that never bloomed.

"I don't think a song can re-educate anyone. People who laugh at *Alice* have come to these things themselves. They already know; if they didn't understand it, it would not be funny.

Experiences

"Only experiences can re-educate. You can read a book twenty times and not understand what it's saying and then get it, or you can read it once and get it, or some don't even have to read the book at all to get it. So *Alice* can only do things that have been done, it may be an experience if someone is ready for that experience, or is in a position to understand it, to make some kind of sense out of it.

"I don't believe in the Generation Gap at all. My grandmother is 85 and she told me she was a hippie and she is, she's very groovy. The Generation Gap has to do with law and order and the Establishment. The Generation Gap is a religious feeling, that something is about to happen that is totally different from all other things that have happened. A lot of people don't know what it is, nevertheless they feel it. Some people try to forget it. Those people that don't feel it are naturally separated from those people who do feel it. This is the Generation Gap between people that feel change and people that don't."

KRLA ARCHIVES

Six O'clock Younger Generation
Money Old Folks
She Is Still A Mystery

AVAILABLE AT
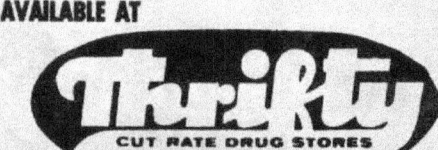

"You Can Get Anything You Want At Alice's Restaurant"

VELVET NANCY

AVAILABLE AT:

KRLA ARCHIVES

THERE ARE BUT FOUR SMALL FACES

Now Available At:
MONTGOMERY WARD DEPARTMENT STORES

WANTED: The Notorious Byrd Brothers

KRLA ARCHIVES

How I Won The War Premiere Revisited

POLICE HAVE HANDS full holding back thousands of teenagers on hand to catch a glimpse of their favorite recording star during KRLA's live broadcast of the "How I Won the War" premiere in Beverly Hills.

KRLA'S REB FOSTER arrives with actress Carla Green at American premiere of Beatle John Lennon's "How I Won the War" at Fine Arts Theatre in Beverly Hills. Hundreds of pop stars attended the charity event sponsored by KRLA.

CHEETAH

1 NAVY STREET — **VENICE** 392-4501

THE No. 1 DISCOTHEQUE

Presents

ITS PROGRAM OF No. 1 ATTRACTIONS

Feb. 23-24   IKE AND TINA TURNER REVUE AND THE VISIONS

Mar. 1st   BLUE CHEER AND MUSIC MACHINE

Mar. 2nd   PAUL BUTTERFIELD BLUES BAND
BLUE CHEER AND MUSIC MACHINE

Mar. 8-9   **1st L.A. APPEARANCE**
QUICKSILVER MESSENGER SERVICE
STEPPEN WULF & KALEIDOSCOPE

Mar. 15-16   THE SOUL SOUNDS OF JACKIE WILSON AND HIS REVUE

Mar. 22-23   COUNTRY JOE AND THE FISH AND PACIFIC GAS AND ELECTRIC CO.

KRLA ARCHIVES

Unique Interpreters Of Pop
USA, Leonard Cohen, Van Dykes Parks

by Jacoba Atlas

The revolution in pop music has produced some extraordinary people. Attracting poets, jazz musicians and classical music enthusiasts, the field has now expanded into a multifaced creative venture embracing all forms of music.

Because of the top forty dominence of most radio stations and the limited time devoted to LP selections, the average record buyer finds it difficult to hear the new material that is constantly being produced. Buying a record, without hearing cuts from the album can be an expensive mistake, but unless this chance is taken, many people will miss out on what is truly worthwhile in pop music.

This article will attempt to bridge that gap, in the case of three new artists representative of the new order in pop music. The *United States of America*, a new electronic rock group with a solid background in classical music, *Leonard Cohen* a poet from Canada whose work has been recorded by Judy Collins and Buffy Saint-Marie, and *Van Dyke Parks*, a young, proclaimed genius who worked with Brian Wilson of the Beach Boys.

USA

The USA has its basis in a fantastic combination of hard rock and intricate modern electronics. Using such diverse devices as synthesizers and ring modulators they are able to distort voices and music to create a whole new sound.

The group consists of six people: Joseph Byrd who studied music and composition at both Sanford University and UCLA; Dorothy Maskowitz who attended Barnard College and sang avant-garde concerts; Gordon Marron who began playing the violin at the tender age of four; Craig Woodson who studied at UCLA, and participated in a New Musical workshop; and Rand Forbes who majored in music at UCLA and once toured Great Britain and Scandinavia with a Youth Symphony.

Although their music has been put forth as "avant garde" and "art rock" the group itself dislikes this pseudo-intellectual label. Gordon explains, "we're not really far out and freaky. We play really good rock. We're not like the Mothers of Invention at all. We have the best rhythm section (Craig and Rand) and they play really hard."

Working with a young engineer named Durett they developed a ring modulator, a synthesizer and an electric violin. Together they make up a completely unique unit which transforms normal instruments into geniunely new sounds. Echoes, wa-wa peddles, fuzz tape echoes are all used to create their sound. In fact, the whole unit takes about four hours to set up.

Although all the electronic devices might indicate an inability to produce their sound live, just the opposite is true. With Joseph Byrd working the electronics, Dorothy singing led, and Gordon on electric violin, their complicated music is reproduced to the letter. In fact, Gordon insists, they are better live. "All the music, all the effects are done live. We don't believe in being a studio group. Some of us even play more than one instrument at a time. We're much more exciting live."

With their amazing background in what is commonly called 'serious music' the group has earned a pre-release reputation as being far out and classical. But although they cut their musical teeth on everything from Bartok to Cage and Stockhausen their present interest is in good rock.

Their lead singer, Dorothy, is an interesting looking blonde without any of the affectations usually associated with singers. Straightforward, talented, she is a major participant in all of the groups creative endeavors. When a national magazine recently did a story on the problems of girl singers with all male group, Dorothy was amazed at some of their reactions. She herself has found no difficulty with the group. "Once I decided to stop trying to set up the equipment everything worked out fine."

She has held many jobs including working for the Time-Life complex. But as she says, "everybody now wants to sing with a rock band, I know a girl who outwardly has everything anybody could want, and she told me she'd change places with me in a minute."

It is Dorothy's voice which ties the USA together and adds to its dramatic appeal. Although she states she doesn't have any trouble sustaining her sound, the one difficulty is when the band gets "sometimes overpowering."

The United States of America is a group you will be hearing about. They are an important combination of two schools of music united into one tight sound. Listen to their album and try to see them live.

Leonard Cohen

Into a totally different sound is poet Leonard Cohen. Well known in Canada for his love poetry and for his movie scoring, the writer is gaining importance in this country with the release of his first album and a novel entitled "Beautiful Loosers."

One criticism of Cohen's album rests with the poets voice: it is really non-existant. What carries the record along is the meaning of the words and not his ability to sing them. Judy Collins is able to give much more musical tone to *Sisters of Mercy* or *Suzanne*, but hearing a composer perform his own words always gives an added dimension that cannot be subverted by a weak voice.

Cohen is a modern day Homer. Maintaining a house on the Greek Island of Hydra without benefit of electricity or running water, holding up at the Chelsea Hotel in New York, dropping into his home town of Montreal Cohen is a man who rarely stays put. US college campuses have been demanding his services in concert appearances to read his own poetry and at 33 he has become a spokesman for a whole generation of people newly vocal in their aspirations.

His music and his poetry is liberally sprinkled with religious images. Allegorical tales of God and salvation run throughout his work. Once Cohen volunteered the battle cry "God is alive. Magic is afoot!"

"Everybody I meet wipes me out. Here are all these people plugging away at their roles. Being producers and policemen and bishops. It knocks me out, and all I can do is get down on my knees. I don't even think of myself as a writer, singer or whatever. The occupation of being a man is so much more. In spite of all the philosophical encouragement about hanging loose and all that Sunday School stuff, I admit I'm confused. I can't begin to locate my head. It has a life of its own."

Concerned with salvation, with finding a 'state of grace' (harmony with the rest of the world) or a deeper meaning to life, Cohen has gone through many devices that were to help bring him closer to

(Continued on Page 15)

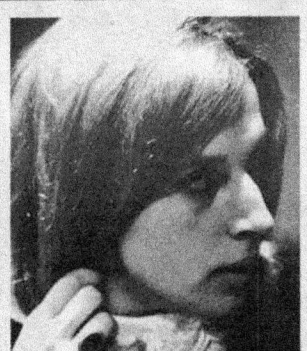
DOROTHY MOSKOWITZ of the USA

The USA in concert

LEONARD COHEN

KRLA ARCHIVES

OH WHAT CHANGES TIME HAS WROUGHT!

The inevitable time does many things to many people. Some become better, some worse. Some learn how to shave and others become proficient at growing beards.

Entertainers are no less effected by time than florists or garbage collectors or used car salesmen. Consequently, while looking through our photograph files we came upon several marked changes over the past few years in pop personalities.

You know their names, you know what they looked like "then" . . . you know what they look like "now."

Did you ever stop to ponder what changes time has wrought?

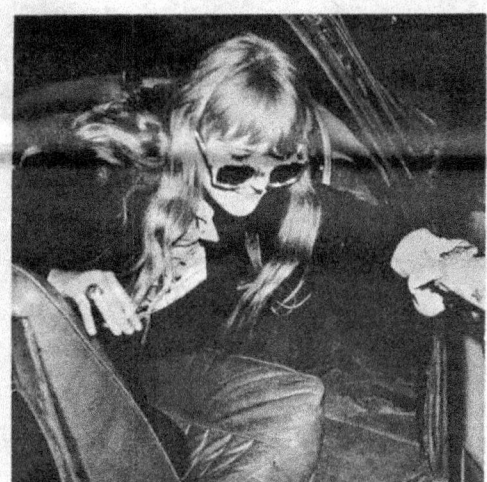  

KRLA ARCHIVES

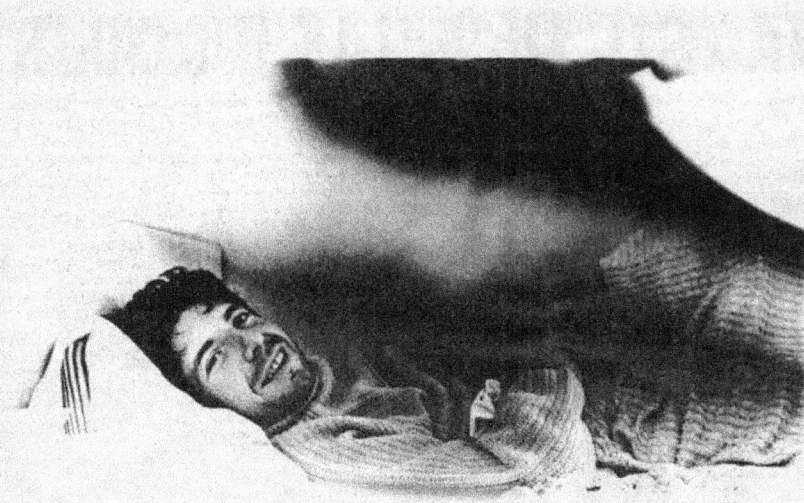
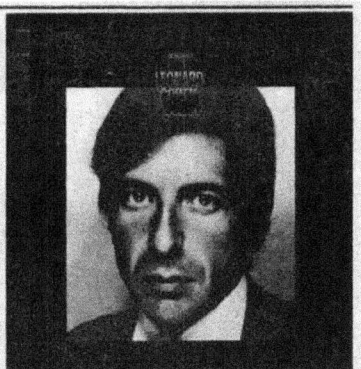

"I've been on the outlaw scene since I was 15. I had some things in common with the Beatniks, and even more things with the hippies. The next thing may be even closer to where I am."

AVAILABLE AT

From Flint Hill near Shelby, North Carolina to the Avalon Ballroom in San Francisco, Flatt and Scruggs have been playing their banjo and guitar. They even made the get-away faster for "Bonnie and Clyde." Now see what they can do for you!

AVAILABLE AT

KRLA ARCHIVES

FRANKIE VALLI "WE STILL LIGHT CANDLES"

Tony Leigh

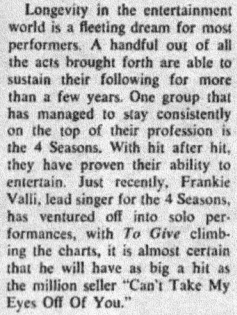

Longevity in the entertainment world is a fleeting dream for most performers. A handful out of all the acts brought forth are able to sustain their following for more than a few years. One group that has managed to stay consistently on the top of their profession is the 4 Seasons. With hit after hit, they have proven their ability to entertain. Just recently, Frankie Valli, lead singer for the 4 Seasons, has ventured off into solo performances, with *To Give* climbing the charts, it is almost certain that he will have as big a hit as the million seller "Can't Take My Eyes Off Of You."

"Many people ask me the question am I planning on leaving the group. No, I am not planning on leaving the group ever, because the group is really what gave birth to all the things that are beginning to happen — all the extra things — and there's a very soft spot in my heart for the group and all the members in it," explained Valli, in Los Angeles to promote his new single on the Joey Bishop show.

"I guess to a certain extent I will solo on television, but as far as concerts go, we will keep the group intact. While I'm doing these single records, the rest of the group keeps itself occupied by soliciting people to buy my records."

Actually, the rest of the 4 Seasons have been doing a good deal more than that, as Frankie well knows. A new 4 Seasons record has been released this week, a cover of the old Shirells record. "Will You Still Love Me Tomorrow."

Although most people assume that "Can't Take My Eyes Off Of You" was Valli's first venture into the solo field, this is not quite true. "I had a couple of records out before that. One record being cut six months before my record was cut was "The Sun Ain't Gonna Shine Anymore" — the Walker Bros. had a hit recording of it. I'm very sorry that we didn't have the hit recording of it, but they did do it exactly as we had done it. And I had one previous to that which was a regional hit, in about four markets called "You're Gonna Hurt Yourself."

"The reason I decided to do some solo recording is first of all it offered me a challenge and it gave me the opportunity to do some things that I had always wanted to do that I would not be able to do with the group."

Challenge

"Even when we started I think we had that in mind, for me to do some solo work. But at that particular time, it was more important for a 4 Seasons success and then go on to other things.

"'Can't Take My Eyes Off Of You' was written for me. 'Your Gonna Hurt Yourself' was written for the group but in a different concept than anything we had ever done. After we started running it down to record we decided that it would be my record. 'To Give' was written specifically for me.

"The whole group takes part in my records in one way or another. Joe plays bass on 'Can't Take My Eyes Off Of You' and he also acts as my musical director whenever I got out and do TV shows. Bobby also takes care of the musical end of it, contracting the musicians. Bob does the writing and arranging and assists Joe in many ways. Tommy is basically the businessman of the group, he's in the background."

Although Valli is aware of their popularity throughout the years, he has no ready explanations for their success. "I think we still all light candles. Say prayers and we all have very large families. But I can remember the very early days when we had decided we wanted to go into the record business. The very first 4 Seasons record was a bomb called 'Bermuda' — it sold three records. We all bought one, except Tommy who didn't like it."

The 4 Seasons concert performances are always sold out. People seem to enjoy hearing their hits and their new interpretations of old standards. But although many groups complain of having to sing their old songs, the 4 S e a s o n s readily comply. "I can't understand how somebody could not want to do something that gave them their start, I don't know if they're ashamed of it or whatever. But if you do make a record that sells a million copies you should be thrilled to do it.

"We do hits and melodies and we also do songs all the way through. I enjoy it thoroughly. I think in concert you can do your hits and also do some new things, you can even do comedy. There is so much to do, you don't have to take your hits and throw them out, many people come just to hear that.

"I think in our particular case one of the reasons that we have achieved the longevity that we have had is that we sincerely have a feeling for our audience. I know there are many groups that get carried away after a few hits and get to the point where they don't care less what the audience wants. I think this is wrong. You really do owe an obligation to the people who buy your records to come to see you. Once you loose site of that you're done."

Gimmicks aren't part of the scheme for long life in the record business a l t h o u g h many new groups seem to be relying heavily on just that.

"These groups will never last, especially they're instruments. I don't know, if they sincerely get something out of it, if they're not putting anybody on, that's great. But if they're not, they're just doing it to spoof the audience then it's an insult. To anyone's intelligence to listen to it. I can't for the life of me understand how anyone could get any enjoyment out of destruction. Artistry is one thing, but that's something else.

"But on a whole, I think music is getting better. There are so many kids today interested in music. I also find that with the more orchestration on albums it is leading back to a more classical form of music. But of course, that is not new. The average listener who is not familiar with classical music might think this is brand new, and that this is a new stroke of genius, but actually the genius came centuries before."

USA, COHEN and PARKS

(Cont. from page 12)

his goals, he tried astrology, "I Ching," a phase where he only ate meat (radishes screamed when they were pulled from the earth) a phase where he only ate vegetables (animals are alive), his quest for finding a way not to harm the universe in its complexity has only brought him m o r e problems. Cohen considers himself a rebel, but like Camus he is an anarchist unable "to throw the bomb." He is the personification of the person who sees both sides in trying to see the world, both sides of any political endeavor are evil, both are holy.

He himself seems to write from a constant state of pain, and his work reflects that feeling. "The best products of our time are in agony. The finest sensibilities of the age are convulsed with pain. That means a change is at hand.

"People keep saying India, India, India. But the Indian vocabulary is much too precise for us. Our natural vocabulary is Judeo-Christian. That is ours. We have to rediscover law from our own heritage."

Van Dykes Parks

Away from the agonized pain that Leonard Cohen puts into his music, is the rather interesting phenomenon of Los Angeles known as Van Dyke Parks. A young man, of about 23, who looks 12, and has been called a genius by some and a put-on by others. It is almost impossible to tell where one aspect lets off and the other begins.

Van Duke has worked on songs for the Beach Boys — songs like Heroes and Villains (along with Brian Wilson, of course), he also worked with the Byrds during their *Eight Miles High* period. His new album is called "Song Cycle" and interpretations of the work have absolutely covered the gamut of what can be said about any record.

What is apparent from this album is an amazing knowledge of musical arrangements. The songs flow into one another in what one critic describes as the place the Beatles will eventually have to end up.

Van Dyke like most people into music dispises categories. "Rock and roll, pop music, the Beach Boys are rock and roll for me. *Pet Sounds*, that's the ultimate with all these instruments and rhythms."

In his album Parks uses every sound from electronics to Busby Berkeley musical n u m b e r s. He nails Hollywood in his music, talks about 20th century man, has fleeting reverences to politics and ends one song with "Dust Off Pearl Harbor Time."

Van Dyke, like many people in this town, is convinced that he is miles ahead of other people. "I mean to stand right up there with the best of em," he recently told a national magazine, "and let's just say that it'd be a good thing if after this record come out, a lot of people have to start running to catch up. A *lawhit* of people are gonna have to catch up."

Parks maintains that Song Cycle was impossibility hard to record. Speaking of it he says, "we worked like hell to make it. We had staff musicians there, and those musicians really played. And we had Russian cats playing there. And their hands were shaking. The finest balalaika player and he doesn't even have a record player. I'm gonna give him mine — it's not important, I can get another one — so he can hear the record."

As for the future, Parks isn't really sure. He's expressed a wish to go to Europe and travel all over by car making his living by playing in little clubs. But on the other hand he has a wife to support, he might go back to doing studio work. Then again with *Song Cycle* taking off, someone might just let him record another album.

Send a 1 Year BEAT

Subscription to

ANY Serviceman

for only $1.00

(to cover mailing costs)

NAME..

ADDRESS...

CITY.. ZIP..........

KRLA ARCHIVES

KRLA ARCHIVES

1967 Grammy Award Nominations

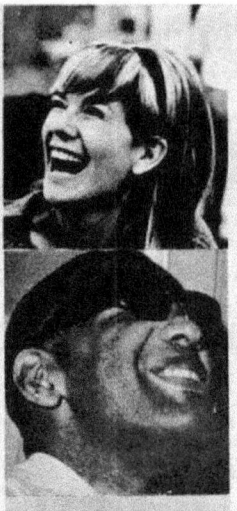

Record of the Year

By the Time I Get to Phoenix—Glen Campbell
My Cup Runneth Over—Ed Ames
Ode to Billie Joe—Bobbie Gentry
Somethin' Stupid—Nancy and Frank Sinatra
Up, Up and Away—5th Dimension

Album of the Year

Francis Albert Sinatra/Antonio Carlos Jobim—Sinatra/Jobim
It Must Be Him—Vikki Carr
My Cup Runneth Over—Ed Ames
Ode to Billie Joe—Bobbie Gentry
Sgt. Pepper's Lonely Hearts Club Band—The Beatles

Song of the Year

By the Time I Get to Phoenix—songwriter Jim Webb
Gentle On My Mind—songwriter John Hartford
My Cup Runneth Over—songwriter Tom Jones, Harvey Schmidt
Ode to Billie Joe—songwriter Bobbie Gentry
Up, Up and Away—songwriter Jim Webb

Best Vocal Female Performance (solo performance either single, album)

Alfie—Dionne Warwick
Don't Sleep in the Subway—Petula Clark
It Must Be Him—Vikki Carr
Ode to Billie Joe—Bobbie Gentry
Respect—Aretha Franklin

Best Male Vocal Performance

By the Time I Get to Phoenix—Glen Campbell
Can't Take My Eyes Off of You—Frankie Valli
Francis Albert Sinatra/Antonio Carlos Jobim—Sinatra
My Cup Runneth Over—Ed Ames
Yesterday—Ray Charles

Best Instrumental Performance

Casino Royale—Herb Alpert & the Tijuana Brass
Chet Atkins Picks the Best—Chet Atkins
Mercy, Mercy, Mercy—Cannonball Adderley
Mission: Impossible—Lalo Schifrin
Music to Watch Girls By—Bob Crew Generation

Best Performance by a Vocal Group

I'M a Believer—The Monkees
The Letter—The Box Tops
Never My Love—The Association
Sgt. Pepper's Lonely Hearts Club Band—The Beatles
Up, Up and Away—5th Dimension

Best New Artist

Lana Cantrell
5th Dimension
Bobbie Gentry
Harpers Bizarre
Jefferson Airplane

Best Contemporary Single

By the Time I Get to Phoenix—Glen Campbell
Don't Sleep in the Subway—Petula Clark
Ode to Billie Joe—Bobbie Gentry
Up, Up and Away—5th Dimension
Yesterday—Ray Charles

Best Contemporary Album

Insight Out—The Association
It Must Be Him—Vikki Carr
Ode to Billie Joe—Bobbie Gentry
Sgt. Pepper's Lonely Hearts Club Band—The Beatles
Up, Up and Away—5th Dimension

Best Contemporary Female Vocal Solo Performance

I Say A Little Prayer—Dionne Warwick
Don't Sleep in the Subway—Petula Clark
It Must Be Him—Vikki Carr
A Natural Woman—Aretha Franklin
Ode to Billie Joe—Bobbie Gentry

Best Contemporary Male Solo Performance

By the Time I Get to Phoenix—Glen Campbell
Can't Take My Eyes Off of You—Frankie Valli
Child of Clay—Jimmie Rodgers
San Francisco—Scott McKenzie
Yesterday—Ray Charles

Best Contemporary Group Performance (vocal or instrumental)

I'm A Believer—The Monkees
The Letter—Box Tops
Sgt. Pepper's Lonely Hearts Club Band—The Beatles
Up, Up and Away—5h Dimension
A Whiter Shade of Pale—Procol Harum
Windy—The Association

Best Rhythm and Blues Recording

Dead End Street—Lou Rawls
Respect—Aretha Franklin
Skinny Legs and All—Joe Tex
Soul Man—Same and Dave
Try a Little Tenderness—Otis Redding

Best Rhythm and Blues Solo Vocal Performance — Female

I Heard It Through the Grapevine—Gladys Knight and The Pips
The Queen Alone—Carla Thomas
Respect—Aretha Franklin
Tell Mama—Etta James
Go to Hell—Nina Simone

Best Rhythm and Blues Group Performance, Vocal or Instrumental

Ain't No Mountain High Enough—Marvin Gaye and Tammi Berrell
Hip Hug-Her—Booker T. and The M.G.'s
The King and Queen—Carla Thomas and Otis Redding
Soul Man—Sam and Dave
I Second That Emotion—Smokey Robinson and The Miracles

Best Rhythm and Blues Solo Performance — Male

Dead End Street—Lou Rawls
Funky Broadway—Wilson Pi.kett
Higher and Higher—Jackie Wilson
Skinny Legs and All—Joe Tex
Try a Little Tenderness—Otis Redding

Best Folk Performance

Album 1700—Peter Paul and Mary
Alice's Restaurant—Arlo Guthrie
Gentle On My Mind—John Hartford
In My Life—Judy Collins
Janis Ian—Janis Ian
Waist Deep in the Big Muddy—Peter Seeger

KRLA ARCHIVES

Please Love Me Forever

Now Available At:
MONTGOMERY WARD DEPARTMENT STORES

Meet The Board

Love Rhapsodies

The Mission: Impossible

Now Available At:
MONTGOMERY WARD DEPARTMENT STORES

SUBSCRIBE NOW

GET ONE ALBUM FREE WITH A 1 YEAR SUBSCRIPTION TO THE BEAT AT ONLY $3.00. THIS OFFER DOES NOT APPLY TO RENEWALS — ONLY NEW SUBSCRIBERS.

Mail to: BEAT PUBLICATIONS
  9000 Sunset Blvd.
  Los Angeles, California 90069

☐ NEW SUBSCRIPTION

We want BEAT for ☐ 1 year at $3.00; ☐ 2 years $5.00

Please print your name and address

Name .... Name ....
Address .... Address ....
City............... State............... Zip........... City............... State............... Zip...........

ENCLOSED IS $3.00 for a 1 year BEAT subscription
             $5.00 for a 2 year BEAT subscription

Payment is in ☐ cash ☐ check ☐ money order

—CLASSIFIED—

My buddy's buddy loves his buddy.

Bumblebee reigns!

George—I still love you. Call me, Karla

People is coming.

Congratulations Sherrieann — President of Dino, Desi and Billy National Fan Club, and popular Teen-age Model.

Neil Young. Where's your reservation? I'm expecting to fly there.

Let the Blue Jay of love guide your way to peace and eternal bliss.

Monkee National Fan Club, Illinois Chapter, c/o Beat Publications, 9000 Sunset Blvd., Suite 1000, Los Angeles, California.

Happy birthday Larry (Standell) Tamblyn. Love me.

Gene — thanks for anoutasite January 12. Nora

The Thunderwords, join their fan club and receive a membership card, picture and news letter. Write Dorothy Ricks, c/o Beat Publications, 9000 Sunset Blvd., Suite 1000, Los Angeles, Calif.

Bank Without a name fan club, c/o Beat Publications.

Lucy Swartz is an overgrown flower child.

Who has a Denver Raiders Fan Club?

Gary Lee I love you.

H and L commands the universe.

Beware of March! The Fountain of Youth is coming.

Bill Walz.

Chapter seventeen.

Martin Erwin!!

Join the John Hartwich Fan Club.

dearjim beaminglyyours—revae

Happy birthday Peter Scott—Karen

Pete — special birthday Happiness love and peace your Phoenix friend.

Wanted: Prince and the Paupers back in Ortonville — Cathi Dawson

Happy (March 9) Birthday to the one and only ponytail wonder, Mark Lindsay! Love, Your Jersey East Coast Fan Club Ellie

The Midnight Raiders!... Tom, Mike, Jamie, Dave, Keith, Chuck (Janesville, Wisconsin).

Mizergivesbjs

Hello Fellow Walruses, Terry S.

Lary Larden, Happy Birthday—Lia

Barbara loves Chuck.

Support the Scaffold.

Teddy Boys where are you?

Ralph, Ronnie, Peppy, Mike Geoff: Chicago is waiting for you.

Beatles abide — Monkees subside.

To Twila, hello friend from Allan.

Tiger + pussycat = true love.

THE CREAM SHOWS EVERYDOBY.

The second and the twenty-fourth of 1944,
Began his life, and road of stife,
  the opening of a door.
His first breath came,
His first note rang.
Soon people came to hear
The mellow beauty from his throat
To soothe a longing ear
The second and the twenty-fourth of 1968.
He's now a man, the one who can—

If be the will of fate—
Become the best above the rest,
The world will hear the call
Of talent bathed in splendor:
The Voice, the voice of Paul.
Wishing happiness on his day
   to Paul Jones.
            The Moon (Diana)

Donovan, Dylan and Manfred —Baby, I'm a rich man, too.
            Diana

THE BEAT will accept only personal messages in the classified section. We will print names but not addresses or phone numbers.
  We will also accept Fan Club addresses in care of The Beat.
  Rates are cheap! Only 10 cents per word.
  Your deadline for the next issue is: March 1, 1968.

KRLA ARCHIVES

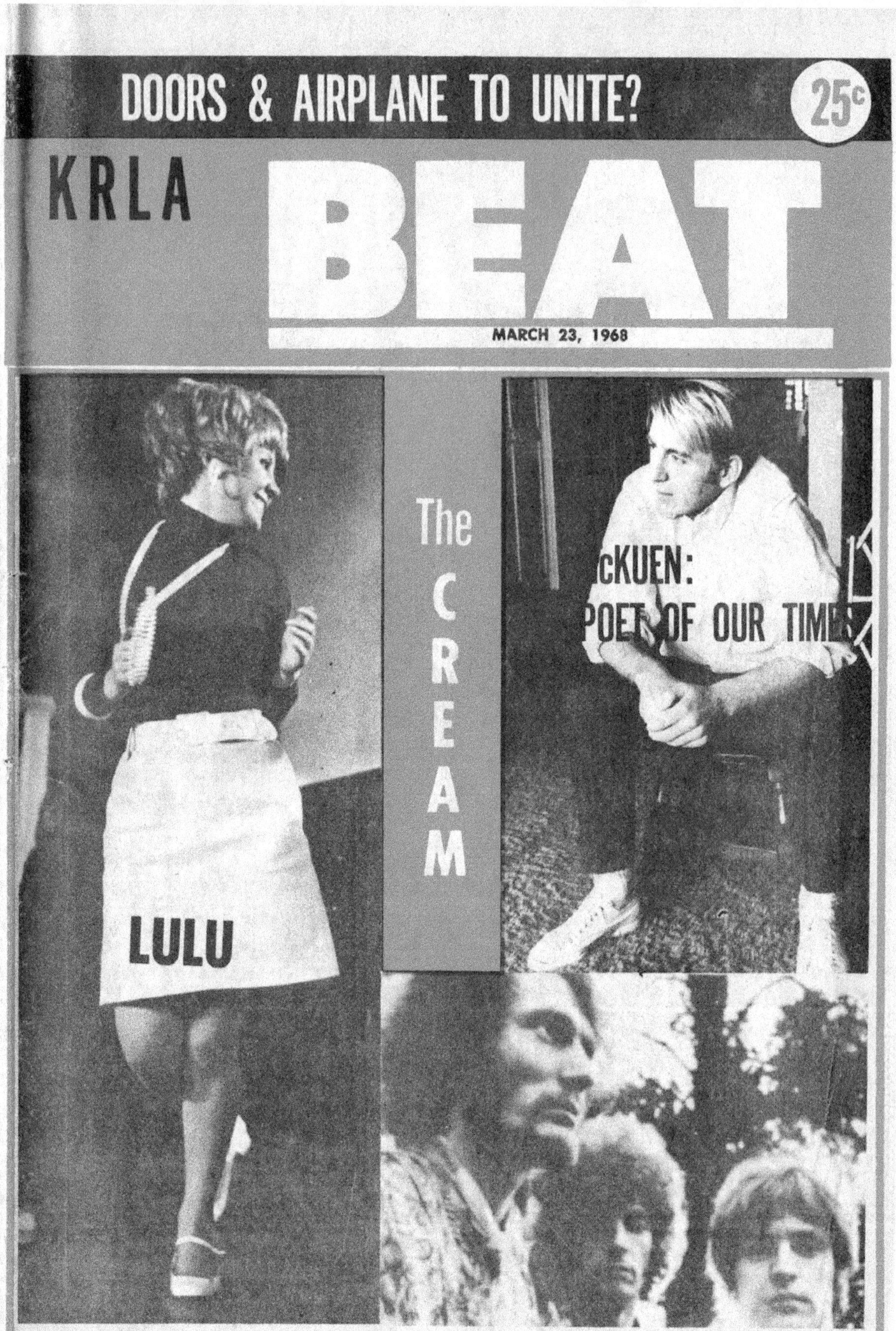

KRLA ARCHIVES

DOORS & AIRPLANE TO UNITE?

KRLA BEAT

MARCH 23, 1968

25¢

LULU

The CREAM

McKUEN: POET OF OUR TIMES

KRLA BEAT

Volume 4, Number 1 — March 23, 1968

Mamas And Papas Bag Another One

The Mamas and Papas have been awarded another Gold Record for their latest album, "Farewell to the First Golden Era".

The group, which made a rather dramatic exit from the country a few months ago, has returned to the United States. Although all parties concerned are giving little information as to the future of the group, singly the Mamas and Papas are still active. Cass Elliot has produced a few records and will be the subject of a television documentary. Michelle Philips has given birth to their first child, a daughter. The two "papas" of the group have not made any public pronouncements lately.

BEAT Photo: Rich Schor

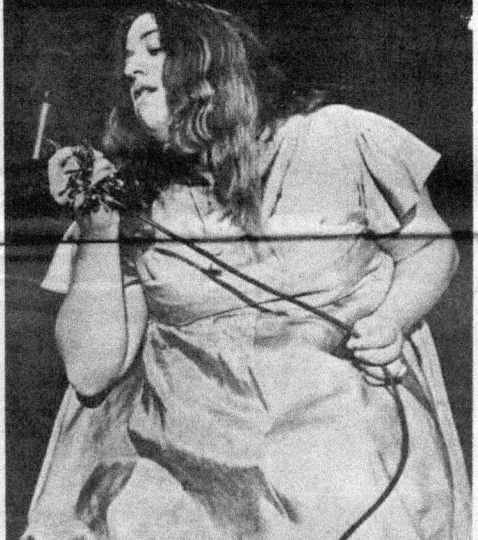

MAMA CASS will go it alone on the "Andy Williams Special."

Pop To Quell Riots?

Civic leaders have hit upon a new idea to help quell the threat of riots this summer. The pop festival is being considered as a possible deterrent to chaos in the streets.

The latest move in this direction comes from Philadelphia scene of racial trouble a couple of summers back. With the cooperation of the Department of Recreation, a local advertising firm will produce at 17-date al fresco concert series to run between the Fourth of July and Labor Day.

Plans call for nine concerts to be staged in the John F. Kennedy Stadium where the 100,000 seating capacity will be sliced to 55 thousand for a special stage and seating re-arrangement which, the producers claim, will bring performer and audience into close proximity.

Using a similar idea to New York's Central Park concerts, these nine concerts will only cost $1 with no free tickts being given ao the press or city dignitaries. There are also plans for block parties to play throughout the city and these will be free.

NEW YORK — Rascals manager, Sid Bernstein, is currently holding meetings with New York City mayor, John Lindsay, for an official go-ahead on plans for a pop festival in Sheep Meadow, Central Park, New York.

The festival will be held the last weekend in June, 1968. Volunteers from ovr 200 schools across the nation have already written to Bernstein offering their help for the festival.

Other festivals are being planned throughout the world. The First European Pop Festival didn't quite get off the ground as planned, and has been postponed from their original date of mid-February to the beginning of May.

In another festival, this one sponsored by Leonard Bernstein, will begin on May 1 and run for that weekend. Although no talent, other than the Cream, has been set, the festival is definite.

Sid Bernstein, who presented the Beatles in Shea Stadium, is also planning a pop festival to be held in Central Park in New York. The only definite plans concerning this festival is the singing of the Young Rascals to the fest's board of directors.

Doors/Airplane For UK Concert

LONDON — The Jefferson Airplane and the Doors have been set for an Easter concert at London's famed Royal Albert Hall.

From this end comes word from both the Doors and the Airplane that U.K. tour plans are still only in the discussion stage. But both groups are enthusiastic about working together.

Can you imagine Grace & Marty singing "Light My Fire" or Jim Morrison doing "White Rabbit." Incredible.

DOORS TAKE A rest before scheduled British tour.

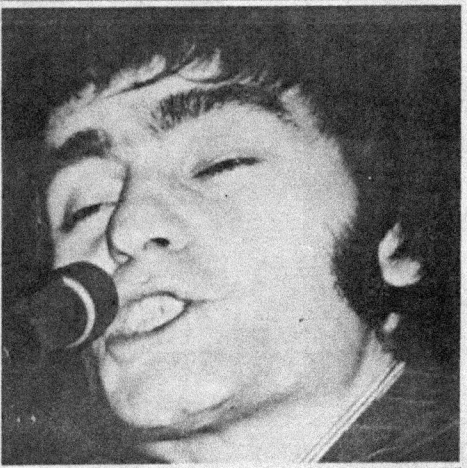

BEAT Photo: Ed Caraeff

MARTY, AIRPLANE pilot, to sing "Light My Fire?"

ALL THAT HAIR

Dear BEAT:

Upon having read the Letters to the Editor, I am deeply disappointed over the redundancy of the long-hair controversy. In fact, I don't believe it to be a controversy, rather the majority persecuting the minority for displaying their eccentrisities via long hair. Many readers have questioned the right of groups who display themselves in the so-called sloppy manner; these readers are questioning the group's right to freedom of expression. I'm sure no reader would ask the group to re-write their music because it didn't appeal to that particular individual.

Then the majority would argue, "well, I still think a sloppy group is too repulsive for my straight eyes, I can't groove on weirdness." But, all I could say, it's just as much a stomach turner to see a short-haired, single breasted dude perform completely chained and inhibited by his culture to the degree where he is no longer entertaining me.

Raitis Lablaiks

All very well and good, Mr. Lablaiks, but would we not be violating freedom of expression ourselves by not printing the "majority" letters as wel as the "minority" rebuttals? Airing both sides of any question is what the editorial staff of this newspaper believes freedom of expression is all about.

The Editor

Dear BEAT:

I think it is time that someone (namely me) stood up and supported the so-called "filthy looking groups."

Most people really dig the music that groups play. Physical appearance of a group is a trival matter. One does not attend pop concerts to see what kind of clothes a group is wearing or what the group looks like. It's the talent and good music that the groups produce that attracts the crowd.

I feel that such great groups as Cream, Grateful Dead, Doors and Canned Heat (to name a few) should not suffer a lack of popularity just because they are not "clean cut" in appearance.

It's the music that makes them great.

Steve Aldunda

MORE AND MORE FOR THE ASSOCIATION

Dear BEAT:

What's happening with the Association? They are my favorite people, but it's so hard to know what's going on with them because you never print anything on them, just once in awhile. C'mon, let's see more on the Association! They are what's happening.

Do you know when the Association will be back in San Francisco? I saw them the last time they were in San Francisco and I thought they were so fabulous. I'm just dying to see them again.

Just like their song "Everything That Touches You," they say "Everything is love." The Association are LOVE.

Thank you for listening, it's nice being "associated" with The BEAT.

Delores DeMartini

The Association have no definite date for San Francisco at this time.

The Editor

Dear BEAT:

I certainly agree with the person who wrote in the last issue that there should be more printed on the Association.

Terry Kirkman and the Association are the most talented and most clever group there is! Many groups look up to them as I'm sure they have inspired many.

The Association are beautiful—doesn't The BEAT realize this?

Vicky Seaman

As far as we can recall, not one of us has ever called the Association beautiful. Guilty as charged.

The Editor

FILTHY LOOKS

Dear BEAT:

I used to think I was the only teenagr who disliked the looks of many pop groups, but now I see I'm not alone. Some of these groups look so filthy and cheap that its hard to believe that they're the same ones creating such beautiful music.

I also agree with the people who say The BEAT should bring back Shirley Poston!

Chris Hudson

Whatever Happened To The East Side Kids

Dear BEAT:

I am as yet undecided on how to word this, so please bear with my erratic noises. They are sincere.

I recently saw the East Side Kids perform and they raised my curiosity. I recalled having read about them somewhere and spent two hours or thereabouts grovelling through my past issues of THE BEAT in search of this memory. What I found was July 9, 1966, the so-called "Jewish funky sound" and a picture with two excess members.

Understandably, they've changed in two years. They now have a good sound and . . . well, a strange act. Original, anyway. I won't say I like it but I am interested in who they are. Is there any possibility of information concerning them in the future?

Peace to you, brothers, for your patience.

George

Due to the ever-growing number of pop groups and the equally diminishing space in The BEAT, we've had to adhere to a policy of doing articles only on those entertainers who have hits rapidly moving up the national charts. Which means that we probably won't be printing anything further on the East Side Kids until they get a hit record.

The Editor

Beat Publications, Inc.

Executive Editor .... Cecil J. Tuck
Publisher .... Gayle Tuck
Editor .... Louise Criscione
Assistant Editor .... Jacoba Atlas

Staff Writers
Bobby Bovino, Ron Koslow
Tony Leigh, Shirley Poston

Contributing Writers
Tony Barrow, Sue Barry
Eden, Bob Levinson
Jamie McClusky III, Mike Masterson

Photographers
Ed Caraeff, Jerry Hass

National Advertising Representative
Sam Chase Assoc., Inc.
527 Madison Avenue
New York, New York 10022
(212) PL. 5-1668

Business Manager .... Judy Felice
Subscriptions .... Judy Worth

Distribution
Miller Freeman Publications
500 Howard Street, San Francisco, Calif.
The BEAT is published bi-weekly by BEAT Publications, Inc., editorial and advertising offices at 9000 Sunset, Suite 1000, L.A., California 90069. U.S. bureaus in Hollywood, San Francisco, New York, Chicago and Nashville; overseas correspondents in London, Liverpool and Manchester, England. Sale price 25 cents. Subscription price: U.S. and possessions $5 per year; Canada and foreign rates, $9 per year. Second class postage prepaid at Los Angeles, California.

How About The Movies

Dear BEAT:

I realize that The BEAT is a pop music newspaper and that's fine. But I was thinking how much better it would be if you could include articles on young actors and actresses in both television and movies, I mean, all your readers watch TV and go to the movies and are interested in what's going on there as well as what's going on in the music field. At least I know I am.

You already do movie reviews, which I think is great. Now, why not branch off into the personalities who make the movies and television shows? I really believe young people are interested and, to my knowledge, no other publication continually includes all these areas of the entertainment business.

So, how about it BEAT?

Interested Reader

We publish The BEAT for our readers and for no one else. We started out as a pop music newspaper and have kept it that way; however, if the majority of our readers would like us to include young television and motion picture artists as well as the pop personalities, we'd be most willing to do so. All you have to do is let us hear from you. Just send us a "yes" or "no" on TV and films and we'll let the majority rule.

The Editor

AROUND the WORLD

Citizens Of Monterey Vote 'No' On Festival

MONTEREY—The Monterey County Fair Board has cancelled plans for a 2nd annual Monterey International Pop Festival because of civic opposition.

The fair board had previously authorized manager George Wise to negotiate with John Phillips, of the Mamas and the Papas. The negotiations were cancelled because of civic protest.

The second music festival had tentatively been scheduled for June 21-23.

The first festival drew nearly 40,000 persons to Monterey. The police made few arrests, and in the press after the festival everyone concerned seemed more than pleased.

But since that time of mutual understanding the civic groups have reversed their feelings. The Health Board, the Sheriff Department, the chief of police in two cities, the Mayor of Monterey and at least one county supervisor protested holding the event again.

The civic groups charged that the last festival led to widespread marijuana smoking, violations of public morals and general disorders in open air sleeping accommodations by hitch-hiking groups on the fair grounds.

Who said all you need is love.

BEAT Photo: Rich Schor
THERE WILL BE NONE OF THIS in 1968; Monterey will have no festival.

Bonnie, Clyde Cult Growing

Is there no end to the off springs of "Bonnie and Clyde"? From the film has come a cult, from the cult has emerged new folk heroes, from the heroes come the fashions, songs and commercials that have jumped on to the colossal bandwagon.

Flatt and Scruggs find themselves with a hit record of the "Foggy Mountain Breakdown" — the theme song from the film; and Georgie Fame has also found fortune with a ballad about the exploits of this criminal pair.

The latest entry to the disc success of the story of Bonnie and Clyde, is an RCA Victor album featuring Billie Jean Parker, sister of Bonnie Parker. The album is called "The Truth About Bonnie and Clyde," it is in a question and answer format, with WSM-TV Nashville directory of news, Jud Collins, questioning the sister.

In the album, Miss Parker makes no claims to her sister's innocence, but does make the customary extenuating a r g u e m e n t that the Depression forced her sister into a life of crime. Miss Parker depicts Bonnie and Clyde as being simply "run-of-the-mill folk" who just happened to rob banks and kill people.

One notable exclusion from the album is any reference to the accuracy of the film. Curious in fact, since law suits and threats of law suits have been pending since the release of the fantastically popular film.

Gold Records For Warwick

NEW YORK — Dione Warwick's single of "I Say A Little Prayer" and "The Theme From the Valley of the Dolls" have both been certified million sellers by RIAA.

"I Say A Little Prayer" went as high as number 4 on the national charts, last year. "The Theme From the Valley of the Dolls" is number 2 this week.

ONE MILLION FOR BEE GEES

LONDON — The Bee Gees have been set for a 25 city tour of the United States during the month of July. They will open at the Hollywood Bowl on July 26th.

Robert Stigwood, the group's manager, has already predicted that the Bee Gees will earn a *minimum* of 1 million dollars for the seven week tour. It has been reported that the group grossed $70,000 for two shows in Anaheim, California, just last month. One other comforting factor is that the Bee Gees have sold over 1,500,000 single records plus another 500,000 album sales.

JACK of the Airplane

BEAT Photo: Ed Caraeff
NEW JOB for Paul

Airplane To Go Beatles

SAN FRANCISCO—The Jefferson Airplane have followed the lead of the Beatles by deciding to be their own managers. They have broken with their long-term manager Bill Graham founder of the Fillmore Auditorium in San Francisco. Their new manager is one of "themselves," Bill Thompson.

One of the reasons for the split, was that Graham expected the group to come up with new material even when they were on tour.

The Airplane are also very dissatisfied with the way in which RCA handled the merchandising for the group's last album "After Bathing At Baxter's." The Airplane feels that RCA did little to promote their album perhaps in the hope of retaliation for the months spent by the group in the recording studio. This allegation was unconfirmed by either party concerned.

The Airplane is not the only group to be dissatisfied with RCA's handling of their records. A few other new and talented groups are also feeling RCA's neglect. They are now in the process of talks to see if a more applicable agreement can't be worked out.

GRACE, voice of Airplane

Beatle Bio For Fall

The first "authorized" biography of the Beatles will be published this fall by Heinemann's.

The book has been written by novelist Hunter Davies, noted for his novel "Here We Go Round the Mulberry Bush". Mr. Davies spent many months traveling with the Beatles on tour. He has also been given the complete cooperation of John, Paul, George and Ringo, plus their immediate families, their business associates and even their financial advisors.

HARPERS BIZARRE ride on the Girl Wagon with lovely Ramp Girls.

ABC TO PRESENT TEEN SPECIAL

HOLLYWOOD — Every so often one of the major television networks agrees to air a special dedicated to the young people of America. On Sunday, April 21 from 7 to 8 p.m. the ABC network will present just such a special.

Titled "Romp," the hour-long show will be co-hosted by the perennial "Peyton Place" man, Ryan O'Neal, and popular singer, Michelle Lee. Talent lined up for the special is wide-spread enough to offer something for everyone's taste.

Set to appear are James Darren, Lesley Ann Warren, the Harpers Bizarre, Spanky & Our Gang, Jimmy Rodgers and that man who is everyone's favorite, Jimmy Durante.

"Romp" will be an excursion into the current fads and fancies of the U.S. teen world, a composite of music, fashion, dance and laughs.

Be sure to watch it, pull up the ratings and, hopefully, make the network see that youth specials do garner large audiences across the country.

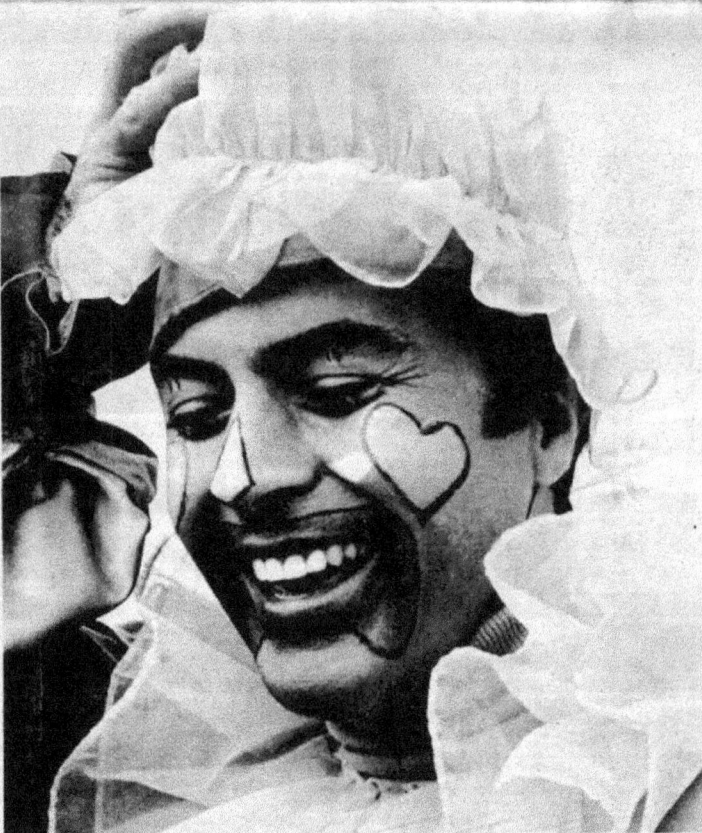

JAMES DARREN dons clown face for ABC-TV's "Romp" special.

ON THE BEAT
BY LOUISE CRISCIONE

Arlo Guthrie's hilarious story of "Alice's Restaurant," the title cut off his album, has now been made into a 96 page paperback book with illustrations by Marvin Glass. Grove Press is handling the distribution throughout the country.

Peter, Paul and Mary obviously impressed the people from the "Jonathan Winters Show" when they made their first appearance on the show February 28 because they've been asked back for a guest spot in April.

Gentry All Over

Bobbie Gentry is one performer who doesn't believe in leaving anything to chance. Consequently, she has formed her own publishing and production company for music, films and television properties.

Rod McKuen, currently America's best-selling poet, has his finger in so many pies it's impossible to list them all . . . latest is penning songs with Petula Clark and scoring the film, "Joanna." All of this is, of course, in addition to composing, producing, recording, writing poetry and forming his own production company.

Big surprise in the city of Los Angeles, where just about no one can sell-out a concert . . . the Cream managed to sell-out *two* shows. An indication of things to come for the Cream?

Airplane Out

Jefferson Airplane say they bowed out of their scheduled appearance in the film "Petula" because they objected strenuously to being merely a backdrop for a scene in a topless restaurant in San Francisco's North Beach. They figured at this stage of their career, who needs it? And they're probably right.

You can now add the name of the 5th Dimension to the list of top 40 groups currently involved in singing the title songs in motion pictures. They're just been signed to sing the title tune from "East Of Java," starring Maximilian Schell and Brian Keith.

New Springfield

The Buffalo Springfield have acquired a new bass guitarist in the form of Jim Messina. The group is currently on a 38 day tour along with the Beach Boys.

QUICK ONES: Despite the fact that "I Spy" has apparently received the ax for next season, Bill Cosby is shedding no tears. Among other things, he's set for ten one night gigs beginning on March 29th in Denver . . . John Lennon is teaming up with Charles Aznavour for a songwriting stint . . . Rumor has it that Country Joe and the Fish will call their next album, "Hello To The First Golden Era" . . . The Rascals are set to sing several songs from their new album on the March 13th "Kraft Music Hall" on NBC.

Fish Influence

Country Joe and the Fish are extending their sphere of influence by playing the Cheetah in Los Angeles (March 22 & 23), the Fillmore in San Francisco (March 27 & 28) and the Grand Ballroom in Detroit (April 26). Also coming up in April, gigs in Dallas, Denver and Chicago.

Lulu opened to a full house and rave reviews at the Cocoanut Grove in Los Angeles. The young lady from Scotland shows more professionalism in her act than some entertainers who have been in the business for 20 years. Tommy Smothers was on hand to introduce Lulu and seated in the audience were such people as Davy Jones, Nancy Sinatra, Nilsson and Lee Hazelwood.

However, it was not all sweetness for Lulu's opening . . . her back-up orchestra was less than sensational causing Lulu to come off worse than she should have. But she needn't worry . . . at the party after the show the general concensus of opinion was that she was fantastic and no one placed the band's poor showing on her.

March 23, 1968 — THE BEAT — Page 5

PICTURES IN THE NEWS

CROWD GATHERS IN ROME to welcome America's Cowsills.

"WHAT DO YOU MEAN WE'RE OFF???" Yes, it's true, the Monkees appear to have had the knife comed own on their television show. At least, the official list of next season's shows has come out of NBC minus the Monkees. "Star Trek" is taking over the Monkees' time slot . . . 7:30 p.m. on Mondays.

EIGHT OF THE COWSILLS take a stroll outside of Rome during their smash European tour. Meanwhile, they're not doing badly Stateside with their current hit, "We Can Fly."

THE RASCALS TAKE SOME TIME OFF before the "Joey Bishop Show" to fill Sammy Davis Jr. in on their up-coming schedule which includes their first movie (to be released thru Warner Bros./7 Arts) as wel as their first major world tour coming up this summer.

EVERYONE IS CURRENTLY TALKING about the so-called "Boston Sound" and the group which is the forerunner of the sound, the Ultimate Spinach. "We're not strictly interested in hitting the Top 40," admits the group, "but in just striving to further expand pop music. The Spinach is not necessarily a dance or a rock group, in fact we'd rather have people listen to the words of our songs and be turned on." So speaks the Ultimate Spinach.

CREAM IN CONCERT

Tony Leigh

SANTA MONICA—The audience was a show in themselves. Long satin dresses, ringlet curls, rahja jackets and brightly colored blouses dominated the scene. For the first half of the concert, it was almost as if the audience only came to be on display. They talked, ate and walked around as Steppenwolf opened the show. They squirmed a little as Penny Nichols went through wishy song after wishy song. They paid little attention as the Electric Prunes gave a loud electronic performance. If they couldn't hear the Cream they wouldn't hear anyone.

By the end of the intermission, the audience was more than ready for the Cream. As the curtains parted and then came together again almost in a teasing manner, sporadic applause broke out. Then the Cream came on in full force. Clapton, Baker and Bruce. The best that England has to offer there could be no disputing that fact.

Improvisation

They played for a little over an hour for the second sell-out show at Santa Monica. The audience broke out in applause as familiar songs were played. With a strong blues orientation and a jazzman's ear for improvisation, the Cream created some of the most dynamic music heard anywhere.

When the group first started out, music critics in England gave them little chance for success. All three members had been formerly with other groups — Clapton with the Yardbirds and Mayhall, Bruce with Manfred Mann and Baker with Graham Bond — and the critics were positive three such 'solo' performers could never come together in a cohesive trio.

Critics in their infinite wisdom have been known to be wrong before — and the Cream's performance proved that. Their original concept behind the formation of the group was to eliminate any weak links and to obtain maximum personal freedom within the confines of a group.

Although this concept could have resulted in exhibitionist performances by the three, it in fact did not. Solo performances by each member of the group were beautifully in evidence, but they were still always part of the greater whole.

Drum "Monster"

What was particularly interesting to note Saturday was the musicality of their driving sound. After listening to the Prunes and Steppenwolf who have their own brand of loudness which thinely veils music, it was heartening to listen to sound combined with music form an exciting and dynamic performance.

Ginger Baker who plays drums is a self confessed "monster" who violently and emotionally attacks his drums. His special style and amazing energy was fantastically displayed during his solo on "Toad". And it was Baker's drums who throughout the evening kept the excitement growing.

Jack Bruce who sings lead and plays bass guitar offered an incredible tour de force on the harmonica. His whole body rocking with the sound, the sound of the harmonica broken by the yell of his voice, Bruce had the audience jumping from their seats.

Eric Clapton who is perhaps the most well known of the three offered beautiful guitar solo which definitely explained why he is considered the finest lead guitarist in the world. Clapton is somewhat of a perfectionist who once told a reporter that listening to something the Cream did just few months before wasn't really 'their sound'.

"We're changing all the time," Eric insists. "I have got to the point now where my playing satisfies me technically, and I am now realizing the importance of visual impact in the same way Pete Townsend has.

"I also want to try a few new recording effects and I've got a few ideas for the guitar, I want to get a guitar with tow necks. I saw one in an Elvis Presley film poster, It's a guitar with a 12-string nect and a six-string neck on the same body."

In a three man group no one can compensate for another member. With the Cream no one has to try. They are the best England has to offer, perhaps the best in the world. They proved that in two concerts Saturday night in Santa Monica. As Clapton says, "we're the only group where we all work to knock each other out as well as the audience." They succeeded.

SHOUTS FROM GENE

By Gene Cornish

Many of our fans have asked me to go through some of the early years we spent before we became The Rascals. My career as a guitarist began when I was 7 years old — the first instrument I ver owned was a push-button ukelele (that I immediately took apart and put back together again). The next was a one-string banjo that I played over and over until mother was urging me to go outside and "play baseball like your buddies..."

Ancient Guitar

And, finally it came — an ancient guitar that my grandfather handed to me . . . and around then, I saw Elvis Presley on the old Tommy Dorsey Show . . . Elvis is one of the few people I'd like to meet today . . . he became an idol as soon as I caught a glimpse of his workmanship and style . . . But my secret ambition is still to be a topnotch recording engineer . . . I've just built a recording studio in my house on Long Island and I'm helping to produce records for groups managed by friends of mine . . .

Summer World Tour

Our thanks to Tom Moffat of K-POI in Hawaii for making our recent vacation there absolutely outasite . . . and to Steve Corey, who our manager, Sid Bernstein, and all The Rascals feel is one of the finest young promoters in the Southeastern United States. We plan to return to New York via Hawaii once again after the first leg (Instanbul, Stockhoim and South Africa) in our world tour is finished early this summer . . .

Steve Allen now writing the script for our first feature-length movie . . . to star filming late spring.

Greetings To Mitch

A special greeting to Mitch Ryder and all our friends at The Scene, one of our favorite New York nite places . . .

The new album, "Once Upon a Dream," is flying along . . . but the key to the meaning of the items in the photograph of Dino's sculpture on the cover is still a mystery to most everybody but The Rascals themselves . . . a key is in the works now and will be published very soon . . .

Television Special

Really enjoyed BEAT's 1968 Calendar . . . it doubles a groovy poster! . . . We'll be recording a new single very soon . . . and our promotion film for our last single, "It's Wonderful, is being lengthened and will be distributed nationally as a theatrical short by Youth Concepts, Ltd. . . . We're also putting together an hour-long TV special on the beginnings and the growth of The Rascals from 1965 to the present! Also, two new songbooks coming out soon — one for the "Groovin" album and one for "Once Upon A Dream" and all the songs we wrote for that LP . . .

Right now I'm busy gathering anecdotes about our vacation in Hawaii . . . will fill you in more on what happened there (it's unbelievable!) when I talk to you next tife . . . CHOW, for now . . .

Love, *Gene*

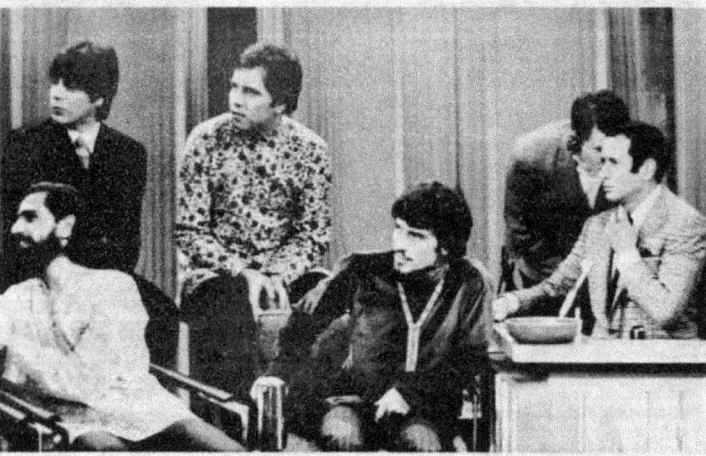

ROD McKUEN
"We're Being Bombarded With Love"

Jacoba Atlas

Are we rushing headlong into another Romantic Era? The Doors, the Stones, Allen Ginsberg and Andy Warhol all belie that fact, but other trends seem to point in that direction. One of the biggest hits of last year was syrupy love story "A Man And A Woman" and this year's run away film is another love story "Elvira Madigan". Added to that is the poetry and songs of Rock McKuen. The age of super cool is on the way out. Does that then mean that honest commitment is becoming the new thing? Perhaps. The second fastest selling book last year was McKuen's book of poetry "Stanyan Street and Other Sorrows," if that is an indication.

"The popularity of the book boils down, I think, to the fact that I'm talking in simple language, the language of today. Then too, I'm not ashamed of my feelings or expressing them. I think one of the problems today is that we lack directness in our lives.

"That's one of the reasons for kids rebellion. They can't find the straight answers at home. They can't find them on the street either, but at least on the street there aren't the same old stories, the same old lies.

"I believe we are on the threshold of a brand new romantic era. People are tired of bull, they're tired of the manufactured. Do you realize we have raised the first generation in history who have been taught to do nothing but consume? Well, they don't want to consume anymore. That's one of the reasons they escape from reality — either by drugs or with movies or whatever.

"I myself, don't reject reality completely. I try to balance them both. I have to be completely against the drug thing — even aspirin gives me a headache. That's why I have trouble respecting anything that's created under the influence of drugs. It lacks a valid well-spring from the person.

"But I don't believe that one person should try to enforce his code of ethic on another. It is important that a man come up with his own code of ethic that fits himself and doesn't turn off the rest of society."

Paying Off

After years of working, Rod's labors are finally paying off. A list of just completed and future projects would make anyone's head spin. He has just finished the score for an interesting English film called "Joanna;" he has written the music for TV special called "Travel with Charley"; he is presently working on a musical with Maurice Jarre ("Doctor Zhivago") and Dale Wasserman ("Man of La Mancha") concerning the Montparnesse clown Chi Chi who was immortalized by Henri Toulose-Latrec. He is also now working on the screenplay for his third book "Lonesome Cities", and is writing songs with Petula Clark.

"I like working against time. I like the feeling that this has to get done, I like pressure. I occasionally get mentally tired of writing, and then I try to do something else like play with my animals.

"It's hard for me to take a vacation. I tried to take one in Italy a few months ago. But I went crazy. I invented things to do. I guess I have some deep rooted fear of not being busy.

Success Isn't Money

"Even now that I'm financially secure, and I know I'll never be poor again, even if I never did another thing, residuals would keep me from starving, but I can't slow up.

"But the object isn't to reach a certain point to give up working. I work as hard as I do, to do good things. To do everything to the best of my ability. The idea is to do the job well, not just to get by.

"On my albums I try to do as many tracks as possible. I think it's cheating if you don't. You should give people more than enough.

"I measure success not by money but how well I sleep."

With the resurgence in pop music there seems to be more and more composers everyday. But the problem has arisen that there are so many singer-composers that the straight writer can't get his songs sung.

"There's more opportunity for songwriters today in one area. But there's also more competition and with so many people singing their own material, it's hard for some writers to get through.

"There are many fine writers today, many who will get even better as they get older. People like Paul Simon, Leonard Cohen, Bob Dylan, Judy Collins, They're all saying important things. But the real object in songwriting is not just to say important things, but to say them well.

"I think a song has to be a unity. It has to have a beginning, a middle and an end. It's harder to write a song well, then a book or a movie. With a book you have perhaps 800 pages to tell your story, or a film 24 reels, but not with a song.

"The reason I think kids buy so much of the music that's bad today — look at some of the songs on the top forty — is that they have been trained to consume what people tell them to consume. Kids today keep a pretty close eye on the charts and if they say something is a hit, the kids will buy it regardless."

Success has brought many things to Rod for which he didn't bargain. His anonimity has been taken away. In airports, at dinner, just walking around, people come up to him and ask for autographs and stare. It is not that Rod isn't friendly, it is just that a certain amount of his privacy has been taken from him.

Since his poems deal with love and communication people naturally, looking for an expert on everything, seek out his views on those subjects.

Disturbing

"People keep asking me if I'm married, and then they seem disturbed to find out that I'm not. For a long time I didn't want to feel the need for marriage. It's not that I'm tired of being a loner it's just that you can't be alone in everything. It's difficult for me though, because a woman would have to take second place to my work. And that most women aren't really willing to do. It's hard for anyone to understand that I can work 14 to 18 hours without stopping."

Even with the hippie concept of Universal love, people today still seem to feel afraid of it. The age old fear of being hurt has not been subverted.

"I still think it's important to get stepped on occasionally, it makes us grow. Hurt isn't always bad. It's sometimes difficult for people to respond to love, that's one of the reasons, I like animals so much. I've never known an animal that wouldn't respond to love.

"But there is the danger of spreading oneself too thin. Also it gets difficult to recognize true love. We're bombarded with love. Love this, love that. There's even a group called Love. And so you get wary of it, you ask 'what do they want from me'.

"It's like when people ask me if I'm against the war in Viet Nam, I have to say no, I'm not just against the war in Viet Nam, I'm against all wars, all killing. It's all done in the name of humanity too, which has to be so ridiculous. How can killing ever benefit humanity?"

Last year brought him a certain amount of notoriety and attention. He bought a house in the Hollywood Hills, his books began to sell well at first and then sensationally. He worked out of his office with relatively few people helping him. Now all that has changed. His house is too small, he wants more room for animals — perhaps a horse this time — and with success has come a publishing firm, a production company, a public relations firm and managers. But Rod still insists "I only make more money to get more animals."

Photos: Jerry Hass

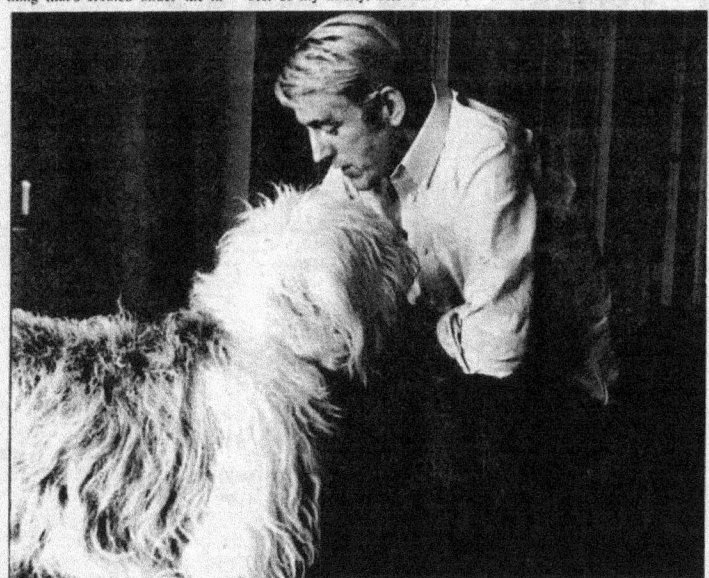

"Do you realize this is the first generation in history who have been taught to do nothing but consume? Well, they don't want to consume anymore."

THE BEAT — March 23, 1968

LULU ON HER MUSICAL SUCCESS: 'IT HAS SOUL'

The girl born as Marie McDonald McLaughlin Lawris and known around the world as simply Lulu has made a name for herself in the United States on the strength of the title song from a gold-plated Sidney Poitier film.

The petite redhead began singing so young that she remembers "the old 78's my father used to buy — Connie Francis, Kay Starr, Teresa Brewer — and I used to sit right up against the gramophone listening until he swore I'd go deaf."

Awareness

It didn't happen that way. Instead of going deaf she became acutely aware of the particular types of rhythmic and lyric stylization, making it possible for Lulu to make her singing debut at the Bridgeton Public Hall at the age of nine.

While still in school, Lulu had her first record, "Shout", released and duly marked in the British Top Ten. Her second disc, "Satisfied", established the fact that Lulu was one up on the "one-hit-wonders." But in America no one had yet heard of the big voice encased in the tiny body.

Simple Soul

Analyzing her musical success in Britain was easy: "It has soul," determined Lulu, "it's as simple as that. And the singers I enjoy have more soul than all the balladeers put together. Their songs are personal things. They're real. They need attention, demand it."

Lulu's popularity with British audiences continued to grow but her name in America remained equally unknown. In 1966 Lulu became the first female British artist to be allowed behind the Iron Curtain in Poland.

Likes It Alive

Asked about it later, Lulu answered with the complete frankness that had come to be synonymous with her. "I like everything to be alive, with ears screaming down the road and people and lights and things. And it's not like that over there. Just big buildings and people working in them. But when we got to the shows it was marvelous. Fantastic! Because we played to audiences of over six thousand and they went absolutely mad. Because they just don't get that sort of entertainment. I felt a bit sad over there, but I got a tremendous kick out of the way they reacted to the shows."

It was not until the tail end of 1967 that Lulu managed to get a number one single in the U.S. The song was, of course, "To Sir With Love" from the movie of the same name. It's true that a popular movie can bolster the sales of its title song, but it's impossible to blindly say that a song reach the top position on the nation's charts. And even if people did maintain that position, how could they explan the success of "Best Of Both Worlds?"

Professional

Lulu is finally being given the recognition she deserves. It's as simple as that. Her vocal talents are obvious, her years of experience in show business have made hers a tightly professional performance.

She has just opened at the Cocoanut Grove, the top prestige club the City of Los Angeles can offer. Can there be any real doubt that Lulu has made a niche for herself in show business . . . a niche which she fully and rightly intends to keep?

TURNING ON

VINGEBUS ERUPTUM (Philips) Blue Cheer, *Summertime Blues, Rock Me Baby, Doctor Please, Out of Focus, Parchment Farm* and *Second Time Around.* This is the first album for a San Francisco group who is getting a rather large "push" from their record company. They sound all right, although I really wouldn't say they were at the tops of their field. They play loud, screech a lot, but they simply can't compare to their competition, Hendrix and the Cream outclass them no end. This is not to say that they won't get better, or that they aren't any good at all, it's just that in comparison to what other people are doing, the Blue Cheer don't hold up. One interesting and perhaps noteworthy sideline to this album is the fact that Summertime Blues has been picked as a single from the album and is getting to 40 airplay. The record has also reached the national charts. If this single is well accepted it may pave the way for other electronic sounds to be played on the top 40 stations, and some of us will be reprived from a constant diet of the American Breed and Jay and the Techniques.

★ ★ ★

THE DELTA SWEETE (Capitol) Bobbie Gentry, *Big Boss Man, Sermon, Tobacco Road,* plus eight other tracks. Amazingly enough, this album is much better than her first attempt. Staying totally within the frame work of the Mississippi Delta, Miss Gentry begins with a marvelous self-penned tune about a River Bottom Band — the one that everyone wants to join. From there she moves on the blues with *Big Boss Man.* Her voice and manner are perfectly suited to the 'down home' sound of the blues. With *Reunion,* Bobbie returns to the idea of her "Ode" — the family setting, this time getting together for the first time after a few months. Gentry also includes a song by Mose Allison, *Parchman Farm.* One in an interview with The BEAT, Miss Gentry said that the only other person who songs she would really like to record would be Mose Allison's. She does well by him.

★ ★ ★

THE HUMAN BEINZ (Capitol) *Nobody But Me, Foxy Lady, It's Fun to Be Clean, Serenade to Sarah* plus nine other tracks. The Human Beinz have a hit with their single release of Nobody But Me which is also included in this album. There is always a danger of recording other people's material, especially when that material has previously been recorded and released by the original. The case and point here, is Jimi Hendrix, Foxy Lady — somehow the Human Beinz just don't make it with this song. They are an interesting group, the only real problem is that you've heard it all before. The lead singer bears a striking resmeblance to early Mick Jagger, without his special something-or-other, The group does come through with some good harmony. And the slightly sarcastic song "It's Fun To Be Clean" is fun if not really subtle commentary, Unfortunately they also come up with a rather pretentious version of "Black is the Color of My True Loves' Hair."

KRLA ARCHIVES

March 23, 1968 — THE BEAT — Page 9

WE'RE THE WINNERS

For once the public seems to have been successful in influencing the programming of a national network. Star Trek will return next season.

KRLA is proud to have played even a small part in bringing this popular show back on the air. With fortitude that would impress even the stalwart Mr. Spock, the students of CAL Tech picketed, complained, and generally made bloody nuisances of themselves. But it all paid off.

NBC has finally agreed to putting the show back on the air. The students have won. The show which takes all of us into the future will be able to continue in the future. The Star Ship Enterprise will ride again.

Glen Campbell's latest hit album

Glen will appear at Anaheim Convention Center

Saturday, March 9

The GIRL who made 'ALFIE' has done it again with the theme from VALLEY Of The DOLLS

Now Available At:
MONTGOMERY WARD DEPARTMENT STORES

PINK FLOYD IS READY NOW...ARE YOU?

THE FOLK POETS: HARDIN BUCKLEY, IAN & COLLINS

Jacoba Atlas

Music has become a very personal thing. With the advance of the writer-singer, songs have become an expression of internal feelings mirrored for everyone. These young writers are not talking in generalities, although the songs may affect several thousand people. They are writing about their own feelings, their own times, their own life styles. And people are responding.

Top forty records seem, in most cases, to elude them. Yet large followings that pack concert halls, coffee houses, and wait patiently for each new recording do measure their success. In the large coastal cities, most people know their names, in the vast country between New York and Los Angeles those who value good sounds and beautiful lyrics know their names. They are important.

Tim Hardin

Tim Hardin, is perhaps the most well known and the one who has had the most success on the charts thnks to Bobby Darin. Darin's versions of Hardin's "If I Were A Carpenter" and "The Lady Came From Baltimore" brought both tunes to the foreground. However, the writer of those beautiful songs became known through Darin's rendition of the songs.

Hardin was born in Oregon, a descendant of John Wesley Hardin the outlaw (Wonder about Dylan's title?). Both his parents were classical musicians. He was in the Marine Corps, studied acting in New York City but latter quit because he didn't like school.

He then turned to writing. Becoming somewhat of a legend among New York musicians, Hardin held court at the Night Owl Cafe in Greenwich Village. At that time everyone was playing acoustic guitar except Hardin; he was playing electric and singing the kind of jazz flavored blues that has become totally accepted today. Before that time he sang country and western, and before that folk.

Stories out of New York say that Tim Hardin is one of the few writers that Bob Dylan respects.

Hardin now lives in Colorado, in semi-seclusion. Venturing out occasionally to New York and Los Angeles to see his friends, he retreats almost instantly to the privacy of the Rockies. He doesn't talk about his music, he sings it.

Phil Ochs, fellow folk singer once wrote about his friend in the "Village Voice", "If such a form as folk rock does exist, the nuances and phrasing qualities of his (Hardin's) voice easily make him the master interpreter. Hardin can takes the rhythm and blues idiom and handles its guttural intonations without any unnatural strain on his voice, which at the same time has enough depth and feeling to simulate the sweet lyrical sound of a stringed instrument. His vocal attack is always to the point, and his off-beat syncopation is enough to jeep the most balse listener continually interested. When he does a song, he makes his version, THE version."

Tim Buckley

Another Tim that has just recently entered the ranks of folk poet is Tim Buckley. A young, 19 year old resident of Venice, California. If one had to classify Venice as an area it would be best to say simply that it is the area where artisans, singer, writers and musicians sprinkled with students here and there live together in relative inexpense. It is the area where musicians rehearse, where the Doors can be seen, where beautiful shops run by hard working artists stay open half the night. It's where the ocean is only a few blocks away, it's where there is a section of Jews who still speak nothing but Yiddish, and it's where Tim Buckley calls home.

It is impossible to describe Buckley to anyone who has not seen him. His appearance is belied in pictures and his sound is diminished on records. He is a live person, someone who needs personal contact with another to come on himself. He is beautiful to look at with the kind of tender good looks one expects, and rarely finds, in poets. And his songs reflect his appearance.

"My only goal in music is that it's true when I write it and true when I sing it," he stated.

Although he is unavoidibly part of what the magazines call the Love Generation, he stands apart from it, balancing more than just easy phrases of philosophy.

"I wrote a song about love since everyone's still into the love ting. I was reading Corinthinas. It's from the Bible so they can't keep it off the radio.

"I like love" he added, "but I also like hate."

He loves Venice and claims he wouldn't live anywhere else. "It's a mental thing. Just walking down the street is a wonderful put-on. I was walking down the street one day and I past a bar, and one of the people there said to me, 'what do you know for sure'."

Listen to his albums. Especially "Hello-Goodbye". You'll learn what he knows for sure. See him in person, it's an incredible experience, he sings for himself, and he lets you come along.

Judy Collins

One new comer to the composing end of folk is Judy Collins for long one of the finest singer anywhere. She has recently branched out of the restricted shell of what used to be termed folk. The single guitar, with accompaniment by Bruce Langhorn has given way to complicated arrangements by Joshua Rifkin.

On her first break-away album "In My Life" she proved herself to be the finest singer of her genre. With her second album "Wildflowers" she proved herself to be a fine composer.

Perhaps it was inevitable, Miss Collins once stated "When I sing I expose myself. I want the audience to take the trip with me to expand their experience." She has done that with other's song she has recorded and now she is doing that with her own, A fine new talent has emerged to heightened the already noted one.

Janis Ian

Janis Ian who made a country-wide splash with her controversial "Societoes Child" is still great attraction in her hometown of New York City and the Eastern Seaboard. Leonard Bernstein attempted to immortalize her with his interpretation of her musical abilities. But time will tell whether or not his prophecy was correct.

As for now, she is an interesting composer, one who cannot be passed over. It is difficult to estimate how advanced her songs are compared to other people of her age. It is almost unfair to compare with her competition who are many years older. Certainly, Ian displays an unusual maturity in some situations and an amazingly direct view of her world.

"In Vietnam, adults know a war is going on. But they don't really know. Hatred is the ultimate insanity.

"You know, poverty. There are families who can't afford milk for their kids, and a vast rich middle class society who buy their kids $300 guitars. I would like to be rich in a society where everybody's rich."

She too looks for maturity and growth in her songs, and states that she won't be writing about the cold war between the generations forever.

These people demand a commitment from the listener. It is not so much a sensual commitment, as it is an intellectual commitment, an emotional commitment that says you're willing to take in what they're putting down. It's their own way and as Buffy Sainte-Marie, one of the foremost poets anywhere said, it can't be our way too. But we can listen, we can learn and we can feel.

TIM HARDIN

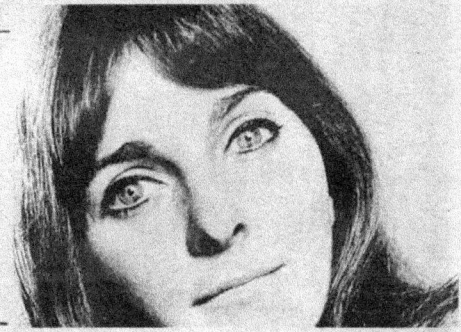
JUDY COLLINS

JANIS IAN

TIM BUCKLEY

GEORGIE FAME: Pop Singer With A Jazz Orientation

By Tony Leigh

Georgie Fame is not very well known in America — his appeal has been sporadic at best. In 1964, with the British wave his recording of "Yea, Yea" hit the American charts. But since that time he has not been able to sustain his English following in this country. Now, back on the top of the charts with 'Ballad of Bonnie and Clyde" Georgie Fame is concentrating on cultivating America.

Our knowledge of this very talented artist is unfortunately quite sketchy. Although many Americans know his present hit, and others recall "Yea, Yea," most do not know of Fame's work as a rhythm and blues singer, his love for jazz or his instrumental leanings.

"I wasn't really oriented in jazz, I more or less progressed to jazz. I guess I was oriented in rock and roll.

"I did a concert with Count Bassie in Europe when he came over with Tony Bennett, I had always admired Bassie and when Bennett couldn't make a couple of dates I said, 'please Mr. Bassie let me play with your band' and he did.

Big Bands

"I like playing with big bands. I like the sound. I have recorded an album with a big band in England — with some of the best jazz musicians around. It started out as just a hobby — this singing with a big band, but I hope it will come to something more."

Fame himself is a fine musician, specializing in the organ. "I started playing when I bought my first organ in Christmas 1962. That's one of the first electronic instruments. One the 'B' side of "Bonnie and Clyde" is an instrumental that I wrote."

Although those hearing Georgie Fame for the first time singing "Bonnie and Clyde" may think this is Fame's style, nothing could be further from the truth. His style is jazz and rhythm and blues.

"I started out singing rhythm and blues. That's why I had the 'ivy league' look at the start of the Beatles' thing. The only place I would work was at clubs that catered to the American GIs. And at that time they liked to see ivy league clothes. I also played at American Air Force bases.

"It was the English kids who first really appreciated the rhythm and blues sound. They made it more popular in this country too. Then a lot of the spade guys started realizing their kind of music was commercial, and a lot of them lost their sound. They sold out. Everything began sounding mass produced."

Musical Synthesis

With his love of jazz and his interest in R&B Georgie is a perfect example of what could be called the synthesis of pop music. The clear cut decisions that once dictated every record now seem to be disappearing as styles and genres overlap.

"It would be a good deal better for everyone concerned if all the styles of music did come together. R&B, jazz all the progressive forms can be fused together.

"When I started out, people would say to me 'you can't sing R&B because you're not black', but I didn't care. You have to go into different things. Look at Charles Lloyd. A lot of people in jazz don't like what he's doing because they say he's too mass oriented. But a lot of people are listening to what Lloyd is doing that would never listen to jazz. The minute they hear that word, they refuse to listen.

"Not everybory who is listening to Charles Lloyd can understand what he is doing, but even though they may not understand musically, they can get the atmosphere.

"I am very interested in putting words to jazz instrumental. A friend of mine is doing that with me. My first hit, 'Yea, Yea' was originally an instrumental and John Hendrix put the words to it. I'm now in the process of putting words to a couple of Charles Lloyd things. I hope to have an album of them out soon."

The time certainly seems to be right for an album of that type. The record buying public no longer seems to pigeoned holed into categories. A pop star could come out with jazz interpretations in 1968. Could that have happened in 1964? Fame is not the same person that sang on Hullabaloo in New York. Nor is he solely the singer of "Bonnie and Clyde" — it would appear that he is definitely a part of the best trends in popular music today. The trends that are lifting the caliber of music far above the Herman Hermit's syndrome.

"When I started out, people would say to me 'you can't sing R&B because you're not black,' but I didn't care. You have to go into different things."

The GRADUATE

ORIGINAL SOUND TRACK FROM THE YEAR'S MOST TALKED ABOUT MOVIE... THE GRADUATE

AVAILABLE AT

Now On Columbia Records

March 23, 1968 — THE BEAT — Page Fifteen

please send me **BEAT**

26 issues only

$3 per year

Mail to: BEAT Publications
9000 Sunset Blvd.
Los Angeles, California 90069

☐ New Subscription

I want BEAT for ☐ 1 year at $3.00 or ☐ 2 years at $5.00
I enclose ☐ cash ☐ check ☐ money order
Outside U.S.—$9 per year

*Please print your name and address.

Name_____

Street_____

City_____

State_____ Zip_____

—CLASSIFIED—

Beautiful birthday, beautiful George Harrison.

Love 'ya Jim.

Wayne — What's the matter? Johnny — You got a question? Sue — My leg.

To Dorothy from Wonderful me.

Happiest Ever, George Harrison, luv.

The PAGE V are bitchen.

Happy birthday Mike Magoo.

Newark loves WACK's Ray Ross.

Happy belated India George. Steve . . .

Mickey — My love on your birthday—Cinde.

Soul Inc. Belong to the World! —Pat.

Love Exists!—Pat.

Donovan, Dylan and Manfred — I sleep, almost dead. Bigdaddy teach you truth. You wake me, help me live. But "Theoneinthemiddle"? He now Santa in red suit. Boes he know Bigdaddy? He must come to Moon with us! —Diana

Stephen Shorter for prexy!

Official Scott Walker Fan Club of North America. Write to Scott Walker Fan Club c/o BEAT Publications, 9000 Sunset Blvd., Los Angeles, California.

Happy birthday Pete—Bonnie.

Graham Nash is love.

Happy St. Patick's Day, Derf! —Barb.

"Love is Blue" by "Sight and Sounds" happens.

Dee + Mark = Luv.

Pooh on Pegleg!

Happy Birthday Mark Lindsay.

Happy Birthday Mark, Jim, Smitty, Micky, Dean, Jeremy, Tom Murphy and me! Sue, Calif.

Happy Birthday George Harrison. Peace and bliss be yours. — Jen.

Watch out South Western Michigan "Reality" is coming, says Paul, their singer.

To Judy — GET WELL.

Richie Havens on Review

Tony Leigh

LOS ANGELES — For a long time Richie Havens only belonged to New York, now he will belong to everyone. Havens opened on the West Coast for the first time at the Troubador Cafe. He was outstanding.

He began with Bob Dylan's "All Along the Watchtower." It was almost unbelievable. Havens voice is rich and strong, and he uses it as one would an instrument, changing the tone and pattern to heighten the song.

He sits on a stool on the stage, with a bongo player and another guitarist. He himself plays guitar, beautifully. With his entire body rocking to the music, his foot tapping strongly with the beat, his is a total performance that commands attention and respect.

Havens breezed into a New York favorite, "High Flying Bird." It was stupendous. The audience which was primarily dominated by Hollywood pop elite went wild. The applause seemed like it just wouldn't stop. Two people from the Jimi Hendrix Experience were there, Eric Burton was there, and members of practically every other Los Angeles group around. They came and were completely conquered.

Havens combines all genres of music. He is a totally unrestricted artist who goes from jazz to blues to folk to rock without anyone noticing the transition. He is very near brilliant for he forces you to become involved in what he is singing—in what he is trying to say.

The highlight of the evening came when Havens sang Bob Dylan's "Just Like A Woman." The beauty of that song was clearly felt by everyone. When Dylan sings "Just Like A Woman" you come away hating the girl, when Havens' sings it, you come away loving her and pitying her. He is able to convey great humanity in his songs. They relate to people without malice, without hatred.

He finished the set with a song about war and about the inevitability of war as long as people stay the way they are. The audience loved him. He is an exceptional singer who should be heard.

BEAT SHOWCASE
LEE MICHAELS

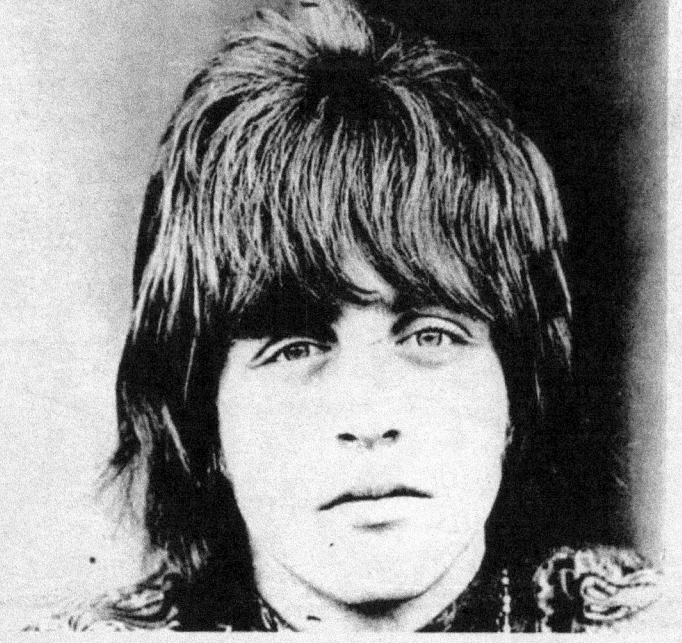

Lee Michaels is a person to watch. Californian, Saggitarian, young, musical, and imaginative. Michaels has been carving a name for himself among people who appreciate good new talent from San Francisco to Los Angeles. In a short time he will be known among the music followers on the East Coast too.

He is part of a sub-culture of the music world. A culture sometimes dubbed the underground, sometimes not. It is a world that belongs to people like Van Dyke Parks, Billy James, Penny Nichols, Andy Wickham and other people directly and indirectly involved in the creation of good music.

He was reluctant to join a record label, he missed appointment after appointment with A&M because he said he forgot. One day he decided to remember and walked into their offices. A little while later his first album was cut. It contains the songs of Michaels, songs that he believes imitate no one.

He admires the Cream, listens attentively to the Beatles, and respects the Byrds. Yet he insists upon remaining his own person. His own singer. His own composer.

KRLA ARCHIVES

Monkees Cancelled?

KRLA ARCHIVES

DONOVAN WRITES FILM

KRLA BEAT Edition

25¢

MAY 4, 1968

RASCALS TIMES TWO

Also In This Issue:
Ladies Of Pop
Otis Redding
Monkees

KRLA BEAT

Volume 4, Number 2   May 4, 1968

A Tribute To Spanky

NEW YORK — Perhaps the most unique tribute in pop music has just been recorded by Margo Guryan. The song, "Spanky And Our Gang," was written as well as recorded by Margo and the concensus of opinion seems to be that this is the first time that a pop artist has composed, recorded and titled a song after another pop artist.

Although Bob Dylan recorded "Like A Rolling Stone" and the Supremes cut "The Happening," neither song made any reference to either the Rolling Stones or the Happenings.

The key to the unique tribute may lie in the fact that Margo's first hit as a songwriter occurred when Spanky And Our Gang recorded her "Sunday Morning."

SPANKY AND OUR GANG garner a first in pop music.

THE LATE OTIS REDDING receives recognition from his native state.   BEAT Photo: Ed Caraeff

The Georgia Senate Honors Otis Redding

ATLANTA — Members of the Georgia State Senate meeting here unanimously passed a resolution honoring the memory of the state's most renowned musical native son, the late Otis Redding of Macon, Ga.

The senators praised Redding as one "who rose from poverty and obscurity to become one of the most famous entertainers in the United States."

Redding's dedication to the welfare of youth and his active participation in Vice President Hubert H. Humphrey's "Stay In School" campaign were also cited in the lengthy resolution.

The Georgia Senate then, as a body, expressed its condolences to the widow of the great blues singer who died in the crash of his private airplane in Wisconsin on December 10th of last year.

Meanwhile, sales of Otis Redding's last single, "Sittin' On The Dock Of The Bay," continue to climb and are expected to past the million and a half mark very shortly. It has, of course, already been certified a million-seller by the RIAA. The Gold Record marked the first time that the RIAA had presented a posthumous Award.

The Cowsills Go Into Fashion Design World

NEW YORK — It's not enough that the Cowsills have made a name for themselves in pop music. They are now entering into the world of fashion.

"We have been observing the fashion trends very closely for some time now," said Barbara Cowsill, "and we think we have hit upon what might be termed 'the fashions of today'."

The plan is this: Bill (20), Bob (18) and Paul (16) will design and market the clothes they feel will be accepted and liked by today's young adult men and woman. Barry (14) and John (12) will do their part to offer for approval their concepts in what teen and pre-teen fashions of today should be.

The Cowsills' mom, Barbara, will design clothes for housewives, working mothers and career woman and daughter Susan will join the act by sketching in her views on what the well-dressed young lady should wear.

The Cowsills have contracted the services of young London fashion designer, 23 year old Angela King. Miss King will personally design and supervise many of the fashion lines for the Cowsills and act as general fashion consultant for the company. The Cowsills and Miss King will have the entire winter line ready for preview in June.

FASHION for the women.

WEEKLY BANQUET will now be replaced by specials.

Monkee Specials

LOS ANGELES—The Monkees, Screen Gems and NBC-TV have agreed upon a three special deal instead of the weekly series.

The reason for the new programming is due to the Monkees' popularity, e x p l a i n e d Screen Gems studio boss, Jackie Cooper. "The Monkees grossed $2,000,000 on their last tour. They've sold 21,000,000 records. Now that's more than we're going to make in a 26-week, half-hour series that ties you up for so much time."

The Monkees plan to go on two one nighter tours next year and will produce more records. The group is presently involved in their first feature motion picture for Columbia called "Untitled."

Donovan Writes Film

LONDON—Donovan has written the script and entire musical score for a film in which he plans to star. Paul McCartney has also agreed to play a part in the movie.

No director has yet been set for the production, but discussion has involved Sweden's famed director, Ingmar Bergman.

The film is a "fairy-tale musical" in which Donovan will play a wandering minstrel. McCartney will be featured as a Court minstrel.

Donovan's manager stated, "the film is definitely going ahead. We have had offers from three companies who are anxious to make it. The delay so far has been in finding the right director, but only this week Ingmar Bergman has expressed interest in the project."

Donovan is currently in India for four weeks to study with the Maharishi.

DONOVAN to secure McCartney?

Letters to the Editor

'Sir' Left Out Cold

Dear BEAT,

Again this year it seems that the Academy Awards has ignored all pop songs. Instead of nominating songs like "The Happening" and "To Sir With Love," they continue to stay within the safe bounds of the Hollywood musical. I think it's about time that the various Establishment industries woke up to the fact that pop music is not only here to stay, but that it is getting better all the time. Certainly better than any of the older forms of popular music.

Terry Marshall

"SIR" GOT LEFT OUT

East, West Coverage

Dear BEAT,

I enjoy reading your paper very much, but I still have one suggestion. I would like to see a column originating from different cities across the country where interesting things are occurring. Particularly New York and San Francisco.

Also I enjoyed reading Tony Barrow who wrote from London, and have missed him greatly in the last few issues. Is he coming back?

Paul Sterns

Yes, we plan to have Tony Barrow back within the next couple of issues. As to your request to have articles coming from other cities . . . we are now planning on doing just that. Keep watching in the upcoming issues of the BEAT for columns written directly from and about both San Francisco and New York.

GUTHRIE REFRESHES

Dear BEAT,

It was refreshing to hear Arlo Guthrie say, "No one can ever be a spokesman for someone other than himself." I get very tired of people thinking that they can influence everyone who listens to their music. Although, I may agree with many of the pop singers and their views on life, I resent their thinking that they are my spokesman. I appreciate honesty, and is gratifying to hear someone speak his mind without assuming he is becoming "our leader."

George Rodgers

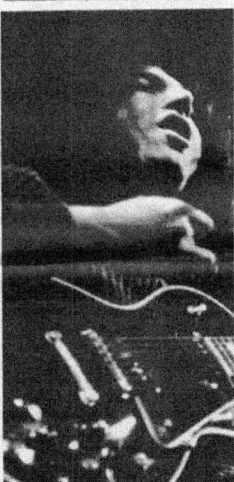

DEAD HAPPENING in San Francisco.

GUTHRIE A REFRESHING CHANGE

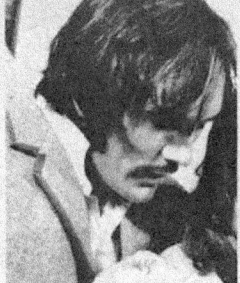

TERRENCE STAMP certainly rising.

The Boston Credibility

Dear BEAT,

After seeing the build up given to the so-called "Boston Sound" it makes me wonder about the credibility of many publications. If there is a "Boston Sound" it is still totally restricted to that area. It seems to me that promoters should not get so eager over something that isn't any good. I was glad to see that the BEAT did not go overboard with calling the Boston sound the wave of the future.

Jane Freidman

MICHELLE IN 1967

Where's Tony?

Dear BEAT,

I like your newspaper very much, but I have one complaint. For the past few issues Tony Barrow has not be included. Will he continue to write in the future, or has he been permanently discontinued? I really appreciated finding out what is happening in England, and hearing the truth about all those Beatle rumors.

Carol Davies

The Majority Rules!

Dear BEAT,

I am an avid BEAT reader who agrees with Interested Readers letter in the March 23, 1968 issue. I, too, believe that rising young actors and actresses, in both television and the movies should be included in future issue of your newspaper.

I truly believe that this would be of interest to many people as it is a field of entertainment widely followed. Also it certainly would make a unique publication as no others contain such a wide coverage. Possibly, you could include interviews of young dancers and tour reviews such as Job Corps and USO. These, too, would surely have a great deal to offer in modern entertainment.

Thank you for listening and for writing an extremely objective paper. Yours sincerely,

Nancy Lowe

The majority of letters we've received have favored including television and motion picture entertainers in The BEAT. Now, we only have one future question for you . . . which ones would you like featured in the paper? Please send your suggestions to us as soon as possible.

ULTIMATE SPINACH A CREDIBILITY GAP?

Why Disenchantment?

Dear BEAT,

I was extremely unhappy to hear that the people of Monterey do not want another pop festival held in their city. It seems incredible to me that after many years of holding the Jazz Festival in that city, that the people should become so disenchanted with a Festival devoted to Pop.

However, if nothing can be done to change their minds I suggest holding the Festival in another city, maybe in Los Angeles or Laguna by the Sea.

I was glad to hear that many public officials are realizing that pop concerts made available to kids at little to no cost would help keep everyone 'cool' this summer. Giving people something to do is always useful in cooling tempers.

Sandra Kellogg

RINGO STARR

Beat Publications, Inc.

Publisher .... Michael Curb
Editor .... Louise Criscione
Assistant Editor .... Jacoba Atlas

Staff Writers
Bobby Bovino .... Angel Lansing
Tony Leigh .... Tammy Hitchcock
Marty Schaffner .... Jim Pewter

Contributing Writers
Tony Barrow .... Sue Barry
Eden .... Bob Levinson
Jamie McClusky III .... Mike Masterson

National Advertising Representative
Sam Chase Assoc., Inc.
527 Madison Avenue
New York, New York 10022
(212) PL. 5-1668

Advertising Director .... Dick Stricklin
Business Mgr. & Circulation .... Judy Felice
Complaints .... Dick Whitehouse

Distribution
Miller Freeman Publications
500 Howard Street, San Francisco, Calif.

The BEAT is published bi-weekly by BEAT Publications, Inc., editorial and advertising offices at 9000 Sunset Blvd., Suite 1000, L.A., California 90069. U.S. bureaus in Hollywood, San Francisco, New York, Chicago and Nashville; overseas correspondents in London, Liverpool and Manchester, England. Sale price 25 cents. Subscription price: U.S. and possessions $3.00 per year; Canada and foreign rates, $9 per year. Second class postage pre-paid at Los Angeles, California. Send Form 3579 to 9000 Sunset Blvd., Los Angeles, Calif. 90069.

KRLA ARCHIVES

BEATLES BACK TWIGGY FILM

LONDON — Twiggy is venturing forth into new areas of exploration. Deciding that modeling was too limiting for the slender 18 year old, her friend and mentor, Justin de Villneuve announced that Twiggy is embarking on a movie career.

Her first film will be a fairy tale based on Nobel Prize winner William Faulkner's short stories called *The Wishing Tree*. In the film, Twiggy is reported to be playing a very young boy. The film is being produced by the Beatles new corporation, Apple.

Arlo Guthrie Films 'Alice'

NEW YORK — Arlo Guthrie probably had no idea in the world that his "Alice's Restaurant" would become such a gigantic and widespread smash. The composition has already been made into a book and now it's about to become a motion picture.

Arthur Penn ("Bonnie & Clyde" director) has acquired the film rights to "Alice" and intends to use it as his next feature. Filming will begin in August and Arlo will play himself in the film version as will Chief of Police William J. Obanheim. The scene of the story is Stockbridge, Mass. and Penn already has permission to shoot the film on location there.

"Alice's Restaurant" is the title of Guthrie's first album and occupies one entire side of the LP.

Cream Will Sing Title

LOS ANGELES — The Cream has been signed by Dick Clark to sing the title tune in his forthcoming American International film, "The Savage Seven." The song will be released as a single by Atco Records and is, surprisingly enough, entitled "The Savage Seven Theme (Anyone For Tennis)."

The film, a contemporary western, stars Robert Walker, Jr.

Dylan Nabs Fifth Goldie

NEW YORK — Bob Dylan, whose influence of pop music cannot be passed over lightly, has earned himself another Gold Record for his latest album, "John Wesley Harding."

The Dylan album, the first to be released since his accident over eighteen months ago, achieved unprecedented success in an unusually short amount of time, earning a Gold Record faster than any of his other LP's. "Harding" sold over a quarter-million copies in the first week alone.

This marks Dylan's fifth million-selling album; the others were for "Blonde on Blonde," "Highway 61 Revisited," "Bringing It All Back Home" and "Bob Dylan's Greatest Hits."

GOLD 'HONEY'

NEW YORK — Bobby Goldsboro recording of "Honey" has been certified a million seller by the RIAA.

United Artist for whom the record was released stated that "Honey" is the fastest selling single in the company's ten-year history. "Honey's" writer has also written the new Roger Miller hit, "God Didn't Make Little Green Apples."

PEOPLE ARE TALKING ABOUT the Monkees' "Valleri" debuting on the national charts and selling a million all in the first week out . . . Georgie Fame saying his "Bonnie And Clyde" song is only loosely based on the real Bonnie and Clyde — question is "how loosely?" . . . what Murray Roman's point is . . . the fact that Bob Dylan is the author of the Manfred Mann's "Mighty Quinn" . . . why Simon and Garfunkel steadfastly refuse to be interviewed

. . . whether or not the Blue Cheer are really the "breakthrough" some people think they are . . . why the Union Gap have suddenly switched their name to "and featuring Gary Puckett" . . . ditto for Linda Ronstadt and the Stone Poneys . . . O.C. Smith's "Son Of Hickory Holler's Tramp" being one of the most original songs to come along in a long time . . . The 5th Dimension getting so many Grammy Awards on the strength of only one song

. . . why Monkee Davy Jones felt compelled to give his opinion to the audience while reading his batch of nominated songs at the Grammy affair . . . the fact that Ira S. Mothner is a very funny man . . . Ringo Starr and his wife cutting short their Indian stay with the Marharishi due, in part, to the fact that they dislike spicy food . . . the Byrds wanting to set everything straight . . . why the Rolling Stones have been keeping so quiet lately . . . what a smash Petula Clark is going to be in the film, "Peter Pan"

. . . Lulu being upset about "To Sir With Love" failing to grab an Academy Award nomination . . .

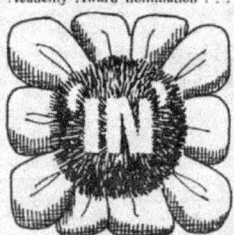

how nice it was to see Glen Campbell finally recognized by the recording industry . . . who the Montanas are . . . Gladys Knight and the Pips getting a certified million for sales of "The End Of Our Road" . . . bets being taken on when (if ever) the 4 Seasons are going to miss getting a hit single

. . . the fact that Sly and the Family Stone have a monster of a hit without having any publicity whatsoever and what a neat trick that is . . . ditto for the Delfonics and "La-La Means I Love You" . . . Fat Albert turning into a star in his own right thanks to the talent of Bill Cosby . . . whether or not Donovan will really get his movie produced and will convince Paul McCartney to take a cameo role

. . . the predictions that pop music will shortly go back to hard core rock with a heavy drum and wondering what that will do to at least half the groups now making records . . . the Association's new album being a gas . . . the Scaffold's record not making it very big after all . . . the fact that "Judy In Disguise" is still hanging on the charts after 17 weeks . . . what the Vanilla Fudge had in mind when they cut their latest album

. . . Bobby Vee making it back and wondering if Ronnie Dove can do the same . . . Tony Barrow going on his own after all this time with NEMS and wishing him the very best of luck . . . the fact that no one dances at the Fillmore and the jazz clubs in San Francisco are having a difficult time meeting their overhead . . . who decided to ban the new Beatle song because of one line and what their reasoning behind it was.

KRLA ARCHIVES

FIRST DATES FOR THE BEE GEES' STATESIDE TOUR have been announced. They are: August 1, Memorial Aud., Sacramento, Calif.; August 2, Hollywood Bowl, Hollywood, Calif.; August 3, Cow Palace, San Francisco, Calif.; August 4, Sports Arena, San Diego, Calif.; August 10, Forest Hills, Long Island, New York; August 11 (afternoon), rain date for Forest Hills; August 11 (evening), Civic Light Opera, Pittsburgh, Pa.; August 24, Stadium, Detroit, Mich.

THE UNION GAP MAKE IT TWO IN A ROW with their second Gold Record.

Union Gap - A Gold Record

NEW YORK — The Union Gap, who earlier this year received their first Gold Record for "Woman, Woman," has just been awarded another Goldie for their follow-up single, "Young Girl."

The group's first album, "The Union Gap," is rapidly climbing the LP charts, selling over 100,000 copies during the first week of its release, making a third Gold Record more than a slim possibility.

THE GRATEFUL DEAD

Lampert Forms Publishing Company

LOS ANGELES — Popular songwriter, Diane Lampert, has joined forces with publicist, Fred Stuart, to form Annadiane Music Publishing Co., a BMI affiliate. Annadiane's first release will be "Let No One Love You."

Miss Lampert is now in London working on songs with Tom Springfield; the title song for a Boulting Brothers' film; and a Broadway show with composer Bernard Herrmann.

Englebert Humperdinck and Jimmy Durante are two of the artists which currently have Lampert singles out.

Airplane-Dead Open Carousel

SAN FRANCISCO — The Jefferson Airplane and the Grateful Dead have joined forces to open a new rock hall in San Francisco. The new hall called Carousel has been planned as a showcase for groups preferred by the Airplane and the Dead.

This marks the first time that two top groups have formed their own club and have become involved in bookings. A spokesman for the two groups stated that they plan to open Carousels across the country.

The hall is larger than the Fillmore and the Avalon, and unlike the Wintergarden (the largest rock hall in San Francisco) the Carousel will stay open during the summer months.

ON THE BEAT
BY LOUISE CRISCIONE

Lulu, who made her major film debut in Columbia's "To Sir, With Love," has just been signed for her second movie with the same studio. Titled "Goodbye, Summer" the film will be shot in Blackpool in July and will be directed by Jim Frawley, the man who directed the Monkees' television show.

Frankie Valli, lead singer for the Four Seasons and a recording artist in his own right, is set to try his hand in the movies. His first appearance will be in "Black Mountain."

Association Form Firm

In addition to having their fourth album ("Birthday") released, the Association has formed their own music publishing firm, Ferris Wheel Music. The company will be affiliated with BMI and will have Association manager, Pat Colecchio, direct the firm.

Bobbie Gentry and Glen Campbell, two of 1967's biggest hits, are going to combine forces by cutting an album together. Not terribly surprising since both artists record for Capitol Records.

Bill Cosby received such high ratings and rave notices for his first NBC-TV special that the network has already signed him for another special to air next season. Meanwhile, he's not doing too badly in the concert arena either . . . the mighty Cos grossed a neat $127,700 in six appearances.

Maharishi With Beach Boys

Maharishi Mahesh Yogi, Indian spiritual leader, is set to begin a tour of the United States on May 3 in New York and will end up on May 20 in Los Angeles. This time around the Maharishi is taking the Beach Boys along with him in sort of a package deal. Beach Boy Mike Love has been in India taking instruction from the Maharishi and the rest of the Beach Boys are expected to follow suit in September.

Mike Neshmith is going into the car business with engineer Dean Jeffries. They'll come up with a line of dune-buggy-type cars for street driving and will give the line a nice piece of promotion via the Monkees' first film, "Untitled."

Add Eric Burdon and the Animals to the list of pop groups signed for motion pictures. They're all set for "The Death Of Harry Farmer," which begins filming in June . . . And then there's the Stone Country who will work for Otto Preminger in his currently-filming "Skiddo." Nilsson, RCA's prolific songwriter, is doing the music for the film, his first movie-scoring venture.

Webb Scoring Film

Jim Webb, the 21 year old songwriter who penned "Up, Up And Away" as well as "By The Time I Get To Phoenix" is following Nilsson's lead by writing the music and lyrics for Universal's big-moneyed musical which has not yet been titled.

Buffy On 'Virginian'

It looks as if everyone in the music business is branching out into either films or television. Folk singer, Buffy Sainte Marie has chosen television over movies and will make her debut next season on "The Virginian" in an episode entitled "The Heritage."

Herbie Alpert and the Tijuana Brass are heading out on yet another college tour. It kicks off on May 9 at the University of San Diego and wins itself up on May 18 at Brigham Young. Other stops on the tour include Minnesota, Nebraska, Butler, Bradley, Wichita State, Wyoming, Colorado State and Montana State.

Never under-estimate word of mouth — Traffic opened in Los Angeles to a mere 300 and came back the next night to a pleasantly-surprising audience of 1200 . . . Glen McKay's Headlights (the light show which once backed the Airplane) are now set to go to Europe with the Airplane and the Doors in September. They'll be the first American light show to ever tour Europe.

COS COMES UP A WINNER on two more entertainment fronts.

KRLA ARCHIVES

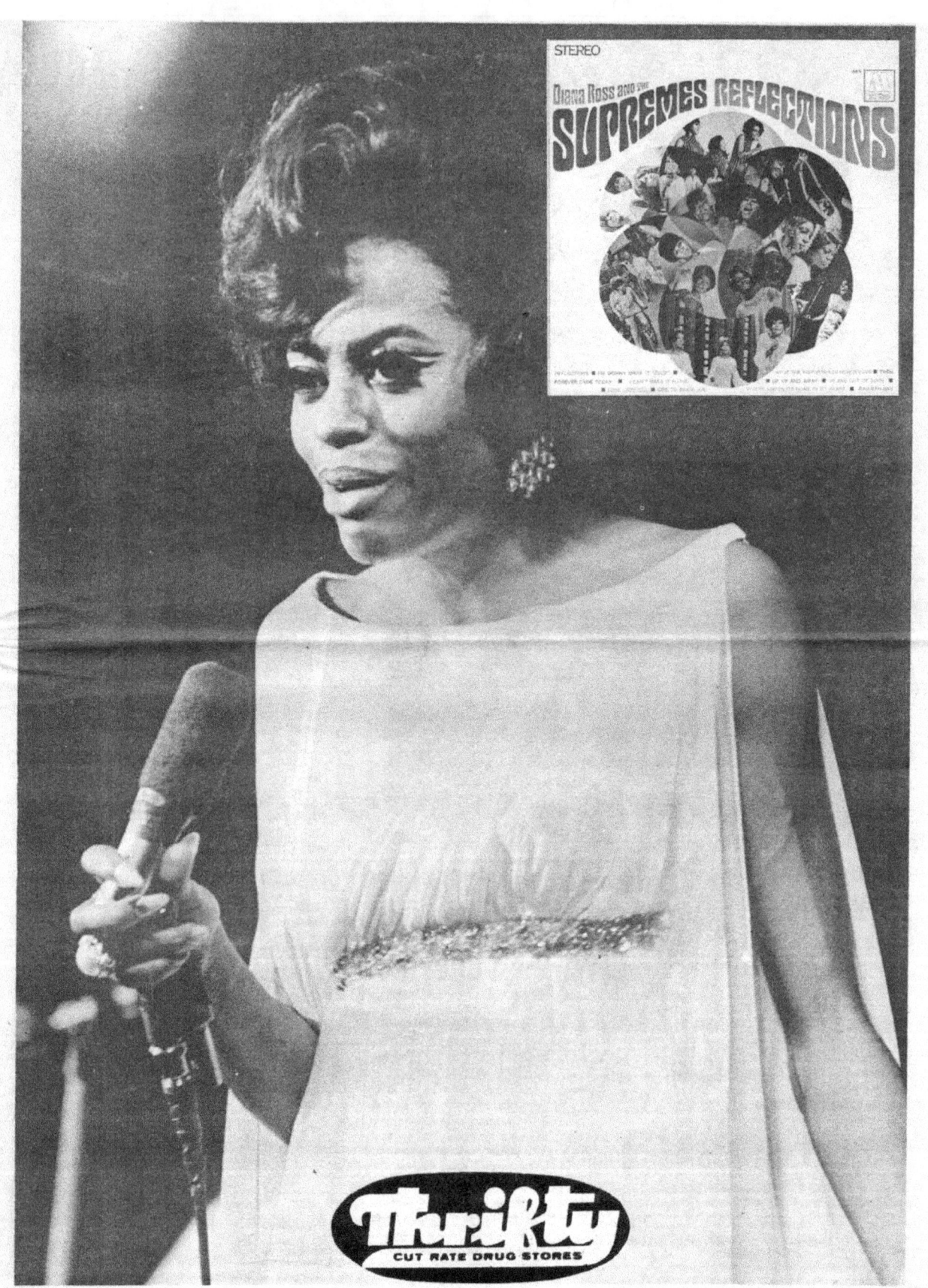

KRLA ARCHIVES

Now Available At:

The Moby Grape is one of the most talented groups out of the San Francisco scene. Voted by one rock paper as the most significant new group of 1967, the Grape envision even better things for 68. One of those things is their latest album entitled appropriately enough **WOW**. If that isn't enough, the Grape have done something many groups say they would like to do, but don't. They have added an album of their jam sessions —spontaneous, unrehearsed, the rock musician at his best. Don't miss this breakthrough in pop albums.

The Four Rascals Two Years Later

By Angel Lansing

A little over two years ago, the calm cool of The BEAT offices was shattered by an unpredictable foursome who then called themselves the Young Rascals. The "Young" has now gone the way of the knickers but the foursome are still unpredictable in a rather predictable sort of way.

Take promptness . . . a safe bet says that the Rascals have never been anywhere on time and probably never will. They managed to be three hours late for their first interview with The BEAT, once they never showed up at all and the rest of the time they just "drop in" completely unannounced.

Take appearance . . . they began in knickers, switched to a mod potpourri and are now well into the Indian-influenced outfits. The once clean-shaven, long-but-not-too-long length of hair has now lost out to a beard on Felix, an on-again-off-again beard on Eddie, an American flag shirt on Dino and a weight loss on Gene.

Take music . . . in the very early part of 1966 they first became known to the nation with "I Ain't Gonna Eat Out My Heart Anymore." If not a number one effort, it did tie for longest title of the year. They followed that up with an impressive string of hit singles, probably the best known is the mini-classic, "Groovin'." Their first album, called simply "The Young Rascals," was succeeded by "Collections" and "Groovin'." Their latest, "Once Upon A Dream," hits the high — a total concept throughout an entire album.

The Rascals have never been "bad." If their first musical outings were not brilliant, neither were they embarrassingly poor. I doubt whether anyone has ever called Eddie a prophet. I doubt seriously that he is. He did, however, make a prophetic statement two years ago. He said that the Rascals would never fall into the pain of sameness . . . would never release one carbon-copied record after another. "I think there is too much talent in this group to do something like that — too many ideas to fall into that bag." (BEAT, Feb. 12, 1966) Now, in 1968, he's still right . . . the Rascals have done a lot of things (some good, some not so good) but they have never released a second-time-around record.

Not every one of their records has made the top ten . . . not every one of their personal appearances has been sold-out. But they have gone further than any other contemporary group in America because they have changed and evolved; they've tried new techniques in music, new sounds, new ideas. They played the Madison Square Garden with a full orchestra; they had Eddie's brother, Dave, sing the title song from their "Dream" album . . . and (will wonders never cease?) they even went so far as to include his name on their album jacket.

On the subject of films, nothing concrete has come to pass. They've steadfastly refused to appear in the dime-a-dozen "teen" films, but they have set out to make their own motion picture. No one has seen fit to reveal the contents of the script (if such a thing even exists) and although a shooting date has supposedly been set, the movie has yet to begin filming. No doubt it will occur sooner or later, but just as no one bets on the Rascals being prompt, so no one will bet on when the movie will become reality.

But, as with just about everything they do, it is certain not to be an imitation . . . it will undoubtedly be different, if not totally unique.

Personality-wise, it's hard to pinpoint any individual changes, except the obvious fact that Dino is doing more talking today than he did two years ago. Conceit, if it has touched them at all, is not discernible on the surface. Fans who travel out to airports to welcome the Rascals to their part of the country are still rewarded with autographs and amicable greetings. Friends they made two years ago when they didn't have much going for them are still friends today. Because they're considerably busier now, visits are not as frequent as they once were but the Rascals still remember how to use a telephone, so in many cases a phone call has replaced a personal call.

Still, the Rascals are not impossible to reach; guards do not block their entrance, hotels do not receive the "complete secrecy" command from Rascal headquarters and armies of press agents, managers, secretaries, road managers and hangers-on have failed to substantially materialize.

This, then, is what the Rascals are all about in 1968 . . . musically and professionally more mature, but in total concept — exactly the same.

RASCALS REGARD promptness as a vice rather than a virtue.

KNICKERS GONE, replaced by beard.

"...too many ideas to fall into that bag"

PHONE CALLS take the place of personal visits.

BUT AUTOGRAPHS are still as abundant as they ever were.

AND FANS are not shoved aside.

KRLA ARCHIVES

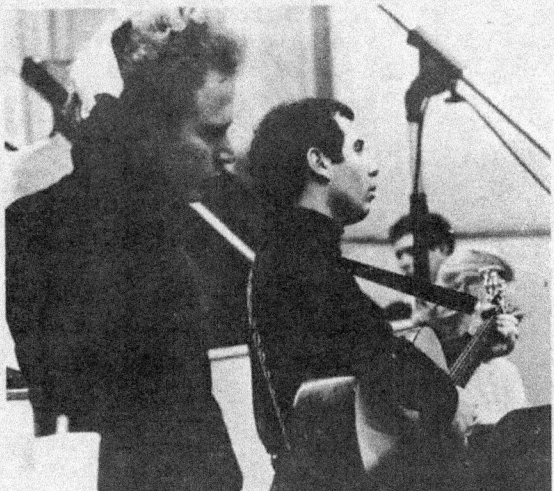

SIMON AND GARFUNKLE sing Paul's songs for Mike Nichols' "The Graduate." "Parsley, Sage, Rosemary and Thyme" and "Sound of Silence" are used throughout the film.

THE FUGS sing in Conrad Rooks' "Chappaqua" with a score written by Ravi Shankar. The music combined the styles of rock, Indian and classical influences.

A New Trend for Films: The Pop Composer's Score

By Jacoba Atlas

Music for motion pictures has undergone change after change. Before the advent of sound, a piano player often sat in the orchestra pit plunking out tunes which tried to correspond with the action on the screen. Usually the music was left to the discretion of the piano player, but with such grand epics as "Birth of a Nation" special scores were created. When sound came into fashion, all music was written directly for a particular motion picture. However, this didn't always denote good scoring. Try watching some of the old movies on the late show, as good as the acting is, as good as the direction is, the music is usually terrible. Even the classic "Gone With The Wind" despite the beautiful and universally acclaimed "Tara's Theme" over-all it seems over-orchestrated and unduly loud.

It has really only been in the last 15 years that the score to a film has been given as much and as close attention as any other aspect of film making. Using familiar themes interwoven with new music, such composers as Aaron Copeland (The Heiress) and Dimitri Tiomkin (Giant) sought to bring the flavor of the country and the heritage of the people into their scores.

Authentic Sounds

Today, this of course, is taken for granted in films. The use of the balalika in "Doctor Zhivago" by Maurice Jarre, the banjo scoring of "Bonnie and Clyde" as played by Flatt and Scruggs, the plantive and soulful string instruments employed by Alex North to underscore the meaning of "Who's Afraid of Virginia Wolfe". These have all helped to create the climate in which movie makers now seek scores for their films. Today, more than ever before, they are looking for authenticity in music. Music that will be an integral part of the film, instead of just background music.

This trend has finally led producers to recognize the talents of pop composers. For many years overlooked as any real source for creative talent the pop composers have now come into their own, as critics acclaim the new art of pop music. Suddenly it has become more than chic to have a pop artist score a movie — it has become acceptable. It has become the norm.

Spoonful Beginning

Perhaps it all started with John Sebastian of the Lovin' Spoonful. First he scored the music for Woody Allen's film "What's Up Tiger Lily" and then he wrote the songs for Francis Ford Coppola's "You're A Big Boy Now". The race was on. Suddenly producers realized that a score like a hit single would help their film to success. As most of the movie going public is under thirty, having their pop idols write the music for a film seemed like good box-office. The bonus came when people realized these very same pop idols wrote good scores.

It is impossible to say how much "You're A Big Boy Now" was helped by Sebastian's score. Certainly, the air play given to "Amy's Theme" and "Darling Be Home Soon" was a large factor in publicizing this first major film for Coppola.

Jumping on the bandwagon and capitalizing on the popularity of the Beatles, Paul McCartney was set to score the music for the Bolting Brothers' "The Family Way." The score itself was not very impressive . . . nice, yes, but not up to Beatles standards. A rather lukewarm score, which only really employed one major theme, it nevertheless helped to sell that picture too. In the advertising campaign, Paul "Beatle" McCartney was given as large a billing as the film's stars.

Perhaps the most famous pop scoring for a film, is the one currently playing — "The Graduate." Written by Paul Simon and performed by both he and his partner, Art Garfunkel. It seems the perfect score for that funny-sad film. It is doubtful that any other use of music could have underlined the picture's meaning with the effectiveness of Simon's songs. Pop tunes were perfect to give added dimension to the popular film. Although these songs were not written directly for the film, but were off an earlier album, the use of "Sound of Silence", "Parsley, Sage, Rosemary and Thyme" and "April, Come She Will" contributed immensely to the tone of the film.

Donovan Too

Just recently, Donovan has ventured into the realm of motion picture scoring with the Joseph Janni production of "Poor Cow". His plaintive song about human condition is said to help clarify the poignant outlook of that film.

Ravi Shankar who only recently fits into the category of a pop musician has scored the music for Conrad Rook's "Chappaqua" (see BEAT, February 24, 1968). His score for the film combined classical, rock and Indian music to heighten the internal contradictions of the film. However, Mr. Shankar is no newcomer to movie scoring, in his native India he has fulfilled that capacity many times before.

Harrison Now

George Harrison is the latest pop star to enter the ranks of movie scorer. He is now completing work on the music for "Wonderwall" a film which, quite naturally, takes place in India.

Producers have long noted the worth of a popular song to sell a movie. It is only recently that they realized that a modern film demands modern music.

GEORGE HARRISON has written the score for "Wonderwall" thus joining Paul McCartney in the film scoring business.

JOHN SEBASTIAN, possibly the man who started the trend with his scores for "What's Up Tiger Lily" and "You're A Big Boy Now."

KATHERINE ROSS, nominated for an academy award for her portrayal of Elaine in "The Graduate"—score by Paul Simon.

PAUL McCARTNEY received top billing for his luke-warm scoring of the Bolting Brothers "The Family Way."

KRLA ARCHIVES

the LADIES infiltrate POP MUSIC

GLADYS KNIGHT leads the Pips for Motown

GRACE SLICK synonymous with Airplane

By Louise Criscione

Pop music is a male medium . . . owing, perhaps, to the long-held belief that females buy the large majority of records. But at last it appears that females are obtaining, if not equal, then certainly greater rights on the nation's record charts. Just as segregation is gradually being torn away in our school systems, so is it incinerating in pop music.

Today females are being allowed to sing along with males in integrated groups. In fact, three of the bigger groups in pop music find themselves not only with incidental female members but with females who share and at times even *steal* the all-important spotlight.

"Unmistakably Loud"

Although she is not the group's leader, Grace Slick has become synonymous with the name Jefferson Airplane. The daughter of an investment banker who is "nonplussed" by her activities, Grace describes her untrained voice as "loud, unmistakably loud. I have a lot to learn, including how to sing without hearing my own voice. Sometimes, after four hours of this, I long for a minuet."

Grace was not the original girl in the Airplane, but it was not until after she joined the group that they began reaching out from San Francisco to the rest of the nation. Following a stint at modeling, Grace and her husband formed a group called the Great Society. They failed to set the music world on fire, so when Grace received the chance she boarded the Airplane and became the first of the current crop of females to stand alongside her male counterparts in the center of the pop stage.

Presently Spanky

From San Francisco's thin Grace Slick, we go to Chicago's round Elaine McFarlane, now making her presence known as Spanky, leader of Our Gang. Long before Spanky and Our Gang and "Sunday Will Never Be The Same" Spanky was fairly well-known in folk circles. But in early 1966 she decided to leave Chicago and move to Florida.

If the truth were known, Spanky did not live the life of a jet-setter in Miami . . . rather she rented a one-room converted chicken coop *near* Miami and, as will happen in that area, one night a hurricane hit. Despite the fact that a hurricane is not generally considered a lucky omen, it was because of nature's wrath that Spanky met up with two young men who later became members of Our Gang.

Refuge Seekers

Taking refuge in her somewhat shaky "house," Nigel Pickering, Oz Bach and Spanky passed the time by singing. "I told them that I might leave Miami soon and that if they ever got to Chicago to look me up," recalls Spanky.

As in all good success stories, they did get to Chicago, did look her up and, in due time, did form a group called Spanky and Our Gang.

"Actually, I guess you could say we play good-time music," deduces Spanky. "We just have a lot of fun and we want everyone around us to have fun. We want the audience to relax. We're always looking for new tunes and we're always searching for new comedy bits. We want to blow people's minds. We want to give something to everybody. That's why we make use of such a variety of material."

Spanky McFarlane, lady in pop, leader (even if in name only) of an integrated and successful group.

Defiantly Short

Thelma Camacho is the latest female to nab a spot in a top group. But she is neither new to the music business nor new to the public. In the age of long-haired pop, Thelma defiantly sports a hair cut which lacks an inch or two of being categorized as a "butch."

In addition to the hair cut, Thelma is probably the only female pop singer who has made the transition from opera to rock. Four years of vocal training led her to roles in San Diego, California opera and light opera. She played Tuptin in "The King And I," Tatiyana in "The Forest Prince" and Jilda in "Rigoletto."

Following a year of San Diego State College, Thelma found herself immersed in the world of folk music. She spent six months touring with the Young Americans and then switched her loyalty to the Kids Next Door. After being a "Kid," Thelma became one of the New Christy Minstrels. It was, of course, as a Minstrel that she met Mike Settle, Kenny Rogers and Terry Williams.

The Big One

When it was time to leave the Minstrels, the foursome formed their own group and called it the First Edition. Instantaneous success was not theirs but it came very close to being the case. With an already road-proven manager and a national television debut on none other than the "Smothers Brothers Show," not too many months elapsed before the First Edition (with Thelma very much present) began their climb up the charts with "Just Dropped In (To See What Condition My Condition Was In)."

Grace Slick, Spanky McFarlane and Thelma Camacho are not the only three to make their way among the pop boys. There are several others (Janis Joplin with Big Brother and the Holding Company, Gladys Knight with the Pips and Linda Ronstadt with the Stone Poneys) who are attempting to dent the male monopoly in pop. It's more than doubtful that the ladies will completely triumph, but one can never be sure. After all, women gained the right to vote.

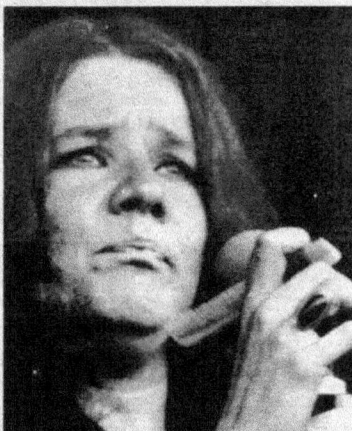

JANIS JOPLIN, voice of Holding Company

SPANKY thanks to a hurricane

LINDA RONSTADT led Poneys to top

KRLA ARCHIVES

Waiting for a new sensation?
Meet England's...
Wayne Thomas

And his first...
"I'll Be Yours"
ABC 11058
Orchestra conducted by Alyn Ainsworth. Produced by Bill Landis for Tito Burns.

Great first album coming up soon!

Bookings: U.S.A. - G.A.C.   Outside U.S.A. - Harold Davison Agency.

ABC RECORDS, INC.
NEW YORK/BEVERLY HILLS
DIST. IN CANADA BY SPARTON OF CANADA

KRLA ARCHIVES

NITTY GRITTY DIRT BAND HOLD-UP THE ICE HOUSE

By Patti Johnson

Could it be that some of the glamour and excitement that once set show business apart from the rest of the world is not dead, after all? At a gangster-type Bonnie and Clyde affair to launch their third album, "Rare Junk", the Nitty Gritty Dirt Band reached into the past for more than music, humor, and wardrobe. The group returned to the past and borrowed part of that gimmicky craziness of days gone by.

Contributing to the over-all effect, the Nitty Gritty Dirt Band and their famous (and infamous) guests arrived on-the-scene, the Ice House in Glendale, in a regal caravan of shiny, black cars including an antique English taxi, three antique Mercedes, an antique Cadillac, a Rolls-Royce, and a Lincoln limousine. Emerging from this impressive-looking collection of vehicles were Pat Paulsen, shaking hands and campaigning for the presidency; the Standells; folk singer, Wahler; Tim Morgon; Dough Dillard; and a group called the David with body guards who were whisked in and out so fast that no one caught more than a glimpse of them! The Sourbridge Lion made their appearance on a bicycle, apparently by choice and not because of a shortage of cars.

There was a restored, brightly painted airplane, reminiscent of the one that Lindberg flew over the Atlantic, on hand for pictures and to generally add to the whole special atmosphere of the evening. Of course, the lively, hammy Nitty Gritty mounted it for the benefit of all the photographers on the scene.

The costumes were elaborate and kooky. They ranged from the dapper dan attire of the Dirt Band to the "Baby Face Nelson" look of the mysterious David to the Scottish kilts of the Stourbridge Lion. One of the Standells made his appearance dressed like a flag! Even the waitresses got in on the act, wearing midi, half-calf length, low-belted dresses reminiscent of those worn in the era in question.

It was hard to believe that after all of the goings on outside that there could still be more to come inside. Folk singer, Tim Morgon, opened the show with a collection of traditional folk and pop songs. Pat Paulsen, hilarious comedian of the Smothers Brothers Show, then got up and made his pitch for the presidency. His speech was followed by an open press conference in which he was forced to voice his opinions on the pressing problems of our time, like "Are you an athletic supporter?" After a brief intermission, the scheduled show began with the baroque-rock sounds of the Fantasy World Orchestra, a quintet that returns to the traditional instruments such as flutes, cellos, etc. to create the sounds of today's psychedelic rock.

The zany Nitty Gritty Dirt Band capped the show with their old-timer swing sounds and their side-splitting, knee-slapping h u m o r. They previewed some of the material from their LP, "Rare Junk" and were met with overwhelming approval. After the show, the room began to clear but there was still a little excitement in the air. The evening had served its purpose: to introduce the press and the public to the group's new album and it had been alot of fun as well!

PAT PAULSON arrives in Lindburg type airplane.

THE NITTY GRITTY DIRT BAND with folk singer Waller.

BLUE CHIP STAMPS TO REPLACE GOLD

Los Angeles pop music station KRLA, long established as a national leader in the use of satirical comedy via the station's widely acclaimed on-air promotional drives, took to the air last week with a series of editorial spoofs suggesting a sure-fire solution to the world monetary crisis.

"Where others have failed, KRLA has found the answer," droned an on-the-air station spokesman, tongue thrust deeply in cheek. Calling on world monetary power to "stamp out speculation and lick the gold crisis" by eliminating the gold standard entirely, KRLA suggests that member nations switch to the "Blue Chip Stamp standard."

"This would end the threat of devaluation since trading stamps cannot be devalued below their present level," the station pointed out. "The Blue Chip Stamp standard would promote world peace," intoned KRLA. "If we cannot bring the communists to the bargaining table, we could at least bring them to the redemption center."

KRLA followed up the spoof editorials with a series of equally satirical slogans backing its campaign. Included were "nations that lick together stick together." Another obvious advantage to the Blue Chip Stamp standard is the immediate solution to the balance of payments problem. "All a nation faced with a balance of payments deficit need do is declare a double stamp day," advised the KRLA editorial.

STEP OUT WITH
spirit"
BY STEVENS

at only
50¢
the pair*

*sold two pairs in a box

Everyone makes the scene in Spirit
the stockings from famous Stevens...
priced to save you a fortune.

They're made for high voltage legs, non-stop action. Stockings to wear anytime, any place without worry at only 50¢ the pair. Spirit—in shades that swing with the maddest mini-skirt or the smartest designer suit. You'll flip at the sleek way they fit. You'll want a pair with plenty of spares in lively "go" shades.

Flash: Boy's school wins girls stockings.

Webb School of California at Claremont is the winner of the school spirit contest with a winning petition containing 99.52% of the student body.

Congratulations from Spirit Hosiery (by J. P. Stevens and Company) and KRLA.

But don't all run out to Claremont to see those boys in silk stockings. They are donating the Spirit Hosiery to Girls Collegiate School, also in Claremont.

KRLA ARCHIVES

KENNY ROGERS: "Since we've all been in a successful group we've had a taste of what it's like to be on top — but now we want it in our own way, with our own music."

TERRY WILLIAMS: "I'm the kind of guy who in a single day lost on 'The Dating Game' and was beaten up at a Love-In." Once he even worked in record distribution and promotion!

The First Edition: Chemistry Of Combining Five Talents

By Tommy Smothers

Sometimes I think that I'd like to let my hair grow long (an unlikely occurrence as it currently requires all of my efforts merely to maintain the status quo), electrify my guitar and join a rock group. I really think that today's music is the most creative and interesting any generation has produced and I would like to be a part of it.

Short-Circuited

Unfortunately, however, my conversation somehow gets short-circuited every time I mention an electric guitar so it appears that I will have to content myself with telling you about a group that is performing my kind of music.

Not long ago I dropped into a small night club in Los Angeles to see a new folk-rock group known as the First Edition. The four kids who put the group together are former members of the New Christy Minstrels and I was anxious to see what they had come up with. Well, I was gassed! The First Edition is the finest, most entertaining new group of its kind. One of the things that impressed me most about the First Edition is the individual talents that it contains.

Pouring It On

Rhythm guitarist Mike Settle has written nearly all of the groups' music and he's the one who really pours it on in "I've Found A Reason" and "Church Without A Name."

Then there's Thelma Camacho —what can I say but that I love her. Unfortunately for me the line forms at the right and about six

THELMA CAMACHO: "Although every area of music is different, each has the same standard of quality."

miles down the road. But just let her smile or sing "I Get A Funny Feeling" and I don't mind waiting.

Terry Williams plays great guitar, has a fine voice and all the girls love him. You don't expect me to add anything to that list of accomplishments do you?

Kenny Rogers really wails on the bass and when you hear him sing "Conditioned" you will have no doubts at all about what condition his condition is in.

Chosen Carefully

Backing the group is drummer Mickey Jones whose list of credits proves that he picks his company carefully. He provided the beat for Trini Lopez, Johnny Rivers and Bob Dylan before joining the First Edition.

But as great as the individuals in the group are, it is the chemistry that takes place when their talents combine that is most exciting. Their music can't be pigeon-holed—there's some folk in there somewhere, but there's also the influence of hard rock and a touch of the blues. There's certainly some of the musical sophistication of jazz, but there is the earthy kind of integrity that only country music can provide.

But most of all there is the First Edition, sounding new and special and very much themselves. And I can't think of anyone else I'd rather have singing my song for me.

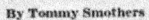

MIKE SETTLE has the look and the soul of a gypsy. When he opens his mouth music pours out in a lusty, earthy torrent, and music pours from his pen in the same unquenchable flow.

MICKEY JONES: the man who provides the beat for the group. Before the First Edition, he played for Bob Dylan, Trini Lopez and Johnny Rivers. When not drumming, he's an actor.

MOVING?

Writing about a subscription?
Be sure to fill out this form

For FASTEST service on address change, missing copies, etc., attach old mailing label in first space below. Otherwise please print clearly your address as we now have it.

OLD ADDRESS (Attach old label here if available)

NAME
ADDRESS
CITY
STATE   ZIP CODE

NAME
ADDRESS
CITY   STATE   ZIP CODE

MAIL TO: BEAT PUBLICATIONS
Circulation Dept.
9000 Sunset Blvd., Suite 1000,
Los Angeles, Cal. 90069

Please allow 3 weeks for change to take effect.

KRLA ARCHIVES

BOOKENDS / SIMON & GARFUNKEL

Simon And Garfunkel

Loosely described, their songs are in the mold of traditional folk with rock overtones and at their center are preoccupations with loneliness, illusory existence, the pain of time passing and lack of communication.

AVAILABLE AT

CUT RATE DRUG STORES

KRLA ARCHIVES

O. C. SMITH: LONG ROAD TO SUCCESS

Controversy and social comment rarely appear at the top of the charts, but just recently O. C. Smith has put a song of purpose to the top. "The Son of Hickory Holler's Tramp" is not what most people would call 'easy listening.'

O. C. was born in Los Angeles to a musically oriented family. His mother, Ruth Shoater Smith was his first music instructor and accompanist. While attending Jeffferson High School and Los Angeles City College O.C. played as many times as he could, but his first real professional break came when he joined the United States Air Force. His work was so well received by service and civilian audiences all over the world, that O.C. made his final decision to sing professionally after leaving the armed services.

Final Decision

After his tour of duty was completed, O.C. went to New York and a job singing at the Club Baby Grand. It was there that O.C. was spotted by Sy Oliver. This led to an introduction to Sid Bernstein—manager of the Young Rascals—who booked him into the Catskills.

From there O.C. took over for Joe Williams with Count Basie. "The Count had heard one of my 'dubs'," recalls O.C. "I met him in a hotel room one night, and he played piano for my audition. Next day, without rehearsal, I was on."

Europe

While with Basie's organization, O.C. traveled thousands of miles and made five trips to Europe. "I really dig Europe," says O.C. "And someday I hope to be able to spend a long vacation there."

O.C. Smith is no over night pop singer. He has earned his success. As Tony Bennett says, "O.C. Smith is a singer's singer."

O. C. SMITH'S "Son of Hickory Holler's Tramp" was originally a C&W song

BEAT Goes To The Movies
'WILL PENNY'

Paramount Pictures believes that "Will Penny" is a "thinking man's western." Yet the audience is not required to delve deeply into their minds to determine the film's outcome. "Will Penny" is, however, an experimental western if only in plot and characterization.

Will Penny (aptly portrayed by a beardless Charlton Heston) is an aging cowboy who is neither a fast-draw nor a flawlessly super-hero. Penny does not own his own spread, does not claim to have had one stolen from him, is not the marshal of Dodge City and doesn't ride upon a white horse.

He is, in fact, a rather ordinary cowhand who, in order to exist through an 1886 Montana winter, takes a job riding the grub line on a ranch. The isolated liner's shack Penny is to occupy during the long winter months is already inhabitated by a young wife (sensitively played by Joan Hackett) and her ten year old son.

It is at this point that "Will Penny" makes a radical departure from the common western film in which the hero must always remain purely heroic and idealistically "good." Penny and the woman fall in love. If this is not enough to shake up western-buffs, the woman goes so far as to suggest leaving her husband and marrying Penny.

Director Tom Gries (who also wrote the screenplay) and producers Fred Engel and Walter Seltzer apparently felt the need to have at least some of the stock western apparel in "Will Penny" and, consequently, we do have a group of "bad guys" out to kill the hero. The climax of the film, again, reverts back to the usual western fare.

In addition to Miss Hackett, Heston is given ample support from co-stars Donald Pleasence, Lee Majors (from TV's "Big Valley") and Anthony Zerbe. Pleasence is especially marvelous as the horribly "bad" man.

The film, on the whole, is certainly far above average, unusually authentic and highly entertaining, appealing to even those who do not normally enjoy westerns.

—*Louise Criscione*

UNBEARABLE AGONY of a hot bath

INTRODUCING Lee Majors

KRLA ARCHIVES

KRLA ARCHIVES

Stevie Wonder's Greatest Hits

ALEXANDER'S TIMELESS BLOOZBAND

Now Available At:
MONTGOMERY WARD DEPARTMENT STORES

KRLA ARCHIVES

Now Available At:
MONTGOMERY WARD DEPARTMENT STORES

I HAVE SAT IN THE REALM OF
HEAVEN (mind)
all my days (periods of accomplishments)
to catch a crooked day
here and there
manifesting experience after
experience
Dodging sounds
hollow ones (vibrations)
simply by not being there....
Recording since the beginning of
illusive time
My childhood in the cave
weighing and watching all the
energies to the point of
acceptance

I AM ACCEPTANCE

I HAVE WAITED LONG IN THE REALM OF
SILENCE (the loudest sound there is)
all my days
to see many faces
in the earth
dust to dust
yesterday's people all yawning
that
the children know
yet go on slaying them at the
feet of existence
like
tiny fingers on the fence
soft and wrinkled with love
biting
D..I..S..A..P..P..E..A..R??
slowly into my eyes
somewhere
everywhere
there ... there and there

I HAVE WAITED LONG TO SEE
PATIENCE
I HAVE UNDERSTOOD
I AM PATIENCE IS

Richie Havens

KRLA ARCHIVES

please send me
BEAT

26 issues only

$3 per year

Mail to: **BEAT Publications**
9000 Sunset Blvd.
Los Angeles, California 90069

☐ New Subscription

I want BEAT for ☐ 1 year at $3.00 or ☐ 2 years at $5.00
I enclose ☐ cash ☐ check ☐ money order
Outside U.S.—$9 per year

* Please print your name and address.

Name_____

Street_____

City_____

State_____ Zip_____

BEAT SHOWCASE

TURNING ON

THE DOCK OF THE BAY (Volt) Otis Redding. *Open the Door, Tramp, Glory of Love* plus nine other tracks. Otis Redding never achieved the success in life that he has with death. Although he spread his special brand of soul music throughout the world, in this country the people for whom he laid the ground work achieved more popular acclaim than the originator. For years Redding worked to fill the gap left by Sam Cooke, to open doors otherwise closed to soul music. He did that and more. In this his last album, we are given a fitting testimony to the talents of one of our greatest singers. Using his full range of extraordinary talent he goes from the plaintive ballad, *I Love You More Than Words Can Say* to the driving, rocking sound of *I'm Coming Home*. This album contains eight selections that have never appeared previously on any album. If this album points up any aspect in particular it is Redding's universality. He belonged as much to the Europe who loved him as the America who produced him.

ONCE UPON A DREAM (Atlantic) The Young Rascals. Following the lead of such groups as the Beatles, Rolling Stones and the Jefferson Airplane, the Rascals have produced an album that sets out to be a total entity with the careful planning of a full length film. Every detail of this album was meticulously considered. In the introduction and dedication Felix states, "Dreams are messages . . . they can occur in all types of shapes and forms from beauty to bizarre . . . the dream of mankind is peace on earth good will towards men. This album is dedicated to that dream." However the dream is only partially realized. Possibly because we live in a world that has already produced A "Sgt. Pepper's Lonely Hearts Club Band" we tend to judge all other recordings by that standard. Somehow, although the Rascals try very hard and produced some beautiful sounds, they don't quite measure up to their promise. However, the Rascals are a very talented group much more so than most people in this country credit them. One interesting aspect of this album is the extensive use of sound effects. Rain storms, babies' voices, thunder and over conversation are all woven into their material. The Rascals stated that they put their dreams into this album. At least they dream high, but as often happens with reality, the dream falls a little short.

THE BEAT GOES ON (Atlantic) The Vanilla Fudge. There are no cuts per se in this album. It is instead a complete, stylized testimony to time and the world and the people who inhabit it. Beginning with some very beautiful classical music, going into an early voice recording, on to a futuristic voice booming "Phase One" this album includes the music of Beethoven, of the Beatles, of Sony Bono. There is also the voice of Neville Chamberlain proclaiming the end of all wars to come as the chanting of "Heil Hitler" is heard in the background, the voice of Winston Churchill committing Great Britain to war, the voice of Franklin Roosevelt informing the American people of the attack on Pearl Harbor. All told to the strains of the *Beat Goes On* . . . and on. The record also contains a survey of music from the middle ages with a lovely 15th century rendition of "Old Black Joe" to the Beatles. If you're one of those people who first heard Elvis when you were just what is now called a teeny-bopper, and if you were just seventeen when the Beatles immortalized that particular age in "I Saw Her Standing There" the nostalgia brought about by "Phase One" is wonderful. Amazingly enough the Fudge have combined the most familiar with the most well known. The rush of electronic sound is heard through the electric organ interpretation of Beethoven's Moonlight Sonata. The surging broken chords of that classic suddenly take on new meaning. Incredible. It is without a doubt that this is a different album, one to which people will react strongly. No apathy sold here.

BOSTON TEA PARTY

Most people think the Boston Tea Party happened in Boston in 1775, but actually it happened in Burbank, California in 1963 when five young men came together to form a non leader group. With Richard DePerna on bass guitar, Mike Stevens on lead guitar, Robert DePerna on organ, Travis Fields as lead singer and Dave Novogroski on drums, they have combined for a total sound that aims at "having something for everyone."

The most accomplished musician of the group is Rich who works out most of the group's arrangements. He prides himself and the group on the fact that their recorded sound is identical to their live performance. Mike, who insists his musical ability is inherited writes most of the material for the group. Rob who plays organ is admittedly responsible for the "tight sound" of the Tea Party while on stage. Along with Dave's drumming, Rob sets the pace for the group. Travis who was born in Chicago sings the lead. And although they would be the first to admit all recording is a growing process, Travis invites everyone to listen to the group's new album saying "We've done the very best we can."

In the future the group is looking forward to appearing in American International's forthcoming film, tentatively entitled, *Free Grass*.

CLASSIFIED

HAPPY BIRTHDAY—Zuch of the Sunliners. Love Chrissie

Denver welcomes Zuch. Love from all

Zuch is an outasite drummer

The Stingrays! . . . Larry, Mike, Thomas, Donny. (Center Point, Texas)

The Gables are on top. They reign Supremely. (Jayton, Texas)

Official Interstate Chapter BR/AM Dave Clark Five Fan Club. Contact: Dawn Lee c/o BEAT Publications, 9000 Sunset Blvd., Suite 1000, Los Angeles, Calif.

Raylene love Francis

Happy Birthday to Mike Love of the Beach Boys

RAIDERS — Chicago concert was positively outasite! I love you —Paula

Monthly newsletters and photos. Join the F.L.M.C. Beatle Club, send self-addressed, stamped envelope to Barb Fenick c/o BEAT Publications, 9000 Sunset Blvd., Suite 1000, Los Angeles, Calif.

Groovy Monkees International. For information send self-addressed, stamped envelope to Sue Petro c/o BEAT Publications, 9000 Sunset Blvd., Suite 1000, Los Angeles, Calif.

Happy Birthday Leona Aina—Tina

OBNN; people fan club

Happy Birthday Mark Lindsay from the Kaleidoscope Kids.

Happy Anniversary Painted Doll. 4-19-67

THE WHO ARE

Happy 17th Birthday Chris and Bob! Vicki

Bob, Jack WOW!!

Happy birthday — Darryl Hooper and Rick Andridge—SEEDS

Daryl Hooper is

Rick Andridge grooves

SEEDS—Sky-Jan-Rick-Daryl

Happy seventeenth Sassafras! May your window into the future always be stained glass. Love, Mum-sis

Live for today Steve, 'cause tomorrow ain't comming. Baby Cakes

How does your grass grow Allison? D. Sino

Younger girl loves Rick

Davy—Memories of our night . . . Lunda

Cat Stevens Fan Club. Please send a self-addressed, stamped envelope in care of BEAT Publications, 9000 Sunset Blvd., Suite 1000, Los Angeles, Calif.

Join the BOTTLES OF GOODNESS National Fan Club, Pontiac, Michigan Chapter. C/o BEAT Publications, 9000 Sunset Blvd., Suite 1000, Los Angeles, Calif.

SMOKESTACK BANANA — BEWARE

KEITH + LOLL = LUV
LUV = LOLL + KEITH

HI KEITH AND LOLL from DANNY and RANDI

KRLA ARCHIVES

SIMON & GARFUNKEL UP ANOTHER LADDER

BEAT Photos: Ed Caraeff

www.ingramcontent.com/pod-product-compliance
Lightning Source LLC
Chambersburg PA
CBHW080433190426
43202CB00038B/2931